unclouded; apparent, audible, coherent, comprehensible, conspicuous, evident, explicit, intelligible, manifest, obvious, palpable, plain, pronounced, recognizable, unambiguous, unmistakable; empty, free, open, smooth, unhindered, unimpeded, unobstructed; crystalline, glassy, pellucid, see-through, transparent; certain, decided, definite, positive, resolved, sure; clean, innocent, pure, stainless, unblemished, undefiled, untarnished.

clearly adv *lit:* beyond doubt, distinctly, evidently, markedly, obviously, seemingly, undeniably.

cleft n *lit:* crack, crevice, chink, fissure, split; dimple.

clergyman n *lit:* chaplain, cleric, curate, father, minister, padre, parson, pastor, priest, rabbi, rector, reverend, vicar.

clever adj *lit:* able, adroit, astute, bright, canny, capable, dexterous, gifted, intelligent, keen, knowledgeable, quick-witted, resourceful, shrewd, skilful, smart, talented.

client n *lit:* applicant, buyer, customer, patient, shopper.

clientèle n *lit:* business, clients, customers, market, regulars, trade.

cliff n *lit:* crag, face, overhang, precipice, rock face, scarp.

climate n *lit:* clime, region, temperature, weather; disposition, feeling, mood, temper, tendency.

climax n *lit:* acme, culmination, head, height, highlight, orgasm, peak, summit, zenith. **vb** *lit:* culminate, peak.

climb n *lit:* ascent, rise, slope, steep part; increase, progression. **vb** *lit:* ascend, clamber, mount, scale; increase, soar, top.

clinic n *lit:* medical centre, surgery; seminar, tutorial.

cling vb *lit:* adhere, attach to, be true to, clutch, embrace, fasten, grip, stick, twine round.

clip n *lit:* blow, box, clout, punch, smack, whack; rate, speed, velocity; fastener, holder, pin, staple. **vb** *lit:* crop, cut, pare, prune, shear, shorten, trim; blow, box, cuff, knock, punch, smack, thump, wallop; attach, fasten, fix, hold, staple.

cloak n *lit:* cape, coat, cover, mantle, wrap; blind, front, mask, pretext, shield. **vb** *lit:* camouflage, cover, disguise, hide, mask, screen, veil.

clock n *lit:* chronometer, repeater, timepiece, watch; dial, gauge, meter, speedometer; milometer, odometer; *fig:* face, phizog. **vb** *lit:* pace, rate, time; report (in), sign (on); knock (off), sign (off); *fig:* look at, see, tour, visit; punch the face of.

cloister n *lit:* covered walk; convent, monastery; den, retreat.

close **vb** *lit:* bar, block, clog, cork, lock, plug, seal, secure, shut, stop up; cease, complete, conclude, discontinue, finish, terminate, wind up; grapple (with), wrestle (with); connect, join. **adj** *lit:* adjacent, approaching, handy, imminent, impending, near, neighbouring; compact, congested, cramped, dense, impenetrable, packed, short, thick, tight; accurate, conscientious, exact, literal, precise; alert, assiduous, careful, detailed, dogged, earnest, intense, intent, keen, minute, painstaking, rigorous, searching, thorough; attached, devoted, familiar, intimate, loving; airless, heavy, oppressive, stale, stifling, stuffy, suffocating, unventilated; hidden, private, reticent, secluded, secretive, taciturn, unforthcoming; mean, miserly, niggardly, parsimonious, stingy, ungenerous. **adv** *lit:* near.

closet n *lit:* cabinet, cupboard, locker; private room. **vb** *lit:* admit, shut.

cloth n *lit:* fabric, material, textile.

clothe **vb** *lit:* accoutre, attire, cover, drape, dress, equip, fit out, garb, outfit, rig, robe.

clothes/clothing n *lit:* apparel, attire, costume, dress, garb, garments, gear, outfit, vesture, wardrobe, wear.

cloud n *lit:* billow, gloom, haze, mist, murk, nebula, vapour; dense mass, horde, multitude, swarm, throng. **vb** *lit:* darken, dim, eclipse, obscure, overcast, shade, shadow, veil; confuse, disorient, distort, impair, muddle.

club n *lit:* bat, bludgeon, cosh, cudgel, stick, truncheon; association, circle, clique, fraternity, group, guild, lodge, order, set, society, union. **vb** *lit:* bash, batter, beat, bludgeon, clobber, clout, cosh, pummel, strike.

clue **n** *lit:* hint, indication, inkling, intimation, lead, sign, suspicion, tip-off, trace.

clumsy **adj** *lit:* awkward, blundering, bungling, clownish, gauche, gawky, inept, lumbering, maladroit, uncoordinated, uncouth, ungainly, unskilful.

coach **n** *lit:* bus, carriage, vehicle; instructor, trainer, tutor. **vb** *lit:* cram, drill, instruct, train, tutor.

coarse **adj** *lit:* boorish, brute, gruff, loutish, rough, rude, uncivil; bawdy, earthy, improper, indelicate, offensive, ribald, smutty, vulgar; coarse-grained, crude, homespun, unpolished, unrefined.

coarseness **n** *lit:* bawdiness, boorishness, indelicacy, offensiveness, ribaldry, roughness, smut, uncouthness.

coast **n** *lit:* beach, coastline, littoral, seaside, shore, strand. **vb** *lit:* cruise, drift, freewheel, get by, sail, taxi.

coat **n** *lit:* fleece, fur, hair, hide, skin, wool; coating, covering, overlay. **vb** *lit:* apply, cover, smear, spread.

coin **n** *lit:* cash, change, copper, money, silver. **vb** *lit:* issue, mint, mould; conceive, create, forge, formulate, invent, make up, think up.

coincide **vb** *lit:* be concurrent, occur simultaneously, synchronize; accord, harmonize, match, tally; acquiesce, concur, correspond.

coincidental **adj** *lit:* accidental, chance, unintentional; coincident, concurrent, simultaneous, synchronous.

cold **n** *lit:* chill, coldness, frigidity, frostiness, inclemency; catarrh, coryza, flu, influenza, rheum, rhinitis. **adj** *lit:* arctic, biting, bitter, bleak, boreal, chilly, freezing, frosty, gelid, raw, wintry; chilled, numbed, shivery; aloof, dead, distant, frigid, indifferent, phlegmatic, reserved, standoffish, stony, unmoved, unsympathetic.

collaborate **vb** *lit:* cooperate, join forces, participate, team up, work together; collude, conspire, fraternize.

collapse **n** *lit:* breakdown, cave-in, disintegration, downfall, subsidence; exhaustion, failure, faint, flop.   **vb** *lit:* break down, cave in, crack up, crumble, fail, faint, fold, founder, give way, subside.

colleague n *lit:* ally, associate, companion, comrade, confederate, partner, team-mate, workmate.

collect vb *lit:* accumulate, aggregate, amass, gather, heap, hoard, stockpile; assemble, cluster, coacervate, congregate, convene, converge, rally; acquire, obtain, raise, secure.

collection n *lit:* accumulation, anthology, coacervation, compilation, heap, hoard, mass, set, stockpile, store; assembly, assortment, company, congregation, crowd, gathering, group; contribution, offering.

college n *lit:* body of colleagues; academy, campus, institute, polytechnic, seminary, university.

collide vb *lit:* clash, conflict, crash, meet head-on.

colour n *lit:* coloration, dye, hue, paint, pigment, shade, tincture, tinge, tint; bloom, blush, brilliance, flush, glow, vividness; *fig:* appearance, disguise, façade, guise, pretence, pretext, semblance.   **vb** *lit:* dye, paint, stain, tinge, tint; *fig:* disguise, distort, embroider, exaggerate, falsify, garble, misrepresent, prejudice, slant, taint; blush, flush, redden.

colourful adj *lit:* bright, brilliant, intense, motley, multicoloured, psychedelic, variegated, vibrant, vivid; characterful, distinctive, lively, picturesque, rich, stimulating, unusual.

combination n *lit:* amalgamation, blend, composite, mixture; alliance, association, cartel, coalition, compound, confederation, consortium, merger, syndicate, union.

combine vb *lit:* amalgamate, associate, bind, blend, compound, connect, fuse, incorporate, integrate, link, merge, put together, synthesize, unify.

come vb *lit:* appear, approach, arrive, enter, move towards, near, occur, show up, turn up; attain, materialize, reach; fall, happen, take place; emanate, emerge, flow, issue, result, turn out; be available, be made, be produced.

comedian n *lit:* clown, comic, funny man, jester, joker, wit.

comedy n *lit:* drollery, farce, hilarity, humour, joking, light entertainment, slapstick, wisecracking.

comfort n *lit:* alleviation, cheer, consolation, ease, enjoyment, help, relief, succour, support; cosiness, opulence, snugness, wellbeing. **vb** *lit:* alleviate, assuage, cheer, commiserate with, console, ease, enliven, hearten, reassure, relieve, soothe, strengthen.

comfortable adj *lit:* adequate, agreeable, ample, convenient, cosy, homely, loose-fitting, pleasant, restful, snug; contented, happy, relaxed; affluent, prosperous, well-off, well-to-do.

comical adj *lit:* absurd, amusing, diverting, droll, entertaining, farcical, funny, hilarious, ludicrous, ridiculous, side-splitting.

coming n *lit:* accession, advent, arrival. **adj** *lit:* approaching, due, forthcoming, imminent, impending, near, next; aspiring, future, promising, up-and-coming.

command n *lit:* behest, bidding, commandment, directive, edict, injunction, instruction, order, precept, requirement, ultimatum; authority, control, domination, government, grasp, management, power, rule, supervision, sway. **vb** *lit:* bid, charge, compel, demand, enjoin, require; control, dominate, govern, head, manage, rule, supervise, sway.

comment n *lit:* observation, remark, statement; annotation, commentary, criticism, explanation, exposition, note. **vb** *lit:* interpose, mention, note, observe, point out, remark, say; annotate, criticize, elucidate, explain, interpret.

commission n *lit:* appointment, charge, duty, employment, errand, function, mandate, task, warrant; allowance, brokerage, compensation, cut, fee, percentage; board, commissioners, committee, delegation, representative. **vb** *lit:* appoint, authorize, contract, delegate, empower, nominate, order, send.

commitment n *lit:* duty, liability, obligation, responsibility; dedication, devotion, involvement, loyalty; assurance, guarantee, pledge, undertaking, word.

common n *lit:* green, heath.   **adj** *lit:* average, commonplace, customary, daily, familiar, frequent, habitual, humdrum, ordinary, plain, routine, standard, stock, usual; accepted, general, popular, prevailing, universal, widespread; communal, community, public, social; coarse, hackneyed, inferior, low, pedestrian, stale, undistinguished, vulgar.

communal **adj** *lit:* collective, community, general, joint, neighbourhood, public.

communicate **vb** *lit:* acquaint, be in contact, be in touch, convey, disclose, divulge, inform, make known, pass on, publish, report, reveal, ring up, spread, transmit, unfold.

communication n *lit:* connection, contact, conversation, correspondence, link, transmission; announcement, disclosure, dispatch, intelligence, message, news, report, statement.

community n *lit:* commonwealth, general public, people, residents, society; affinity, identity, likeness, similarity.

companion n *lit:* accomplice, ally, associate, colleague, comrade, crony, mate, partner; aide, assistant, attendant, chaperon, escort; counterpart, match.

company n *lit:* assembly, band, body, circle, group, party, set, troop; association, business, concern, corporation, firm, house, partnership, syndicate; callers, guests, presence, visitors.

compare **vb** *lit:* balance (with), collate (with), contrast (with), juxtapose (with); equate (to), liken (to), parallel (to); approach, approximate to, come up to, equal, match.

comparison n *lit:* collation, contrast, distinction, juxtaposition; analogy, comparability, correlation, resemblance, similarity.

compartment n *lit:* alcove, berth, booth, carriage, chamber, cubicle, niche, pigeonhole; category, department, section, subdivision.

compassion n *lit:* charity, commiseration, compunction, condolence, humanity, kindness, mercy, pity, sympathy, tenderness.

compensate **vb** *lit:* atone, indemnify, make good, recompense, refund, reimburse, remunerate, repay, requite, satisfy; balance, cancel (out), counteract, make amends, make up for, offset.

compensation n *lit:* amends, atonement, damages, indemnity, payment, recompense, reimbursement, remuneration, reparation, restitution, satisfaction.

competent adj *lit:* able, adequate, capable, endowed, fit, proficient, qualified, sufficient, suitable.

competition n *lit:* contention, contest, one-upmanship, opposition, rivalry, strife; championship, event, quiz, tournament; challengers, field, rivals.

competitor n *lit:* adversary, antagonist, challenger, competition, contestant, emulator, opponent, rival.

compilation n *lit:* anthology, collection, compendium, compiling, miscellany, selection.

complacent adj *lit:* contended, gratified, pleased with oneself, satisfied, self-righteous, smug, unconcerned.

complain vb *lit:* beef, bemoan, carp, deplore, find fault, gripe, groan, growl, grumble, kick up a fuss, moan, whine, whinge.

complaint n *lit:* accusation, criticism, dissatisfaction, fault-finding, grievance, grumble, moan, remonstrance; affliction, ailment, disease, disorder, illness, indisposition, sickness.

complete vb *lit:* accomplish, achieve, cap, conclude, discharge, do, execute, finalize, finish, realize, round off, settle, wrap up. adj *lit:* all, entire, full, integral, unabridged, undivided, whole; accomplished, achieved, concluded, finished; absolute, consummate, perfect, thorough, total, utter.

completely adv *lit:* absolutely, altogether, entirely, from beginning to end, fully, in full, quite, solidly, thoroughly, totally, utterly, wholly.

complex n *lit:* network, organization, scheme, structure, system; fixation, obsession, phobia, preoccupation. adj *lit:* circuitous, complicated, intricate, involved, knotty, labyrinthine, mingled, tangled, tortuous; composite, compound, heterogeneous, manifold, multiple.

complicate vb *lit:* confuse, entangle, involve, muddle, snarl up.

complicated adj *lit:* complex, elaborate, interlaced, intricate, involved, labyrinthine; difficult, perplexing, problematic, puzzling.

compliment n *lit:* admiration, commendation, congratulations, courtesy, eulogy, flattery, honour, praise, tribute. vb *lit:* commend, congratulate, extol, felicitate, laud, praise, salute, speak highly of.

comply vb *lit:* abide by, accord, acquiesce, adhere to, agree to, consent to, defer, discharge, follow, observe, respect, satisfy, submit.

component n *lit:* constituent, element, ingredient, part, unit.
adj *lit:* composing, inherent, intrinsic.

composition n *lit:* arrangement, configuration, design, form, layout, make-up, organization, structure; compilation, creation, fashioning, formulation, invention, making, production; essay, exercise, opus, piece, study, work, writing; balance, concord, harmony, proportion, symmetry.

compound n *lit:* alloy, blend, combination, composite, conglomerate, fusion, medley, mixture. vb *lit:* amalgamate, blend, combine, concoct, fuse, intermingle, mix, unite; add to, aggravate, complicate, exacerbate, intensify, magnify, worsen; adjust, settle a dispute. adj *lit:* complex, composite, intricate, multiple.

comprehension n *lit:* conception, discernment, grasp, intelligence, perception, realization, understanding; compass, field, limits, range, reach, scope.

comprehensive adj *lit:* all-inclusive, blanket, broad, complete, exhaustive, extensive, inclusive, sweeping, thorough, wide.

compromise n *lit:* accord, adjustment, agreement, concession, middle ground, settlement, trade-off. vb *lit:* adjust, agree, arbitrate, compound, concede, meet halfway, settle; discredit, embarrass, expose, implicate, jeopardize, prejudice.

compulsory adj *lit:* binding, imperative, mandatory, obligatory, requisite.

conceal vb *lit:* camouflage, cover, disguise, hide, keep secret, mask, obscure, screen, secrete.

conceited adj *lit:* arrogant, bigheaded, cocky, egotistical, immodest, puffed up, swollen-headed, vainglorious.

conceive vb *lit:* appreciate, apprehend, comprehend, fancy, grasp, imagine, suppose, understand; contrive, create, design, develop, formulate, produce, think up; become pregnant.

concentrate n *lit:* distillate, essence, extract. vb *lit:* be engrossed in, focus attention on, put one's mind to, rack one's brains; centre, cluster, converge, focus; accumulate, collect, congregate, gather.

concentration n *lit:* absorption, application, single-mindedness; centralization, compression, consolidation, convergence, intensification; accumulation, aggregation, collection, horde, mass.

concern n *lit:* affair, business, field, interest, involvement, matter, mission, responsibility, task; bearing, importance, reference, relevance; anxiety, apprehension, attention, consideration, disquiet, distress, heed, worry; company, corporation, enterprise, firm, organization. vb *lit:* affect, apply to, be relevant to, involve, pertain to, regard; bother, disquiet, disturb, make uneasy, perturb, trouble, worry.

concerned adj *lit:* active, implicated, involved, mixed up, privy to; anxious, bothered, distressed, troubled, uneasy, upset, worried; attentive, caring, interested, solicitous.

concerning prp *lit:* about, apropos of, as to, in the matter of, on the subject of, regarding, relating to, touching, with reference to.

concert n *lit:* accord, agreement, concordance, harmony, unanimity, unison; in collaboration, in league.

concise adj *lit:* brief, compact, compressed, condensed, laconic, pithy, summary, terse, to the point.

conclude vb *lit:* cease, come to an end, complete, draw to a close, finish, round off, wind up; assume, deduce, gather, infer, reckon, sum up, suppose; accomplish, carry out, decide, determine, effect, fix, pull off, settle, work out.

conclusion n *lit:* close, completion, end, finish, result; consequence, culmination, issue, outcome, upshot; agreement, conviction, deduction, judgement, opinion, resolution, settlement.

condemn vb *lit:* blame, denounce, reprehend, reproach, upbraid; convict, damn, doom, sentence.

condescending adj *lit:* disdainful, lofty, patronizing, snooty, supercilious, toffee-nosed.

condition n *lit:* circumstances, plight, predicament, situation, state of affairs; demand, limitation, modification, prerequisite, provision, qualification, requirement, restriction, stipulation, terms; fettle, fitness, health, shape, trim; ailment, complaint, malady, problem; class, grade, order, position, rank, status. vb *lit:* accustom, adapt, prepare, ready, tone up, train, work out.

conditional adj *lit:* contingent, dependent, provisional, qualified, subject to.

conduct n *lit:* administration, direction, leadership, management, organization, running; attitude, bearing, behaviour, demeanour, manners, ways. vb *lit:* administer, control, direct, handle, lead, manage, preside over, regulate, supervise; accompany, attend, convey, escort, guide, steer, usher; acquit, act, behave, carry.

confer vb *lit:* accord, award, bestow, give, grant, present; consult, converse, deliberate, discourse, parley.

conference n *lit:* congress, convention, discussion, meeting, seminar, symposium.

confess vb *lit:* acknowledge, admit, blurt out, come clean, confide, disclose, divulge, get off one's chest, grant, own up, reveal; affirm, assert, confirm, declare, profess, prove.

confession n *lit:* acknowledgement, admission, disclosure, exposure, revelation.

confidence n *lit:* belief, faith, reliance, trust; assurance, boldness, courage, nerve, self-reliance.

confident adj *lit:* certain, convinced, counting on, secure, sure; assured, bold, dauntless, positive, self-assured.

confidential adj *lit:* classified, hush-hush, intimate, off the record, private, secret; faithful, trusted, trustworthy.

confirm vb *lit:* assure, clinch, fix, fortify, reinforce, strengthen; approve, authenticate, bear out, corroborate, endorse, ratify, sanction, substantiate, verify.

confirmation n *lit:* authentication, corroboration, proof, substantiation, validation, verification; acceptance, approval, assent, endorsement, ratification, sanction.

conflict n *lit:* battle, clash, collision, combat, contention, contest, encounter, fight, fracas, strife, warfare; antagonism, disagreement, discord, dissension, friction, hostility, opposition. vb *lit:* clash, collide, combat, contend, contest, disagree, interfere, strife, struggle.

confuse vb *lit:* baffle, bemuse, bewilder, mystify, perplex, puzzle; confound, disarrange, disorder, mingle, mistake, mix up, muddle, tangle; abash, addle, demoralize, discompose, disconcert, discountenance, disorient, embarrass, fluster, mortify, rattle, upset.

confusion n *lit:* befuddlement, bewilderment, disorientation, perplexity, puzzlement; bustle, chaos, clutter, commotion, disorder, jumble, mess, muddle, shambles, tangle, turmoil, upheaval; abashment, chagrin, discomfiture, distraction, embarrassment, fluster.

congratulate vb *lit:* compliment, felicitate, wish joy to.

congratulations n *lit:* best wishes, compliments, good wishes, greetings.

congregate vb *lit:* assemble, come together, concentrate, convene, converge, flock, gather, mass, muster, rally, throng.

congregation n *lit:* assembly, brethren, flock, host, multitude, parishioners.

connect vb *lit:* affix, ally, associate, combine, join, link, unite.

connection n *lit:* alliance, association, attachment, junction, link, tie, union; affinity, bond, communication, correlation, correspondence, intercourse, relationship, relevance; context, reference; acquaintance, ally, associate, contact, friend, sponsor; kin, kindred, relation, relative.

conquer vb *lit:* beat, crush, defeat, humble, master, overcome, prevail, quell, rout, subdue, subjugate, surmount, vanquish; acquire, annex, occupy, seize, win.

conquest n *lit:* defeat, overthrow, rout, triumph, victory; acquisition, annexation, appropriation, invasion, occupation, subjection, takeover; captivation, enchantment, enthralment, enticement; admirer, catch, fan, prize, supporter, worshipper.

conscience n *lit:* moral sense, principles, scruples.

conscientious adj *lit:* careful, diligent, exact, meticulous, painstaking, particular, punctilious, thorough; high-minded, honourable, incorruptible, just, scrupulous, strict, upright.

conscious n *lit:* awareness, perception; ego, mind. adj *lit:* alert, alive to, awake, aware, responsive; calculated, deliberate, intentional, rational, reasoning, responsible, wilful.

consecutive adj *lit:* chronological, following, running, succeeding, successive, uninterrupted.

consequence n *lit:* effect, issue, outcome, repercussion, result; account, importance, note, portent, significance, value, weight; distinction, eminence, repute, standing, status.

consequently adv *lit:* accordingly, hence, subsequently, therefore, thus.

conservative n *lit:* middle-of-the-road, moderate, right-winger, Tory, traditionalist. adj *lit:* cautious, conventional, die-hard, moderate, quiet, sober, traditional.

consider vb *lit:* cogitate, contemplate, deliberate, examine, meditate, mull over, ponder, reflect, ruminate, study, weigh; believe, deem, judge, rate, think; bear in mind, care for, reckon with, regard, remember, take into account.

considerable adj *lit:* abundant, ample, comfortable, goodly, large, lavish, noticeable, plentiful, sizable, substantial, tidy; noteworthy, significant.

considerate adj *lit:* attentive, concerned, kind, mindful, obliging, tactful, thoughtful, unselfish.

considering prp *lit:* all in all, insomuch as, in view of.

consignment n *lit:* assignment, committal, dispatch, distribution, entrusting, handing over, sending, transmittal; batch, delivery, shipment.

consistent adj *lit:* constant, dependable, persistent, regular, steady, undeviating; accordant, coherent, compatible, congruous, harmonious, logical.

conspiracy n *lit:* confederacy, frame-up, intrigue, machination, plot, treason.

conspire vb *lit:* confederate, contrive, devise, intrigue, machinate, plot, scheme; combine, contribute, cooperate, tend.

constant adj *lit:* continual, even, fixed, habitual, invariable, permanent, regular, stable, steady, unbroken, unvarying; ceaseless, continuous, endless, everlasting, incessant, interminable, never-ending, nonstop, persistent, relentless, sustained, uninterrupted, unrelenting; determined, dogged, persevering, resolute, unwavering; attached, devoted, faithful, staunch, true, trustworthy, unfailing.

constitution n *lit:* charter, statute; composition, establishment, formation; build, character, disposition, form, health, make-up, nature, physique, structure, temperament.

construct vb *lit:* assemble, build, create, design, engineer, erect, fabricate, formulate, found, make, manufacture, organize, raise, set up.

construction n *lit:* building, composition, edifice, erection, fabrication, formation, shape, structure; explanation, inference, interpretation, rendering.

constructive adj *lit:* helpful, practical, productive, useful.

consult vb *lit:* ask advice of, consider, debate, deliberate, question, refer to, turn to; have regard for, respect, take account of.

consultation n *lit:* conference, council, deliberation, dialogue, examination, interview, meeting, session.

consume vb *lit:* absorb, deplete, drain, exhaust, expend, fritter away, lavish, spend, squander, use, vanish, waste; devour, eat up, gobble, guzzle, polish off, put away; decay, demolish, destroy, devastate, ravage.

contact n *lit:* association, communication; approximation, contiguity, junction, union; acquaintance, connection. **vb** *lit:* approach, call, communicate with, phone, speak to, write to.

contain vb *lit:* accommodate, hold, seat; comprise, include, involve; curb, hold back, repress, restrain, stifle.

contemplative adj *lit:* deep in thought, meditative, musing, pensive, rapt, reflective, thoughtful.

contemporary n *lit:* compeer. **adj** *lit:* coexisting, concurrent, synchronous; current, latest, modern, newfangled, present-day, up-to-date, with it.

contempt n *lit:* derision, disdain, disregard, disrespect, hauteur, mockery, scorn, slight.

content n *lit:* comfort, contentment, ease, pleasure, satisfaction; essence, gist, meaning, substance, thoughts; capacity, size, volume. **vb** *lit:* delight, gratify, humour, placate, please, satisfy, suffice. **adj** *lit:* agreeable, comfortable, contended, fulfilled, satisfied.

contest n *lit:* competition, game, match, tournament, trial; affray, battle, combat, conflict, discord, dispute, fight, struggle. **vb** *lit:* compete, contend, fight, strive; argue, challenge, debate, dispute, object to, oppose.

context n *lit:* background, connection, framework; ambience, circumstances, situation.

continual adj *lit:* constant, continuous, endless, frequent, incessant, perpetual, repetitive, uninterrupted.

continue vb *lit:* carry on, endure, last, persist, remain, stay on, survive; go on, keep at, maintain, persevere, pursue, stick to, sustain; extend, lengthen, prolong; proceed, resume, take up.

continuous adj *lit:* constant, continued, extended, prolonged, unceasing, uninterrupted.

contract n *lit:* agreement, arrangement, commission, compact, covenant, deal, engagement, treaty, understanding. **vb** *lit:* compress, condense, constrict, lessen, narrow, reduce, shrink, tighten, wither; agree, arrange, clinch, engage, enter into, negotiate, pledge; catch, develop, go down with.

contradict vb *lit:* contravene, counteract, deny, dispute, negate, oppose.

contradictory adj *lit:* antagonistic, conflicting, discrepant, incompatible, inconsistent, irreconcilable, opposite, paradoxical.

contrast n *lit:* comparison, difference, disparity, dissimilarity, divergence, foil, opposition. **vb** *lit:* compare, differentiate, distinguish, oppose, set off.

contribute vb *lit:* add, bestow, chip in, donate, give, provide; be instrumental, conduce, help, tend.

control n *lit:* authority, charge, command, discipline, guidance, management, oversight, rule, supervision; check, curb, limitation, restraint. **vb** *lit:* command, conduct, direct, manage, oversee, rule, supervise; check, constrain, curb, hold back, limit, master, restrain, subdue.

controversial adj *lit:* contended, debatable, disputable, disputed.

convenient adj *lit:* beneficial, commodious, handy, helpful, laboursaving, opportune, suitable, useful, well-timed; accessible, at hand, nearby, within reach.

conventional adj *lit:* common, customary, formal, habitual, normal, proper, regular, standard, traditional, usual; bourgeois, commonplace, hackneyed, pedestrian, routine, stereotyped.

conversation n *lit:* chat, communication, dialogue, discourse, discussion, gossip, talk.

convert n *lit:* disciple, proselyte. **vb** *lit:* alter, change, transform, turn; adapt, apply, modify, reorganize, revise; baptize, convince, proselytize, regenerate.

convict n *lit:* criminal, culprit, felon, prisoner. **vb** *lit:* condemn, find guilty, imprison, sentence.

conviction n *lit:* assurance, certainty, confidence, firmness, reliance; belief, creed, faith, opinion, persuasion, view.

convince vb *lit:* assure, persuade, prevail upon, prove to, sway.

cool n *lit:* calmness, composure, poise, self-control, temper. vb *lit:* chill, freeze, refrigerate; abate, allay, calm (down), dampen, lessen, moderate, quiet. **adj** *lit:* chilled, chilling, nippy, refreshing; calm, collected, composed, level-headed, placid, unemotional, unruffled; aloof, apathetic, indifferent, lukewarm, reserved, unconcerned, uninterested; bold, brazen, cheeky, impertinent, impudent; *fig:* cosmopolitan, sophisticated, urbane.

co-operate vb *lit:* aid, assist, collaborate, contribute, co-ordinate, help, join forces, work together.

co-ordination n *lit:* balance, coherence, integration, organization, synchronization.

copy n *lit:* counterfeit, duplicate, imitation, replica, reproduction, transcription. vb *lit:* counterfeit, duplicate, photocopy, reproduce, transcribe; ape, emulate, follow, imitate, mimic, repeat, simulate.

core n *lit:* centre, gist, heart, kernel, medulla, nub, pith.

corner n *lit:* angle, bend, joint; cavity, cranny, niche, nook, recess; pickle, predicament, tight spot. vb *lit:* bring to bay, trap.

corpse n *lit:* body, cadaver, carcass, remains.

correspond vb *lit:* accord, agree, compare, conform, correlate, harmonize, tally; exchange letters (with), keep in touch (with).

correspondence n *lit:* agreement, comparability, conformity, congruity, correlation, harmony, similarity; letters, post, postbag.

corrupt vb *lit:* debauch, deprave, pervert; bribe, fix, nobble, square, suborn, subvert; contaminate, debase, defile, doctor, interfere with, spoil, tamper with; decay, putrefy, rot. **adj** *lit:* debased, degenerate, depraved; bent, crooked, dishonest, unprincipled, unscrupulous; contaminated, defiled, polluted, spoiled, tainted; decayed, decaying, putrescent, putrid, rotten, rotting.

cost n *lit:* charge, expense, outlay, price; damage; harm, injury, loss, penalty, sacrifice.

cottage n *lit:* but-and-ben, cabin, chalet, hut, shack; thatched house.

couch n *lit:* bed, divan, settee, settle, sofa; chaise longue; bench, seat. **vb** *lit:* express, frame, phrase, word.

cough n *lit:* bark, hack, wheeze; chill, hoarseness, huskiness. **vb** *lit:* bark, hack, wheeze; gob (up), hawk (up), spew (up), vomit (up); *fig:* pay (up); give (up).

council n *lit:* assembly, board, chamber, committee, conference, congress, diet, panel, tribunal; conclave, synod.

councillor n *lit:* alderman, committee member, congressman, elder, representative, senator.

counsel n *lit:* advice, direction, guidance, information, recommendations, suggestions; advocate, barrister, lawyer; adviser, consultant. **vb** *lit:* advise, advocate, recommend, urge.

counsellor n *lit:* adviser, barrister, consultant; doctor, specialist, therapist.

count n *lit:* calculation, computation, reckoning; amount, sum, total; poll; charge, item, unit. **vb** *lit:* add (up), calculate, compute, number, reckon (up), score, tally, total (up); consider, deem, judge, regard as, think; include (among); *fig:* be of account, matter, signify.

country n *lit:* kingdom, land, nation, state, territory; area, region, zone; geography, terrain; countryside, farmland, provinces, rural areas; *fig:* electors, populace, voters.

couple n *lit:* brace, duet, duo, pair, twosome; few. **vb** *lit:* clasp, connect, hitch, join, link, yoke; marry, unite; copulate, have intercourse, mate.

courage n *lit:* audacity, boldness, bottle, bravery, daring, gallantry, grit, guts, nerve, pluck, valour.

course n *lit:* bearing, channel, direction, heading, line, path, route, track, trajectory, way; advancement, progress, progression, sequence, succession; manner, mode, policy, procedure; duration, elapsing, passing, term, time; classes, curriculum, lectures, programme, studies;

circuit, lap, links, track; layer, stratum; *spec:* peal, set (of changes in bell-ringing). **vb** *lit:* dash, flow, race, scud, scurry, stream, surge; chase, hunt, pursue.

court **n** *lit:* cloister, quadrangle, square, yard; hall, manor; assizes, bar, bench, lawcourt, tribunal; attendants, cortège, entourage, retinue, suite; homage. **vb** *lit:* date, go steady with, take out, woo; attract, draw upon oneself, invite, provoke; curry favour with, fawn upon, flatter, solicit.

cover **n** *lit:* canopy, cap, coating, dress, envelope, jacket, lid, sheath, top, wrapper; camouflage, concealment, protection, shelter; cloak, disguise, mask, screen, veil; *fig:* indemnity, insurance. **vb** *lit:* clothe, coat, dress, envelop, wrap up; camouflage, cloak, conceal, enshroud, hide, house, mask, obscure, screen, veil; defend, protect, shelter, shield; engulf, flood, immerse, submerge; *fig:* guarantee, indemnify, insure; comprehend, contain, embrace, encompass, include, incorporate, involve, take account of; describe, detail, recount, relate; double for, stand in for, substitute for; counterbalance, make up for; pass through, travel over.

cowardly **adj** *lit:* chicken-hearted, craven, faint-hearted, gutless, lily-livered, pusillanimous, spineless, timid, timorous, weak, yellow-bellied.

crack **n** *lit:* chink, cleft, cranny, crevice, fissure, rift, split; defect, flaw, weakness; detonation, firing, report, shot; bang, blow, clip, thump, whack; *fig:* bit of fun, jape, lark, laugh; gag, joke, quip; dig, gibe, sneer; attempt, bash, go, try; *spec:* cocaine, first light (of dawn). **vb** *lit:* chip, fracture, split; crash, make a sharp noise, snap; bang, buffet, clip, thump, whack; *fig:* give way, yield; break down, collapse, go to pieces; decipher, resolve, solve, work out; become shrill, break, falter; *spec:* break open (a safe).

craft **n** *lit:* art, artistry, dexterity, expertise, know-how, skill, workmanship; handiwork, work; calling, line, occupation, trade, vocation; cunning, guile, subterfuge, subtlety, trickery; aeroplane, aircraft, airship, boat, ship, spaceship, vessel.

crane **n** *lit:* boom, derrick, hoist, winch; outlet pipe; egret, heron, stork; *spec:* (camera) platform. **vb** *lit:* raise, stretch.

crash n *lit:* bang, detonation, explosion, loud noise, thud; accident, collision, pile-up, smash; collapse, depression, disaster, failure, fiasco. **vb** *lit:* bang, clash, detonate, explode, make a loud noise, thunder; break, fracture, shatter, shiver, smash; fall headlong (into), hurtle (into), pitch (into), plunge (into); drive (into), have an accident, plough (into), wreck; smash (through); collapse, fold up, go bust, go under; *fig:* flop (out on a bed).

crate n *lit:* box, case, packing-case, tea-chest; *fig:* kite, plane; banger, heap, rust-bucket. **vb** *lit:* box (up), encase, pack (up).

craving n *lit:* desire, hunger, longing, lust, thirst, yearning.

crawl n *lit:* shuffle, slither, wriggle; dawdle, plod; *spec:* freestyle (swimming stroke). **vb** *lit:* creep, move on all fours, shuffle, slither, wriggle; dawdle, inch along, move at a snail's pace; move furtively, move stealthily; swarm (with), teem (with); abase oneself, grovel, toady.

crazy adj *lit:* demented, deranged, insane, lunatic, mad, mental, unbalanced, unhinged; bananas, barmy, bats, bonkers, certifiable, cracked, crackers, cuckoo, loony, not all there, nuts, off one's rocker, potty, round the twist, touched; absurd, asinine, bird-brained, cockeyed, half-baked, idiotic, inane, irresponsible, ludicrous, nonsensical, preposterous, scatterbrained, senseless, unworkable; bizarre, eccentric, odd, outrageous, peculiar, weird; *fig:* fanatical (about), wild (about); berserk (about), hysterical (about), spare; *spec:* asymmetrical, irregular (paving).

crease n *lit:* fold, tuck; furrow, groove, wrinkle; corrugation; *spec:* (lacrosse-player's) circle; (batsman's/hockey-player's) line. **vb** *lit:* crinkle, crumple, fold, ruck up, rumple, wrinkle; *spec:* fold (up with laughter); graze (with a bullet).

create **vb** *lit:* bring about, bring into existence, cause, devise, dream up, form, generate, invent, make, originate, produce; constitute, dub, establish, found, set up; coin, initiate; *fig:* rant, rave.

creation n *lit:* cosmos, life, nature, universe, world; formation, generation, making, origination, production; constitution, establishing, foundation, laying down, setting up; achievement, invention, mode, piece, style, work.

creative adj *lit:* fertile, imaginative, ingenious, inventive, original, productive.

creature n *lit:* being, living thing, organism; animal, beast, brute.

credit n *lit:* belief, confidence, faith, trust; clout, influence, position, prestige, standing; esteem, regard, repute; acclaim, acknowledgement, approval, commendation, honour, merit, thanks; source of pride (to); (on) account, (on) hire-purchase; plus balance, (in) the black. vb *lit:* accept, believe, buy, fall for, swallow; acknowledge (as being), honour (with being); ascribe (to), attribute (to), chalk up (to).

creditor n *lit:* investor, lender, mortgagee.

crew n *lit:* company, complement, hands; oarsmen; personnel, staff; band, gang, squad, team; bunch, crowd, horde, lot, mob, pack.

crime n *lit:* felony, malfeasance, misdeed, misdemeanour, offence, transgression; lawbreaking, misconduct, villainy; evil, sin, wickedness, wrong.

criminal n *lit:* crook, felon, lawbreaker, offender, transgressor, villain; con, convict, jailbird, lag. adj *lit:* bent, crooked, felonious, illegal, unlawful; *fig:* deplorable, outrageous, scandalous.

crisis n *lit:* climax, crunch, crux, culmination, point of no return, turning-point; situation, emergency, exigency, extremity, plight, predicament, straits.

critic n *lit:* commentator, pundit, reviewer; authority, connoisseur, expert; detractor, fault-finder, knocker.

critical adj *lit:* climactic, dire, emergency, exigent, extreme, grave, hairy, precarious, urgent; crucial, decisive, pivotal, psychological, vital; analytical, diagnostic; derogatory, disparaging.

criticism n *lit:* analysis, appreciation, assessment, commentary, critique, notice, review; censure, flak, knocking, strictures.

criticize vb *lit:* analyse, appreciate, assess, comment upon, pass judgement on, review; censure, disparage, find fault with, knock, pan, pick to pieces, slate.

croak n *lit:* caw, squawk, wheeze. vb *lit:* caw, grunt, squawk, wheeze; *fig:* complain, grouse, grumble, moan; die, expire, kick the bucket, pass over.

crooked *adj lit:* bent, curved, hooked, looped, meandering, tortuous, winding; bowed, crippled, hunched; deformed, disfigured, distorted, misshapen, warped; askew, at an angle, awry, lopsided, slanting, uneven; *fig:* deceitful, dishonest, fraudulent, treacherous, underhand, unscrupulous.

crop *n lit:* fruits, harvest, produce, yield; riding whip; *spec:* craw (of certain birds); handle (of a whip). **vb** *lit:* clip, cut, lop, mow, shear, shorten, snip, trim; browse on, graze; *fig:* come (up), pop (up), turn (up).

cross *n lit:* crucifix, rood; crossing, intersection, junction; halfbreed, hybrid, mixture, mongrel; *fig:* affliction, burden, grief, trial. **vb** *lit:* intersect, meet; bridge, extend over, pass over, span; ford, go over, get over, traverse; hybridize, interbreed, mix; foil, frustrate, impede, oppose, thwart. **adj** *lit:* oblique, transverse; adverse, opposing; *fig:* angry, annoyed, grumpy, ill-humoured, impatient, peeved, snappish, sullen, surly, testy, waspish.

crowbar *n lit:* hook, jemmy, lever.

crowd *n lit:* army, flock, herd, host, mass, mob, multitude, pack, press, swarm, throng; bunch, clique, group, set; attendance, gate, spectators; masses, populace, public; plebs, proletariat, rabble. **vb** *lit:* assemble, cluster, congregate, flock, muster, swarm, throng; cram, huddle, mass, press, push, surge; congest, pack, pile into, squeeze into; elbow, jostle, shove.

crucial *adj lit:* critical, decisive, pivotal, vital.

cruel *adj lit:* barbarous, bloodthirsty, brutal, callous, fierce, hard-hearted, harsh, heartless, implacable, inhuman, inhumane, merciless, pitiless, relentless, ruthless, sadistic, savage, unfeeling, unnatural, vicious.

cruelty *n lit:* barbarity, bloodthirstiness, brutality, callousness, ferocity, fiendishness, harshness, heartlessness, inhumanity, murderousness, ruthlessness, sadism, savagery, viciousness.

crumb *n lit:* morsel, scrap; bit, shred, snippet.

crumble vb *lit:* break up, decompose, disintegrate, fall apart; crush, fragment, grind, triturate; *fig:* collapse, go to pieces.

crumple vb *lit:* crease, rumple, scrumple, wrinkle; break, collapse, give way; *fig:* cave in, yield; break down, go to pieces.

crush n *lit:* crowd, jam, press, squash, surge, throng. vb *lit:* compact, compress, crumble, crumple, grind, mangle, mash, mill, pound, squeeze; embrace, hug, press; conquer, overpower, overwhelm, rout, trounce; oppress, put down, quell, subdue, suppress; *fig:* abash, chagrin, humiliate, mortify, shame.

crust n *lit:* coating, covering, skin, surface; scab; mantle; dough, pastry; *fig:* effrontery, gall, impudence, nerve.

cry n *lit:* bellow, holler, scream, screech, shout, shriek, whoop, yell; bawl, weep; petition, prayer, supplication; proclamation; slogan, watchword; *spec:* call, sound (of an animal). vb *lit:* bellow, call out, holler, scream, screech, shout, shriek, sing out, ululate, whoop, yell; advertise, announce, broadcast, hawk, proclaim, publish, trumpet; bawl, blubber, greet, shed tears, weep.

cuddle n *lit:* embrace, hug; kiss, pet, smooch, snog. vb *lit:* embrace, hug; nestle, snuggle; fondle, pet, smooch, snog.

cuff n *lit:* wristband; turn-up; box on the ear, clip, smack; *fig:* bracelet(s), handcuff(s). vb *lit:* box the ears of, clip round the ear, smack one's head.

culprit n *lit:* guilty party, malefactor, miscreant, offender, transgressor.

cultivate vb *lit:* farm, tend, till, work; grow, plant; *fig:* civilize, develop, elevate, enrich, foster, improve, refine, train; associate with, consort with, court.

culture n *lit:* civilization, life-style, society, way of life; arts; education, enlightenment, erudition, polish, refinement, taste; agronomy, cultivation, farming, tillage; *spec:* growth (of bacteria etc. for experiment).

cultured adj *lit:* civilized, enlightened, genteel, lettered, polished, refined; erudite, highbrow, scholarly, well-read, well-versed.

cunning adj *lit:* artful, canny, crafty, devious, foxy, sharp, shrewd, smart, subtle, wily; clever, deft, dextrous, ingenious.

cup n *lit:* beaker, glass, mug, teacup; chalice, goblet; trophy, vase; bra, support.

cupboard n *lit:* cabinet, closet, dresser, press.

cure n *lit:* antidote, medicine, remedy, specific, treatment; spiritual care; *spec:* preservation (of meats). **vb** *lit:* correct, heal, mend, remedy, restore; *spec:* dry, pickle, salt, smoke.

curious adj *lit:* enquiring, inquisitive, questioning, searching; meddling, nosy, prying; novel, quaint; bizarre, extraordinary, odd, peculiar, singular, strange, unorthodox, unusual.

current n *lit:* draught, drift, flow, stream, tide; *fig:* mood, tendency, trend. **adj** *lit:* contemporary, ongoing, popular, present, present-day, up-to-the-minute; in, in fashion, trendy; circulating, common knowledge.

curse n *lit:* execration, expletive, oath, obscenity, swear-word; anathema, evil eye, hex, jinx, malediction; affliction, calamity, disaster, misfortune, plague; *fig:* menstrual period, menstruation. **vb** *lit:* blaspheme; cuss, swear; anathematize, damn, excommunicate; *fig:* blight, burden, plague, torment.

curved adj (pa.pt) *lit:* bent, bowed, hooked, humped, looping, rounded, sinuous, tortuous, winding.

custody n *lit:* care, charge, guardianship, keeping, perservation, protection, ward; confinement, detention, remand; ownership, possession.

custom n *lit:* convention, fashion, form, observance, practice, rule, usage; habit, routine, wont; clientèle, goodwill, patrons, trade.

customary adj *lit:* accepted, common, conventional, established, general, normal, ordinary, regular, routine, usual.

customer n *lit:* buyer, client, patron, purchaser, shopper; habitué, regular; *fig:* character, citizen.

cut n *lit:* gash, incision, laceration, nick, rip, slash, slit; chop, joint, steak; blow, knock, hit, slice; fashion, mode, shape, style; percentage, portion, rake-off, ration, share; decrease, economy, reduction, saving; *fig:* dig, gibe, slight; *spec:* (short) way.   **vb** *lit:* gash, incise, lacerate, nick, rip, slash, slit; chop, dice; carve, chisel, engrave, saw, sculpt, whittle; clip, dock, hack, hew, lop, mow, reap, shear, trim; divide, sever, slice (through), split (off); axe, decrease, economize on, reduce, save on; abbreviate, curtail, edit out, shorten, truncate; *fig:* cold-shoulder, ignore, ostracize, send to Coventry, snub.   **adj (pa.pt)** *lit:* incised, lacerated, ripped, slit; chopped; carved, engraved, sculpted, whittled; clipped, docked, lopped, shorn, trimmed; culled, harvested, mown, reaped; cleft, divided, severed, sliced, split; axed, decreased, reduced; abridged, curtailed, edited, shortened, truncated; *fig:* cold-shouldered, ostracized, slighted, snubbed.

cut off   vb *lit:* excise, remove, sever; amputate; isolate, separate; disconnect, interrupt, obstruct; bring to a halt, discontinue, suspend; *fig:* disinherit, disown.

cylinder   n *lit:* pipe, tube; drum, revolving chamber, roller; piston chamber.

cynic   n *lit:* misanthrope; disbeliever, sceptic; pessimist.

cynical   adj *lit:* misanthropic; disbelieving, distrustful, sceptical; ironic, sarcastic, sardonic, scornful; pessimistic.

D

dad n *lit:* da, daddy, father, guv'nor, old man, pa, papa, pater.

dam n *lit:* barrage, barrier, dyke, embankment, wall; reservoir, water supply; mother. **vb** *lit:* barricade, block up, hold back, hold in, restrain, restrict, stem.

damage n *lit:* harm, hurt, impairment, injury; destruction, devastation; *fig:* cost, expense, price, sum; reparation(s).
vb *lit:* harm, hurt, impair, injure; mutilate, ruin, spoil, vandalize, wreck.

damp n *lit:* clamminess, dankness, humidity, moisture; dew; *fig:* chill, gloom, restraint. **vb** *lit:* moisten, wet; water (down); *fig:* chill, deject, depress, dispirit, inhibit, restrain, stifle. **adj** *lit:* clammy, dank, humid, moist, muggy, wet; dewy, soggy.

dance n *lit:* ball, dinner, disco, hop, party, social, thé-dansant; measure, step; ballet. **vb** *lit:* take the floor, trip the light fantastic; boogie, bop, frug, jive, rock, shimmy; cavort, jig, leap, pirouette, prance, spin, sway, swing; *fig:* dart, flicker, flit, twinkle.

danger n *lit:* peril; hazard, jeopardy, risk; menace, threat.

dangerous adj *lit:* dicy, perilous; hairy, hazardous, precarious, risky; menacing, nasty, threatening, ugly.

daring n *lit:* audacity, boldness, bravery, courage, dauntlessness, derring-do, grit, guts, intrepidity, nerve, spirit, temerity, valour. **adj (pr.pt)** *lit:* audacious, bold, brave, courageous, dauntless, gritty, gutsy, intrepid, nerveless, spirited, temerarious, venturesome.

dark adj *lit:* brunette, dusky, ebony, swarthy; black, night-time, nocturnal, unlit; dim, dingy, murky, threatening; gloomy, grim, sombre; *fig:* doleful, morbid, mournful; cryptic, deep, enigmatic, mysterious, obscure, occult; diabolical, evil, foul, hellish, infernal, satanic, sinister, wicked; forbidding, glowering, ominous; ignorant, unenlightened, untaught.

darken vb *lit:* blacken, cloud over, dim; shadow; eclipse; *fig:* cast a pall over, depress, sadden; become harsh.

darling n *lit:* adored, apple of one's eye, angel, beloved, chérie, dearest, light of one's life, love, precious, sweetheart, treasure; blue-eyed boy, favourite, pet.

dash n *lit:* élan, flair, panache, style; dart, race, run, sprint; hint, pinch, smack, suggestion, touch. **vb** *lit:* fling, hurl, sling, throw; dart, fly, race, run, speed, sprint; shatter, shiver, smash; *fig:* blight, confound, disappoint, foil, frustrate, spoil, thwart.

data n *lit:* facts, figures, information, statistics.

dawn n *lit:* daybreak, sunrise, sunup; morning; *fig:* advent, birth, genesis, origin, outset, rise. **vb** *lit:* break, brighten, lighten; *fig:* begin, develop, emerge, originate, rise; hit, strike.

day n *lit:* 24 hours; date, hours of daylight, time; age, era, generation, period.

dead n *lit:* deceased, defunct, departed; *spec:* depth, middle (of night, of winter). **adj** *lit:* deceased, defunct, departed, perished; inanimate, lifeless, still; extinct, past; barren, inactive, obsolete, sterile; *fig:* inoperative, unproductive, useless; apathetic, indifferent, numb, paralysed, soulless, wooden; shattered, spent, worn out; empty; not in play; dull, flat, uninteresting; absolute, complete, total; certain, sure.

deadly adj *lit:* deathly, fatal, lethal, mortal; destructive, pernicious, poisonous, venomous; *fig:* grim, implacable, relentless, ruthless; accurate, precise, unerring; boring, tedious, uninteresting.

deaf adj *lit:* hard of hearing, unable to hear; *fig:* indifferent (to), oblivious (to), unresponsive (to).

deal n *lit:* agreement, arrangement, contract, transaction, understanding; amount, degree, extent, portion, proportion, share; distribution. **vb** *lit:* bargain, do business (with), trade (in), traffic (in); allot, dispense, distribute, divide, give (out), share (out); cope (with), have to do (with).

dealer n *lit:* merchant, trader, wholesaler; peddler, pusher; dispenser, distributor.

dear   n *lit:* angel, beloved, darling, love, precious, sweetheart, treasure.   **adj** *lit:* beloved, cherished, darling, precious, treasured; close, familiar, intimate; esteemed, respected, valued; costly, expensive.   **adv** *lit:* at a high price; considerably, very much.

death   n *lit:* decease, demise, departure, expiration, passing, release; bereavement, loss; mortality; grim reaper; *fig:* annihilation, destruction, end, extermination, extinction, ruination, undoing; *spec:* (in at the) kill.

debate   n *lit:* consideration, deliberation; dialogue, discussion, talk; argument, contention, dispute.   **vb** *lit:* consider, deliberate; discuss, talk over; argue, contend, dispute, wrangle over.

debt   n *lit:* arrears, due, liability, obligation, owed amount; debit, overdraft; (in) the red.

decay   n *lit:* atrophy, wasting, withering; decomposition, mortification, putrefaction, putrescence, rot, rotting; caries; mould; decadence, decline, degeneracy, degeneration, deterioration, disintegration.   **vb** *lit:* atrophy, waste, wither; corrode, decompose, mortify, putrefy, putresce, rot; crumble, decline, degenerate, deteriorate, disintegrate, moulder.

deceitful   adj *lit:* crafty, cunning, deceptive, dishonest, dissimulating, duplicitous, false, fraudulent, sly, treacherous, underhand, untrustworthy.

deceive   vb *lit:* bamboozle, cheat, con, double-cross, dupe, fool, hoax, swindle, take in, trick.

deception   n *lit:* cheating, chicanery, dissimulation, duplicity, fraudulence, legerdemain, swindling, treachery, trickery; artifice, fake, feint, fraud, hoax, imposture, lie, pretence, ruse, stratagem, subterfuge, swindle, trick.

deceptive   adj *lit:* ambiguous, ambivalent, fallacious, illusory, misleading, specious, unreliable, untrustworthy.

decide   vb *lit:* conclude, determine, make up one's mind, resolve; adjudicate, arbitrate, choose, elect, settle.

decision   n *lit:* conclusion, resolution; arbitration, choice, judgement, settlement; ruling, verdict; firmness, finality, resolve, strength of purpose.

decisive **adj** *lit:* conclusive, definite, definitive, final, positive; firm, forceful, resolute, strong; critical, crucial, fateful.

declare **vb** *lit:* affirm, announce, assert, depone, proclaim, pronounce, state, testify.

decline **n** *lit:* declivity, depression, downward slope; *fig:* decrease, diminution, downturn, falling off, recession, reduction; decay, degeneration, deterioration, weakening, worsening. **vb** *lit:* descend, dip, sink, slope downwards; *fig:* decrease, diminish, fall off, lessen, shrink, take a downturn; decay, degenerate, deteriorate, weaken, worsen; forgo, reject, say no to, turn down.

decoration **n** *lit:* adornment, elaboration, embellishment, garnish, ornamentation, tinsel, trimmings; bauble, flourish, frill, ornament; award, colours, medal, order, ribbon.

decrease **n** *lit:* abatement, decline, diminution, drop, easing, falling off, lessening, reduction, shrinking, slackening, subsidence, waning. **vb** *lit:* abate, decline, diminish, drop, ease, fall off, lessen, shrink, slacken, subside, wane; make less, reduce.

deduce **vb** *lit:* conclude, derive, gather, infer, understand; extrapolate.

deduction **n** *lit:* conclusion, corollary, extrapolation, inference, reasoning, rider; debit, decrease, reduction, subtraction, withdrawal.

deep **adj** *lit:* abyssal, yawning; broad, wide; *fig:* extreme, great, intense, profound; abstruse, cryptic, esoteric, mysterious, obscure; absorbed, engrossed, immersed, rapt; discerning, penetrating, sagacious, wise; erudite, learned; artful, canny, cunning, devious, knowing, shrewd; *spec:* bass, low, resonant (voice); dark, rich, strong (colour).

defeat **n** *lit:* beating, overthrow, rout, thrashing, trouncing; discomfiture, failure, rebuff, repulse, reverse, setback; strategic withdrawal. **vb** *lit:* beat, crush, overthrow, rout, thrash, trounce; confound, discomfit, foil, stop, thwart.

defect n *lit:* blemish, fault, flaw, imperfection; error, inaccuracy, mistake; absence, deficiency, inadequacy, lack, weakness.
vb *lit:* change sides, desert, go over (to), run (to).

defective adj *lit:* broken, faulty, imperfect, incomplete, inoperative, out of order; lacking, scant, short; retarded, subnormal.

defence n *lit:* barricade, bastion, bulwark, fortification; cover, guard, protection, security, shelter, shield; alibi, denial, excuse, explanation, justification, rebuttal, refutation, vindication; *spec:* backs (in field games).

defend vb *lit:* barricade, fortify; cover, guard, keep safe, preserve, protect, shelter, shield; champion, justify, speak up for, support, uphold, vindicate.

defensive adj *lit:* covering, guarding, preserving, protective, sheltering, shielding; precautionary; hunted, wary; apologetic, explanatory, justificatory.

defiant adj *lit:* contumacious, disobedient, insubordinate, mutinous, rebellious, recalcitrant, refractory, truculent, wilful; bold, challenging, daring.

deficiency n *lit:* absence, deficit, inadequacy, incompleteness, insufficiency, lack, scarcity. shortage; failing, shortcoming, weakness.

deficit n *lit:* shortage, shortfall; overdraft; arrears.

define vb *lit:* describe, designate, explain, gloss, interpret, specify, spell out; circumscribe, delineate, limit, mark, set the parameters of.

definite adj *lit:* clear, exact, explicit, express, fixed, precise; certain, positive, settled, sure.

deflect vb *lit:* avert, edge, fend off, parry, ward off; glance off, ricochet; slew, swerve, turn, veer.

deformity n *lit:* abnormality, defect, disfigurement, malformation; distortion, mutilation; ugliness.

defy vb *lit:* brave, challenge, confront, face; baffle, defeat, foil, frustrate, resist, thwart; be contumacious towards, be recalcitrant towards, be refractory towards, be truculent towards, disobey, flout, mutiny against, rebel against.

degree n *lit:* extent, intensity, level, measure, quality, quantity, rate, scale, standard; division, gradation, grade, mark, point, rung, step, unit; class, position, rank, standing, status; *spec:* (university) honour, qualification.

delay n *lit:* adjournment, deferment, postponement; stay, suspension; hold-up, interval, stoppage, wait. **vb** *lit:* adjourn, defer, postpone, put off, suspend; check, detain, hold up, retard, slow, stop; dally, dawdle, linger, tarry.

delete vb *lit:* cut out, edit out, erase, expunge, rub out; cancel, cross out, obliterate, strike out; leave out, omit.

deliberate vb *lit:* consider, debate, meditate (over), mull (over), ponder (over), think (over). **adj** *lit:* calculated, conscious, considered, intentional, premeditated, studied, voluntary; measured, methodical, prudent, unhurried.

delicacy n *lit:* daintiness, elegance, lightness; fastidiousness, finesse, precision; subtlety; fragility, frailty, infirmity; refinement, sensibility, taste; cake, dainty, savoury, sweet, titbit.

delicate adj *lit:* dainty, elegant, exquisite, fine, graceful, light; deft, expert, fastidious, precise; diplomatic, discreet, subtle, tactful; fragile, frail, sickly, squeamish, weak; discriminating, prudish, refined, sensitive; critical, difficult, ticklish, touchy; faint, muted, soft, subdued.

delicious adj *lit:* appetizing, delectable, luscious, mouthwatering, scrumptious, tasty; delightful, exquisite, pleasing, pleasurable.

delight n *lit:* gratification, happiness, pleasure, rapture; gem, joy, prize, treasure. **vb** *lit:* captivate, charm, enchant, gratify, make happy, please, ravish; amuse, divert, entertain.

delightful adj *lit:* agreeable, captivating, charming, enchanting, gratifying, pleasant, pleasing, pleasurable; amusing, diverting, entertaining.

deliver vb *lit:* bear, bring, carry, convey, transport; provide, supply; dispense, distribute, give out; give (to), hand over, transfer, turn over (to); cede (to), grant (to), yield (to); administer, deal, inflict; liberate, loose, release, save, set free; present, proclaim, publish, read; strike, throw.

delivery n *lit:* consignment, dispatch, distribution; conveyance, transmittal; supply, transmission; ceding, surrender; liberation, release, rescue; elocution, enunciation, intonation; birth, childbirth, labour; bowl, pitch.

delusion n *lit:* hallucination, misapprehension, misbelief, misconception, self-deception.

demand n *lit:* call, need, request, requirement; charge, claim, order, requisition. **vb** *lit:* claim, exact, insist on, request, require; call for, necessitate, need; entail, involve.

demolish **vb** *lit:* bulldoze, destroy, flatten, level, pull down, raze, tear down; *fig:* annihilate, defeat, drub, thrash, trounce; confound, overturn, totally disprove, undo; devour, gobble up, put away, stuff away.

demolition n *lit:* bulldozing, destruction, levelling, pulling down, wrecking.

demonstrate **vb** *lit:* illustrate, show, teach by example; display, evince, exhibit, make clear, manifest; march, picket, rally.

demonstration n *lit:* display, exhibition, exposition, illustration, manifestation, presentation; evidence, proof, testimony; march, parade, protest.

density n *lit:* consistency; body, compactness, homogeneity; bulk, solidity, thickness; *fig:* imbecility, obtuseness, slowness, stupidity; *spec:* specific gravity.

dent n *lit:* bend, buckle, concavity, depression, imprint, pit, stamp; notch. **vb** *lit:* bend, buckle, crease, gouge, imprint, push in.

deny **vb** *lit:* disclaim, disown, renounce, repudiate; contradict, gainsay, rebuff, refute; forbid, refuse; begrudge; negate.

depart **vb** *lit:* blow, evaporate, exit, go, go away, leave, move out, scarper, set out, take one's leave, vamoose; disappear, vanish; retire, withdraw; deviate, diverge, stray; swerve (from), veer (from).

department n *lit:* bureau, division, office, section; *fig:* business, domain, line, look-out, province, responsibility, sphere.

departure n *lit:* exit, going, leaving, moving out, setting out; retiring, withdrawal; deviation, divergence, straying; change, difference, innovation, novelty; *fig:* death, decease, demise; *spec:* latitudinal distance.

depend vb *lit:* bank (on), count (on), lean (on), rely (on); calculate (on), reckon (on); be based (on), be contingent (upon), hinge (upon).

dependent adj *lit:* conditional (on), contingent (on); based (on), calculated (on); reliant; feudal, liege.

deposit n *lit:* alluvium, dregs, lees, sediment; precipitate; loess, silt; down payment, premium, retainer, stake. vb *lit:* lay, place, put, set; drop, settle; bank, lodge, pay in, put in.

depravity n *lit:* amorality, debauchery, degeneracy, lasciviousness, licentiousness, perversion, vice, wickedness.

depress vb *lit:* lower, press down, push down; cast down, desolate, grieve, sadden; daunt, discourage, dispirit, put off; hinder, retard, slow, weaken; cheapen, debase, devalue, downgrade, reduce.

depression n *lit:* basin, bowl, concavity, dell, dip, hollow, indentation; dejection, desolation, despair, despondency, hopelessness, melancholia, sadness; decline, recession, slump, stagnation.

deprivation n *lit:* bereavement, confiscation, dispossession, lack, loss, removal, withdrawal; destitution, hardship, need, privation.

deprive vb *lit:* bereave, dispossess, divest; rob, strip; withhold the benefit (of), withhold the use (of).

depth n *lit:* breadth, drop, profundity, vertical measure, width; *fig:* intensity, strength; complexity, intricacy, involvement; insight, penetration, perception, sagacity, wisdom; erudition, learning, scholarship; (in the) middle (of), (in the) midst (of); *spec:* low pitch, profundo (of voice); darkness, richness, vibrance (of colour).

deputy n *lit:* agent, delegate, locum, proxy, representative; assistant, lieutenant, second-in-command; relief, stand-in, substitute, understudy; *spec:* legislator, member of the assembly (in certain countries); safety inspector (in a coal-mine).

derelict n *lit:* down-and-out, no-hoper, tramp, vagrant; hulk, skeleton, wreck; abandoned vessel. **adj** *lit:* abandoned, deserted, forsaken; dilapidated, skeletal, ruined, wrecked; failing, lax, negligent, remiss.

descend vb *lit:* go down, sink, subside; drop, fall, plummet, plunge; alight, climb down, dismount; pounce (upon), swoop (upon); dip, slant down, slope down; decrease, diminish, lessen, reduce; *fig:* be handed down, be passed on; be derived (from), originate (from), spring (from); lower oneself (to), stoop (to); degenerate, deteriorate.

descendants n *lit:* children, grandchildren, heirs, inheritors, issue, offspring, posterity, progeny, scions, successors.

describe vb *lit:* delineate, draw, limn, mark out, outline; characterize, depict, detail, portray, represent; give an account of, relate, tell.

description n *lit:* characterization, depiction, portrayal, representation, verbal sketch; account, narration, report, story; appearance, character, look, manner, mien, type, variety.

desert n *lit:* waste, wasteland; dunes, sand; maquis, outback, pampas, scrub, veldt, wilderness; tundra; isolation, remoteness, solitude. **vb** *lit:* abandon, forsake, walk out on; jilt, leave in the lurch, maroon, rat on, strand; leave, quit, vacate; abscond, defect, run away.

deserve vb *lit:* be worthy of, justify, merit, rate, warrant.

design n *lit:* draft, drawing, elevation, outline, plan, sketch; blueprint, pattern, template; configuration, figure, form, motif; architecture, graphics, technical drawing; *fig:* aim, end, goal, intention, object, objective, target; enterprise, project, scheme; intrigue(s), machination(s). **vb** *lit:* draft, draw, outline, plan, sketch; contrive, devise, fashion, invent; aim, intend, mean, propose, purpose.

desirable adj *lit:* alluring, seductive, sexy, tempting; advantageous, beneficial, good, preferable, profitable, useful, welcome.

desire n *lit:* ambition, aspiration, hope, wish; craving, hunger, longing, yearning; lechery, libido, lust, orexis, sex drive. **vb** *lit:* entreat, petition, request, solicit; aspire to, hope for, wish for; fancy, set one's heart on, want; crave, hunger for, long for, yearn for; lust after.

desk n *lit:* bureau, escritoire, secretary, writing-table; lectern, pulpit; counter, department, kiosk, office, stall; stand.

despair n *lit:* depression, hopelessness, futility, misery, utter dejection, wretchedness; great disappointment. **vb** *lit:* be depressed, be suicidal; abandon hope (of), give up, lose hope (of).

desperate adj *lit:* forlorn, hopeless, suicidal, wretched; critical, dire, drastic, urgent; dangerous, daring, hazardous, risky, wild; determined; frantic.

desperately adv *lit:* forlornly, hopelessly, suicidally, wretchedly; critically, direly, drastically, urgently; dangerously, gravely, seriously, severely; *fig:* extremely, very.

despise vb *lit:* deride, disdain, look down on, look upon with contempt, scorn, spurn.

despite prp *lit:* in spite of, notwithstanding, regardless of.

dessert n *lit:* afters, pudding, sweet; last course; blancmange, cream, fool, jelly, trifle, whip.

destination n *lit:* journey's end, goal, stop, target; *fig:* aim, end, object, objective, purpose.

destroy vb *lit:* abolish, annihilate, dash to pieces, demolish, dismantle, do away with, exterminate, extirpate, kill, pull down, put an end to, ravage, raze, ruin, shatter, smash, tear down, wipe out, wreck.

destruction n *lit:* abolition, annihilation, demolition, dismantling, eradication, extermination, extinction, extirpation, killing, massacre, pulling down, ruin, shattering, slaughter, smashing, tearing down, undoing, wreckage.

detach vb *lit:* disconnect, disengage, disunite, free, loosen, separate, sever, tear off, unfasten, unhitch; demarcate, designate, pick out, single out.

detachment n *lit:* disconnection, disengagement, separation, unfastening; distance, non-involvement; aloofness, remoteness, unconcern; impartiality, neutrality, objectivity; demarcation, designation, selection; *spec:* detail, party, squad, unit (of the armed forces).

detail n *lit:* particular(s), small point(s), specific(s), technicality; component, element, factor, item; nicety, trivium; *spec:* detachment, party, squad, unit (of the armed forces). **vb** *lit:* catalogue, enumerate, itemize, list, specify; describe, give an account, narrate, recount; designate, detach, pick out, single out.

detect vb *lit:* discern, distinguish, identify, make out, notice, perceive, scent, spot, spy; discover, find, find out, track down, uncover; *spec:* demodulate (a signal from its carrier wave).

deterioration n *lit:* decline, degeneration, degradation, detriment, downturn, fall, impairment, regression, slide, worsening.

determine vb *lit:* decide, make up one's mind, purpose, resolve; ascertain, calculate, discover, establish, find out, learn, work out; condition, control, dictate, govern, regulate, rule; conclude, end, finish, settle, terminate.

detour n *lit:* deviation, diversion; circumnavigation, digression, excursion, roundabout way. **vb** *lit:* circumnavigate, deviate round, digress, find a way round, make a diversion.

devalue vb *lit:* cheapen, debase, degrade; depreciate, weaken; inflate, make worthless.

develop vb *lit:* begin, commence, establish, generate, invent, originate, start; evolve, form, grow, mature, progress; breed, cultivate, foster, promote, rear; contract; *spec:* elaborate on, take further (a musical theme, a chess manoeuvre); print (a photograph).

development n *lit:* advance, evolution, growth, increase, maturation, progress; circumstance, event, happening, occurrence, situation; serial expression.

device n *lit:* apparatus, appliance, contraption, gadget, instrument, tool; artifice, contrivance, dodge, gambit, manoeuvre, ploy, stratagem, strategy, wile; badge, colophon, emblem, logo, motif, trademark.

devious adj *lit:* artful, calculating, cunning, indirect, scheming, sly, underhand, wily; circuitous, erratic, rambling, roundabout, twisting, winding.

devise vb *lit:* contrive, design, dream up, frame, invent, plan, think up, work out; compose, write; bequeath, leave.

devoted adj (pa.pt) *lit:* committed, consecrated, dedicated, pledged; ardent, caring, loving, loyal, true.

devout adj *lit:* ardent, devoted, earnest, fervent, passionate, sincere, zealous; godly, holy, pious, religious; solemn.

diagram n *lit:* artwork, chart, graphic, layout, outline, plan; cross-section, exploded view, representation.

dialogue n *lit:* conversation, discourse, discussion; two-way communication; *fig:* lines, script, words.

dictator n *lit:* absolute ruler, autocrat; despot, tyrant.

dictatorial adj *lit:* autocratic, despotic, tyrannical; authoritarian, disciplinarian, imperious, magisterial, oppressive, totalitarian.

die n *lit:* mould, stamp, template; dice; *spec:* basis, pedestal (for a sculpture or column). vb *lit:* breathe one's last, depart this life, expire, fall asleep, give up the ghost, pass away, pass over; cash in one's chips, croak, kick the bucket, peg out, pop one's clogs, snuff it; be killed, be slain, fall, lay down one's life, perish; *fig:* decline, dwindle, ebb, fade, fizzle out, lapse, pass, peter out, run down, sink, stop, subside, wane, wilt, wither; ache (for), hunger (for), long (for).

diet n *lit:* fare, food, nourishment, nutriment, subsistence; controlled intake, course of regulated meals, fast, regimen. vb *lit:* fast, lose weight, slim.

differ vb *lit:* be distinct (from), depart (from), diverge (from), vary (from); contend (with), contrast (with), demur (with), take issue (with).

difference n *lit:* contrast, disparity, dissimilarity, variation; change, discrepancy, divergence; distinction, exception, particularity, singularity; clash, conflict, contention; contretemps, disagreement, dispute, squabble; balance, remainder, rest; *spec:* modification (on a coat of arms).

different adj *lit:* at odds, at variance, contrasting, disparate, diverse, miscellaneous, varied, various; changed, divergent; atypical, distinctive, exceptional, particular, singular, uncommon, unique; clashing, contentious, conflicting, opposed, opposite; additional, distinct, individual, new, other, separate.

difficult adj *lit:* complicated, demanding, intricate, involved, problematical, taxing; arduous, burdensome, hard, laborious, painstaking, strenuous; knotty, thorny, ticklish, uphill; awkward, grim, straitened, trying; fractious, obstreperous, refractory, troublesome, unmanageable; fastidious, fussy, hard to please, pedantic, tiresome.

difficulty n *lit:* burden, hardship, labour, strenuousness, toil; complication, hurdle, impediment, obstacle, pitfall, stumbling-block; dilemma, enigma, intricacy, problem, predicament, quandary; fix, jam, mess, pickle, plight, spot of trouble; danger, distress, jeopardy, peril.

dig n *lit:* archaeological site, excavation; jab, poke, prod, thrust; *fig:* gibe, sarcastic remark, sneer, taunt, wisecrack. vb *lit:* burrow, delve, excavate, mine, quarry, scoop, tunnel; break up, fork, hoe, spade over, till, turn over; jab, poke, prod, thrust; *fig:* go (into), probe (into), research (into); find (out), root (out); appreciate, enjoy, like, understand.

digest n *lit:* abstract, condensation, paraphrase, précis, résumé, summary, synopsis. vb *lit:* absorb, assimilate, metabolize; abridge, condense, paraphrase, reduce, shorten, summarize; *fig:* consider, contemplate, meditate over, ponder, take in, understand; bear, brook, endure, stand, stomach, tolerate.

digestion n *lit:* absorption, assimilation, incorporation, metabolism; *fig:* consideration, contemplation, meditation, pondering; stomach.

dignified   adj (pa.pt) *lit:* august, decorous, formal, grave, imposing, noble, solemn, stately; lofty, lordly; exalted.

dignity   n *lit:* decorum, grandeur, majesty, nobility, solemnity, stateliness; hauteur, loftiness; eminence, honour, importance, rank, standing, status; pride, self-esteem.

dilute   vb *lit:* thin, water down; adulterate, cut, weaken; *fig:* attenuate, mitigate, temper; decrease, lessen, reduce.   adj *lit:* thin, watered down, watery; adulterated, cut, weakened; insipid, tasteless; *fig:* attenuated, mitigated, tempered; decreased, lessened, reduced.

dim   vb *lit:* dull, fade out, turn down; become obscure, blur, darken, obscure; tarnish.   adj *lit:* cloudy, grey, overcast, shadowy; blurred, dark, fuzzy, indistinct, obscure; dingy, dull, opaque, tarnished; pale, weak; *fig:* confused, hazy, vague; depressing, discouraging, gloomy, sombre; dense, obtuse, slow, stupid, thick.

dine   vb *lit:* eat, feed; have dinner, have lunch, have supper; banquet, feast.

dinner   n *lit:* lunch, supper, tea; banquet, feast, spread; meal, repast.

diploma   n *lit:* certificate, charter, document; degree, doctorate; honour.

diplomat   n *lit:* ambassador, attaché, chargé d'affaires, consul, envoy, foreign office official, government spokesperson, legate, representative, statesman; mediator, negotiator.

diplomatic   adj *lit:* ambassadorial, consular, governmental, official, state; politic, prudent; discreet, subtle, tactful.

direct   vb *lit:* guide, indicate how to get (to), lead, point the way (to), show (towards), usher; administer, conduct, control, govern, manage, oversee, rule, run, superintend; command, instruct, order; address, aim, level, point, train; post, route, send.   adj *lit:* straight, undeviating; face-to-face, head-on, immediate; nonstop, through; blunt, explicit, outspoken, plain, straightforward, unambiguous, unequivocal; candid, frank, honest, open, sincere; *spec:* quoted, verbatim (speech, words).

direction n *lit:* bearing, compass-point, course, line, orientation; guidance, indication, lead; administration, control, governing, management, ruling, running, superintending, supervision; commands, instruction, orders; address, destination.

directly adv *lit:* straight, without deviation; face-to-face, in person; at once, immediately, instantly, promptly, right away, straight away; bluntly, plainly, straightforwardly, unambiguously, unequivocally; candidly, frankly, honestly, openly, sincerely.

director n *lit:* administrator, governor, manager, member of the board, organizer, supervisor; boss, chief, controller, head, leader.

dirt n *lit:* filth, grime, mud, slime; excrement, faeces, muck, prurience, scatology; earth, soil; foreign body, impurity; *fig:* concupiscence, obscenity, pornography, salacity, smut; gossip, low-down, scandal.

dirty vb *lit:* befoul, defile, mess up, soil, stain. adj *lit:* filthy, foul, grimy, grubby, mucky, muddy, polluted, slimy, soiled; dingy, discoloured, dusty, murky, shabby, squalid, tarnished; *fig:* blue, faecal, coprological, indecent, obscene, pornographic, prurient, salacious, scabrous, scatalogical, smutty; corrupt, dishonest, fraudulent, illegal; mean, treacherous; rainy, squally.

disable vb *lit:* cripple, debilitate, hamstring, handicap, incapacitate, put out of action, render incapable; paralyse; disqualify, invalidate.

disabled adj (pa.pt) *lit:* crippled, debilitated, hamstrung, handicapped, incapacitated, out of action; bedridden, in a wheelchair; paralysed; disqualified, invalidated.

disadvantage n *lit:* burden, handicap, hardship, impediment, inconvenience, liability; flaw, minus, trouble, weakness; detriment, loss. vb *lit:* burden, create problems for, handicap, hinder, impede, inconvenience.

disagree vb *lit:* be opposed, clash, conflict, contradict, differ, diverge; argue, bicker, dispute, dissent, quarrel, wrangle; cause trouble (with oneself), cause problems (with oneself); be different, be unequal, be unmatching.

disagreeable adj *lit:* bad-tempered, churlish, cross, difficult, ill-natured, peevish, unfriendly, unlikable; disgusting, distasteful, nasty, obnoxious, offensive, repellent, repulsive.

disappear   vb *lit:* evanesce, fade out, melt away, vanish; be lost to view, go, leave, pass from one's sight; escape, flee, fly; be lost; die, ebb, peter out, taper off, wane.

disappearance   n *lit:* evanescence, evaporation, vanishing; departure, desertion, going, leaving; escape, flight; absence, eclipse, loss; end, passing, petering out, tapering off, waning.

disappoint   vb *lit:* chagrin, dash, dismay; fail, let one down; foil, frustrate, thwart.

disappointment   n *lit:* chagrin, dismay; dejection, discouragement; disillusion, letdown; frustration, misfortune, setback.

disapprove of   vb *lit:* deplore, deprecate, dislike, frown on, take exception to; condemn, object to.

disaster   n *lit:* calamity, cataclysm, catastrophe, ruination, tragedy; blow, misfortune, reverse, trouble.

disastrous   adj *lit:* calamitous, cataclysmic, catastrophic, ruinous, tragic; devastating, dire; ill-starred, unlucky.

discard   vb *lit:* chuck out, dispense with, dispose of, ditch, drop, dump, get rid of, jettison, throw away.

discern   vb *lit:* distinguish, make out, observe, perceive, recognize, see, sense; discriminate (between), judge (between), tell.

discharge   n *lit:* emission, flux, oozing, secretion, seepage, suppuration; emptying, evacuation, unburdening, unloading; demobilization, dismissal, ejection, release; acquittal, freeing, liberation, remission; payment, settlement; accomplishment, execution, fulfilment, observance; blast, detonation, firing, shooting.   vb   *lit:* emit, exude, give off, leak, ooze, secrete, seep, suppurate; empty, evacuate, unburden, unload; cashier, demobilize, dismiss, eject, expel, release, remove, sack; acquit, clear, free, liberate, remit; pay, settle; accomplish, do, execute, fulfil, observe, perform; blast, detonate, fire, set off, shoot.

discipline   n *lit:* control, order, regulation; practice, regimen,

training; chastisement, correction, punishment, strictness; area, branch, field, specialism, specialty; *spec:* (sports) event.
vb *lit:* chastise, correct, punish; be strict with, break in, control, drill, educate, exercise, regulate, train.

discolour **vb** *lit:* soil, stain, tarnish; bleach, etiolate, fade, lighten, pale, yellow; darken.

disconnect **vb** *lit:* detach, disengage, put asunder, separate, take apart, uncouple, undo; free, loosen, release; cut off, switch off, turn off.

discount **n** *lit:* concession, cut, price-cut, rebate, reduction.
vb *lit:* disbelieve, disregard, ignore, let pass, take with a pinch of salt; give a reduction, mark down, reduce.

discover **vb** *lit:* come across, find, light upon; bring to light, dig up, reveal, turn up, uncover, unearth; ascertain, detect, discern, find out, learn; notice, perceive, realize, see, spot; conceive, devise, invent, make, originate.

discovery **n** *lit:* digging up, finding, turning up, unearthing; ascertaining, detection, discerning, learning; noticing, perceiving, realization, seeing, spotting; conception, creation, introduction, invention, origination.

discreet **adj** *lit:* diplomatic, tactful; judicious, politic, sensible; cautious, guarded, prudent, wary.

discriminate **vb** *lit:* differentiate (between), distinguish (between), draw a distinction (between); act unjustly (against), be biased (against), be prejudiced (against).

discuss **vb** *lit:* confer about, consult about, converse about, debate, go into, talk over.

discussion **n** *lit:* conference, consultation, conversation, debate, talk; dialogue, exchange of views; negotiation, talks.

disease **n** *lit:* ailment, complaint, disorder, illness, malady, sickness; blight, contagion, infection, infestation; condition; *fig:* failing, vice, weakness.

disfigurement n *lit:* blemish, deformity, malformation, mutilation, scar; blot, blotch, mark, spot, stain.

disgrace n *lit:* dishonour, ignominy, odium, opprobrium; humiliation, shame; degradation; aspersion, reproach, slur, stain, stigma. **vb** *lit:* bring shame upon, discredit, dishonour, sully; humiliate, mortify, shame; expose, show up.

disgraceful adj *lit:* appalling, contemptible, detestable, disgusting, infamous, outrageous, scandalous, shameful, shocking; dishonourable, ignominious, opprobrious, unworthy.

disguise n *lit:* façade, front, imposture, semblance, simulation; costume; camouflage, cover. **vb** *lit:* dress up (as), make up (as); camouflage, hide, mask, screen, veil; dissimulate, falsify.

disgust n *lit:* abhorrence, aversion, detestation, distaste, loathing, nausea, repugnance, revulsion. **vb** *lit:* fill with loathing, nauseate, offend, outrage, repel, revolt, sicken, turn one's stomach.

dish n *lit:* plate, platter; bowl, saucer; course, preparation, recipe. **vb** *lit:* foil, frustrate, mess up one's chances, ruin, spoil, thwart, wreck.

dishonest adj *lit:* bent, corrupt, crooked, false, lying, mendacious, perfidious, treacherous, unscrupulous, untrustworthy, untruthful; deceitful, dissimulating, economical with the truth, sham.

disillusion n *lit:* disappointment, disenchantment; true perception, undeception; anticlimax. **vb** *lit:* bring down to earth, disabuse, disenchant, open one's eyes, undeceive; disappoint, fail, let down.

disintegration n *lit:* break-up, collapse, crumbling, decomposition, destruction, falling apart, fission, fragmentation, shattering; *spec:* (radioactive) decay.

dislike n *lit:* antipathy, aversion, disapproval, disfavour, distaste.
vb *lit:* be antipathetic towards, be averse to, be disinclined to, disapprove of, disfavour, have a distaste for, object to.

dismal adj *lit:* bleak, cheerless, dark, depressing, discouraging, gloomy, lowering, lugubrious, sombre; boring, dreary, dull, tedious.

dismiss   vb *lit:* discharge, give one's leave, send away; axe, cashier, chuck out, expel, fire, give the boot, give the sack, lay off, make redundant, remove, sack, send down, send packing; banish, dispel, shelve.

dismissal   n *lit:* discharge, dispatch, leave to go, marching orders, release; expulsion, laying off, notice, redundancy, removal, sacking.

disorder   n *lit:* chaos, confusion, disarray, disorganization, disruption, untidiness; anarchy, lawlessness; derangement, dishevelment, dislocation.

disperse   vb *lit:* broadcast, diffuse, disseminate, scatter, spread, strew; break up, separate; dispel, dissipate, dissolve.

display   n *lit:* exhibition, parade, show; array, presentation, spectacle; façade, imposture, ostentation, pretence.
vb *lit:* demonstrate, evince, exhibit, parade, present, reveal, show; betray, disclose; boast, flaunt, flourish, vaunt.

displease   vb *lit:* annoy, be disagreeable to, exasperate, gall, irk, irritate, offend, put out, upset, vex.

dispose   vb *lit:* adjust, arrange, group, marshal, order, place, put, set, stand; bias (towards), condition (to), incline (to), influence (towards), move (to), prompt (to); make an end (of), free oneself (of); get rid (of), rid oneself (of).

dispute   n *lit:* argument, contention, debate, disagreement, dissension; altercation, conflict, discord, friction, quarrel, wrangle.   vb *lit:* argue with, contend with, challenge, contradict, debate, disagree with, dissent to, quarrel with, question; clash with, squabble with, wrangle with.

disqualification   n *lit:* disbarment, disentitlement, elimination, exclusion, expulsion; incapacitation, ineligibility.

disregard   n *lit:* heedlessness, ignoring, neglect, negligence; disdain, disrespect, indifference.   vb *lit:* discount, ignore, neglect, pass over, pay no attention to, take no notice of, turn a blind eye to; brush aside, laugh off, make light of; cut dead, snub, walk straight past.

disrespectful   adj *lit:* cheeky, discourteous, impertinent, impudent, insolent, irreverent, rude; irreverent, sacrilegious.

disruptive adj *lit:* anarchic, destructive, disorderly, distracting, obstreperous, troublesome, unruly, upsetting.

dissolve vb *lit:* deliquesce, liquefy, melt, thaw; break down, break up, crumble, decompose, disintegrate, disperse, dissipate, evaporate, fade away, vanish; dismantle, dismember, disunite, loose, separate; *fig:* adjourn, discontinue, suspend; annul, cancel, conclude, end, finish, terminate.

dissuade vb *lit:* deter, disincline, put off; discourage.

distance n *lit:* extent, range, reach, remove, separation, space, stretch; gap, interval; *fig:* coldness, coolness, reserve, restraint. vb *lit:* leave behind, outrun, outstrip; dissociate (oneself from), separate (oneself from).

distant adj *lit:* faraway, far-flung, far-removed, remote; apart, disparate, distinct, outlying, scattered, separate; faint, indistinct, obscure; *fig:* cold, cool, formal, reserved, restrained, reticent, withdrawn.

distinct adj *lit:* detached, discrete, separate, unconnected; different, individual; apparent, clear, evident, manifest, marked, noticeable, patent, plain, recognizable, unmistakable, well-defined.

distinction n *lit:* contrast, difference; differentiation, discernment, discrimination, separation; characteristic, idiosyncrasy, individuality, particularity, peculiarity, singularity, uniqueness; celebrity, credit, eminence, fame, honour, note, prominence, worth; award, prize.

distinctive adj *lit:* different, distinguishable, extraordinary, individual, original, particular, peculiar, singular, special, unique.

distinguish vb *lit:* differentiate, discriminate, tell apart; discern, make out, perceive, pick out, recognize, see; individualize, label, mark out, separate, single out; glorify, make famous.

distort vb *lit:* bend, bow, buckle, deform, twist, warp; *fig:* misrepresent, pervert, slant.

distress n *lit:* discomfort, misery, suffering, wretchedness; anguish, grief, pain, torment, woe; blow, calamity, difficulty, hardship, misfortune, privation, trial. vb *lit:* pain, torment, trouble, upset; bother, disturb, harass, worry; grieve, sadden, wound.

distribution n *lit:* allocation, allotment, apportionment, dispensing, dispersion, dissemination, division, doling out, giving out, handing out, measuring out, scattering, spreading; dispersal, extent, range, scope, spread; arrangement, disposition, grouping; delivery, dispatch, handling, transportation.

distrust n *lit:* chariness, doubt, scepticism, suspicion, wariness. vb *lit:* be chary of, be suspicious of, have doubts about, suspect.

disturb vb *lit:* bother, disrupt, distract, inconvenience, interrupt, intrude on; trouble; annoy, harass, pester, plague, worry; discompose, distress, fluster, perturb, ruffle, shake, unsettle; derange, disorder, interfere with, touch.

disturbance n *lit:* agitation, disorder, distraction, upset; interruption, intrusion, interference; barney, bother, broil, commotion, demo, fracas, hubbub, ruckus, ruction, rumble, rumpus, stramash, tumult, uproar.

ditch n *lit:* channel, drain, dyke, fosse, gully, trench, verge. vb *lit:* dig a channel in, drain, excavate, irrigate; land on water; *fig:* discard, drop, dump, get rid of, jettison; abandon, maroon, leave in the lurch.

diversion n *lit:* detour, deviation, digression; amusement, delectation, enjoyment, entertainment, gratification, pleasure, recreation, sport.

divert vb *lit:* avert, deflect, fend off, parry, redirect, turn aside, ward off; distract (from), draw away (from), lead away (from), sidetrack; *fig:* amuse, delight, entertain, gratify.

divide n *lit:* border, division, margin, partition; *spec:* border hills, watershed. vb *lit:* bisect, halve, split in two; cut (up), disconnect, part, segregate, separate, sever, sunder; arrange, order, sort; allot, dispense, distribute, measure out, share; alienate, break up, come between, disrupt, estrange, interpose between.

divine n *lit:* churchman, clergyman, cleric, minister, priest, reverend; doctor of divinity, theologian. vb *lit:* apprehend, deduce, discern, infer, perceive, understand; conjecture, foretell, predict; dowse. adj *lit:* godly, hallowed, holy, religious, sacred, spiritual; celestial, godlike, heavenly; beatific, mystic, numinous, transcendental;

fig: angelic, beautiful, lovely, perfect, wonderful.

division n *lit:* bisection, halving, splitting in two; disconnection, parting, segregation, separation, severing, sundering; ordering, sorting; allocation, dispensing, distribution, measuring out, sharing; alienation, break-up, disruption, divorce, estrangement, interruption.

divorce n *lit:* break, disunion, estrangement, parting, rupture, separation, splitting, sundering; annulment, decree nisi. **vb** *lit:* dissociate, disunite, divide, part, separate, sever, split up, sunder; be separated from; have one's marriage dissolved.

do n *lit:* celebration, banquet, dance, event, feast, function, occasion, party. **vb** *lit:* accomplish, carry out, execute, perform, render, undertake, work at; bring about, cause, effect; create, make, produce; achieve, complete, conclude, empty, exhaust, finish; cover, go, proceed, travel; journey through, look at, tour, visit; act, behave, conduct oneself; mount, play, present, put on; arrange, deal with, fix, look after, organize, prepare, see to; be responsible for, take over; bestow on, confer on, give, grant; be, get on, make out, manage; answer, be adequate, be usable, be useful, serve, suffice; figure out, resolve, solve, sort out; cook; *fig:* cheat, con, dupe, swindle, take for a ride; raid, rob; beat up, thrash; *spec:* spend time (in prison).

dock n *lit:* basin, channel, harbour, quay, wharf; stump; accused's enclosure, bar, pulpit; hospital. **vb** *lit:* berth, moor, put in, tie up; couple, hook up, join, link up; amputate, cut off; *fig:* curtail, cut short, reduce, subtract from.

doctor n *lit:* consultant, general practitioner, GP, physician, specialist; casualty officer, houseman; father of the Church, theologian; don; *spec:* cook (on a ship). **vb** *lit:* apply treatment to, treat; mend, patch up, repair; alter, change, falsify, tamper with; adulterate, dilute, nobble, spike.

dog n *lit:* hound, mutt, pooch, pup; *fig:* blackguard, cur, scoundrel, villain. **vb** *lit:* follow, hound, pursue, shadow, tail, track, trail.

domestic adj *lit:* indigenous, internal, national, state; domiciliary, residential; family, household, private; house, pet, trained; homely.

dominate vb *lit:* control, have the ascendancy over, lead by the nose, monopolize, prevail over, rule; be predominant in, loom over, overshadow, tower above; eclipse, outshine, upstage.

domination n *lit:* ascendancy, authority, control, mastery, power, supremacy; oppression, repression, subjection, tyranny.

donate vb *lit:* contribute, gift, give, present; bequeath, leave.

donation n *lit:* alms, contribution, gift, present; gratuity; collection, offering.

donor n *lit:* contributor, giver; benefactor, philanthropist; *spec:* source of organ(s) for transplant surgery.

doom n *lit:* decree, destiny, fate, judgement, lot, verdict; catastrophe, condemnation, death, destruction, disaster, ruination; end of the world, last trump. vb *lit:* destine (to be), foreordain (to be); condemn (to), consign (to), damn (to), sentence (to).

door n *lit:* entrance, entry, way in; egress, exit, ingress, way out; flap, gate, lintel, opening, port, portal, threshold, trap.

dose n *lit:* dosage; amount, measure, quantity; medication, medicament, medicine, placebo, tincture, treatment; *fig:* bout, session.

dot n *lit:* jot, point, spot, stop; fleck, mark, speck. vb *lit:* dab, fleck, spot, stipple, stud; *fig:* hit, smack; disperse, scatter, spread.

doubt n *lit:* distrust, dubiety, lack of faith, mistrust, suspicion, uncertainty, vaccilation; misgiving, qualm, reservation; ambiguity, confusion, perplexity; hesitancy, indecision, irresolution, wavering; *spec:* (without) question. vb *lit:* be uncertain, distrust, have little faith in, mistrust, suspect; query, question; be hesitant, be irresolute, vacillate, waver.

doubtful adj *lit:* distrustful, dubious, hesitant, irresolute, suspicious, uncertain, unconvinced, unsure; ambiguous, debatable, indeterminate, obscure, problematical, questionable, vague; disreputable, shady, suspect.

down n *lit:* descent, drop, fall; dejection, depression, mood; failure, reversal, setback; knock-down, tackle; scrimmage, scrummage; dune, grassy undulation, hill, knoll, mound; feathers, fluff, hair. vb *lit:*

fell, floor, knock down, tackle, trip; drink, gulp, knock back, quaff, put away, toss off. **adv** *lit:* to a lower position, below; to the ground; on the ground; downstairs; to the present time; to a smaller state; to a defeated state; at a disadvantage, behind; in black and white, on record; in cash, on the spot; to leeward. **prp** *lit:* in a descent along/by/through; on/to a lower position in/on; along, with the current of.

drag **n** *lit:* bore, bother, burden, chore, effort, nuisance, pain; friction, resistance; trawl; scent; inhalation, pull; *spec:* (man in) woman's clothing. **vb** *lit:* draw, haul, heave (along), pull, tow, tug; crawl, creep, dawdle, go slowly; draw (out), spin (out), stretch (out); get left behind, lag behind, straggle; *spec:* dredge, trawl (under water).

drain **n** *lit:* conduit, culvert, ditch, outlet, sewer; drag (on), strain (on). **vb** *lit:* draw off, empty, evacuate, pump out; milk, tap; discharge, exude, flow (out), ooze (out), seep (out); deplete, exhaust, sap, strain, use up.

dramatic **adj** *lit:* histrionic, theatrical, Thespian; affecting, moving, powerful, striking; expressive, forceful, vivid; climactic, electrifying, exciting, sensational, tense, thrilling.

drape **n** *lit:* curtain, hanging; cloth, fold. **vb** *lit:* cover, curtain, enfold, hang; arrange in folds, pleat.

draught **n** *lit:* breeze, current, gust, wind; drawing, haul, pull, traction; drink, swallow, swig; dose, measure; catch, trawl; *spec:* displacement (of a ship).

draw **n** *lit:* attraction, enticement, lure; dead heat, stalemate, tie; choosing, picking, selection. **vb** *lit:* drag, haul, pull, tow; approach, come, get; allure, attract, elicit, entice, induce, invite, seduce, tempt; infuse; extract, pull out, unsheathe; disembowel, eviscerate; extend (out), lengthen (out), spin (out), stretch (out); deduce, infer, make; breathe in, inhale, take a pull; delineate, depict, design, map out, outline, portray, sketch; choose, pick, select; *spec:* be biased, lean (of a bowls wood); extrude (plastics, wire); pull away, pull together (curtains); pull back (a bowstring); shed, spill (blood); write out (a cheque).

drawer n *lit:* shelf; box, chest; bartender, tapster; artist, draughtsman.

drawing n *lit:* delineation, outline; illustration, representation; pencil sketch.

dreadful adj *lit:* alarming, formidable, frightening, ghastly, shocking, tragic; *fig:* abysmal, appalling, awful, terrible, useless, worthless.

dream n *lit:* delusion, fantasy, illusion, reverie, vision; ambition, aspiration, hope, wish; *fig:* beauty, gem, joy, treasure.
vb *lit:* fantasize, imagine; *fig:* conceive (of), think (of).

dreamy adj *lit:* calming, lulling, relaxing, soothing; absent, abstracted, faraway, preoccupied; fanciful, impractical, quixotic, vague; fantastic, intangible, misty, unreal; *fig:* attractive, exciting.

dress n *lit:* attire, clothes, clothing, costume, garments, get-up, outfit, rig; apparel, garb, raiment; frock, gown, robe. vb *lit:* change, put one's clothes on; clothe, put clothes on; drape, furbish, rig out; do (up); comb, groom; align, arrange, set, straighten; bandage, plaster, put medication on; garnish, season.

dressmaker n *lit:* couturier, modiste, seamstress.

drill n *lit:* auger, bit, borer, gimlet; ridge of soil; discipline, exercise, training; *fig:* method, procedure, routine. vb *lit:* bore, make a hole in, pierce; sow in rows; discipline, exercise, instruct, train; rehearse (in), teach (in).

drink n *lit:* beverage, liquid refreshment; bumper, draught, gulp, sip, snort, swallow, swig; cup, dram, glass, mouthful, mug, tot, peg; alcohol, liquor, spirits; booze, hard stuff, hooch, plonk, rotgut, vino; cocktail, brew, infusion, tipple, poison; *fig:* briny, ocean, sea.
vb *lit:* down, imbibe, partake of, quaff, sip, sup, swallow; gulp, guzzle, knock back, swig, swill down, toss off; booze, carouse, drown one's sorrows, hit the bottle, tope; absorb, suck up.

drive n *lit:* avenue, entrance, pathway; excursion, jaunt, outing, run, spin, trip; campaign, crusade, effort, push; hit, stroke; power, transmission; *fig:* ambition, dynamism, energy, enterprise, initiative, motivation, pep, vigour, zip.   **vb** *lit:* herd, impel; compel, constrain, force, hammer, oblige, prod, spur; plunge, ram, stab; power, propel, push; hit, strike; control, direct, operate, steer; go, motor, travel; cause to become, make, send; *fig:* aim (at), get (at).

driver   **n** *lit:* chauffeur, motorman, navigator, pilot, steersman; cowboy, drover, herder, herdsman, shepherd; *spec:* wood (golf-club).

drop   **n** *lit:* bead, drip, globule; mouthful, nip, pinch, sip, taste, trace; abyss, chasm, height, precipice; fall, lowering; *fig:* decline, decrease, deterioration, downturn, reduction, slump.   **vb** *lit:* dive, fall, plummet, plunge, sink; bag, shoot; descend, droop, tumble; give birth to, lay; decline, diminish; abandon, deposit, desert, disown, omit, reject, relinquish, renounce, throw over; let (off), set down; cease, forsake, give up, quit; *spec:* send (a line, a note).

drought   **n** *lit:* dry spell; aridity, dehydration; *fig:* deficiency, inadequacy, scarcity, shortage.

drum   **n** *lit:* percussion instrument, tambour; typanum; barrel, cylinder; pad, residence.   **vb** *lit:* beat rhythmically, tattoo, throb; *fig:* din (into), drive (into), instil (into).

drunk   **adj** *lit:* inebriated, intoxicated, maudlin; blotto, boozed up, canned, legless, paralytic, pickled, pie-eyed, pissed as a newt, plastered, stewed, stoned, tight, well oiled.

drunkard   **n** *lit:* alcoholic, dipsomaniac, drunk, lush, soak, sot, toper, wino.

dry   **vb** *lit:* dehydrate, desiccate; parch; shrivel (up), wizen (up).
adj *lit:* arid, dehydrated, desiccated, moistureless, parched, torrid; *fig:* formal, official; dull, monotonous, tedious; deadpan, laconic, sardonic, sharp; teetotal; brut, sugarless.

duck   **n** *lit:* drake, waterfowl; nil score, zero; dip, plunge; dodge; *fig:* love, pet, sweet.   **vb** *lit:* bob down, dodge, drop; dive, plunge, submerge; dunk, immerse; avoid, elude, evade, sidestep.

due   **n** *lit:* deserts, merits; privilege, right.   **adj** *lit:* appropriate, deserved, fitting, just, merited, rightful; adequate, enough, sufficient; outstanding, owed, payable; awaited, expected, scheduled.

dull vb *lit:* cloud, dim, obscure; sully, tarnish; *fig:* alleviate, assuage, blunt, mitigate, palliate, soften; dampen, depress.   **adj** *lit:* blunt, unhoned; cloudy, dim, gloomy, overcast; drab, faded, indistinct, murky, sombre, uninteresting; dense, dim, slow, stolid, thick; apathetic, blank, indifferent, insensitive, lifeless, sluggish; boring, dreary, flat, monotonous, plain, tedious, tiresome, unimaginative.

durable adj *lit:* hard-wearing, long-lasting, permanent, resistant, strong, substantial, tough; lasting, sound, stable; dogged, hardy, persevering.

duration n *lit:* continuance, continuation, existence, length, persistence; period, term, time.

during prp *lit:* throughout, through the entire time of; at some time in, in the course of.

dusk n *lit:* eventide, gloaming, nightfall, twilight; gloom, murk, shadiness, shadow.

dust n *lit:* ash, fluff, grains, grit, particles, powder; dirt, earth, ground, soil; cloud, fumes; *fig:* commotion, fuss, row, to-do.
vb *lit:* brush, brush off, clean, clear, polish, wipe; *fig:* powder, scatter, sprinkle.

dusty adj *lit:* dirty, grimy, grubby; tarnished, unpolished, unswept; crumbly, friable, gritty, powdery; *fig:* dismissive, negative.

duty n *lit:* allegiance, loyalty, obedience; deference, homage; charge, obligation, office, responsibility, service; assignment, function, mission, role, task; (off) operations, (off) work; *fig:* effectiveness, utility; *spec:* (customs/inland revenue) excise, impost, tax, toll.

dye n *lit:* colorant, colouring, pigment, stain.   **vb** *lit:* colour, pigment, stain, tint.

dying adj (pr.pt) *lit:* declining, expiring, fading, going, passing, sinking; final, last.

dynasty n *lit:* family, house, line, succession.

E

each   adj *lit:* every, every single.   adv *lit:* apiece, individually, per capita, per person.   prn *lit:* every one, one and all.

earnest   n *lit:* gravity, seriousness, sincerity, solemnity; collateral, guarantee, pledge, security, surety.   adj *lit:* grave, serious, sincere, solemn; determined, fixed, intent, resolute, steady; ardent, devoted, eager, fervent, passionate, vehement, zealous.

earth   n *lit:* globe, planet, world; clay, loam, mould, soil; clod, sod.

easy   adj *lit:* effortless, light, painless, simple, smooth, undemanding; gentle, leisurely, unhurried; carefree, comfortable, cushy, peaceful, relaxed, tranquil; affable, amiable, casual, genial, informal, natural, sociable, unpretentious; flexible, indulgent, liberal, tolerant; amenable, biddable, docile, pliant, submissive, tractable.

eat   vb *lit:* consume, devour, digest, ingest, swallow; bolt, chomp, masticate, munch, scoff, dine, feed; abrade (away), corrode, dissolve, erode, wear (away); *fig:* take back (one's words).

economic   adj *lit:* lucrative, profitable, solvent, viable; budgetary, fiscal, monetary, pecuniary; commercial, financial, mercantile, trade; cheap, inexpensive, low-priced.

economy   n *lit:* budgetary management, finance, financial organization, profit-and-loss margin, turnover; cost-efficiency, frugality, parsimony, thrift; saving.

edict   n *lit:* command, decree, law, mandate, order, ordinance, proclamation, regulation, rule, statute.

edition   n *lit:* impression, issue, printing; copy, volume; programme.

educate   vb *lit:* bring up, civilize, cultivate, enlighten, inform, rear; coach, drill, instruct, school, teach, train, tutor; indoctrination; *fig:* bring round (to), persuade (to).

education   n *lit:* civilizing, culture, enlightenment, informing; coaching, drill, instruction, learning, schooling, teaching, training, tuition, tutelage.

effect n *lit:* aftermath, consequence, outcome, result; impact, importance, meaning, significance; action, force, implementation, operation; clout, influence, power, weight; (in) fact, (in) reality. **vb** *lit:* accomplish, achieve, bring about, cause, create, make, perform, produce.

effective adj *lit:* active, causative, operative, productive; compelling, consequential, efficacious, emphatic, forceful, important, impressive, influential, powerful, significant, striking, telling; able, competent, energetic, useful, vigorous; contemporary, current, in force, in operation.

efficient adj *lit:* able, businesslike, competent, effective, productive, proficient, skilled; deft, dextrous, neat, tidy.

effort n *lit:* energy, exertion, force, pains, power, work; strain, stress, struggle, travail; attempt, bash, endeavour, go, shot, stab, try.

electric adj *lit:* charged, live; power; *fig:* sparkling, stimulating, stirring, tense, thrilling.

element n *lit:* component, constituent, factor, ingredient, item, member, part, unit; domain, field, habitat, medium; coil, filament, resistance, wire; electrode; rudiment(s).

else adv *lit:* additionally, also, as well, besides, in addition; if not, instead, otherwise.

embarrassment n *lit:* awkwardness, bashfulness, chagrin, discomfiture, humiliation, mortification, shame; excess, superabundance, surfeit, surplus; *fig:* difficulty, predicament, problem.

embassy n *lit:* legation, mission; ambassador's residence, consulate; agency, ministry.

embrace n *lit:* clasp, clinch, hug, squeeze. **vb** *lit:* clasp, cuddle, enfold, hold, hug, squeeze; comprehend, contain, enclose, encompass, include, take in; accept, receive; *fig:* adopt, espouse, take up.

emergency n *lit:* crisis, crunch, crux, exigency, extremity, matter of life and death; danger, urgency, vicissitude.

emission n *lit:* discharge, ejaculation, emanation, exudation, issue, radiation, transmission; escape, leak; secretion.

emit   vb *lit:* broadcast, diffuse, discharge, eject, ejaculate, emanate, exhale, exude, give off, give out, issue, radiate, scatter, secrete, send out, shed, throw out, transmit.

emotion   n *lit:* disposition, feeling, mood, sensation, sentiment; ardour, fervour, passion, vehemence.

emphasize   vb *lit:* accent, accentuate, give priority to, highlight, play on, stress, underline.

employee   n *lit:* hand, staff-member, worker; wage-earner.

enamoured   adj (pa.pt) *lit:* bewitched (by), captivated (by), enraptured (by), fascinated (by), infatuated (by), in love (with), smitten (by).

enclose   vb *lit:* comprehend, contain, embrace, hold, include; circumscribe, encircle, encompass, hedge in, hem in, shut in; add in, insert, put in.

end   n *lit:* cessation, close, closure, completion, conclusion, dénouement, expiry, finale, finish, halt, resolution, stop, termination, winding up; boundary, edge, extremity, limit, terminus, tip; death, decease, demise; abolition, annihilation, cancellation, destruction, dissolution, downfall, extinction, scrapping; aim, aspiration, goal, intention, objective, purpose; leftover, remainder, remnant, scrap; behind, bottom, bum, posterior, rear, stern; final blow, last straw, worst.   vb *lit:* cease, close, come to a halt, conclude, expire, finish, halt, stop, terminate, wind up; bound; decease, die, pass away; be cancelled, be destroyed, be extinguished, be scrapped; abolish, cancel, destroy, extinguish, kill, scrap.

endanger   vb *lit:* compromise, hazard, imperil, jeopardize, put at risk.

endure   vb *lit:* bear, brook, put up with, stand, stomach, swallow, take, tolerate, withstand; experience, go through, suffer, undergo; abide, continue, last, live on, persist, remain, survive.

enemy   n *lit:* adversary, antagonist, foe; competitor, rival; opposition.

energy n *lit:* animation, drive, fire, force, life, liveliness, power, stamina, strength, verve, vigour, vim, vivacity, zest, zip.

engagement n *lit:* betrothal; agreement, bond, contract, oath, pledge, understanding, vow; appointment, date, meeting, rendezvous, tryst; commission, employment, gig, job, post, situation; action, battle, conflict, encounter, fight, skirmish.

engineer n *lit:* mechanic, physicist, technician, technologist; designer, inventor, planner.

enjoy vb *lit:* appreciate, delight in, like, relish, revel in, take pleasure in; experience, have, own, possess, use.

enjoyable adj *lit:* amusing, delightful, entertaining, gratifying, pleasant, pleasurable.

enough adj *lit:* adequate, sufficient. adv *lit:* adequately, satisfactorily, sufficiently.

ensure vb *lit:* confirm, guarantee, make sure.

enter vb *lit:* come in, go in, pass into, penetrate, pierce; enlist, enrol, join, sign up for; list, log, note, record, register, take down; put forward, submit, tender.

entrance n *lit:* door, doorway, ingress, way in; gate, opening, port, trap; mouth; admittance, entry; access, avenue; appearance, arrival, introduction. vb *lit:* bewitch, captivate, charm, enchant, enrapture, enthral, fascinate, infatuate; hypnotize, mesmerize, spellbind.

entry n *lit:* appearance, entrance, introduction; door, doorway, ingress, way in; avenue; access, admission, admittance, entrée; candidate, competitor, contestant, entrant, player; item, minute, note, record; plea, submission.

envious adj *lit:* covetous, green, jealous.

environment n *lit:* background, context, milieu, setting, surroundings; countryside, landscape, nature; domain, habitat.

episode n *lit:* adventure, affair, event, happening, incident, occurrence; chapter, instalment, part.

equal n *lit:* compeer, counterpart, equivalent, fellow, match,

peer. **vb** *lit:* agree with, balance with, be level with, equate with, match, parallel, rival, tie with; amount to, come to, total.
adj *lit:* alike, balanced, commensurate, corresponding, even, level, like, uniform; up (to).

equally **adv** *lit:* alike, evenly, identically, proportionately, regularly, symmetrically, uniformly; fairly, impartially, justly, squarely.

equivalent **n** *lit:* counterpart, equal, opposite number, parallel.
adj *lit:* comparable (to), equal (to), tantamount (to).

erect **vb** *lit:* build, construct, pitch, put up, raise, set up; establish, found, institute; harden, stiffen, tumesce. **adj** *lit:* perpendicular, upright, vertical; haughty, proud; hard, ithyphallic, rigid, standing, stiff, tumescent.

error **n** *lit:* bloomer, boob, corrigendum, erratum, fault, inaccuracy, literal, mistake, slip.

especially **adv** *lit:* expressly, mainly, markedly, notably, outstandingly, particularly, peculiarly, principally, singularly, specifically, unusually.

essay **n** *lit:* article, composition, dissertation, paper, piece.
vb *lit:* attempt, have a go at, try; gauge, test, try out.

estate **n** *lit:* domain, holdings, lands, property; assets, effects, possessions, wealth; condition, position, rank, standing, station, status; caste, class, order.

ethics **n** *lit:* conscience, integrity, morality, moral values, principles, scruples, standards.

evaporate **vb** *lit:* vaporize; desiccate, dry up; *fig:* disappear, dissipate, dissolve, fade away, vanish.

even **vb** *lit:* balance (up), equal (up), level (out), match (up), square (up); settle (the score). **adj** *lit:* flat, flush, level, parallel, steady, uniform; balanced, drawn, equal, tied; constant, regular, unbroken, unwavering; calm, composed, cool, placid, serene, stable, tranquil, unruffled; **adv** *lit:* evenly; exactly (as), just (as); indeed, nay, veritably; fully, quite, right; surprisingly; still, yet.

ever adv *lit:* at all, at any time, on any occasion; always, constantly, continually, eternally, incessantly, perpetually, unceasingly.

everybody prn *lit:* each one, each person, the world; everyone.

evil n *lit:* badness, immorality, iniquity, malevolence, malice, malignity, sin, sinfulness, vice, wickedness, wrongdoing; blasphemy, sacrilege, ungodliness; calamity, catastrophe, disaster, injury, misfortune, pain, suffering. adj *lit:* bad, immoral, iniquitous, malicious, malignant, sinful, wicked; blasphemous, sacrilegious, ungodly; calamitous, catastrophic, disastrous, injurious; foul, noxious, offensive, putrescent, vile.

evolve vb *lit:* advance, develop, form, grow, metamorphose, progress, transform.

exactly adv *lit:* accurately, carefully, faithfully, faultlessly, meticulously, precisely, punctiliously, rigorously, scrupulously, specifically, unerringly.

exaggerate vb *lit:* amplify, embellish, emphasize, enlarge, inflate, magnify, overstate.

exaggeration n *lit:* amplification, embellishment, emphasis, enlargement, inflation, overstatement.

except vb *lit:* bar, exclude, leave out, omit, pass over; absolve, exempt. prp *lit:* apart from, bar, barring, but, excluding, omitting, other than, save, saving; absolving, exempting, not including.

exceptional adj *lit:* abnormal, atypical, extraordinary, singular, special, strange, uncommon, unusual; excellent, outstanding, prodigious.

excitement n *lit:* activity, ado, agitation, commotion, flurry, furore; animation, elation, exaltation, fever, heat, passion; kick, thrill; impulse, stimulation, urge.

exciting adj *lit:* electrifying, exhilarating, galvanizing, rousing, sensational, stimulating, thrilling.

exclamation n *lit:* cry, ejaculation, interjection.

exclusive adj *lit:* private, sole, unshared; chic, classy, fashionable, posh, restricted, select.

executive n *lit:* administrator, manager, official; administration, directorate, government, leadership, management.

exemption n *lit:* absolution, dispensation, exception, immunity.

exercise n *lit:* activity, effort, exertion, movement; discipline, drill, training, work-out; employment, practice, use, utilization; problem, task, work. **vb** *lit:* discipline, drill, practise, train, work out; apply, employ, exert, use, utilize; burden, preoccupy.

exhaust n *lit:* emission, waste; carbon monoxide. **vb** *lit:* be emitted, discharge, escape; consume, dissipate, finish, run through, spend, use up; drain, empty, void; bankrupt, disable, fatigue, sap, tire out, weaken, wear out.

exhaustion n *lit:* debilitation, fatigue, prostration, tiredness.

existence n *lit:* actuality, being, life, reality; creation.

expect **vb** *lit:* anticipate, forecast, foresee, foretell, predict; contemplate, hope for, look for, watch for; demand, insist on, rely upon.

expenditure n *lit:* costs, expenses, outgoings, outlay, payment; application, consumption.

expense n *lit:* cost, disbursement, expenditure, outlay, payment; sacrifice.

expensive adj *lit:* costly, dear, exorbitant, extortionate, extravagant, overpriced, steep.

experience n *lit:* familiarity, involvement, knowledge, observation, practice, trial, understanding; adventure, affair, episode, event, incident, occurrence. **vb** *lit:* encounter, face, go through, know, meet, observe, sample, suffer, taste, try, undergo.

experienced adj *lit:* adept, competent, expert, knowledgeable, practised, qualified, seasoned, trained, veteran; mature, sophisticated, worldly-wise.

explain **vb** *lit:* clarify, elucidate, illustrate, interpret, resolve; account for, excuse, justify; rationalize.

explanation n *lit:* clarification, elucidation, illustration, interpretation, resolution, solution; account, answer, excuse, justification, reason; rationalization.

explore   vb *lit:* enquire into, examine, investigate, look into, probe, research, search; reconnoitre, scout; sightsee, tour, travel.

expose   vb *lit:* disclose, display, exhibit, present, reveal, show, uncover; betray, denounce, divulge, lay bare, make known, unmask; endanger, imperil, jeopardize, leave open (to).

expressive   adj *lit:* eloquent, forceful, lively, moving, poignant, telling, vivid; allusive (of), indicative (of), meaningful (of), suggestive (of); pointed, pregnant, significant.

external   adj *lit:* exterior, outer, outward; apparent, surface, visible; alien, exotic, foreign.

extra   adj *lit:* accessory, additional, ancillary, auxiliary, fresh, more, new, supplementary; excess, redundant, spare, superfluous, surplus, unneeded, unused.

extract   vb *lit:* cull, draw, pluck out, pull out, take out, uproot; bring out, elicit, evoke; gather, glean, reap; distil, express, press out, squeeze out; abstract, cite, quote.

extravagant   adj *lit:* excessive, lavish, profligate, wasteful; exaggerated, extreme, fanciful, fantastic, immoderate, inordinate, unreasonable, wild; flamboyant, flashy, garish, gaudy, ostentatious; costly, exorbitant, expensive, extortionate, steep.

eye   n *lit:* orb, optic, peeper; *fig:* appreciation, discernment, discrimination, perception, vision; (keep a) watch (on).   vb *lit:* contemplate, gaze at, look at, regard, stare at, study, watch; leer at, ogle.

F

fable n *lit:* story, tale, yarn; legend, myth; allegory, par`ble; fabrication, fiction, invention.

face n *lit:* countenance, features, physiognomy; clock, dial, kisser, mug, mush, phizog; air, appearance, expression, look; frown, girn, grimace, pout, scowl; exterior, front, obverse, outside, surface, top; façade, outward appearance; character, disposition, physical form; font, print, type; cliff-edge, edge, sheer side, wall; aspect, facet, plane; *fig:* audacity, cheek, effrontery, gall, nerve; dignity, image, prestige, status; cutting-surface; striking-surface. **vb** *lit:* look towards, turn to; front on to, give on to, overlook; anticipate, be confronted by, have to cope with, look forward to; encounter, experience, present oneself to, stand before; brave, confront, defy, overcome, stare (down); clad, coat, cover, laminate, sheathe, veneer; edge, line, trim; *spec:* dress (stone).

facilities n *lit:* amenities, equipment, services; accommodation, buildings, rooms; arrangements, means, opportunities, resources; aid, assistance.

fact n *lit:* actuality, reality, truth; act, action, circumstance, event, happening, incident, occurrence; factor.

factor n *lit:* component, consideration, constituent, element, ingredient, part, unit; multiplicand; agent, bailiff, estate manager, steward.

factory n *lit:* plant, works; makers'; depot, warehouse; assembly line.

factual adj *lit:* accurate, actual, authentic, detailed, exact, faithful, objective, real.

fade vb *lit:* blanch, dim, discolour, dull, pale; bleach, etiolate, wash out; decline, die, dwindle, ebb, fail, flag, wane, wilt, wither; disappear, vanish.

fail vb *lit:* be unable (to), be unsuccessful (in); flub, flunk; neglect (to); be useless to; be in vain, come to nothing, fall through, flop, go wrong, miscarry; be absent, be lacking, be missing; decline, deteriorate, fade, sink, wane; break down, cease, conk out, die, disappear, give out, give up, go out, peter out, stop; go bankrupt.

failure　**n** *lit:* unsuccessful attempt; inability (to), neglecting (to); absence, breakdown, deficiency, deterioration, lack, loss, negligence, omission; defeat, disaster, fiasco, non-starter; collapse, disintegration; bankruptcy, crash, ruin; dud, flop, incompetent, lame duck, loser, no-hoper, washout.

faint　**n** *lit:* blackout, dizzy spell, swoon, syncope.　**vb** *lit:* become dizzy, black out, flake out, keel over, lose consciousness, pass out, swoon.　**adj** *lit:* dizzy, giddy, light-headed, muzzy, woozy; exhausted, fatigued, worn to a frazzle; feeble, halfhearted, slight, weak; fearful, timid, timorous; dim, dull, faded, hazy, indistinct, light, soft, vague; distant, faltering, low, muffled, subdued.

fair　**n** *lit:* amusement park, carnival, funfair; bazaar, market; exhibition, show.　**adj** *lit:* blond, blonde, flaxen, light, yellow; bright, clear, cloudless, dry, sunny; beautiful, bonny, handsome, lovely, pretty; error-free, fine, legible, presentable; civil, courteous, gentle, polite; favourable, likely, promising; adequate, all right, average, moderate, not bad, okay, passable, reasonable, satisfactory; above-board, equitable, honest, impartial, judicial, judicious, just, square, unbiased, unprejudiced; open, unobstructed.

fairy　**n** *lit:* brownie, fay, peri, pixie, sprite; leprechaun.

faith　**n** *lit:* belief, confidence, conviction, reliance, trust; Church, communion, creed, religion, theology; allegiance, constancy, fidelity, loyalty.

faithful　**n** *lit:* adherents, believers, devotees, followers; Church; communicants, congregation.　**adj** *lit:* devoted, loyal, steadfast, true; dependable, reliable, trusty; accurate, actual, authentic, detailed, exact, factual, precise, truthful.

faithfulness　**n** *lit:* constancy, devotion, fidelity, loyalty; dependability, reliability; accuracy, authenticity, exactitude, precision, truth.

fake n *lit:* copy, counterfeit, forgery, imitation, reproduction, sham, simulation; fraud, impostor; charlatan, mountebank. vb *lit:* copy, counterfeit, forge, reproduce; feign, rig, sham, simulate. adj *lit:* copied, counterfeit, forged, phoney, reproduced, sham, simulated; affected, assumed, false, feigned, imitation, pretended.

fall n *lit:* dive, drop, plunge, slip, tumble; collapse, defeat, destruction, overthrow, ruin, surrender; death; descent, incline, slant, slope; precipitation; depth, height; *fig:* decline, decrease, dip, lessening, lowering, reduction, slump; lapse, sin, transgression; *spec:* hold, throw (in wrestling). vb *lit:* dive, drop, plunge, slip, tumble; keel over, topple, trip; be defeated, be destroyed, be overthrown, collapse, surrender, yield; be lost, die, perish; descend, incline downwards, slant, slope; be precipitated, cascade, rain, shower down; *fig:* abate, be reduced, decline, decrease, diminish, dip, flag, go down, lessen, lower, slump; backslide, commit a sin, lapse, transgress; become, get, happen, occur, turn; be drawn (into); *spec:* be thrown (in wrestling).

false adj *lit:* erroneous, fallacious, inaccurate, incorrect, invalid, untrue, wrong; lying, mendacious, untruthful; deceitful, dishonest, disloyal, faithless, perfidious, traitorous, unfaithful, unreliable, untrustworthy; deceiving, deceptive, misleading; artificial, counterfeit, fake, feigned, forged, sham, simulated, synthetic, trumped up; ersatz, imitation, substitute; ill-founded, misconceived; bum, off, out of tune.

fame n *lit:* celebrity, distinction, eminence, illustriousness, name, note, renown, reputation, repute, stardom; infamy, notoriety.

family n *lit:* folks, household, people, relations, relatives; clan, kindred, kinsmen, tribe; children, issue, offspring, progeny; ancestry, blood, descent, genealogy, house, line, lineage, parentage, pedigree; class, genre, group, kind.

famous adj *lit:* celebrated, distinguished, eminent, illustrious, legendary, noted, renowned, reputed, well known; infamous, notorious.

fan n *lit:* air conditioner, blower, vane, ventilator; aficionado, buff, devotee, enthusiast, freak, supporter. vb *lit:* air-condition, blow, ventilate; *fig:* arouse, excite, kindle, provoke, stir up; *spec:* spread out (cards).

fanatic   n *lit:* activist, extremist, militant, zealot; addict, devotee, enthusiast.

fantasy   n *lit:* daydream, dream, image, mental picture, vision; nightmare; fairy story; fancy, imagination; invention, originality; fiction, lie, untruth.

far   adj *lit:* distant, remote; outlying; farther, hinder, other.
adv *lit:* a long way, deep, distantly, remotely; considerably, definitely, much, positively.

fare   n *lit:* passenger, pick-up, traveller; fee, price, ticket money, transportation cost; food, provisions, rations, sustenance.   **vb** *lit:* be, do, go, get along, make out, proceed, turn out, work out; be fed, eat, feed.

farewell   n *lit:* adieu, goodbye, valediction; leave-taking, parting, send-off, well-wishing.

farm   n *lit:* croft, homestead, plantation, ranch, smallholding; acreage, fields; battery, beds, breeding-station, piggery, stud; treatment plant, works.   **vb** *lit:* cultivate, till, work; breed, raise, rear, tend; contract (out), subcontract (out).

farmer   n *lit:* crofter, homesteader, rancher, smallholder; agriculturalist, agronomist; grower, planter, producer; breeder, cattleman, dairyman, shepherd; contractor, subcontractor.

fascinate   vb *lit:* allure, attract, bewitch, captivate, enchant, enrapture, enthrall, entrance, infatuate, mesmerize, put a spell on, ravish, spellbind; intrigue.

fascination   n *lit:* allure, attraction, charm, enchantment, magic, magnetism, spell; captivation, infatuation.

fashion   n *lit:* convention, custom, usage; craze, fad, rage, trend, vogue; creation, cut, form, line, make, mode, pattern, shape; manner, style, way; appearance, description, kind, sort, type; high society, jet set.   **vb** *lit:* build, create, form, make, mould, knead, shape, work.

fashionable   adj *lit:* à la mode, chic, modish, snappy, snazzy, stylish, trendy; current, in, in vogue, latest, popular, up-to-the-minute.

fast **n** *lit:* abstinence; period of abstinence; hunger-strike. **vb** *lit:* abstain, go hungry, refrain from eating, take no food. **adj** *lit:* brisk, fleet, hasty, hurried, nippy, quick, rapid, swift; fixed, secure, tight; *fig:* close, firm, loyal, steadfast; dissolute, licentious, loose, promiscuous; intemperate, rash, reckless, wild; *spec:* before time, early (of a clock); permanent, unfading (colours); sound (asleep). **adv** *lit:* briskly, hastily, hurriedly, quickly, rapidly, speedily, swiftly; fixedly, securely, tightly; *fig:* firmly, loyally, steadfastly, unflinchingly; close (by), near (by); *spec:* sound, soundly (asleep).

fasten **vb** *lit:* attach, connect, join, link, secure, unite; bind, chain, tie; affix, bond, cement, glue; nail, rivet, tack, weld; buckle, button, do up, hook up, lace, pin (on), zip; *fig:* aim (on), concentrate (on), focus (on); latch (on to), seize (on); push (on to).

fat **n** *lit:* adipose tissue, carbohydrate; blubber, flab; grease, oil; butter, lard, margarine, polyunsaturates; *fig:* body, fullness, richness, substance. **adj** *lit:* adipose; blubbery, corpulent, flabby, fleshy, obese, overweight, plump, portly, roly-poly, rotund, stout, tubby; greasy, oily, oleaginous; broad, bulky, enormous, great, huge, jumbo, massive, vast, wide; *fig:* fertile, fruitful, lush, rich.

fatal **adj** *lit:* deadly, lethal, mortal; incurable, terminal; *fig:* calamitous, catastrophic, disastrous; critical, decisive, fateful, portentous.

fate **n** *lit:* destiny, predestination, providence; lot, portion; forecast, future, horoscope, stars; luck, fortune.

father **n** *lit:* begetter, progenitor, sire; dad, guv'ner, old man, pa, papa, pater, pop; elder, senator; abbot, confessor, priest, prior, vicar; *fig:* author, creator, discoverer, founder, inventor, maker. **vb** *lit:* beget, sire; engender, generate; adopt, foster; *fig:* establish, found, institute, originate.

fault **n** *lit:* defect, deficiency, flaw; blunder, error, inaccuracy, lapse, mistake, slip; omission; blemish, imperfection; blame, culpability, guilt, responsibility; offence, sin, transgression, trespass. **vb** *lit:* find a flaw in, pick holes in; blame.

faultless **adj** *lit:* exemplary, flawless, immaculate, impeccable, irreproachable, perfect, spotless, unblemished.

faulty adj *lit:* blemished, broken, defective, deficient, flawed, imperfect; inaccurate, incorrect, invalid, wrong; malfunctioning.

favour n *lit:* approbation, approval, esteem, good books, goodwill, patronage, support; bias, partiality; good turn, kindness, service; keepsake, kerchief, ribbon, token. **vb** *lit:* approve of, commend, fancy, support; be biased towards, have a soft spot for, prefer, side with; grace (with), oblige (with); *fig:* look like, resemble, take after.

favourable adj *lit:* approving, encouraging, positive, welcoming, well-disposed; advantageous, beneficial, good, helpful, opportune, propitious; clement, suitable.

favourite n *lit:* best, choice, pick, preference; cert, certainty, cinch, hot tip, sure thing, tip.

fear n *lit:* anxiety, apprehension, dread, foreboding, fright, misgiving, panic, terror, timidity, trepidation, unease; horror, phobia; reverence, veneration. **vb** *lit:* apprehend, be afraid of, be apprehensive (that), be frightened of, be terrified of, dread (that); suspect (that); be anxious (for), tremble (for); respect, revere, reverence, venerate.

fearless adj *lit:* bold, daring, dauntless, heroic, indomitable, intrepid, unafraid, unflinching.

feasible adj *lit:* achievable, possible, practicable, realizable, viable, workable.

feast n *lit:* banquet, beano, blow-out, slap-up meal, spread; meal, repast; celebration, festival, saint's day; *fig:* delight, pleasure, treat. **vb** *lit:* banquet, gorge (on), stuff, wine and dine; entertain sumptuously; *fig:* delight, gladden, gratify.

federation n *lit:* alliance, association, combination, confederacy, league, syndicate, syndication.

fee n *lit:* charge, cost, hire, payment, price, toll; emolument, remuneration.

feeble adj *lit:* debilitated, doddering, failing, frail, puny, sickly, skinny, slight, thin, weak; delicate, effete, faint, indecisive, ineffectual, insignificant; *fig:* flimsy, inadequate, lame, poor, tame, threadbare.

feed vb *lit:* cater for, provision, seat, victual; provide for, supply to; exist (on), live (on), subsist (on); devour, eat; crop, graze; *fig:* foster, fuel, nourish, strengthen; channel, duct, pipe, supply; be straight-man to, cue.

feel vb *lit:* caress, finger, fondle, fumble over, grasp, grope, handle, paw, stroke, touch; be aware of, experience, notice, perceive, sense; test (out), try (out); believe (that), consider (that), hold (that), think (that); agonize (for), be sorry (for), bleed (for); have great sympathy (for).

feeling n *lit:* consciousness, impression, perception, presentiment, sensation, sense; air, atmosphere, aura, mood; idea, notion, suspicion; consensus, opinion, view; affection, fondness, sentimentality, warmth; emotion, fervour, passion; compassion, empathy, sympathy, understanding.

feminine adj *lit:* female, womanly; girlish, ladylike; delicate, graceful, soft, tender; effeminate, womanish.

fence n *lit:* barrier, hedge, hurdle, palings, palisade, railings, stockade, wire, wire netting; receiver of stolen property. vb *lit:* barricade, hedge (in), pen (in); fortify, secure, shield; dispose of stolen property; *spec.* fight (with swords).

ferry vb *lit:* chauffeur, convey, drive, escort, run, see (to), ship, transport.

fertile adj *lit:* fecund, fruitful; arable, cultivable; abundant, luxuriant, productive, prolific, rich, teeming.

fertilize vb *lit:* impregnate, inseminate, make pregnant; pollinate; compost, dress, manure, mulch.

festival n *lit:* feast, saint's day; anniversary; commemoration programme, season; celebration, gala, party.

festive adj *lit:* celebratory, convivial, festal, happy, holiday, jolly, joyous, merry; bright, colourful, decorative, gay.

fetch vb *lit:* bring, carry, convey, deliver, get, obtain, recover, retrieve, take; escort, guide, lead; draw out, elicit; bring in, earn, make, produce, sell for.

fever n *lit:* heat, high temperature; *fig:* delirium, ferment, flush, frenzy, passion.

feverish adj *lit:* burning, febrile, flushed, hectic, hot, inflamed; *fig:* delirious, frenetic, frenzied, impassioned, passionate.

few n *lit:* couple, handful, scattering.   adj *lit:* hardly any, not many; meagre, scanty, scarce, sparse.

fiancé(e) n *lit:* affianced, betrothed, intended.

fiasco n *lit:* catastrophe, debacle, disaster, rout, ruin.

fibre n *lit:* filament, strand, thread; nap, pile, texture; *fig:* being, nature, spirit, soul; (moral) strength.

fiction n *lit:* narrative, story, tale, yarn; fantasy, imagination, invention; fabrication, fib, imposture, lie, simulation, untruth.

fictitious adj *lit:* imaginary, invented, made-up, unreal, untrue; imagined, make-believe; affected, assumed, counterfeit, feigned, sham, simulated.

fiddle n *lit:* violin; *fig:* con, fraud, graft, ramp, rip-off, swindle. vb *lit:* play the violin, scrape the strings; *fig:* fidget (with), mess about (with), play (with), tamper (with), toy (with); cheat, con, rip off, swindle.

field n *lit:* lea, meadow, pasture; acreage; *fig:* area, confines, domain, province, territory; line, sphere; bounds, limits, range, scope; department, discipline, specialty; competitors, contestants, entrants, runners; applicants, candidates.   vb *lit:* catch, retrieve, throw back; *fig:* cope with, deal with, handle; deflect, parry, turn aside.

fierce adj *lit:* dangerous, fell, feral, ferocious, murderous, predatory, savage, tigerish, untamed, wild; furious, raging, tempestuous, violent; *fig:* blazing, fiery, hot; cut-throat, intense, strong.

fight n *lit:* affray, altercation, brawl, clash, conflict, fracas, free-for-all, melee, punch-up, riot, row, scrap, scrimmage, scuffle, set-to, tussle; bout, boxing-match, contest; action, battle, engagement, skirmish, struggle, war; *fig:* aggression, belligerence, militancy;

gameness, mettle, spirit. **vb** *lit:* brawl, clash, come to blows (with), cross swords (with), do battle (with), scrap (with), scuffle (with), tussle (with), wrestle (with); box (with), spar (with); combat, engage, skirmish (with), struggle against, wage war against; bicker, squabble, wrangle; contest, dispute, oppose, resist against.

fill **vb** *lit:* cram, crowd, pack; charge (up), replenish, restock; suffuse; supply; sate, satiate, satisfy, stuff; saturate; bung, cork, plug, seal, stop; cover, occupy, take up; *fig:* discharge, execute, fulfil; belly out, extend, inflate.

film **n** *lit:* coating, integument, layer; membrane, skin, tissue; dusting, powder; blur, cloud, haze, mist; celluloid, feature, movie, tape, video. **vb** *lit:* photograph, shoot, take; blur (over), cloud (over), haze (over), mist (over).

final **adj** *lit:* closing, concluding, last, terminal, terminating, ultimate; conclusive, decisive, definitive, irrevocable.

finally **adv** *lit:* in conclusion, lastly, to end with; at last, eventually, in the end, ultimately; conclusively, decisively, definitively, irrevocably, once and for all.

finance **n** *lit:* banking, commerce, economics, investment; bourse, money market, stock market; asset(s), backing, capital, fund(s), funding, money, resource(s). **vb** *lit:* back, bankroll, float, fund, guarantee, put up the money for, sponsor, support, underwrite.

financial **adj** *lit:* commercial, economic, fiscal, monetary.

find **n** *lit:* catch, discovery; acquisition, bargain. **vb** *lit:* chance upon, come across, discover, encounter, light upon, meet, stumble on; acquire, gain, get hold of, lay one's hands on, locate, obtain, procure, run down, spot, track down, turn up, uncover; recover, regain, retrieve; bring to light, detect, reveal; furnish, provide, supply; *fig:* become aware, note, notice, observe, perceive, realize; declare, proclaim, pronounce.

finding **n** *lit:* detection, discovery, location, recovery, retrieval, tracking down; conclusion, decision, judgement, verdict; answer, result, total.

fine **n** *lit:* forfeit, penalty; fee, price, toll. **vb** *lit:* mulct, penalize;

compel to pay. **adj** *lit:* admirable, attractive, beautiful, bonny, excellent, exquisite, magnificent, smart, splendid, striking, stylish; dainty, delicate, elegant, fragile, slender; slight, thin, tenuous; diaphanous, gauzy, gossamer, light, sheer; crushed, powdery, pulverized, refined; clear, pure, unadulterated, unalloyed; bright, dry, fair, sunny; agreeable, all right, good, okay, suitable; critical, discriminating, fastidious, keen, precise, sensitive, sharp; cutting, razor-edged; brilliant, polished.

finish n *lit:* close, completion, conclusion, culmination, end, ending, stop, termination, winding-up; bankruptcy, liquidation, ruin; death, demolition, destruction; defeat; lustre, patina, polish, shine, surface texture; *fig:* culture, refinement, sophistication. **vb** *lit:* accomplish, achieve, cease, close, complete, conclude, culminate (in), do, end, round off, stop, terminate, wind up; drain (off), drink (up), eat (up), use (up); destroy, ruin; kill (off); defeat; coat, face, lacqueur, polish, texture, wax; *fig:* perfect, refine.

fire n *lit:* combustion; blaze, conflagration, inferno; coals, embers, flames, sparks; barbecue, beacon, brazier, grate, hob, oven, stove; bombardment, fusillade, shelling, sniping; *fig:* brightness, brilliance, flare, intensity, lustre, radiance, scintillation, sparkle; ardour, fervour, force, heat, passion, zeal; animation, dash, eagerness, enthusiasm, excitement, life, spirit, verve, vigour, vivacity; creativity, inspiration; danger, hardship, ordeal, trial, tribulation. **vb** *lit:* ignite, kindle, light, set ablaze, set alight to, set on fire; bake; cauterize; detonate, explode, touch off; discharge, let off, shoot; *fig:* arouse, electrify, galvanize, inflame, inspire, rouse, stir; fuel; boot out, cashier, dismiss, give the sack, lay off; *spec:* catch, start (of a car engine).

firm n *lit:* business, company, organization, outfit. **adj** *lit:* fast, fixed, immovable, rooted, secure, solid, stable, steady, strong, sturdy, unshakable; compact, dense, hard, rigid, stiff; *fig:* adamant, inflexible, obdurate, resolute, steadfast, unfaltering, unflinching, unswerving.

firmness n *lit:* fixity, immobility, security, solidity, stability, steadiness, strength, sturdiness; compactness, density, hardness, rigidity, stiffness, tensile strength; *fig:* inflexibility, obduracy, resolve, steadfastness, strength of purpose.

first adj *lit:* dawn, earliest, initial, opening, original, primary, primeval; foremost, leading; chief, head, highest, prime, principal, top; basic, cardinal, elementary. adv *lit:* at the outset, beforehand, initially, in the beginning, to start with; liefer, rather, sooner.

fish n *fig:* character, individual, person, type; bracket, plate, stay. vb *lit:* angle (for), bait a line (for), net, trawl (for); dive (for); *fig:* be on the lookout (for), try (for); fumble (for), search (for).

fit n *lit:* dimensions, shape, size; appropriateness, aptitude, rightness, suitability; attack, bout, convulsion, seizure, spasm; outbreak, spell; humour, mood. vb *lit:* be appropriate for, be apt for, be right for, conform to, correspond to, match, suit, tally; equip (out), kit (out), rig (out); slot (in), sort (in); frame (up). adj *lit:* able, adequate, competent, deserving, equipped, good enough (to), qualified (for), right, suitable, well-suited; athletic, hale, healthy, in condition, in good shape, in rude health, robust, trim, well.

fitness n *lit:* appropriateness, aptitude, aptness, correspondence, eligibility, match, suitability; athleticism, good condition, health, shape.

flag n *lit:* arms, banner, colours, ensign, jack, standard; burgee, gonfalon, pennant. vb *lit:* be fatigued, droop, ebb, fade, fail, sag, slump, taper off, tire, wane, weary, wilt, wither; label, mark, tab; hail, salute, wave (down).

flair n *lit:* ability, aptitude, feel, genius, gift, knack, talent; dash, elegance, panache, savoir-faire, style, virtuosity.

flamboyant adj *lit:* extravagant, florid, grandiose, ornate, ostentatious, swaggering, theatrical; garish, gaudy, loud, showy.

flame n *lit:* fire; light; *fig:* amour, boyfriend, girlfriend, love, sweetheart; ardour, fervency, intensity, passion. vb *lit:* blaze, burn, flare, flash, glow, shine; blush, flush, suffuse.

flap n *lit:* apron, cover, fold, lappet, lid, tab; aerofoil, aileron, beat, flail, flutter, threshing; *fig:* commotion, fluster, panic, state, tizzy. vb *lit:* bang, beat, flail, flutter, swing, thresh, wave; *fig:* be flustered, get into a state, panic.

flash n *lit:* beam, blaze, burst, flare, flicker, gleam, glow, glint, glistening, scintillation, spark, sparkle; cascade, deluge, flood, spurt; *fig:* blur, streak; instant, moment, second, trice; display, exposure, show; news headline. **vb** *lit:* beam, blaze, burst, flare, flicker, gleam, glint, glisten, glow, scintillate, spark, sparkle; *fig:* blur, shoot, streak; dash, speed, sprint, zip; display, expose, let one see, show.

flashy adj *lit:* garish, gaudy, loud, ostentatious, showy; cheap, tasteless, vulgar.

flask n *lit:* bottle, canteen, carafe, decanter; powder-horn; retort.

flat n *lit:* apartment, room, storey; lowland, plain; marsh, swamp; shallow, shoal; backdrop, prop; *fig:* dupe, gull, john, mark. **adj** *lit:* horizontal, level, plane, uniform; at full length, prone, prostrate, recumbent, supine; burst, collapsed, deflated, empty, punctured; *fig:* boring, colourless, dead, insipid, lifeless, stale, vapid, watery; blue, dejected, depressed, morose; absolute, categorical, fixed, positive, unequivocal, unqualified; *spec:* back, short (vowel, diphthong); below the right (musical) pitch; defunct (battery). **adv** *lit:* horizontal, in a heap, to the ground; *fig:* absolutely, categorically, positively, unequivocally, utterly; *spec:* below the right (musical) pitch.

flatter vb *lit:* be sycophantic towards, butter up, crawl to, fawn over, soft-soap, toady to, truckle to; be over-complimentary about; humour (into), wheedle (into); become, enhance, set off, show to good advantage.

flattery n *lit:* fawning, obsequiousness, servility, soft-soaping, sycophancy, toadying.

flavour n *lit:* essence, piquancy, savour, smack, tang, taste; *fig:* character, feel, quality, stamp, tone; hint, suggestion, tinge, touch. vb *lit:* imbue (with), infuse (with); season, spice; *fig:* add interest to, ginger up.

flee vb *lit:* beat it, bolt, fly, make off, run away, run for it, scarper, scram, split, take a powder, take off; abscond, escape, get away; hurtle, race, speed, sprint; disappear, fade away, vanish.

fleet n *lit:* armada, flotilla, navy; company, force, team.

adj *lit:* fast, nimble, rapid, speedy, swift; ephemeral, evanescent, fast-fading, transient.

flesh **n** *lit:* meat, muscle; brawn, fat, gristle, tissue; food; *fig:* body, physical self; carnality, physical urges; humanity, humankind, human nature, humans, mankind.

flexible **adj** *lit:* elastic, plastic, pliable, pliant, springy, tensile; ductile, mouldable; agile, limber, lithe, loose-limbed, nimble, supple; *fig:* adaptable, adjustable, variable; amenable, compliant, responsive, tractable.

flight **n** *lit:* aircraft, aeroplane; journey; flying; air travel, flying time; collection, flock, swarm; squadron, wing; aeronautics, aviation; escape, fleeing, getaway; rout, scattering, stampede; *fig:* digression, foray, sally; staircase; salvo, volley; hurdle, jump; *spec:* feathering (on a dart or arrow).

flimsy **adj** *lit:* delicate, frail, insubstantial, slight, chiffon, diaphanous, gauzy, gossamer, light, sheer, thin; rickety, shaky, unsteady; *fig:* feeble, implausible, shallow, trivial, unconvincing, weak.

flippant **adj** *lit:* disrespectful, facetious, frivolous, impertinent, impudent, irreverent, pert, saucy, smart-aleck.

flirt **n** *lit:* coquette, gadabout, minx, tease; philanderer, rake. **vb** *lit:* be coquettish (with); *fig:* play (with), toy (with), trifle (with).

float **n** *lit:* bobber, cork, quill; pontoon, raft; ballcock; blade, paddle; spatula, trowel; cart, dray, flat lorry; cash in hand, petty cash, small change. **vb** *lit:* be buoyant, stay up; bob, drift, glide, slide; hover, levitate; *fig:* establish, launch, set up; circulate, divulge, publish; sell shares in.

flock **n** *lit:* nap, pile, tuft, wool; colony, flight, rookery, skein; *fig:* collection, company, crowd, group, herd, mass, throng; assembly, congregation. **vb** *lit:* assemble, collect, congregate, crowd, gather, mass, throng.

flood **n** *lit:* deluge, inundation, spate, tide, torrent; immersion, overflow, submersion; *fig:* glut, plethora, profusion, rush.

vb *lit:* drown, engulf, immerse, inundate, overflow, submerge, swamp; drench, saturate, soak; flow, gush, rush, surge; *fig:* fill, glut.

floor **n** *lit:* base, bed, bottom, ground, surface; level, storey, tier. **vb** *lit:* fell, flatten, knock down, level, raze; put down, set down; *fig:* confound, defeat, discomfit, nonplus, perplex, puzzle, stump, throw.

flourish **n** *lit:* flatfish, fluke. **n** *lit:* gesticulation, gesture, wave; display, parade, show; fanfare, tucket; decoration, embellishment, ornamentation; curlicue, kern, loop, sweep. **vb** *lit:* bloom, blossom, burgeon, flower, grow, thrive; do well, get on, increase, prosper; brandish, gesture with, swish, wave, wield; display, parade, show, vaunt.

flow **n** *lit:* circulation, current, drift, spate, stream, tide; bleeding, dripping, oozing, trickling; effusion, emanation, emission, escape, leak; cascade, deluge. **vb** *lit:* circulate, course, gush, pour, run, surge; bleed, drip, ooze, trickle; be emitted, emanate, emerge, escape, issue, leak; cascade, deluge, flood, inundate, stream, teem.

flower **n** *lit:* bloom, blossom, efflorescence; *fig:* best, cream, elite, pick. **vb** *lit:* bloom, blossom, burgeon, effloresce, open; mature, ripen; flourish, prosper, thrive.

fluctuate **vb** *lit:* alternate, go up and down, oscillate, seesaw, swing, undulate, vary; vacillate, waver.

fluid **n** *lit:* liquid; liquor; *spec:* gas (physics). **adj** *lit:* flowing, gaseous, liquid; melted, runny; aqueous, watery; *fig:* mellifluous, smooth, soft, tender; changeable, fluctuating, mercurial, volatile; elegant, graceful, sinuous.

flush **n** *lit:* blush, reddening, ruddiness; freshness, prime. **vb** *lit:* blush, burn, colour hotly, crimson, go red, redden, suffuse; douche, flood, rinse out, wash; *fig:* beat (out), hunt (out), nose (out), sniff (out). **adj** *lit:* even, flat, level, parallel, square; abundant, overflowing; rich, wealthy, well off. **adv** *lit:* evenly (with), level (with), parallel (with), squarely (against).

flustered **adj (pa.pt)** *lit:* agitated, bothered, distracted, disturbed, excited, hurried, nervous, perturbed, rattled, upset.

flute   n *lit:* fife, pipe, whistle; groove; *spec:* shuttle (in weaving).
vb *lit:* pipe, whistle; sing shrilly; carve a groove in.

fly   n *lit:* aphis, bluebottle, cleg, gnat, housefly, insect, midge; fish-hook; awning, flap, tent-door; trouser-buttons, zip.   **vb** *lit:* flutter, glide, hover, sail, soar, take wing; control, operate, pilot; have at the masthead, hoist, raise, wave; *fig:* bolt, dart, dash, race, shoot, speed, sprint, tear, zip; go (at), hurl oneself (at), rush (at); elapse, pass rapidly, roll past, vanish.   **adj** *lit:* canny, knowing, sharp, shrewd, smart.

fold   n *lit:* crease, pleat, turn-over, turn-up; furrow, wrinkle; flock of sheep, sheep-pen; *fig:* congregation, parish.   **vb** *lit:* bend over, crease, double, pleat, tuck, turn under; envelop (in), wrap (in); collapse, crumple, drop in a heap, fall over, keel over; *fig:* crash, fail, go bankrupt, go bust.

follow   **vb** *lit:* dog, pursue, shadow, stalk, track, trail; be after, look for, search for; be next, come after, succeed, supersede, tag on behind; develop, ensue, issue (from), proceed (from), result; *fig:* copy, emulate, imitate, model oneself on; adhere to, be a devotee of; conform to, keep, obey, observe; catch on, comprehend, fathom, get, grasp, see, understand; appreciate, keep up with.

follower   n *lit:* adherent, believer, devotee, disciple, fan, supporter, worshipper; attendant, henchman, retainer; hanger-on, sidekick.

following   n *lit:* acolytes, adherents, aficionados, desciples, devotees, fans, neophytes, public, supporters; crew, entourage, retinue, staff, suite.   **adj (pr.pt)** *lit:* ensuing, later, next, subsequent, succeeding, successive.

fond   **adj** *lit:* enamoured (of); adoring, devoted, doting, indulgent, loving; cherished, favourite, pet.

fondness   n *lit:* affection, devotion, love; liking (for), partiality (for), predilection (for), soft spot (for), taste (for), weakness (for).

food   n *lit:* chow, diet, fare, grub, nosh, nourishment, pabulum, provisions, rations, sustenance, tuck, victuals; cooking, cuisine, menu; feed, fodder, provender; *fig:* energy-source, fuel.

fool n *lit:* ass, blockhead, chump, clod, cretin, dolt, dunce, fathead, halfwit, idiot, imbecile, moron, nincompoop, nitwit, numbskull, simpleton, twit; butt, dupe, gull, john, mark, mug, sucker; clown, comic, jester, merryman. **vb** *lit:* bamboozle, deceive, dupe, gull, have on, hoodwink, put one over on, take in, trick; antic (about), lark (about), mess (about); play (about with), toy (with), trifle (with).

foolish adj *lit:* asinine, barmy, batwitted, brainless, cretinous, daft, fatheaded, fatuous, half-baked, idiotic, imbecile, inane, mad, moronic, senseless, stupid; absurd, ill-advised, imprudent, indiscreet, injudicious, unintelligent.

foot n *lit:* base, bottom, end, leg, podium, stanchion; 12 inches; *fig:* infantry, infantrymen; *spec:* metrical unit (in verse). **vb** *lit:* pace (out), stride (out), walk; *fig:* pay, settle.

forbid vb *lit:* ban, interdict, outlaw, prohibit, proscribe, rule out, veto.

forbidden adj (pa.pt) *lit:* banned, interdicted, outlawed, out of bounds, prohibited, proscribed, ruled out, taboo, vetoed.

force n *lit:* army, body, brigade, corps, patrol, service, squad, troop; dynamism, energy, impulse, life, momentum, power, strength, vigour; coercion, compulsion, duress, pressure, violence; emphasis, fervour, intensity, vehemence; effectiveness, efficacy, punch, weight. **vb** *lit:* compel, constrain, drive, impose (upon), oblige, pressurize; break open, prise apart, strong-arm, wrench open; extort (from), wring (from).

forceful adj *lit:* dynamic, effective, effectual, potent, powerful, weighty; cogent, compelling, telling.

forcible adj *lit:* aggressive, armed, forceful, violent; *fig:* compelling, potent, powerful.

forecast n *lit:* haruspication, prediction, prognosis, projection, prophecy. **vb** *lit:* augur, foresee, foretell, haruspicate, predict, prognosticate, prophesy.

foreign adj *lit:* alien, exotic, imported, outlandish, strange, unfamiliar; extraneous (to), irrelevant (to), unrelated (to).

foreigner n *lit:* alien, immigrant, outlander, stranger.

foreman n *lit:* gaffer, governor, overseer, superintendent, supervisor; convener, spokesman.

foresee vb *lit:* anticipate, forecast, foretell, predict, prognosticate, prophesy.

foresight n *lit:* anticipation, far-sightedness, forethought, preparedness, prescience.

forest n *lit:* woodland, woods; copse, coppice, heath, moor, scrub, thicket, undergrowth, wilderness; national park, nature reserve, parkland.

forestry n *lit:* arboriculture, silviculture, woodcraft; dendrology.

forever adv *lit:* eternally, evermore, permanently; always, continually, incessantly, perpetually.

forfeit n *lit:* fine, penalty; loss, surrendering. vb *lit:* be mulcted of, be obliged to give up, have to relinquish, lose, surrender.

forgery n *lit:* copy, counterfeit, fake, phoney, sham; copying, counterfeiting, faking.

forget vb *lit:* fail to think of, neglect, omit, overlook; leave behind; dismiss from one's mind, put behind one.

forgetful adj *lit:* absent-minded, inattentive, neglectful, oblivious, unmindful.

forgive vb *lit:* absolve of, pardon for, remit; excuse of, overlook; grant pardon.

forgiveness n *lit:* absolution, pardon, remission; grace, mercy.

forgotten adj (pa.pt) *lit:* neglected, omitted, overlooked; forlorn, forsaken, left behind; behind one, dismissed from one's mind.

fork n *lit:* pronged instrument; rake, trident; branch, prong, tine; bifurcation, divergence, divide, division, ramification, split; zigzag. vb *lit:* impale, prong, stab; dig up, rake, turn over; bifurcate, branch, diverge, divide, ramify, split; zigzag.

form n *lit:* mould, template; configuration, outline, pattern, shape; body, build, construction, figure, frame, physique, structure; framework, order, organization, plan, system; character, description, guise, mode, sort, style; fashion, manner, method, way; application, document, schedule, slip; bench, seat, settle; *fig:* condition, health, spirits, trim; behaviour, conduct, etiquette, manners, protocol; class, grade, year; background, history, record. **vb** *lit:* create, fashion, forge, make, model, mould, shape; build, construct; establish, found, set up; appear, come into being, emerge, evolve, manifest oneself, materialize, take shape; arrange, dispose, draw up, organize; *fig:* contract, cultivate, develop.

formal adj *lit:* approved, conventional, correct, decorous, prescribed, punctilious, set, solemn; ceremonial, official.

formality n *lit:* convention, correctness, decorum, etiquette, punctilio, punctiliousness, solemnity; ceremony, protocol; custom, matter of form, observance.

formation n *lit:* compilation, composition, creation, fashioning, modelling, moulding, shaping; building, construction; development, establishment, foundation; evolution, manifestation, materialization; arrangement, configuration, disposition, form, grouping, organization.

former adj *lit:* earlier, erstwhile, one-time, past, previous, prior, quondam; above, above-mentioned, aforesaid, preceding; ancient, bygone, old.

fortunate adj *lit:* favoured, lucky; convenient, opportune, timely; advantageous, favourable, felicitous.

fortune n *lit:* chance, destiny, fate, luck, providence; circumstance(s), event(s), happening(s), occurrence(s); prosperity, riches, success, treasure, wealth; bomb, mint, packet, tidy sum.

forward vb *lit:* dispatch, freight, remit, send, send on, ship; advance, aid, expedite, further, promote, speed on, support. **adj** *lit:* advance, first, foremost, leading; early, precocious, premature; bold, brazen, cheeky, familiar, fresh, impudent, officious, pert, presumptuous, pushy. **adv** *lit:* ahead, on, onward(s); into the open, into view, out; in the open, on the table.

foul n *lit:* breach of the rules, illegality, misdemeanour, villainy.
vb *lit:* contaminate, defile, dirty, pollute, smear, soil, stain; catch on, choke up, clog, entangle in, jam, obstruct, snarl up in; break the rules, commit an illegality. **adj** *lit:* contaminated, defiled, dirty, polluted, soiled, stained; disgusting, filthy, noisome, offensive, putrescent, revolting, scabrous, squalid, stinking; disgraceful, dishonourable, iniquitous, scandalous, wicked; underhand, against the rules, illegal, unfair, unscrupulous, unsportsmanlike; blasphemous, blue, coarse, gross, indecent, obscene, scatological; blustery, rough, stormy, unfavourable, wild.

found **vb** *lit:* base, ground, support; establish, inaugurate, institute, originate, set up, start. **adj (pa.pt)** *lit:* discovered, located, situated; brought to light, detected, spotted, tracked down; acquired, obtained, procured, run down.

foundation **n** *lit:* base, basis, footing, grounding; establishment, institution, origination, setting up.

founder **n** *lit:* initiator, originator, patriarch. **vb** *lit:* go to the bottom, sink; collapse, lurch, subside; go lame, stumble, trip; *fig:* break down, come to nothing, fall through.

fraction **n** *lit:* bit, fragment, part, section; chip, particle, scrap, shred, sliver; factor, multiplicand; division, sector, segment.

fragile **adj** *lit:* breakable, brittle, delicate, fine, slight, weak; *fig:* feverish, hungover, ill, liverish, nauseous, sick.

fragment **n** *lit:* bit, fraction, part, section; chip, particle, scrap, shard, sherd, shred, sliver. **vb** *lit:* break up, come apart, disintegrate, shatter, shiver, splinter, split up; disperse, divide, separate, sever.

fragrance **n** *lit:* aroma, bouquet, perfume, scent; *fig:* beauty, radiance, sweetness.

fragrant **adj** *lit:* aromatic, perfumed, scented, sweet-smelling; *fig:* beautiful, radiant.

frail **adj** *lit:* decrepit, delicate, feeble, flimsy, infirm, rickety, slight, unsteady, weak.

frame n *lit:* cross-members, form, girdering, shell, skeleton, struts, system; casing, mounting, setting, surround; cradle, support, trestle; body, build, figure, morphology, physique, shape; *fig:* mood, temper. **vb** *lit:* build (on), construct (around), fashion, form, invent, make, model, put together; case, mount, set, surround; codify, compose, couch, define, draft, express, formulate; *fig:* fit (up), fix the blame on.

frank **vb** *lit:* postmark, stamp. **adj** *lit:* blunt, candid, forthright, honest, open, outspoken, plain-spoken, sincere, straightforward, uninhibited.

frankly **adv** *lit:* bluntly, candidly, forthrightly, honestly, openly, outspokenly, plain-spokenly, sincerely, straightforwardly, uninhibitedly.

fraud n *lit:* chicanery, con, deceit, deception, duplicity, forgery, hoax, swindle, trick, trickery; charlatan, con artist, counterfeit, crook, fake, forger, impostor, mountebank, phoney, quack, sham, swindler.

fraudulent **adj** *lit:* counterfeit, crooked, deceitful, deceptive, dishonest, duplicitous, phoney, sham, spurious, swindling.

free **vb** *lit:* emancipate, let go, let out, liberate, loose, redeem, release, turn loose, unleash, untie; disentangle, extricate, relieve, rescue; clear (of), rid (of). **adj** *lit:* complimentary, for nothing, gratis, gratuitous, on the house; at large, loose, on the loose; at leisure, available, idle, spare, uncommitted, unrestricted; empty, unengaged, uninhabited, unused, vacant; casual, easy, familiar, informal, laid-back, liberal, relaxed, uninhibited; generous, lavish, munificent, open-handed, unsparing; open, unimpeded, unobstructed, unrestrained; allowed, permitted; at liberty, emancipated; autonomous, democratic, independent.

freedom n *lit:* autonomy, independence; emancipation, liberty; release; ease, familiarity, frankness, informality, openness; laxity, licence, presumption; exemption (from), immunity (from); ability (to), discretion (to), facility (to), latitude (to), leeway (to), opportunity (to), power (to), scope (to).

freely **adv** *lit:* cleanly, easily, readily, smoothly; candidly, frankly,

openly, sincerely, straightforwardly, uninhibitedly; of one's own
volition, spontaneously, voluntarily; unchallenged, unrestrainedly,
unrestrictedly; abundantly, copiously, lavishly, liberally, open-
handedly.

freeze vb *lit:* chill, frost, ice, ice over, refrigerate; numb; *fig:* fix,
peg, stiffen, stop dead, stop in one's tracks, suspend, transfix.

freight n *lit:* cargo, consignment, goods, load, payload, shipment;
carriage, transportation.

frequent vb *lit:* be a regular at, hang out at, haunt, patronize, visit
often; be most often found at. **adj** *lit:* constant, continual,
customary, familiar, habitual, persistent, recurrent, repeated.

fresh adj *lit:* green, hand-picked, natural, new, verdant; raw,
uncured, unprocessed; latest, modern, novel, recent, up-to-date;
additional, auxiliary, different, further, supplementary; bracing, brisk,
clean, crisp, invigorating, pure, spanking; blooming, glowing, healthy,
rosy, wholesome; *fig:* alert, bright, energetic, invigorated, keen, lively,
revived, spry, young; callow, inexperienced, untrained, youthful; bold,
brazen, cheeky, familiar, impudent, pert, presumptuous, saucy.

friend n *lit:* confidant, confidante, crony, intimate; buddy, china,
chum, mate, mucker, pal; ally, associate, colleague, companion,
comrade, partner.

friendly adj *lit:* affable, amiable, amicable, companionable, cordial,
genial, kindly, matey, neighbourly, sociable, well-disposed;
affectionate, attached, chummy, close, familiar, fond, intimate;
benevolent, benign, generous, good, helpful, kind, sympathetic.

friendship n *lit:* amity, concord, rapport, regard; affection,
attachment, fondness, goodwill, love; alliance, association,
companionship, comradeship, partnership.

fright n *lit:* alarm, apprehension, dread, fear, panic, terror,
trepidation; heart attack, scare, shock, start; *fig:* apparition, eyesore,
mess, scarecrow, sight.

frighten vb *lit:* alarm, petrify, put the wind up, scare, startle, terrify,
unnerve; cow, daunt, intimidate, menace, threaten; scare (away/off).

frightening   adj (pr.pt) *lit:* alarming, dreadful, fearsome, horrendous, petrifying, scary, startling, terrifying, unnerving; daunting, intimidatory, menacing, threatening; creepy, dark, eerie, ghastly, macabre, sinister, spooky.

frightful   adj *lit:* awful, dreadful, ghastly, grim, horrible, lurid, terrible; *fig:* appalling, insufferable, unpleasant, very bad.

fringe   n *lit:* border, edging, trimming; tassel; edge, freeze, limits, margin, periphery, rim.   **vb** *lit:* border, edge, hem, march on, skirt.   **adj** *lit:* alternative, unconventional, unorthodox.

frivolous   adj *lit:* dizzy, flighty, fun-loving, irresponsible, nonsensical, silly, trivial; childish, insignificant, juvenile, minor, paltry, shallow, trifling, unimportant.

from   prp *lit:* off, out of; out of the possession of; beginning at, starting at; because of, by reason of; caused by; in comparison with.

frost   n *lit:* freezing, hoar, rime; *fig:* chill, coldness, frigidity, hauteur; failure, flop.

frosty   adj *lit:* chilly, frozen, gelid, hoary, icy, wintry; *fig:* grey, white; cold, frigid, unfriendly, unapproachable.

frown   vb *lit:* glare, glower, scowl; *fig:* look askance (upon).

fruit   n *lit:* produce, product; berry, drupe, pome; grain, nut, pod, seed; crop, harvest, yield; *fig:* issue, offspring, progeny, young; advantage, benefit, profit, return; consequence, effect, outcome, result.

frustrate   vb *lit:* baffle, block, bring to nothing, counter, defeat, foil, forestall, nullify, prevent, stymie, thwart; discourage, dishearten; leave unsatisfied.

frustration   n *lit:* bafflement, blocking, bringing to nothing, countering, defeating, foiling, forestalling, nullification, prevention, thwarting; discouragement; dissatisfaction.

fuel   n *lit:* kindling, tinder; fodder, food, nourishment; ammunition, material; *fig:* encouragement, support; incitement, provocation.
vb *lit:* arm, charge, feed, fill up, load, prime, stoke; *fig:* encourage, intensify, provoke.

fulfil vb *lit:* accomplish, achieve, attain, complete, conclude, execute, keep, observe, perform, realize, satisfy.

full adj *lit:* brimming, filled, loaded; chock-a-block, crammed, crowded, jammed, packed; gorged, replete, sated, satiated, satisfied; complete, entire, intact; broad, comprehensive, detailed, extensive; exhaustive, maximum, thorough; abundant, copious, plentiful; baggy, capacious, voluminous; buxom, curvaceous, rounded; deep, loud, resonant, rich. adv *lit:* completely, entirely, thoroughly; to the brim; directly, straight; perfectly, very.

fully adv *lit:* abundantly, amply, comprehensively, sufficiently; absolutely, completely, entirely, thoroughly, totally, utterly; altogether, perfectly.

fume n *lit:* gas, smoke, vapour; *fig:* fury, heat, passion, rage. **vb** *lit:* exude, smoke; *fig:* chafe, fret, rage, seethe, smoulder.

fun n *lit:* amusement, diversion, enjoyment, entertainment, excitement, pleasure, recreation, sport; high jinks, japes, jocularity, jollity, larks, skylarking; buffoonery, clowning, teasing; horseplay, playfulness; (in) jest; (make) game (of), (make) sport (of). **adj** *lit:* amusing, enjoyable, entertaining, exciting, pleasurable.

function n *lit:* business, charge, duty, employment, job, mission, office, post, responsibility, role, task; activity, faculty, operation, purpose, service; equation; *fig:* affair, do, reception, party, thrash. vb *lit:* go, operate, run, work.

fund n *lit:* capital, exchequer, finance(s), resource(s), saving(s), treasury, kitty, pool, reserve, stock, store, vein. vb *lit:* bankroll, endow, finance, float, pay for, stake.

fundamental adj *lit:* basic, elementary, essential, indispensable, key, primary, underlying.

funeral n *lit:* memorial service, obsequies, requiem; burial, cremation, interment.

funnel n *lit:* chimney, smoke outlet, stack; cone, filter; channel, cylinder, tube. vb *lit:* channel, convey, duct, pass; filter, stream.

funny adj *lit:* amusing, choice, comic, delirious, farcical, hilarious, humorous, killing, rib-tickling, riotous, side-splitting, waggish; curious, odd, peculiar, queer, strange, suspicious, weird; eccentric, quirky; devious, tricky, underhand.

furious adj *lit:* angry, beside oneself, boiling, enraged, fuming, incensed, livid, maddened, raging; fierce, stormy, tempestuous, tumultuous, turbulent, violent; boisterous, frenzied, unrestrained, wild.

furniture n *lit:* appliances, equipment, fittings, household effects, movables; accessories, accoutrements, decor, decoration, trappings.

further vb *lit:* advance, aid, assist, expedite, forward, foster, promote, speed. **adj** *lit:* additional, extra, more, supplementary; hinder, more distant, remoter. **adv** *lit:* additionally, again, more, more deeply; at a greater distance, to a greater distance; also, besides, moreover.

fury n *lit:* anger, ire, passion, rage; ferocity, storminess, tempestuousness, turbulence, violence; frenzy, wildness.

fuss n *lit:* bother, bustle, commotion, dust, flap, flurry, fluster, furore, stir, tumult. **vb** *lit:* be flustered, fidget, flap, fret, worry; bustle (about); create a scene (about), make a song and dance (about).

fussy adj *lit:* choosy, discriminating, finicky, particular, pernickety, picky, selective; difficult, exacting, hard to please; delicate, nice, squeamish; busy, over-detailed, over-elaborate.

future n *lit:* days to come, hereafter; outlook, way ahead. **adj** *lit:* coming, prospective; later, subsequent; destined, eventual; unborn.

G

gain n *lit:* accretion, enlargement, growth, increase, rise; acquisition, earnings, emolument, increment, profit, return, winnings, yield; advance, advantage, benefit, headway, improvement, progress, victory, win. **vb** *lit:* build up, enlarge, grow, increase, rise; acquire, be paid, bring in, capture, earn, get, glean, make, net, obtain, pick up, profit by, receive, secure, take, win; advance, arrive at, attain to, benefit, catch up (on), improve, make headway, progress; *spec:* stall for (time).

gale n *lit:* cyclone, hurricane, storm, tempest, tornado, typhoon; *fig:* burst, explosion, howl, outburst, peal.

gallant n *lit:* adventurer, cavalier, daredevil, hero, buck, Corinthian, dandy, gentleman; admirer, beau, escort, suitor. **adj** *lit:* audacious, bold, brave, daring, dashing, dauntless, fearless, heroic, intrepid, manly, noble, valiant; chivalrous, courteous, gentlemanly, gracious; grand, imposing, magnificent, splendid.

gallop **vb** *lit:* hurry, race, run, speed; dash, fly, sprint.

gamble n *lit:* bet, flutter, speculation, wager; chance, lottery, risk, venture. **vb** *lit:* bet (on), have a flutter, play (at), stake, wager; chance, risk, venture.

game n *lit:* competition, contest, match, tournament; leisure activity, pastime, recreation, sport; diversion, joke, lark, romp; chase, prey, quarry; *fig:* plan, ploy, scheme, stratagem, tactic; business, line, métier; prostitution; (make) fun (of), (make) sport (of). **adj** *lit:* brave, dogged, fearless, intrepid, persistent, spirited; prepared (for), ready (for), willing (for).

gang n *lit:* band, clique, crew, group, party, ring, set, squad, team. **vb** *lit:* combine (together), come (together), team (up).

gangster n *lit:* bandit, brigand, desperado, hood, hoodlum, mobster, racketeer.

gap n *lit:* break, discontinuity, hiatus, intermission, interstice, interval, lacuna, pause, space, vacuum, void; chink, crack, crevice, hole, opening, recess, rent, rift; *fig:* difference, disparity, divergence.

gape vb *lit:* open, widen, yawn; goggle, stare.

gardening n *lit:* cultivation, horticulture; growing, planting, sowing; landscaping.

garnish n *lit:* adornment, decoration, embellishment, ornament, trimming; relish. vb *lit:* adorn, bedeck, decorate, embellish, ornament, trim; flavour, spice.

gate n *lit:* barrier, boom, grille, wicket; doorway, entrance, exit, portal; channel, passage; lock, sluice, valve; *fig:* attendance, spectators; frame, framework. vb *lit:* confine, curfew, detain, keep in, restrict.

gather vb *lit:* accumulate, amass, assemble, coacervate, expand, grow, heap up, increase, rise, thicken; collect, convene, group, hoard, muster, pile up, stack up, stockpile; clasp, embrace, enfold, hug; fold, pleat, ruffle, tuck; crop, cull, garner, harvest, pick, pluck, reap; *fig:* conclude, deduce, infer, presume, surmise, understand.

gauge n *lit:* dial, indicator, measure, meter; criterion, example, exemplar, guideline, model, pattern, sample, standard, touchstone, yardstick; bore, calibre, magnitude, span, thickness, width. vb *lit:* ascertain, assess, compute, count, determine, evaluate, judge. measure, value, weigh; estimate, guess.

gay n *lit:* homosexual, lesbian. adj *lit:* carefree, cheerful, festive, frolicsome, fun-loving, happy, jovial, joyous, light-hearted, merry, sportive, sunny; bright, colourful, flamboyant, flash, gaudy, showy; homoerotic, homosexual, lesbian, sapphic.

gaze n *lit:* gape, look, regard, stare. vb *lit:* gape, look, stare.

gear n *lit:* cog, cogwheel; linkage, machinery, mechanism, transmission, work(s); accessories, apparatus, equipment, implements, instruments, tackle, tools; accoutrements, paraphernalia, rigging, supplies, trappings; belongings, effects, kit, stuff, things; attire, clothes, clothing, garments. vb *lit:* connect, link, mesh; equip (up), fit (up), harness (up), rig (up); adapt (to), adjust (to).

gem n *lit:* jewel, precious stone, stone; *fig:* flower, masterpiece, prize, treasure.

general n *lit:* head, leader, officer; common, ordinary, usual.
adj *lit:* accepted, accustomed, common, conventional, customary, everyday, habitual, ordinary, popular, prevailing, regular, typical, universal, usual, widespread; all-inclusive, blanket, catholic, collective, comprehensive, sweeping, total; ill-defined, imprecise, indefinite, inexact, unspecific, vague.

generally adv *lit:* as a rule, commonly, conventionally, customarily, habitually, largely, mainly, mostly, normally, ordinarily, predominantly, regularly, typically, usually; extensively, popularly, universally, widely.

generate vb *lit:* breed, cause, create, engender, initiate, make for, originate, produce, stir up.

generation n *lit:* creation, engendering, genesis, origination, procreation, production, propagation; age-group, family group; *fig:* age, day, era, period, time.

generosity n *lit:* beneficence, bounty, charity, kindness, liberality, munificence; altruism, unselfishness; leniency, magnanimity.

generous adj *lit:* beneficent, bounteous, bountiful, charitable, free, kind, lavish, liberal, munificent, open-handed, unstinting; abundant, ample, copious, full, rich; altruistic, unselfish; lenient, magnanimous.

genius n *lit:* brain, intellect, mastermind; expert, master, natural, virtuoso; brilliance, flair; faculty, gift, knack, talent.

gentle adj *lit:* benign, bland, meek, mild, moderate, peaceable, placid, quiet, temperate; biddable, docile, manageable, tame, tractable; compassionate, humane, lenient, merciful; calm, easy, light, low, serene, slight, soft, tender; gradual, imperceptible, muted, slow; aristocratic, noble, patrician, refined.

genuine adj *lit:* authentic, bona fide, legitimate, real, true, veritable; honest, sound, sterling; natural, original, pure, unadulterated; heartfelt, sincere, unaffected, unfeigned.

germ n *lit:* bacterium, microbe, microorganism, virus; bud, corm, seed, spore; egg, gamete, nucleus, ovum; *fig:* beginning, origination.

gesture n *lit:* gesticulation, motion, signal; action, deed, demonstration. **vb** *lit:* beckon, gesticulate, motion, signal.

get vb *lit:* acquire, come by, come into possession of, inherit, obtain, pick up, receive, succeed to; bring, fetch, procure, secure, win; earn, gain, make, net, realize; arrest, collar, entrap, grab, seize, take; hit, shoot, strike; become, come to be, grow, turn; catch, come down with, contract; contact, reach; *fig:* comprehend, follow, hear, learn, perceive, see, understand; arrange, contrive, fix, organize, wangle; induce, influence, persuade, prevail upon; arrive, come to; affect, stimulate; annoy, irritate; confound, mystify, stump; begin, start; go, leave.

ghost n *lit:* phantom, spectre, wraith; spirit; apparition, spook; pseudonymous author; *fig:* glimmer, hint, merest possibility, shadow, suggestion. **vb** *lit:* appear suddenly, flit; author, pen, write for somebody else.

giant n *lit:* colossus, titan; ogre; enormous person; *spec:* large star. **adj** *lit:* colossal, enormous, gargantuan, huge, immense, mammoth, titanic, vast.

gift n *lit:* contribution, donation, present; gratuity, tip; bequest, legacy; oblation, offering, sacrifice; *fig:* attribute, faculty, flair, genius, talent.

gifted adj (pa.pt) *lit:* brilliant, clever, expert, masterly, superb, talented.

girl n *lit:* damsel, gal, lass, lassie, maid, maiden; daughter; miss.

give n *lit:* bend, elasticity, flexibility, resilience, resistance.
vb *lit:* bestow, confer, donate, hand over, impart, issue, present; bring, deliver, fetch, let have, provide with, supply; award, contribute, pay, return; accord, cause, create, grant; administer, deal, dole out, mete out; emit, render, transmit, utter, vent; devote, entrust with, lend; demonstrate, display, evidence, furnish, manifest, show; carry out, do, make, perform; cede, relinquish, surrender, throw (in) the towel, yield; be elastic, bend; open (on to), lead (out to).

glad　adj *lit:* delighted, gratified, happy, pleased; willing; cheerful, cheering, gratifying, pleasing.

glamour　n *lit:* allure, charisma, enchantment, fascination, magnetism, mysterious quality, spell; gloss, luminescence, radiance.

glare　n *lit:* dirty look, frown, gaze, glower, scowl; blaze, brilliance, brightness, dazzle; *fig:* garishness, gaudiness, loudness, showiness.　vb *lit:* frown, give a dirty look, gaze, glower, lower, scowl; blaze, dazzle, flare, shine brightly.

glaze　n *lit:* gloss, lacquer, varnish; slip; finish, lustre, polish, shine.　vb *lit:* gloss, lacquer, varnish; coat, laminate; fit windows, glass; *fig:* become vacant, dull, glass over, go blank.

glide　vb *lit:* plane, skate, skim, slide, slip; drift, float, sail; coast, freewheel, roll.

glimpse　n *lit:* glance, look, peek, peep; flash, sight, view.
vb *lit:* glance, look quickly, peek, peep, squint; catch sight of, espy, sight, spot.

gloom　n *lit:* darkness, dimness, dusk, murk, obscurity, shadow, umbra; *fig:* dejection, depression, despair, despondency, hopelessness, low spirits, unhappiness.

gloomy　adj *lit:* cloudy, crepuscular, dark, dim, dusky, murky, obscure, shadowy, sombre; *fig:* blue, dejected, depressed, despondent, downcast, glum, in low spirits, morose, unhappy; black, depressing, dismal, dispiriting, doleful, joyless, pessimistic.

glorious　adj *lit:* beautiful, bright, brilliant, divine, excellent, fine, gorgeous, great, heavenly, marvellous, radiant, resplendent, splendid, superb, wonderful; celebrated, distinguished, eminent, honoured, illustrious, magnificent, noted, triumphant.

glory　n *lit:* adoration, beatification, blessing, eulogy, homage, honour, praise, reverence, veneration, worship; magnificence, majesty, pomp, splendour; distinction, eminence, illustriousness, renown; beauty, brightness, brilliance, radiance, resplendence; *fig:* aura, halo.　vb *lit:* delight (in), exult (in), pride oneself (in), rejoice (in), revel (in).

glow **n** *lit:* brightness, gleam, glimmer, lambency, light, phosphorescence, radiance; *fig:* blush, flush, reddening; ardour, fervour, heat, passion, warmth. **vb** *lit:* gleam, glimmer, light, radiate, shine; be red-hot, be white-hot, burn, smoulder; be suffused, blush, colour, flush, redden, tingle.

glue **n** *lit:* adhesive, gum; tack; cement. **vb** *lit:* gum, paste; affix, cement, stick, tack.

glum **adj** *lit:* blue, dejected, depressed, despondent, doleful, downcast, gloomy, in low spirits, morose, unhappy; dismal, joyless, pessimistic.

go **n** *lit:* attempt, bash, crack, shot, stab, try, turn, whirl; drive, dynamism, energy, life, spirit, verve, vigour, vivacity. **vb** *lit:* advance, fare, move, pass, proceed, repair, travel; depart, leave, set off, withdraw; be spent, elapse, flow, lapse, slip away; die, expire, pass away, perish; break down, fail, give way; function, operate, perform, run, work; be, become; attend, be present; develop, fall out, happen, result, turn out; be acceptable, be permitted; extend (between), lead (to), reach (to), span (over), spread (over), stretch (to); refer (to), take (to); contribute (towards), serve (to), tend (towards); blend (together), chime (together), fit (together), harmonize (together).

goal **n** *lit:* mark, net, target; objective; *fig:* aim, end, object; design, intention, purpose.

god **n** *lit:* deity, divinity; fetish, idol, image; *fig:* celebrity, hero.

gold(en) **adj** *lit:* aureate, gilded, gilt, yellow; blond, blonde, flaxen; *fig:* best, glorious, happy, prosperous, rich, successful; excellent, favourable, promising, propitious.

gone **adj (pa.pt)** *lit:* absent, away, departed, vanished; lost, missing; elapsed, finished, over, past; dead, deceased, done; exhausted, spent, used.

good **n** *lit:* merit, morality, probity, righteousness, virtue; advantage, benefit, gain, profit, use, usefulness, wellbeing.
adj *lit:* acceptable, capital, commendable, fine, first-rate, great, pleasing, satisfactory, valuable, worthy; fair, halcyon, pleasant, sunny; admirable, beneficent, benevolent, charitable, estimable,

humane, honourable, kindly, praiseworthy, upright, virtuous; dutiful, mannerly, obedient, polite, proper, well-behaved; agreeable, congenial, convivial, enjoyable, gratifying; authentic, bona fide, genuine, legitimate, real, true, valid; accomplished, adept, adroit, clever, competent, dextrous, efficient, expert, proficient, skilled, useful; advantageous, beneficial, favourable, helpful, opportune, propitious; healthy, salubrious, sound, untainted, wholesome; adequate, ample, considerable, extensive, large, long, solid, substantial; (for) ever.

goods n *lit:* commodities, merchandise, stock, wares; belongings, chattels, effects, gear, paraphernalia, possessions, property, things.

gossip n *lit:* backbiter, busybody, chatterbox, scandalmonger; chitchat, hearsay, idle talk, scandal, tittle-tattle. **vb** *lit:* chat, mind other people's business, prattle, tattle, tell tales.

govern vb *lit:* administer, command, control, direct, manage, oversee, pilot, rule, steer; decide, determine, influence; check, contain, curb, discipline, master, restrain, tame.

government n *lit:* administration, authority, execution, rule; assembly, congress, diet, parliament, senate; regime; command, control, direction, management.

grab n *lit:* clutch, grasp, snatch; take-over bid, seizure, sequestration; scoop. **vb** *lit:* capture, catch, clutch, grasp, grip, nab, seize, snatch.

grace n *lit:* ease, elegance, finesse, panache, poise, polish, style, taste; attractiveness, charm; benevolence, charity, favour, goodwill, kindness; clemency, forgiveness, lenience, mercy, pardon; benediction, prayer, thanksgiving; divine influence, salvation; allowance, amnesty, interval, time in hand. **vb** *lit:* adorn, bedeck, decorate, dignify, distinguish, embellish, enhance, honour, ornament.

graceful adj *lit:* elegant, fine, flowing, gracile, natural, smooth, symmetrical.

gradual n *lit:* antiphon, canticle, processional; antiphonal, missal. **adj** *lit:* continuous, gentle, progressive, slow, steady.

grand adj *lit:* august, dignified, elevated, exalted, glorious, imposing, impressive, lofty, lordly, luxurious, magnificent, majestic, opulent, palatial, splendid, stately, sumptuous; highest, main, principal, supreme.

grant n *lit:* allowance, award, endowment, subsidy; allocation, donation. **vb** *lit:* accede to, agree to, cede, concede, consent to; accord, assign, bestow, confer, convey, give, transfer, vouchsafe, yield; acknowledge, admit.

grasp n *lit:* clasp, clutch, grip, hold, possession; *fig:* control, range, reach, scope; comprehension, perception, realization, understanding. **vb** *lit:* catch, clasp, clutch, grab, grip, hold, seize; *fig:* comprehend, get, realize, see, understand.

grass n *lit:* greenery, herbage, pasturage, verdure; sward, lawn, turf; cannabis, ganja, hemp, marijuana, pot. **vb** *lit:* lay out a lawn, turf; *fig:* inform (on), sneak (on), tell (on).

grate n *lit:* bars, griddle, grill, grille; fireplace; mesh, screen. **vb** *lit:* mince, shred; abrade, file, grind, rasp, rub, scrape, scratch; *fig:* chafe (on), get (on) one's nerves, jar (on).

grateful adj *lit:* appreciative, thankful; obliged (to).

grave n *lit:* last resting-place; crypt, tomb, vault; headstone. adj *lit:* grim, sedate, serious, sober, solemn, sombre; critical, dangerous, perilous, severe, threatening, urgent, weighty.

gravity n *lit:* force, weight; *fig:* dignity, earnestness, sobriety, seriousness, solemnity, thoughtfulness; grimness, perilousness, severity; consequence, importance, moment, significance.

graze n *lit:* abrasion, scrape; scratch; cannon, glance, kiss. **vb** *lit:* abrade, brush, chafe, scrape; cannon off, glance off, shave, skim, touch.

grease n *lit:* fat, lard; lubricant, oil; lanolin; perspiration, sweat. **vb** *lit:* lard, lubricate, oil, rub fat over, smear; *fig:* bribe with, put money in (one's palm).

greasy adj *lit:* fatty, oily; slick, slippery; *fig:* fawning, ingratiating, slimy, smarmy, unctuous.

great adj *lit:* big, bulky, expansive, extensive, immense, large, long, protracted, vast; considerable, decided, extreme, high, pronounced, strong; critical, crucial, grave, heavy, momentous, serious, significant, solemn; absolute, complete, positive, total; chief, grand, leading, main, principal; august, dignified, idealistic, impressive, lofty, noble; celebrated, distinguished, eminent, illustrious, notable, outstanding, prominent, remarkable; active, enthusiastic, keen; adept, adroit, expert, skilled; excellent, marvellous, terrific, tremendous, wonderful.

greed n *lit:* covetousness, cupidity, desire, longing, rapacity, selfishness; esurience, gluttony, insatiability, voracity.

green n *lit:* common, heath; lawn, turf; putting area. vb *lit:* blooming, flourishing, grassy, leafy, verdant; immature, unripe; pliable, supple, tender, unseasoned; ill, nauseous, pallid, sick, unhealthy; environmental, environmentalist; *fig:* callow, inexperienced, new, raw, unpractised, untrained; credulous, gullible, innocent, naive, unsophisticated; envious, jealous.

greet vb *lit:* address, hail, salute, welcome; *fig:* meet (with), react to (with), respond to (with).

greeting n *lit:* hail, salutation, salute, welcome; compliment(s), regard(s), respect(s).

grey adj *lit:* cloudy, dark, dim, dismal, drab, gloomy, murky, overcast; ashen, bloodless, pale, pallid, sallow, wan; elderly, hoary, old; *fig:* characterless, colourless, dull, neutral; indistinct, misty, vague; *spec:* white (horse).

grief n *lit:* mourning, sadness, sorrow; heartache, heartbreak, misery, wretchedness; (come to) nothing, (come to) ruin.

grievance n *lit:* beef, complaint, gripe, moan; grounds for complaint, hardship, wrong.

grieve vb *lit:* keen, lament, mourn, sorrow, weep (for); distress, hurt, pain, sadden, wound.

grill n *lit:* grate, grid, gridiron, griddle, rack; barbecue; broilery, dining-room, kitchen, restaurant; bars, lattice, mesh.
vb *lit:* barbecue, broil, roast, toast; *fig:* interrogate, pump, quiz.

grim **adj** *lit:* fierce, forbidding, formidable, sinister, terrible; frightful, ghastly, gruesome, hideous, horrible; harsh, implacable, merciless, ruthless, unrelenting; dark, gloomy, menacing, sullen, threatening.

grip **n** *lit:* clasp, clutch, grasp, hold, possession; footing, leverage, purchase; hold-all, travelling bag; clip; handle, haft; *fig:* clutches, control, influence, mastery, power; comprehension, perception, understanding. **vb** *lit:* clasp, clutch, grasp, hold, latch on to, seize; *fig:* absorb, engross, enthral, entrance, fascinate, rivet.

groan **n** *lit:* moan, sigh. **vb** *lit:* moan, sigh; call painfully, utter despairingly; *fig:* be burdened, be laden.

groove **n** *lit:* channel, cutting, furrow, rift, score, trench; *fig:* routine, rut. **vb** *lit:* channel, flute, furrow, rifle, score.

gross **n** *lit:* bulk, entirety, whole. **vb** *lit:* bring in, earn, make, take. **adj** *lit:* bulky, corpulent, fat, hulking, massive, thick; coarse, crude, improper, indecent, indelicate, offensive, ribald, rude, vulgar; boorish, crass, ignorant, insensitive, unfeeling, unsophisticated; blatant, flagrant, glaring, manifest, plain, utter; outrageous, shocking; *spec:* (earnings, income) before tax.

ground **n** *lit:* earth, land, soil, terra firma; arena, field, park, pitch; floor; *spec:* (electrical) earth, earthing. **vb** *lit:* lay down, put down; base, establish, pitch, set; coach (in), educate (in), initiate (in), instruct (in), teach (in), tutor (in). **adj (pa.pt)** *lit:* crushed, milled, powdered, pulverized; filed (down), sanded (down); eroded (away); *fig:* oppressed.

group **n** *lit:* band, bunch, cluster, collection, company, gang, gathering, pack, party, set; class, category. **vb** *lit:* assemble, associate, cluster, collect, gather, get together; arrange, assort, bracket together, classify, marshal, order, put together, sort.

grow **vb** *lit:* develop, germinate, shoot, sprout; breed, cultivate, farm, produce, propagate; arise (from), spring (from), stem (from); augment, enlarge, expand, extend, get bigger, increase, spread, stretch, swell; advance, flourish, multiply, progress; *fig:* become, come to be, get, turn.

growth n *lit:* development, germination, shoot, sprout; cultivation, propagation; evolution; augmentation, enlargement, expansion, extension, increase, spread, stretching, swelling; cancer, lump, tumour; advance, flourishing, multiplication, progress, proliferation.

gruelling adj *lit:* arduous, backbreaking, demanding, exhausting, grinding, laborious, punishing, stiff, taxing.

gruesome adj *lit:* bloody, ghastly, gory, grim, grisly, horrible, horrific, macabre, sickening, terrible.

guarantee n *lit:* assurance, collateral, pledge, security, warranty. **vb** *lit:* answer for, insure, pledge, promise, stand behind, vouch for, warrant.

guard n *lit:* defender, lookout, sentinel, sentry, warder, watchman; custodian, jailer, screw; escort; buffer, bumper, pad, safety screen, shield; vigilance, wariness, watchfulness. **vb** *lit:* defend, patrol, police, protect, secure, watch over; escort, mind, tend.

guardian n *lit:* keeper, protector, trustee, warden; curator, custodian, escort, guard, warder.

guess n *lit:* conjecture, hypothesis, speculation, supposition, surmise, theory. **vb** *lit:* conjecture, estimate, fancy, hazard, hypothesize, imagine, reckon, surmise.

guest n *lit:* caller, visitor; boarder, lodger; *spec:* inquiline.

guide n *lit:* beacon, key, landmark, pointer, sign, signal, signpost; directory, handbook, manual; chaperon, conductor, escort, leader, pilot, usher; *fig:* master, paradigm; example, inspiration. **vb** *lit:* control, direct, handle, manoeuvre, steer; conduct, escort, lead, shepherd, usher; advise, counsel.

guilt n *lit:* blameworthiness, culpability; misconduct, wrongdoing; bad conscience, self-condemnation, shame; dishonour.

guilty adj *lit:* culpable, responsible, wrong; ashamed, contrite, hangdog, remorseful, rueful, sorry.

gun n *lit:* firearm; cannon, gat, rod; pistol, revolver, rifle, shotgun; starting pistol; *fig:* nozzle, spray, syringe; accelerator, throttle.

vb *lit:* hunt (down), shoot (down); *fig:* hunt (for), look (for); accelerate, race.

gutter **n** *lit:* conduit, drain, pipe; ditch, groove, scuppers, trench, trough. **vb** *lit:* flicker, smoke.

guts **n** *lit:* bowels, intestines; entrails, tripes, viscera; *fig:* backbone, bottle, bravery, courage, fortitude, nerve, pluck, spunk; insides, machinery, works.

guy **n** *lit:* bloke, geezer, man; chap, fellow, lad. **vb** *lit:* caricature, make fun of, send up, take off.

gypsy **n** *lit:* Romany, tinker, traveller; rover; vagrant.

H

habit n *lit:* custom, fashion, practice, routine, rule, tendency, way; idiosyncrasy, mannerism, proclivity, trait, wont; consuetude, usage; addiction, dependence; composition, constitution, frame, make-up, nature, structure; apparel, costume, dress, garb, garment.

hail n *lit:* call, cheer, greeting, shout, yell; greetings, salutation; bombardment, rain, shower, volley; *fig:* shouting-distance; *spec:* frozen rain, ice. **vb** *lit:* address, call to, greet, shout to, yell at; accost, flag down, wave down; acclaim, applaud, glorify, honour, salute; cascade (down), pelt, pour (down), rain; come (from), have started (from), originate (from).

hair n *lit:* locks, mane, mop, tresses; filament, strand, thread, villus; down, fluff, fur; *fig:* fraction, narrow margin, whisker; split second.

hairy adj *lit:* hirsute, shaggy, woolly; bearded, bewhiskered, stubbly, unshaven; downy, fleecy, flocculent, furry; awned, tufted; *fig:* chancy, dicey, hazardous, risky.

hall n *lit:* corridor, passageway; entrance, entry, foyer, lobby, vestibule; auditorium, chamber, meeting-place, nave, salon; dormitory, residence; manor-house, mansion.

halt n *lit:* pause, standstill, stop; impasse; close, end, termination. **vb** *lit:* draw up, hold still, pause, pull up, stop; break off, cease, desist, take a rest; arrest, check, curb, terminate; block, obstruct.

hammer n *lit:* gavel, mallet, striking head; clapper. **vb** *lit:* bang, beat, hit, strike; drive; fashion, forge, make, shape; *fig:* clobber, defeat, drub, thrash, trounce; din (into), drum (into), grind (into); beaver (away at), drudge (away at), keep (on at), plug (on away at), work (away at).

hamper n *lit:* basket. **vb** *lit:* delay, encumber, handicap, hinder, hold back, hold up, impede, obstruct.

hand n *lit:* mitt, paw; assistance, help, support; influence, part, role, share; crewman, employee, labourer, operative, sailor, worker; clap, ovation, round of applause; artistry, deftness, dexterity, skill; calligraphy, handwriting, longhand, script, writing; *fig:* (in) order, (in) progress, (in) readiness, (in) reserve; (at) one's command, (on) tap.   **vb** *lit:* deliver, give, pass; assist, help.

handicap   **n** *lit:* defect, disability, impairment; disadvantage, difficulty, drawback, encumbrance, hindrance, impediment, limitation, penalty, restriction, stumbling-block; edge, head start.   **vb** *lit:* encumber, hamper, hinder, hold back, hold up, impede, limit, restrain, restrict, retard.

handle   **n** *lit:* grip, haft, hilt, knob, lever, stock, switch; *fig:* agnomen, cognomen, name, nickname, praenomen, title. **vb** *lit:* feel, grasp, hold, pick up, touch; control, direct, manage, manipulate, manoeuvre, use, wield; cope with, deal with, take care of, treat; deal in, trade in, traffic in.

handsome   **adj** *lit:* attractive, becoming, comely, fine, good-looking, personable; ample, bountiful, large; generous, liberal, magnanimous.

happen   **vb** *lit:* befall, come about, come to pass, eventuate, occur, pass, take place; fall out, turn out; be done (to), transpire (to); appear, arise, crop up, materialize.

happily   **adv** *lit:* cheerfully, contentedly, delightedly, gaily, gladly, joyfully, pleasurably, willingly; appropriately, suitably; felicitously, harmoniously, successfully; fortunately, luckily, providentially; blithely, casually, unwittingly.

happiness   **n** *lit:* cheerfulness, contentment, delight, enjoyment, gaiety, gladness, harmony, joy, joyfulness, joyousness, light-heartedness, pleasure; beatitude, blessedness, jubilation; bliss, ecstasy.

happy   **adj** *lit:* cheerful, contented, delighted, gay, glad, gratified, joyful, joyous, pleased, sunny; blissful, ecstatic, elated, exultant, overjoyed, rapturous; over the moon, thrilled, walking on air; beatific, blessed, rapt; appropriate, apt, opportune, timely; favourable, felicitous, promising, successful; fortunate, lucky, providential; blithe, casual, unwitting.

harass   **vb** *lit:* badger, beleaguer, chivvy, harry, hassle, hound, pester, plague, trouble, vex, worry; annoy, bug, exasperate, torment.

harbour n *lit:* anchorage, marina, port, quay, wharf, yacht-basin; *fig:* haven, mooring, shelter; asylum, refuge, retreat, sanctuary.
vb *lit:* accommodate, lodge, provide refuge for, shelter; conceal, hide, protect, shield; entertain, foster, hold, nurse, retain.

hard adj *lit:* compact, firm, inflexible, rigid, solid, stiff, strong, tough, unyielding; bare, indisputable, physical, plain, practical, real, unvarnished; arduous, backbreaking, complex, complicated, difficult, formidable, intricate, involved, knotty, laborious, rigorous, strenuous, thorny, uphill; bad, disagreeable, distressing, grievous, harsh, painful, ugly, unpleasant; fierce, forceful, powerful, violent; cold, grim, implacable, mean, near, obdurate, pitiless, ruthless, stern, strict, stingy, unfeeling, unsparing; acrimonious, bitter, hostile, rancorous; *spec:* alcoholic (drinks); calciferous (water); penetrative (rays).
adv *lit:* assiduously, determinedly, diligently, energetically, forcefully, industriously, intensely, intently, keenly, persistently, powerfully, strenuously, strongly, vigorously, violently; badly, harshly, laboriously, painfully, roughly, slowly, with difficulty; completely, fully; firmly, solidly, tightly; close, near; *spec:* (frozen) fast, solid; (hold) tight.

harden vb *lit:* set, solidify, stiffen; cake, congeal, gell, freeze; anneal, temper; *fig:* brace, fortify, nerve, steel, strengthen; accustom, habituate, inure, season, train; brutalize, toughen; *spec:* (share prices) rise.

hardly adv *lit:* barely, just, only just, scarcely; probably not, surely not; with difficulty.

hardship n *lit:* burden, difficulty, encumbrance, labour, oppression, privation, suffering, trial, tribulation, trouble.

harm n *lit:* damage, hurt, ill, impairment, injury; detriment, disservice, mischief. **vb** *lit:* damage, hurt, ill-treat, ill-use, impair, injure, maltreat, spoil.

harmful adj *lit:* damaging, hurtful, impairing, injurious, noxious; baneful, deleterious, detrimental, malignant, mischievous, pernicious; destructive, ruinous.

harmless adj *lit:* innocuous; not poisonous, safe; gentle, inoffensive, mild.

harmony n *lit:* euphony, mellifluousness, musicality; arrangement, chord-structure, part-writing; *fig:* accord, agreement, balance, compatibility, concord, consonance, correspondence, rapport, unanimity, unity; amicability, friendship, sympathy, understanding.

harsh adj *lit:* discordant, dissonant, strident; grating, jarring, rasping, raucous, rough; brutal, cruel, dour, draconian, hard, pitiless, relentless, ruthless, stern, strict, unfeeling, unpleasant; austere, grim, severe, spartan; bleak, cold, sharp, unrelenting; acrid, astringent, bitter, pungent, sour.

harvest n *lit:* gathering, gleaning, reaping; crop, produce, yield; *fig:* fruits, result, return; effect, product. **vb** *lit:* gather, glean, reap; pick, pluck; mow; *fig:* accumulate, amass, collect, garner, take in.

haste n *lit:* dispatch, expedition, hurrying, urgency; hustle, impetuosity, rush.

hasty adj *lit:* impetuous, impulsive, precipitate, rash, thoughtless; cursory, fleeting, perfunctory, short, superficial; brusque, fiery, impatient, irascible, quick-tempered.

hate n *lit:* abhorrence, detestation, loathing, odium, repugnance, revulsion; animosity, antagonism, antipathy, dislike. **vb** *lit:* abhor, be repelled by, detest, have an aversion to, loathe; be antagonistic towards, dislike intensely; be loath (to), be sorry (to), be unwilling (to).

haul n *lit:* drag, heave, pull; distance, journey, trip; catch, harvest, yield; *fig:* booty, loot, spoils, swag, takings. **vb** *lit:* drag, heave, pull, tug; draw, tow, trail; carry, hump, lug; cart, convey, move, transport; *spec:* turn, veer (of a sailing-ship, of the wind).

haunt n *lit:* base, habitat, hangout, patch, stamping-ground, territory; den, hidey-hole, lair, refuge, retreat, sanctum. **vb** *lit:* come back, frequent, return, visit; beset, obsess, prey on, weigh on.

have vb *lit:* hold, keep, own, possess, retain; carry, stock, store; comprehend, contain, include, take in; accept, get, obtain, receive, secure, take; acquire, gain; enjoy, experience, feel, meet with, suffer, sustain, undergo; allow, consider, endure, entertain, permit, put up with, tolerate; be a parent of, bear, bring forth, deliver, give birth to; be a relative of; assert, declare, maintain; engage in, carry on; cheat, deceive, fool, hoax, outwit, swindle, trick; be compelled (to), be forced (to), be obliged (to), be required (to), ought (to); cause to, force to, oblige to, require to; cause to be, require to be.

head n *lit:* brain-case, cranium, skull; block, bonce, loaf, noddle, nut, poll; apex, crest, crown, peak, summit, tip, top; climax, crisis, culmination, dénouement, turning-point; cape, foreland, promontory; boss, captain, chief, commander, director, leader, manager, master, principal; fore, forefront, front, van; beginning, origin, rise, source, start; ability, aptitude, brains, flair, intelligence, mentality, mind, understanding; capacity, faculty; division, section, subject, topic; lavatory, toilet, WC; individual, person, soul; *spec:* chuck (on a drill, a lathe); cluster (of flowers); froth (on beer); pick-up (on a tape-head); pressure (of steam in a steam-engine); (lose one's) self-control; striking end (of a hammer). **vb** *lit:* be on top of, cap, crown, top; go first of, lead; excel, outdo, outstrip; be in charge of, command, control, direct, govern, manage, rule, run; aim (for), make (for), set off (for), steer (for); go, move, travel, turn; decapitate, lop, poll; butt; cut (off), fend (off), ward (off).

heading n *lit:* headline, rubric, title; division, section; bearing, compass-point, direction; *spec:* drift, exploratory tunnel (in a mine), hitting a ball with one's head (soccer), leading (a group, revolt, etc.).

headquarters n *lit:* base, barracks, camp, command centre, home, living quarters, main office, offices, post, residence, station.

heal vb *lit:* cure, remedy, restore; knit, mend, regenerate; *fig:* patch up, reconcile, settle, smooth over.

healing n *lit:* curing, officinal, remedying, restoration; knitting, mending, regeneration; *fig:* reconciliation, smoothing things over. **adj (pr.pt)** *lit:* curative, medicinal, remedial, restorative, therapeutic; comforting, soothing.

health n *lit:* condition, fitness, shape, soundness, well-being.

healthy adj *lit:* fit, hale and hearty, in fine fettle, in good condition, in the pink, sound, well; active, flourishing, robust, strong, sturdy; beneficial, bracing, invigorating, nourishing, wholesome; hygienic, sanitary.

hear **vb** *lit:* listen to; attend to, hearken to, heed, take in; catch, pick up; be informed, be told, find, gather, learn, understand; examine, judge, try.

heart **n** *lit:* cardiac muscle; centre, core, hub, kernel, middle, nucleus; *fig:* mind, soul; affection, love; feeling, sentiment, sympathy; disposition, nature, temperament; bottle, courage, fortitude, guts, nerve; determination, resolution, spirit; energy, enthusiasm; crux, essence, marrow, pith, root; (by) memory, (by) rote.

heartless **adj** *lit:* brutal, callous, cold, cruel, harsh, merciless, pitiless, unfeeling.

heat **n** *lit:* high temperature, temperature, warmth; torridity; febrility, fever; blaze, fire, flame; *fig:* intensity, fervour, vehemence; agitation, excitement, passion; pressure; *spec:* oestrus (in female mammals); eliminator, preliminary race, qualifier.   **vb** *lit:* keep warm, make hot, warm (up); cook, microwave, put on the boil; *fig:* excite, inflame, rouse, stimulate.

heave **n** *lit:* haul, pull, tow, tug; fling, pitch, throw; convulsion, surge, swell; *spec:* dislocation, displacement (of a geological stratum).   **vb** *lit:* drag, haul, pull, tow, tug; hoist (up), lift (up); fling, hurl, pitch, throw, toss; billow, convulse, rise, surge, swell; breathe heavily, give vent to, pant, utter, wheeze; gag, retch.

heaven **n** *lit:* garden of Eden, paradise; life to come, next world, Nirvana; Elysian fields, happy hunting-ground, place of the dead, Valhalla; firmament, sky; *fig:* bliss, ecstasy, joy, rapture.

heavy **adj** *lit:* hefty, massive, ponderous, weighty; burdened, encumbered, loaded, pregnant; bulky, portly, stout; extra-large, giant, jumbo; broad, coarse, thick; awkward, clumsy, lumbering, slow, sluggish, torpid, wooden; dull, gloomy, leaden, lowering; burdensome, difficult, hard, laborious, onerous, severe, taxing; complex, deep, grave, profound, serious; boisterous, stormy, tempestuous, turbulent, violent; abundant, copious, excessive, profuse.

hectic adj *lit:* excited, feverish, frantic, frenetic, frenzied; flushed, rosy; fevered; atrophied, consumptive, painfully thin, wasted.

height n *lit:* altitude, elevation; tallness; crag, fell, rocky point; hill, mountain, peak, summit; apex, crest, crown, pinnacle, top, zenith; climax, culmination, limit, maximum, ultimate; acme, embodiment, epitome; eminence, grandeur.

hell n *lit:* Gehenna, Hades, infernal regions, nether world, Tartarus, underworld; abyss, bottomless pit, eternal fires, fire and brimstone, weeping and wailing and gnashing of teeth; purgatory; *fig:* agony, martyrdom, nightmare, ordeal, torment; commotion, din, uproar; deuce, dickens, heck.

help n *lit:* aid, assistance, succour, support; avail, benefit, use; collaboration, co-operation; amelioration, facilitation, improvement; balm, relief, remedy; assistant, worker. **vb** *lit:* aid, assist, lend a hand, succour, support; abet, be with, collaborate with, co-operate with; serve; ameliorate, facilitate, improve; alleviate, cure, remedy; avoid, prevent oneself from; abstain from, keep from, refrain from, resist.

helpful adj *lit:* accommodating, considerate, cooperative, kind, neighbourly; beneficial, profitable, serviceable, useful; constructive, practical, productive, supportive, timely.

helpless adj *lit:* defenceless, exposed, unprotected, vulnerable; feeble, incapable, weak; impotent, powerless; incompetent.

hence adv *lit:* and so, ergo, for which reason, therefore; from now, from this time; from here, from this place; from that source.

herald n *lit:* announcer, crier, messenger; forerunner, harbinger, precursor, token; *spec:* member of the Royal College of Arms. **vb** *lit:* pave the way, precede, presage, usher in; announce, broadcast, proclaim, publish, trumpet.

hereditary adj *lit:* congenital, genetic, inheritable, transmissible; ancestral, bequeathed, family, handed down, inherited, patrimonial.

hero n *lit:* popular figure; conqueror, victor; celebrity, demigod, idol, star, superstar; champion; lead, principal character, protagonist.

heroic adj *lit:* audacious, bold, brave, courageous, daring, fearless, gallant, intrepid, valiant; epic, legendary, mythological; *fig:* elaborate, exaggerated, extravagant, grandiose, inflated.

hesitant adj *lit:* reluctant, unwilling; diffident, halting, irresolute, timid, uncertain, vacillating, wavering.

hesitate vb *lit:* be reluctant (to), be unwilling (to), scruple (to); delay, pause, wait; dither, falter, shillyshally, vacillate, waver.

hidden adj (pa.pt) *lit:* cloaked, concealed, covert, masked, shrouded, veiled; cryptic, occult, secret; dark, obscure; ulterior, clandestine, furtive, underhand.

hide n *lit:* concealment, hiding-place. **vb** *lit:* conceal, cover, mask, screen, shroud, veil; bury, cache; hush up, keep secret, suppress; camouflage, disguise; go to ground, go underground, hole up, lie low.

hideous adj *lit:* frightful, grotesque, gruesome, horrible, monstrous, ugly, unsightly; appalling, awful, dreadful, repulsive, sickening, terrible.

high adj *lit:* lofty, tall; elevated, soaring, towering; chief, eminent, exalted, important, main, noble, prominent, ruling, superior; capital, grave, serious; extreme, great, powerful; dear, expensive, steep, stiff; extravagant, grand, lavish, rich; arrogant, domineering, haughty, lofty, overbearing, proud; latest, most advanced; acute, piercing, sharp, shrill, soprano, treble; gamy, niffy, putrescent, rancid, slightly off, whiffy; elated, exhilarated, merry, tipsy; euphoric, freaked out, inebriated, intoxicated, legless, pissed as a newt, spaced out, stoned, turned on. **adv** *lit:* aloft, far up, way above.

hill n *lit:* down, fell, tor; hummock, knoll, kopje, mound; gradient, incline, rise, slope.

hindrance n *lit:* check, encumbrance, handicap, impediment, limitation, restriction; barrier, hurdle, obstacle, obstruction, stumbling-block; difficulty, drawback, snag.

hint n *lit:* clue, intimation, pointer, suggestion, tip, whisper, word, wrinkle; implication, innuendo, insinuation; allusion, mention; dash, speck, suspicion, taste, tinge, trace, whiff. **vb** *lit:* give a clue, suggest, tip off; imply, insinuate; allude, mention.

hire   n *lit:* rent, rental; charge, fee, payment, price, wages.
vb *lit:* charter, lease, rent; lease out, let, rent out; employ, engage, sign up, take on.

historic   adj *lit:* earth-shattering, epoch-making; great, important, momentous, significant; consequential, seminal; famous, illustrious.

historical   adj *lit:* chronicled, documented, recorded; attested, authentic, factual, verified; antiquated, archaic, old-fashioned, outmoded; of olden days.

history   n *lit:* ancient days, antiquity, olden days, past, yesterday; annals, archives, chronicles, records; account, recital, story; autobiography, biography.

hit   n *lit:* blow, buffet, impact, knock; clout, cuff, punch, rap, slap, smack, swipe, tap, thump, thwack, wallop, whack; cannon, collision; shot, stroke; *fig:* fluke, lucky chance; sensation, smash, success, triumph, winner; dig, sarcasm, thrust, witticism; assassination, murder.   **vb** *lit:* bang, bash, beat, belt, buffet, clobber, clout, cuff, knock, punch, slap, smack, strike, thump, wallop, whack; bang into, bump, cannon into, collide with, crash into, run into; damage, devastate, overwhelm; *fig:* affect, influence, leave a mark on, touch; attain, gain, reach; accomplish, achieve; come across, encounter; assassinate, murder.

hoard   n *lit:* cache, stockpile, treasure-trove; heap, mass, pile, store.   **vb** *lit:* cache, garner, lay up, put by, stash away, stockpile; amass, heap up, pile up, store.

hobby   n *lit:* avocation, leisure activity, pastime, pursuit, sideline; amusement, entertainment.

hold   n *lit:* clutch, grasp, grip; footing, leverage, purchase; *fig:* dominance, influence, power, pull, sway; *spec:* cargo space (on a ship); fermata, pause (in musical dynamics).   **vb** *lit:* clasp, cling to, clutch, grasp, grip; have, keep, retain; be in possession of, occupy, possess; bear, carry, support, sustain, take; accommodate, be large enough for, contain, seat; arrest, detain, restrain, stop; confine, imprison; *fig:* believe, consider, deem, judge, reckon, think; be in force, continue, exist, last, operate, persist, remain, stand; call, conduct, convene, convoke, organize, run; be enough for, satisfy; adhere (to), stick (to).

hole n *lit:* aperture, crack, fissure, opening, orifice, outlet, puncture, rent, tear; cavity, gap; excavation, hollow, pit, shaft; burrow, den, earth, lair, scrape, sett; *fig:* dive, dump, joint; fix, jam, mess, spot; discrepancy, fallacy, fault, flaw, inconsistency.   **vb** *lit:* sink.

holiday n *lit:* break, furlough, leave, leisure-time, time off; feast, festival, saint's day; statutory day off.

hollow n *lit:* basin, bowl, concavity, crater, dell, depression, dingle, hole, pit, trough; crease, dimple; palm; channel, groove.   **adj** *lit:* empty, vacant; deep-set, indented, sunken; *fig:* booming, deep, dull, resonant, sepulchral; empty, meaningless, pointless, specious, useless; artificial, false, flimsy, insincere.   **adv** *fig:* dully, resonantly, sepulchrally; falsely, insincerely; completely, thoroughly, totally, utterly.

holy adj *lit:* consecrated, hallowed, sacred, sacrosanct; divine, godly, numinous; pious, religious, saintly; blessed, venerable; *fig:* awesome, dreadful, unearthly; unholy.

home n *lit:* fireside, hearth, household; abode, domicile, dwelling, habitation, place, residence; habitat, nest; base; asylum, hall of residence, institution, refuge, sanatorium; *fig:* (at) ease (in); *spec:* plate (in baseball).   **vb** *lit:* be directed (in on), be guided (in on).   **adj** *lit:* domiciliary, household, residential; own, private; familiar, normal, usual; national; local.   **adv** *lit:* to one's domicile, to one's household, to one's residence, to one's country; *fig:* to one's destination, to one's goal, to where one belongs.

homosexual n *lit:* gay; lesbian.   **adj** *lit:* gay, homoerotic; lesbian, sapphic.

honest adj *lit:* ethical, honourable, straight, true, truthful, veracious; decent, law-abiding, reputable, upright, virtuous; reliable, trustworthy; authentic, bona fide, genuine, real; candid, frank, open, sincere; equitable, fair, good, just.

honesty n *lit:* ethics, honour, truthfulness, veracity; faithfulness, fidelity; decency, integrity, legality, morality, probity, uprightness, virtue; authenticity, genuineness, good faith, straightforwardness, trustworthiness; candour, frankness, openness, sincerity; equity, fairness, goodness, justice.

honour n *lit:* credit, esteem, fame, glory, kudos, prestige, repute; commendation, glorification, homage, recognition, reverence, veneration; dignity, high rank; decency, honesty, integrity, morality, probity, uprightness, virtue; chastity, modesty, purity, virginity; compliment, grace, privilege; decoration, distinction, title; *spec:* high trump (in cards). **vb** *lit:* acclaim, celebrate, glorify, pay homage to, venerate; adore, hallow, revere, worship; dignify, ennoble, exalt; decorate; compliment, grace; commend, praise; be faithful to, discharge, fulfil, keep, perform; acknowledge, credit; *spec:* accept, cash, clear, pass, pay (a monetary transaction).

honourable adj *lit:* decent, law-abiding, reputable, upright, virtuous; equitable, ethical, fair, good, honest, just, moral, principled, reliable, trustworthy; creditable, estimable, noble, proper, right.

hop n *lit:* jump, skip, step; twitch; leg, short flight; dance, dancing party. **vb** *lit:* jump on one leg; bound, skip, spring; fly across, take a short flight; *fig:* beat (it), get out of (it).

hope n *lit:* desire, dream, expectancy, wish; ambition; anticipation, expectation; optimism; grounds for optimism, promise. **vb** *lit:* aspire (to), long (to), look forward (to); long (for), wait (for); earnestly wish, trust.

hopeful adj *lit:* expectant, optimistic, sanguine; auspicious, encouraging, heartening, promising, propitious.

hopeless adj *lit:* irreparable, irreversible; futile, impossible, impracticable, pointless, useless, vain; incompetent, inferior, worthless; despairing, desperate.

horrible adj *lit:* awful, dreadful, frightful, ghastly, grim, gruesome, hideous, repugnant, repulsive; beastly, disagreeable, mean, nasty, unkind.

horrid adj *lit:* awful, beastly, disagreeable, malevolent, malignant, mean, nasty, offensive, spiteful, unpleasant.

horrify vb *lit:* appal, outrage, shock; disgust, nauseate, revolt, sicken.

horror n *lit:* abhorrence, disgust, nausea, repugnance, revulsion; dread, fright; *fig:* disgusting thing, loathsome creature, monster.

hospitable adj *lit:* generous, gracious, liberal, receptive, welcoming.

hospitality n *lit:* welcome; reception; generosity, liberality, kindness.

host n *lit:* guest-master, inviter; innkeeper, landlord, proprietor; anchor man, master of ceremonies, presenter; parasiticized object; army, horde, mass, mob, multitude, vast number; *spec:* bread (at Communion services). vb *lit:* compere, introduce, present; entertain.

hostage n *lit:* captive, pawn; security.

hostile adj *lit:* adverse, antagonistic, bellicose, belligerent, inimical, opposed, unfriendly.

hot adj *lit:* boiling, scorching, searing, sultry, sweltering, torrid, tropical; burning, fiery, flaming, heated, roasting, scalding; curried, peppery, spicy; *fig:* ardent, fervent, intense, passionate, vehement; fierce, fiery, impetuous, lustful, stormy; approved, popular. adv *lit:* close, immediately.

hotel n *lit:* boarding-house, caravanserai, guest-house, hostel, rooming-house; hospice, inn; chalet, motel.

house n *lit:* building, dwelling, edifice, residence; abode, domicile, home; clan, family, line, lineage; business, company, establishment, firm, organization. vb *lit:* accommodate, contain, cover, harbour, keep, put up, sheathe, shelter, take in.

household n *lit:* family, folks, home, ménage, people; establishment. adj *lit:* domestic, family; about the house.

however adv *lit:* by what means, how on earth, in what way; no matter how, to whatever extent. cnj *lit:* all the same, at all events, but, despite this, nevertheless, nonetheless, still, yet.

hug n *lit:* clasp, clinch, embrace, squeeze; grip, hold. vb *lit:* clasp, embrace, enfold, hold, squeeze; *fig:* cleave to, skirt, stay close to; be protective towards, cling on to, guard, hang on to, nurse.

huge   adj *lit:* colossal, cyclopean, enormous, gargantuan, gigantic, immense, mammoth, massive, monumental, prodigious, titanic, tremendous, vast.

human   n *lit:* individual, man, person, woman; mortal, soul.
adj *lit:* anthropoid; mortal; approachable, kindly, understanding; forgivable, natural, understandable; fallible, vulnerable.

humane   adj *lit:* benign, compassionate, gentle, good-natured, kindly, sisterly love, sympathetic, understanding; charitable, forgiving, lenient, merciful.

humanity   n *lit:* human race, mankind, people everywhere; benevolence, brotherly love, compassion, generosity, gentleness, kindliness, kindness, sympathy, toleration, understanding; leniency, mercy.

humble   vb *lit:* abase, degrade, demean, humiliate; bring down, chasten, disgrace, mortify, shame, subdue, take down a peg.
adj *lit:* modest, self-effacing, unassuming; deferential, obsequious, respectful, subservient; common, lowly, obscure, ordinary, simple, undistinguished, unpretentious; commonplace, insignificant, low, mean, plebeian, poor, unimportant.

humid   adj *lit:* muggy, steamy, sticky, sultry; damp, moist.

humorous   adj *lit:* amusing, comical, funny, waggish, witty; droll, facetious, jocose, playful.

humour   n *lit:* mood, spirits, state of mind, temper; caprice, fancy, freak, vagary, whim; comedy, drollery, jocularity, joking, pleasantries, wit, witticisms.   **vb** *lit:* accommodate, gratify, indulge, pander to; acquiesce in, flatter.

hunger   n *lit:* ravening, starvation; appetite; emptiness; craving, desire, longing, need, yearning.   **vb** *lit:* raven (for), starve (for); have an appetite (for); crave, long, lust, pine, yearn.

hungry   adj *lit:* ravening, starved, starving, empty, famished, peckish; *fig:* eager (for), greedy (for).

hunt n *lit:* chase, pursuit; quest; search; *spec:* pack (of hounds).
vb *lit:* chase, harry, hound, pursue; follow, stalk, track down; forage (for), look (for), search (for), seek.

hurricane n *lit:* cyclone, gale, storm, tempest, tornado, typhoon.

hurry n *lit:* dash, rush; flurry, haste, speed; dispatch, urgency; commotion. **vb** *lit:* dash, fly, race, run, rush; accelerate, expedite, hasten, quicken, speed; hustle, push on, spur on.

hurt n *lit:* injury, lesion, sore, trauma, wound; bruise; distress, pain; damage, mischief, wrong. **vb** *lit:* injure, wound; bruise, damage, harm, impair; ache, be sore, pain, sting, throb; *fig:* aggrieve, cut to the quick, distress, pain, sadden. **adj (pa.pt)** *lit:* injured, wounded; bruised, damaged, harmed, impaired; in pain, sore; *fig:* aggrieved, cut to the quick, distressed, miffed, offended, pained, piqued, saddened.

husband n *lit:* man, partner; hubby, old man; spouse. **vb** *lit:* conserve, garner, hoard, save, store; be steward over, be thrifty with, manage carefully.

hut n *lit:* cabin, hogan, lean-to, shack, shanty, shed.

hypnotic n *lit:* anaesthetic, sedative; narcotic, opiate; drug.
adj *lit:* mesmerizing, spellbinding, trance-inducing; narcotic, opiate; sedative, soporific.

hypocrisy n *lit:* double standards, inconsistency; cant, duplicity, insincerity, speciousness.

hypocrite n *lit:* charlatan, faker, fraud, Holy Joe, impostor, mountebank, sham.

hypothesis n *lit:* postulate, premise, proposition, supposition, theory; conjecture, possibility, suggestion.

hypothetical adj *lit:* academic, conjectural, posited, postulated, putative, speculative, theoretical; proposed, supposed.

I

icy adj *lit:* arctic, biting, bitter, boreal, cryogenic, freezing, frosty, frozen, gelid, raw; glassy, slippery, slippy, wintry; *fig:* cold, distant, frigid, glacial, hostile, inimical, stony.

idea n *lit:* hypothesis, suggestion, supposition, theory; design, plan, scheme; concept, conception, thought; fancy, notion, whim; belief, conviction, opinion, view, viewpoint; aim, end, intention, meaning, object, objective, purpose; import, reasoning, significance; clue, hint, inkling, suspicion; feeling, impression; essence, form, gist, nub.

ideal n *lit:* paragon, perfection; example, exemplar, model, paradigm, pattern; embodiment, epitome; standard(s); principle(s), value(s). adj *lit:* consummate, optimal, perfect; exemplary, model; classic, compleat, quintessential, supreme; conceptual, hypothetical, imaginary, notional, paradisial, theoretical, unattainable, utopian.

idealistic adj *lit:* optimistic, romantic; moral, principled; naive, impracticable, impractical; ambitious, hopeful; perfectionist.

identical adj *lit:* alike as two peas, congruent, duplicated, exactly the same, geminate, indistinguishable, twin; corresponding, equal, equivalent, like, matching.

identify vb *lit:* know, place, recognize; discern, diagnose, name, pick out, pinpoint, single out, tag; catalogue, classify, label; associate (with), categorize (with), relate (with); empathize (with), sympathize (with).

identity n *lit:* name, particulars; individuality, particularity, singularity, uniqueness; equality, identicality, sameness, unity; empathy, rapport, sympathy, unanimity.

idiot n *lit:* cretin, duffer, dunce, imbecile, mental defective, moron, twerp; *fig:* blockhead, clod, dimwit, fool, halfwit, lunatic, simpleton; ass, chump, twit.

idiotic adj *lit:* asinine, blockheaded, cretinous, daft, dimwitted, fatuous, feeble-minded, halfwitted, insane, lunatic, moronic, stupid, witless.

idle vb *lit:* do nothing, laze, loaf, shirk, skive, slack, take it easy; fritter (away), while (away); dawdle, drift, tick over, vegetate.
adj *lit:* indolent, lazy, loafing, shirking, skiving, slack, slothful; inactive, inoperative, out of action, stationary, unoccupied, unused; jobless, redundant, unemployed; abortive, futile, groundless, pointless, unproductive, useless, vain, worthless; frivolous, irrelevant, trivial, unnecessary.

idleness n *lit:* indolence, laziness, loafing, shirking, skiving, slacking, sloth, time-wasting; inactivity, inertia, sluggishness, torpor; joblessness, unemployment.

if cnj *lit:* in the event that; assuming, on condition that, on the assumption that, provided, supposing; whether; admitting that, although, even though; albeit, though.

ignorance n *lit:* lack of education, unenlightenment, unknowing; inexperience, innocence, unawareness.

ignorant adj *lit:* uneducated, unlearned, unlettered, untaught, untrained; boorish, crass, gross, lumpen, uncomprehending; green, inexperienced, innocent, naive, unaware, unconscious, uninformed, unwitting.

ignore vb *lit:* be oblivious to, dismiss, disregard, neglect, take no notice of, turn one's back on; overlook, turn a blind eye to; cold-shoulder, cut dead, ostracize, shun.

ill n *lit:* affliction, misfortune, suffering, trial, tribulation, trouble; hurt, injury; evil, mischief, unkindness, wrong. adj *lit:* indisposed, infirm, off colour, poorly, sick, unwell; damaging, detrimental, harmful; bad, evil, wicked, wrong; acrimonious, hostile, inimical, malevolent, unfriendly; inauspicious, ominous, sinister, unfavourable. adv *lit:* badly, hard, poorly, unfavourably; barely, hardly, only just, scarcely; insufficiently.

illegal adj *lit:* criminal, felonious, illicit, prohibited, proscribed, unlawful, wrong; bootleg, unauthorized; actionable.

illegible adj *lit:* indecipherable, undecipherable, unreadable; faint, impossible to make out, obscure.

illegitimate **adj** *lit:* bastard, born out of wedlock, natural; illegal, unauthorized; inconsistent, illogical, invalid, specious, spurious, unwarranted; improper, incorrect.

illness **n** *lit:* ailment, cachexia, complaint, disease, disorder, indisposition, infirmity, malady, sickness.

illusion **n** *lit:* misapprehension, misconception, mistaken impression; apparition, daydream, figment of the imagination, magic, mirage.

illusory **adj** *lit:* deceptive, false, unreal, untrue; figmentary, imaginary, nonexistent; erroneous, fallacious, misleading.

illustration **n** *lit:* picture; artwork, chart, drawing, figure, graphic, halftone, line-drawing, map, photo, plate, print; demonstration, example, instance, specimen; analogy, comparison.

image **n** *lit:* effigy, figure, likeness, picture, representation, statue, statuette; appearance, reflection; conception, idea, mental picture, notion, perception; *fig:* double, same.

imaginary **adj** *lit:* fictitious, illusory, imagined, invented, made-up; nonexistent, unreal; hypothetical, supposed, theoretical.

imagination **n** *lit:* conception, invention, insight, originality; creativity, ingenuity, resourcefulness, vision, wit.

imaginative **adj** *lit:* creative, inventive, ingenious, original; fanciful, lively, vivid, witty.

imagine **vb** *lit:* conceptualize, create, devise, dream up, invent, picture, plan, think up, visualize; believe, comprehend, realize, think; assume, deem, gather, infer, surmise; conjecture, fancy.

imitate **vb** *lit:* copy, duplicate, echo, emulate, mirror, repeat, simulate; ape, impersonate, mimic; caricature, do, parody, take off.

imitation **n** *lit:* copy, counterfeit, duplicate, echo, fake, forgery, impersonation, mirror-image, replica, reproduction, sham; duplication, emulation, mimicry, simulation; caricature, parody, take-off. **adj** *lit:* artificial, counterfeit, duplicate, ersatz, fake, forged, reproduction, sham, simulated, synthetic.

immediate **adj** *lit:* direct, instant; closest, nearest; most recent;

current, present, prevailing; urgent; *spec:* intuitive, self-evident (knowledge, in philosophy)

immediately adv *lit:* at once, instantly, instantaneously, now, straight away, without delay; directly, promptly, on the spot, there and then; at first hand.

immobile adj *lit:* fixed, motionless, rigid, stationary, stiff, still, unmoving; square, stable, static, steady.

immobilize vb *lit:* freeze, halt, paralyse, stop, transfix; brace, splint; cripple, disable, put out of action; withdraw from circulation.

immoral adj *lit:* debauched, degenerate, depraved, indecent, lewd, licentious, obscene, pornographic, prurient, scabrous, smutty; corrupt, dishonest, evil, sinful, unethical, unprincipled, wicked, wrong; dissolute, profligate, reprobate.

immorality n *lit:* debauchery, degeneracy, depravity, indecency, lewdness, licentiousness, obscenity, pornography; corruption, dishonesty, evil, sinfulness, unethical behaviour, vice, wickedness; dissoluteness, profligacy.

impact n *lit:* concussion, contact, shock; bang, blow, crash, jolt, smash; force, power; momentum; *fig:* burden, impression, thrust; brunt, weight; consequences, effects, influence, repercussions, significance. vb *lit:* crash (on), hit, strike; impinge on, press together; compact, harden.

impair vb *lit:* damage, harm, injure; debilitate, hinder, mar, spoil, weaken; decrease, deteriorate, lessen, reduce, worsen.

impassable adj *lit:* impenetrable, unnavigable; insurmountable, unscalable.

impatience n *lit:* hastiness, impetuosity, intolerance; shortness of temper, snappishness; anxious expectancy, eagerness, restlessness; fretfulness, nervousness.

impatient adj *lit:* brooking no delay, hasty, impetuous, over-eager, rash; short-tempered, snappish; anxiously expectant, eager, restless; fretful, nervous.

impenetrable adj *lit:* dense, impassable, impermeable, solid, thick; *fig:* baffling, incomprehensible, inexplicable, inscrutable, mysterious, unfathomable.

imperative adj *lit:* compulsory, indispensable, obligatory, vital; crucial, essential, necessary, urgent; authoritative, commanding, exigent, imperious, insistent, peremptory.

imperceptible adj *lit:* indiscernible, infinitesimal, invisible, microscopic, minute, subtle, undetectable, unnoticeable; faint, fine, tiny; gradual.

imperfect adj *lit:* defective, deficient, faulty, flawed, incomplete, unfinished; broken, damaged, impaired; underdeveloped; abnormal, deformed, misshapen, subnormal.

imperil vb *lit:* endanger, hazard, jeopardize, put at risk, risk.

impersonal adj *lit:* detached, dispassionate, formal; bureaucratic, businesslike, disinterested, neutral; cold, inhuman.

impersonate vb *lit:* imitate, masquerade as, pass oneself off as, pose as; act as, mimic, play the part of, take the role of; ape, take off.

impetuous adj *lit:* hasty, impulsive, precipitate, rash, unthinking; eager, headlong, unrestrained.

implausible adj *lit:* doubtful, dubious, incredible, inconceivable, suspect, suspicious, unbelievable, unconvincing, unlikely, unreasonable.

implement n *lit:* instrument, piece of equipment, tool, utensil; appliance, device. vb *lit:* carry out, discharge, execute, perform, put into effect.

implementation n *lit:* carrying out, discharge, execution, fulfilment, performance, putting into effect.

implication n *lit:* conclusion, corollary, inference, meaning, ramification, significance; association, connection, entanglement, involvement.

implicit adj *lit:* contained, included, inherent; inferred, tacit, understood, unspoken; absolute, complete, steadfast, total, unqualified, unreserved, unshakable; *spec:* invisible (response, in psychiatry).

imply vb *lit:* hint, insinuate, intimate, suggest; connote, denote, mean, signify; entail, involve, presuppose.

impolite adj *lit:* bad-mannered, discourteous, ill-mannered, rude, ungracious, unmannerly; ungentlemanly, unladylike; abusive, boorish, impudent, insolent, insulting.

importance n *lit:* significance, usefulness, value; consequence, distinction, mark, note, standing; concern, influence, interest; eminence, moment, substance, weight.

impose vb *lit:* apply, enforce, establish, institute, ordain; fix (on), inflict (on), lay (on), place (on), put (on), set (on); *fig:* butt in (upon), intrude (upon), trespass (upon); play (upon), presume (upon); palm off (on); *spec:* set up (type for printing).

imposition n *lit:* application, enforcement, establishment, institution, ordinance; fixing on, inflicting on, laying-on, placing on; *fig:* burden, hardship; charge, duty, tax, toll; encroachment, intrusion, presumption.

impossible n *lit:* unattainable; inconceivable, unthinkable; insoluble, unanswerable; unendurable; unacceptable. adj *lit:* impracticable, not feasible, not viable, out of the question, unattainable; inconceivable, unthinkable; insoluble, unanswerable, unworkable; god-awful, unendurable; hopelessly unsuitable, outrageous, unacceptable.

imprecise adj *lit:* approximate, inexact, rough, vague; ambiguous, equivocal, indefinite, indeterminate, loose; careless, inaccurate, sloppy.

impress vb *lit:* emboss, imprint, print, stamp; *fig:* have an effect upon, influence, make an impression on, move, reach; emphasize (on), stress (upon).

impression n *lit:* brand, dent, imprint, indentation, mark, print, stamp; edition, issue, printing; *fig:* effect, impact, influence; conviction, feeling, idea, memory, notion, opinion, reaction, recollection; *spec:* model, mould (of dentition).

impressionable **adj** *lit:* easily influenced, responsive, sensitive, suggestible, susceptible; gullible.

impressive **adj** *lit:* affecting, commanding, imposing, moving, powerful, stirring, striking.

imprison **vb** *lit:* confine, gaol, immure, incarcerate, intern, jail, lock up, put away, send down, shut up.

improbable **adj** *lit:* far-fetched, implausible, unlikely; doubtful, questionable, uncertain; unforeseeable, untoward.

improper **adj** *lit:* erroneous, false, incorrect, wrong; inapposite, inappropriate, infelicitous, out of place, uncalled for, unsuitable, unwarranted; impolite, indelicate, unbecoming, unseemly, vulgar; bawdy, indecent, pornographic, rude, smutty.

improve **vb** *lit:* ameliorate, better, enhance, make better; advance, develop, gain in strength, grow, increase, pick up, progress, rise; amend, correct, mend, polish up, rectify, reform; get better, rally, recover, recuperate.

improvement **n** *lit:* amelioration, betterment, enhancement; advance, development, gain, growth, increase, pick-up, progress, rise; correction, emendation, polishing, rectification, reformation; rally, recovery.

impulse **n** *lit:* force, impetus, momentum, pressure; push, stimulus, thrust; *fig:* drive, motivation, urge; passion, spark, spirit; fancy, inclination, whim, wish, yen.

impunity **n** *lit:* immunity, licence; without punishment; without restriction.

inability **n** *lit:* incapacity, incompetence; helplessness, impotence, powerlessness.

inaccurate **adj** *lit:* erroneous, faulty, incorrect, out, wrong; imprecise, inexact; defective, unreliable.

inactive **adj** *lit:* immobile, inert, inoperative, out of service; idle, unoccupied, unused; dormant, in abeyance, latent; indolent, lazy, lethargic, sluggish, torpid; passive, sedentary.

inadequate adj *lit:* deficient, incomplete, insufficient, meagre, scanty, sparse, too few, too little; incompetent, not up to it, unfitted, unsatisfactory.

inappropriate adj *lit:* inapposite, inapt, incongruous, unfitting, unsuitable, unsuited; infelicitous, unbecoming, unseemly; untimely, wrong; disproportionate.

inattentive adj *lit:* absent-minded, distrait, dreamy, preoccupied, vague; paying no heed (to).

inaudible adj *lit:* silent, unheard; incomprehensible, muffled, mumbling.

inaugurate vb *lit:* begin, commence, initiate, launch, open, usher in; commission, dedicate, induct, install.

inauspicious adj *lit:* black, ill-omened, ominous, unfortunate, unlucky, unpromising.

incapable adj *lit:* helpless, powerless, unfit; incompetent, ineffectual, inefficient, inept; not capable (of); not admitting (of).

incense n *lit:* fumes, heady aroma, scented smoke; aroma, fragrance, perfume, scent; *fig:* homage; adulation, praise. vb *lit:* anger, enrage, inflame, infuriate, madden, make one's blood boil, rile.

incentive n *lit:* inducement, motivation, stimulus; bait, carrot, enticement, lure.

inchoate adj *lit:* early, imperfect, incipient, incomplete, rudimentary, undeveloped.

incident n *lit:* circumstance, episode, event, happening, occasion, occurrence; action, clash, commotion, crime, disturbance, scene.

incidental adj *lit:* accompanying, ancillary (to), concomitant, lesser, minor, secondary (to); subordinate (to); accidental, chance, coincidental, fortuitous, random.

inclination n *lit:* angle, gradient, lean, slant, slope; heel, list; bending, bow, nod; *fig:* bent, disposition, fondness, liking, partiality, propensity, tendency.

include *vb lit:* contain, cover, embrace, enclose, encompass, incorporate, take in; comprehend, comprise, embody; add (in), enter, insert (in); count (in), reckon (in).

incognito *adj lit:* anonymous, under an assumed name, unknown; in disguise, unrecognizable. *adv lit:* anonymously, under an assumed name, without being recognized; in disguise, unrecognizably.

income *n lit:* earnings, gains, pay, proceeds, receipts, revenue.

incompatible *adj lit:* conflicting, contradictory, irreconcilable, mutually antipathetic; inconsistent (with); at odds, inharmonious, unsympathetic.

inconceivable *adj lit:* unimaginable, unthinkable; incredible, mind-blowing, unbelievable; impossible.

inconclusive *adj lit:* indecisive, indeterminate; arguable, debatable, unfinished, unsettled.

inconsistent *adj lit:* changeable, fickle, inconstant, unpredictable, variable; conflicting, contradictory, contrary, different, incompatible, incongruous, irreconcilable.

inconvenience *n lit:* bother, disturbance, nuisance, upset.
vb lit: bother, discommode, disrupt, disturb, put to trouble.

incorrect *adj lit:* erroneous, inaccurate, out, wrong; defective, faulty, flawed; mistaken.

increase *n lit:* addition, augmentation, extension, gain, increment; development, enlargement, expansion, growth; escalation, rise, upsurge; amplification, enhancement, intensification; multiplication, propagation. *vb lit:* add on to, augment, extend, prolong; develop, enlarge, expand, gain, grow, spread; escalate, rise, surge; amplify, enhance, intensify; multiply, propagate.

incredible *adj lit:* beyond belief, unbelievable, unimaginable; amazing, astonishing, astounding, mind-boggling.

incur *vb lit:* bring upon oneself, draw down, evoke, invoke, provoke; earn, gain; be liable to.

incurable *adj lit:* inoperable, irremediable; fatal, mortal, terminal; *fig:* incorrigible, inveterate.

indecision n *lit:* doubt, hesitancy, hesitation, irresolution, vacillation.

indeed adv *lit:* certainly, definitely, positively, undoubtedly, veritably; actually, in fact, really.

indefinite adj *lit:* boundless, indeterminate, limitless, unbounded, unlimited; imprecise, inexact, loose, vague.

indent n *lit:* dent, impression, notch; niche, nook, recess; demand, order, requisition; *spec:* space (at the head of a paragraph).
vb *lit:* cut, make an impression, nick, notch, penetrate (into); serrate; leave space.

independence n *lit:* autonomy, self-determination, self-rule, sovereignty; self-reliance, self-sufficiency; freedom, liberty; impartiality, objectivity; *fig:* private income.

independent n *spec:* non-party MP, unaffiliated politician; nonconformist (cleric or congregation). adj *lit:* autonomous, non-aligned, self-determining, self-governing, sovereign; self-reliant, self-sufficient; free, liberated, unaffiliated; impartial, objective.

indestructible adj *lit:* imperishable, incorruptible, indissoluble, permanent, unbreakable; immortal; *fig:* durable.

indicate vb *lit:* display, point out, point to, show (to); mark, signal, single out; betoken, denote, express, reveal, signify; read, register; imply, suggest.

indication n *lit:* mark, pointer, sign, signal, token; evidence, symptom; implication, inkling, suggestion.

indifference n *lit:* detachment, disinterest, unconcern; apathy, inattention, negligence; insignificance, unimportance.

indignant adj *lit:* angry (at), annoyed (at), exasperated (at), full of wrath (at).

indignation n *lit:* anger, annoyance, exasperation, wrath; pique, resentment.

indirectly adv *lit:* circuitously, in a roundabout way, obliquely; deviously; at second-hand; by implication; fortuitously, incidentally.

indiscreet　adj *lit:* tactless, undiplomatic; ill-judged, impolitic, imprudent, incautious, injudicious; scandalous.

indiscretion　n *lit:* tactlessness; folly, impetuosity, imprudence; act of folly, gaffe, impropriety, peccadillo; betrayal, disclosure, leak.

indispensable　adj *lit:* crucial, essential, key, necessary, vital.

individual　n *lit:* one, unit; being, creature; mortal, party, person, soul; character, nonconformist, one-off, original.　adj *lit:* discrete, distinct, particular, respective, separate, single, unique; characteristic, distinctive, idiosyncratic, peculiar, personal, singular, special.

induce　vb *lit:* get (to do), impel, influence, move, persuade, prompt; bring about, cause, effect, lead to, occasion; deduce, derive, infer; *spec:* produce (an electric current, radioactivity).

industry　n *lit:* commerce, manufacturing, trade; business; hard work, labour, toil; application, diligence, effort, perseverance, zeal.

inebriated　adj (pa.pt) *lit:* blind drunk, drunk, intoxicated, merry, tipsy; blotto, boozed up, half cut, legless, paralytic, pickled, plastered, smashed, sozzled, squiffy, stoned, three sheets to the wind, under the influence.

inefficient　adj *lit:* wasteful; incapable, incompetent, inept, sloppy; feeble, weak.

inequality　n *lit:* difference, disparity, irregularity, variation; disproportion; unevenness, variability; deviation.

inert　adj *lit:* idle, immobile, inactive, inanimate, lifeless, motionless, static, still, unconscious, unmoving; dead; passive, quiescent, unresponsive.

inertia　n *lit:* immobility, inactivity; passivity, unresponsiveness; apathy, idleness, indolence, lassitude, lethargy, sloth, torpor.

inevitable　adj *lit:* automatic, inescapable, inexorable, necessary, unavoidable.

inexperienced　adj *lit:* callow, green, immature, raw, unpractised, unschooled, untried, unversed.

infallible *adj lit:* inability to be wrong; dependability, reliability; omniscience.

infamous *adj lit:* disreputable, heinous, iniquitous, notorious, opprobrious, scandalous, shocking; disgraceful, dishonourable, outrageous.

infant *n lit:* babe, baby, neonate, toddler, tot.

infantile *adj lit:* babyish, childish, juvenile, puerile; *fig:* early, primary.

infect *vb lit:* blight, contaminate, poison, pollute, taint; affect, spread to.

infer *vb lit:* conclude, deduce, derive, gather, presume, reason, surmise, take as read, understand.

inference *n lit:* conclusion, corollary, deduction, presumption, reasoning, surmise, understanding.

inferior *adj lit:* junior, lesser, secondary, subordinate, subsidiary; lower; poor, second-rate, shoddy, substandard, worse.

infiltrate *vb lit:* filter through into, penetrate, percolate through, pervade; get into, pass into, slip into, sneak into.

infinite *adj lit:* boundless, endless, illimitable, immeasurable, inestimable, inexhaustible, limitless, measureless, unbounded, untold; countless, numberless; eternal, everlasting, perpetual; *fig:* immense, vast.

infirm *adj lit:* ailing, debilitated, decrepit, frail, weak; shaky, wobbly; indecisive, irresolute, vacillating.

inflate *vb lit:* blow up, puff out, pump up; balloon, bloat, dilate, distend, expand, swell; *fig:* aggrandize, exaggerate; be devalued, be worth less.

inflict *vb lit:* impose (upon), place (upon), visit (upon), wreak (upon); exact (upon).

influence *n lit:* ascendancy, domination, spell, sway; effect, force, pressure, weight; control, direction; authority, clout, hold, leverage,

power; connections, pull; *spec:* (electrostatic) induction.   **vb** *lit:*
affect, dispose, incline, have an effect on, induce, lead (to), move,
persuade, predispose, sway; have a bearing on; carry weight with, pull
strings with.

influential   **adj** *lit:* effective, efficacious, important, significant,
telling, weighty; moving, persuasive; powerful, well-connected.

inform   **vb** *lit:* advise, apprise, enlighten, let know, notify, tell; blab,
grass, peach, sneak, tell; *spec:* animate, illuminate, permeate (in
archaic senses).

informal   **adj** *lit:* casual, easy, familiar, unceremonious, unofficial;
colloquial, idiomatic.

information   **n** *lit:* data, facts, gen, info; advice, intelligence, news,
word; bulletin, message, printout, report.

ingredient   **n** *lit:* component, constituent, element, factor.

inhabit   **vb** *lit:* abide in, dwell in, live in, occupy, reside in; people,
populate.

inhabitant   **n** *lit:* denizen, dweller, inmate, native, occupant,
occupier, resident, tenant.

inhibit   **vb** *lit:* constrain, hold back, restrain; check, discourage,
hinder; prevent, stop.

inhuman   **adj** *lit:* barbaric, barbarous, bestial, brutal, cruel,
heartless, ruthless, unfeeling; diabolical, fiendish; abnormal,
subhuman; superhuman.

initial   **n** *lit:* character, letter.   **vb** *lit:* endorse, sign;
countersign.   **adj** *lit:* beginning, first, inaugural, introductory,
opening; early, primary, rudimentary.

initiative   **n** *lit:* drive, dynamism, enterprise, get-up-and-go,
gumption, resourcefulness; leadership; advantage, control, dominance,
lead.

inject   **vb** *lit:* jab, syringe; mainline, shoot; immunize, inoculate;
infuse; *fig:* insert, introduce; throw in, toss in; force in.

injustice n *lit:* inequity, wrong; bias, discrimination, inequality, prejudice, unfairness.

inn n *lit:* hospice, hostel, hostelry, pub, public house, tavern; bar, boozer, local, oasis, watering-hole.

innocence n *lit:* blamelessness, guiltlessness; chastity, purity, virginity, virtue; artlessness, ingenuousness, naiveté, simplicity; inexperience, unsophistication, unworldliness; credulousness, gullibility; ignorance, unawareness.

innocent adj *lit:* blameless, faultless, guiltless, not guilty; chaste, immaculate, pure, spotless, unblemished, virgin; artless, ingenuous, naive, open, simple; harmless, innocuous, inoffensive; ignorant (of), unaware (of).

inoffensive adj *lit:* harmless, innocuous, mild, peaceable, quiet, unobtrusive, unprovocative.

inquisitive adj *lit:* curious, enquiring, investigative; intrusive, nosy, prying, snooping.

insane adj *lit:* certifiable, mentally disordered; crazy, demented, deranged, lunatic, mad, mental, unbalanced, unhinged.

insanity n *lit:* dementia, mental derangement, mental illness; lunacy, madness; *fig:* folly, senselessness, stupidity; irresponsibility.

insecure adj *lit:* defenceless, exposed, open to attack, unprotected, unsafe, vulnerable; flimsy, precarious, rickety, rocky, shaky, unreliable, unsteady, wobbly; anxious, diffident, unsure.

insensitive adj *lit:* callous, hardened, indifferent, tough, unfeeling; indifferent, uncaring, unconcerned; dull, obtuse.

insert n *lit:* additional material, inset, interpolation; addendum, corrigendum; tip-in. vb *lit:* implant, interpolate, interpose, introduce, put in, tuck in, work in.

inside n *lit:* interior; contents; bowels, entrails, guts, innards, viscera. adj *lit:* inner, interior, internal; *fig:* confidential, exclusive, private, restricted; limited, small; in prison. adv *lit:* in, indoors. prp *lit:* in, into, within.

insight n *lit:* acumen, comprehension, discernment, penetration, perspicacity, vision; understanding, wisdom; perception, realization, solution.

insignificant adj *lit:* inconsequential, meaningless, negligible, nugatory, unimportant; extraneous, irrelevant; minor, paltry, petty, trifling, trivial.

insincerity n *lit:* dissimulation, duplicity, hypocrisy, perfidy, pretence; dishonesty, mendacity, untruthfulness.

insist vb *lit:* demand (that); maintain (that), repeat (that); stand firm (on), take a stand (on).

insistent adj *lit:* compulsive, demanding, emphatic, importunate, persistent, pressing.

insoluble adj *lit:* undissolvable; *fig:* indecipherable, inexplicable, mystifying, unfathomable.

inspect vb *lit:* examine, go over, look over, scan, scrutinize, survey, vet.

inspiration n *lit:* creativity, insight, muse, stimulus.

inspire vb *lit:* arouse, enkindle, excite, fire, spur, stimulate, stir.

install vb *lit:* lodge, place, position, settle, set up; establish, inaugurate, institute, introduce.

instant n *lit:* flash, jiffy, moment, second, time, trice, twinkling of an eye. adj *lit:* immediate, prompt, rapid; *fig:* imperative, pressing; *spec:* convenience (food).

instead adv *lit:* alternatively, in lieu; preferably, rather; in place (of).

instinctive adj *lit:* inborn, inherent, innate, involuntary, natural, reflex, spontaneous.

institute n *lit:* academy, college, foundation, school, society; decree, doctrine, law, precept, principle, rule. vb *lit:* establish, found, initiate, introduce, launch, originate, set up, start.

instruct vb *lit:* coach, direct, drill, educate, school, teach, train; command, order; advise, apprise, counsel, inform, notify, tell.

instruction   n *lit:* coaching, direction, drill, education, schooling, teaching, training; command, order; advice, counsel, information.

instructor   n *lit:* coach, director, mentor, teacher, trainer; commander; adviser, counsel.

instrument   n *lit:* device, gadget, implement, tool, utensil; appliance, mechanism; dial, meter, read-out; agent, factor; channel, means, medium, vehicle; contract, deed, legal document, writ; *fig:* pawn, puppet.

insult   n *lit:* affront, incivility, offence, rudeness, scurrility, slight; abuse, invective, vituperation.   vb *lit:* abuse, affront, be rude to, be offensive to, call names, offend, outrage, slight.

insurance   n *lit:* assurance, cover, guarantee, indemnity, safeguard, security, warranty; policy; premium.

integrate   vb *lit:* absorb, accommodate, assimilate, blend in, fuse, harmonize, incorporate, merge, mesh, mingle; connect up, put together, unify.

integrity   n *lit:* completeness, homogeneity, totality, unity, wholeness; *fig:* honesty, honour, incorruptibility, principle, probity, sincerity, virtue.

intellectual   n *lit:* thinker; academic, philosopher, scholar; highbrow.   adj *lit:* cerebral, mental, rational; academic, bookish, philosophical, scholarly.

intelligence   n *lit:* brains, grey matter, mind; acumen, discernment, discrimination, intellect, nous, perception, reason, wit; data, facts, gen, information, knowledge, news, notification, word; secret service.

intelligent   adj *lit:* brainy, bright, clever, penetrating, perceptive, quick-witted, reasoning, smart, thinking.

intelligible   adj *lit:* comprehensible, decipherable, legible, lucid, simple, understandable.

intend   vb *lit:* aim (to), be determined (to), mean (to), propose (to), purpose (to); destine (for), earmark (for), have in mind (for), mean (for).

intense   **adj** *lit:* acute, concentrated, deep, extreme, great, powerful, profound, severe; burning, consuming, fanatical, fervent, impassioned, passionate, vehement; earnest, fierce, haunted, strained; bright; dense.

intention   **n** *lit:* aim, design, idea, objective, plan, purpose, target; *spec:* concentration (of a priest in administering a sacrament); concept (in logic).

interest   **n** *lit:* concern, importance, moment, pertinence, relevance, significance, weight; curiosity; attention, notice, regard; activity, hobby, occupation, pastime, pursuit; claim, commitment, influence, involvement, stake; benefit, gain, profit; affair, business, matter; (in the) cause (of).   **vb** *lit:* affect, concern, involve; absorb, engross, fascinate, grab the attention of, intrigue; amuse, divert, entertain.

interesting   **adj (pr.pt)** *lit:* affecting, compelling, gripping, riveting, thought-provoking; absorbing, engrossing, fascinating, intriguing, stimulating; amusing, diverting, entertaining, pleasing; curious, strange, unusual.

interfere   **vb** *lit:* butt in, intervene, intrude, meddle, stick one's oar (in); clash (with), conflict (with); react (with); take a liberty (with).

interior   **n** *lit:* inside; centre, core, heart; heartland; contents; domestic scene.   **adj** *lit:* inside, internal, inward; inner, mental, personal, private; domestic, home.

interlude   **n** *lit:* break, breathing-space, halt, intermission, pause, respite, rest, stoppage; diversion, interim entertainment, voluntary.

intermediate   **adj** *lit:* in-between, intervening, transitional; medium, middle.

interminable   **adj** *lit:* endless, everlasting, infinite, perpetual; boring, long-drawn-out, long-winded, protracted, tedious, wearisome.

intermittent   **adj** *lit:* discontinuous, fitful, periodic, spasmodic, sporadic.

internal   **adj** *lit:* inside, interior; inner, private, secret; domestic, home; company, in-house, personnel, staff.

interpret vb *lit:* decipher, decode, make sense of, translate; elucidate, explain; bring out the meaning of, render; read, understand.

interpretation n *lit:* decipherment, decoding, translation; elucidation, exegesis, explanation; analysis, diagnosis, reading, understanding; performance, rendition, version; meaning.

interrogate vb *lit:* cross-question, examine, grill, pump, question, quiz; ask.

interrupt vb *lit:* break into, butt into, cut off, disturb, hold up, intrude into, punctuate; check, cut short, stop; break off, discontinue, suspend; interfere with, obstruct.

interval n *lit:* break, distance, gap, hiatus, period, space, term, time; intermission, pause; interim, meantime, meanwhile.

interview n *lit:* audience, consultation, meeting, talk; examination, interrogation. vb *lit:* examine, interrogate, question, quiz.

intestines n *lit:* guts, tripe, viscera; bowels, entrails, innards.

intimidate vb *lit:* browbeat, bully, cow, lean on, menace, terrorize, threaten; daunt, dishearten, frighten, overawe, scare, terrify.

intolerance n *lit:* impatience; dogmatism, fanaticism, illiberality, narrow-mindedness; discrimination, prejudice; chauvinism.

intolerant adj *lit:* impatient, uncharitable; dogmatic, fanatical, illiberal, narrow-minded; discriminating, prejudiced; chauvinistic.

intone vb *lit:* chant, recite, warble; sing.

intoxication n *lit:* drunkenness, inebriety; poisoning; *fig:* delirium, euphoria, exaltation, exhilaration.

intransigent adj *lit:* intractable, obdurate, obstinate, stubborn, tenacious, uncompromising, unyielding.

intrepid adj *lit:* audacious, bold, brave, daring, dauntless, fearless, heroic, nerveless, stout-hearted, undaunted, valiant.

intricate adj *lit:* complex, complicated, elaborate, involved, labyrinthine, tangled, tortuous.

intrigue n *lit:* complot, conspiracy, machination, plot, scheme, stratagem, trick; amour, liaison, romance. **vb** *lit:* fascinate, interest; perplex, puzzle; connive, conspire, plot, scheme.

intriguing **adj (pr.pt)** *lit:* fascinating, interesting; perplexing, puzzling.

introduce **vb** *lit:* acquaint, make known, present; bring in, establish, inaugurate, institute, launch, pioneer, usher in; announce, bring up, broach, lead off, preface, put forward; add, insert, interpolate, put in; put next to.

introduction n *lit:* presentation; debut, establishment, inauguration, institution, launching, pioneering; foreword, opening statement, overture, preamble, preface, prelude, prologue; addition, insertion, interpolation.

introverted **adj** *lit:* indrawn, introspective; reserved, withdrawn; self-contained; self-centred.

intruder n *lit:* burglar, prowler, raider; gate-crasher, interloper, trespasser; invader.

intuition n *lit:* awareness, feeling, hunch, instinct, presentiment, sense.

intuitive **adj** *lit:* instinctive; penetrative, percipient; innate, instinctual, involuntary, natural, reflex, spontaneous.

invade **vb** *lit:* burst in, encroach upon, infringe, occupy, raid; infect, infest, overrun, penetrate, permeate; assault, attack.

invalid n *lit:* convalescent, patient. **adj** *lit:* bedridden, disabled, frail, ill, sick, sickly; inoperative, not in service, null, void; fallacious, false, incorrect, irrational, untrue.

invaluable **adj** *lit:* precious, priceless; *fig:* essential, indispensable, necessary, vital.

invariably **adv** *lit:* always, consistently, every time, regularly, rigidly, unfailingly.

invasion n *lit:* encroachment, infringement, intrusion, occupation, penetration, permeation; infestation; assault, attack, incursion, raid.

invent vb *lit:* come up with, create, construct, devise, formulate, originate; conceive, imagine, make up, think up; concoct, cook up, fabricate.

invention n *lit:* creativity, genius, imagination, ingenuity, originality; construction, devising, formulation, origination; brainchild, creation, discovery, innovation, novelty; fabrication, fantasy, fiction, story; falsehood, lie, untruth.

inventive adj *lit:* creative, imaginative, ingenious, original, resourceful; constructive, practical; innovative.

invest vb *lit:* authorize, empower, license; consecrate, dedicate, induct, install, ordain; endow, provide, supply; put (money in), sink (funds in); devote, lay out, spend; beset, besiege, lay siege to, surround.

investigate vb *lit:* enquire into, examine, explore, go into, look into, probe, study.

invisible adj *lit:* imperceptible, indiscernible; inconspicuous, unseen; infinitesimal, microscopic; concealed, hidden.

invitation n *lit:* call, request, suggestion; hospitality, welcome; *fig:* allurement, come-on, glad eye, inducement, temptation.

invite vb *lit:* ask, bid, call, request, summon, welcome; *fig:* ask for, court, look for, provoke, tempt; attract, draw.

inviting adj (pr.pt) *lit:* appealing, attractive, captivating, welcoming, winning; alluring, enticing, seductive, tempting.

invoke vb *lit:* appeal to, call upon, pray to; beg, petition, supplicate; call up, conjure; apply, implement, put into effect; call in, resort to.

involuntary adj *lit:* automatic, instinctual, reflex, spontaneous, uncontrolled; accidental, unintended, unintentional; reluctant, unwilling.

involve vb *lit:* entail, imply, mean, necessitate; contain, cover, include, incorporate, take in; absorb, engross, grip, hold, rivet; affect, concern, touch; connect with, implicate; complicate, embroil, enmesh, entangle.

involved adj (pa.pt) *lit:* complex, complicated, elaborate, intricate, labyrinthine, tangled; concerned (in), implicated (in), mixed up (in), occupied (in).

irony n *lit:* dissimulation, paradox, sarcasm.

irrational adj *lit:* absurd, crazy, illogical, insane, mindless, nonsensical, silly, senseless, unreasonable.

irregular n *lit:* reservist, volunteer; part-timer, temporary.
adj *lit:* amorphous, asymmetrical, crooked, lopsided, lumpy, shapeless, unequal, uneven; fitful, intermittent, odd, patchy, spasmodic, sporadic, unsteady, variable; eccentric, erratic, haphazard; fluctuating, oscillating, varying; abnormal, exceptional, extraordinary, peculiar, queer, unorthodox, unusual; part-time, temporary, unauthorized, unofficial; *spec:* strong (verb).

irrelevant adj *lit:* extraneous, immaterial, inappropriate, not pertinent, unconnected, unrelated; inadmissible, inapplicable.

irrepressible adj *lit:* bright, bubbling, buoyant, cheery, ebullient, effervescent; cheeky, impudent, incorrigible; uncontrollable, unstoppable.

irresistible adj *lit:* compelling, compulsive, overpowering, overwhelming; inescapable, inexorable; *fig:* enchanting, fascinating, ravishing.

irresponsible adj *lit:* ill-advised, ill-judged, reckless, wild; undependable, unreliable, untrustworthy; feckless, flighty, giddy.

irreverent adj *lit:* impious, irreligious, sacrilegious; cheeky, disrespectful, impertinent, impudent, saucy.

irritate vb *lit:* annoy, be trying, bother, exasperate, get on one's nerves, offend, pester, provoke, rub up the wrong way; inflame; chafe, rub; itch, tickle.

isolate vb *lit:* detach, divorce, keep separate, segregate, separate; quarantine.

isolation n *lit:* detachment, insularity, seclusion, segregation, separation; loneliness, solitude.

issue n *lit:* child, children, offspring, progeny; delivery, dissemination, distribution, publication, supplying; edition, impression, instalment; affair, concern, matter, point, question, subject; argument, bone of contention, controversy, problem; conclusion, culmination, finale, outcome, result, upshot. **vb** *lit:* arise, come (forth), emanate, emerge, flow, rise, spring, stem; deliver, disseminate, distribute, emit, publish, put out; announce, broadcast, circulate, release.

itch n *lit:* irritation, tickling, tingling; *fig:* craving, desire, longing, lust, yearning. **vb** *lit:* irritate, tickle, tingle; *fig:* ache, crave, long, lust, pine, yearn.

item n *lit:* article, object, thing; component, detail, particular, unit; entry, matter, point, subject, topic; article, feature, notice, piece, report.

J

jab n *lit:* dig, poke, prod, stab; lunge, nudge, thrust; blow, punch; *fig:* injection, inoculation, vaccination. **vb** *lit:* dig, poke, prod, stab; lunge, nudge, thrust.

jacket n *lit:* blazer, body-warmer, bolero, coat; case, casing, covering, lagging, sheath, wrapper, wrapping; outside, skin, surface; dustcover, envelope, folder. **vb** *lit:* case, cover, lag, sheathe, wrap; enclose, enfold, envelop.

jail n *lit:* lockup, prison; brig, clink, jug, nick, penitentiary, stir; detention centre, remand centre; internment. **vb** *lit:* detain, imprison, lock up, send down; confine, immure, incarcerate.

jam n *lit:* conserve, preserve; crush, press, queue, squeeze, tailback, throng; blockage, congestion, obstruction; *fig:* dilemma, predicament, quandary; bit of bother, fix, hole, pickle, scrape, spot. **vb** *lit:* cram, crush, force, pack, press, push, ram, shove, squeeze, stuff, wedge; block, clog, congest, obstruct; bring to a standstill, halt, stick fast.

jar n *lit:* amphora, crock, flagon, jug, pitcher, urn, vase; pint-glass, pint-mug, tankard; container, pot, vessel; bump, jerk, jolt, knock, nudge, percussion, shock, start, vibration, wrench; clash, grating; *fig:* conflict, disagreement, quarrel. **vb** *lit:* bump, jerk, jolt, knock, nudge, rock, shake, vibrate, wrench; clash, grate, rasp; *fig:* agitate, disturb, irritate, rattle; annoy, irk, nettle, touch on the raw; bicker, disagree, quarrel, wrangle; clash, jangle, stick out like a sore thumb.

jargon n *lit:* patter, private vocabulary, technical terminology; cant, idiom, usage; *fig:* argot, patois, slang; *spec:* creole, pidgin.

jaunt n *lit:* excursion, tour, trip; expedition, trek; airing, outing, promenade, ramble, stroll; ride, spin. **vb** *lit:* go on an excursion, make a trip, tour; promenade, ramble, saunter, stroll; go for a spin, ride.

jaw n *lit:* mandible, maxilla; pincer; *fig:* chat, chew the rag, gossip, natter; conversation, dialogue, talk; chattiness, talkativeness;

scolding.　**vb** *lit:* chat, chatter, go on, gossip, natter, rabbit; censure, criticize, find fault, lecture, scold.

jealous **adj** *lit:* covetous, envious, green-eyed; grudging, resentful; possessive, protective, solicitous, vigilant; anxious, mistrustful, suspicious, wary, watchful.

jealousy **n** *lit:* covetousness, enviousness; resentment; possessiveness, protectiveness, solicitousness, vigilance; anxiety, distrust, mistrust, suspicion, wariness, watchfulness.

jeans **n** *lit:* denims.

jeering **n** *lit:* barracking, boos, catcalls, gibes, heckling, hisses, mockery, obloquy, ragging, raillery, ridicule, scoffs, sneers, taunts; abuse, derision.　**adj (pr.pt)** *lit:* barracking, booing, catcalling, gibing, heckling, hissing, hooting, mocking, ridiculing, scoffing, sneering, taunting; abusive, deriding.

jerk **n** *lit:* jolt, pull, tug, tweak, twitch, wrench, yank; lurch, twist; spasm, start, tic.　**vb** *lit:* jar, jolt, pull, tug, tweak, wrench, yank; lurch, twist, veer; go into spasm, start, twitch; bounce, bump, rattle, shake, tremble, vibrate; *fig:* force out, say brokenly, stammer, stutter; *spec:* slice and dry (meat to preserve it).

jet **n** *lit:* gush, spray, stream; fountain, geyser; atomizer, nozzle, rose, spout, sprinkler; aeroplane, jumbo, plane; *spec:* black lignite (stone).　**vb** *lit:* gush, issue, rush, shoot, spew, spout, spray, squirt; fly (by jet aircraft).　**adj** *lit:* black, ebony, glossy black; *fig:* moneyed, rich, wealthy.

jewel **n** *lit:* gemstone, precious stone; brilliant, rock, sparkler; *fig:* gem, paragon, pearl, prize, treasure; find, marvel, rarity, wonder.　**vb** *lit:* adorn, beautify, bejewel, deck, decorate, ornament.

jewellery **n** *lit:* gems, gemstones, precious stones; brilliants, rocks, sparklers; finery, ornaments, regalia, trinkets; bracelets, brooches, pendants, rings, tiaras; diamonds, pearls.

jittery **adj** *lit:* jumpy, nervous, shaky; anxious, worried; agitated, flustered; fidgety, in a state.

job **n** *lit:* appointment, assignment, calling, career, charge, duty,

employment, function, livelihood, métier, occupation, office,
position, post, profession, role, situation, task, vocation, work; affair,
business, concern, responsibility; enterprise, piece of work,
undertaking, venture; finished product, output, product; act, deed,
feat; criminal act, felony; *fig:* embezzlement, fraud.   **vb** *lit:* buy and
sell, deal in, trade in; hire out, let, rent.

jockey   **n** *lit:* horse-rider, rider; presenter, player; operator.
vb *lit:* jostle, nudge, ride against; *fig:* engineer, manage, manipulate,
manoeuvre; finagle, inveigle, worm.

jocular   **adj** *lit:* amusing, cheerful, comical, droll, funny, gay, genial,
good-humoured, humorous, jocose, jocund, joking, jolly, jovial,
merry, waggish, witty; facetious, flippant, jokey, mischievous,
playful, roguish, teasing, tongue-in-cheek, whimsical.

jog   **n** *lit:* canter, slow run, trot; excursion, outing, short trip.
vb *lit:* bounce, jar, jerk, jiggle, joggle, jolt, jostle, jounce, knock,
nudge, prod, push, rock, shake, vibrate; canter, lope, trot; *fig:* arouse,
prompt, stimulate, stir; urge.

join   **n** *lit:* junction, seal, seam, suture, union; overlap.
vb *lit:* cement, combine, connect, couple, fasten together, knit, link,
put together, tie together, unite, yoke together; accompany, affiliate
with, associate with, converge, get together with, move to be with;
adhere, stick together; add, annex, append; enlist, enrol, enter, sign;
abut, border on, meet, reach, touch.

joint   **n** *lit:* articulation, hinge; connection, interface, intersection,
junction, node, seam, union; section, segment; cut, roast; *fig:* dive,
low dive; marijuana cigarette, reefer.   **vb** *lit:* articulate, connect,
couple, fasten together, fit together, link, unite; butcher, carve,
cleave, cut up, disarticulate, dismember, dissect.   **adj** *lit:* collective,
combined, communal, concerted, co-operative, shared, united;
mutual.

joke   **n** *lit:* gag, jest, pun, quip, wisecrack; bit of fun, jape, lark,
prank; butt, laughing-stock, target; absurdity, nonsense.   **vb** *lit:*
banter, be amusing, be funny, be witty, jest, quip, tell gags, wisecrack;
be facetious, chaff, kid, lark about, tease.

joker n *lit:* buffoon, clown, jester; comedian, comic, humorist, wag, wit; prankster, trickster; wild card; *fig:* contingency, unforeseen factor.

jolly n *lit:* festivity, jollification, merriment; *fig:* flattery, gratification, humouring; *spec:* marine (soldier). vb *lit:* flatter, gratify, humour; coax, wheedle; kid, tease. adj *lit:* cheerful, convivial, frolicsome, gay, genial, jocund, jovial, merry, mirthful; carefree, playful; agreeable, delightful, pleasant. adv *lit:* extremely, very.

jostle vb *lit:* bump, collide with, elbow, jar, jiggle, jog, joggle, press against, push against, shove, squeeze; crowd, hustle, throng.

journal n *lit:* magazine, monthly, periodical, weekly; daybook, diary, log, record, register; newspaper.

journalist n *lit:* columnist, correspondent, editor, feature-writer, hack, newspaperman, reporter, scribe, stringer, subeditor; broadcaster, commentator, newscaster; chronicler, diary-writer, record-keeper.

journey n *lit:* excursion, expedition, jaunt, odyssey, outing, tour, trek, trip, voyage; pilgrimage, peregrination, ramble, travels, wanderings. vb *lit:* drive, go, move, ride, tour, travel, trek, voyage, wend; ramble, roam, rove, wander; make one's way, proceed, progress.

joy n *lit:* delight, elation, exultation, felicity, gladness, happiness, pleasure, satisfaction; bliss, ecstasy, exaltation, rapture.
vb *lit:* delight, exult, rejoice; enrapture, gladden, please.

joyful adj *lit:* delighted, elated, exultant, happy; blissful, ecstatic, exalted, enraptured, jubilant, rapturous, transported; glad, gratified, pleased, satisfied; delightful, gladdening, gratifying, pleasing, ravishing.

joyous adj *lit:* beatific, ecstatic, exalted, jubilant; cheerful, joyful, rapturous; festive, gladsome, merry; elating, gladdening, heartening, pleasing.

jubilant adj *lit:* elated, euphoric, exultant, joyous, triumphal, triumphant; rejoicing, shouting for joy, thrilled; cock-a-hoop, over the moon.

jubilation n *lit:* celebration, elation, euphoria, exultation, festivity, joy, rejoicing, triumph; applause, cheering, clapping, ovation.

judge n *lit:* beak, bench, deemster, justice of the peace, magistrate, m'lud; appraiser, arbiter, assessor, evaluator; adjudicator, arbitrator, authority, referee, umpire; moderator. **vb** *lit:* dispense justice, hear, sit in judgement on, try; decree, deem, declare, find, pass sentence of, pronounce sentence, rule, sentence; adjudge, appraise, assess, conclude, consider, deduce, determine, discern, estimate, evaluate, rate, suppose, think, value, weigh up; adjudicate, arbitrate, decide, distinguish, differentiate, mediate, referee, settle, umpire.

judgement n *lit:* reason, reasoning; acumen, common sense, discernment, discretion, discrimination, penetration, percipience, prudence, sense, shrewdness, taste, understanding, wisdom; appraisal, assessment, conclusion, consideration, deduction, estimation, evaluation, valuation; arbitration, decision, decree, finding, opinion, view; ruling, sentence, settlement, verdict; doom, fate; punishment, retribution.

jug n *lit:* crock, ewer, pitcher; carafe, jar, urn; pot; coffee-pot; mug, tankard; *fig:* cells, jail, prison. **vb** *lit:* boil, steam, stew; *fig:* imprison, incarcerate, jail.

juice n *lit:* sap; extract, liquor, nectar; enzyme, secretion, serum; fluid, liquid; petrol; current, electricity; *fig:* piquancy; crux, essence, nub. **vb** *fig:* brighten (up), liven (up).

juicy adj *lit:* sappy, succulent, watery, wet; *fig:* colourful, lively, racy, sensational, spicy, vivid; lurid, provocative, risqué, suggestive; lush, richly textured.

jumble n *lit:* clutter, disarray, disorder, hodgepodge, hotchpotch, mess, mishmash, muddle; confusion, farrago, mixture; bric-a-brac, rummage. **vb** *lit:* disarrange, disorder, mix, shuffle; confuse, disorganize, muddle; dishevel, entangle, tangle; be mixed, be shuffled.

jumbo adj *lit:* elephantine, mammoth; extra-large, giant, outsized; colossal, enormous, gigantic, huge, immense, massive; *spec:* Boeing-747 aircraft.

jump n *lit:* bound, leap, spring, vault; hop, skip; bounce, jerk, jolt, lurch, start; ditch, fence, hurdle, obstacle; break, gap, hiatus, interval, space; boost, hike, increase, rise, upturn; *fig:* advantage. **vb** *lit:* bound, clear, leap, spring, vault; hop, hurdle, skip; bounce, jerk, jolt, kangaroo, lurch, start; avoid, dodge, evade, get away from, leave, run away from; leave out, miss, omit, pass over; ascend, be boosted, escalate, increase, mount, rise, surge; ambush, pounce on, surprise; *fig:* agree (with), coincide (with); *spec:* raise (in poker).

jumpy adj *lit:* jittery, nervous, on edge, tense; anxious, worried; agitated, fidgety, flustered, in a state, nervy; highly-strung, restless.

junction n *lit:* joint, seal, seam, suture; connection, coupling, join, linking; crossing, crossroads, intersection; convergence, merging, union; contact, node; border, edge, interface.

junior n *lit:* adolescent, child, juvenile, minor, young person; younger person; assistant, trainee; inferior, subordinate. **adj** *lit:* younger; inferior, lesser, lower, minor, subordinate.

junk n *lit:* bric-a-brac, odds and ends, rummage, scrap, trash; clutter, debris, litter, refuse, rubbish, waste; *fig:* nonsense, old rope; *spec:* Chinese vessel; drugs, narcotics; salt tack. **vb** *lit:* scrap, throw away; abandon, discard, reject.

just adj *lit:* equitable, fair, honest, impartial, right, unbiased, unprejudiced; appropriate, apt, deserved, due, fitting, merited, proper, suitable; accurate, correct, exact, precise, true; decent, good, honourable, righteous, upright; lawful, legal, legitimate. **adv** *lit:* but, merely, only, simply, solely; barely, hardly, scarcely, with difficulty; in the immediate past, lately, recently; absolutely, entirely, exactly, perfectly, precisely, positively, quite, truly; a little, slightly.

justice n *lit:* equity, fairness, honesty, impartiality, rightness; integrity, reason, rectitude, truth; judge, judiciary, law, magistrate; integrity; amends, compensation, correction, recompense, redress, reparation.

justification n *lit:* grounds, rationale, reason, warrant; defence, excuse, explanation, rationalization; vindication; *spec:* alignment, ranging (lines of type); redemption, salvation (in theology).

justify vb *lit:* explain, prove reasonable, validate, warrant; defend, excuse, legitimize, uphold; clear, exculpate, vindicate; *spec:* align, range (lines of type); be the salvation of, redeem (in theology); prove acceptable (in law).

K

keen vb *lit:* bewail, lament, mourn, wail. **adj** *lit:* avid, eager, enthusiastic, fervent, intense, zealous; ardent, devoted, impassioned, passionate; cutting, edged, honed, incisive, penetrating, piercing, pointed, sharp; biting, bitter; acute, astute, canny, clever, discerning, discriminating, perceptive, perspicacious, quick, shrewd; sensitive; *fig:* sardonic, satirical, tart, trenchant.

keep n *lit:* board, livelihood, living, maintenance, subsistence; castle, donjon, fastness, fortress, stronghold, tower. **vb** *lit:* carry, conserve, have, hold, possess, reserve, retain, stock, store, own; accumulate, heap, pile, stack; care for, defend, guard, look after, maintain, mind, preserve, protect, shelter, shield, tend, watch over; conduct, manage, operate, run; board, foster, nurture, support, sustain; arrest, constrain, detain, hold back, impede, prevent, refrain, restrain, stall; block, check, curb, delay, deter, hamper, hinder, inhibit, limit, obstruct, retard; be, carry (on), continue, endure, persevere, persist, remain, stay; last, survive; *fig:* adhere to, celebrate, commemorate, observe, perform; comply with, fulfil, honour, obey, respect.

keeper n *lit:* attendant, caretaker, curator, custodian, guardian; gaoler, guard, jailer, overseer, superintendent, warden, warder; defender, preserver; owner, possessor, proprietor; *spec:* armature; clasp, catch, socket.

keeping n *lit:* care, charge, custody, guardianship, possession, preservation, protection, reservation, retention; accord, accordance, agreement, conformity, consistency, correspondence, harmony, proportion; adherence, celebration, commemoration, observance, performance.

key n *lit:* doorkey, latchkey, opener, winder; spanner, tuner; ivory, lever, note; bolt, filler, pin, wedge; capstone; character, letter; octave, register, scale, tonal system; caption, explanation, legend, scheme; answer, interpretation, solution, translation; clue, cue, hint, indicator, lead, pointer, sign, signal; focus, hub, pivot. **vb** *lit:* fasten, lock;

adjust, loosen, tighten, tune, turn, wind up; differentiate, distinguish, encode, identify, mark, mark out, mark up; align, attune; excite, nerve, stimulate.   **adj** *lit:* controlling, crucial, deciding, decisive, essential, pivotal, vital; basic, fundamental, major, principal.

kick   **n** *lit:* boot, punt; hack, hoof; jerk, jolt, jump; *fig:* drive, force, power, punch, strength, verve, vigour, zest; opposition, resilience, resistance; potency, pungency; boost, buzz, excitement, fillip, stimulation, stimulus, thrill; enjoyment, gratification, pleasure; binge, craze, fad, phase, vogue; *spec:* recoil (of a gun).   **vb** *lit:* boot, hack, hoof, sidefoot, toe; jerk, jolt, jump, thresh; *fig:* complain, gripe, grumble, protest, rebel; abandon, break, give up, leave off, quit.

kid   **n** *lit:* child, infant, tot, young goat, youngster; boy, girl; bairn; teenager; *spec:* goat-leather.   **vb** *lit:* bamboozle, deceive, delude, fool, hoax, hoodwink, pretend, trick; banter, joke, rag, tease.

kidnap   **vb** *lit:* abduct, hijack, hold to ransom, skyjack, take hostage; carry off, seize, steal.

kill   **n** *lit:* game, prey, quarry; death, destruction, elimination, end; *fig:* coup de grâce, end-play, final stroke.   **vb** *lit:* assassinate, butcher, dispatch, do away with, execute, extirpate, massacre, murder, put down, put to death, slaughter, slay; bump off, do in, get rid of, knock off, liquidate, neutralize, rub out, terminate with extreme prejudice, waste; annihilate, destroy, eliminate, eradicate, exterminate, obliterate; *fig:* cancel, quash, scotch, suppress, veto; bring to an end, end, halt, stall, still, stop, terminate; quell, smother, stifle; delete, discard, reject; defeat, overcome, overwhelm, ruin, spoil; fritter away, spend, use up, waste, while away; *spec:* reduce (in metal refining).

killer   **n** *lit:* assassin, cutthroat, gunman, hitman, murderer, slayer; butcher, slaughterer; executioner; destroyer, exterminator, liquidator, neutralizer.

killing   **n** *lit:* assassination, carnage, cull, execution, extirpation, fatality, genocide, homicide, massacre, murder, slaughter, slaying; annihilation, destruction, elimination, extermination, obliteration; game, prey, quarry; *fig:* cancellation, quashing, scotching, suppression, vetoing; ending, halting, stopping, termination; bomb, coup, fortune, gain, profit.   **adj** *lit:* deadly, deathly, fatal, lethal, mortal, murderous; destructive; *fig:* arduous, debilitating, exhausting, fatiguing, gruelling, punishing, strenuous, tiring; hilarious, uproarious; fascinating, irresistible.

kin n *lit:* clan, family, folks, kith, relations, relatives, stock, tribe; blood, connections; affinity, consanguinity, relationship.
adj *lit:* consanguine, related, tied; akin, allied, cognate.

kind n *lit:* brand, category, class, make, sort, style, type, variety; breed, family, genus, ilk, race, species, strain; character, description, fashion, manner, nature, stamp; *spec:* goods, produce (in bartering). **adj** *lit:* beneficent, benevolent, benign, charitable, generous, liberal, munificent, philanthropic; compassionate, considerate, friendly, humane, humanitarian, loving, obliging, sympathetic, tender, thoughtful, understanding; affectionate, amicable, congenial, cordial, courteous, gentle, good, gracious, indulgent.

kindly adj *lit:* benevolent, charitable, compassionate, considerate, friendly, helpful, humane, humanitarian, loving, sympathetic, tender, thoughtful, understanding, warm; agreeable, amiable, amicable, congenial, cordial, courteous, genial, gentle, good, indulgent, pleasant. **adv** *lit:* affectionately, benevolently, benignly, compassionately, congenially, considerately, helpfully, humanely, sympathetically, tenderly, thoughtfully, warmly; agreeably, genially.

kindness n *lit:* altruism, beneficence, benevolence, benignity, charity, generosity, goodness, hospitality, liberality, magnanimity, munificence, philanthropy; compassion, consideration, friendliness, friendship, humanitarianism, humanity, love, sympathy, tenderness, thoughtfulness, understanding; affection, indulgence; favour, good deed, good turn, kindly act, service.

king n *lit:* head of state, monarch, ruler, sovereign; emperor, overlord, prince; his majesty; *fig:* best, greatest; magnate, supremo, tycoon.

kingdom n *lit:* dominion, nation, realm, state, territory; monarchy, reign, sovereignty; *fig:* area, classification, division, domain, field, province, sphere.

kiosk n *lit:* bookstall, booth, newsstand, stall, stand; callbox, telephone box; information bureau; ticket office.

kiss n *lit:* osculation; peck, smacker; greeting, salutation; *fig:* caress, contact, glance, graze, touch. **vb** *lit:* osculate; give a peck, peck; greet, salute; neck, smooch, snog; *fig:* alight on, land on; brush, caress, contact, glance off, graze, touch gently.

kit n *lit:* apparatus, gear, impedimenta, outfit, paraphernalia, rig, tackle, trappings; accoutrements, effects, equipment, implements, instruments, tools, utensils; materials, parts, pieces, set; *spec:* bucket, pail, tub. **vb** *lit:* accoutre, equip, fit, rig, tool, set; furnish, provide, provision, supply.

knack n *lit:* bent, facility, flair, gift, propensity, talent, trick; adeptness, aptitude, art, skill, technique, touch; ability, capacity; adroitness, dexterity.

knickers n *lit:* panties, underwear, undies; bloomers, camiknickers, drawers, pants, smalls.

knife n *lit:* blade, cutter, scalpel, steel; dagger, dirk, poniard, sgian-dhu, stiletto. **vb** *lit:* cut, lacerate, pierce, slash, stab, wound; *fig:* betray, undermine; impale, penetrate, slice.

knit **vb** *lit:* interlace, intertwine, link up, loop together, tie, weave; affix, bind, cement, connect, join, secure, unite; heal, mend; consolidate, firm up; *fig:* crease, furrow, wrinkle.

knob n *lit:* doorhandle, handle, projection; boss, button, stud; bump, lump, nodule, protrusion, protuberance, swelling; knot.

knock n *lit:* blow, box, buffet, hit, punch, rap, smack, thump; *fig:* censure, criticism; rebuff, reversal, setback; arrest; *spec:* bat, innings (in cricket); pinking, rattle (of an engine). **vb** *lit:* box, buffet, clap, clip, cuff, drive, hammer, hit, punch, rap, smack, strike, thump, whack; daze, stun; *fig:* belittle, disparage, run down; censure, criticize, condemn; *spec:* pink, rattle (of an engine).

knot n *lit:* bond, bow, joint, ligature; aggregation, assembly, band, bunch, circle, clique, clump, cluster, collection, company, gang, group, squad; mare's nest, mess, tangle; complexity, focus, node;

bulge, bump, concretion, knob, lump, swelling; *spec:* nautical mile per hour, type of wading bird.   **vb** *lit:* bind, knit, loop, secure, tether, tie, weave; entangle, snarl, tangle, twist; bunch, harden, tighten.

know   **vb** *lit:* be acquainted with, be familiar with, recognize; be assured of, be aware of, be certain of, be informed of, be sure of, comprehend, have learned, have memorized, realize, understand; apprehend, grasp, learn, perceive, see; differentiate, discern, distinguish, identify, make out, tell; experience, feel, undergo; *spec:* have sexual intercourse with.

knowing   **adj (pr.pt)** *lit:* aware, conscious, deliberate, intended, intentional; competent, enlightened, expert, qualified, skilful, well-informed; acute, astute, clever, cunning, intelligent, perceptive, shrewd; eloquent, expressive, meaningful, significant.

knowledge   **n** *lit:* enlightenment, experience, learning, wisdom; education, instruction, scholarship, schooling, tuition; erudition, intelligence, science; ability, acquaintance, awareness, certainty, comprehension, consciousness, discernment, familiarity, grasp, intimacy, perception, recognition, understanding; cognizance, information, notice; *spec:* sexual intercourse.

knowledgeable   **adj** *lit:* competent, educated, enlightened, experienced, expert, familiar, qualified, skilful, well-informed; astute, clever, intelligent; aware, conversant, erudite, learned, scholarly.

known   **adj (pa.pt)** *lit:* acknowledged, admitted, avowed, overt, patent; celebrated, commonplace, famous, noted, popular, recognized, well-known; common, familiar, obvious, plain; certain, distinct, established, factual, sure; called, named.

L

label   n *lit:* marker, name-tag, tab, tag, ticket, trademark; *fig:* category, classification, description, designation, name, stamp; *spec:* codicil (to a legal document); dripstone (in architecture). **vb** *lit:* brand, identify, mark, name, tag; *fig:* characterize, categorize, classify, describe, designate; *spec:* irradiate (in physics).

lace   n *lit:* braid, chiffon, crochetwork, netting, tatting; cord, string, thong, tie.   **vb** *lit:* braid, do up, entwine, fasten, interweave, string, thread, tie; *fig:* thrash; *spec:* add in, drug, fortify, mix in, nobble, spike (food or drink).

lack   n *lit:* absence, dearth, deficiency, deficit, deprivation, famine, need, scarcity, shortage, shortfall, want.   **vb** *lit:* be without, do without, fail, miss, need, want.

lacking   adj (pr.pt) *lit:* absent, defective, deficient, inadequate, missing, short, wanting.

lad   n *lit:* boy, chap, fellow, guy, son, youngster, youth; *fig:* rebel, reveller, roisterer, wide boy.

laden   adj (pa.pt) *lit:* burdened, encumbered, full, loaded, lumbered, oppressed, weighed down.

lag   vb *lit:* dawdle, drop back, fall back, fall behind, linger, loiter, straggle, tarry, trail; *spec:* insulate.

lair   n *lit:* den, nest, refuge, retreat; *fig:* base, harbour, haven, hideaway, home, sanctuary, shelter, stronghold.

lake   n *lit:* dam, loch, mere, pond, pool, tarn; *fig:* reservoir, store.

lame   vb *lit:* cripple, disable, injure, maim, nobble, wound. **adj** *lit:* crippled, disabled, game, gammy, halt, handicapped, hobbling, injured, limping, maimed, wounded; *fig:* defective, feeble, flimsy, imperfect, inadequate, insufficient, pathetic, poor, unconvincing, weak.

lament   n *lit:* complaint, moan; dirge, elegy, threnody, wake.

vb *lit:* bemoan, bewail, cry about, keen, mourn, sorrow, wail; *fig:* deplore, regret.

lamentable **adj** *lit:* deplorable, distressing, pathetic, pitiable, pitiful, regrettable, tragic; distressed, miserable, low, meagre, poor, unfortunate, wretched.

lamentation **n** *lit:* complaining, crying, grieving, keening, lament, moan, moaning, mourning, sorrowing, wailing, weeping.

lamp **n** *lit:* flashlight, headlight, lantern, light, sidelight, torch; *fig:* eye.

land **n** *lit:* country, district, nation, realm, region; countryside, ground, soil, terrain, tract; domain, estate, grounds, property, real estate, territory. **vb** *lit:* alight, disembark, dock, touch down; *fig:* arrive, end up; acquire, attain, gain, get, obtain, secure, win; *spec:* get in, plant (a punch).

landlord **n** *lit:* lease-holder, owner, proprietor; host, hotel-keeper, innkeeper.

landmark **n** *lit:* indicator, marker, milestone, pointer, signpost; feature, monument; *fig:* event, happening, turning-point.

landslide **n** *lit:* avalanche, landslip, rockfall. **adj** fig: decisive, overwhelming, runaway.

lane **n** *lit:* alley, passage, path, road, sidestreet, street, track; channel, course.

language **n** *lit:* argot, dialect, jargon, lingo, patois, tongue; diction, expression, idiom, phraseology, phrasing, speech, terminology, vocabulary, wording, words; oratory, rhetoric, semantics, style; *fig:* alphabet, cipher, code, system.

languid **adj** *lit:* faint, feeble, flagging, inert, limp, listless, slack, spiritless, torpid, weak, wearied; *fig:* apathetic, lethargic, unenthused.

lank **adj** *lit:* drooping, flabby, flaccid, limp, straggling; gaunt, lean, scrawny, skinny, slender, slim, thin.

lanky **adj** *lit:* gangling, long, tall, ungainly, weedy; lean, scrawny, skinny, thin.

lap **n** *lit:* circuit, loop, orbit, round, tour; *fig:* part, section, stage. **vb** *lit:* circle, make a circuit, loop, orbit; gently splash, ripple, slap, wash against; lick up, suck up, sip, sup; *fig:* enjoy, love.

lapse **n** *lit:* error, failure, fault, faux pas, mistake, slip; indiscretion, solecism; duration, interval, period; apostasy. **vb** *lit:* become invalid, become void, expire, pass, run out, stop, terminate; decline, drop, fail, fall away, fall into disuse, stop going, tail off; fall back, sink back; apostasize.

lapsed **adj (pa.pt)** *lit:* discontinued, invalid, expired, run out, stopped, terminated; former, past; gone, over, passed.

large **adj** *lit:* big, colossal, enormous, extensive, giant, gigantic, great, huge, immense, massive, monumental, substantial, vast; *fig:* expansive, grand; *spec:* fair, favourable (for ships at sea).

lark **n** *lit:* antic, caper, escapade, frolic, fun, jape, joke, prank, romp; type of bird. **vb** *lit:* antic, be mischievous, cavort, frolic, play, rollick, romp.

lascivious **adj** *lit:* concupiscent, lecherous, lewd, libidinous, lustful, wanton; promiscuous; *fig:* erotic.

lash **n** *lit:* blow, hit, stroke; stripe, weal; *spec:* ferocity, force, severity (of a person's tongue); sweep, swing, swirl, swish (of an animal's tail). **vb** *lit:* attach together, bind, fasten, join, secure, tie up; beat, birch, flagellate, flog, lay into, scourge, thrash, whip; *fig:* castigate, censure, criticize, lambast, rebuke, scold, upbraid; *spec:* beat down, cascade, pour (with rain); sweep, swing, swirl, swish (of an animal's tail).

last **n** *lit:* concluding one, ending one, final one, terminating one; close, conclusion, end, final time, termination; *spec:* final breath (at death). **vb** *lit:* continue, endure, go on, hold out, keep going, persist, remain, survive; be enough, suffice. **adj** *lit:* closing, concluding, ending, extreme, final, latest, lattermost, rearmost, terminal, ultimate, utmost. **adv** *lit:* afterwards, finally, most recently, ultimately.

lasting **adj (pr.pt)** *lit:* durable, enduring, indelible, long-standing, perennial, permanent, remanent, undying; abiding, consistent, continual, continuous, ongoing, perpetual, viable.

late adj *lit:* behindhand, overdue, slow, tardy, unpunctual; dead, deceased, departed, erstwhile, former, last, old, past, preceding, previous; fresh, modern, new, recent. adv *lit:* after hours, behindhand, belatedly, dilatorily, over time, tardily, unpunctually.

lately adv *lit:* freshly, just now, newly, recently.

later adj *lit:* following, next, subsequent, succeeding, successive. adv *lit:* afterwards, subsequently, thereafter.

latest adj *lit:* contemporary, current, modern, most recent, newest, topical, up-to-date; fashionable, in, modish, trendy.

laudable adj *lit:* admirable, commendable, creditable, estimable, meritorious, praiseworthy.

laugh n *lit:* cackle, chortle, chuckle, giggle, guffaw, roar, titter; *fig:* bit of fun, hoot, joke, lark, scream; card, clown, comedian, comic, wag, wit. vb *lit:* be amused, be convulsed, cackle, chortle, chuckle, crease up, giggle, guffaw, roar, split one's sides.

laughable adj *lit:* absurd, ludicrous, nonsensical, preposterous, ridiculous; *fig:* contemptible, derisory.

laughter n *lit:* cachinnation, cackling, chortling, chuckling, giggling, guffawing, hilarity, jocularity, laughing, mirth, tittering.

launch n *lit:* boat, cutter, dinghy, shallop, sloop, vessel; beginning, commencement, debut, establishing, floating, flotation, inauguration, send-off, setting out, start; discharge, firing off. vb *lit:* despatch, discharge, fire, fling, project, propel, push out, put forth, send off, send out, set going, throw, throw out; begin, commence, embark upon, inaugurate, initiate, open, set off, set out, start, take off; dive, jump, rush at; *spec:* promote, publish (a new book or programme).

lavatory n *lit:* bathroom, bog, cloakroom, convenience, gents, ladies, little room, loo, powder room, privy, public convenience, toilet, washroom, water closet, WC; *spec:* heads (on navy ships).

lavish vb *lit:* deluge, heap, pour, shower, spare no expense with, surround with; expend, use to the full; *fig:* squander, waste.
adj *lit:* abundant, bountiful, copious, effusive, generous, liberal, plentiful, profuse, prolific; *fig:* exaggerated, excessive, extravagant,

immoderate, improvident, intemperate, overdone, prodigal,
superfluous, unrestrained, wasteful.

law   n *lit:* act, canon, codex, jurisprudence, ordinance, regulation,
rule, statute; axiom, precept; commandment, decree, edict, order;
fig: legal proceedings, police; *spec:* Mosaic code (of the Pentateuch);
principle (in science).

law-abiding   adj *lit:* decent, dutiful, honest, lawful, obedient,
orderly, peaceable, upright.

lawful   adj *lit:* allowed, authorized, constitutional, legal, legitimate,
licit, permissible, permitted, rightful, sanctioned, statutory.

lawless   adj *lit:* anarchic, disorderly, insurgent, rebellious, riotous,
seditious, ungovernable, unruly, wild; criminal, nefarious, outlawed,
shady; uncontrolled, unrestrained.

lawyer   n *lit:* advocate, attorney, barrister, counsel, solicitor;
spec: bramble, trailing briar; scribe (interpreter of Mosaic law).

lax   adj *lit:* casual, lenient, overindulgent, unfussy; careless, slipshod;
flabby, loose, shapeless, slack, soft; imprecise, indefinite, nonspecific,
vague.

lay   n *lit:* arrangement, disposition, positioning, site; chant, hymn,
lyric, poem, song; *spec:* plaiting (of a rope); (female) sexual
partner.   vb *lit:* apply, arrange, burden, charge, cover, deposit,
dispose, impose, locate, position, put, set down, spread over, station;
stake, wager; *fig:* ascribe, assign, attribute, impute; contrive, design,
devise, plan, plot; *spec:* bury (one deceased); exorcize; have sex with;
plait (a rope); produce (an egg).   adj *lit:* laic, nonclerical, secular;
fig: amateur, nonprofessional; *spec:* not trumps (in cards).

layer   n *lit:* bed, ply, stratum, thickness; course, row, seam; coat,
coating, covering, film, mantle; *spec:* chicken, hen (of eggs); rooting
shoot (of a plant).

layout   n *lit:* arrangement, geography, scenario, set; display,
presentation; design, draft, outline, plan.

laziness   n *lit:* idleness, inactivity, indolence, inertia, slackness, sloth,
sluggishness, torpor.

lazy   *adj*   *lit:* idle, inactive, indolent, inert, shiftless, slothful, sluggish, torpid, workshy; *spec:* weak (of heart or eye muscles).

lead   *n*   *lit:* advantage, first place, front, precedence, primacy, priority; first player, principal, star, starring role, title part; clue, direction, guidance, guide, hint, suggestion; example, leadership, model, path; *spec:* channel (in ice-field); (electrical) conductor, connection, wire; first play (in cards); leash, rein, string (on a pet); lode (in mining).   **vb**   *lit:* be ahead, be first, be in front, excel, outdo, outstrip, pass, precede, surpass; command; direct, govern, head, manage, preside over; conduct, convey, escort, guide, pilot, show, steer, usher; cause, draw, induce, influence, persuade, produce, prompt; begin, commence, initiate, open; *fig:* experience, go forward, go on, live, pass, spend, undergo; *spec:* take the offensive (in a game or sport).

leader   *n*   *lit:* captain, chief, commander, conductor, director, guide, head, ruler, superior; first, forerunner, guide, vanguard; principal, star; *spec:* bargain offer; channel (from or in a waterway); editorial (in a periodical).

leadership   *n*   *lit:* authority, captaincy, chieftancy, command, control, direction, directorship, guidance, management, organization, regulation, rule, supremacy.

leading   *adj (pr.pt)*   *lit:* chief, dominant, main, primary, principal, ruling, superior; first, foremost, pre-eminent; celebrated, important, famous, noted, significant.

leaf   *n*   *lit:* blade, bract, frond, petal; *fig:* folio, page, sheet, side; *spec:* board, lath, slat (detachable from window, door or table); lamina (of gold or silver).   **vb**   *lit:* flip, riffle, skim, thumb, turn; *spec:* bud, put out leaves (of trees).

league   *n*   *lit:* alliance, association, cartel, compact, confederacy, confederation, federation, partnership, society, union; collaboration; category, class, group; cahoots, conspiracy.

leak   *n*   *lit:* discharge, drip, emission, escape, oozing, percolation, seepage, spill, spillage; breach, crack, fissure, hole, opening, puncture; *fig:* informant, informer, mole, sneak, telltale; *spec:* urination.

vb *lit:* discharge, emit, exude, let out; drip out, escape, get out, issue, ooze, percolate, seep, spill, trickle out; get in, infiltrate; *fig:* admit, disclose, divulge, give away, inform, reveal, tell.

lean **vb** *lit:* heel, incline, list, slant, slope, tilt, tip; be supported, be propped up, rest, weigh; bend down; *fig:* favour, incline, prefer, tend; depend, rely, trust; coerce, intimidate, pressurize. **adj** *lit:* bony, gaunt, skinny, slender, slim, thin; barren, inadequate, insufficient, meagre, mean, poor, scanty, spare, sparse, unproductive, weak; *fig:* unprofitable.

leaning **n** *lit:* bent, bias, favouritism, inclination, partiality, penchant, predilection, preference, proclivity, taste; aptitude, propensity, tendency.

leap **n** *lit:* bound, hop, jump, skip, spring, vault; escalation, hike, increase, rise, upsurge; *fig:* distance, journey; enterprise, undertaking; gap, interval; *spec:* jump-off point. **vb** *lit:* bound, caper, hop, jump, skip, spring, vault; clear; cavort, frisk, gambol; escalate, increase, rise, rocket, soar, surge; *fig:* fly, hasten, hurry, run, rush; *spec:* jump (to a conclusion).

learn **vb** *lit:* apprehend, be taught, comprehend, grasp, master, memorize, study; ascertain, be informed, be told, come to know, determine, discern, discover, find out, gather, hear, pick up.

learned **adj (pa.pt)** *lit:* cultured, educated, erudite, lettered, literate, scholarly, well-informed, well-read; expert, skilful, skilled, well-versed.

learning **n** *lit:* education, erudition, knowledge, letters, literacy, scholarship; culture, understanding, wisdom; expertise, lore, skill.

leash **n** *lit:* chain, lead, line, rein, strap, string, tether, thong; curb; *fig:* control, restraint; *spec:* group of three, trio (of animals, in hunting or judging). **vb** *lit:* chain, fasten, put on a lead, secure, tether, tie up; *fig:* check, control, curb, restrain.

least **n** *lit:* fewest, minimum, most minute, slightest, smallest, tiniest; *fig:* lowest, meanest, poorest; most feeble. **adj** *lit:* fewest, minimal, most minute, slightest, smallest, tiniest; *fig:* lowest, meanest, poorest, most feeble. **adv** *lit:* by the tiniest amount, minimally, to the slightest degree, to the smallest extent.

leave n *lit:* authorization, consent, dispensation, permission, sanction; freedom, holiday, liberty, time off, vacation; departure, going, parting, withdrawal; farewell, goodbye. **vb** *lit:* depart, exit, go, move off, pull out, quit, retire from, set out, vacate, withdraw; abandon, cede, desert, evacuate, forget to take, go off without, relinquish, surrender; cease, desist, drop, give up, refrain, stop; assign, commit, give over; *spec:* bequeath to, hand on to, will to.

lecture n *lit:* address, discourse, disquisition, exegesis, lesson, talk; *fig:* admonition, censure, dressing-down, rebuke, scolding, talking-to, telling-off. **vb** *lit:* address, expound, give a talk, instruct, teach; *fig:* admonish, berate, censure, chide, reprimand, reprove, scold, tell off.

ledge n *lit:* shelf, sill, step; ridge; *spec:* lode, vein (in geology).

leech n *lit:* bloodsucker; *fig:* hanger-on, parasite, sponger; *spec:* doctor, physician.

leer n *lit:* hot glance, smirk, stare. **vb** *lit:* give the eye, make sheep's eyes, ogle, smirk, stare.

leg n *lit:* limb, member, pin; basis, brace, prop, support, upright; episode, lap, part, section, stage; *spec:* on side (in cricket); tack (in sailing).

legality n *lit:* law, lawfulness, legitimacy; permissibility, validity.

legalize **vb** *lit:* authorize, legitimate, legitimize, license; allow, make official, permit, sanction, validate.

legend n *lit:* fable, folklore, myth, saga, story, tale, tradition; caption, device, inscription, key, motto, table of symbols, wording; *fig:* celebrity, hero, prodigy; *spec:* hagiography.

legendary **adj** *lit:* apocryphal, fabulous, mythical, traditional; epic, heroic, prodigious; celebrated, famous, illustrious, renowned; fictitious, untrue.

legitimate **adj** *lit:* lawful, legal, licit, statutory; authorized, official, rightful, sanctioned; authentic, correct, fair, genuine, justifiable, logical, normal, proper, real, true, valid, warranted; *spec:* by right of heredity.

leisure   n *lit:* freedom, holiday, liberty, spare time, time off, vacation; recreation, relaxation, rest, taking it easy.   **adj** *lit:* free, holiday, spare, unoccupied.

leisurely   **adj** *lit:* comfortable, deliberate, easy, relaxed, restful, slow, unhurried.   **adv** *lit:* comfortably, deliberately, easily, relaxedly, restfully, slowly, unhurriedly.

lend   **vb** *lit:* advance, give temporarily, loan; *fig:* afford, bestow, confer, give, impart.

length   n *lit:* distance, extent, measure, reach, span; piece, portion, section, segment; duration, period, stretch, term, time; extensiveness, prolixity, protractedness; *spec:* end-to-end distance (in rowing and horse races); quantity (of a vowel in phonetics).

lengthy   **adj** *lit:* drawn-out, extended, long, prolix, protracted; interminable, long-drawn-out, tedious.

less   **adj** *lit:* lower, inferior, slighter, smaller; not so much; minor, secondary, subordinate.   **adv** *lit:* not so much, not so well, to a lower degree, to a smaller extent.   **prp** *lit:* lacking, minus, sans, subtracting, without.

lessen   **vb** *lit:* abate, decrease, die away, diminish, dwindle, ease, lighten, moderate, reduce, slow, wind down; become smaller, contract, erode, shrink; *fig:* belittle, disparage, minimize.

lesson   n *lit:* coaching, instruction, lecture, school period, teaching, tuition; exercise, reading, subject, study; *fig:* example, inspiration, model, moral; admonition, rebuke, reprimand, reproof, scolding, warning; *spec:* reading.

let   n *lit:* hindrance, impediment, interference, obstruction; *spec:* net, net cord ball (in tennis).   **vb** *lit:* allow, authorize, enable, give leave, give permission, grant, permit, sanction; assume, suppose; contract out, hire, lease, rent.

lethal   **adj** *lit:* deadly, fatal, mortal, murderous; dangerous, devastating, poisonous, virulent.

let on   **vb** *lit:* dissemble, give the impression, pretend, simulate; disclose, divulge, manifest, reveal, show.

let off **vb** *lit:* excuse, exempt, release, reprieve, spare; absolve, forgive, pardon; detonate, discharge, explode, fire; emit, exude, give off, release; allow to alight.

let out **vb** *lit:* discharge, free, liberate, release, set free; augment, enlarge, make larger; emit, sound, voice; betray, disclose, leak, reveal; contract out, hire, lease, rent.

letter **n** *lit:* character, sign, symbol; communication, despatch, document, epistle, message, missive, note; *fig:* expression, language, literal meaning, wording.

level **n** *lit:* altitude, elevation, grade, height, position, rank, standing, status; flat surface, floor, layer, plane, storey, stratum; degree, standard; *spec:* ditch, channel (for drainage in fen country); gallery (in a mine). **vb** *lit:* even out, flatten, plane, smooth; bulldoze, pull down, raze, tear down; equalize; *fig:* aim, direct, focus, point, train; be candid, reveal all, tell the truth; *spec:* measure height (in surveying). **adj** *lit:* even, flat, horizontal, plain, plane, smooth, stable, steady, uniform; balanced, commensurate, equable, equal, equivalent, even, flush, parallel; sound; *spec:* equipotential (in physics).

lever **n** *lit:* bar, crowbar, handle, jemmy, switch; *fig:* hold, threat. **vb** *lit:* force, jemmy, prise.

leverage **n** *lit:* power, purchase; *fig:* advantage, ascendancy, clout, influence, pull, weight.

lewd **adj** *lit:* bawdy, blue, dirty, erotic, indecent, lascivious, libidinous, licentious, obscene, pornographic, salacious, smutty; debauched, lecherous, lustful.

lewdness **n** *lit:* bawdiness, carnality, debauchery, depravity, indecency, lasciviousness, lechery, licentiousness, lubricity, obscenity, pornography, salaciousness, smut.

liar **n** *lit:* deceiver, fabricator, falsifier, perjurer, storyteller; fibber, libeller, prevaricator, slanderer; double-crosser, fraud, impostor.

libel **n** *lit:* calumny, defamation, smear, vilification; slander; *spec:* accusation, charge, complaint (in law) **vb** *lit:* calumniate, defame, malign, smear, traduce, vilify; slander.

liberal adj *lit:* beneficent, bounteous, bountiful, charitable, generous, kind, munificent, philanthropic; abundant, ample, copious, lavish, plentiful, profuse, prolific; broad, easy-going, flexible, free, general, indulgent, lenient, loose, magnanimous, open, tolerant; broad-minded, catholic, disinterested, humanitarian, unbiased, unprejudiced; progressive, radical, reformist; *spec:* cultural, intellectual (as opposed to practical).

liberation n *lit:* deliverance, emancipation, enfranchisement, freedom, freeing, letting go, loosing, release, releasing, rescue, setting free, unbinding, untying; *spec:* disestablishment (of the Church); manumission, redemption (of a slave, of sinners); political reform, social reform (theology).

liberty n *lit:* emancipation, enfranchisement, freedom; autonomy, independence, power, right, self-determination; carte blanche, dispensation, exemption, immunity; authorization, franchise, leave, licence, permission, sanction; leisure, spare time; *fig:* breach of good manners, familiarity, impertinence, impropriety, impudence, insult, presumption.

licence n *lit:* accreditation, certificate, charter, permit, warrant; authority, power, privilege, right; authorization, dispensation, entitlement, leave, permission, sanction; carte blanche, freedom, independence, latitude, liberty; exemption, immunity; excess, immoderation, indulgence, irresponsibility, laxity, profligacy; abandon, anarchy, debauchery, lawlessness, unruliness, wantonness.

license vb *lit:* accredit, certify, warrant; authorize, commission, empower; allow, permit, sanction.

lick n *lit:* lap, slurp; sample, sip, taste; saliva; *fig:* bit, dab, little, speck, spot, touch; clip, pace, rate, speed, velocity; *spec:* anacrusis, intro, riff (in jazz); salt-pan. vb *lit:* lap, slurp, taste, tongue; *fig:* ripple against, touch, wash; beat, conquer, defeat, rout, trounce; beat, drub, flog, spank, thrash; beat, excel, outdo, surpass; *spec:* dart, flicker, play over (of flames).

lie n *lit:* deception, fabrication, falsehood, falsification, fiction, invention, perjury, story, untruth; fib, libel, prevarication, slander; arrangement, disposition, positioning, site; geography, terrain;

aspect. **vb** *lit:* deceive, fabricate, falsify, invent, perjure, tell an untruth; be economical with the truth, equivocate, fib, libel, mislead, misrepresent, prevaricate, slander, tell a story; abide, be, be arranged, be found, be located, be placed, be positioned, be prone, be recumbent, be set, be situated, extend, lean, recline, remain, repose, rest, stretch out; be constituted, consist; be buried, be interred; *spec:* be admissible, be sustainable (in law).

life **n** *lit:* being, being alive, being awake, being conscious, breath, existence, living; biosphere, creatures, human, human being, organisms, person, soul; animation, heart, lifeblood, soul, spirit, vitality; activity, brio, energy, liveliness, verve, vigour, vivacity, zest; duration, lifetime, span, time; autobiography, biography, career, history, memoirs; *fig:* power, validity; period, term.

lift **n** *lit:* elevation, hoisting, raising; rising; advancement, boost, fillip, progress, rise, uplift; drive, ride, transport; crane, elevator, hoist, tow-bar track; *spec:* catch (of fish); masthead rope (in sailing); upward force (in aeronautics). **vb** *lit:* elevate, hoist, hold up, pick up, pull up, raise, support, uplift, upraise; ascend, go up, rise; advance, boost, elate, enhance, exalt, promote, upgrade; cancel, countermand, end, relax, rescind, revoke, terminate; be dispelled, disperse; *fig:* appropriate, purloin, rob, steal, take; arrest, detain; copy, pirate, plagiarize; harvest, reap; *spec:* approach (at sea); catch (fish); mine (ore).

light **n** *lit:* brightness, brilliance, gleam, glint, glow, illumination, incandescence, luminosity, radiance; blaze, effulgence, flash, luminescence, ray, scintillation, sparkle; dawn, daylight, daytime, morning, sun, sunshine; beacon, candle, flame, flare, lighter, match, taper; bulb, lamp, lantern, torch; lighthouse; window; *fig:* aspect, context, interpretation, slant, view; angle, approach, viewpoint; awareness, comprehension, elucidation, enlightenment, explanation, insight, understanding; example, exemplar, model; clue, hint; *spec:* traffic signal. **vb** *lit:* brighten, illuminate, illumine, irradiate; put on, switch on, turn on; fire, ignite, kindle, set ablaze, set on fire, touch a match to; alight, come down, get off, land, perch, settle; chance, come across, encounter, happen, stumble; *fig:* clarify, expose; inflame, intoxicate; animate, cheer up. **adj** *lit:* bright, brilliant,

glowing, illuminated, luminous; sunny; fair, pale, whitish; blond;
clear; delicate, easy, insubstantial, not heavy, portable, slight, thin,
underweight; faint, gentle, indistinct, mild, soft, weak; unchaste;
facile, frivolous, idle, inconsequential, insignificant, paltry, petty,
superficial, trifling, trivial, unimportant; effortless, manageable,
undemanding; amusing, entertaining, funny, pleasing, witty; agile,
airy, athletic, graceful, lithe, nimble; blithe, carefree, cheerful;
fig: dizzy, giddy, delirious; less, minus, short; *spec:* bland, digestible,
frugal (diet); friable, loose, sandy (soil).

like n *lit:* favourite, partiality, predilection, preference; match,
resemblance; counterpart, equal, fellow, parallel. **vb** *lit:* be fond of,
care for, enjoy, love, relish; be partial to, choose to, fancy, prefer,
select, take to; appreciate, approve of, esteem; **adj** *lit:* alike,
corresponding, equal, equivalent, identical, matching, parallel,
resembling, similar. **adv** *lit:* in the same way (as), just (as). **prp** *lit:*
similar, similar to, resembling; befitting, characteristic of; namely,
such as; as much as.

likely **adj** *lit:* anticipated, expected, probable; believable, credible,
feasible, plausible, reasonable; appropriate, fitting, suitable; fair,
favourite, pleasing, promising. **adv** *lit:* doubtless, in all probability,
probably.

likeness n *lit:* correspondence, resemblance, similarity; appearance,
form, guise, semblance, simulation; copy, facsimile, image, model,
replica, representation; photo, picture, portrait.

liking n *lit:* bias, inclination, partiality, penchant, predilection,
preference, taste, tendency; affection, fancy, fondness, love;
appreciation, approval, esteem, satisfaction, pleasure.

limit n *lit:* border, boundary, confines, edge, end, extent, frontier,
perimeter, periphery; ceiling, maximum, termination, ultimate;
restriction, stop, terminus. **vb** *lit:* bound, circumscribe; demarcate,
fix, set, specify; check, confine, hinder, ration, restrict.

limited **adj (pa.pt)** *lit:* bounded, circumscribed, defined, fixed;
cramped, confined, hampered, hemmed in, hindered, restricted;
diminished, inadequate, insufficient, minimal, narrow, reduced, short,
unsatisfactory; *fig:* dull, unintelligent; *spec:* assigned (in law); of
restricted liability (in company law).

line n *lit:* cable, cord, filament, rope, strand, string, thread, wire; bar, dash, rule, streak, stripe, stroke; crease, crow's foot, furrow, groove, score, wrinkle; column, crocodile, procession, queue, rank, row, sequence, series, succession; border, boundary, edge, limit, mark; configuration, contour, figure, outline; course, direction, path, route, trajectory; transport system; rail, track; hose, tube; *fig:* approach, method, policy, procedure; business, field, forte, interest, job, occupation, profession, speciality, trade; brand, make; card, letter, note, postcard; clue, hint, indication, lead, pointer; plot, story; accordance, correspondence, parallel. **vb** *lit:* draw, inscribe, mark, rule; hatch; crease, furrow, score; align, form a column, range; border, fringe, hem round, skirt, surround; cover, face; fill, reinforce, stuff.

link n *lit:* connection, contact, coupling, tie; attachment, bond, joint, relationship; *spec:* (electrical) fuse; hoop, loop, ring (of a chain). **vb** *lit:* connect, contact, couple, join, liaise between, make contact between, tie together, unite; attach, bind, bracket, fasten, relate, yoke.

lip n *lit:* labium; brim, flange, rim; edge, margin, welt; *fig:* cheek, impertinence, impudence, insolence, sauce; *spec:* embouchure (in playing a wind instrument).

liquid n *lit:* fluid, moisture; liquor. **adj** *lit:* flowing, fluid, melted, moist, molten, runny, wet; aqueous, watery; juicy; *fig:* dulcet, mellifluous, smooth, soft, sweet; bright, clear, limpid, translucent; graceful; *spec:* disposable, encashable, realizable (assets).

liquor n *lit:* alcohol, grog, hard stuff, hooch, moonshine, spirits, strong drink; broth, gravy, juice, stock; infusion, solution, suspension.

list n *lit:* catalogue, enumeration, inventory, record, register, roll, tally; file, print-out, schedule, tabulation; series; lean, slant, slope, tilt; *spec:* stock quotation (on the stock market). **vb** *lit:* catalogue, enrol, enter, enumerate, inventory, itemize, note down, record, register, write down; file, schedule, tabulate; arrange in order, serialize; cant, heel, incline, lean, slant, slope, tilt, tip.

listen vb *lit:* attend, be attentive, hear, hearken, pay attention; be advised, heed, mind, take notice.

listless adj *lit:* apathetic, enervated, impassive, indifferent, languid, spiritless, supine, uninterested, vacant; indolent, lethargic, lifeless, limp, torpid.

literally adv *lit:* accurately, exactly, faithfully, precisely, strictly, to the letter, verbatim, word for word; actually, in reality, really, truly; *fig:* as it were, in a way, virtually.

litter n *lit:* debris, garbage, muck, refuse, rubbish, trash; brood, children, cubs, family, kittens, offspring, progeny, pups, young; palanquin, stretcher, travois; bed, couch, palliasse; mulch; clutter, disorder, jumble, mess. vb *lit:* leave lying around, scatter, strew; make a mess; disarrange, disorder, jumble; *spec:* give birth to (a litter of animals); make a straw bed.

little n *lit:* bit, bite, dab, dash, fraction, lick, modicum, morsel, pinch, small amount, spot, taste, touch, trace, trifle; short time. adj *lit:* miniature, petite, short, small; diminutive, dwarf, infinitesimal, minute, tiny, wee; meagre, scant, skimpy, sparse; insignificant, minor, paltry, trifling, trivial, unimportant; mean, narrow-minded, petty, small-minded. adv *lit:* barely, hardly, scarcely; rarely, seldom; only just, slightly.

live vb *lit:* be, be alive, breathe, exist, have life, subsist; continue, endure, last, lead, pass, persist, remain, survive; abide, dwell, inhabit, lodge, occupy, reside, stay; be remembered; eat, feed; enjoy life, flourish, revel, thrive; *fig:* accept, put up with, tolerate. adj *lit:* alive, animate, breathing, living; active, awake, alert, dynamic, energetic, vigorous; ablaze, alight, burning, connected, glowing, hot, ignited, on, switched on; contemporaneous, current, pertinent, pressing, topical, up-to-date, vital; in play; unexploded, unignited; natural, real, unquarried.

lively adj *lit:* active, brisk, energetic, quick, sprightly, spry, vigorous; agile, alert, animated, chirpy, perky, spirited, vivacious; bright, colourful, exciting, fresh, invigorating, refreshing, stimulating, stirring, vivid; bustling, busy, crowded, eventful.

livid adj *lit:* anaemic, ashen, grey, leaden, pale, pallid, sallow, wan, waxen, white; black and blue, bruised, contused, discoloured, purple; angry, enraged, fuming, furious, hopping mad, incensed, infuriated, irate.

living n *lit:* job, livelihood, occupation, work; employment, means, income; support; lifestyle, way of life; being, existence, life, subsistence; *spec:* benefice (for clergymen). **adj** *lit:* alive, being, existing, live, organic, subsisting; active, contemporary, current, extant, ongoing, operative; continuing, persisting, remaining; strong, vigorous; lifelike, vivid; dwelling, lodging, occupying, residential, residing, staying.

load n *lit:* burden, cargo, charge, weight; consignment, freight, shipment; *fig:* encumbrance, millstone, onus, pressure; affliction, busyness, trouble, worry; amount, host, lot, mass, multitude, quantity; *spec:* output (in power, of an engine); force, power, work (in physics). **vb** *lit:* burden, charge, put in, put on, weigh down; cram, fill, heap, pack, pile on, stack, stuff; encumber; *fig:* oppress, trouble, worry; bias, prejudice, slant, weight; *spec:* adulterate, drug, fortify (wine); charge, prime (a firearm); fix, rig (dice).

loaded **adj (pa.pt)** *lit:* burdened, charged; crammed, filled, heaped, packed, piled, stacked, stuffed; encumbered, laden; *fig:* anxious, oppressed, troubled, worried; biased, leading, slanted, weighted; affluent, moneyed, rich, wealthy, well-heeled, well off, well-to-do; drunk, inebriated, intoxicated, legless, stoned; *spec:* adulterated, drugged, fortified; charged, primed; fixed, rigged.

loan n *lit:* advance, credit; mortgage, overdraft; accommodation, use. **vb** *lit:* advance, give temporarily, let someone have for a time, lend.

local n *lit:* inhabitant, native, resident; bar, hostelry, inn, pub, tavern. **adj** *lit:* community, district, neighbourhood, parish, parochial, provincial, regional, suburban; confined, limited, restricted; *spec:* topical (in medicine); slow (train).

locate vb *lit:* establish, fix, found, place, put, seat, set, site, situate; detect, discover, find, pin down, pinpoint, trace, track down.

lock n *lit:* bolt, clasp, fastening, latch, padlock, snib; clutch, embrace, grapple, grasp, hold, hug; linkage, mesh; curl, ringlet, strand, tress; *spec:* (airtight) chamber (on a space-ship); firing mechanism (on a gun); turning-circle (on a car). **vb** *lit:* bar, bolt, close, fasten, latch, seal, secure, shut, snib; engage, entwine, link, mesh, unite; clasp, clutch, embrace, enclose, grapple, grasp, hold, hold fast, hug, jam together, press.

lodge n *lit:* cabin, chalet, cottage, house, hut, log-cabin, shelter, villa; den, haunt, lair, retreat; gatehouse, porter's room, reception; wigwam, teepee; meeting-place; *fig:* assembly, branch, chapter, club, society. **vb** *lit:* accommodate, billet, board, harbour, put up, quarter, shelter; dwell, room, spend the night, stay, stop, temporarily reside; adhere, catch, embed, get stuck, implant, stick; deposit, file, lay, make, place, put, record, register, submit; be vested (in); *spec:* flatten (a field of grain); flush out (a deer).

lodger n *lit:* boarder, paying guest, roomer, tenant; guest, inhabitant, occupant, resident.

lodgings n *lit:* accommodation, board, boarding, digs, place to stay, quarters, room, rooms, shelter; abode, dwelling, residence; harbour.

lofty adj *lit:* high, soaring, tall, towering; *fig:* dignified, elevated, exalted, lordly, majestic, noble, stately, superior; grand, illustrious, sublime; arrogant, disdainful, haughty, overweening, patronizing, proud, snooty, supercilious.

loiter vb *lit:* amble, dawdle, idle, loaf, stroll; hang about, skulk; delay, linger.

loneliness n *lit:* desolation, forsakenness, solitude; aloneness, isolation, seclusion, solitariness.

lonely adj *lit:* abandoned, alone, deserted, desolate, forsaken, friendless, solitary, unaccompanied; apart, isolated, remote, secluded, single, unfrequented, uninhabited, withdrawn.

long vb *lit:* crave, hunger, lust, pine, wish, yearn. **adj** *lit:* elongated, extended, extensive, far-reaching, lengthy, stretched; interminable, prolonged, protracted, slow, sustained; distant, remote; *spec:* accented, stressed (syllable). **adv** *lit:* continually, through; extendedly, extensively, for years; distantly, remotely.

longing n *lit:* covetousness, craving, desire, hunger, itch, lust, thirst, yearning; ambition, aspiration, urge, wish, yen. **adj** *lit:* covetous, desirous, hungry, lustful, wishful, wistful, yearning; avid, eager.

look n *lit:* air, appearance, aspect, bearing, cast, complexion, demeanour, expression, manner, mien, semblance; examination, inspection, review, search, survey, view; gaze, observation, stare; dekko, eyeful, gander, glance, glimpse, once-over, peek, sight, squint. **vb** *lit:* behold, contemplate, examine, gaze, inspect, observe, regard, scan, scrutinize, see, stare, study, survey, view, watch; gawp, glance, goggle; appear, seem; display, evince, exhibit, manifest, show; face, give (on to); hope.

look after vb *lit:* attend, care for, mind, nurse, tend; guard, protect, supervise, watch over; attend to, take care of.

look forward to vb *lit:* anticipate, await, be eager for, expect, wait for; hope for, long for, wish for, yearn for.

look into vb *lit:* check, examine, go into, inspect, scrutinize, study; check out, explore, follow up, investigate, probe, research.

lookout n *lit:* guard, sentinel, sentry, watchman; alert, guard, vigil, watch; crow's nest, observation post, tower, watchtower; *fig:* affair, business, concern, department, worry; outlook, prospect.

loop n *lit:* doubling, coil, convolution, curl, eyelet, hoop, noose, ring, whorl; bend, curve, spiral, twist; *spec:* antinode (in physics); closed (electrical) circuit; intra-uterine (contraceptive) device.
vb *lit:* circle, coil, curl, encircle; bend, curve, spiral, turn; braid, connect, double over, fold, join, knot, twist, wind round.

loose vb *lit:* detach, disconnect, disengage, free, let go, liberate, release, set free, unbind, undo, unfasten, unleash, untie; hurl, shoot, throw; relax, slacken. **adj** *lit:* detached, disconnected, free, mobile, open, unattached, unconfined, unrestricted, unsecured, untied; flexible, free-moving, lithe, relaxed, slackened, wobbly; baggy, hanging, slack, sloppy; diffuse, ill-defined, imprecise, indefinite, inexact, vague; careless, inattentive, lax, negligent, thoughtless; *fig:* disreputable, dissolute, fast, immoral, promiscuous, wanton.

loosen vb *lit:* let out, open, relax, slacken, untense, untighten; *fig:* ease up, let up, moderate, soften, weaken.

lord n *lit:* liege, master, owner, ruler; king, monarch, prince, sovereign; noble, nobleman, peer; commander, governor, leader, superior; *spec:* dominant planet (in astrology).

lose vb *lit:* forget, mislay, misplace, miss; be defeated, capitulate, fail, give up, surrender, yield; default on, forfeit, pass up; be depleted by, be deprived of, be drained of, exhaust, expend, use up; be bereaved of; squander, waste; stray from, wander from; dodge, elude, escape, evade, give the slip, shake off.

loser n *lit:* capitulator, defeated party, yielder; defaulter, sufferer; also-ran, dud, failure, flop, has-been, lame duck, no-hoper, nonstarter, second-rater.

loss n *lit:* decrease, depletion, deprivation, diminution, reduction, shrinkage; bereavement; cost, debit, debt, expenditure, forfeiture; defeat; disappearance, forgetting, mislaying, misplacing; squandering, wastage, waste; damage, impairment, ruin, wreck.

lost adj *lit:* mislaid, misplaced, missing; disappeared, vanished; adrift, astray, baffled, bewildered, clueless, disoriented, perplexed, puzzled; destroyed, ruined, wrecked; conceded, forfeited; abstracted, engrossed, entranced, preoccupied, rapt; dissipated, misapplied, misspent, misused, squandered, wasted; *fig:* dead, gone, lapsed, over, past; abandoned, depraved, dissolute, fallen, promiscuous, wanton.

lot n *lit:* abundance, amount, deal, heap, host, mass, multitude, plenitude, plethora, quantity, stack; batch, bunch, collection, crowd, group, set; chance, destiny, doom, fate, kismet, hazard, portion; choice, lucky dip, random selection, selection; allocation, cut, part, piece, quota, ration, share; plot, property, site; *fig:* character.

loud adj *lit:* blaring, clamorous, deafening, ear-splitting, forte, fortissimo, noisy, piercing, resounding, sonorous, stentorian, thunderous; brash, raucous, rowdy, strident; *fig:* blatant, brassy, coarse, crass, flashy, garish, gaudy, lurid, obtrusive, ostentatious, showy, tasteless, vulgar.

love n *lit:* adoration, affection, attachment, devotion; adulation, infatuation; ardour, passion; amity, fancy, fondness, friendship, liking, regard, soft spot, tenderness, warmth, weakness; *fig:* nil, nought, zero; free, nothing; *spec:* angel, beloved, darling, dear, dearest, sweetheart. vb *lit:* adore, be affectionate towards, be attached to, be devoted to, be very fond of, cherish, dote on, hold dear; adulate, idolize, worship; appreciate, enjoy, fancy, have a soft spot for, have a weakness for, like very much, prize, relish, savour, take great pleasure in, treasure.

lovely   adj *lit:* beautiful, exquisite, gorgeous, ravishing; captivating, delightful, enchanting, eye-catching, fascinating, stunning; alluring, bewitching, desirable; appealing, attractive, charming, engaging, fair, handsome, lovable, pleasing, pretty, sweet, winning.

lover   n *lit:* friend, guy, man, mistress, paramour, woman; admirer, beau, boyfriend, fiancé, fiancée, girlfriend, suitor, sweetheart; aficionado, connoisseur, devotee, fan; adulator, idolizer, worshipper.

low   n *lit:* depression, hollow; bottom level, minimum; *spec:* depression, cyclone (in meteorology).   **vb** *lit:* moo, ululate.
adj *lit:* deep, depressed, ground-level, prone, prostrate, sunken; little, shallow, short, small, squat, stunted; deficient, depleted, inadequate, meagre, primitive, reduced, scant, sparse; inferior, insignificant, mediocre, paltry, poor, shoddy, trifling; coarse, common, disreputable, rough, rude, vulgar; base, contemptible, degraded, depraved, gross, ignoble, ill-bred, servile, sordid, undignified; humble, mean, obscure, plebeian; cheap, economical, inexpensive, modest; debilitated, feeble, frail, ill, weak; gentle, hushed, muted, quiet, soft, subdued; blue, dejected, depressed, despondent, disheartened, down, forlorn, glum, miserable, morose, sad, unhappy; *spec:* less ornate, less rigorous, simplified (Church, or mass).   **adv** *lit:* down, short, to a depressed level, under; to the horizon; humbly, meanly; gently, mutedly, quietly, softly.

lower   vb *lit:* drop, haul down, let down, pull down; fall, sink, submerge; depress; abate, curtail, cut, decrease, diminish, lessen, moderate, reduce, slash; belittle, bring down, debase, degrade, demean, devalue, disgrace, dishonour, humble, humiliate; condescend, deign, stoop; dilute, mute, quieten, soften, subdue, tone down.
adj *lit:* closer to the ground; nearer to the horizon; cut, decreased, diminished, lessened, reduced, slashed; inferior, lesser, minor, smaller, subordinate.   **adv** *lit:* below, beneath, closer to the ground, further down, further below, further under, under, underneath; nearer to the horizon.

loyal   adj *lit:* devoted, faithful, staunch, steadfast, true, trusty;

attached, constant, dependable, trustworthy, unswerving; dutiful, patriotic.

loyalty n *lit:* allegiance, devotion, faithfulness, fealty, fidelity, staunchness, steadfastness, trustiness; attachment, constancy, dependability, trustworthiness; patriotism, sense of duty.

luck n *lit:* chance, fortuitousness, happenstance, hazard; good fortune, serendipity; accident; destiny, fate, lot.

luckless adj *lit:* ill-fated, ill-starred, unfortunate, unlucky, unpropitious; doomed, jinxed, star-crossed; hapless, unhappy, wretched.

lucky adj *lit:* fortuitous, fortunate, serendipitous; blessed, charmed; auspicious, propitious.

lull n *lit:* calming, let-up, interval, pause, respite, subsiding; calm, quiet, silence, stillness. **vb** *lit:* allay, calm, pacify, soothe, still, subdue, tranquillize; hush, quieten; abate, decrease, diminish, ease off, let up, moderate, slacken, subside, wane.

lump n *lit:* bulge, bump, growth, protrusion, protuberance, swelling, tumour; bit, chunk, clod, gobbet, hunk, mass, piece; gross, whole; deadweight, lot, mass. **vb** *lit:* aggregate, batch, bunch, combine, conglomerate, group, mass, pool, put together; endure, put up with, stand.

lunatic n *lit:* madman, madwoman, maniac, psychopath; loony, nutcase, nutter, psycho; *fig:* idiot, imbecile; ass, fool, moron; crank, eccentric, weirdo; berserker. **adj** *lit:* crazy, demented, deranged, insane, mad, maniac, psychotic, raving, unbalanced; barmy, bananas, bats, bonkers, crackers, cuckoo, gaga, loony, nuts, nutty, potty, round the bend, touched, unhinged; asinine, crackbrained, daft, foolish, idiotic, imbecilic, inane, moronic; cranky, dotty, eccentric, weird; berserk; reckless, wild.

lunge n *lit:* jab, pass, stab, swing, swipe, thrust; charge, pounce; lurch, plunge. **vb** *lit:* hit out, jab, poke, stab, strike out, swing out, swipe, thrust; bound, charge, jump, leap, pounce; drop, fall, lurch, plunge.

lurch n *lit:* dip, drop, fall, plunge, slump; roll, stagger. vb *lit:* dip, drop, fall, plummet, plunge, sink, slump, tumble; pitch, reel, roll, stagger, stumble, totter, veer.

lure n *lit:* bait, carrot, decoy; attraction, enticement, inducement, temptation; allure, charm. vb *lit:* decoy, ensnare, inveigle, seduce; attract, draw, entice, invite, lead on, tempt; allure, charm; *spec:* recall (a hawk).

lurk vb *lit:* be furtive, be stealthy, creep, hide, lie in wait, loiter with intent, prowl, skulk, slink, steal; be hidden, lie low.

lush adj *lit:* densely-growing, flourishing, green, juicy, luxuriant, succulent, tender, verdant; *fig:* lavish, luxurious, opulent, rich, sumptuous; abundant, prolific, teeming; extravagant, flowery, ornate.

lust n *lit:* desire, libido, passion; carnality, concupiscence, lasciviousness, lewdness, sensuality, wantonness; appetite, craving, cupidity, greed, longing, thirst; relish. vb *lit:* be aroused, feel desire; crave, hunger, long, thirst, yearn.

lustre n *lit:* gleam, glistening, glitter, gloss, sheen, shimmer, shine, sparkle; brilliance, dazzle, radiance, resplendence; *fig:* fame, glory, honour, illustriousness, renown, splendour; *spec:* glass pendant (of a chandelier); glaze (on ceramics).

lusty adj *lit:* brawny, healthy, powerful, robust, stalwart, stout, strapping, strong, sturdy, vigorous; manly, red-blooded, virile; energetic, hearty.

luxuriant adj *lit:* densely-growing, flourishing, lush, prolific, rich, teeming, thriving, verdant; fecund, fertile, fruitful; abundant, copious, lavish, plentiful, profuse; elaborate, excessive, extravagant, florid, flowery, ornate, superabundant.

luxurious adj *lit:* costly, expensive, grand, lavish, magnificent, opulent, rich, sumptuous; cushy, epicurean, pampered, self-indulgent, sybaritic; comfortable, palatial, plush, richly-furnished, well-appointed.

luxury n *lit:* grandeur, magnificence, richness, sumptuousness; affluence, expense, opulence; comfort, gratification, indulgence, pleasure, satisfaction; extra, extravagance, self-indulgence, treat.

lying   **n** *lit:* deceit, deception, dissimulation, fabrication, falsehoods, falsification, mendacity, perjury, storytelling, untruthfulness; fibbing, libel, prevarication, slander; fraud, imposture, misrepresentation.
adj (pr.pt) *lit:* deceitful, dishonest, dissembling, double-crossing, false, mendacious, perjuring, two-faced, untruthful; devious, perfidious, treacherous; fibbing, prevaricating; fraudulent.

M

machine n *lit:* apparatus, appliance, device, gadget, mechanism, tool; engine, generator, motor; aeroplane, aircraft, car, motorbike, vehicle; *fig:* infrastructure, organization, set-up, system; android, automaton, robot, workaholic. **vb** *lit:* cut, finish, heat, make, manufacture, print, saw, sew, turn.

macho adj *lit:* aggressive, dominant, domineering, he-man, male, muscular, powerful, strong, strong-willed, tough, virile.

mad adj *lit:* certifiable, insane, mentally disordered, psychopathic, psychotic; crazy, deranged, demented, lunatic, mental, unbalanced, unhinged; *fig:* asinine, half-baked, daft, idiotic, irrational, irresponsible, ludicrous, nonsensical, preposterous, senseless, unworkable; dotty (about), fanatical (about), wild (about); agitated, excited, frantic, hectic, hysterical, riotous; berserk, furious, hysterical, incensed, spare.

made vb (pa.pt) *lit:* built, composed, constituted, constructed, fashioned, formed, generated, invented, manufactured, originated, produced, shaped; designed, devised, drafted, drawn up, framed; enacted, passed; appointed, elected, installed, ordained; had (one do something); added up to, amounted to, came to, totalled; earned, gained, netted, received; reckoned to be; arrived in time for, caught, got, reached; knew, recognized.

madly adv *lit:* crazily, dementedly; idiotically, irrationally, irresponsibly, nonsensically, senselessly; agitatedly, excitedly, frantically, frenziedly, hectically, hysterically, recklessly, riotously, wildly; desperately, devotedly, intensely, passionately.

madness n *lit:* insanity, lunacy, mental derangement, psychopathy, psychosis; dementia, irrationality; aberration, craziness, daftness, folly, recklessness, wildness; passion; rage; excitement, fever, frenzy, intoxication.

magazine n *lit:* journal, monthly, paper, periodical, weekly; ammunition dump, arsenal, powder store.

magic n *lit:* black arts, necromancy, sorcery, spells, witchcraft, wizardry; paranormal, supernatural; conjuring, hocus-pocus, legerdemain, sleight of hand, trickery; *fig:* charisma, enchantment, fascination, magnetism, power; fire, life, spark.

magician n *lit:* enchanter, enchantress, sorcerer, warlock, witch, wizard; conjuror, illusionist, prestidigitator; *fig:* miracle-worker, wonder-worker; genius, expert, virtuoso.

magnetic adj *lit:* attractive; *fig:* captivating, charming, enchanting; fascinating, hypnotic, mesmerizing.

magnificence n *lit:* glory, grandeur, lavishness, luxury, opulence, pomp, resplendence, splendour, sumptuousness.

magnificent adj *lit:* exalted, fine, glorious, grand, grandiose, imposing, lavish, luxurious, majestic, opulent, princely, resplendent, splendid, sumptuous, superb.

magnify vb *lit:* amplify, blow up, enlarge, expand; heighten, increase, intensify; laud, praise, worship; *fig:* exaggerate, inflate, overdo, overstate.

magnitude n *lit:* amplitude, capacity, dimensions, extent, immensity, measure, proportions, quantity, scale, size, volume; *fig:* consequence, eminence, importance, note, significance, weight; *spec:* brightness, brilliance (of a star).

mail n *lit:* correspondence, letters, post; armour, chain-link.
vb *lit:* dispatch, post, send.

main n *lit:* might, power, strength, weight; cable, channel, duct, pipe; high sea, ocean.   adj *lit:* cardinal, chief, critical, essential, important, leading, pre-eminent, primary, principal, vital; extensive, great, large, strong; mere, pure, sheer.

mainly adv *lit:* chiefly, for the most part, largely, mostly, predominantly, primarily, principally, substantially; generally, on the whole, usually.

maintain vb *lit:* care for, foster, keep up, look after, nurture, preserve, provide for, take care of; carry on, conserve, continue, keep, retain, sustain; allege, assert, aver, claim, contend, declare, hold, insist, state; defend, stand by, uphold.

maintenance   n *lit:* care, fostering, looking after, nurturing, preservation, provision, upkeep; conservation, continuance, retention, sustaining; defence, protection; allowance, grant, keep, living, support; alimony, award.

majestic   adj *lit:* august, dignified, exalted, grand, imperial, imposing, lofty, magnificent, princely, regal, royal, stately.

majesty   n *lit:* dignity, glory, grandeur, greatness, loftiness, magnificence, pomp, splendour, state, stateliness.

major   adj *lit:* great, important, leading, main, notable, outstanding, pre-eminent, significant, weighty; elder, senior.

majority   n lit: best part, bulk, preponderance; adulthood, maturity, seniority.

make   n *lit:* brand, design, form, kind, marque, model, shape, sort, style, type, variety; constitution, manufacture; build, composition. vb *lit:* build, construct, create, fabricate, fashion, form, generate, invent, manufacture, originate, produce, put together, shape; design, devise, draft, draw up, frame; conclude, contract; enact, pass; convert, turn; appoint, elect, install as, ordain; have (one do something); add up to, amount to, come to, total; score; contribute, put forward; earn, gain, net, realize, receive; reckon to be; arrive in time for, catch, get, reach; know, recognize.

make do   vb *lit:* cope, get by, manage (with), scrape by; be content (with).

make out   vb *lit:* detect, discern, distinguish, perceive, see; decipher, read; comprehend, grasp, understand; allege, assert, claim, maintain, suggest; feign, pretend; complete, draft, draw up, fill out, write out; cope, fare, get by, get on, manage; prosper, succeed.

make-up   n *lit:* cosmetics, face, warpaint; grease-paint; composition, constitution, construction, formation, structure; layout; *fig:* character, disposition, nature, temperament.

make up   vb *lit:* compose, comprise, constitute, form; compensate for, complete, fill, supply; come up with, concoct, create, devise, dream up, fabricate, hatch, invent, write; atone (for), make amends (for); mend, repair; become friends again, be reconciled, make peace; make overtures (to); settle in (one's mind).

male　n *lit:* boy, man; lad; boar, buck, bull, cock, dog, jack, ram, tom.　**adj** *lit:* manly, masculine, virile; butch, macho.

maltreat　vb *lit:* abuse, be cruel to, be rough with, bully, ill-treat; damage, hurt, injure.

man　n *lit:* male; person; human, individual; *Homo sapiens,* humanity, humankind, human race, people; gentleman; bloke, chap, geezer, guy; boyfriend, husband, lover, spouse; attendant, employee, hand, retainer, servant, valet, worker; soldier; follower; team-member; *spec:* piece (chess/draughts).　vb *lit:* crew, garrison, people, staff.

manage　vb *lit:* administer, be in charge of, control, direct, oversee, run, superintend, supervise; manipulate, operate, use, wield; carry out, cope with, do, execute, handle, perform; accomplish, bring off, effect; contrive, engineer, orchestrate; cope, fare, get by, get on, make out, survive; have time for.

manageable　adj *lit:* amenable, compliant, controllable, docile, submissive, tractable; achievable, attainable, possible; easy; convenient.

management　n *lit:* administration, board, directors; charge, control, government, handling, running, supervision; manipulation, use, wielding.

mangled　adj (pa.pt) *lit:* pressed, wrung; bent, broken, crooked, crushed, deformed, disfigured, distorted, lamed, maimed, mutilated, ripped, torn; *fig:* garbled, misrepresented, travestied.

manhandle　vb *lit:* haul, heave, lug, manoeuvre, pull, push, roll, shove; fondle, grope, maul, paw; abuse, knock about, rough up.

manifest　n *lit:* bill of lading, cargo checklist; passenger-list. vb *lit:* demonstrate, display, evince, exhibit, make evident, make visible, reveal, show; announce, declare.　**adj** *lit:* apparent, clear, evident, obvious, patent, plain, visible.

manifestation　n *lit:* appearance, demonstration, display, exhibition, revelation, show; evidence, indication, sign, symptom; example, instance; apparition, materialization.

manipulation   n *lit:* command, control, direction, driving, guidance, handling, management, manoeuvring, piloting, steering, use, wielding; arrangement, contrivance, engineering, orchestration, organization.

manliness   n *lit:* machismo, maleness, masculinity, muscularity, power, strength, strength of will, toughness, virility; bravery, courage, hardihood, intrepidity, valour; chivalry, gallantry, gentlemanliness.

manner   n *lit:* approach, means, measures, method, mode, procedure, process, steps, way; custom, fashion, habit, practice, routine, style, usage; air, appearance, comportment, demeanour, mien, tone; attitude, behaviour; category, form, kind, nature, sort, strain, type, vein.

mannerism   n *lit:* characteristic, foible, habit, idiosyncrasy, quirk, trait; affectation, distortion.

manners   n *lit:* courtesy, decorum, etiquette, good form, proprieties, protocol, refinement, social graces; behaviour, conduct, mores.

mantle   n *lit:* cape, hood; cloak, redingote; *fig:* covering, curtain, screen, shroud, veil; *spec:* feathers; incandescing mesh (in a gas lamp); lining (of a mollusc's shell); stratum (of rock between the earth's core and crust).   **vb** *lit:* blanket, cloak, cover, envelop, mask, screen, shroud, veil.

manual   n *lit:* bible, compendium, guidebook, handbook, instruction-book, textbook, vade mecum, workshop reference; keyboard.   **adj** *lit:* hand-cranked, hand-operated.

manufacture   n *lit:* assembly, construction, mass-production, production; end-product, product.   **vb** *lit:* assemble, build, construct, make, mass-produce, process, produce, put together, turn out; *fig:* come up with, concoct, devise, fabricate, make up, think up.

manure   n *lit:* droppings, dung, muck; fertilizer, mulch.

march   n *lit:* haul, hike, tramp, trek, walk, yomp; advance, development, progress; (on the) way; demo, demonstration, parade, procession; military tune; border, boundary; borderland, edge, frontier, margin. **vb** *lit:* hike, step out, stride out, traipse, tramp, tread, trek, walk, yomp; abut, adjoin, border, bound.

margin　**n** *lit:* border, boundary, edge, limit, perimeter, periphery, verge; allowance, elbow-room, latitude, leeway, play, room, surplus.

marginal　**adj** *lit:* bordering, peripheral; insignificant, minimal, negligible, outside, slight, tiny.

marijuana　**n** *lit:* cannabis, ganja, grass, hash, hashish, hemp, pot, smoke, weed.

mark　**n** *lit:* blot, splodge, spot, stain; badge, brand, device, emblem, logo, signature, symbol, token; label, tag; blemish, dent, nick, scar, scratch; footprint, sign, trace, vestige; criterion, level, line, norm, yardstick; aim, goal, jack, objective, target; dupe, greenhorn, innocent, patsy, sucker; model, type; consequence, distinction, eminence, note, standing; point, unit. **vb** *lit:* blot, splodge, spot, stain; sign, write on; brand, label, tag; blemish, dent, nick, scar, scratch; exemplify, illustrate, register, show; attend to, mind, note, pay heed to, watch; assess, evaluate, grade.

marked　**adj (pa.pt)** *lit:* splodged, spotted, stained; branded, identified, indicated, labelled, tagged; blemished, dented, imperfect, nicked, scarred, scratched; clear, conspicuous, distinct, manifest, obvious, patent, pronounced, striking; emphatic, extreme, great, surprising, unexpected; suspected, threatened, watched; dead, doomed, ill-fated.

market　**n** *lit:* bazaar, mart; souk, town square; stock exchange; buying public, consumers, purchasers; demand. **vb** *lit:* hawk, peddle, sell, vend; advertise, hype, plug, promote, push.

maroon　**vb** *lit:* abandon, cast away, desert, isolate, leave high and dry, rat on, run out on, strand. **adj** *lit:* chestnut, red-brown; mauve, violet.

married　**adj (pa.pt)** *lit:* hitched, spliced, wed, wedded; conjugal, connubial, marital.

marrow　**n** *lit:* core, pith, substance; *fig:* crux, heart, kernel, nub; essence, gist, spirit; best part, juice.

marry vb *lit:* be wed, get hitched, get spliced, take the plunge, tie the knot, wed; ally, join, link, match, put together, unite.

marvel n *lit:* phenomenon, prodigy, wonder; expert, genius, virtuoso. vb *lit:* be awed, gape, wonder; be astonished, be overwhelmed.

marvellous adj *lit:* amazing, astonishing, astounding, phenomenal, prodigious, wonderful; fabulous, fantastic, incredible, unbelievable.

mask n *lit:* domino; visor; *fig:* camouflage, cloak, cover, disguise, front, veil. vb *lit:* camouflage, cloak, conceal, cover, disguise, screen, veil.

mass n *lit:* entirety, sum, totality, whole; body, bulk, matter, substance; dimensions, magnitude, scale, size; block, chunk, lump, piece; accumulation, amount, collection, heap, load, lot, pile, quantity; crowd, horde, host, mob, multitude, throng; majority; lower class(es); *spec:* communion service, Eucharist, holy communion, the Lord's supper. vb *lit:* accumulate, assemble, collect, congregate, muster, rally; concentrate (together), flock, swarm.

master n *lit:* captain, chief, commander, head, lord, principal, skipper; overseer, owner; boss, director, employer; guide, instructor, teacher, tutor; guru, swami; ace, adept, expert, virtuoso; *fig:* model, mould, original, pattern. vb *lit:* command, control, dominate, rule; become good at, grasp, learn; break, bridle, curb, domesticate, overpower, subdue, subjugate, tame. adj *lit:* chief, foremost, grand, main, prime, principal; adept, expert, skilled, virtuoso; *fig:* model, original; *spec:* skeleton (key).

mastermind n *lit:* brains, engineer, genius, organizer, planner. vb *lit:* arrange, be the brains behind, engineer, orchestrate, organize, plan.

mastery n *lit:* authority, control, domination, dominion, rule, supremacy, whip hand; triumph, victory; command, grasp, knowledge, understanding; ability, dexterity, expertise, skill, virtuosity.

match n *lit:* complement, counterpart, equal, equivalent; copy, duplicate, lookalike, replica, ringer, twin; competitor, rival; bout, competition, contest, game; alliance, marriage, pairing, partnership; light, lucifer; fuse. **vb** *lit:* compare, equal, parallel, rival; oppose (against), pit (against); agree with, blend with, go with, harmonize with, suit; ally, couple, marry, pair, partner, put together.

matchless **adj** *lit:* incomparable, inimitable, peerless, perfect, superior, unequalled, unique, unrivalled.

mate **n** *lit:* partner, spouse; husband, lover, wife; buddy, china, chum, pal; associate, companion, comrade, crony; colleague, co-worker, partner; aide, assistant, henchman, second-in-command; complement, counterpart, fellow, match, twin. **vb** *lit:* match, pair; marry, wed; breed, copulate, couple.

material **n** *lit:* matter, substance; constituents, element(s); cloth, fabric; data, evidence, information, schema; apparatus, implement(s), instrument(s), tool(s). **adj** *lit:* concrete, corporeal, palpable, physical, tangible; essential, important, key, significant, vital; applicable (to), germane (to), pertinent (to), relevant (to).

matter **n** *lit:* material, substance; affair, case, circumstance, concern, event, incident, occurrence, question, situation, subject, thing; argument, gist, point, purport, sense; contents, copy, text; consequence, importance, moment, significance; amount, quantity; difficulty, problem, trouble; *spec:* (discharge of) purulence, pus. **vb** *lit:* be important, count, make a difference, signify; *spec:* suppurate (pus).

mature **vb** *lit:* be fully developed, come of age, grow up, reach adulthood; bloom, blossom, mellow, ripen, season; *fig:* become payable, fall due. **adj** *lit:* adult, full-grown, grown-up, of age; fully fledged, mellow, ready, ripe, seasoned; *fig:* due, payable; practical, prudent, wise.

maturity **n** *lit:* adulthood, age of reason, majority, manhood, womanhood, years of discretion; bloom, blossoming, mellowness, ripeness; *fig:* common sense, nous, poise, practicality, prudence, wisdom.

maul **n** *lit:* loose scrimmage, ruck. **vb** *lit:* claw, lacerate, mangle; batter, beat, knock (about), thrash; manhandle, treat roughly; abuse, fumble, grope, molest, paw.

maximum n *lit:* best, chief, greatest, highest, largest, most; apogee, ceiling, crest, height, peak, pinnacle, summit, top, zenith.

maze n *lit:* labyrinth; *fig:* complex, mesh, system, tangle, web; puzzle, state of bewilderment.

mean n *lit:* average, intermediate, median, medium, middle; norm, par, standard. **vb** *lit:* betoken, connote, denote, express, indicate, signify, stand for; drive at, imply, insinuate, refer to, say, suggest; entail, involve, lead to, result in; aim (to), be resolved (to), intend (to), plan (to), propose (to), purpose (to); design (to), destine (to), fate (to), foreordain (to), make (to), predestine (to). **adj** *lit:* average, intermediate, median, medium, middle; normal, standard; close-fisted, miserly, near, parsimonious, penny-pinching, stingy, tight; beggarly, contemptible, low, seedy, shabby, sordid, squalid, wretched, base, degenerate, degraded, dishonourable, shameful; common, humble, inferior, low-born, menial, ordinary, plebeian; *fig:* bad-tempered, cantankerous, disagreeable, ornery, rude, sour; dangerous; clever, shrewd, tricky; tasty.

meaning n *lit:* connotation, import, interpretation, purport, significance; drift, gist, implication, insinuation, point, sense, substance, suggestion; force, thrust, validity, value; aim, design, intention, object, purpose. **adj** *lit:* eloquent, expressive, pregnant, significant, speaking.

meaningless adj *lit:* aimless, empty, hollow, pointless, purposeless, useless, worthless; garbled, incomprehensible, unintelligible.

means n *lit:* agent, instrument, medium, method, mode, process, way; agency, instrumentality, methodology, procedure; capital, funds, income, property, resources, substance, wealth, wherewithal; (by) dint (of).

meanwhile adv *lit:* at the same time, concurrently, contemporaneously, simultaneously; for the duration, for the moment, in the interim, in the meantime.

measure n *lit:* gauge, meter, rule, ruler, scale, scoop, tape; optic; benchmark, criterion, line, norm, standard, touchstone, unit, yardstick; allocation, proportion, quota, ration, share; amount,

quantity; degree, extent, range, scope; dimensions, magnitude, size; column-width, page-width; action, course, manoeuvre, ploy, step; act, bill, law, resolution, statute; beat, cadence, rhythm; dance; foot, metre; *fig:* moderation, restraint; *spec:* (geological) bed(s).
vb *lit:* calibrate, determine, gauge, mark (off/out), quantify, value; deal (out), dole (out), mete (out).

measurement n *lit:* calibration, gauging, quantifying, valuation; amplitude, dimensions, extent, magnitude, proportions, size.

meat n *lit:* flesh, viands; brawn, muscle; chow, food, grub, nourishment, provisions, rations, subsistence, victuals; *fig:* essence, heart, marrow, nub, pith, substance.

meaty adj *lit:* beefy, brawny, burly, hulking, muscular, strapping; nourishing, rich; *fig:* concentrated, meaningful, pithy.

mechanical adj *lit:* automated, automatic, machine-operated; emotionless, impersonal, machine-like, unfeeling; constant, habitual, mindless, monotonous, perfunctory, reflex, routine, unchanging, unthinking.

mechanism n *lit:* apparatus, appliance, device, gadget, machine; action, cogs, machinery, works; functioning, operation, performance, working; means, method, procedure, system, technique.

medicine n *lit:* medicament, medication, therapy, treatment; drug; capsule, pill, tablet; linctus; pathology; *fig:* punishment; charm, magic, spell.

mediocre adj *lit:* average, commonplace, medium, ordinary, undistinguished; indifferent, less than ordinary, pedestrian, second-rate, uninspired.

mediocrity n *lit:* ordinariness, undistinguished nature; lack of inspiration, pedestrianism; lightweight, nonentity, second-rater.

medium n *lit:* average, middle; compromise, midpoint; agency, channel, instrument, means, organ, vehicle; method, mode, process, way; mouthpiece, spiritist, spiritualist, transmitter; atmosphere, conditions, environment, milieu, setting. adj *lit:* average, intermediate, median, middle, middling.

meek   **adj** *lit:* docile, gentle, humble, mild, submissive, unassuming; deferential, modest, peaceable; spineless, tame, weak.

meet   **vb** *lit:* come across, encounter, find, happen on, run into; greet, welcome; assemble, congregate, convene, gather, muster, rally; compete with, confront, contend against, do battle with, face, line up against; adjoin, connect, converge, join, merge, touch; *fig:* come up to, comply with, fulfil, match, measure up to, satisfy; bear, endure, experience, undergo.   **adj** *lit:* appropriate, correct, fitting, proper, right, seemly, suitable.

meeting   **n** *lit:* encounter; assignation, rendezvous, tryst; conclave, conference, convention, convocation, gathering, get-together, rally; service; concourse, confluence, conjunction, convergence, junction, merging; crossing.

mellow   **vb** *lit:* age, mature, ripen, soften, sweeten.   **adj** *lit:* full, juicy, mature, rich, ripe, soft, sweet; *fig:* mellifluous, rounded, smooth, tuneful; elevated, expansive, happy, jolly, merry.

melodramatic   **adj** *lit:* exaggerated, histrionic, overdone, sensational, stagy, theatrical.

melody   **n** *lit:* air, theme, tune; lay, song, strain; tunefulness.

melt   **vb** *lit:* deliquesce, dissolve, fuse, liquefy, thaw; fade (away), vanish (away); *fig:* disarm, charm, soften.

member   **n** *lit:* associate; representative; appendage, component, constituent, element, limb, organ, part; *fig:* clause.

memoirs   **n** *lit:* autobiography, diaries, history, life, life-story; experiences, reminiscences; documents, journals, papers, records, transactions.

memorable   **adj** *lit:* emotive, impressive, indelible, moving, notable, remarkable, striking, unforgettable; extraordinary, odd, strange; historic, important; catchy, haunting.

memory   **n** *lit:* recall, recollection; powers of retention; remembrance, reminiscence; commemoration, memorial; fame, renown, reputation; data-bank, data-base, data-store.

menace n *lit:* threat; danger, hazard; *fig:* nuisance, pain, pest.
vb *lit:* bully, frighten, intimidate, terrorize, threaten; loom over, overshadow.

mend vb *lit:* fix, patch up, repair, replace; renovate, restore; better, correct, rectify; heal, improve, knit, recover.

mental adj *lit:* intellectual; psychological; internal, notional; *fig:* deranged, insane, psychotic, unbalanced.

mention n *lit:* acknowledgement (of), allusion, citation, plug, reference, tribute. **vb** *lit:* acknowledge, allude to, bring up, cite, make known, name, refer to, touch upon.

mercenary n *lit:* dog of war, freelance, hired soldier, soldier of fortune. **adj** *lit:* hired, paid; avaricious, greedy, money-grubbing, venal.

merchant n *lit:* dealer, retailer, seller, shopkeeper, trader, tradesman, wholesaler.

merciful adj *lit:* clement, compassionate, humane, lenient, magnanimous; forgiving.

merciless adj *lit:* callous, cruel, hard-hearted, harsh, heartless, implacable, inhumane, pitiless, ruthless; strict, unforgiving.

mercy n *lit:* clemency, compassion, grace, humanity, leniency, magnanimity, pity, quarter; forgiveness; *fig:* blessing, godsend, relief; (at the) disposition (of).

mere adj *lit:* plain, pure, sheer, simple, stark, unadulterated, unmitigated; callow, green, young; insignificant, trifling, trivial, unimportant.

merit n *lit:* credit; excellence, meed, quality, value, virtue, worth; advantage, strong point. **vb** *lit:* be worthy of, deserve, rate, warrant; earn.

merry adj *lit:* blithe, carefree, convivial, droll, fun, happy, jolly, waggish; *fig:* fuddled, high, mellow, sozzled, tiddly, woozy.

mesh n *lit:* net, network, plexus, reticulation; lattice, web, webbing; tangle, toils. **vb** *lit:* ensnare, entangle, net, snare, tangle; connect, coordinate, dovetail, engage, interlock; heal, knit.

mess n *lit:* clutter, confusion, jumble, mishmash, shambles; chaos, disarray, untidiness; blot, blotch, smear, smudge, splodge; bungle, cock-up, dog's dinner, hash; *fig:* fix, jam, muddle, pickle, predicament, spot; *spec:* dining-room, refectory, sitting (in the armed forces). **vb** *lit:* clutter (up), disorganize, jumble (up); blot, smear, smudge; foul (up), hash (up), muck (up), muddle; dirty, foul, pollute, soil; fiddle (with), interfere (with), meddle (with), tinker (with); fiddle (with), play (with).

message n *lit:* communiqué, dispatch, memo, news, word; import, meaning, moral, point, sense, theme.

messenger n *lit:* bearer, carrier, courier, emissary, envoy, go-between.

messy adj *lit:* cluttered, disorganized, jumbled, muddled,; blotchy, smeared, smudged; dirty, muddied, muddy, polluted, soiled; dishevelled, matted, slovenly, tangled, unkempt.

method n *lit:* approach, fashion, manner, mode, practice, procedure, process, routine, system, technique, way; form, order, planning, structure; classification.

methodical adj *lit:* businesslike, disciplined, efficient, orderly, planned, regular, systematic, tidy.

microscopic adj *lit:* minuscule, minute, tiny; infinitesimal.

middle n *lit:* centre, midpoint; mean, medium; midriff, stomach, waist; (in the) midst (of). **adj** *lit:* central; mean, median, medium; intermediate.

midget n *lit:* person of restricted growth; dwarf; homunculus, pygmy; manikin; halfpint, shrimp, titch. **adj** *lit:* dwarf, miniature, pocket, pygmy, tiny.

mighty adj *lit:* forceful, powerful, strong, vigorous; brawny, muscular, stalwart, strapping; colossal, enormous, gigantic, huge, immense, massive, vast.

migrate vb *lit:* journey, move on, shift camp, travel, trek, voyage; move elsewhere, pass (through).

mild   adj *lit:* easy-going, gentle, meek, peaceable, placid, serene, temperate, tender, tranquil; moderate, pleasant, warm; bland, soothing.

mildness   n *lit:* gentleness, meekness, placidity, serenity, temperateness, tenderness, tranquillity; moderation, warmth; blandness.

military   n *lit:* armed forces, army, services, war office.
adj *lit:* army, service.

milk   n *lit:* lactation; juice, sap.   **vb** *lit:* cream, draw off, express, extract, tap; *fig:* bleed, drain, wring; exploit, impose upon, take advantage of.

mill   n *lit:* crusher, grinder; factory, plant, processing plant, works   **vb** *lit:* crush, granulate, grind, powder, press, pulverize, punch, stamp; crowd (around), swarm (about), throng (around).

mind   n *lit:* brain, grey matter, intellect, intelligence, reason; consciousness, psyche, subconscious; marbles, rationality, sanity, wits; memory, recollection; thoughts; *fig:* genius, thinker; attitude, judgement, opinion, thoughts, way of thinking; imagination; attention, concentration; fancy (to), urge (to), wish (to).   **vb** *lit:* care, disapprove, feel strongly about, object, take offence; attend to, heed, listen to, mark, note; comply with, follow, obey; ensure that, make certain that, take care that; keep an eye on, look after, take care of, watch over; beware of, look out for; *fig:* recall, remember.

mindless   adj *lit:* automatic, mechanical; casual, gratuitous, incidental, indifferent, unreasoning; careless, forgetful, negligent, unmindful; asinine, idiotic, moronic, obtuse.

mine   n *lit:* bomb, explosive device, shell; excavation, gallery, pit, quarry, shaft, tunnel; *fig:* fund, hoard, stock, store, wealth.
vb *lit:* lay a bomb, sink a bomb; dig (for), excavate (for), quarry (for); subvert, tunnel under.

minimal   adj *lit:* infinitesimal, minuscule, minute, tiny; invisible, virtually nonexistent; nominal, token.

minimize   vb *lit:* deprecate, make light of, play down, tone down;

keep as small as possible, reduce as much as possible; *fig:* decrease, diminish, shrink.

minimum   n *lit:* least, lowest, slightest, smallest; bottom, nadir.

minister   n *lit:* clergyman, cleric, padre, parson, preacher, priest, vicar; cabinet/government member, consul, diplomat, envoy; agent, lieutenant, official, subordinate.   **vb** *lit:* attend to, serve, take care of.

minor   adj *lit:* immature, juvenile, under-age; inconsequential, insignificant, negligible, petty, slight, trifling, trivial, unimportant; junior, subordinate; younger.

minority   n *lit:* lesser number, smaller group; losing voters; childhood years.

mint   n *lit:* coin factory, herb; *fig:* origin, source; bomb, fortune, king's ransom, packet, tidy sum.   **vb** *lit:* cast, coin, punch, stamp, strike; *fig:* come up with, create, devise, invent, make up, produce, think up.   **adj** *lit:* brand-new, fresh, perfect, undamaged, unused.

minute   n *lit:* agendum, memorandum, note(s), record(s); *fig:* flash, instant, jiffy, moment, second, tick.   **vb** *lit:* log, make a transcript of, record, register, take notes of.   **adj** *lit:* diminutive, fine, microscopic, minuscule, tiny; insignificant, negligible, trifling, trivial, unimportant; detailed, exhaustive, meticulous, precise, punctilious, scrupulous.

miraculous   adj *lit:* divine, providential; supernatural; extraordinary, incredible, inexplicable, phenomenal, unaccountable, unbelievable; magic, magical, wondrous.

mirror   n *lit:* glass, looking-glass; double, image, likeness, reflection, twin.   **vb** *lit:* depict, display, reflect, show; echo, emulate; copy, simulate.

misapprehension   n *lit:* error, false impression, misconception, misconstruction, misunderstanding.

misbehave   vb *lit:* act up, be disobedient, be naughty, be mischievous, be rude, get into trouble, muck about.

mischief n *lit:* disobedience, misbehaviour, mucking about, naughtiness; boisterousness, devilment, horseplay, shenanigans; damage, harm, hurt, injury, trouble; *fig:* devil, nuisance, pest, rogue, scamp.

mischievous adj *lit:* badly behaved, disobedient, impish, misbehaving, mucking about, naughty, troublesome, vexatious; boisterous, careless, riotous, rough; deleterious, detrimental, malign, spiteful; destructive, evil, harmful, injurious, pernicious, wicked.

miser n *lit:* hoarder, niggard, penny-pincher, Scrooge, skinflint.

miserable adj *lit:* blue, broken-hearted, dejected, depressed, desolate, despondent, dismal, doleful, down, gloomy, grief-stricken, heartbroken, melancholy, sorrowful, suffering, unhappy, wretched; bankrupt, destitute, impoverished, penniless, poor; base, deplorable, low, mean, pitiable, shabby, shameful, sordid, sorry, squalid.

miserly adj *lit:* avaricious, close-fisted, grasping, mean, niggardly, parsimonious, penny-pinching, stingy, tight.

misery n *lit:* dejection, depression, despair, distress, grief, melancholy, sadness, sorrow, suffering, unhappiness, wretchedness; destitution, pennilessness, penury, poverty; meanness, shabbiness, sordidness, squalor; burden, hardship, misfortune, trial, tribulation, woe.

misgiving n *lit:* anxiety, apprehension, fear, qualm, reservation, scruple, suspicion, worry.

misguided adj *lit:* deluded, ill-advised, led astray, misled; imprudent, injudicious, indiscreet, misplaced, unwise; mistaken.

misinterpret vb *lit:* misapprehend, misconstrue, misread, misunderstand; distort, falsify, garble, misrepresent, pervert, travesty.

misleading adj (pr.pt) *lit:* ambiguous, confusing, deceptive, fallacious, false, inaccurate, specious, unrepresentative.

miss vb *lit:* be late for, forgo, lose; fail to grasp, let slip; fail to notice, pass over, overlook; jump, leave out, neglect, omit, skip; long for, pine for, yearn for.

missing adj *lit:* absent, gone astray, lacking, lost, mislaid, misplaced, not there, unaccounted for.

mist n *lit:* fog, haar, smog, vapour; condensation, drizzle, spray.

mistake n *lit:* blunder, botch-up, clanger, error, fault, gaffe, howler, inaccuracy, miscalculation, misconception, misunderstanding, oversight, slip. **vb** *lit:* get wrong, misinterpret, misunderstand; miscalculate, misjudge.

mistaken adj (pa.pt) *lit:* misguided, misinformed, wide of the mark; inaccurate, incorrect, wrong; ill-advised, ill-judged, imprudent, unwise.

mix n *lit:* assortment, blend, compound, medley, mixture, variety; combination, proportions, ratio; mixture, paste. **vb** *lit:* blend, combine, compound, diffuse, fuse, intermingle, merge, stir together; shuffle; associate (with), get on (with), hang out (with), mingle (with), socialize (with).

moan n *lit:* groan, lament, sob, wail; *fig:* beef, complaint, gripe, grouse. **vb** *lit:* groan, keen, lament, sob, whine; beef, carp, complain, gripe, grouse, grumble.

mob n *lit:* crew, crowd, flock, herd, gang, group, horde, host, mass, multitude, press, set, throng; hoi polloi, masses, proles, rabble, riffraff, scum. **vb** *lit:* crowd, jostle, surround.

mock vb *lit:* deride, insult, jeer at, laugh at, ridicule, scoff at, sneer at, taunt; ape, burlesque, caricature, lampoon, send up, take off. **adj** *lit:* artificial, bogus, counterfeit, ersatz, fake, false, imitation, phoney, sham, spurious.

mockery n *lit:* contumely, derision, gibes, insults, ridicule, scorn; farce, travesty.

model vb *lit:* archetype, example, exemplar, mould, original, pattern, prototype; copy, dummy, mock-up, replica, reproduction; design, plan, representation; kind, make, marque, sort, style, type, version; poser, sitter, subject; mannequin. **vb** *lit:* construct, design, devise, fashion, form, mould, pattern, shape, style; display, exhibit, show off. **adj** *lit:* facsimile, imitation; miniature, scaled-down; exemplary, ideal, perfect.

moderate **vb** *lit:* calm, control, curb, mitigate, repress, restrain, soften, tame, tone down; chair, preside over; arbitrate (between), mediate (between). **adj** *lit:* average, fair, medium, middling, passable, reasonable, tolerable; indifferent, mediocre, ordinary; medium-sized; equable, mild, peaceable, restrained, temperate.

modern **adj** *lit:* contemporary, current, latest, new, novel, present day, recent, state-of-the-art, twentieth-century, up-to-date.

modernize **vb** *lit:* bring up to date, renovate, revamp, update.

modest **adj** *lit:* bashful, diffident, humble, meek, reserved, retiring, self-effacing, shy; chaste, decent, demure; fair, moderate, reasonable, unpretentious.

modesty **n** *lit:* bashfulness, diffidence, humility, meekness, reserve, reticence, self-effacement; chastity, decency, demureness; moderation, unpretentiousness.

modification **n** *lit:* adjustment, alteration, change, refinement; modulation; lessening, lowering, moderation, reduction.

modify **vb** *lit:* adjust, alter, change, convert, refine, revise; modulate; lessen, lower, moderate, reduce, tone down.

moist **adj** *lit:* clammy, damp, dank, humid, sodden, soggy, sweaty, wet; rainy, watery.

moisture **n** *lit:* damp, dampness, dankness, humidity; fluid, liquid.

molest **vb** *lit:* abuse, fondle, grope, interfere with, maltreat, manhandle; badger, bother, harass, harry, hound, importune, pester, plague, worry; annoy, irritate, vex.

moment **n** *lit:* instant, second, split second, twinkling of an eye; juncture, point, time; concern, consequence, historicity, importance, significance, weight.

momentous **adj** *lit:* consequential, crucial, decisive, fateful, historic, important, significant, weighty.

momentum **n** *lit:* drive, energy, force, impetus, motion, thrust.

money **n** *lit:* assets, capital, cash, currency, finances, funds, legal tender, liquidity, riches, sterling, wealth.

monitor   n *lit:* invigilator, overseer, supervisor, warden; prefect; alarm, detector, gauge, meter, scanner, tester; screen.
vb   *lit:* observe, oversee, supervise, watch over; keep track of, record, scan, screen.

monkey   n *lit:* primate, simian; ape; *fig:* imp, jackanapes, rascal, rogue, scamp, scapegrace; (make a) fool (of); ass, laughing-stock; *fig:* £500, $500; hammer, pile-driver.   **vb**   *lit:* fiddle (with), meddle (with), tamper (with); fool (about), mess (about), play (about).

monotonous   adj *lit:* constant, continual, mindless, relentless, repetitious, repetitive, uniform, unvarying; boring, humdrum, soporific, tedious, wearisome.

monster   n *lit:* freak, mutant, obscenity; animal, beast, brute, savage; demon, devil, fiend; colossus, giant, jumbo, mammoth, whopper.
adj   *lit:* colossal, enormous, giant, huge, immense, jumbo, mammoth, massive, vast, whopping.

monstrous   adj *lit:* abnormal, deformed, freakish, grotesque, malformed, mutant, obscene, teratological, unnatural; bestial, brutal, brutish, savage; cruel, demonic, diabolical, evil, fiendish, inhuman, loathsome, satanic, vicious; frightful, gruesome, hideous, horrible; colossal, enormous, giant, huge, immense, jumbo, mammoth, massive, vast, whopping.

monumental   adj *lit:* commemorative, memorial; columnar, monolithic, statuary; awesome, classic, epoch-making, historic, lasting, outstanding, significant; *fig:* colossal, enormous, giant, huge, immense, jumbo, mammoth, massive, vast, whopping.

mood   n *lit:* disposition, humour, state of mind, temper; bad temper, melancholy, moroseness, sulkiness.

moody   adj *lit:* capricious, changeable, erratic, fitful, mercurial, temperamental, unpredictable, volatile; bad-tempered, broody, crotchety, gloomy, ill-humoured, melancholy, morose, petulant, sulky, sullen, touchy.

mop   n *lit:* sponge, squeegee, swab; cloth, rag; brush, shock, tangle, thatch; face, grimace.   **vb**   *lit:* absorb, soak (up), stem; sponge, swab, wipe (up).

moral　n *lit:* lesson, message, point; envoi; ethic(s), ideal(s), principle(s), scruple(s).　adj *lit:* ethical, principled; decent, good, honest, honourable, proper, upstanding, virtuous; intellectual, mental; likely, probable.

morality　n *lit:* ethics, ideals, integrity, principles, standards; decency, goodness, honesty, honour, propriety, virtue.

morbid　adj *lit:* downcast, melancholy, pessimistic; brooding, gloomy, grim, sombre; ghastly, ghoulish, gruesome, macabre, sick, unhealthy; diseased, ill, infected, sickly; fatal, malignant, necrotic, terminal.

more　adj *lit:* additional, extra, further, supplementary; different, fresh, new, other; of greater size; of greater quantity.　adv *lit:* to a greater degree, to a greater extent; further; longer; additionally, again.

moreover　adv *lit:* additionally, also, besides, further, furthermore, in addition, likewise, too.

mortal　n *lit:* human being, individual, person.　adj *lit:* human; corporeal, temporal; impermanent, transient, waxing and waning; deadly, fatal, lethal, terminal; deathly; to the death.

most　adj *lit:* (the) greatest amount of, (the) greatest degree of, (the) greatest measure of, (the) greatest number of; nearly all, the great majority of.　adv *lit:* extremely; principally; to the greatest degree, to the greatest extent.

mother　n *lit:* ma, mama, mater, mum, mummy, old lady; dam, matron, parent, protectress; abbess, prioress, superior.　vb *lit:* bear, engender, give birth to, produce; care for, cherish, foster, nurture, raise, rear, tend; *fig:* baby, fuss over, make a fuss of, mollycoddle, pamper.

motion　n *lit:* advance, movement, passage, progress, travel, way; proposal, proposition, subject, submission, theme, topic; gesticulation, gesture, signal, wave; bowel movement, defecation, evacuation.

motionless　adj *lit:* at rest, immobile, inert, static, stationary, still, unmoving; fixed, frozen, paralysed, stopped, transfixed; crouched, in wait, tensed.

motivate vb *lit:* act as an incentive, bring (to), cause (to), drive (to), induce (to), inspire (to), instigate, prompt (to), stimulate (to), stir (to).

motive n *lit:* aim, design, intention, object, purpose, rationale, reason, reasoning, thinking; incentive, inducement, stimulus.
adj *lit:* activating, driving, impulsive, operative, propelling.

motto n *lit:* catch-phrase, inscription, logo, slogan; maxim, precept, watchword; caption, headline, legend.

mould n *lit:* fungus, mildew, saprophyte; dust, earth, loam, soil; die, matrix, pattern, stencil, template; cast; blancmange, jelly; *fig:* build, configuration, fashion, form, kind, shape, style, type; calibre, character, quality, stamp. **vb** *lit:* cast, model, sculpt; create, fashion, form, shape; *fig:* control, direct, guide, influence, inform.

mount n *lit:* backing, frame, setting; slide; base, plinth, podium, stand; gun-carriage; horse, nag, ride, steed. **vb** *lit:* frame, put in a frame; put on a slide; fix on a base, set; ascend, climb, go up, scale; climb on to, climb up on, get on to, get up on; accumulate, build (up), escalate, grow, increase, intensify, pile (up); organize, produce, put on, stage; deliver, launch, make, put into effect; install, place, position; *spec:* keep, stand (guard).

mountain n *lit:* crag, fell, height, peak, summit; *fig:* heap, mass, pile, stack.

mountainous adj *lit:* alpine, highland, upland; craggy, precipitous, rocky, serrated, sheer, soaring, towering; *fig:* enormous, giant, huge, immense, mammoth, massive, vast.

mourn vb *lit:* bewail, grieve (for), lament, sorrow (for), weep for; miss; deplore, regret.

mournful adj *lit:* disconsolate, grief-stricken, heartbroken, heavy-hearted, inconsolable, melancholy, miserable, sad, sorrowful, unhappy, wretched; affecting, elegiac, piteous, plaintive, tragic.

mourning n *lit:* bereavement, grief; grieving, lamentation, sorrowing, weeping; black, widow's weeds.

mouth n *lit:* jaws, lips; aperture, entrance, inlet, opening, stoma; estuary; *fig:* backchat, cheek, insolence, lip, sauce; chatter, gab, talk;

boasting, bragging, hot air; spokesperson. **vb** *lit:* mime; declaim, orate, spout; *spec:* train (a horse) to the bit.

move n *lit:* go, play, turn; action, manoeuvre, motion, shift, stroke; gambit, initiative, ploy, strategy; change of address, relocation, transfer; campaign, plan, proposal, suggestion. **vb** *lit:* advance, budge, go, pass, proceed, progress, shift, travel; change address, relocate, transfer; depart (from), go away, leave, migrate (from); bring, carry, convey, fetch, take, transport, transpose; activate, drive, propel, power, push; affect, agitate, excite, stir, touch; *fig:* cause (to), induce (to), influence (to), inspire (to), lead (to), prompt (to), stimulate (to); advocate, propose, recommend, suggest.

movement n *lit:* activity, agitation, development, progress, shift, stirring; manoeuvre, operation, progression; action, mechanism, works; exercise, gesture, motion; current, drift, flow, tendency, trend; campaign, caucus, drive, organization, party; beat, metre, pace, rhythm, tempo; *spec:* division, section (of a musical work).

moving adj (pr.pt) *lit:* mobile; portable; powering, propelling; *fig:* affecting, emotive, pathetic, piteous, poignant, touching; dynamic, exciting, inspiring, motivating, stimulating.

much n *lit:* a good deal, a great deal, a lot, lots, the majority. **adj** *lit:* abundant, copious, plenteous; considerable, great, substantial. **adv** *lit:* considerably, exceedingly, greatly; approximately, nearly; indeed, to a great degree, to a great extent.

muddled adj (pa.pt) *lit:* chaotic, confused, disordered, disorganized, jumbled, mixed, scrambled, tangled; bewildered, disoriented, perplexed, vague, woolly.

muddy vb *lit:* bespatter, dirty, get mud on, smear, soil; *fig:* blur, cloud, confuse, obscure. **adj** *lit:* bespattered, dirty, miry, slimy, slushy, wet; boggy, marshy, swampy; foul, impure, turbid; *fig:* dingy, dull, flat; blurred, cloudy, confused, obscure, vague, woolly.

muffle vb *lit:* cloak, conceal, cover, envelop, hood, mask, swathe; deaden, dull, mute, quieten, silence, stifle, suppress.

muggy adj *lit:* close, humid, oppressive, sticky, stifling, sultry.

multiple **adj** *lit:* manifold, numerous, sundry, various; collective, compound; repeated.

multiply **vb** *lit:* accumulate, expand, increase, spread; repeat; breed, proliferate, propagate, reproduce.

multitude **n** *lit:* army, crowd, horde, host, legion, mass, sea, swarm, throng; herd, mob, proletariat, rabble.

mundane **adj** *lit:* banal, boring, commonplace, everyday, humdrum, ordinary, platitudinous, prosaic, trite; earthly, human, mortal, secular, temporal, worldly.

murder **n** *lit:* assassination, homicide, killing; carnage, massacre, slaughter; *fig:* agony, hell, torture. **vb** *lit:* assassinate, do to death, kill; bump off, do in, hit, rub out, waste; massacre, slaughter, slay; *fig:* abuse, mangle, ruin, spoil; drub, hammer, thrash out of sight, trounce.

murky **adj** *lit:* black, dark, dim, dusky, gloomy; grey, hazy, misty; *fig:* obscure, shady.

murmuring **adj (pr.pt)** *lit:* babbling, droning, humming, purring, rippling, rumbling, rustling, trickling, whispering; listless, muttering, restive, restless, unquiet, unsatisfied.

muscle **n** *lit:* ligament, sinew, tendon; extensor, flexor; *fig:* brawn, power, stamina, strength; clout, force, weight. **vb** *lit:* butt (in), elbow (in), force a way (in), thrust one's way (in).

muscular **adj** *lit:* brawny, lusty, powerful, robust, stalwart, strapping, strong; athletic, vigorous.

musical **adj** *lit:* euphonious, harmonious, melodic, melodious, orchestral, symphonic, tuneful.

musician **n** *lit:* bandsman, orchestra-member, performer, player, singer; arranger, composer; conductor.

must **n** *lit:* essential, imperative, necessity, prerequisite, requirement, sine qua non; semi-fermented juice. **vb** *lit:* be obliged to, have to; ought to, should.

musty **adj** *lit:* damp, dampish, mildewed, moth-eaten, mouldering, mouldy, stale.

mute vb *lit:* dampen, deaden, hush, muffle, silence, soften, tone down, turn down. **adj** *lit:* aphonic, dumb, silent, speechless, voiceless; mum, unspoken, wordless.

mutilate vb *lit:* cripple, damage, deform, disfigure, lame, maim, mangle; *fig:* abbreviate, abridge, butcher, censor, cut, distort, spoil.

mutiny n *lit:* defiance, disobedience, insurrection, rebellion, revolt, riot, rising, uprising. **vb** *lit:* rebel, revolt, rise up.

muzzle n *lit:* mouth, snout; cage, clamp, guard; mouthpiece, respirator; barrel. **vb** *lit:* curb, gag, silence; *fig:* censor, restrict, suppress.

mysterious adj *lit:* cryptic, enigmatic, incomprehensible, inexplicable, insoluble, obscure, perplexing, puzzling, strange, uncanny, weird; furtive, secretive; concealed, covert, hidden, secret.

mystery n *lit:* enigma, puzzle, riddle, secret; obscurity, secrecy; rite, ritual, sacrament.

mystical adj *lit:* cabalistic, esoteric, metaphysical, occult, paranormal, preternatural, supernatural, transcendental; ritual, symbolic.

N

nab vb *lit:* catch, grab, grasp, seize suddenly; snatch away, steal; *fig:* apprehend, arrest.

nag n *lit:* hack, horse, jade; scold, shrew, termagant. vb *lit:* goad, henpeck, scold, upbraid; annoy, badger, chivvy, harass, pester; irritate, plague, provoke, vex.

nagging adj (pr.pt) *lit:* bothersome, distressing, irritating, painful, vexatious, worrisome; continuous, persistent; scolding, shrewish.

nail n *lit:* peg, pin, tack; horn, keratin. vb *lit:* pin, tack; attach, fasten, fix, join, secure; hammer; fig: catch, seize.

naive adj *lit:* artless, frank, guileless, ingenuous, innocent, jejune, unsophisticated, unworldly; childlike, natural, open, simple, trusting; unaffected, unpretentious; callow, credulous, green, gullible.

name n *lit:* agnomen, appellation, cognomen, handle, moniker, sobriquet; denomination, designation, title; celebrity, personality; reputation; epithet, nickname. vb *lit:* call, designate, dub, entitle, style, term; baptize, christen, denominate, label; identify, specify; cite, mention, nominate.

nap n *lit:* doze, kip, siesta, sleep, snooze; rest; pile, shag; down, fibre; cert, dead cert, hot tip, winner. vb *lit:* doze, drop off, drowse, sleep, snooze; tip a winner.

narrate vb *lit:* recite, recount, relate, set forth, tell; describe, detail, report; chronicle.

narrator n *lit:* commentator, reporter, storyteller, voiceover; raconteur, speaker; author, chronicler, novelist, writer.

narrow vb *lit:* constrict, reduce, straiten, tighten; decrease, diminish; *fig:* limit, simplify. adj *lit:* attenuated, fine, slim, thin; close, confined, constricted, tight; meagre, restricted, scanty; *fig:* biased, dogmatic, partial, prejudiced; exclusive, select; avaricious, mean, niggardly.

narrowly   adv *lit:* barely, by a whisker, just, only just; carefully, closely, painstakingly.

narrow-minded   adj *lit:* petty, illiberal, insular, short-sighted, strait-laced; biased, intolerant, prejudiced; bigoted, opinionated.

nastiness   n *lit:* malevolence, malice, malignity, meanness, offensiveness, spitefulness, viciousness; defilement, filth, foulness, squalor, uncleanliness, vileness; indecency, licentiousness, obscenity, pornography.

nasty   adj *lit:* dirty, disgusting, filthy, foul, loathsome, nauseating, objectionable, obnoxious, odious, offensive, repellent, repugnant, sickening, vile; bad, dangerous, serious, severe; abusive, despicable, disagreeable, mean, spiteful, unpleasant, vicious; gross, indecent, lewd, obscene, pornographic.

national   n *lit:* citizen, compatriot, native; inhabitant, resident, subject.   adj *lit:* civil, governmental, public, state; nationwide; patriotic; domestic, internal.

nationwide   adj *lit:* countrywide, national; general, overall, universal.

native   n *lit:* aborigine, inhabitant; citizen, dweller, national, resident.   adj *lit:* domestic, indigenous, local, born (to); inborn, inbred, innate, intrinsic; mother, vernacular.

natter   n *lit:* chat, confabulation, conversation, gossip, talk; blather, chitchat, jabber.   vb *lit:* blather, chat, chatter, gabble, gossip, jabber, jaw on, prate, prattle, rabbit on, talk, witter on.

natty   adj *lit:* snappy, snazzy; chic, elegant, fashionable, stylish, well-dressed; dapper, neat, smart, spruce, trim.

natural   n *lit:* genius; *fig:* cert, certainty; *spec:* white note (on a piano).   adj *lit:* common, logical, normal, ordinary, typical, usual; characteristic, inborn, inherent, instinctive, native; artless, genuine, ingenuous, simple, spontaneous, unpretentious, unsophisticated; organic, plain, pure, unrefined, whole.

naturally   adv *lit:* congenitally, essentially, inherently, innately, instinctively; artlessly, genuinely, ingenuously, simply, spontaneously, unpretentiously; organically; normally, typically; fig: certainly, of course; absolutely.

nature n *lit:* character, constitution, essence, make-up, quality; category, kind, sort, style, type, variety; cosmos, earth, environment, universe; disposition, outlook, temper, temperament; country, countryside, scenery.

naughty adj *lit:* bad, disobedient, misbehaving, mischievous, refractory, roguish, wayward, wicked; ribald, vulgar.

navigate vb *lit:* plot a course, steer; manoeuvre, pilot, sail; *fig:* direct, guide, skipper; find one's way (through), make one's way (to).

near vb *lit:* approach, close on, draw up towards, get closer to. adj *lit:* close, close by;, adjacent, adjoining, at close quarters, nigh; approaching, imminent, impending, looming, threatening; *fig:* closely-related, dear, familiar, intimate; close-fisted, mean, miserly, parsimonious, stingy, tight. adv *lit:* close, nigh; into proximity, within reach; almost, close on. prp *lit:* close to, nigh unto; adjacent to, alongside, not far from.

nearby adj *lit:* adjacent, adjoining, neighbouring; *fig:* convenient, handy.

near by adv *lit:* close by, close at hand, not far away.

neat adj *lit:* accurate, fastidious, methodical, nice, orderly, precise, shipshape, smart, straight, systematic, tidy, trim; adroit, deft, dexterous, handy, nimble, skilful, stylish; pure, straight, unadulterated, undiluted.

neatness n *lit:* accuracy, fastidiousness, orderliness, smartness, tidiness, trimness; adroitness, deftness, dexterity, handiness, nimbleness, preciseness, skilfulness, stylishness.

necessarily adv *lit:* by definition, inescapably, inevitably, inexorably, of necessity, perforce, unavoidably, willy-nilly; certainly, without question.

necessary adj *lit:* essential, imperative, indispensable, mandatory, obligatory, vital; compulsory, de rigueur, required; inevitable, unavoidable.

necessity n *lit:* essential, indispensability, prerequisite, requirement, want; demand, need; compulsion, obligation; extremity, penury, privation.

need n *lit:* deprivation, lack, inadequacy, insufficiency, paucity, privation, shortage, want; penury, poverty; demand, exigency, requirement, urgency. **vb** *lit:* call for, demand, necessitate; lack, miss, require, want.

needle n *lit:* point, prong, spicule, spike, tine; stylus; hypodermic syringe; gnomon, pointer; obelisk. **vb** *lit:* aggravate, bait, goal, provoke, spur; annoy, harass, irk, nag, nettle, pester, prick, prod, ruffle, sting.

needless adj *lit:* causeless, gratuitous, groundless, pointless, superfluous, uncalled-for, unnecessary, unwanted, useless.

needy adj *lit:* deprived, impecunious, indigent, poor, poverty-stricken; friendless, homeless.

negative n *lit:* no; contradiction, denial, refusal, veto; *spec:* reversed-out image (on film). **adj** *lit:* contradictory, contrary, dissenting, opposing, rejecting, resisting; antagonistic, counteractive; gloomy, pessimistic, unenthusiastic, unwilling; colourless, insipid.

neglect n *lit:* disregard, inattention, indifference, unconcern; default, dereliction, forgetfulness, laxity, oversight, remissness, slackness. **vb** *lit:* disregard, ignore, overlook, pass over; evade, forget, omit, shirk, skimp.

negotiate vb *lit:* bargain, deal, haggle; debate, discuss, parley, work out; get over, get past, get round, pass through.

nerve n *lit:* neural tract; sinew, tendon; *fig:* bravery, courage, determination, firmness, grit, guts, intrepidity, mettle, pluck, resolution, will; audacity, brazenness, cheek, effrontery, impudence, temerity. **vb** *lit:* brace, encourage, fortify, steel.

nervous adj *lit:* agitated, anxious, edgy, fidgety, flustered, highly strung, jittery, jumpy, on edge, shaky, tense, uneasy, uptight.

nervousness n *lit:* agitation, anxiety, edginess, jumpiness, tension, uneasiness.

nest n *lit:* hatchery, home; *fig:* den, hideaway, lair; haunt, refuge, retreat; hotbed; *spec:* set (of tables).

net   n *lit:* mesh, trawl; lacework, lattice, reticulum; web.   **vb** *lit:* capture, catch, enmesh, ensnare, nab, trap; *fig:* bring in, gain, earn, make, realize.   **adj** *lit:* after taxes, clear, take-home; closing, final.

network   n *lit:* grid, grille, mesh; organization, structure, system; circuitry, complex, labyrinth, maze, plexus, web.

neutral   adj *lit:* disinterested, even-handed, impartial, non-aligned, noncommittal, unbiased, uncommitted, uninvolved; achromatic, colourless, dull, expressionless, indistinct, toneless, undefined.

new   adj *lit:* fresh, latest, novel, original, pristine, unused, virgin; advanced, contemporary, current, modern, modish, recent, topical, ultra-modern, up-to-date; added, additional, extra, supplementary; altered, different, improved, redesigned, reissued, restored; unexperienced, unexpected, unfamiliar, untried.

news   n *lit:* information, intelligence, tidings, word; gen, latest; account, bulletin, communiqué, dispatch, report, statement, story; advice, disclosure, release; gossip, hearsay, rumour.

next   adj *lit:* ensuing, later, subsequent, succeeding; consequent, resulting; adjacent, closest, nearest.   **adv** *lit:* afterwards, later, subsequently, thereafter, thereupon; in turn.

nice   adj *lit:* agreeable, amiable, charming, courteous, delightful, friendly, likable, pleasant, well-mannered; dainty, neat, tidy, trim; accurate, careful, delicate, exacting, fastidious, meticulous, precise, scrupulous, subtle; cultured, respectable, well-bred.

niche   n *lit:* alcove, aumbry, hollow, nook, recess; *fig:* calling, position, slot, vocation.

nick   n *lit:* chip, dent, groove, mark, notch, scar, score, scratch; eleventh hour, last moment; cells, jail, police station, prison.
vb *lit:* chip, damage, dent, mark, notch, scar, score, scratch; glance, snick; filch, nab, pilfer, pinch, steal, whip; arrest, capture, take; jail, imprison.

nickname   n *lit:* agnomen, familiar name, moniker, pet name, sobriquet; diminutive; kenning; epithet.

night n *lit:* dark, darkness, early hours, evening, hours of darkness, moonlight hours, night-time, small hours. **adj** *lit:* nocturnal; after dark, late; *spec:* sleeper (train).

nil n *lit:* nought, none, no score, nothing, zero, zilch; duck; love.

nimble adj *lit:* agile, limber, lithe; active, brisk, lively, quick, sprightly; dexterous, proficient.

nip n *lit:* dram, draught, drop, finger, mouthful, sip, taste, tot; bite, chill, frost. **vb** *lit:* bite, nibble, snap; clip, pinch, squeeze, tweak; *fig:* check, thwart.

nippy adj *lit:* biting, chilly, sharp; agile, fast, lively, nimble, quick, spry.

nit-picking adj (pr.pt) *lit:* carping, fault-finding, finicky, hairsplitting, pedantic, quibbling.

nobility n *lit:* aristocracy, high society, nobles, society, upper class; dignity, excellence, greatness, illustriousness; honour, integrity, uprightness.

noble n *lit:* aristocrat, patrician, peer. **adj** *lit:* aristocratic, blue-blooded, high-born, titled; dignified, eminent, excellent, impressive, splendid; honourable, magnanimous, upright.

nobody n *lit:* lightweight, nonentity. **prn** *lit:* none, no one.

nod n *lit:* bob, bow, duck; acknowledgement, indication, sign. **vb** *lit:* bob, bow, duck one's head; acknowledge, indicate, signal; agree, assent, concur; doze, droop, drop off.

noise n *lit:* sound; clamour, clatter, commotion, din, pandemonium, racket, tumult; babble, hubbub, outcry, uproar.

noiseless n *lit:* inaudible, silent, soundless; hushed, muted, quiet.

noisy adj *lit:* clamorous, deafening, ear-splitting, loud, piercing, tumultuous, uproarious, vociferous; cacophonous, strident.

nominate vb *lit:* appoint, assign, choose, designate, name, propose, recommend, select.

nominee n *lit:* choice, proposal, suggestion; aspirant, candidate, contestant, entrant, runner.

nondescript adj *lit:* commonplace, dull, mousy, ordinary, undistinguished, uninteresting, unremarkable, vague.

none adv *lit:* in no way, not at all, to no extent. **prn** *lit:* nobody, no one; not any, not one; not a bit, no part, nothing.

nonplus vb *lit:* baffle, bewilder, confound, discomfit, disconcert, discountenance, dumbfound, mystify, perplex, puzzle, take aback.

nonsense n *lit:* absurdity, blather, bunk, claptrap, double Dutch, drivel, fatuity, folly, gibberish, inanity, rot, rubbish, trash, twaddle, waffle.

nonstop adj *lit:* direct; ceaseless, constant, continuous, endless, incessant, relentless, uninterrupted, unremitting. **adv** *lit:* ceaselessly, constantly, continuously, endlessly, incessantly, relentlessly, steadily, uninterruptedly, unremittingly.

nook n *lit:* alcove, corner, cranny, crevice, niche, recess.

normal adj *lit:* average, common, natural, ordinary, regular, run-of-the-mill, standard, usual; rational, reasonable, well-adjusted.

nose n *lit:* proboscis; hooter, snout, trunk; front; *fig:* smell, sensitivity; aroma, bouquet, fragrance. **vb** *lit:* smell, sniff (out); nudge, push, shove; *fig:* meddle, pry, snoop.

notable adj *lit:* distinguished, eminent, famous, outstanding, remarkable; conspicuous, evident, marked, striking, unusual; manifest, noticeable.

notably adv *lit:* especially, particularly; conspicuously, distinctly, manifestly, markedly, outstandingly, strikingly; remarkably, uncommonly.

note n *lit:* jotting, memo, memorandum, minute; communication, letter, message, reminder; aside, comment, observation, remark; mark, sign, symbol, token; heed, notice; distinction, prestige, renown. **vb** *lit:* notice, perceive, see; mention, observe, remark; jot down, record.

noted adj (pa.pt) *lit:* acclaimed, celebrated, distinguished, eminent, illustrious, prominent, renowned, well-known; logged, minuted, recorded, registered.

notice n *lit:* attention, consideration, heed, note, regard; announcement, intelligence, news, notification; advertisement, poster; critique, review; advice, forewarning, warning; dismissal, eviction order. **vb** *lit:* detect, discern, note, observe, perceive, see, spot; heed, mind.

noticeable adj *lit:* discernible, perceptible; clear, conspicuous, evident, manifest, obvious, plain, striking.

notification n *lit:* advice, information, intelligence, message, notice, warning; announcement, declaration, statement.

notify vb *lit:* advise, inform, send word to, tell, warn; announce to, declare to, proclaim to.

notion n *lit:* brainwave, idea, thought; belief, concept, impression, opinion, understanding; inkling, knowledge; desire, fancy, inclination, sentiment, wish.

notwithstanding adv *lit:* however, nevertheless, nonetheless, still, yet. **prp** *lit:* despite, in spite of. **cnj** *lit:* although, though.

nourish vb *lit:* feed, nurture, sustain, tend; comfort, cultivate, encourage, foster, promote, supply.

nourishing adj (pr.pt) *lit:* healthful, nutritious, nutritive, sustaining; beneficial, wholesome.

novel n *lit:* story, tale; book, volume, work; romance; narrative. **adj** *lit:* fresh, innovative, new, original; different, rare, singular, strange, unusual.

novelty n *lit:* freshness, innovation, newness, originality; oddity, strangeness, unfamiliarity; curiosity, gimmick; knick-knack, trifle, trinket; memento, souvenir.

now adv *lit:* at once, immediately, instantly, promptly, straight away; any more, nowadays, these days; once. **cnj** *lit:* in that; since; for, the fact is, well.

nude n *lit:* naked figure; altogether, birthday suit. **adj** *lit:* au naturel, bare, in the altogether, in the buff, naked, starkers, stark-naked, stripped, uncovered, undressed.

nuisance n *lit:* annoyance, bore, bother, inconvenience, irritation, pest, plague, trouble, vexation.

numb adj *lit:* dead, frozen, immobilized, insensible, insensitive, paralysed, unfeeling; *fig:* dazed, overwhelmed, shocked, stunned.

number n *lit:* digit, figure, integer, numeral, unit; amount, quantity, sum, total; company, multitude, throng; copy, edition, issue; fig: aria, song, tune; item, product. **vb** *lit:* count, include in, total; classify, designate, label, rank.

numbered adj (pa.pt) *lit:* categorized, classified, designated; limited, totalled.

numbness n *lit:* deadness, dullness, immobilization, insensibility, insensitivity, paralysis, unfeeling; *fig:* daze, shock, torpor.

numerous adj *lit:* many, plentiful; abundant, copious, profuse; myriad, countless, host of, multitude of.

nursery n *lit:* crèche, play-room; allotment, garden, garden centre, kitchen garden, orchard, plantation.

nut n *lit:* seed; drupe, kernel, stone; *fig:* bonce, head; brain, intelligence, mind; problem; buff, enthusiast, fanatic; crank, eccentric, lunatic; ball, bollock, testicle; *spec:* (ginger) biscuit; knob, lump (of coal); screw. **vb** *lit:* gather nuts; *fig:* butt, head-butt (a person); head (a ball).

O

oaf n *lit:* blockhead, clod, dolt, dunce, fool, halfwit, imbecile, lout, lummox, moron, nincompoop, simpleton.

oafish adj *lit:* blockish, bovine, dim, dull, dumb, loutish, obtuse, slow on the uptake, stupid, thick; clumsy, lubberly.

oar n *lit:* pole, scull; blade; paddle. **vb** *lit:* paddle, row, scull.

oath n *lit:* promise, vow, word; bond, pledge; curse, expletive, imprecation, profanity, swearword.

obedience n *lit:* compliance, conformability, docility, dutifulness, submission, submissiveness, subservience, tractability; acquiescence, demureness, readiness, willingness; accordance.

obedient adj *lit:* compliant, conformable, docile, dutiful, submissive, subservient, tractable; acquiescent, amenable, biddable, demure, ready, willing; law-abiding.

obese adj *lit:* chubby, corpulent, fat, gross, overweight, paunchy, plump, podgy, portly, roly-poly, rotund, stout, tubby.

obey vb *lit:* be ruled by, bow to, serve, take orders from; comply, do what one is told, submit; act upon, carry out, discharge, execute, fulfil, perform; abide by, follow, heed, keep, mind, observe; truckle to.

object n *lit:* article, body, item, thing; phenomenon; fact, reality; design, intention, point, purpose; aim, end, goal, target; butt, focus. **vb** *lit:* demur, protest; be opposed (to), take exception (to).

objection n *lit:* demur, exception, opposition, protest, remonstration; counterargument.

objectionable adj *lit:* disagreeable, displeasing, distasteful, obnoxious, offensive, repugnant, unpleasant, unseemly.

objective n *lit:* aim, end, goal, target; aspiration, intention; design, purpose. **adj** *lit:* detached, disinterested, dispassionate, equitable, fair, impartial, impersonal, just, unbiased, uninvolved, unprejudiced.

obligation n *lit:* duty, liability, responsibility; burden, charge, commitment, requirement; must; debt, promise, trust, understanding.

oblige vb *lit:* do a favour, gratify, indulge, please; favour, serve; compel, constrain, force, impel, require.

obliged adj (pa.pt) *lit:* beholden, grateful, indebted, thankful; appreciative, gratified, pleased; bound, compelled, forced, required.

obliging adj (pr.pt) *lit:* accommodating, good-natured, helpful, willing; considerate, eager to please, generous, kind, open-hearted; agreeable, amiable, civil, courteous, friendly.

oblivion n *lit:* insensibility, unawareness, unconsciousness; blackness, darkness, nothingness, vacuum, void; extinction; abstraction, forgetfulness, negligence; abeyance, limbo.

oblivious adj *lit:* blithe, heedless, uncaring, unconcerned; forgetful, inattentive, negligent, unmindful, unobservant.

obscene adj *lit:* bawdy, blue, filthy, perverted, pornographic, smutty; coarse, dirty, gross, immoral, improper, indecent, lewd, licentious, ribald, salacious, suggestive; *fig:* disgusting, horrible, sickening, vile.

obscenity n *lit:* bawdiness, filthiness, perversion, pornography, smut; coarseness, dirtiness, grossness, immorality, lewdness, licentiousness, suggestiveness, vileness; expletive, four-letter word, profanity, swear-word; *fig:* atrocity, offence, outrage, vileness.

obscure vb *lit:* adumbrate, blur, cloud, dim, dull, obfuscate; conceal, cover, disguise, eclipse, hide, mask, screen, shade, shroud, veil. adj *lit:* abstruse, ambiguous, cryptic, enigmatic, esoteric, mysterious, opaque, recondite, vague; concealed, hidden, veiled; blurred, clouded, dim, faint, hazy, murky, shady, sombre; humble, lowly, minor, nameless, remote, undistinguished, unheard-of, unimportant, unknown.

obscurity n *lit:* abstruseness, ambiguity, complexity, incomprehensibility, mysteriousness, opacity, vagueness; dimness, gloom, haziness, murkiness, shadows; insignificance, lowliness, unimportance.

observant   adj *lit:* alert, eagle-eyed, vigilant, wary, watchful, wide awake; attentive, insightful, penetrative, perceptive, percipient, quick on the uptake; heedful, mindful.

observation   n *lit:* inspection, monitoring, scrutiny, study, surveillance, watch; comment, finding, note, opinion, reflection, thought; *spec:* reading (on an instrument, dial).

observe   vb *lit:* espy, notice, perceive, see, spot; keep an eye on, keep under observation, look at, monitor, regard, study, view, watch, witness; comment, mention, note, remark, state; abide by, adhere to, comply with, follow, heed, obey; celebrate, commemorate, keep.

obsessed   adj (pa.pt) *lit:* consumed, dominated, fixated, gripped, haunted, infatuated, manic, monopolized, one-track-minded, possessed.

obsession   n *lit:* bee in one's bonnet, fixation, hang-up, infatuation, mania, phobia, thing; fanaticism; preoccupation, ruling passion.

obsessive   adj *lit:* compulsive, fixated, manic, paranoid, phobic; consuming, dominating, fanatical, haunting, passionate, overwhelming; constant, persistent.

obstacle   n *lit:* barrier, blockage, impediment, obstruction; check, hindrance, hitch, hurdle, pitfall, stumbling-block; difficulty, snag.

obstinate   adj *lit:* dogged, immovable, persistent, pertinacious, steadfast, tenacious; headstrong, inflexible, intractable, mulish, pig-headed, recalcitrant, stubborn, wilful; firm, strong-minded.

obstruct   vb *lit:* bar, barricade, block, prevent; check, curb, delay, hinder, hold up, impede, interfere with, interrupt, slow down, stall; hamstring, inhibit, restrict; foil, frustrate, parry, thwart; get in the way of, obscure.

obstruction   n *lit:* bar, barricade, barrier, blockage; check, hindrance, hold-up, impediment, stop; difficulty, snag.

obtain   vb *lit:* acquire, come into possession of, get, get hold of, procure; attain, gain, secure, win; catch, hold on to, possess oneself of, take; be, exist, prevail, remain, stand.

obvious adj *lit:* clear, conspicuous, distinct, evident, indisputable, manifest, marked, palpable, patent, plain, pronounced, self-evident, straightforward, undeniable, unmistakable; apparent, noticeable, overt, perceptible, recognizable, visible.

occasional adj *lit:* desultory, infrequent, intermittent, irregular, odd, rare, sporadic; ceremonial, formal.

occasionally adv *lit:* at times, every now and then, from time to time, infrequently, intermittently, irregularly, on and off, once in a while, periodically, sometimes, sporadically.

occupation n *lit:* craft, employment, job, line of work, profession, trade, work; activity, pursuit; métier, vocation; incumbency, habitation, possession, residence, tenancy, tenure; conquest, domination, invasion, subjugation; sit-in, squat, take-over.

occupied adj (pa.pt) *lit:* busy, hard at it, tied up, working; inhabited, lived-in; engaged, full, taken, unavailable.

occur vb *lit:* befall, come to pass, eventuate, happen, pass, take place, transpire; fall out, turn out; appear, arise, be, crop up, exist, materialize, turn up; be suggested (to one), come (to one).

odd adj *lit:* abnormal, bizarre, extraordinary, freakish, outlandish, peculiar, strange, unusual, weird; curious, funny, quaint, singular; exceptional, rare; mysterious, uncanny; casual, incidental, occasional, random; miscellaneous, sundry, various; alternate, uneven; leftover, remaining, single, solitary, spare, surplus.

odds n *lit:* chances, likelihood, probability; difference, disparity, distinction; *fig:* (at) loggerheads, (at) variance.

odour n *lit:* aroma, bouquet, fragrance, perfume, scent; redolence, smell, stench, stink; air, atmosphere, aura, quality, spirit.

off adj *lit:* finished, unavailable; absent, on holiday, on leave; deferred, postponed; free, quiet, slack; bad, below par, poor, substandard; decomposed, mouldy, rancid, rotten. adv *lit:* apart, aside, away, elsewhere, out.

offence n *lit:* crime, misdemeanour, transgression, trespass; affront, insult, slight, snub; harm, hurt, wrong; hard feelings; anger, annoyance, displeasure, indignation, pique, resentment, umbrage.

offend vb *lit:* affront, insult, outrage, slight, snub; anger, annoy, disgruntle, irritate, miff, provoke, rile, upset, vex; disgust, nauseate, repel, sicken; be repugnant to, be unacceptable to; commit a crime (against), transgress (against), trespass (against).

offender n *lit:* criminal, law-breaker, transgressor; sinner, wrongdoer; culprit, guilty party, malefactor, miscreant.

offensive n *lit:* attack, onslaught, push; invasion; warpath. **adj** *lit:* affronting, insulting, insolent, rude; abusive, discourteous, objectionable, unacceptable; aggressive, attacking, belligerent, intrusive, provocative; angering, enraging, infuriating, outrageous, riling; disgusting, nauseating, obnoxious, revolting, vile.

offer n *lit:* bid, proposition, tender; proposal, suggestion; suit. **vb** *lit:* display to, hold out to, make available to, present to, proffer, put to, show to; bid, tender; propose, put forward, submit, suggest; put on the market, put up for sale; come forward, volunteer.

office n *lit:* capacity, function, role; appointment, employment, occupation, post, situation, station; bureau, department, section; business premises, company address, working environment; employees, staff, workers; act of worship, service.

officer n *lit:* person of rank, person of authority; executive, official; agent, functionary, representative; dignitary.

official n *lit:* person of authority, officer; executive; agent, functionary, representative; dignitary. **adj** *lit:* authoritative, authorized, sanctioned; certified, endorsed, legitimate; accredited, authentic, bona fide, formal, proper.

offset vb *lit:* cancel out, counteract, counterbalance, make up for. **adj** *lit:* contrasted, highlighted; balanced, equipoised.

offspring n *lit:* child, descendant, heir; children, descendants, heirs, progeny, issue, seed; successors.

often adv *lit:* frequently, repeatedly, time after time; commonly, generally.

oily *adj lit:* greasy, well-lubricated; sebaceous; black, inky, sticky, tarry; *fig:* fawning, smooth, slippery, unctuous.

okay *n lit:* approval, assent, consent; authorization, go-ahead, green light, permission. **vb** *lit:* agree to, approve, authorize, pass, permit, sanction. **adj** *lit:* acceptable, adequate, all right, good enough, in order, not bad, passable, satisfactory, tolerable; correct; fine, good. **adv** *lit:* adequately, passably, satisfactorily, well enough; correctly.

old *n lit:* aged, elderly, pensioners, senior citizens. **adj** *lit:* of age; advanced in years, elderly, getting on, past one's prime; in one's dotage, senile; aboriginal, age-old, ancient, antediluvian, primeval, primordial; experienced, practised, veteran; customary, familiar, habitual, long-established, time-honoured, traditional; clichéd, hackneyed; antique, archaic, obsolete, out of date, unfashionable; earlier, erstwhile, ex-, former, last, original, previous; dead, empty, rejected, worn-out.

old-fashioned *adj lit:* antiquated, archaic, dated, obsolescent, obsolete, outmoded, out of date, passé, unfashionable; fuddy-duddy, fusty, musty, stick-in-the-mud.

omission *n lit:* exclusion, leaving out; jump, skip; gap, hiatus, interval; negligence, oversight; avoidance, inaction.

omit *vb lit:* drop, exclude, leave out; delete, eliminate, erase; jump, pass over, skip; neglect, miss, overlook.

on *adj lit:* active, functioning, operative, performing, working; available; happening, occurring, taking place; allowable, permissible. **adv** *lit:* ahead, forward, further, more; during, in, when, while; into activity, into functioning, into operation. **prp** *lit:* atop; adhering to, stuck to; in regard to, with reference to; by means of, through, with.

once *adj lit:* erstwhile, former, prior, sometime. **adv** *lit:* at one time, formerly, in the past, long ago, previously; on a single occasion, just one time. **cnj** *lit:* any time, when, whenever; if, if ever.

one *adj lit:* a, a certain, an, a single, a sole; joined, united.
prn *lit:* anybody, somebody; an example, a sample.

only *adj lit:* lone, single, sole, unique. *adv lit:* just, merely; purely; at most.

ooze *n lit:* ebb, gentle flow; dregs, grounds, lees; alluvium, mud, silt, slime; discharge, dribble, drip, exudation, seepage, weeping. *vb lit:* dribble, drip, exude, leak, seep, weep; discharge, drain, emit.

open *vb lit:* throw wide, uncover, unlock, unseal; uncork, unwrap; expand, spread out, unfold; disclose, divulge, reveal; begin, commence, inaugurate, kick off, launch, set in motion, start; come apart, separate, split. *adj lit:* ajar, gaping, revealed, spread out, unclosed, unfolded, unlocked; bare, exposed, undefended, unfortified, unprotected; accessible, public, spacious, sweeping, unenclosed, unfenced, wide-open; unengaged, unoccupied, vacant; blatant, clear, flagrant, overt, plain, unconcealed; arguable, debatable, undecided, unsettled; impartial, objective, uncommitted; liable (to), susceptible (to), vulnerable (to); candid, frank, guileless, honest, sincere; generous, liberal, munificent.

opening *n lit:* aperture, fissure, fistula, gap, hole, orifice, perforation, rupture, slot, vent; break, chance, opportunity, vacancy; beginning, commencement, inauguration, kickoff, launch, onset, start. *adj (pr.pt) lit:* commencing, first, inaugural, initial, introductory.

openly *adv lit:* candidly, forthrightly, frankly, plainly, unreservedly; blatantly, flagrantly, overtly, publicly.

operate *vb lit:* act, function, go, perform, run, work; be in charge of, handle, manage, manoeuvre, use, wield; perform surgery.

operation *n lit:* action, functioning, performance, running, working; activity, movement; handling, management, manipulation, manoeuvring, use, wielding; affair, campaign, exercise, procedure; deal, proceeding, undertaking; surgical procedure.

operative *n lit:* employee, hand, worker; executive; shopfloorman. *adj lit:* active, functioning, on, performing, running, working; effective, efficient, functional, usable, serviceable, workable; crucial, influential, key, relevant, significant.

operator n *lit:* button-pusher, driver, handler, user, wielder, worker; administrator, agent, contractor, franchise-holder, representative, trader; chief, manipulator, wheeler-dealer.

opinion n *lit:* assessment, estimation, impression, judgement, point of view, view; belief, conception; ideas, sentiments, thoughts; supposition, theory.

opponent n *lit:* adversary, antagonist, challenger, co-contestant, disputant; enemy, foe, rival.

opportunity n *lit:* break, chance, opening; convenient moment, occasion, time.

oppose vb *lit:* act against, be against, counter, dispute, fight, resist, speak against, take issue with; contradict, defy, stand up to; confront, face; bar, hinder, obstruct; contrast, counterbalance.

opposing adj (pr.pt) *lit:* alternative, contesting, other, rival; confronting, facing; antipathetic, conflicting, contrary, hostile, incompatible, irreconcilable.

opposite n *lit:* antithesis, contrary, converse, reverse.
adj *lit:* alternate, facing, other; contradictory, contrary, different, reverse; adverse, antagonistic, irreconcilable.

opposition n *lit:* counteraction, defence, resistance; blocking, obstruction; antagonism, hostility; antagonist, rival; competition, opponent, other side.

oppressive adj *lit:* burdensome, grinding, onerous, severe; despotic, overbearing, repressive, tyrannical; close, heavy, overpowering, stifling, suffocating.

oppressor n *lit:* despot, dictator, persecutor, subjugator, tyrant; bully, martinet, ogre, slave-driver.

optimistic adj *lit:* hopeful, inclined to look on the bright side, Micawberish; confident, positive; buoyant, cheerful.

option n *lit:* alternative, choice; decision, preference, selection.

optional adj *lit:* discretionary, noncompulsory, voluntary; additional, extra, supplementary.

orb n *lit:* ball, globe, sphere; *fig:* celestial body, celestial sphere; world; eyeball; time-cycle.

orbit n *lit:* circumnavigation, encircling motion, revolution, rotation; circle, cycle; course, path; *fig:* ambit, compass, range, scope, sphere; *spec:* socket (for each eyeball). **vb** *lit:* circle, circumnavigate, encircle, revolve around.

ordeal n *lit:* labour, nightmare, torment, tribulation, uphill struggle; test, trial.

order n *lit:* command, decree, directive, injunction, mandate, ordinance, rule; application, booking, request, reservation; alignment, arrangement, line, organization, regularity, symmetry, tidiness; calm, control, discipline, peace, propriety, quiet; categorization, classification, codification, grouping, progression; breed, family, genre, ilk, kind, sort, type; caste, class, grade, hierarchy, position, rank; association, brotherhood, company, fraternity, guild, league, lodge, society; (in) place, (in) sequence, (in) turn; (in) commission, (in) service; (out of) operation, (out of) repair. **vb** *lit:* command, decree, direct, instruct, ordain, prescribe, require; apply for, book, contract for, request, reserve; adjust, align, arrange, marshal, regulate; catalogue, classify, sort out.

orderly adj *lit:* methodical, neat, regular, shipshape, systematic, tidy, trim; businesslike, controlled, formal, restrained; calm, disciplined, law-abiding, quiet, well-behaved.

ordinarily adv *lit:* as a rule, commonly, generally, habitually, in general, normally, usually.

ordinary adj *lit:* common, everyday, habitual, humdrum, normal, regular, standard, typical, usual; common or garden, customary, familiar, household, humble, plain, prosaic, simple, unpretentious, unremarkable; average, clichéd, commonplace, hackneyed, indifferent, mediocre, pedestrian, unexceptional.

organic adj *lit:* biological, biotic, living, natural; anatomical, constitutional, inherent, integral, structural; integrated, ordered, structured, systematic.

organism n *lit:* animal, being, creature, living thing; integrated structure.

organization n *lit:* assembly, composition, construction, coordination, design, formation, framework, plan, planning, structure, structuring; alignment, arrangement, conformation, grouping, make-up; association, body, company, concern, consortium, corporation, group, institution, syndicate.

organize vb *lit:* assemble, compose, construct, coordinate, design, form, frame, plan, structure; combine, join together, unite; align, arrange, group, line up, marshal, put in order, set up; classify, codify; be responsible for, manage, orchestrate, run, see to, take care of.

orgy n *lit:* bacchanal, carousal, debauch, revelry; binge, splurge, spree; *fig:* fit, frenzy, storm.

origin n *lit:* roots, source; beginning, commencement, outset, start; basis, creation, derivation, emergence, foundation, fount, genesis; ancestry, extraction, lineage, pedigree, provenance, stock.

original n *lit:* first, master, true one; archetype, model, paradigm, pattern, prototype; *fig:* anomaly, character, eccentric, oddity, weirdo. **adj** *lit:* early, first, initial, starting; authentic, first-hand, genuine, master, true; creative, fresh, imaginative, ingenious, innovatory, inventive, new, novel, unprecedented, unusual.

originally adv *lit:* at first, first, initially, in the first place, to begin with; prehistorically, primordially; imaginatively, ingeniously, innovatively, inventively.

originate vb *lit:* arise, begin, come, derive, emanate, emerge, spring, start; bring about, create, evolve, initiate, pioneer, set up.

originator n *lit:* architect, author, creator, designer, deviser, founder, inventor, pioneer.

ornament n *lit:* decoration, jewel, trinket; adornment, embellishment, frill, garnish, trimming; *fig:* flower, glory, pride, treasure. **vb** *lit:* adorn, decorate, embellish, festoon, garnish, trim; *fig:* grace, honour.

ornamental adj *lit:* decorative, embellishing; artistic, picturesque, scenic; extra, inessential, supplementary.

ornate adj *lit:* bedecked, elaborate, florid, ornamented, showy; lavish, rich, sumptuous.

other adj *lit:* additional, ancillary, auxiliary, extra, further, more, remaining, spare, supplementary; alternative, contrasting, different, dissimilar, diverse, separate, variant.

otherwise adj *lit:* different. adv *lit:* alternatively, differently; apart from this, except for this. cnj *lit:* if not, or else.

out adj *lit:* absent; dismissed, disqualified, eliminated; at fault, incorrect, in error, wrong; striking, on strike; exposed, in the open, public; blooming, in bloom. adv *lit:* away, elsewhere, outside; not allowed, not on, unacceptable; antiquated, behind the times, dated, old-fashioned; at an end, dead, exhausted, expired, finished; completely, thoroughly, unreservedly; in society; lengthways; from a total (of), from the midst (of). prp *lit:* outside.

outbreak n *lit:* epidemic, upsurge; burst, eruption, explosion, flare-up, rash.

outburst n *lit:* discharge, eruption, outpouring, surge; explosion, fit of temper, storm, tantrum; interpolation, interruption, intrusion.

outcome n *lit:* conclusion, consequence, end result, result, upshot; aftermath.

outcry n *lit:* complaint, howl, hullabaloo, protest, screech; commotion, uproar, yell.

outdated adj *lit:* antiquated, archaic, behind the times, out of date, passé, unfashionable.

outdo vb *lit:* beat, excel, surpass, transcend, outstrip; get the better of, outmanoeuvre, overcome.

outer adj *lit:* cortical, exterior, external, outlying, outside, peripheral, superficial.

outfit n *lit:* clothes, costume, dress, get-up, suit; accoutrements, gear, trappings; clique, company, crew, group, organization, set, squad, team, unit. vb *lit:* equip, fit out, kit out, stock, supply.

outgoing adj *lit:* approachable, easy, extrovert, friendly, gregarious, open, sociable; departing, ex-, former, past, retiring.

outing   n *lit:* airing, excursion, expedition, jaunt, spin, trip.

outlaw   n *lit:* criminal, malefactor, miscreant; bandit, brigand, desperado, marauder; fugitive, outcast.   **vb** *lit:* ban, banish, bar, exclude, make illegal, proscribe.

outline   n *lit:* contour, delineation, form, profile, shape, silhouette; draft, framework, layout, plan, sketch; bare facts, rough idea, summary, synopsis; silhouette.   **vb** *lit:* delineate; draft, plan, sketch, summarize.

outlook   n *lit:* attitude, frame of mind, standpoint, view; expectations, forecast, prospect; aspect, panorama, scene, vista.

outrage   n *lit:* atrocity, barbarism, enormity, inhumanity; affront, insult, profanation; injury, offence, rape, violation; anger, fury, indignation, resentment.   **vb** *lit:* affront, incense, infuriate, madden, offend, shock; injure, insult.

outrageous   adj *lit:* atrocious, barbaric, infamous, monstrous, unspeakable; disgraceful, iniquitous, scandalous; exorbitant, immoderate, preposterous, shocking.

outright   adj *lit:* definite, direct, straightforward; absolute, arrant, complete, downright, out-and-out, thorough, total, unqualified, utter.   **adv** *lit:* absolutely, completely, explicitly, overtly, thoroughly, without hesitation; at once, immediately, instantaneously, instantly, straight away, there and then.

outside   n *lit:* cortex, exterior, façade, front, surface; topside; hide, peel, skin; extreme, most.   **adj** *lit:* exterior, external, outdoor, outer, outermost, outward, surface; extramural; extraneous; distant, marginal, negligible, slight, slim, small, unlikely.   **adv** *lit:* on the exterior, to the exterior.   **prp** *lit:* beyond, excluded from, the far side of; excepted from, exempt from; apart from.

outspoken   adj *lit:* blunt, candid, direct, forthright, frank, free; explicit.

outstanding   adj *lit:* arresting, conspicuous, eye-catching, noteworthy, prominent, striking; eminent, excellent, exceptional, great, pre-eminent, superlative; due, owing, payable, remaining, unpaid, unsettled.

outward adj *lit:* exterior, external, outer, outside, surface; apparent, evident, ostensible, overt, superficial, visible.

outwardly adv *lit:* apparently, as far as one can see, externally, on the face of it, ostensibly, overtly, seemingly, supeficially, to all intents and purposes, visibly.

outweigh vb *lit:* be more important than, be preponderant over, eclipse, have more clout than, predominate over, prevail over, take precedence over.

over adj *lit:* accomplished, ancient history, completed, concluded, finished, past, settled; closed, done; left, remaining, spare, surplus. adv *lit:* above one, overhead; across. prp *lit:* above, atop, on, on top of, superior to; exceeding, in excess of, more than.

overall adj *lit:* all-embracing, complete, comprehensive, general, inclusive, long-term, total. adv *lit:* generally speaking, in general, in the long term, on the whole.

overbearing adj *lit:* arrogant, autocratic, bossy, dictatorial, domineering, haughty, high-handed, officious, peremptory, supercilious, superior.

overcast adj *lit:* clouded, cloudy, dismal, dull, grey, leaden, lowering, threatening.

overcome vb *lit:* beat, conquer, crush, defeat, get the better of, overpower, prevail over, subdue, vanquish; be victorious over, rise above, surmount; come through, survive, weather. adj *lit:* affected, bowled over, overwhelmed, speechless; ecstatic, elated; horrified, terrified; awestricken; dumbstruck, flabbergasted.

overcrowded adj (pa.pt) *lit:* choked, congested, crammed, full, overpopulated, packed.

overdo vb *lit:* overwork at; exaggerate, overact; belabour, take to extremes, overstate; overuse.

overdue adj *lit:* behind schedule, behind time, late, unpunctual; outstanding, owing.

overeat vb *lit:* binge, eat like a horse, gorge, guzzle, make a pig of oneself, pack it away, pig out, stuff oneself.

overflow n *lit:* discharge, flood, inundation; surplus. **vb** *lit:* flood, pour over, run over, spill over; drown, immerse, inundate, submerge, swamp.

overhang n *lit:* projection, protrusion. **vb** *lit:* bulge over, jut over, loom over, project over, protrude over, stick out over; *fig:* be imminent over, loom over, threaten.

overindulgence n *lit:* excess, immoderation, intemperance, surfeit.

overlook **vb** *lit:* command a view of, front on, look over; fail to notice, forget, miss, pass over; disregard, ignore, let one off with, let pass, omit, skip, turn a blind eye to.

overtake **vb** *lit:* get past, outdistance, outdo, pass; catch unprepared, engulf, overwhelm, strike, take by surprise.

overthrow n *lit:* deposing, dethronement, downfall, ejection, expulsion, ouster, removal, undoing; defeat, destruction, rout, ruin, subjugation, suppression. **vb** *lit:* bring down, depose, dethrone, eject, expel, oust, remove, undo; defeat, destroy, rout, ruin, subdue, subjugate, suppress; abolish, do away with, demolish, overturn, put an end to, topple, raze.

overturn **vb** *lit:* capsize, keel over, knock over, tip over, topple, tumble, upend; annul, countermand, invalidate, repeal, reverse; depose.

overweight adj *lit:* bulky, chubby, corpulent, fat, gross, heavy, hefty, massive, obese, plump, podgy, portly, stout, tubby.

owe **vb** *lit:* be in arrears; be under an obligation to pay, have to give, should give.

owing adj *lit:* due, outstanding, unpaid, unsettled.

own **vb** *lit:* have, hold, possess, retain; acknowledge, admit (to), avow, concede (to), confess (to), go along with, grant. **adj** *lit:* individual, personal, private.

owner n *lit:* landlord, proprietor; possessor, retainer; master.

P

pace n *lit:* step, stride; gait, tread, walk; momentum, motion, rate, speed, tempo, velocity. **vb** *lit:* march, pound, stride; patrol; count (out), mark (out), measure (out).

pack n *lit:* bale, bundle; burden, load; haversack, knapsack, rucksack; band, bunch, crowd, gang, group, herd, troop; collection, deck, kit, set; application; carton, packet. **vb** *lit:* batch, bundle, parcel up; burden, load, store, stow; cram, fill, jam, press, ram, stuff; crowd, mob, throng; compact, compress.

package n *lit:* box, carton, packet, parcel; amalgamation, combination; unit, whole; deal, enterprise, transaction; product. **vb** *lit:* batch, box, pack, parcel up, wrap up; assemble, make, manufacture, put it all together.

pact n *lit:* agreement, arrangement, bargain, contract, deal, entente, treaty, understanding; alliance, coalition.

pad n *lit:* buffer, cushion, guard, protection, shield, wad; block, jotter, notepad; paw, sole; apartment, flat, room; heliport, launching platform. **vb** *lit:* cushion, fill, line, stuff; *fig:* digress, draw (out), fill (out), prevaricate.

pagan n *lit:* barbarian, heathen, unbeliever; infidel; atheist. **adj** *lit:* barbaric, godless, heathen, unbelieving; irreligious, profane, unchristian, ungodly.

page n *lit:* folio, leaf, sheet, side; attendant, boy, servant, squire; *fig:* epoch, era, period, phase, stage, time. **vb** *lit:* call for, have called for, send to find.

pain n *lit:* ache, agony, discomfort, pang, smarting, soreness, throb; anguish, distress, suffering, woe; grief, sadness; *fig:* bore, bother, nuisance, pest. **vb** *lit:* hurt, smart, wound; chafe, discomfort, torment; *fig:* afflict, aggrieve, agonize, distress; annoy, gall, harass, irritate, vex, worry.

painful **adj** *lit:* aching, agonizing, excruciating, hurting, raw, smarting, sore, throbbing; abhorrent, awful, distressing, dreadful, nasty, terrible, unpleasant; arduous, difficult, hard, tedious, trying.

painstaking adj *lit:* assiduous, careful, conscientious, meticulous, punctilious, scrupulous, thorough.

paint n *lit:* colour, dye, pigment, tint, wash; emulsion, enamel; cosmetics, make-up. **vb** *lit:* colour, dye, enamel, tint; depict, draw, picture, portray, represent, sketch; brush (on), coat, daub, decorate, put (on), slap (on); *fig:* describe, evoke, picture.

pair n *lit:* brace, couple, doublet, duo, twosome. **vb** *lit:* bracket, couple, match, put together, yoke; marry, mate, wed.

pale **vb** *lit:* blanch, blench, go white, whiten; dim, dull, fade; *fig:* decrease, diminish, lessen. **adj** *lit:* anaemic, ashen, bleached, faded, pallid, sallow, wan, washed-out, whitish; dim, faint, feeble, thin, weak.

palm n *lit:* hand, paw; coconut tree, date tree; *fig:* glory, laurels, success, triumph, trophy, victory. **vb** *lit:* conceal in one's hand; steal, thieve, walk off with; *fig:* fob (off with); pass (off as).

pampered adj (pa.pt) *lit:* babied, coddled, cosseted, indulged, mollycoddled, spoilt.

pan n *lit:* cooking tray, pot, saucepan, vessel; toilet bowl; basin, concavity, depression, hollow; *fig:* face, features; *spec:* drum (in a steel band); floe (of ice); priming area (on a flintlock). **vb** *lit:* search (for), sift, wash; *fig:* scan, sweep, track; censure, criticize, flay, knock, slate; come (out), turn (out).

panel n *lit:* oblong, rectangle; board, lath, plank, strip; fencing, hurdle, paling; dashboard, instrument board, switchboard; painting, picture; saddle-pad; *fig:* discussion group, jury, quiz team; *spec:* box, frame, inset, key (on a page); division, section (of a coalmine, of a hull); list (of clients, of consultants, of doctors, of jurors, of patients).

pang n *lit:* gripe, pain, prick, stab, twinge; stitch; ache; *fig:* qualm, scruple.

panic n *lit:* alarm, consternation, fear, fright, hysteria; red-alert, scare. **vb** *lit:* become hysterical, go to pieces, lose one's nerve, overreact; alarm, frighten, put the wind up, scare; unnerve.

pant **vb** *lit:* blow, gasp, heave, puff, wheeze; *fig:* hunger (for), long (for), pine (for), yearn (for).

pants **n** *lit:* bloomers, briefs, drawers, knickers, panties, shorts, slacks, trousers, underpants, Y-fronts.

paper **n** *lit:* document(s); certificate, deed, instrument; dossier(s); file(s); account(s), receipt(s); daily, journal, newspaper, organ, periodical, tabloid; article, dissertation, essay, monograph, study, thesis, treatise; examination; wrapping.

par **n** *lit:* average, norm, standard, usual; balance, equality, equilibrium, level, parallel.

parade **n** *lit:* array, cavalcade, pageant, procession; march-past, military display, trooping; display, exhibition, flaunting, ostentation, show; esplanade, promenade; *spec:* defence, parry (in fencing). **vb** *lit:* march past, process; brandish, display, flaunt, show off, vaunt; troop.

paradise **n** *lit:* garden of Eden, heaven; life to come, next world; Elysian fields, happy hunting-ground, Promised Land, Utopia; *fig:* bliss, ecstasy, joy, rapture.

parallel **n** *lit:* analogy, comparison, correlation, likeness, resemblance, similarity; analogue, counterpart, duplicate, equal, equivalent, match. **vb** *lit:* agree with, be alike with, correlate to, correspond with, equal, match; balance, complement. **adj** *lit:* aligned, alongside, side by side; analogous, compatible, complementary, uniform.

paralyse **vb** *lit:* anaesthetize, benumb, immobilize; cripple, debilitate, disable, lame; *fig:* arrest, halt, stop, transfix.

paralysis **n** *lit:* ataxia, paresis; immobility, numbness, palsy; *fig:* disruption, shutdown, stasis, stillness, stoppage.

parasite **n** *lit:* bloodsucker; *fig:* hanger-on, leech, scrounger, sponger; drone.

parcel n *lit:* carton, package, packet; batch, bunch, bundle; bit, portion, part; area, lot, plot, site. **vb** *lit:* do (up), pack (up), wrap (up); apportion (out), deal (out), mete (out), share (out).

parched adj *lit:* arid, dehydrated, desiccated, dry; thirsty; scorched, shrivelled, withered.

pardon n *lit:* forgiveness; absolution, mercy, remission, reprieve; amnesty, grace; acquittal, clearance, discharge, exculpation, exoneration; *spec:* (papal) indulgence. **vb** *lit:* forgive; absolve, free, let off, release from, remit, reprieve; acquit, clear, exculpate, excuse, overlook.

parent n *lit:* dam, father, mother, procreator, progenitor, sire; guardian; author, creator, generator, originator, source; derivation, prototype.

park n *lit:* estate, garden, grounds, nature reserve, reservation, woodland; playground, playing-field, recreation ground; funfair. **vb** *lit:* dump, leave, put down; pull up, station, stop.

part n *lit:* bit, fraction, fragment, piece, portion, scrap, section, sector, segment, share; component, constituent, element, ingredient, module, unit; limb, member, organ; area, district, region, territory, vicinity; behalf, cause, concern, interest; duty, function, involvement, say, task; character, role, voice; conduct, disposition, temperament. **vb** *lit:* detach, disconnect, disjoin, divide, put asunder, rend, separate, sever, split, tear; break up, go separate ways, leave, quit, split up, withdraw.

partial adj *lit:* biased, discriminatory, one-sided, partisan, prejudiced, unfair; incomplete, part, unfinished.

participant n *lit:* competitor, contestant, contributor, member, partaker; partner, shareholder.

particle n *lit:* atom, bit, grain, ion, iota, jot, mite, molecule, scrap, shred, speck; crumb; prefix, suffix.

particular n *lit:* circumstance(s), detail(s), fact(s), specification(s). **adj** *lit:* choosy, fastidious, finicky, fussy, meticulous, painstaking, thorough; detailed, itemized, minute;

distinct, exact, special, specific; distinctive, remarkable, singular, unusual.

particularly adv *lit:* decidedly, distinctly, especially, explicitly, expressly, intimately, markedly, notably, outstandingly, specifically; individually, peculiarly, singularly, uncommonly, unusually.

partition n *lit:* barrier, divider, fence, screen, septum, wall; division, segregation, separation; apportioning, distribution, rationing out; allocation, portion, ration, share. vb *lit:* divide, fence (off), screen, wall (off); cut up, segment, separate, split up, subdivide; allocate, apportion.

partner n *lit:* ally, associate, collaborator, colleague, co-founder, confederate; abetter, accomplice; companion, comrade, mate; bedfellow, boy-friend, consort, girl-friend, husband, spouse, wife.

party n *lit:* celebration, do, festivity, gala, get-together, reception, social gathering, soirée, thrash; band, body, bunch, company, detachment, group, squad, team, unit; alliance, association, clique, coalition, confederacy, faction, grouping, set, side; individual, person; contractor, defendant, litigant, plaintiff.

pass n *lit:* canyon, col, defile, gap; authorization, identification, permit, safe-conduct, warrant; free ticket, season ticket, voucher; advances, approach, overture, sexual advance; plight, predicament, situation, state of affairs; lunge, push, thrust; brandishing, gesticulation, wave; *spec:* success (in an examination). vb *lit:* depart, elapse, go by, leave, move, proceed; beat, exeed, excel, outdo, surmount, surpass, transcend; get through, graduate, qualify; do, suffice; fill, occupy, spend, while away; befall, happen, occur, take place; convey, give, hand, kick, throw, transfer, transmit; accept, approve, authorize, enact, legislate, ratify, sanction, validate; declare, pronounce; disregard, ignore, miss, omit, overlook, skip; defecate, discharge, evacuate, excrete, micturate, urinate; blow over, cease, die, dwindle, ebb, expire, fade, vanish, wane; be seen (as), be taken (for).

passage n *lit:* corridor, doorway, entrance, exit, hall, lobby, vestibule; crossing, journey, tour, trek, trip, voyage; avenue, course, lane, path, road, route, thoroughfare, way; advance, flow, passing, progress, transition; clause, excerpt, extract, piece, quotation, reading, section, text; acceptance, enactment, legislation, ratification.

passing n *lit:* death, decease, demise, end; overhauling, overtaking. **adj** *lit:* incidental, fortuitous; casual, cursory, hasty, shallow, superficial; brief, ephemeral, fleeting, momentary, transitory.

passion n *lit:* ardour, eagerness, emotion, ferocity, fervour, fire, intensity, spirit, vehemence, voracity, zeal; craving, desire, lust; enthusiasm, fondness, infatuation, love; craze, mania, obsession; anger, ire, rage, resentment, wrath; frenzy, storm.

passionate **adj** *lit:* amorous, ardent, erotic, hot, loving, lustful, sensual, sexy; aflame, eager, enthusiastic, excited, fervent, fiery, heartfelt, intense, spirited, vehement, zealous; emotional, wild; hot-headed, irascible, irritable, quick-tempered, stormy, tempestuous, violent.

passive **adj** *lit:* inactive, inert; long-suffering, patient, resigned, submissive, unresisting; acquiescent, compliant, docile.

past n *lit:* days gone by, former times, good old days, times past; background, experience, history, life, particulars, previous life, record. **adj** *lit:* completed, done, extinct, finished, gone, over; ancient, bygone, old, previous; earlier, erstwhile, former, preceding, quondam. **adv** *lit:* by, on; beyond, to the far side of; over. **prp** *lit:* beyond, farther than, outside, over; after, subsequent to.

patch n *lit:* darn, reinforcement, replacement; bit, fragment, scrap, shred; area, ground, land, manor, stretch, vicinity; period; time; *spec:* cover, pad (over an eye); false mole (as facial decoration); overlay (in printing). **vb** *lit:* cover over, darn, fix (up), mend, treat; put (together), reconnect (together); *fig:* make (up).

paternal **adj** *lit:* fatherly, parental; avuncular, benevolent, protective, solicitous; family, hereditary, patrimonial.

path n *lit:* alley, footway, gangway, kerb, passage, pavement, sidewalk, track, trail, walk, walkway; course, direction, line, route, way.

pathetic **adj** *lit:* affecting, distressing, heart-rending, moving, pitiable, sad, touching; *fig:* abysmal, feeble, lamentable, petty, weak, wet; hopeless, useless, worthless.

patience n *lit:* endurance, forbearance, perseverance, sufferance, tolerance; calmness, composure; diligence, fortitude, persistence.

patient n *lit:* invalid, sufferer; victim; case, client. **adj** *lit:* enduring, forbearing, long-suffering, persevering, resigned, stoic, suffering, tolerant; calm, composed, cool; diligent, persistent; lenient, magnanimous, understanding.

patrol n *lit:* policing, rounds, safeguarding, reconnaissance, watch; guard, sentinel, watchman. **vb** *lit:* guard, inspect, keep watch over, make the rounds, police, reconnoitre.

patron n *lit:* benefactor, sponsor; angel, backer; champion, defender, guardian, protector; client, customer, shopper.

patronize vb *lit:* be condescending to, be lofty with, look down on, talk down to; fund, sponsor; back, support; be a client of, buy from, do business with, frequent, trade with.

pause n *lit:* break, breather, delay, gap, halt, interlude, intermission, interval, lull, respite, stoppage; hesitation; interruption, suspension. **vb** *lit:* break off, delay, halt, have a breather, rest, stop briefly; falter, hesitate, waver.

paw n *lit:* foot, hand; pad; claws; mitt. **vb** *lit:* finger, fondle, grope, maul, molest; feel, grab, handle roughly, manhandle; *spec:* kick, strike (the ground restlessly).

pawn n *lit:* collateral, deposit, pledge, security; bond, hock; cat's-paw, dupe, instrument, puppet, stooge, tool. **vb** *lit:* deposit, hock, pledge, stake.

pay n *lit:* earnings, fee, hire, remuneration, salary, stipend, wages; emolument, income, takings; reimbursement. **vb** *lit:* cough up, foot, settle; clear, honour; recompense, reimburse, remunerate; be advantageous, benefit, be worthwhile, repay; bring in, return, yield; be profitable, make a return, provide a living; bestow, extend, give, present, proffer, render; *fig:* answer (for), make amends (for), suffer (for).

payment n *lit:* emolument, fee, hire, remuneration, salary, stipend, wages; advance, deposit, outlay, premium; remittance, settlement.

peace n *lit:* calm, hush, quiet, repose, restfulness, serenity, silence, stillness, tranquillity; amity, concord, friendliness, harmony; armistice, cessation of hostilities, non-aggression, non-violence, treaty, truce; *spec:* ease (of mind).

peaceful adj *lit:* calm, hushed, placid, quiet, restful, serene, silent, still, tranquil, undisturbed, unruffled; amicable, friendly, harmonious, on good terms; non-military.

peak n *lit:* apex, crest, pinnacle, point, summit, tip, top; *fig:* climax, culmination, high point, maximum, zenith. **vb** *lit:* climax, come to a head, reach a maximum.

peal n *lit:* chime, chiming, clangour, resonance, reverberation, ringing, sounding, tolling; *spec:* carillon, set (of bells); grilse, sea-trout. **vb** *lit:* chime, clang, resonate, resound, reverberate, ring, sound, toll.

peculiar adj *lit:* abnormal, bizarre, freakish, funny, odd, outlandish, strange, weird; curious, extraordinary, quaint, singular, unusual; characteristic, distinctive, idiosyncratic, individual, own, particular, private, specific, unique.

pedestrian n *lit:* walker; footslogger, hiker; passer-by. **adj** *lit:* on foot, walking; *fig:* boring, dull, long-winded, prosaic, slow, tedious, trite, unimaginative.

peel n *lit:* rind, skin; bark; outer layer. **vb** *lit:* pare, skin, strip (off); flake off.

peep n *lit:* glance, glimpse, look, peek; cheep, chirp, chirrup, squeak, twitter. **vb** *lit:* glance, peek, sneak a look; appear briefly, be partly visible; cheep, chirp, chirrup, squeak, twitter.

peer n *lit:* aristocrat, lord, noble, nobleman; equal. **vb** *lit:* gaze, look (at), take a close look (at); look (out), peep (out).

peerage n *lit:* aristocracy, lords, nobility, peers.

peevish adj *lit:* cantankerous, cross, crusty, fretful, grumpy, ill-tempered, irascible, petulant, short-tempered, snappy, sulky, surly, testy, touchy, waspish.

peg n *lit:* bolt, pin, stake; hook, key; dram, drink, tot; *fig:* degree, step; leg; *spec:* wooden leg. **vb** *lit:* attach, fasten, fix, join, secure; freeze, hold, limit, set; *fig:* beaver (away at), plug (away at), work (away at).

pelt n *lit:* fell, fur, hide, skin; (at full) speed. **vb** *lit:* assail (with), bombard (with), pepper (with), shower (with); bucket down, pour, rain; career, dash, race, rush, speed, tear.

pen n *lit:* ballpoint, biro, felt-tip, marker, nib, quill; cage, coop, enclosure, hutch, sty; *fig:* prison; *spec:* female swan. **vb** *lit:* be the author of, jot down, write; cage, confine (in), coop up, enclose (in), fence (in), hedge (in), shut (in).

penalize **vb** *lit:* discipline, fine, imprison, punish; handicap, put at a disadvantage.

penalty n *lit:* punishment; fine, forfeit, imprisonment; disadvantage, handicap; free kick, spot kick.

pending **adj** *lit:* hanging fire, remaining, undecided, unsettled, up in the air. **prp** *lit:* awaiting, until; during.

penetrate **vb** *lit:* enter, go through, perforate, pierce; get (into), infiltrate, permeate, seep, suffuse; *fig:* get through to, impress, reach, touch; comprehend, fathom, figure out, unravel, work out.

penetrating **adj** *lit:* biting, pervasive, piercing, pungent, sharp, shrill; *fig:* acute, astute, discerning, incisive, keen, perceptive, quick, searching, sharp, shrewd.

pension n *lit:* allowance, benefit; annuity, superannuation; *spec:* boarding-house, guest-house.

people n *lit:* human beings, mankind, persons; citizens, community, inhabitants, nation, population, tribe; general public, laity, masses, mob, populace, voters; family, folks, household, kinfolk, parents; party, side, team; employees, staff. **vb** *lit:* inhabit, occupy, settle; populate.

peppery **adj** *lit:* fiery, hot, piquant, pungent, spicy; *fig:* hot-tempered, irascible, irritable, snappy, touchy, waspish; biting, caustic, sarcastic, sharp, stinging.

perceive vb *lit:* become aware of, discern, notice, recognize, spot; be aware of, behold, distinguish, observe, see; apprehend, comprehend, conclude, deduce, gather, get, grasp, realize, understand.

perception n *lit:* apprehension, discernment, grasp, recognition; awareness, observation, sense; impression, notion, understanding; consciousness, sensation.

perceptive adj *lit:* acute, alert, astute, discerning, observant, percipient, quick, sharp, shrewd.

perch n *lit:* branch, pole, resting-place, roost; seat; bar, peg.
vb *lit:* alight (on), land (on), rest, settle; sit (on); balance (on).

perfect vb *lit:* complete, consummate, effect, finish, fulfil; accomplish, carry out, perform; cultivate, develop, improve, polish up. adj *lit:* absolute, complete, consummate, entire, finished, unadulterated, utter, whole; excellent, faultless, flawless, ideal, impeccable, sublime, superb, unblemished, untarnished; accurate, correct, exact, precise, spot-on, unerring; accomplished, adept, expert, masterly, polished, skilful.

performance n *lit:* accomplishment, achievement, carrying out, completion, discharge, execution, exploit, feat; action, behaviour, conduct, efficiency, functioning, operation, practice, working; acting, appearance, exhibition, interpretation, portrayal, presentation, production, representation; act, carry-on, fuss, palaver, to-do.

period n *lit:* span, spell, time, while; interval, season, stage, stretch, term; cycle, revolution; age, epoch, era; dot, full stop, point; *spec:* menstruation; lesson time.

perish vb *lit:* be killed, die, expire, lose one's life, pass away; be destroyed, go under, vanish; decay, decompose, rot, waste, wither.

perky adj *lit:* brisk, jaunty, pert, saucy, self-assertive.

permanent adj *lit:* fixed, immutable, imperishable, indelible, indestructible, invariable, lasting, perpetual, persistent, steadfast, unchanging.

permit n *lit:* authorization, documentation, licence, papers, pass, ticket, visa, warrant. vb *lit:* allow, authorize, consent to, endorse, give leave to, grant, licence, sanction; acquiesce in, submit to, tolerate.

perpetual *adj lit:* eternal, everlasting, never-ending, undying, unending; constant, continual, endless, incessant, interminable, persistent, recurrent, unceasing, uninterrupted, unremitting.

perplex *vb lit:* baffle, bewilder, confound, confuse, dumbfound, puzzle, stump; complicate, entangle, jumble, mix up, tangle.

persecute *vb lit:* ill-treat, maltreat, oppress, torment, victimize; afflict, molest; harass, hound, hunt, pursue; *fig:* annoy, badger, bother, pester, worry.

persevering *adj (pr.pt) lit:* diligent, dogged, indefatigable, lasting, persistent, pertinacious, tenacious; resolute, steadfast; long-suffering, patient.

persist *vb lit:* be dogged (in), be tenacious (in), persevere (in), stand firm (in); carry on, continue, keep going, keep up, last, remain.

persistent *adj lit:* assiduous, dogged, indefatigable, pertinacious, resolute, steadfast, tenacious, tireless; immovable, obdurate, obstinate, stubborn; constant, continual, continuous, incessant, lasting, perpetual, relentless, remaining, unrelenting, unremitting.

personality *n lit:* appearance, character, disposition, make-up, nature, temper, temperament; identity; attractiveness, charisma, charm, magnetism; dynamism; *fig:* celebrity, household name, personage, star.

personnel *n lit:* employees, hands, members, people, staff, workers, work force.

perspire *vb lit:* sweat, swelter; drip, exude, secrete.

persuade *vb lit:* coax, entice, induce, influence, prevail upon; egg on, incite; convince (that), satisfy (that).

persuasion *n lit:* cajolery, enticement, exhortation, inducement, wheedling; belief, conviction, creed, faith, opinion, tenet, view; cult, denomination, faction, party, school of thought, sect, side.

pert *adj lit:* bold, forward, free-speaking, impudent, provocative, saucy; jaunty, stylish; in good spirits, lively.

perturb vb *lit:* agitate, alarm, bother, disconcert, disquiet, disturb, fluster, ruffle, upset, worry; confuse, disarrange, muddle, unsettle.

perverse adj *lit:* abnormal, depraved, deviant, immoral, unnatural; awkward, argumentative, intractable, mulish, obdurate, obstinate, pig-headed, stubborn, wayward, wilful; cantankerous, fractious, ill-tempered, peevish, refractory, sullen, surly.

pervert n *lit:* debauchee; deviant. vb *lit:* distort, falsify, misinterpret, misrepresent, misuse, twist, warp; corrupt, debase, debauch, deprave, lead astray, subvert.

pest n *lit:* annoyance, bore, bother, irritation, nuisance, pain, trial; blight, curse, infection, infestation, parasite, pestilence, plague.

pet n *lit:* darling, favourite, jewel, treasure; animal; huff, rage, tantrum. vb *lit:* baby, coddle, cosset, pamper, spoil; caress, fondle, pat, stroke; cuddle, kiss, neck, smooch. adj *lit:* cherished, dearest, favoured, particular, preferred, special; caged, domesticated, family, tame, trained.

petition n *lit:* appeal, application, entreaty, plea, request, suit, supplication. vb *lit:* appeal to, ask, beg, beseech, call upon, entreat, plead with, solicit, supplicate; urge.

petty adj *lit:* contemptible, insignificant, little, measly, minor, negligible, paltry, slight, trivial, unimportant; cheap, grudging, mean, shabby, stingy; inferior, lower, subordinate.

phase n *lit:* juncture, period, stage, time; condition, development, state; chapter. vb *lit:* carry out by stages; make regular; synchronize; get (in), move (in); get (out), move (out).

phenomenal adj *lit:* extraordinary, fantastic, miraculous, outstanding, prodigious, remarkable, sensational, singular, unique, unparalleled.

phenomenon n *lit:* circumstance, event, fact, happening, incident, occurrence; exception, marvel, miracle, prodigy, rarity, sensation, wonder.

philistine n *lit:* barbarian, boor, ignoramus, lowbrow. adj *lit:* barbarian, boorish, crass, loutish, lowbrow, unappreciative, uncultivated, uneducated, unrefined.

philosophy n *lit:* logic, metaphysics, rationalism, reasoning, thinking, thought; attitude to life, beliefs, convictions, ideology, principles, tenets, values, viewpoint; composure, coolness, equanimity, resignation, self-possession, stoicism.

phlegmatic adj *lit:* apathetic, cold, dull, frigid, heavy, impassive, lethargic, placid, sluggish, stoic, stolid, undemonstrative, unemotional, unimpressed.

phoney n *lit:* counterfeit, fake, forgery, fraud, impostor, pretender, sham. adj *lit:* affected, assumed, bogus, counterfeit, ersatz, fake, forged, imitation, sham, trick.

photograph n *lit:* halftone, likeness, picture, print, shot, slide, snap, snapshot, transparency. vb *lit:* film, shoot, snap, take a picture of.

phrase n *lit:* clause, expression, motto, proverb, remark, saying, slogan, tag, term. vb *lit:* articulate, couch, express, formulate, frame, put, say, word.

physical adj *lit:* bodily, carnal, corporeal; fleshly, profane, secular, temporal, unspiritual; actual, material, natural, palpable, real, solid, tangible, visible.

pick n *lit:* choice, decision, option, preference, selection; choicest, élite, flower, pride; adze, axe, hammer; hook, spike. vb *lit:* choose, decide upon, elect, opt for, select, settle upon, single out; instigate, provoke, start; nibble (at), peck (at); break open, crack, force, jemmy, open, prise open.

picture n *lit:* depiction, description, image, impression, re-creation, replica, representation, reproduction; artwork, drawing, engraving, illustration, likeness, painting, photograph, portrait, print, sketch; film, motion picture, movie; *fig:* carbon copy, double, duplicate, living image, portrait, twin; archetype, embodiment, epitome, essence, personification. vb *lit:* conceive of, see, visualize; depict, describe, draw, illustrate, map, paint, photograph, plan, portray, render, represent, sketch.

piece n *lit:* bit, chunk, division, fraction, iota, morsel, mouthful, portion, section, segment, slice; fragment, scrap, sherd, smithereen; article, composition, creation, item, production, work of art; example, sample, specimen; fire-arm, gun, pistol, revolver; coin; *fig:* baggage, woman; entity, unity, whole; instance, occurrence, stroke; *spec:* man (in chess, draughts). **vb** *lit:* connect (together), fit (together), fix (together), patch (together).

pier **n** *lit:* breakwater, groyne, jetty, mole, quay, wharf; buttress, column, pile, pillar, upright; stand, support.

pierce **vb** *lit:* drill, penetrate, prick, puncture, run through, spike, stab, transfix; *fig:* cut to the quick, move, pain, sting, strike, thrill, wound.

piercing **adj** *lit:* ear-splitting, high-pitched, shattering, shrill; arctic, biting, bitter, freezing, numbing, raw; acute, agonizing, excruciating, exquisite, intense, racking, sharp, stabbing; *fig:* alert, keen, penetrating, perceptive, probing, searching, shrewd.

pig **n** *lit:* boar, hog, piglet, porker, sow, swine; *fig:* glutton, guzzler; animal, beast, brute, slob; burden, chore, hardship, problem; *spec:* ingot, mould (in an iron foundry).

pile **n** *lit:* accumulation, heap, hoard, mound, stack; building, edifice, structure; beam, column, pier, pillar, support, upright; fibre, hair, nap, shag; battery, generator, reactor; *fig:* large amount, lot, quantity; fortune, mint, packet; *spec:* haemorrhoid. **vb** *lit:* accumulate, amass, gather, heap, hoard, stack, store; crowd, crush, flood, jam, pack, rush.

pillage **n** *lit:* despoliation, looting, plundering, rapine, robbery, sack; booty, loot, plunder, spoils. **vb** *lit:* despoil, loot, maraud, plunder, raid, ransack, ravage, rob, sack, strip.

pilot **n** *lit:* airman, aviator; guide, helmsman, steersman; captain, coxswain, navigator. **vb** *lit:* control, direct, drive, fly, guide, handle, navigate, operate, steer. **adj** *lit:* experimental, initial, introductory, preliminary trial.

pin **n** *lit:* nail, tack; needle, spike; key, peg, rod; axle, bar, cross-piece, lever, spindle, toggle; skittle; *fig:* leg; *spec:* flag (in golf). **vb** *lit:* affix, attach, fasten, fix, nail, secure, tack; *fig:* hold down, immobilize, pinion, restrain.

pinch n *lit:* nip, squeeze, tweak; bit, dash, soupçon, speck, taste; *fig:* crisis, emergency, hardship, plight, predicament. **vb** *lit:* nip, squeeze, tweak; chafe, confine, cramp, crush; afflict, oppress; economize, scrimp; *fig:* filch, pilfer, purloin, snatch, steal; apprehend, arrest, pull in, take into custody.

pine **vb** *lit:* ache, hanker, hunger (for), long, lust, wish, yearn; grieve (for); decline, droop, dwindle, fade, languish, sicken, waste, wilt, wither.

pinnacle n *lit:* acme, apex, crest, height, peak, summit, vertex, zenith; obelisk, spire, steeple.

pioneer n *lit:* colonizer, frontiersman, settler; explorer, leader; deviser, discoverer, founder, innovator, inventor. **vb** *lit:* devise, develop, discover, initiate, instigate, invent, launch, open up.

pipe n *lit:* channel, conduit, cylinder, duct, flue, hose, tube, vessel; briar; fife, flute, penny-whistle, whistle; *spec:* mass, vein (of ore); vent (of a volcano). **vb** *lit:* channel, duct, convey, lead, siphon; play, whistle; *fig:* speak shrilly, trill, tweet, twitter, warble.

pirate n *lit:* brigand, buccaneer, corsair, freebooter, raider; copyright-breaker, plagiarist. **vb** *lit:* copy, lift, plagiarize, poach; appropriate, take over.

pit n *lit:* hole, mine, shaft; abyss, chasm; crater, dent, indentation, trench. **vb** *lit:* dent, gouge, indent, nick, notch, scar; *fig:* match, oppose, set (against).

pitch n *lit:* arena, ground, playing-field, sports-field; gradient, incline, slant, slope, tilt; degree, height, level, point; modulation, sound frequency, tone; *fig:* line, patter, sales talk, spiel.
vb *lit:* cast, chuck, fling, heave, launch, sling, throw, toss; erect, plant, put up, set up, station; flounder, lurch, plunge, wallow; dive, drop, topple, tumble.

pitiful adj *lit:* distressing, heart-rending, pathetic, piteous, sad, wretched; abject, contemptible, despicable, miserable, shabby, sorry, worthless.

pity n *lit:* compassion, empathy, feeling, sympathy; clemency, mercy; commiseration; sad thing, shame.   **vb** *lit:* be compassionate towards, bleed for, commiserate with, empathize with, feel for, sympathize with.

place n *lit:* location, position, site, spot, venue; area, district, locality, manor, neighbourhood, region, vicinity; town, village; accommodation, dwelling, home, house, property, residence; chair, reservation, seat; stead; *fig:* room, space; affair, concern, function, prerogative, responsibility; precedence; office, rank, station, status; appointment, employment, job, post.   **vb** *lit:* deposit, lay, put, rest, set, stand; arrange, dispose, locate, position, situate, station; allocate, appoint, assign, commission, put out; invest; establish, fix; classify, grade, group, order, sort; identify, know, recognize, remember.

plague n *lit:* epidemic, pandemic, pestilence; affliction, blight, contagion, disease, infection, infestation; *fig:* cancer, curse, scourge, trial; aggravation, annoyance, bother, nuisance, pain, pest.   **vb** *lit:* afflict, annoy, badger, bother, fret, harass, hassle, persecute, pester, tease, trouble, worry.

plain n *lit:* plateau, prairie, steppe, tableland; heath, moor, open country.   **adj** *lit:* even, flat, level, smooth; clear, conspicuous, distinct, evident, obvious; comprehensible, legible, unambiguous; blunt, candid, forthright, frank, outspoken, straightforward; common, everyday, homely, ordinary; discreet, modest, restrained, simple, unadorned, unaffected, unpretentious; austere, bare, spartan, stark; ill-favoured, unalluring, unattractive, unprepossessing.

plan n *lit:* design, draft, idea, plot, project, proposal, proposition, scheme, strategy; method, programme, scenario, schema, script; blueprint, chart, diagram, drawing, elevation, layout, map, sketch.   **vb** *lit:* design, devise, draft, formulate, plot, scheme, think up; arrange, contrive, lay out, map out, organize, outline, project, propose; aim (to), intend (to), mean (to), propose (to).

plane n *lit:* flat, level, surface; degree, layer, stratum; aeroplane, aircraft, jet; file, rasp, scraper, shaver, smoother.   **vb** *lit:* glide, skate, skim; carom.   **adj** *lit:* even, flat, flush, level, smooth, uniform.

plant n *lit:* flower, vegetable, vegetation; cutting, offshoot; *fig:* factory, foundry, mill, works; apparatus, equipment, gear, machinery;

plate 298

agent, informer, inside man, mole, spy, undercover agent. **vb** *lit:*
disseminate, embed, put in, scatter, seed, sow; *fig:* establish, found,
institute; place, post, station, settle; convey, deliver, strike.

plate n *lit:* dish, platter; lamina, layer, panel, sheet; badge, panel;
block, mould, stencil; brace, denture; *fig:* illustration, print; cup,
trophy; foot; *spec:* base (in baseball); precious metal, silver; racing
horseshoe. **vb** *lit:* coat, cover, electroplate, gild, laminate, overlay.

platform n *lit:* dais, podium, rostrum, stage; basis, raised surface;
railway station; gun mounting; oilrig; *fig:* manifesto, policy.

play n *lit:* comedy, drama, performance, piece, stage show, tragedy;
diversion, entertainment, fun; leisure activity, pastime, recreation,
sport; gambling, gaming; exercise; *fig:* leeway, margin, movement,
range, room, scope, slack, space; (in) action, (in) function, (in)
operation. **vb** *lit:* amuse oneself, entertain oneself, have fun; frolic,
gambol, revel, romp; toy (with), trifle (with); compete, contend
against, participate, take on, take part in, vie with; act, impersonate,
portray, take the part of; bet on, gamble on, speculate on, wager on;
discharge (over), shower (over), spray (over); make music with,
perform with; allow leeway, give room.

playful adj *lit:* coy, flirtatious, frisky, frolicsome, humorous,
impish, jokey, kittenish, lively, merry, mischievous, roguish, sportive,
sprightly, vivacious, waggish.

plea n *lit:* appeal, entreaty, intercession, petition, request,
supplication; argument, claim, defence, excuse, explanation,
vindication.

plead vb *lit:* appeal, ask, beg, beseech, entreat, implore, petition,
request; argue, assert, claim, give as an excuse, maintain.

pleasant adj *lit:* agreeable, delectable, delightful, enjoyable,
gratifying, pleasurable, refreshing, satisfying, welcome; affable,
amiable, charming, cheerful, congenial, engaging, friendly, good-
humoured, likable, nice.

please vb *lit:* delight, gladden, gratify; amuse, charm, cheer;
humour, indulge, serve; content, satisfy, suit; be inclined, choose,
like, see fit, want, wish.

pleasure n *lit:* delectation, delight, gratification; amusement, contentment, enjoyment, happiness, satisfaction; choice, desire, inclination, preference, will, wish.

pledge n *lit:* assurance, oath, undertaking, vow, word of honour; bail, bond, deposit, guarantee, pawn, security; *fig:* health, toast. **vb** *lit:* contract, give one's word, promise, undertake, vouch, vow; guarantee, mortgage; *fig:* drink the health of, drink to, toast.

plenty n *lit:* ample, heaps, lots, masses, much, oodles, piles, quantities, stacks, superabundance; abundance, copiousness, fruitfulness, profusion; affluence, luxury, opulence, prosperity, wealth.

plot n *lit:* conspiracy, intrigue, machination, plan, scheme; allotment, area, lot, patch, site, stretch, tract; action, gist, scenario, schema, story, story-line, thread. **vb** *lit:* collude, conspire, intrigue, machinate, plan, scheme; calculate, chart, compute, draft, draw, map, outline; concoct, cook up, design, devise, frame; arrange for, organize, set up.

pluck n *lit:* backbone, bravery, courage, grit, guts, mettle, nerve, resolution, spirit. **vb** *lit:* cull, gather, pick, pull out; jerk, pull, snatch, tug, yank; pick, strum, thrum, twang; *fig:* fleece, rob; *spec:* de-feather (a bird to prepare it for eating).

plug n *lit:* bung, cork, spigot, stopper; cake, quid, wad; *fig:* advertisement, mention, puff, push. **vb** *lit:* block, bung, cork, cover, pack, stop, stuff; *fig:* advertise, build up, hype, promote, publicize, push; gun down, pot, put a bullet in, shoot; drudge (away at), grind (away at), peg (away at), slog (away at).

plunge n *lit:* dive, drop, fall, immersion, swoop. **vb** *lit:* dive, drop, fall, lurch, nose-dive, pitch, plummet, swoop, tumble; dip, douse, dunk, immerse, sink, submerge; *fig:* career, dash, hurtle.

ply vb *lit:* carry on, exercise, practise, pursue, work at; employ, use, utilize; handle, manipulate, wield; assail, beset, bombard, deluge, importune; cruise, prowl, sail, travel.

poet n *lit:* lyricist, rhymer, versifier; bard, troubadour, skald; *fig:* aesthete.

poetic adj *lit:* aesthetic, descriptive, sensitive, sensual, sublime, vivid; affecting, ecstatic, moving; elegiac, in verse, lyrical, metrical, rhyming, rhythmical.

point n *lit:* dot, full stop, period, speck; location, place, position, site, spot; apex, end, spike, summit, tine; cape, headland, promontory; mark, score, unit; *fig:* degree, extent, stage; instant, juncture, moment, time; aim, end, goal, intention, motive, object, purpose, reason; core, crux, essence, gist, idea, meaning, theme; aspect, detail, feature, instance, item, particular; attribute, characteristic, peculiarity, trait; *spec:* (compass) bearing; (pen) nib. vb *lit:* call attention (to), direct (to); pick (out), single (out); aim (at), direct (at), level (at), train (at); sharpen, taper, whet; *spec:* arrange, set (canticles to music).

pointless adj *lit:* aimless, futile, inane, irrelevant, meaningless, nonsensical, unproductive, useless, vain, worthless.

poison n *lit:* toxin, venom; *fig:* contamination, corruption, malignancy. vb *lit:* administer a lethal dose to; contaminate, kill, pollute; *fig:* embitter, sour; corrupt, defile, mar, taint, undermine; deprave, pervert, warp.

poisonous adj *lit:* toxic, venomous; corrosive; deadly, fatal, lethal, virulent; *fig:* malicious, pernicious, scathing, vicious.

pole n *lit:* boom, handle, mast, paling, post, rod, shaft, stick; electrode, terminal; *fig:* antipode, extremity.

police n *lit:* constabulary, force, law. vb *lit:* control, guard, monitor, patrol, regulate, supervise, watch.

policy n *lit:* code, line, method, practice, procedure, protocol, rule, strategy; approach, custom; *fig:* discretion, prudence, shrewdness; cunning.

polish n *lit:* varnish, wax; brightness, finish, gloss, lustre, sheen, sparkle; *fig:* class, finesse, panache, refinement, style. vb *lit:* buff, burnish, clean, shine, wax; *fig:* brush (up), touch (up).

polite adj *lit:* civil, courteous, mannerly, well-mannered; civilized, cultured, elegant, genteel, polished, well-bred.

poll n *lit:* ballot, election, plebiscite, referendum, vote; census, survey; count, figures, returns, tally. **vb** *lit:* ballot, hold a referendum, take it to a vote; canvass, register, notch up, tally; interview, question, survey.

pollute **vb** *lit:* contaminate, dirty, foul, infect, soil, taint; *fig:* corrupt, defile, deprave, desecrate, mar, profane, sully.

pompous **adj** *lit:* bloated, grandiose, ostentatious, portentous, pretentious, priggish, self-important, snobbish, vainglorious; boastful, bombastic, inflated, orotund, overblown, turgid.

ponder **vb** *lit:* brood, cerebrate, cogitate, contemplate, deliberate, give thought to, mull (over), muse, puzzle (over), ruminate, think about.

pool n *lit:* lake, mere, pond, puddle, reservoir, tarn; swimming-bath; *fig:* collective, consortium, group, syndicate, team; funds, jackpot, kitty, stakes. **vb** *lit:* amalgamate, combine, group, merge, share.

poor **adj** *lit:* badly off, destitute, hard up, impoverished, needy, penurious, poverty-stricken; deficient, inadequate, insufficient, meagre, niggardly, reduced, scanty, skimpy, sparse, straitened; faulty, inferior, mediocre, rotten, rubbishy, shabby, shoddy, sorry, worthless; bad, bare, barren, depleted, infertile, exhausted, infertile, unproductive; hapless, ill-fated, miserable, pathetic, unfortunate, wretched; humble, insignificant, mean, modest, paltry, trivial.

popular **adj** *lit:* common, conventional, general, prevailing, public, standard, stock, ubiquitous, widespread; approved, famous, fashionable, favourite, in, in demand, sought-after, well-liked.

population n *lit:* community, denizens, inhabitants, natives, people, residents, society.

port n *lit:* anchorage, docks, harbour, haven, marina, mooring, roads; door, doorway, embrasure, gate, outlet, shutter, window; larboard, left-hand side; fortified red wine.

portion n *lit:* bit, morsel, part, piece, segment; allocation, allotment, allowance, lot, quota, ration, share; helping, serving; *fig:* destiny, fate, fortune, luck. **vb** *lit:* dole (out), parcel (out), share (out).

pose n *lit:* attitude, bearing, demeanour, posture, stance; affectation, façade, front, masquerade, pretence, role. **vb** *lit:* model, sit (for); masquerade (as), pass oneself off (as); posture, put on airs, show off, strike an attitude; arrange, position; advance, present, propound, put forward, set.

position n *lit:* bearings, locale, location, place, site, situation, whereabouts; attitude, pose, stance; job, office, post; *fig:* angle, outlook, point of view, standpoint; circumstances, pass, plight, predicament, state, strait(s); caste, class, importance, prestige, rank, standing, status; capacity, function, role. **vb** *lit:* arrange, array, lay out, place, put, set.

positive adj *lit:* categorical, certain, conclusive, decisive, definitive, emphatic, express, firm, indisputable, real, unequivocal; affirmative; beneficial, constructive, efficacious, helpful, practical, progressive, useful; assured, confident, convinced, sure; absolute, complete, consummate, thorough, unmitigated; dogmatic, emphatic, forceful; insistent, obdurate, resolute, stubborn.

possess vb *lit:* be blessed with, enjoy, have, hold, keep, own, retain; acquire, seize, take over, usurp; *fig:* bewitch, enchant, entrance, mesmerize, obsess, put under a spell; control, dominate.

possession n *lit:* asset(s), belonging(s), effect(s), estate, property; control, custody, hold, occupancy, ownership, proprietorship, tenure, title; colony, dominion, protectorate, territory.

possessive adj *lit:* acquisitive, covetous, grasping, greedy; retentive, tenacious; jealous, overprotective.

possible adj *lit:* conceivable, credible, feasible, imaginable, practicable, viable; hypothetical, potential, theoretical; on, realizable, within reach.

post n *lit:* column, pale, pillar, pole, stake, support, upright; mail, postal service; appointment, assignment, job, office, position, situation; beat, place, station; *spec:* (winning-)line; pin (in a lock). **vb** *lit:* assign, establish, place, position, put, station; advertise, display, publicize, publish, put up; dispatch, mail, send; advise, brief, fill in on, notify, report to.

posture   n *lit:* attitude, bearing, pose, position, set, stance; *fig:* disposition, frame of mind, outlook, point of view; circumstance, mode, phase, situation, state.   **vb** *lit:* pose, put on airs, show off, strut, swagger.

pot   n *lit:* bowl, container, dish, jar, pan, urn, vessel; hole, cave; lavatory, po, toilet; cup, trophy; *fig:* kitty, pool, stakes; shot, shy, throw; paunch, potbelly; *spec:* basket, trap (for catching lobsters); cone, stack (on a chimney); large sum (of money); cannabis, marijuana.   **vb** *lit:* turn on the wheel; plant, replant; *fig:* bag, secure, shoot, win; hole, pocket.

potent   adj *lit:* dynamic, effective, efficacious, forceful, mighty, powerful, strong, vigorous; cogent, compelling, impressive, persuasive; authoritative, commanding, dominant, influential.

potential   n *lit:* capacity, power, resources; ability, aptitude, capability, makings.   **adj** *lit:* budding, dormant, future, inherent, latent, possible, undeveloped.

pounce   n *lit:* dart, jump, leap, spring, swoop; ambush.   **vb** *lit:* fall (upon), jump (on), leap (on), swoop down (upon).

pout   n *lit:* cross look, glower, grimace, lowering, moue.   **vb** *lit:* glower, grimace, look petulant, look sullen, mope, pull a long face, sulk.

poverty   n *lit:* beggary, destitution, insolvency, pennilessness, penury, privation; inadequacy, lack, paucity, scarcity, shortage; *fig:* aridity, barrenness, infertility, sterility.

power   n *lit:* brawn, clout, force, might, muscle, strength; ability, capability, capacity, competence, faculty, potential; energy, vigour; authority, command, control, dominance, influence, supremacy, sway; authorization, licence, prerogative, right, warrant.

powerful   adj *lit:* brawny, mighty, muscular, robust, stalwart, strapping, strong, sturdy; energetic, vigorous; authoritative, commanding, dominant, forceful, influential; compelling, convincing, effectual, impressive.

powerless   adj *lit:* defenceless, helpless, impotent, incapable, ineffectual; disabled, incapacitated, paralysed; debilitated, feeble, frail, vulnerable, weak; captive, chained, manacled, shackled.

practical adj *lit:* applied, functional, pragmatic, utilitarian; adept, ingenious, inventive, resourceful; businesslike, down-to-earth, factual, matter-of-fact, mundane, realistic, sensible; feasible, practicable, serviceable, sound, workable; accomplished, efficient, experienced, proficient, skilled, working.

practically adv *lit:* almost, in effect, just about, nearly, to all intents and purposes, virtually; factually, rationally, realistically, reasonably, sensibly; efficiently, ingeniously, inventively, resourcefully.

practice n *lit:* custom, habit, mode, routine, rule, tradition, usage, way; application, experience, operation, use; career, profession, vocation, work; drill, exercise, rehearsal, training, work-out.

practise vb *lit:* drill, exercise, prepare, rehearse, run through, train; apply, carry out, do, follow, live up to, observe; carry on, engage in, ply, pursue, work at.

practised adj (pa.pt) *lit:* able, accomplished, adept, efficient, experienced, proficient, skilled, trained, well-rehearsed.

praise n *lit:* acclaim, accolades, applause, commendation, compliments, congratulation, eulogies, panegyrics, tribute; *fig:* adoration, adulation, homage, worship. vb *lit:* acclaim, applaud, commend, compliment, congratulate, eulogize, extol, honour, pay tribute to; adore, adulate, worship.

preach vb *lit:* deliver a sermon, give an address (on); orate, speak, talk; harangue, lecture; *fig:* moralize.

precaution n *lit:* preventative measure, safeguard, safety measure; contingency plan; anticipation, caution, foresight, forethought, wariness.

precede vb *lit:* come before, go before, herald, introduce, lead; antedate; rank before.

preceding adj *lit:* above, aforementioned, earlier, former, previous, prior.

precious adj *lit:* cherished, favourite, prized, treasured, valued; adored, beloved, dearest; costly, expensive, invaluable, priceless, valuable; *fig:* affected, artificial, camp, naff, overnice, twee.

precipice n *lit:* cliff, cliff face, height, rock face, sheer drop; canyon, chasm, chine, gorge, ravine.

precise adj *lit:* accurate, clear-cut, definitive, exact, express, specific; fastidious, finicky, meticulous, nice, particular, scrupulous; prim, puritanical, strict.

precision n *lit:* accuracy, correctness, exactitude, fidelity, meticulousness, scrupulousness, strictness.

precursor n *lit:* ancestor, forebear, predecessor; forerunner, harbinger, herald, messenger, vanguard; originator, pioneer.

predator n *lit:* carnivore, hunter, raptor; *fig:* marauder, plunderer, vulture.

predatory adj *lit:* carnivorous, rapacious, voracious; *fig:* despoiling, destructive, marauding, plundering, raiding, ravaging.

predecessor n *lit:* antecedent, forerunner, precursor; previous occupant; ancestor, forebear, forefather.

predicament n *lit:* corner, dilemma, jam, mess, pickle, plight, quandary, scrape, situation, spot.

predict vb *lit:* augur, forecast, foresee, foretell, prophesy.

predominant adj *lit:* chief, dominant, leading, main, paramount, preponderant, prime, principal, prominent, ruling, supreme.

prefer vb *lit:* choose, favour, go for, like better, opt for, pick, plump for, select, single out; advance, elevate, promote, upgrade; *spec:* file, lodge, press (charges).

preferable adj *lit:* better, eligible, favoured, more desirable, superior.

preference n *lit:* choice, favourite, first choice, option, pick, selection; advantage, precedence, priority.

pregnant adj *lit:* expectant, expecting, gravid, in the family way, with child; *fig:* charged, expressive, meaningful, pointed, revealing, significant, telling, weighty; creative, imaginative, inventive, original; abundant, fecund, fruitful, productive, prolific, teeming.

prejudiced **adj (pa.pt)** *lit:* biased, discriminatory, influenced, jaundiced, narrow-minded, opinionated, partial, partisan, slanted, swayed, unfair.

preliminary **n** *lit:* beginning, first round, foundation, groundwork, initiation, introduction, opening, preface, preparation, start. **adj** *lit:* beginning, exploratory, first, initial, introductory, opening, pilot, precursory, preparatory, qualifying, trial.

premature **adj** *lit:* early, immature, incomplete, undeveloped, untimely; *fig:* hasty, ill-considered, ill-timed, impulsive, inopportune, precipitate.

premier **n** *lit:* chancellor, head of government, prime minister, secretary of state. **adj** *lit:* first, foremost, leading, main, principal, top; earliest, inaugural, initial.

premises **n** *lit:* building, grounds, property, site.

preoccupation **n** *lit:* absent-mindedness, absorption, abstraction, inattentiveness, oblivion, reverie; fixation, hang-up, hobbyhorse, obsession.

preparation **n** *lit:* anticipation, foresight, precaution, provision, readiness; fundamentals, groundwork, research and development; homework, revision, schoolwork, study; compound, concoction, medicine, mixture, tincture; *spec:* devotions (before a church service).

prepare **vb** *lit:* make ready, prime, put in order; coach, equip, fit out, groom, outfit, supply, train, warm up; concoct, contrive, draw up, fix up, make, put together; brace oneself (for), fortify (oneself for), ready (oneself for), strengthen (oneself for).

prepared **adj (pa.pt)** *lit:* all set, arranged, in order, in readiness, ready, set; able (to), disposed (to), inclined (to), of a mind (to), willing (to).

preposterous **adj** *lit:* absurd, incredible, insane, laughable, ludicrous, monstrous, nonsensical, outrageous, ridiculous, unreasonable, unthinkable.

prescription n *lit:* direction, instruction, specification; formula, recipe.

presence n *lit:* attendance, immediacy; company; occupancy, residence; closeness, propinquity, proximity; *fig:* air, carriage, demeanour, personality, poise, self-assurance; apparition, ghost, manifestation, spectre, spirit, wraith.

present n *lit:* now, this moment, time being; donation, endowment, gift, gratuity. **vb** *lit:* acquaint (with), introduce (to), make known (to); demonstrate, display, exhibit, put on, show; advance, expound, introduce, offer, produce, proffer, raise, relate, state, submit, suggest, tender; award, donate (to), endow (with), give. **adj** *lit:* contemporary, current, existing, immediate; accounted for, at hand, available, near, ready, to hand.

preserve n *lit:* area, domain, realm, sphere; game reserve, reservation, sanctuary; conserve(s), jam, jelly, marmalade, pickle. **vb** *lit:* care for, conserve, keep, pickle, protect, safeguard, save, secure, shelter, store; keep up, maintain, perpetuate, sustain, uphold.

press n *lit:* bunch, crowd, crush, mob, multitude, pack, throng; bustle, hassle, pressure, strain, stress, urgency; printing house, printing machine; bookcase, cupboard; *spec:* Fleet Street, Grub Street, journalism, newsmedia, newspapers; columnists, correspondents, journalists, newsmen, photographers, reporters. **vb** *lit:* compress, condense, crush, jam, push, squeeze; cluster, crowd, flock, gather, mill, push, rush, seethe, swarm, throng; flatten, iron, mangle, smooth, steam; clasp, embrace, enfold, hold close, hug; compel, constrain, demand, enforce, force, insist on; beg, exhort, implore, petition, plead, pressurize, sue, supplicate, urge; afflict, assail, beset, besiege, harass, plague, trouble, vex, worry.

pressure n *lit:* compression, crushing, force, squeezing, weight; *fig:* coercion, constraint, influence, obligation, sway; adversity, affliction, demands, distress, hassle, strain, stress.

prestige n *lit:* cachet, celebrity, distinction, eminence, fame, importance, influence, kudos, renown, standing, stature, status, weight.

prestigious **adj** *lit:* celebrated, eminent, esteemed, exalted, great, illustrious, impressive, influential, prominent, renowned.

presume **vb** *lit:* assume, believe, conjecture, postulate, suppose, take for granted, think; dare (to), go so far as (to), have the audacity (to), make so bold as (to), venture (to); count (on), depend (on), rely (on).

presumption **n** *lit:* audacity, boldness, cheek, effrontery, forwardness, gall, impudence, insolence, nerve, presumptuousness; assumption, hypothesis, presupposition, supposition, surmise; grounds, likelihood, probability.

presumptuous **adj** *lit:* audacious, bold, cheeky, forward, impudent, insolent, pushy, too big for one's boots, uppish.

pretence **n** *lit:* affectation, artifice, charade, cover, deceit, display, fabrication, façade, falsehood, guise, make-believe, pose, pretext, semblance, sham, show, trickery.

pretend **vb** *lit:* affect, dissemble, fake, feign, make out, put on, sham; make believe; purport (to be); aspire (to), lay claim (to).

pretext **n** *lit:* affectation, cloak, cover, device, excuse, mask, ploy, pretence.

pretty **adj** *lit:* appealing, attractive, bonny, charming, comely, cute, good-looking, pleasing, personable; dainty, delicate, neat, nice, trim. **adv** *lit:* fairly, moderately, quite, rather, reasonably, somewhat.

prevent **vb** *lit:* bar, block, debar, foil, frustrate, obstruct, obviate, preclude, stop, thwart; avert, avoid, head off, inhibit, nip in the bud, stave off, ward off.

preventive **n** *lit:* barrier, block, impediment, obstacle, obstruction; precaution, prophylactic, protection, safeguard; condom, rubber. **adj** *lit:* blocking, counteractive, obstructive; deterrent, precautionary, protective.

previously **adv** *lit:* before, beforehand, earlier, in anticipation; formerly, in the past, once; hitherto, until now.

price **n** *lit:* bill, charge, cost, damage, expense, fee, premium, value;

expenditure, outlay; estimate, evaluation; compensation, recompense, reward; odds; *fig:* consequences, penalty, toll.   **vb** *lit:* cost, estimate, evaluate, rate, value.

prick   **n** *lit:* perforation, pinhole, puncture; cock, member, penis, phallus; *fig:* pang, prickle, smart, sting.   **vb** *lit:* drill, jab, perforate, pierce, puncture, stab; bite, prickle, smart, sting, tingle; *fig:* distress, trouble, wound.

prickly   **adj** *lit:* barbed, spiny, thorny; itchy, smarting, stinging, tingling; *fig:* bad-tempered, cantankerous, edgy, grumpy, irritable, peevish, pettish, ratty, snappish, touchy, waspish; complicated, difficult, intricate, involved, knotty, tricky, troublesome.

pride   **n** *lit:* honour, self-esteem, self-respect; arrogance, conceit, egotism, haughtiness, loftiness, presumption, pretention, self-importance; boast, prize, treasure; best, choice, elite, flower, glory; delight, gratification, joy, satisfaction.   **vb** *lit:* be proud of (oneself), congratulate (oneself), flatter (oneself).

primarily   **adv** *lit:* above all, chiefly, for the most part, mainly, mostly, on the whole, principally; basically, essentially, fundamentally; initially, in the first place, originally.

primary   **adj** *lit:* basic, elemental, essential, fundamental, ultimate; capital, cardinal, chief, leading, main, paramount, principal, top; first, initial, introductory; elementary, rudimentary, simple; aboriginal, earliest, primal, primeval; crude, primitive, raw.

prime   **n** *lit:* best, greatest, height, heyday, peak, perfection; *fig:* beginning, opening; spring; *spec:* (musical) keynote, tonic; (musical) octave.   **vb** *lit:* coach, get ready, groom, prepare, train; charge, fuel, fill, load; brief, fill in, inform, tell; size, undercoat, whitewash.   **adj** *lit:* best, choice, excellent, first-rate, highest, perfect, superior, top-grade; basic, fundamental, original, primary, underlying; leading, main, predominant, principal; *spec:* indivisible (number).

primitive   **adj** *lit:* early, prehistoric, primeval, primordial; earliest, first; crude, elementary, rudimentary, unrefined, unsophisticated; barbarian, savage, uncivilized; childlike, naive, simple, untrained.

principal n *lit:* chairperson, chief, director, head, president; dean, director, headmaster, headmistress, rector; guarantor, security; culprit, ringleader; duellist; assets, capital, money; girder, main beam, rafter; *spec:* first violin (in an orchestra); lead, star (of a show). **adj** *lit:* cardinal, chief, crucial, dominant, essential, foremost, key, leading, main, paramount, pre-eminent, primary, prime, vital.

principle n *lit:* axiom, doctrine, dogma, golden rule, law, maxim, precept, rule; belief, code, creed, ethic, tenet; approach, attitude, thesis, way of thinking; conscience, duty, honour, integrity, morality, virtue; *fig:* active ingredient, flavour.

print n *lit:* impression; font, fount, type, typeface; engraving; photograph, positive, reproduction; fingerprint. **vb** *lit:* imprint, press in, stamp; go to press, run off.

priority n *lit:* precedence, pre-eminence, preference, seniority, superiority, supremacy; essential, prerequisite, requirement, sine qua non.

prison n *lit:* gaol, jail, lockup, penal institution, penitentiary; choky, clink, jug, nick, stir.

private adj *lit:* exclusive, individual, intimate, own, personal; confidential, in camera, secret; concealed, isolated, not overlooked, secluded, solitary; independent, non-incorporated, unaffiliated.

prize n *lit:* award, reward, trophy; jackpot, purse, winnings; booty, haul, loot, pickings, plunder, swag; *fig:* aim, ambition, desire, goal. **vb** *lit:* appreciate, esteem, regard highly, treasure, value. **adj** *lit:* award-winning, champion, first-rate, outstanding, top-class.

probably adv *lit:* almost certainly, doubtless, in all likelihood, most likely, presumably, surely.

problem n *lit:* brain-teaser, conundrum, enigma, puzzle, riddle; difficulty, predicament, quandary, snag, trouble; complication, dilemma, doubt. **adj** *lit:* delinquent, difficult, unmanageable, unruly, wayward.

procedure n *lit:* conduct, course, method, modus operandi, plan of action, policy, practice, process, routine, scheme, strategy, way of working.

proceed vb *lit:* carry on, continue, get on (with), go ahead, go on, press on (with); arise (from), come (from), derive (from), emanate (from), issue (from), originate (from), stem (from); ensue, follow, result.

process n *lit:* course of action, means, measure, method, mode, operation, practice; action, case, suit, trial. vb *lit:* deal with, handle, take care of; alter, prepare, refine, transform, treat.

procession n *lit:* cavalcade, cortège, motorcade, parade; crocodile, file, line, queue, sequence, series, succession; course, cycle.

proclaim vb *lit:* advertise, announce, blaze (abroad), circulate, declare, enunciate, give out, make known, promulgate, pronounce, publish, trumpet.

prod n *lit:* elbow, jab, nudge, poke, push, shove; goad, poker, spur, stick; *fig:* cue, prompt, reminder, signal. vb *lit:* dig, elbow, jab, nudge, poke, push, shove; drive, egg on, goad, incite, motivate, prick, prompt, spur, stir, urge.

produce n *lit:* crop, harvest, yield; groceries, products. vb *lit:* come up with, construct, create, devise, invent, make, manufacture, put together, turn out; bear, bring forth, deliver, generate; furnish, render, supply, yield; bring about, cause, effect, give rise to, set off, start; elongate, extend, protract; advance, bring to light, demonstrate, exhibit, offer, put forward, set out; direct, do, mount, perform, present, put on, stage.

production n *lit:* assembly, construction, manufacture, preparation; creation, generation, origination; marketing, presentation, supply; bringing to light, disclosure, revelation; direction, mounting, performance, staging.

productive adj *lit:* creative, inventive; fecund, fertile, fruitful, prolific, vigorous; *fig:* advantageous, constructive, effective, effectual, efficacious, helpful, profitable, rewarding, useful, worthwhile.

profession n *lit:* business, calling, line of work, métier, occupation, vocation; acknowledgement, affirmation, assertion, confession, declaration, statement, testimony; claim.

professional n *lit:* business executive, career man/woman, employee, non-amateur, wage-earner; artist, expert, master, virtuoso; specialist. **adj** *lit:* career-minded, employed, full-time, managerial, non-amateur, salaried, wage-earning; vocational; competent, experienced, expert, polished, proficient, qualified, skilled, trained.

profile n *lit:* contour, outline, side view, silhouette; drawing, figure, portrait, sketch; biography, cameo, character sketch, vignette; *fig:* chart, diagram, graph, table; analysis, study, survey.

profit n *lit:* earnings, gains, proceeds, return, revenue, takings, yield; advantage, benefit, good, help, use, value. **vb** *lit:* aid, benefit, gain, help, improve, serve, stand in good stead; make a killing, make money.

profitable adj *lit:* commercial, cost-effective, lucrative, money-making, remunerative, rewarding; advantageous, beneficial, productive, useful, valuable, worthwhile.

profound adj *lit:* deep, insightful, penetrating, philosophical, sagacious, subtle, thoughtful, wise; erudite, learned, recondite; abstruse, difficult, serious; abyssal, bottomless, cavernous, infernal, yawning; heartfelt, intense, keen, sincere; extensive, extreme, far-reaching, great, immense, vast, wide-ranging.

programme n *lit:* agenda, list, order, plan, procedure, schedule, scheme, sequence, syllabus, timetable; cast-list, line-up; performance, presentation, production, show. **vb** *lit:* arrange, bill, book, line up, schedule, organize; itemize, list, plan; order, put in sequence.

progress n *lit:* advance, journey, movement, passage, way; advancement, betterment, development, growth, headway, improvement, promotion. **vb** *lit:* advance, come on, get farther, get on, make headway, move forward, proceed, travel, work one's way up; develop, grow, improve; blossom, gain, increase.

progressive adj *lit:* accelerating, advancing, developing, increasing, intensifying, worsening; continuous, ongoing; dynamic, enterprising;

fig: advanced, avant-garde, go-ahead, radical, reformist, revolutionary; enlightened, liberal, open.

prohibited adj (pa.pt) *lit:* banned, barred, embargoed, forbidden, illegal, interdicted, proscribed, outlawed; made impossible, precluded, prevented, stopped.

project n *lit:* assignment, enterprise, job, plan, programme, scheme, task, undertaking, venture; proposal, proposition. **vb** *lit:* beetle, extend forward, jut out, overhang, protrude, stick out; fling, hurl; launch, propel, throw; broadcast, radiate, transmit; estimate, forecast, foretell, predict; design, devise, draft, frame, outline, plan, scheme.

projection n *lit:* bulge, extension, overhang, protrusion; jetty, pier; ledge, ridge, shelf, sill; launch, propulsion; radiation, transmission; cinematography, screening; estimate, forecast, prediction, prognosis; blueprint, outline, plan; *spec:* (astral) externalization, independence, transference; (mental) telekinesis, telepathy.

prolong vb *lit:* extend, lengthen, make longer, produce, project, protract; carry on, continue; drag out, stretch.

promenade n *lit:* esplanade, parade; pier, sea-front, terrace; amble, constitutional, saunter, stroll; *fig:* drive, ride; dance. **vb** *lit:* amble, perambulate, saunter, stroll, take a walk; flaunt, parade, show off; *spec:* stand (at a concert).

prominence n *lit:* crag, headland, height, projection, promontory, spur; bulge, hummock, lump, mound, protrusion, protuberance, rise, swelling; conspicuousness, distinctiveness, dominance, salience, visibility; distinction, precedence; celebrity, eminence, fame, importance, prestige, reputation, standing.

prominent adj *lit:* beetling, jutting, protruding, protuberant; conspicuous, eye-catching, noticeable, obvious, pronounced, striking, unmistakable; celebrated, distinguished, eminent, famous, important, leading, main, outstanding, pre-eminent, renowned, top, well-known.

promise n *lit:* assurance, bond, commitment, oath, pledge, undertaking, vow, word of honour; *fig:* ability, aptitude, capability, flair, potential, talent. **vb** *lit:* assure, contract, engage, give an undertaking, give one's word, pledge, plight, take an oath, undertake, vouch; *fig:* augur, be likely (to), betoken, hint at, look like, seem to mean, suggest.

promising adj *lit:* auspicious, bright, encouraging, hopeful, optimistic, propitious, reassuring, rosy; *fig:* gifted, talented; likely, rising, up-and-coming.

promotion n *lit:* advancement, elevation, rise, upgrading; advocacy, backing, boosting, furtherance, support; advocacy, recommendation, sponsorship; advertising, marketing, media hype, plugging, publicity, sales pitch.

prompt n *lit:* cue, hint, prod, reminder, spur. vb *lit:* cue, jog the memory, prod, remind; cause, elicit, evoke, occasion, provoke; induce, inspire, instigate, move, spur. adj *lit:* immediate, instant, instantaneous, punctual, quick, speedy, swift, timely; *fig:* alert; willing.

pronounce vb *lit:* articulate, enunciate, say; accent, emphasize, stress; announce, assert, declare, decree, proclaim.

proof n *lit:* authentication, confirmation, corroboration, substantiation, verification; evidence, testimony; *spec:* galley, ozalid, pull, slip (in publishing). adj *lit:* resistant (against), sealed (against), treated (against).

prop n *lit:* brace, buttress, stanchion, stay, support. vb *lit:* bolster, brace, buttress, hold up, shore up, support, sustain; *fig:* lean (against), put up (against), rest (against), set (against).

propaganda n *lit:* advertisement, hype, marketing, promotion, publicity, slogan; disinformation.

proper adj *lit:* decent, decorous, genteel, mannerly, polite, punctilious, refined; becoming, fitting, legitimate, right; appropriate, apt, suitable; accepted, conventional, established, formal; accurate, correct, exact, precise; characteristic, individual, own, particular, personal, specific.

property n *lit:* assets, belongings, capital, effects, estate, goods, holdings, possessions, resources, wealth; building, grounds, land, premises, territory; *fig:* attribute, characteristic, feature, idiosyncrasy, peculiarity, quality, trait; *spec:* article, bit of scenery (on stage).

prophet n *lit:* augur, oracle, seer, sibyl, soothsayer; astrologer, clairvoyant, crystal-gazer, magus; forecaster, tipster; mouthpiece, spokesperson.

prophetic adj *lit:* oracular, prescient, sibylline, visionary; clairvoyant; apocalyptic, revelatory.

proportion n *lit:* cut, division, fraction, part, percentage, quota, ration, share; dimension(s), measurement(s); distribution, ratio, relationship; (in) agreement, (in) balance, (in) correspondence.

proposal n *lit:* motion, proposition, suggestion; plan, presentation, programme, project, scheme; offer, tender; conditions, terms; *spec:* request for one's hand in marriage.

propose vb *lit:* advance, present, proffer, propound, put forward, submit, suggest, tender; aim, intend, mean, plan; introduce, invite, name, nominate, put up for membership, recommend; *spec:* request one's hand in marriage, pop the question.

propulsion n *lit:* drive, driving force, impulsion, locomotion, power, propelling force, push, thrust.

prosecute vb *lit:* bring an action against, bring to trial, indict, litigate against, prefer charges against, sue, summons, take to court; carry on, discharge, engage in, perform, practise, work at; carry through, continue, persevere in, persist with, pursue, see through.

prospect n *lit:* panorama, scene, sight, view, vista; anticipation, expectation, outlook; chance, likelihood, possibility. vb *lit:* explore, look (for), pan (for), search, sift (for), survey.

prosperity n *lit:* affluence, plenty, riches, success, wealth, wellbeing.

prostitute n *lit:* call girl, harlot, hooker, hustler, streetwalker, tart, trollop, whore. vb *lit:* cheapen, debase, degrade, demean, profane; pimp for, put on the game, sell.

protect vb *lit:* defend, give sanctuary to, keep safe, safeguard, shelter, shield; care for, harbour, look after, support, take under one's wing, watch over; conceal, hide, keep secret; cover up for.

protection n *lit:* armour, defences, guard; barrier, cover, screen, shield; refuge, shelter; preservation, safety, security; care, charge, custody, guardianship, sake keeping.

protest n *lit:* complaint, demur, dissent, objection, outcry, remonstration, resistance. **vb** *lit:* complain, demur, disagree, dissent, expostulate, object, remonstrate; argue, assert, contend, declare, insist on, maintain, profess, testify to.

proud adj *lit:* honoured; basking in the glory (of); gratified, pleased; glorious, gratifying, memorable, pleasing, satisfying; august, distinguished, eminent, grand, noble, splendid; arrogant, boastful, conceited, haughty, presumptuous, self-important, snobbish, snooty, supercilious, vain; *fig:* projecting, swelling.

provide vb *lit:* accommodate (with), contribute, equip (with), furnish, outfit (with), stock up (with), supply (with); afford, give, impart, lend, render, yield; determine, lay down, require, specify, stipulate; arrange (for), plan (for), prepare (for); care (for).

provided cnj *lit:* as long as, given (that), in the event (that), on condition (that), on the understanding (that).

providence n *lit:* destiny, divine intervention, fate, God's will, predestination; caution, foresight, forethought, prudence.

province n *lit:* colony, dependency, dominion, region, territory, zone; *fig:* area, business, duty, employment, field, function, line, responsibility, role, sphere.

provincial adj *lit:* backwoods, parochial, remote, small-town, upcountry; uninformed, unsophisticated; insular, inward-looking, limited, narrow-minded.

provision n *lit:* catering, equipping, furnishing, supplying, victualling; arrangement, plan, preparation; *fig:* agreement, clause, condition, specification, stipulation. **vb** *lit:* stock, supply, victual; accoutre, equip.

provisional adj *lit:* conditional, contingent, interim, stopgap, temporary, tentative, transitional.

provocative   adj *lit:* arousing, erotic, exciting, seductive, sensual, sexy, suggestive, tantalizing, titillating; aggravating, annoying, disturbing, galling, infuriating, offensive.

provoke   vb *lit:* bring about, cause, elicit, evoke, excite, generate, give rise to, incite, induce, inflame, instigate, lead to, occasion, precipitate, promote, prompt, rouse, stir up; annoy, enrage, exasperate, gall, get on one's nerves, incense, infuriate, irk, irritate, madden, offend, pique, rile.

prowess   n *lit:* ability, accomplishment, command, excellence, expertise, facility, mastery, skill; audacity, boldness, bravery, courage, daring, dauntlessness, intrepidity, valour.

prowl   vb *lit:* cruise, lurk, patrol, ply, range, roam (around), skulk, sneak.

prudence   n *lit:* care, caution, circumspection, common sense, discretion, forethought, judgement, judiciousness, precaution, sagacity, vigilance, wariness, wisdom; economy, frugality, husbandry, thrift.

prune   n *lit:* dried plum; purple; *fig:* crone, hag, witch.   vb *lit:* clip, coppie, cut back, lop, pare down, pollard, reduce, shape, trim.

prying   adj (pr.pt) *lit:* inquisitive, nosy, snooping, spying; interfering, intrusive, meddlesome.

psychic   n *lit:* medium; clairvoyant, dowser.   adj *lit:* clairvoyant, ESP, extrasensory, sensitive, supernatural, telekinetic, telepathic; mental, psychological; *fig:* astral.

public   n *lit:* citizens, community, electorate, nation, people, populace, population, society, voters; audience, buyers, clientèle, market, patrons, supporters, trade.   adj *lit:* civic, civil, national, popular, state, universal, widespread; communal, community, open to the public; accessible, unrestricted; exposed, known, open, overt, patent, plain, recognized; celebrated, important, prominent, well-known.

publication   n *lit:* appearance, broadcasting, declaration, disclosure, issue, printing, proclamation, promulgation; launch, marketing; book, brochure, leaflet, pamphlet, periodical.

publish **vb** *lit:* print, produce, put out; bring out, issue, launch, market, sell; advertise, announce, broadcast, communicate, disclose, divulge, impart, leak, promulgate, publicize, spread.

pull **n** *lit:* haul, heave, tow, tug; jerk, twitch, yank; strain, stretching; hit, stroke; row, scull; resistance; drag, inhalation, draught, swallow, swig; *fig:* ascent, climb; attraction, influence, magnetism, power; clout, influence, leverage, weight; *spec:* proof (in publishing). **vb** *lit:* draw, haul, heave, tow, tug; jerk, twitch, yank; strain, stretch; cull, pick, pluck, strip; extract, take out; hit, knock, strike; row, scull; move, steer; drag, inhale, suck; *fig:* attract, entice, lure; arrest, catch; *spec:* hold back (a horse, a punch).

pulp **n** *lit:* flesh, marrow, pith; mash, mush, pap. **vb** *lit:* crush, grind, mash, mill, powder, squash. **adj** *lit:* cheap, trashy; lurid, sensational.

pulse **n** *lit:* heartbeat; beat, beating, rhythm, throbbing, vibration; *spec:* legume, seed vegetable (such as peas, beans or lentils). **vb** *lit:* beat, throb, vibrate.

pump **n** *lit:* compressor, energizer, inflater, pressurizer, siphon, syringe; dancing-shoe. **vb** *lit:* drive, force, siphon, syringe; empty (out), inject (in); blow (up), inflate; energize, excite; *fig:* cross-examine, grill, interrogate, question, quiz; *spec:* contract (muscles).

punch **n** *lit:* bash, blow, buffet, clout, hit, jab, knock, thump, wallop, whack; *fig:* bite, dynamism, energy, force, impact; *spec:* cold chisel; die, stamp; fruit cup; pit-prop. **vb** *lit:* bash, box, buffet, clout, hit, jab, knock, slam, smash, strike, thump, wallop, whack; imprint, indent, stamp; bore (through), drill (through); key, type; *spec:* drive (cattle).

punctual **adj** *lit:* on the dot, on time, prompt, timely.

puncture **n** *lit:* flat tyre; break, hole, rupture, slit; escape, leak. **vb** *lit:* penetrate, perforate, pierce, prick, rupture; go down, go flat; *fig:* deflate, disillusion, humble, take down a peg.

pungent **adj** *lit:* acrid, aromatic, bitter, peppery, piquant, sharp, spicy, strong, tart; *fig:* biting, caustic, cutting, incisive, keen, penetrating, piercing, poignant, pointed, sarcastic, scathing, stinging, trenchant.

punish vb *lit:* castigate, chasten, chastise, correct, discipline, make one sorry, penalize; beat, cane, flog, spank, tan one's hide, whip; batter, hurt, injure, knock about, rough up.

punishment n *lit:* castigation, chastening, chastisement, correction, discipline, penalty, penance; beating, caning, flogging, spanking, tanning, whipping; battering, injury, knocking about, rough treatment.

puny adj *lit:* feeble, frail, pint-sized, runtish, sickly, stunted, undersized, weakly; *fig:* inconsequential, insignificant, paltry, petty, trifling, trivial.

pup n *lit:* cub, whelp, young dog; *fig:* jackanapes, popinjay, whippersnapper; *spec:* (sold a) dud, dummy.

pupil n *lit:* disciple, learner, schoolboy, schoolgirl, student; neophyte, novice, postulant; eye-hole.

purchase n *lit:* buy; acquisition, gain, property; foothold, footing, grasp, grip, toehold; *fig:* edge, hold, influence, leverage. vb *lit:* buy; acquire, come by, invest in, obtain, pick up, procure, secure, shop for.

pure adj *lit:* flawless, perfect, unalloyed; straight, unmixed; authentic, genuine, natural, real, simple, true; immaculate, pristine, spotless, virgin; clean, sanitary, sterile, uncontaminated, unpolluted, untainted, wholesome; *fig:* blameless, chaste, innocent, uncorrupted, virginal, virtuous; absolute, complete, mere, sheer, total, unqualified, utter; academic, hypothetical, speculative, theoretical.

purge n *lit:* aperient, cathartic, emetic, laxative; *fig:* clean-up, clear-out, sorting out, weeding out; pogrom, witch hunt. vb *lit:* absolve, cleanse, expiate, forgive, pardon, purify, wash clean; evacuate, use a laxative; *fig:* clean up, clear out, sort out, weed out.

purity n *lit:* flawlessness, perfection, spotlessness; clarity, cleanness, clearness, opacity; faultlessness, fineness, genuineness; simplicity; *fig:* blamelessness, chastity, innocence, virginity, virtue; piety; sincerity.

purpose n *lit:* aim, design, idea, intention, object, point, reason;

end, goal, objective, target; aspiration, desire, wish; determination, firmness, persistence, resolve, single-mindedness, steadfastness, tenacity, will; avail, benefit, effect, gain, outcome, profit, result, return, use. **vb** *lit:* aim, aspire, commit oneself, determine, intend, mean, plan, propose, resolve.

purse n *lit:* money-bag, pouch; exchequer, funds, money, resources, treasury; award, prize, reward; gift, present. **vb** *lit:* draw tight, pucker, tighten.

pursue **vb** *lit:* chase, follow, go after, hound, hunt, tail, track; *fig:* chase after, court, pay court to, woo; aim for, aspire to, seek, strive for, work towards; apply oneself to, carry on, engage in, perform, ply, practise, work at; adhere to, continue, hold to, keep on, persist in.

push n *lit:* heave, ram, shove, thrust; assault, attack, charge, offensive, onslaught; *fig:* ambition, determination, drive, dynamism, energy, enterprise, vigour; effort, go, try. **vb** *lit:* drive, press, propel, ram, shove, thrust; elbow, jostle, shoulder, squeeze; browbeat, coerce, egg on, encourage, hurry, impel, incite, influence, oblige, persuade, urge; advertise, boost, plug, promote, publicize; hawk, peddle, market; *spec:* approach (in age).

put **vb** *lit:* bring, deposit, lay, place, position, rest, set, settle, situate; push (away), thrust (away); heave, hurl, lob, pitch, throw, toss; *fig:* arrange, fix; commit, condemn, consign, doom; assign (to), constrain (to), employ (to), make (to), oblige (to), require (to); express, phrase, pose, state, word; assess (at), estimate (at); advance, bring forward, posit, present, propose, submit.

puzzle n *lit:* brainteaser, conundrum, dilemma, enigma, problem, quandary, question, riddle; maze, mystery, paradox; difficulty, perplexity, uncertainty. **vb** *lit:* baffle, beat, bewilder, mystify, nonplus, perplex, stump; brood (over), mull (over), muse (over), ponder (over), think long and hard (over); figure (out), sort (out), work (out).

Q

quaint **adj** *lit:* antiquated, archaic, baroque, gothic, old-fashioned, old-world, rococo; picturesque, scenic; curious, eccentric, odd, peculiar, singular, unusual; bizarre, fantastic, grotesque, strange, whimsical.

quake **n** *lit:* convulsion, quiver, shaking, shiver, shudder, spasm, tremor, vibration; earthquake, seismic shock. **vb** *lit:* convulse, go into spasm, quail, quiver, shake, shiver, shudder, tremble, vibrate; flutter, palpitate, throb.

qualification **n** *lit:* authority, capability, eligibility, power; achievements, attainments, background, certificate, experience, history, past, record; attribute, capacity, skill; distinguishing feature, distinction; caveat, exception, limitation, modification, reservation, restriction; condition, proviso.

qualify **vb** *lit:* be accepted, be authorized, be certified, become eligible, be empowered, be entitled, be trained; equip, fit, prepare, ready, school; limit, moderate, modify, restrict, soften, temper; abate, diminish, lessen, mitigate, reduce; characterize, describe, distinguish; have an effect upon.

quality **n** *lit:* character, class, demeanour, description, essence, kind, make, manner, nature, sort, stamp, type; attribute, characteristic, feature, property, trait; timbre, tone; calibre, distinction, merit, standing, value, worth; position, rank, status, superiority; aristocracy, landed gentry, nobility, upper classes.

quantity **n** *lit:* amount, number, sum, total; aggregate, bulk, capacity, extent, magnitude, mass, measure, size, volume; dose, helping, part, portion, ration, share; *spec:* duration, length (of a musical note, of a syllable).

quarrel **n** *lit:* altercation, argument, clash, controversy, difference of opinion, disagreement, discord, dispute, dissension, feud, row, slanging match, squabble, tiff, vendetta, wrangle; *spec:* arrow, bolt, dart (for a crossbow); (stone-mason's) chisel. **vb** *lit:* argue, bandy words, bicker, clash, differ, disagree, dispute, dissent, fall out, feud, have words, row, squabble, wrangle; carp, cavil, decry, demur, find fault, take exception.

quarry   n *lit:* excavation, open-cast mine, pit; game, hunted, kill, prey, victim; *fig:* reservoir, source, well; aim, end, goal, objective. **vb** *lit:* dig out (from), excavate; *fig:* extract.

quarter   n *lit:* fourth; 15 minutes; 3 months; area, district, locality, neighbourhood, place, region, side, territory, zone; compass point, direction; clemency, leniency, mercy; *fig:* authority, source; *spec:* phase (of the moon); staff, upright, vertical (in construction). **vb** *lit:* chop up, divide into fourths; accommodate, billet, house, lodge, post, station; abide, be accommodated, board, put up, stay; range, roam; beat, search thoroughly; *fig:* compartment; impose.

queer   **vb** *lit:* foil, mar, ruin, spoil, wreck; impair, jeopardize. **adj** *lit:* abnormal, anomalous, extraordinary, odd, outlandish, peculiar, singular, strange, uncommon, unnatural, unusual, weird; curious, droll, funny, quaint; unconventional, unorthodox; dubious, fishy, questionable, suspicious; eerie, mysterious, uncanny; dizzy, faint, ill, light-headed, sick, queasy; crazy, touched; counterfeit, fake, sham.

quell   vb *lit:* crush, extinguish, overthrow, put down, quash, suppress; check, curb, repress, stifle, subdue; conquer, defeat, overcome; *fig:* allay, calm, mollify, pacify, quiet, soothe.

quench   vb *lit:* douse, drown, extinguish, put out, smother, snuff out, stifle; dip, plunge; allay, appease, cool, satiate, satisfy, slake; end, finish, stop; die down, fade out, subside.

query   n *lit:* inquiry, question; contention, controversy, debate, doubt, reservation, uncertainty; objection, problem; interrogation mark, question mark.   **vb** *lit:* ask, challenge, debate, dispute, enquire, interrogate, question; doubt, wonder.

question   n *lit:* inquiry, query; contention, controversy, debate; demur, doubt, objection, problem, reservation, uncertainty; examination, interrogation; issue, motion, proposition, subject, topic.   **vb** *lit:* ask, cross-examine, enquire, grill, interrogate, pump, query, quiz; challenge, debate, disbelieve, dispute, doubt, wonder about.

quick   n *lit:* living; flesh, sensitive part; *fig:* heart.   **adj** *lit:* express, fast, fleet, meteoric, rapid, snappy, speedy, swift; abrupt, immediate, prompt, sudden; brief, brisk, cursory, hasty, hurried, perfunctory; active, adroit, alert, animated, energetic, keen, lively, nimble, ready, sharp, spry, vivacious; adept, clever, deft, dextrous, skilful, versatile; acute, intelligent, perceptive, shrewd; excitable, irascible, touchy, volatile.   **adv** *lit:* fast, rapidly, speedily, swiftly; at once, immediately.

quicken   vb *lit:* accelerate, expedite, hasten, hurry up, hustle, speed up; activate, animate, arouse, awaken, excite, fire, kindle, reactivate, reanimate, rekindle, resurrect, revitalize, revive, rouse, stimulate, stir up.

quickly   adv *lit:* at the double, briskly, fast, flat out, rapidly, snappily, speedily, swiftly, with alacrity; abruptly, immediately, instantly, promptly, soon, smartish, suddenly; briefly, cursorily, hastily, hurriedly, perfunctorily.

quiet   n *lit:* peace, silence, stillness, tranquillity; serenity; calm, repose, rest.   **vb** *lit:* hush, silence; calm down, pacify, soothe, still.   **adj** *lit:* noiseless, silent, soundless; hushed, low, peaceful, soft; at rest, calm, motionless, placid, restful, serene, still, tranquil; dumb, mute, unresponsive; private, secluded, secret, undisturbed, unfrequented; modest, plain, restrained, sedate, sober, subdued, unobtrusive, unpretentious; gentle, inoffensive, meek, mild, reserved, retiring, shy.

quietly   adv *lit:* noiselessly, silently, soundlessly; gently, peacefully, softly; complacently, contentedly, placidly, serenely, tranquilly; confidentially, furtively, privately, secretively, secretly; inoffensively, modestly, plainly, sedately, soberly, unobtrusively, unpretentiously; demurely, meekly, shyly.

quite   adv *lit:* fairly, moderately, rather, reasonably, relatively, somewhat; absolutely, completely, entirely, fully, perfectly, totally, wholly; indeed, exactly, precisely; actually, definitely, positively, really, truly.

R

rabble n *lit:* crowd, mob, throng; populace; commoners, hoi polloi, masses, proletariat, riffraff.

race n *lit:* chase, dash, sprint; competition, contest; blood, breed, clan, ethnic group, nation, people, stock. **vb** *lit:* career, dart, dash, fly, gallop, hurtle, speed, tear, zip, zoom; compete (against), contest (against), run (against).

racket n *lit:* ballyhoo, commotion, din, disturbance, fuss, hubbub, hullabaloo, noise, pandemonium, row, tumult, uproar; fraud, ramp, swindle; business, game, line.

radiant adj *lit:* beaming, brilliant, effulgent, gleaming, glittering, incandescent, luminous, resplendent, shining, sparkling; blissful, delighted, ecstatic, glowing, joyful, rapturous.

radical n *lit:* extremist, fanatic, militant, revolutionary. **adj** *lit:* constitutional, innate, natural, organic; basic, fundamental, profound, thoroughgoing; complete, entire, excessive, extreme, severe, sweeping, thorough; extremist, militant, revolutionary.

rag n *lit:* cloth, remnant, scrap, shred, tatter; jape, lark, practical joke, prank; ragtime music; roofing-slate; *fig:* (lose one's) temper. **vb** *lit:* abrade, become frayed, become tattered, fray; *fig:* make fun of, play jokes on, tease; scold.

rage n *lit:* anger, fury, heat, ire, passion, wrath; craze, obsession; fad, latest, mode, vogue. **vb** *lit:* be beside oneself, blow one's top, fume, rave, seethe; blow, rampage, storm, surge.

raid n *lit:* attack, incursion, invasion, onset, onslaught, sally; foray, sortie; break-in; ambush. **vb** *lit:* assault, attack, despoil, invade, maraud, pillage, plunder, rifle, sack; break into, get into.

rail n *lit:* bar, barrier, fence; balustrade, banister; line, railway track. **vb** *lit:* enclose, fence round, hem in; rant (at), shout (at), yell (at).

rain *n lit:* cloudburst, downpour, drizzle, shower; deluge, flood, torrent; cascade, fountain, spray. *vb lit:* bucket down, drizzle, pour, sheet down, shower, teem; cascade, drop, fall, fountain, spray, sprinkle; *fig:* bestow, lavish.

raise *vb lit:* build, construct, erect, put up, set up; heave, hoist, lift; bring up, foster, rear; breed, cultivate, develop, grow, nurture, produce, propagate; augment, boost, enlarge, escalate, heighten, increase, intensify, strengthen; elevate, exalt, promote, upgrade; activate, arouse, excite, foment, incite, instigate, motivate, provoke, stir up, whip up; bring about, cause, create, give rise to, occasion, originate, start; advance, broach, introduce, put forward, suggest; assemble, form, gather, levy, mass, muster, obtain, rally, recruit; *spec:* abandon, give up, relieve, remove (a siege).

rally *n lit:* assembly, congregation, convention, gathering, mass meeting, muster; reformation, regrouping, reorganization, stand; improvement, recovery, renewal, resurgence, revival; road-race. *vb lit:* assemble, convene, gather, get together, mobilize, muster, organize, round up, summon, unite; reassemble, reform, regroup, reorganize; come round, get better, improve, perk up, recover, revive.

ram *n lit:* male sheep; piston, plunger; pump; battering-ram; *spec:* beak (of a warship). *vb lit:* butt, collide with, crash into, drive (home), run into; cram, drum, force, hammer, jam, pack, pound, stamp, thrust.

ramble *n lit:* excursion, hike, perambulation, promenade, saunter, stroll, walk. *vb lit:* amble, perambulate, roam, rove, saunter, stray, stroll, walk, wander; meander, wind; babble, chatter, digress, maunder, rabbit on, rattle on.

rampage *vb lit:* be beside oneself, go berserk, rage, rant, rave, run amok, run riot, storm, tear.

rampant *adj lit:* dominant, raging, riotous, uncontrollable, unrestrained, wild; epidemic, exuberant, profuse, rife, unchecked, widespread; erect, rearing, upright.

range *n lit:* area, bounds, compass, confines, domain, extent, limits, orbit, province, radius, reach, scope, sphere, sweep; chain, file, line, rank, row, series, string; assortment, gamut, kind, lot, selection, sort, variety. **vb** *lit:* align, array, dispose, draw up, order; arrange, bracket, catalogue, classify, file, grade, group, rank; aim, direct, level, point, train; cruise, explore, ramble, roam, straggle, stray, stroll, wander; extend, fluctuate, go, reach, stretch, vary (between).

rank n *lit:* caste, classification, division, grade, level, order, position, quality, standing, station, status, type; column, formation, group, line, row, series. **vb** *lit:* align, arrange, array, classify, grade, line up, marshal, order, position, range, sort. **adj** *lit:* abundant, dense, lush, productive, profuse, vigorous; bad, foetid, foul, fusty, noxious, off, offensive, pungent, rancid, stale, stinking; absolute, blatant, downright, excessive, flagrant, gross, rampant, sheer, total, unmitigated, utter; abusive, atrocious, coarse, filthy, gross, indecent, obscene, outrageous, scurrilous, vulgar.

rap n *lit:* blow, knock, tap; *fig:* blame, punishment, rebuke, reproof; conviction, prison sentence; atom, jot, whit; *spec:* skein (of yarn). **vb** *lit:* knock, tap, strike; censure, condemn, criticize, rebuke, reprove.

rape n *lit:* ravishment, sexual assault, violation; defilement, defloration; abuse, maltreatment; *fig:* depredation, despoliation, looting, pillage, plundering, ransacking, stripping. **vb** *lit:* outrage, ravish, sexually assault, violate; *fig:* despoil, loot, pillage, plunder, ransack, strip.

rare adj *lit:* exceptional, infrequent, scarce, singular, sparse, sporadic, uncommon, unusual; admirable, excellent, exquisite, extreme, fine, incomparable, superb, superlative; invaluable, precious, priceless.

rash n *lit:* eruption, inflammation; outbreak; *fig:* epidemic, flood, plague, series, spate, succession. **adj** *lit:* adventurous, audacious, brash, foolhardy, harebrained, hasty, headstrong, heedless, hot-headed, ill-advised, impetuous, impulsive, indiscreet, injudicious, madcap, premature, reckless, thoughtless, unthinking.

rate n *lit:* degree, percentage, proportion, ratio, scale; charge, cost, duty, fee, price, tariff, tax, toll; gait, pace, speed, time, velocity. **vb** *lit:* adjudge, appraise, assess, classify, count, evaluate, grade, rank, reckon, value, weigh; be worthy of, deserve, merit; admire, respect, think highly of.

ration n *lit:* allotment, allowance, dole, helping, portion, quota, share; provision(s), store(s), victual(s). **vb** *lit:* allocate (out), apportion (out), deal (out), distribute (out), dole (out), give (out), mete (out); budget, control, limit, restrict.

rational adj *lit:* intelligent, judicious, logical, lucid, realistic, reasonable, sensible, sound; cognitive, reasoning, thinking; all there, balanced, conscious, lucid, sane.

rationalize vb *lit:* account for, excuse, extenuate, justify, make allowance for, vindicate; elucidate, reason out, resolve, think through; cut back on, make cost-effective, make cuts in, streamline, trim.

rattle n *lit:* knock, knocking, pinking, rasp, castanet, maracca; clatter, racket, uproar; chatter, gossip, prattle. **vb** *lit:* bang, clatter, jangle; bounce, jiggle, jolt, shake, vibrate; chatter, gabble, prattle, rabbit on, run on, witter; disconcert, discountenance, disturb, perturb, scare, shake, upset; reel (off), recite (off), run (through).

ravage n *lit:* damage, desolation, destruction, devastation, havoc, pillage, plunder, ruin(s), waste. **vb** *lit:* demolish, desolate, destroy, lay waste, loot, pillage, plunder, ransack, raze, ruin, sack, shatter, wreck.

rave n *lit:* acclaim, applause, praise; celebration, do, party, thrash; craze, fashion, vogue. **vb** *lit:* babble, fume, rage, rant, roar, seethe, splutter, thunder; be mad (about), be wild (about), enthuse (about), rhapsodize (over). **adj** *lit:* acclamatory, commendatory, ecstatic, enthusiastic, excellent, laudatory.

ravishing adj (pr.pt) *lit:* bewitching, charming, dazzling, delightful, enchanting, gorgeous, radiant, stunning.

raw adj *lit:* bloody, fresh, uncooked, unprepared; basic, coarse, crude, natural, organic, rough, unrefined, untreated; abraded, grazed, open, scratched, sore, tender; callow, green, ignorant, immature, inexperienced, new, unskilled, untrained; blunt, brutal, candid, frank, naked, plain, realistic, unembellished; biting, bitter, bleak, chilly, cold, freezing, harsh, piercing.

reach n *lit:* capacity, compass, distance, extension, extent, grasp, influence, jurisdiction, power, range, scope, spread, stretch. **vb** *lit:* arrive at, attain, get to, make; extend to, get hold of, grasp, stretch to, touch; hand, hold (out), pass, stretch (out); amount to, come to; go down to, fall to; climb to, rise to; contact, find, get through to, make contact with.

read vb *lit:* look at, peruse, pore over, study; comprehend, construe, decipher, discover, interpret, perceive, see; deliver, recite; display, indicate, record, register, show.

reading n *lit:* examination, perusal, scrutiny, study; concept, grasp, interpretation, rendition, treatment, understanding, version; education, erudition, knowledge, learning, scholarship; homily, lecture, lesson, recital, sermon.

ready vb *lit:* arrange, equip, fit out, organize, prepare, set up (for); nerve (oneself), steel (oneself). **adj** *lit:* arranged, fit, organized, prepared, set; mature, ripe; agreeable, eager, game, glad, inclined, keen, minded, prone, willing; acute, alert, apt, astute, bright, clever, deft, dextrous, perceptive, prompt, quick-witted, resourceful, sharp, skilful; about, close, near; to hand; liable (to), likely (to).

real adj *lit:* absolute, actual, authentic, existent, factual, genuine, heartfelt, intrinsic, legitimate, positive, rightful, sincere, true, unfeigned, valid, veritable.

realistic adj *lit:* businesslike, commonsense, down-to-earth, level-headed, matter-of-fact, practical, rational, sensible, unsentimental; accurate, authentic, lifelike, naturalistic, true-to-life.

really adv *lit:* absolutely, actually, assuredly, categorically, certainly, genuinely, indeed, in fact, positively, truly, undoubtedly.

rear n *lit:* aft, back, back end, stern, tail; backside, behind, bottom, bum, posterior, seat. **vb** *lit:* breed, bring up, care for, cultivate, foster, grow, nurse, nurture, raise, train; build, construct, erect; stand upright; lift up; loom, rise, soar, tower. **adj** *lit:* aft, back, following, hindmost, last.

rearrange vb *lit:* move, realign, redeploy, redispose, relocate, reorder, reposition; alter, change, turn round; decorate, refurnish, renovate; reorganize, reschedule, reset.

reason n *lit:* apprehension, comprehension, intellect, logic, mentality, mind, rationality, reasoning, sanity, soundness, understanding; basis, cause, grounds, occasion, purpose; argument, defence, excuse, explanation, ground, justification, rationale, vindication; aim, end, goal, incentive, inducement, motive, object, target; moderation, propriety, sense, wisdom. **vb** *lit:* conclude, deduce, infer, make out, think, work out; argue (with), debate (with), dispute (with), expostulate (with).

reasonable adj *lit:* advisable, believable, credible, intelligent, justifiable, logical, plausible, practical, rational, sensible, sound, tenable, well-advised, wise; acceptable, equitable, fair, fit, honest, inexpensive, just, moderate, modest, proper, right, within reason.

rebel n *lit:* insurgent, mutineer, revolutionary, secessionist; dissenter, heretic, nonconformist, renegade, schismatic; anarchist; eccentric. **vb** *lit:* mutiny, resist, revolt, rise up, take to the streets; come out against, defy, disobey, dissent; recoil, shy away.

rebellious adj *lit:* defiant, disloyal, insubordinate, insurgent, intractable, mutinous, revolutionary, seditious, subversive; disobedient, naughty; difficult, obstinate, recalcitrant, refractory, wilful.

rebuff n *lit:* brush-off, cold shoulder, discouragement, refusal, rejection, repulse, slight, snub; setback. **vb** *lit:* brush off, cut, discourage, put off, reject, repulse, snub, spurn, turn down.

rebuke n *lit:* carpeting, reprimand, reproach, reproof, telling-off, ticking-off, tongue-lashing. **vb** *lit:* castigate, censure, chide, lecture, reprimand, reproach, reprove, scold, take to task, tell off, tick off, upbraid.

recall n *lit:* summons; memory, recollection, remembrance, retrieval; repeal, retraction, withdrawal. **vb** *lit:* bring back, call back, summon; bring to mind, recollect, remember, reminisce about, revive one's memory of; renew, revive; be reminiscent of, hark back to; repeal, retract, withdraw.

receipt n *lit:* acknowledgement, counterfoil, proof of purchase; acceptance, reception; gain(s), proceed(s), profit(s), taking(s).

receive vb *lit:* accept, acquire, be given, get, obtain, take; have, own, possess; accommodate, admit, entertain, incorporate, meet, take in, welcome; *fig:* sustain, undergo.

recent adj *lit:* contemporary, current, late, new, present-day, up-to-date.

reception n *lit:* acceptance, acquisition, receipt; greeting, recognition, response, welcome; do, function, levée, party, soirée.

recess n *lit:* alcove, bay, cavity, depression, indentation, niche, nook; adjournment, break, holiday, intermission, interval, respite, rest. vb *lit:* set back; adjourn, take a break, take time off.

recipe n *lit:* constituents, formula, ingredients, instructions, method, prescription, procedure, technique.

reckless adj *lit:* careless, daredevil, foolhardy, heedless, imprudent, incautious, indiscreet, madcap, mindless, negligent, precipitate, rash, thoughtless.

reckon vb *lit:* add up, calculate, count, figure, number, tally, total; assess as, consider, deem, evaluate as, hold, judge, regard, think of; assume, believe, conjecture, expect, guess, imagine, suppose, surmise, think; cope (with), deal (with), settle accounts (with); bank (on), count (on), depend (on), rely (on).

recognize vb *lit:* identify, know, make out, place, recall, remember, spot; accept, acknowledge, admit, allow, be aware of, concede, grant, own, perceive, realize, see, understand; appreciate, approve, honour, salute.

recommend vb *lit:* approve, commend, praise, speak well of, vouch for; advise, advocate, counsel, urge; advance, propose, suggest; be in one's favour, promote.

reconstruct vb *lit:* reassemble, rebuild, recreate, renovate, reorganize, restore; build up, deduce, piece together.

record n *lit:* account, annals, archives, chronicle, document, entry, file, log, memorandum, minute, register, report; documentation, evidence, remembrance, testimony, trace; background, curriculum vitae, performance; best performance, best time; album, disc, platter, release, single. **vb** *lit:* chronicle, document, enrol, enter, log, minute, note, put down, register, transcribe, write down; contain, indicate, read, say, show; cut, make a recording of, tape, video-tape.

recover **vb** *lit:* find, get back, recapture, reclaim, recoup, regain, restore, retrieve, win back; come round, get well, heal, improve, mend, pull through, rally, regain one's strength, revive; convalesce, recuperate.

recovery **n** *lit:* recapture, reclamation, repossession, restoration, retrieval; convalescence, healing, mending, recuperation; improvement, rehabilitation, restoration, revival, upturn.

recreation **n** *lit:* amusement, distraction, diversion, enjoyment, entertainment, leisure activity, pastime, pleasure, relaxation.

red **adj** *lit:* carmine, coral, crimson, maroon, pink, ruby, scarlet, vermilion; bay, chestnut, flaming, titian; blushing, embarrassed, flushed, rubicund, shamefaced, suffused; blooming, glowing, healthy, rosy, ruddy; bloodshot, inflamed; bloodstained, gory, sanguine.

redeem **vb** *lit:* buy back, reclaim, regain, repossess, retrieve, win back; cash (in), exchange, trade in; abide by, acquit, adhere to, carry out, discharge, fulfil, keep, meet, satisfy; absolve, rehabilitate, reinstate; atone for, compensate for, make up for, offset, redress; deliver, emancipate, extricate, free, liberate, ransom, rescue, save, set free.

reduce **vb** *lit:* abate, contract, curtail, cut down, decrease, dilute, diminish, impair, lessen, slow down, truncate, weaken; bankrupt, impoverish, ruin; bring, drive, force, subdue, vanquish; lose weight, shed weight, slim; cut, discount, lower, mark down, slash; bring low, degrade, demote, downgrade, humble.

redundant **adj** *lit:* excess, inessential, inordinate, superfluous, surplus, unnecessary, useless; diffuse, repetitious, verbose.

refer **vb** *lit:* allude (to); direct, guide, point, recommend; apply (to), turn (to); be directed (to), pertain (to), relate (to); attribute, credit, impute, put down (to); commit, consign, hand over, pass on, transfer.

referee **n** *lit:* adjudicator, arbitrator, judge, umpire. **vb** *lit:* adjudicate, arbitrate, judge, umpire.

reference n *lit:* allusion (to); applicability, connection, regard, relation; credential(s), endorsement, recommendation, testimonial.

refined adj *lit:* civilized, cultured, genteel, gracious, polished, sophisticated, urbane, well-mannered; discerning, discriminating, exact, fastidious, nice, precise, punctilious, subtle; clarified, distilled, filtered, pure, purified.

refinement n *lit:* clarification, cleansing, distillation, filtering, processing, purification; nicety, nuance, subtlety; civility, courtesy, cultivation, delicacy, discrimination, fastidiousness, finesse, gentility, good manners, graciousness, polish, sophistication, style, taste.

reflect vb *lit:* echo, imitate, mirror; cogitate, contemplate, deliberate, meditate, mull over, ponder, ruminate, think; communicate, demonstrate, display, exhibit, express, indicate, manifest, reveal.

reform n *lit:* amendment, correction, improvement, rectification, rehabilitation. vb *lit:* amend, better, correct, emend, mend, reconstruct, rectify, rehabilitate, renovate, reorganize, repair, restore; go straight.

refreshing adj *lit:* bracing, cooling, fresh, invigorating, thirst-quenching; novel, original, stimulating.

refuse n *lit:* debris, garbage, litter, rubbish, trash, waste; offal; detritus, parings; scrap. vb *lit:* decline, negate, reject, repudiate, spurn, turn down, veto, withhold.

regard n *lit:* gaze, look, scrutiny, stare; attention, heed, notice; affection, attachment, concern, consideration, esteem, love, respect, sympathy, thought; aspect, detail, item, matter, particular, point; bearing, connection, reference, relation, relevance; best wish(es), compliment(s), greeting(s), respect(s). vb *lit:* behold, gaze at, observe, scrutinize, watch; consider, esteem, hold, look upon, rate, think, view; apply to, be relevant to, have to do with, pertain to, relate to; attend, heed, listen to, mind, note, pay attention to, take notice of.

region n *lit:* area, district, division, part, section, sector, territory, zone; locality, range, scope, vicinity; domain, field, sphere.

register n *lit:* annals, archives, chronicle, file, list, memorandum, record, roll, roster, schedule. **vb** *lit:* catalogue, check in, chronicle, enlist, enrol, enter, list, note, record, sign on, take down; display, express, indicate, manifest, record, reflect, reveal, show; *fig:* dawn on, get through, have an effect, sink in.

regret n *lit:* bitterness, compunction, contrition, disappointment, grief, remorse, repentance, ruefulness, self-reproach. **vb** *lit:* bemoan, be upset, deplore, grieve, lament, mourn, repent, rue.

regular adj *lit:* commonplace, customary, everyday, habitual, normal, ordinary, routine, typical, usual; consistent, constant, even, fixed, ordered, periodic, rhythmic, set, steady; dependable, efficient, methodical, orderly, standardized, systematic; balanced, flat, level, smooth, straight, symmetrical; approved, correct, established, formal, official, orthodox, prevailing, proper, standard, traditional.

regulate vb *lit:* adjust, administer, arrange, control, direct, fit, handle, manage, moderate, monitor, organize, rule, run, supervise, systematize.

rehearse vb *lit:* act, drill, go over, practise, prepare, run through, train, try out.

rein n *lit:* bridle, control, curb; check, restraint, restriction. **vb** *lit:* control, curb, steer; hold (back), hold (in).

reinforce vb *lit:* augment, bolster, buttress, fortify, harden, prop, strengthen, supplement, support, toughen.

reject n *lit:* castoff, discard, second. **vb** *lit:* ban, bar, cast aside, discard, eliminate, exclude, rebuff, repulse, scrap, spurn, throw out, turn down, veto.

rejoicing n *lit:* celebration, cheer, elation, exultation, gladness, happiness, jubilation, triumph. **adj (pr.pt)** *lit:* celebrating, elated, exalted, exultant, glad, happy, jotful, joyous, jubilant, triumphant.

relate vb *lit:* chronicle, describe, detail, impart, narrate, present, recite, report, tell; ally, associate, coordinate, correlate, join, link; be allied (to), be cognate (to), be kin (to); appertain, apply, be relevant (to), pertain, refer.

relationship n *lit:* affair, association, bond, connection, exchange, kinship, liaison, parallel, rapport, similarity.

relative n *lit:* kinsman, kinswoman, relation. **adj** *lit:* allied, associated, comparative, contingent, corresponding, dependent, proportionate, reciprocal, related, respective; in proportion (to), proportional (to).

relax vb *lit:* abate, diminish, ease, loosen, lower, mitigate, reduce, relieve, slacken; flop, let oneself go, loosen up, rest, take it easy, unbend, unwind.

relaxation n *lit:* amusement, enjoyment, entertainment, leisure, recreation, refreshment; abatement, easing, let-up, reduction, slackening, weakening.

release n *lit:* acquittal, deliverance, discharge, emancipation, liberation, liberty, relief; absolution, acquittance, dispensation, exemption, exoneration, let-off; announcement, issue, proclamation, publication. vb *lit:* discharge, disengage, drop, emancipate, extricate, let out, liberate, set free, turn loose, unchain, undo, unshackle, untie; absolve, acquit, dispense, excuse, exempt, exonerate, let off; break, circulate, distribute, issue, launch, make public, present, publish, put out.

relentless adj *lit:* fierce, grim, harsh, implacable, inexorable, inflexible, merciless, pitiless, ruthless, uncompromising, unrelenting, unyielding; incessant, persistent, punishing, sustained, unabated, unfaltering, unremitting, unstoppable.

relief n *lit:* abatement, alleviation, comfort, cure, deliverance, easement, mitigation, release, remedy, solace; aid, assistance, help, succour, support, sustenance; break, breather, relaxation, respite, rest; distraction, diversion.

relieve vb *lit:* abate, alleviate, appease, calm, comfort, console, diminish, dull, ease, mollify, palliate, salve, soften, soothe; aid, assist, help, succour, support, sustain; stand in for, substitute for, take over from; deliver, discharge, exempt, release, unburden; break, interrupt, slacken, vary.

religious adj *lit:* devout, doctrinal, faithful, god-fearing, pious, reverent, sectarian, spiritual, theological; *fig:* conscientious, exact, fastidious, meticulous, punctilious, rigid, scrupulous, unswerving.

relish n *lit:* appetite, appreciation, enjoyment, fondness, gusto, liking, partiality, penchant, predilection, taste, zest; flavour, piquancy, savour, smack, tang, trace; appetizer, chutney, condiment, sauce. vb *lit:* appreciate, enjoy, fancy, like, revel in, savour.

remain vb *lit:* continue, go on, last, persist, prevail, stand, stay, survive, wait; dwell, live, stop; be left, be over.

remains n *lit:* crumbs, debris, fragments, leftovers, oddments, pieces, relics, remainder, residue, scraps, vestiges; bones, carcass, corpse, skeleton; hulk, ruins, shell, wreckage.

remark n *lit:* aside, assertion, comment, observation, statement, utterance, word; acknowledgement, attention, consideration, heed, mention, notice, recognition, regard, thought. vb *lit:* comment, mention, observe, say; espy, heed, make out, mark, notice, perceive, regard, see, take note of.

remarkable adj *lit:* conspicuous, distinguished, impressive, notable, noteworthy, outstanding, pre-eminent, prominent; extraordinary, singular, striking, uncommon, unusual.

remedy n *lit:* antidote, cure, medicament, medicine, panacea; corrective, countermeasure, redress, solution. vb *lit:* alleviate, cure, ease, heal, palliate, relieve, restore, soothe; correct, fix, rectify, redress, repair, solve.

remember vb *lit:* look back, recall, recollect, relive, reminisce, retain, think back.

reminder n *lit:* alarm, bleeper; knot; memo, memorandum; keepsake, memento, souvenir.

remiss adj *lit:* careless, culpable, delinquent, derelict, dilatory, forgetful, inattentive, indifferent, lackadaisical, lax, neglectful, slack, slipshod, sloppy, tardy, thoughtless.

remit n *lit:* authorization, brief, guidelines, instructions, orders. vb *lit:* dispatch, forward, mail, post, transmit; cancel, halt, repeal, stop; abate, alleviate, decrease, diminish, dwindle, mitigate, reduce, relax, slacken, soften, wane; defer, delay, postpone, put off, suspend.

remorseful adj *lit:* apologetic, ashamed, conscience-stricken, contrite, guilt-ridden, penitent, regretful, repentant, rueful, self-reproachful, sorry.

remote adj *lit:* distant, faraway, godforsaken, isolated, lonely, secluded; alien, extraneous, extrinsic, immaterial, irrelevant, outside, removed, unrelated; doubtful, dubious, faint, implausible, meagre, negligible, poor, slender, slight, slim, unlikely; aloof, cold, detached, indifferent, introverted, reserved, unapproachable, uninvolved, withdrawn.

remove vb *lit:* abstract, delete, eliminate, extract, get rid of, throw out; amputate, take off; doff; depart, move away, quit, relocate, transfer, transport, vacate; discharge, dismiss, expel, purge, relegate; depose, dethrone, dislodge, eject, oust, unseat; *fig:* assassinate, dispose of, do away with, execute, get rid of, liquidate, murder, wipe out.

render vb *lit:* contribute, furnish, give, make available, present, provide, submit, supply, tender, yield; display, exhibit, manifest, show; exchange, return, swap, trade; cause to become, leave, make; act, depict, do, interpret, perform, play, portray; construe, explain, reproduce, transcribe, translate; cede, give up, hand over, relinquish, surrender, turn over; give back, make restitution, pay back, restore.

rent n *lit:* fee, hire, lease, payment, rental, tariff; break, chink, crack, flaw, gash, hole, rip, slash, split, tear; *fig:* breach, dissension, disunity, division, rift, rupture, schism. vb *lit:* charter, hire, lease, let.

reorganize vb *lit:* adapt, adjust, move, realign, rearrange, redispose, relocate; remodel, restructure, rework; reschedule, re-establish, reset.

repair n *lit:* adjustment, mend, overhaul, patch, restoration; condition, fettle, form, shape, state. vb *lit:* fix, heal, mend, patch, put back together, rectify, renew, renovate, restore; retrieve; compensate for, make up for; betake oneself, go, move, retire; have recourse (to), resort (to), turn (to).

repay vb *lit:* pay back, refund, reimburse, remunerate, square; reciprocate, requite; avenge, get even with, settle the score with.

repeat n *lit:* duplicate, echo, recapitulation, reiteration, repetition, replay, reshowing. vb *lit:* duplicate, echo, iterate, quote, recapitulate, recite, rehearse, reiterate, renew, rerun, reshow, restate.

repel vb *lit:* drive off, fight off, hold off, parry, put to flight, rebuff, reject, repulse, resist, ward off; *fig:* disgust, nauseate, offend, put one off, revolt.

repetition n *lit:* duplication, echo, iteration, recapitulation, recital, recurrence, reiteration, renewal, repeat, restatement, return, tautology.

replace vb *lit:* restock, resupply, substitute, succeed, supersede, supplant, take over from.

reply n *lit:* acknowledgment, answer, comeback, counter, rejoinder, response, retort, return, riposte. vb *lit:* acknowledge, answer, come back, counter, react (to), respond (to), retaliate, retort, riposte, write back.

report n *lit:* account, article, broadcast, bulletin, communiqué, description, dispatch, message, piece, record, statement, story, summary; rumour; fame, reputation, repute; bang, blast, boom, crash, discharge, explosion, noise, sound. vb *lit:* announce, broadcast, communicate, describe, detail, document, inform of, notify of, pass on, publish, record, recount, relay, state, tell; appear, be present, clock in, show up, turn up.

represent vb *lit:* be, correspond to, express, mean, serve as, stand for, symbolize; embody, epitomize, exemplify, personify, typify; denote, depict, describe, designate, illustrate, picture, portray, render, show, sketch.

representative n *lit:* commercial traveller, rep, salesman; archetype, embodiment, epitome, exemplar, personification, type; agent, councillor, delegate, member of parliament, spokesman. adj *lit:* archetypal, characteristic, evocative, exemplary, symbolic, typical; chosen, delegated, elected.

repress vb *lit:* check, control, crush, curb, master, overcome, quash, quell, subdue, subjugate, suppress; bottle up, hold back, inhibit, muffle, restrain, smother, stifle, swallow.

reprieve n *lit:* abeyance, amnesty, deferment, pardon, postponement, remission, stay of execution. vb *lit:* grant a stay of execution to, let off the hook, pardon.

reproach n *lit:* censure, rebuke, reprimand, reproof; discredit (to), disgrace (to). vb *lit:* censure, chide, condemn, rebuke, reprimand, scold, take to task, upbraid; be a discredit to, condemn.

reproduce vb *lit:* copy, duplicate, emulate, imitate, mirror, parallel, print, recreate, replicate, represent; breed, generate, multiply, procreate, proliferate, propagate, spawn.

reproduction n *lit:* copy, duplicate, facsimile, imitation, print, replica; breeding, generation, multiplication, procreation, proliferation, propagation.

repulsive adj *lit:* disgusting, distasteful, foul, hideous, loathsome, nauseating, obnoxious, odious, offensive, revolting, sickening, vile; adverse, antagonistic, incompatible, opposed.

reputable adj *lit:* creditable, estimable, honest, honourable, law-abiding, reliable, respectable, trustworthy, upright.

reputation n *lit:* character, credit, distinction, fame, name, renown, repute, standing, stature.

request n *lit:* appeal, application, call, demand, entreaty, petition, requisition, solicitation, suit, supplication. vb *lit:* appeal for, apply for, ask for, entreat, petition, seek, solicit, sue for, supplicate.

require vb *lit:* call for, demand, necessitate, take; lack, miss, need, want, wish for; bid, call upon, command, compel, constrain, instruct, oblige.

rescue n *lit:* extrication, liberation, recovery, relief, salvage, saving. vb *lit:* deliver, extricate, free, get out, recover, release, salvage, save, set free; redeem.

resemblance n *lit:* affinity, closeness, comparability, conformity, correspondence, likeness, parity, semblance, similitude.

resent   vb *lit:* be angry about, begrudge, be offended by, dislike, grudge, object to, take amiss, take exception to, take umbrage at.

resentment   n *lit:* anger, animosity, bitterness, grudge, ill feeling, indignation, irritation, pique, rancour, umbrage, vexation; envy.

reserve   n *lit:* capital, fund, reservoir, savings, stockpile, supply; asylum, park, reservation, sanctuary; aloofness, constraint, coolness, formality, reluctance, reservation, restraint, reticence, shyness, taciturnity.   vb *lit:* conserve, hoard, hold, keep back, preserve, put by, save, set aside, store, withhold; book, engage, retain, secure; defer, delay, postpone, put off.

residence   n *lit:* abode, domicile, dwelling, habitation, household, lodging, home, quarters; hall, manor, mansion, palace, seat; occupancy, sojourn, stay, tenancy.

resident   n *lit:* citizen, denizen, inhabitant, local, lodger, occupant, tenant.   adj *lit:* local, neighbourhood, settled.

resign   vb *lit:* hand in one's notice; leave, quit, vacate; abandon, relinquish, surrender, yield; commit (oneself to).

resigned   adj *lit:* long-suffering, patient, stoical, subdued, submissive; committed (to); defeatist, fatalistic.

resist   vb *lit:* battle against, combat, contend with, counteract, curb, defy, fight back, hinder, hold out against, oppose, repel, stand up to, struggle against, thwart, weather, withstand; abstain from, avoid, forgo, leave alone, refrain from.

resistance   n *lit:* contention, counteraction, defiance, hindrance, impediment, intransigence, opposition.

resolute   adj *lit:* bold, dedicated, determined, dogged, fixed, inflexible, obstinate, persevering, purposeful, relentless, set, staunch, steadfast, stubborn, tenacious, undaunted, unflinching, unwavering.

resolution   n *lit:* boldness, dedication, determination, doggedness, firmness, fortitude, obstinacy, perseverance, purpose, relentlessness, stamina, steadfastness, stubbornness, tenacity, willpower; aim, intention; decision, declaration, finding, verdict; motion, proposition; settlement; answer, dénouement, outcome, solution, unravelling, working out.

resolve n *lit:* conclusion, decision, design, objective, purpose, resolution, undertaking; boldness, courage, determination, firmness, resoluteness, resolution, steadfastness, willpower. **vb** lit: agree, conclude, decide, design, determine, fix, intend, make up one's mind, settle, undertake; answer, clear up, crack, elucidate, fathom, work out; banish, dispel, explain, remove; analyse, break down, disentangle, disintegrate, dissolve, reduce, separate, solve, unravel; alter, convert, transform, transmute.

resources n *lit:* assets, capital, funds, holdings, means, money, property, reserves, wealth, wherewithal.

respect n *lit:* admiration, appreciation, deference, esteem, recognition, regard, reverence; aspect, characteristic, detail, facet, matter, particular, point, sense; bearing, connection, reference, relation; compliments, good wishes, greetings, regards. **vb** *lit:* admire, adore, appreciate, defer to, honour, look up to, revere, set store by, think highly of, value, venerate; abide by, adhere to, comply with, heed, obey, observe, pay attention to, show consideration for.

respectable adj *lit:* admirable, decent, decorous, estimable, honest, proper, reputable, respected, upright, worthy; ample, appreciable, considerable, fair, goodly, reasonable, sizable, substantial, tidy, tolerable.

response n *lit:* acknowledgment, answer, comeback, feedback, reaction, rejoinder, reply, retort, riposte.

responsible adj *lit:* in authority, in charge, in control; accountable, answerable, bound, liable, under obligation; authoritative, decision-making, executive; at fault, culpable, guilty, to blame; adult, conscientious, dependable, level-headed, mature, rational, reliable, sensible, sober, stable, trustworthy.

rest n *lit:* calm, doze, inactivity, leisure, lie-down, nap, relaxation, relief, repose, siesta, slumber, snooze, standstill, tranquillity; break, breathing space, cessation, halt, interlude, interval, lull, pause, stop, time off, vacation; haven, refuge, retreat, shelter; base, prop, stand, support, trestle; excess, leftovers, others, remainder, remains, residue, surplus. **vb** *lit:* be at ease, doze, have a snooze, idle, laze, lie down, nap, relax, sit down, sleep, slumber; lay, lean, lie, prop, recline, repose, stretch out; break off, cease, come to a standstill, discontinue, halt, knock off, stop, take a breather; be based, be founded, depend, hang, hinge, rely; be left, go on being, keep, remain, stay.

restless   adj *lit:* active, bustling, footloose, inconstant, irresolute, nomadic, roving, transient, unsettled, unsteady, wandering; agitated, anxious, edgy, fidgeting, fretful, ill at ease, jumpy, nervous, on edge, restive, troubled, uneasy, worried.

restoration   n *lit:* reconstruction, recovery, refurbishing, rejuvenation, renewal, renovation, repair, revival; re-establishment, reinstatement, restitution, return.

restraint   n *lit:* coercion, compulsion, confines, control, curtailment, grip, hindrance, hold, inhibition, moderation, restriction, self-discipline, suppression; bonds, captivity, confinement, detention, fetters, imprisonment, manacles, pinions, straitjacket; ban, check, curb, embargo, limitation, rein, taboo.

restrict   vb *lit:* bound, confine, contain, cramp, demarcate, hamper, handicap, hem in, impede, inhibit, limit, regulate, restrain.

restriction   n *lit:* check, condition, confinement, constraint, control, curb, demarcation, handicap, inhibition, limitation, regulation, restraint, rule, stipulation.

result   n *lit:* conclusion, consequence, decision, effect, end, event, issue, outcome, reaction, sequel, termination.   vb *lit:* appear, arise, derive, develop, emanate, ensue, eventuate, follow, happen, issue, spring, turn out; culminate (in), end (in), terminate (in).

resume   vb *lit:* begin again, continue, go on, proceed, recommence, reinstitute, reopen, restart; assume again, reoccupy, take up again.

retain   vb *lit:* absorb, detain, grasp, grip, hang onto, hold fast, keep, maintain, preserve, reserve, save; bear in mind, keep in mind, memorize, recall, remember; commission, employ, engage, hire.

retard   vb *lit:* arrest, check, clog, decelerate, defer, delay, encumber, handicap, hinder, impede, obstruct, set back, slow down, stall.

retire   vb *lit:* be pensioned off, give up work; absent oneself, depart, exit, leave, remove, withdraw; go to bed, go to sleep, hit the sack, turn in; ebb, fall back, give ground, give way, pull out, recede, retreat.

retiring adj *lit:* bashful, coy, demure, meek, modest, quiet, reclusive, reserved, reticent, self-effacing, shy, timorous, unassuming.

retreat n *lit:* departure, ebb, evacuation, flight, withdrawal; den, haunt, hideaway, privacy, resort, sanctuary, seclusion. **vb** *lit:* back away, depart, draw back, ebb, give ground, leave, pull back, recede, retire, turn tail, withdraw.

retrieve vb *lit:* fetch back, get back, recapture, recoup, recover, regain, rescue, restore, salvage, win back.

return n *lit:* homecoming, reappearance, recurrence, retreat, reversion; reestablishment, reinstatement, restoration; advantage, benefit, gain, interest, proceeds, profit, revenue, takings, yield; compensation, reciprocation, recompense, reparation, repayment, retaliation, reward; account, report, statement, summary; answer, comeback, rejoinder, reply, retort, riposte. **vb** *lit:* come back, go back, reappear, recoil, recur, retreat, revert, turn back; convey, give back, re-establish, reinstate, remit, replace, restore, send back, transmit; pay back, reciprocate, recompense, refund, reimburse, repay, requite; bring in, earn, make, net, yield; answer, come back (with), rejoin, reply, retort; choose, pick, vote in; announce, arrive at, deliver, render, report, submit.

reveal vb *lit:* announce, betray, disclose, divulge, give away, impart, leak, let out, let slip, make public, proclaim, tell; bare, display, exhibit, lay bare, manifest, show, uncover, unearth, unveil.

revel n *lit:* bachanal, carouse, celebration, debauch, festivity, merrymaking, saturnalia, spree. **vb** *lit:* bask (in), delight (in), gloat (in), indulge (in), rejoice (in), relish (in), take pleasure (in), wallow (in); carouse, go on a spree, live it up, rave, roister, whoop it up.

revenge n *lit:* reprisal, requital, retaliation, retribution, vengeance, vindictiveness. **vb** *lit:* avenge, repay, requite, retaliate, take revenge for, vindicate.

reverse n *lit:* antithesis, contradiction, contrary, converse, opposite; back, flip side, other side, rear, verso, wrong side; adversity, affliction, blow, check, defeat, disappointment, failure, misadventure, misfortune, mishap, repulse, setback, vicissitude.   **vb** *lit:* invert, transpose, turn over, turn round, upend; alter, annul, cancel, change, invalidate, negate, overrule, overthrow, quash, repeal, retract, set aside, undo; back, backtrack, go backwards, retreat.   **adj** *lit:* back to front, backward, contrary, converse, inverted, opposite.

review   **n** *lit:* analysis, examination, report, scrutiny, study, survey; commentary, criticism, evaluation, judgement, notice; journal, magazine, periodical; fresh look, reassessment, recapitulation, rethink, retrospect, revision; *spec:* inspection, march past, parade, procession.   **vb** *lit:* go over again, reassess, recapitulate, reconsider, re-evaluate, rethink, revise, think over; call to mind, recall, recollect, reflect on, summon up; assess, criticize, discuss, evaluate, judge, read through, scrutinize, study, weigh.

revive   **vb** *lit:* animate, awaken, bring round, cheer, come round, comfort, invigorate, quicken, rally, recover, rekindle, restore, resuscitate, revitalize, rouse.

revolt   **n** *lit:* defection, insurgency, insurrection, mutiny, rebellion, revolution, rising, sedition, uprising.   **vb** *lit:* defect, mutiny, rebel, resist, rise, take up arms (against); disgust, nauseate, offend, repel, repulse, shock, sicken.

revolting   **adj** *lit:* abhorrent, abominable, appalling, disgusting, distasteful, horrid, loathsome, nasty, nauseating, obnoxious, offensive, repellent, repugnant, repulsive, shocking, sickening.

revolution   **n** *lit:* coup d'état, insurgency, mutiny, rebellion, revolt, uprising; drastic change, innovation, metamorphosis, reformation, shift, transformation, upheaval; circle, circuit, cycle, gyration, orbit, rotation, spin, turn, whirl.

revolutionary   **n** *lit:* insurgent, insurrectionist, mutineer, rebel, revolutionist.   **adj** *lit:* extremist, insurgent, mutinous, radical, rebel, seditious, subversive; avant-garde, different, drastic, experimental, fundamental, innovative, novel, progressive, radical, thoroughgoing.

reward   **n** *lit:* benefit, bonus, compensation, gain, merit, payment, premium, profit, recompense, remuneration, requital, return, wages; comeuppance, just deserts, retribution.   **vb** *lit:* compensate, honour, recompense, remunerate, repay, requite.

rich n *lit:* plutocracy; affluent, moneyed, opulent, wealthy, well off.   **adj** *lit:* affluent, loaded, made of money, opulent, prosperous, wealthy, well off, well-to-do; abounding, productive, well-provided, well-stocked, well-supplied; abundant, ample, copious, exuberant, fecund, fertile, fruitful, lush, plentiful, prolific; costly, elaborate, expensive, exquisite, lavish, precious, priceless, splendid, sumptuous, superb, valuable; creamy, fatty, full-bodied, heavy, juicy, luscious, savoury, succulent, sweet, tasty; bright, deep, intense, strong, vibrant, vivid; dulcet, full, mellifluous, mellow, resonant; amusing, funny, hilarious, humorous, ludicrous, ridiculous, side-splitting.

ridicule n *lit:* banter, chaff, derision, gibe, jeer, mockery, raillery, sarcasm, satire, scorn, sneer, taunting.   **vb** *lit:* banter, caricature, deride, humiliate, jeer, lampoon, make fun of, mock, parody, poke fun at, pooh-pooh, satirize, scoff, sneer, taunt.

ridiculous adj *lit:* absurd, contemptible, derisory, farcical, foolish, hilarious, laughable, ludicrous, outrageous, preposterous, silly, unbelievable.

right n *lit:* authority, business, claim, due, interest, liberty, license, permission, power, prerogative, privilege; equity, good, honour, integrity, legality, morality, propriety, reason, rectitude, truth, uprightness, virtue.   **vb** *lit:* compensate for, fix, rectify, repair, settle, sort out, vindicate.   **adj** *lit:* equitable, ethical, fair, good, honourable, just, lawful, moral, proper, righteous, true, upright, virtuous; accurate, admissible, authentic, correct, exact, factual, genuine, precise, satisfactory, sound, spot-on, valid; advantageous, appropriate, becoming, deserved, done, due, fitting, ideal, opportune, propitious, rightful, seemly, suitable; all there, balanced, fit, healthy, normal, rational, reasonable, sane, unimpaired, well; conservative, reactionary, Tory; absolute, complete, out-and-out, thorough, utter.   **adv** *lit:* accurately, exactly, factually, genuinely, truly; appropriately, aptly, fittingly, properly, suitably; directly, immediately, instantly, promptly, quickly, straightaway; bang, precisely, squarely; absolutely, altogether, completely, entirely, quite, thoroughly, totally, utterly; fairly, honestly, justly, morally, virtuously; advantageously, beneficially, favourably, well.

rigorous adj *lit:* austere, challenging, demanding, exacting, firm, hard, rigid, severe, tough; accurate, conscientious, meticulous, nice, precise, punctilious, scrupulous, thorough; bad, bleak, extreme, harsh, inhospitable.

ring n *lit:* band, circle, circuit, halo, hoop, loop, round; arena, circus, rink; association, cabal, cartel, cell, clique, coterie, gang, group, mob, organization, syndicate; chime, knell, peal; buzz, phone call. **vb** *lit:* encircle, enclose, encompass, girdle, hem in, seal off, surround; chime, clang, peal, resound, reverberate, sound, toll.

riot n *lit:* anarchy, commotion, confusion, disorder, disturbance, fray, lawlessness, quarrel, row, strife, tumult, turmoil, uproar; boisterousness, excess, frolic, high jinks, jollification, merry-making, revelry, romp; display, extravaganza, show, splash. **vb** *lit:* go on the rampage, raise an uproar, run riot, take to the streets; carouse, cut loose, frolic, go on a binge, make merry, revel, roister, romp.

rip n *lit:* cut, gash, hole, rent, tear; current, overfall, rough water; cheat (off), con (off), loot (off), rifle (off), strip (off). **vb** *lit:* cut, pull apart, rend, sunder, tear; strip, wrench, wrest; come asunder, open up, split; move fast, rush along.

ripe adj *lit:* fully developed, mature, mellow, ready, ripened; accomplished, complete, finished, in readiness, perfect, prepared; auspicious, favourable, ideal, opportune, right, suitable, timely.

rise n *lit:* advance, ascent, climb, improvement, increase, upsurge, upward turn; advancement, aggrandizement, progress, promotion; acclivity, elevation, hillock, incline, upward slope; increment, pay increase. **vb** *lit:* arise, get out of bed, get up, stand up, surface; ascend, climb, go up, grow, improve, increase, lift, mount, move up, swell, wax; advance, be promoted, get on, get somewhere, go places, progress, prosper, work one's way up; appear, become apparent, crop up, emanate, emerge, happen, issue, occur, turn up; mount the barricades, mutiny, rebel, resist, revolt, take up arms.

rival n *lit:* adversary, antagonist, challenger, contender, contestant, opponent; compeer, equal, equivalent, fellow, match, peer. **vb** *lit:* be a match for, come up to, compare with, compete, contend, emulate, equal, match, measure up to, oppose, vie with. **adj** *lit:* competing, competitive, conflicting, emulating, opposed, opposing.

road n *lit:* avenue, course, direction, highway, lane, motorway, pathway, route, street, thoroughfare, track; *spec:* anchorage, roadstead.

roast vb *lit:* bake, cook; burn, calcine, desiccate, prepare by heating, prefine; *fig:* banter, chaff, make fun of, ridicule; criticize, reprove.

rob vb *lit:* burgle, cheat, con, defraud, deprive, dispossess, hold up, loot, pillage, plunder, raid, ransack, rifle, rip off, sack, strip, swindle.

robbery n *lit:* burglary, depredation, embezzlement, filching, fraud, hold-up, larceny, pillage, plunder, raid, rapine, rip-off, stealing, stick-up, swindle, theft.

robust adj *lit:* athletic, brawny, fit, hale, hardy, hearty, husky, in fine fettle, muscular, rugged, sinewy, sound, staunch, stout, strapping, strong, sturdy, tough, vigorous, well; boisterous, coarse, earthy, raw, roisterous, rollicking, rough, rude, unsubtle; common-sensical, down-to-earth, hard-headed, practical, sensible, straightforward.

rock n *lit:* boulder, stone; anchor, bulwark, cornerstone, foundation, mainstay, protection, support. vb *lit:* lurch, reel, roll, sway, swing, toss, wobble; astonish, astound, daze, dumbfound, jar, shake, shock, stagger, surprise.

rogue n *lit:* blackguard, charlatan, cheat, conman, crook, deceiver, fraud, mountebank, ne'er-do-well, rapscallion, rascal, reprobate, scamp, scoundrel, swindler, villain; mutant, sport, variant. adj *lit:* maverick, outcast, savage, wild; breakaway, disruptive, mischievous; defective, mutant, variant.

roll n *lit:* cycle, gyration, reel, revolution, rotation, run, spin, turn, twirl, wheel, whirl; ball, bobbin, cylinder, scroll, spool; annals, catalogue, census, chronicle, directory, index, inventory, list, record, register, schedule, table; billowing, lurching, rocking, rolling, tossing, undulation, wallowing; boom, drumming, grumble, resonance, reverberation, roar, rumble, thunder. vb *lit:* elapse, flow, go past, gyrate, pass, pivot, reel, revolve, rock, rotate, run, spin, swivel, turn, twirl, undulate, wheel, whirl; coil, curl, enfold, entwine, furl, twist, wind, wrap; even, flatten, level, smooth, spread; billow, lurch, sway, swing, toss, tumble, wallow; lumber, stagger, swagger, waddle.

romantic **adj** *lit:* amorous, lovey-dovey, mushy, passionate, sentimental, sloppy, tender; charming, exciting, fascinating, glamorous, mysterious, nostalgic; dreamy, high-flown, idealistic, starry-eyed, unrealistic, utopian, visionary, whimsical; chimerical, exaggerated, extravagant, fairy-tale, fanciful, fictitious, idyllic, imaginary, legendary, made-up, wild.

root **n** *lit:* radicle, radix, rhizome, tuber; base, cause, core, crux, derivation, essence, foundation, heart, mainspring, nub, nucleus, occasion, source, starting point; beginnings, origins.   **vb** *lit:* anchor, become established, entrench, fasten, fix, ground, implant, moor, set, stick, take root.

rot **n** *lit:* blight, canker, corrosion, decay, decomposition, disintegration, mould, putrefaction; balderdash, bosh, bunkum, claptrap, codswallop, drivel, hogwash, moonshine, nonsense, poppycock, rubbish, tosh, twaddle.   **vb** *lit:* corrode, corrupt, crumble, decay, decompose, deteriorate, disintegrate, fester, go bad, moulder, perish, putrefy; decline, degenerate, languish, waste away, wither away.

rotten **adj** *lit:* bad, corroded, crumbling, decaying, decomposed, disintegrating, festering, fetid, foul, mouldering, putrescent, putrid, rank, sour, unsound; bent, corrupt, crooked, degenerate, dishonest, disloyal, immoral, mercenary, perfidious, treacherous, untrustworthy, venal; base, contemptible, despicable, dirty, disagreeable, filthy, mean, nasty, scurrilous, vile, vicious; deplorable, disappointing, regrettable, unfortunate, unlucky; crummy, inadequate, inferior, lousy, low-grade, poor, sorry, substandard, unacceptable, unsatisfactory; below par, ill, off colour, poorly, ropy, rough, sick, under the weather.

rough **n** *lit:* draft, outline, preliminary sketch; bruiser, bully, ruffian, thug.   **vb** *lit:* block out, draft out, outline, sketch out; bash up, beat up, thrash up.   **adj** *lit:* broken, bumpy, craggy, jagged, rocky, rugged, stony, uneven; bristly, coarse, dishevelled, fuzzy, hairy, shaggy, tangled, tousled, uncut; agitated, boisterous, choppy, stormy, tempestuous, turbulent, wild; bluff, blunt, brusque, churlish, curt, discourteous, ill-mannered, impolite, indelicate, loutish, rude, unceremonious, uncouth, unmannerly, unpolished, unrefined; cruel, drastic, extreme, harsh, nasty, severe, sharp, tough, unjust, violent; below par, ill, off colour, poorly, ropy, rotten, unwell, upset; cacophonous, discordant, grating, gruff, husky, inharmonious, jarring, rasping, raucous; arduous, austere, hard, spartan, uncomfortable; basic, crude, cursory, hasty, incomplete, quick, raw, rudimentary, sketchy, unfinished, untutored; uncut, unprocessed, unwrought; approximate, estimated, foggy, general, hazy, inexact, vague.

roughly *adv lit:* irregularly, unevenly; boisterously, choppily, turbulently, wildly; bluntly, brusquely, coarsely, curtly, impolitely, rudely, unceremoniously, ungraciously; drastically, extremely, hardly, severely, sharply, unjustly, unpleasantly, violently; discordantly, gruffly, harshly, raucously; arduously, toughly, uncomfortably; basically, crudely, hastily, imperfectly, quickly, sketchily; approximately, generally, hazily, inexactly, vaguely.

round *n lit:* circle, disc, globe, orb, ring, sphere; bout, cycle, sequence, series, session; division, lap, level, period, stage; beat, circuit, compass, course, routine, schedule, turn; bullet, cartridge, discharge, shot. **vb** *lit:* bypass, circle, encircle, flank, skirt, turn. **adj** *lit:* annular, bowed, bulbous, circular, curved, cylindrical, disc-shaped, globular, orbicular, rotund, spherical; complete, entire, solid, unbroken, whole; ample, bountiful, considerable, generous, large, substantial; fleshy, full, plump, roly-poly, rounded; mellifluous, resonant, rich, sonorous; blunt, candid, frank, outspoken, plain, straightforward. **adv** *lit:* in a circle, with a whirling motion; around, in every direction, on all sides; in circumference, in distance around; by a longer way; from one to another; through a round of time; about, here and there; for all; in the opposite direction; to the opposite opinion. **prp** *lit:* so as to make a turn to the other side of, so as to encircle; in all directions from, to all parts of; about, around; on all sides of; here and there in; throughout; so as to rotate about.

rouse *vb lit:* awaken, get up, rise, wake up; agitate, animate, bestir, disturb, excite, exhilarate, get going, incite, instigate, move, provoke, startle, stimulate, stir, whip up.

rout *n lit:* beating, debacle, defeat, drubbing, hiding, licking, overthrow, shambles, thrashing, trouncing. **vb** *lit:* beat, chase, conquer, crush, defeat, destroy, dispel, drive off, drub, lick, overpower, overthrow, scatter, thrash, trounce.

routine n *lit:* custom, formula, grind, method, pattern, practice, procedure, usage, way, wont; act, bit, line, performance, piece. **adj** *lit:* conventional, customary, everyday, familiar, normal, ordinary, standard, typical, usual, wonted; boring, dull, hackneyed, humdrum, run-of-the-mill, tedious, tiresome, unimaginative, unoriginal.

row n *lit:* bank, column, file, line, queue, range, sequence, series, string, tier; paddle, scull; altercation, brawl, commotion, controversy, disturbance, fracas, fuss, quarrel, racket, rumpus, slanging match, squabble, tiff, trouble, uproar; castigation, dressing-down, lecture, reprimand, rollicking, telling-off, ticking-off. **vb** *lit:* paddle, scull; argue, battle, dispute, fight, squabble, wrangle.

rub n *lit:* caress, kneading, massage, polish, stroke, wipe; catch, difficulty, drawback, hindrance, hitch, impediment, obstacle, problem, snag. **vb** *lit:* abrade, caress, chafe, clean, grate, knead, massage, polish, scour, scrape, shine, smooth, stroke, wipe; apply, smear, spread.

rubbish n *lit:* debris, dross, garbage, junk, litter, refuse, scrap, trash, waste; balderdash, bunkum, claptrap, codswallop, drivel, gibberish, moonshine, nonsense, piffle, poppycock, rot, twaddle. **vb** *lit:* be caustic about, be scathing about, criticize severely, pan, slate.

rude adj *lit:* abrupt, abusive, blunt, brusque, churlish, curt, ill-mannered, impertinent, impudent, insolent, offhand, peremptory, unmannerly; boorish, brutish, coarse, gross, loutish, oafish, obscene, rough, scurrilous, uncouth, ungracious, vulgar; artless, crude, makeshift, primitive, roughly-made, simple; harsh, sharp, startling, sudden, unpleasant.

ruin n *lit:* bankruptcy, breakdown, collapse, crash, damage, decay, destitution, devastation, disrepair, downfall, failure, havoc, insolvency, overthrow, ruination, the end, undoing, wreckage.
vb *lit:* bankrupt, break, bring down, crush, defeat, demolish, devastate, impoverish, lay waste, overturn, raze, shatter, smash, wreck; botch, damage, injure, make a mess of, mangle, mar, spoil.

rule n *lit:* axiom, canon, criterion, decree, guideline, law, maxim, ordinance, precept, principle, regulation, ruling, standard, tenet; administration, authority, command, control, domination, government, leadership, power, regime, reign, supremacy, sway; condition, convention, custom, habit, practice, procedure, routine, wont; course, formula, method, policy, way. **vb** *lit:* administer, command, control, dominate, govern, lead, manage, regulate, reign; adjudicate, decide, decree, determine, establish, find, judge, pronounce, resolve, settle; be customary, hold sway, predominate, prevail.

rumour n *lit:* buzz, gossip, hearsay, report, talk, tidings, whisper, word. **vb** *lit:* circulate, gossip, pass around, publish, put about, report, say, tell, whisper.

run n *lit:* dash, gallop, jog, race, rush, sprint, spurt; drive, excursion, lift, outing, ride, round, trip; chain, course, cycle, passage, period, season, sequence, series, spell, stretch, string; category, class, kind, sort, type, variety; application, demand, pressure; ladder, rip, snag, tear; current, direction, drift, flow, motion, path, stream, tendency, tide, trend, sway; coop, enclosure, pen. **vb** *lit:* bolt, career, dart, dash, gallop, hasten, hotfoot, hurry, jog, leg it, race, rush, scamper, scurry, speed, sprint; abscond, beat it, clear out, depart, escape, flee, make off, scarper, take off, take to one's heels; course, glide, go, move, pass, roll, skim; bear, carry, drive, manoeuvre, transport; operate, ply; function, perform, tick, work; administer, control, direct, head, look after, manage, mastermind, oversee, regulate, supervise, take care of; continue, extend, last, lie, proceed, range, reach, stretch; cascade, discharge, flow, gush, issue, leak, pour, spill, stream; dissolve, fuse, liquefy, melt, turn to liquid; be diffused, mix, spread; come apart, ladder, tear, unravel; be current, circulate, climb, creep, go round, trail; display, feature, print, publish; be a candidate, challenge, contend, stand, take part; bootleg, deal in, smuggle, sneak, traffic in.

S

sabotage   **n** *lit:* damage, destruction, disruption, subversion, treachery.   **vb** *lit:* cripple, damage, destroy, disable, disrupt, incapacitate, subvert, undermine, vandalize, wreck.

sack   **n** *lit:* bag; bagful; loose-hanging coat, trail; wine; dismissal, termination of employment, the axe, the boot, the chop; *fig:* despoliation, destruction, devastation, looting, pillage, plunder, ravage, ruin.   **vb** *lit:* axe, discharge, dismiss, fire, kick out; *fig:* demolish, despoil, destroy, devastate, lay waste, loot, maraud, pillage, plunder, raid, ravage, rifle, ruin, spoil.

sacred   **adj** *lit:* blessed, consecrated, hallowed, holy, revered, sanctified, venerable; invulnerable, precious, protected, sacrosanct, secure; holy, solemn.

sacrifice   **n** *lit:* burnt offering, hecatomb, immolation, oblation; loss, renunciation, surrender.   **vb** *lit:* immolate, offer, forego, forfeit, give up, immolate, let go, lose, offer, surrender.

sad   **adj** *lit:* blue, cheerless, depressed, disconsolate, dismal, doleful, down, downcast, down in the dumps, gloomy, glum, heavy-hearted, low, lugubrious, melancholy, mournful, sick at heart, sombre, tearful, wistful, woebegone; *fig:* calamitous, dark, depressing, disastrous, grievous, heart-rending, moving, pathetic, pitiful, sorry, tearful, tragic, upsetting; bad, deplorable, distressing, lamentable, miserable, regrettable, serious, unfortunate, unhappy, unsatisfactory, wretched.

saddle   **vb** *lit:* burden, charge, encumber, load, lumber, task, tax.

safe   **n** *lit:* coffer, repository, safe-deposit box, strongbox. **adj** *lit:* impregnable, intact, protected, secure, unharmed, unscathed; harmless, innocuous, nontoxic, pure, unpolluted, wholesome; bearish, cautious, circumspect, conservative, dependable, discreet, prudent, realistic, reliable, sure, trustworthy, unadventurous; certain, risk-free, riskless, secure, sound.

sail   **vb** *lit:* embark, get under way, put to sea, set sail; captain, cruise, navigate, pilot, skipper, steer, voyage; *fig:* drift, float, fly, glide, shoot, skim, soar, sweep, wing.

sailor n *lit:* Jack Tar, lascar, mariner, matelot, navigator, salt, sea dog, seafarer, seaman, tar.

saintly adj *lit:* angelic, blessed, devout, god-fearing, godly, pious, righteous, sainted, virtuous, worthy.

salary n *lit:* earnings, emolument, income, pay, remuneration, stipend.

sally n *lit:* foray, incursion, offensive, raid, sortie, thrust; *fig:* crack, jest, joke, quip, retort, riposte, wisecrack, witticism; escapade, excursion, frolic, jaunt, trip. vb *lit:* erupt, go forth, issue, rush, set out, surge.

salty adj *lit:* brackish, saline, salt, salted; *fig:* colourful, humorous, lively, piquant, pungent, racy, snappy, spicy, tangy, witty, zestful.

salute n *lit:* address, greeting, obeisance, recognition, salutation, tribute. vb *lit:* acknowledge, address, greet, hail, kiss, welcome; *fig:* honour, pay tribute to, recognize.

salvage vb *lit:* glean, recover, redeem, rescue, retrieve, save.

salve n *lit:* ointment, unguent; *fig:* balm, flattery, praise. vb *lit:* anoint; smear; *fig:* make good, smoothe; account for, dispose of, harmonize, vindicate; *spec:* save (cargo).

same adj *lit:* aforementioned, selfsame, very; alike, corresponding, duplicate, equivalent, identical, indistinguishable, interchangeable, synonymous; *fig:* consistent, constant, invariable, unaltered, unchanged, unfailing, unvarying.

sample n *lit:* cross section, example, illustration, indication, instance, model, pattern, representative, sign, specimen. vb *lit:* experience, inspect, partake of, taste, test, try. adj *lit:* illustrative, pilot, representative, specimen, test, trial.

sanction n *lit:* allowance, approbation, approval, authority, authorization, backing, confirmation, endorsement, ratification, seal of approval, support; *fig:* ban, boycott, embargo, penalty.

vb *lit:* allow, approve, authorize, back, countenance, endorse, permit, support, vouch for; confirm, ratify, warrant.

sanctuary n *lit:* altar, church, sanctum, shrine, temple; *fig:* asylum, haven, protection, refuge, retreat, shelter; conservation area, nature reserve.

sane adj *lit:* lucid, normal, of sound mind, rational; *fig:* balanced, judicious, level-headed, moderate, reasonable, sensible, sober, sound.

sanity n *lit:* mental health, normality, rationality, reason, right mind, stability; *fig:* common sense, good sense, judiciousness, level-headedness, sense.

sap n *lit:* essence, life-blood, vital fluid; *fig:* charlie, chump, fool, jerk, nincompoop, ninny, nitwit, noddy, noodle, simpleton, twit, weakling, wet. **vb** *lit:* bleed, deplete, drain, enervate, erode, exhaust, undermine, weaken, wear down.

sarcastic adj *lit:* acerbic, acrimonious, back-handed, biting, caustic, contemptuous, cutting, cynical, derisive, disparaging, ironic, mocking, mordant, sardonic, satirical, sharp, sneering, taunting.

satanic adj *lit:* accursed, black, demoniac, demonic, devilish, diabolic, evil, fiendish, hellish, infernal, iniquitous, malevolent, malignant, wicked.

satisfactory adj *lit:* acceptable, adequate, average, competent, fair, passable, sufficient.

satisfy vb *lit:* appease, assuage, content, fill, gratify, indulge, mollify, pacify, please, quench, sate, satiate, slake, surfeit; answer, be sufficient, fulfil, meet, qualify, serve, suffice; assure, convince, dispel doubts, persuade, quiet, reassure; comply with, discharge, pay off, settle, square up; *fig:* atone, compensate, indemnify, make good, recompense, remunerate, requite.

sauce n *lit:* dressing, gravy, ketchup, relish; custard, topping; *fig:* backchat, brass, cheekiness, disrespect, impertinence, impudence, insolence, lip, nerve, rudeness.

saucy adj *fig:* cheeky, disrespectful, flippant, forward, impertinent, impudent, insolent, pert, presumptuous, rude; dashing, jaunty, natty, perky, rakish, sporty.

saunter n *lit:* amble, constitutional, promenade, ramble, stroll, turn, walk. vb *lit:* amble, dally, linger, loiter, mosey, ramble, roam, stroll, tarry, wander.

savage n *lit:* aboriginal, aborigine, autochthon, heathen, indigene, native, primitive; *fig:* barbarian, boor, roughneck, yobbo; beast, brute, fiend, monster. vb *lit:* attack, lacerate, mangle, maul. adj *lit:* feral, rough, rugged, uncivilized, uncultivated, untamed, wild; *fig:* barbarous, beastly, bestial, blood-thirsty, brutal, brutish, cruel, devilish, diabolical, ferocious, fierce, inhuman, merciless, murderous, ravening, ruthless, sadistic, vicious; primitive, unspoiled.

save vb *lit:* bail out, deliver, free, liberate, redeem, rescue, salvage, set free; be frugal, be thrifty, collect, economize, hide away, hoard, hold, husband, lay by, put by, reserve, set aside, store, treasure up; *fig:* conserve, guard, keep safe, look after, preserve, protect, safeguard, shield; hinder, obviate, prevent, rule out, spare.

say n *lit:* crack, turn to speak, voice, vote; *fig:* authority, influence, power, sway, weight. vb *lit:* add, affirm, announce, assert, declare, maintain, mention, pronounce, put into words, remark, speak, state, utter, voice; answer, disclose, divulge, make known, reply, respond, reveal, tell; allege, claim, noise abroad, put about, rumour, suggest; *fig:* deliver, do, orate, perform, read, recite, rehearse, render, repeat; assume, conjecture, dare say, estimate, imagine, judge, presume, suppose, surmise; communicate, convey, express, imply.

saying n *lit:* adage, aphorism, apophthegm, axiom, byword, dictum, maxim, proverb, saw.

scale n *lit:* flake, lamina, layer, plate; calibration, degrees, gamut, gradation, graduation, hierarchy, ladder, pecking order, ranking, register, sequence, series, spectrum, spread, steps; *fig:* proportion, ratio; degree, extent, range, reach, scope, way. vb *lit:* ascend, clamber, climb, escalade, surmount; *fig:* adjust, calibrate, proportion, regulate.

scamper vb *lit:* dart, dash, fly, hasten, romp, run, scoot, scurry, scuttle, sprint.

scan vb *lit:* browse, check, examine, glance over, investigate, scour, scrutinize, search, size up, survey, sweep.

scandalous adj *lit:* atrocious, disgraceful, disreputable, infamous, monstrous, odious, opprobrious, outrageous, shameful, shocking, unseemly; *fig:* defamatory, libellous, scurrilous, slanderous, untrue.

scanty adj *lit:* bare, deficient, exiguous, inadequate, insufficient, meagre, narrow, poor, restricted, scant, skimpy, slender, sparing, sparse, thin.

scarcely adv *lit:* barely, hardly, only just; *fig:* by no means, hardly, not at all, on no account, under no circumstances.

scarcity n *lit:* dearth, deficiency, famine, insufficiency, lack, paucity, rareness, shortage, undersupply, want.

scare n *lit:* alarm, alert, fright, panic, shock, start, terror.
vb *lit:* alarm, daunt, dismay, frighten, give someone a turn, intimidate, panic, put the wind up someone, shock, startle, terrify, terrorize.

scathing adj *lit:* painful, biting, brutal, caustic, critical, cutting, harsh, mordant, sarcastic, scornful, searing, trenchant, withering.

scatter vb *lit:* broadcast, diffuse, disseminate, fling, litter, sew, shower, spread, sprinkle, strew; *fig:* disband, dispel, disperse, dissipate, separate.

scene n *lit:* display, exhibition, pageant, representation, show, sight, spectacle, tableau; area, locality, place, position, site, situation, spot, whereabouts; backdrop, background, set, setting; act, division, episode, incident, part, stage; landscape, panorama, prospect, view, vista; *fig:* carry-on, commotion, confrontation, fuss, row, tantrum, to-do; arena, business, environment, field of interest, milieu, world.

scent n *lit:* aroma, bouquet, fragrance, nose, odour, perfume, redolence, smell; *fig:* spoor, track, trail. vb *lit:* detect, discern, get wind of, nose out, recognize, sense, smell, sniff, sniff out.

schedule n *lit:* agenda, calendar, catalogue, inventory, itinerary, plan, programme, timetable. vb *lit:* appoint, arrange, be due, book, organize, plan, programme, time.

scheme 356

scheme n *lit:* contrivance, course of action, design, device, plan, programme, project, proposal, strategy, system, tactics, theory; arrangement, blueprint, chart, codification, diagram, disposition, draft, layout, outline, pattern, schedule, system; *fig:* conspiracy, dodge, game, intrigue, machinations, manoeuvre, plot, ploy, ruse, shift, stratagem, subterfuge. **vb** *lit:* contrive, design, devise, imagine, lay plans, project, work out; *fig:* collude, conspire, intrigue, machinate, manoeuvre, plot, wheel and deal.

school n *lit:* academy, alma mater, college, discipline, faculty, institute, institution, seminary; *fig:* adherents, circle, class, clique, denomination, devotees, disciples, faction, followers, following, group, pupils, sect, set; creed, faith, outlook, persuasion, stamp, way of life. **vb** *lit:* coach, discipline, drill, educate, indoctrinate, instruct, prepare, prime, teach, train, tutor, verse.

scintillating adj *lit:* animated, bright, brilliant, dazzling, ebullient, glittering, lively, sparkling, stimulating, witty.

scoff vb *lit:* belittle, deride, despise, flout, gibe, jeer, knock, mock, poke fun at, pooh-pooh, revile, ridicule, scorn, sneer, taunt, twit.

scold n *lit:* nag, shrew, termagant, Xanthippe. **vb** *lit:* berate, blame, bring (someone) to book, castigate, censure, chide, find fault with, lecture, nag, rate, rebuke, remonstrate with, reprimand, reproach, tell off, tick off, upbraid, vituperate.

scope n *lit:* area, capacity, compass, confines, extent, freedom, latitude, liberty, opportunity, orbit, outlook, purview, range, reach, room, space, span, sphere.

scorch vb *lit:* blacken, blister, burn, char, parch, roast, sear, shrivel, singe, wither.

score n *lit:* grade, mark, outcome, points, record, result, total; the facts, the setup, the situation, the truth; crowds, droves, hosts, hundreds, legions, lots, masses, millions, multitudes, myriads, swarms; *fig:* account, basis, ground, reason; a bone to pick, grievance, grudge, injury, injustice, wrong; amount due, bill, charge, debt, obligation, reckoning, tally, total; *spec:* dots, music. **vb** *lit:* achieve, amass, gain, make, notch up, win; count, keep count, record, register, tally; *lit:* crosshatch, cut, deface, gouge, graze, indent, mar, mark, nick, notch, scrape, scratch, slash; cross out, put a line through, strike out; gain an advantage, go down well with (someone), impress, make an impact, make a point, put oneself across, triumph; *spec:* adapt, arrange, orchestrate, set.

scorn n *lit:* contempt, derision, disdain, mockery, sarcasm, scornfulness, slight, sneer. **vb** *lit:* be above, consider beneath one, contemn, deride, disdain, flout, hold in contempt, look down on, make fun of, scoff at, slight, sneer at, spurn.

scotch **vb** *lit:* crush, eradicate, stamp out; foil, frustrate, prevent, thwart; cut, gash, score.

scour **vb** *lit:* abrade, rub, scrape clean, scrub; hose, syringe; cauterize; burnish, polish; *fig:* beat, comb, rake.

scowl n *lit:* frown, glower, grimace, pout. **vb** *lit:* frown, glower, pout, snarl.

scramble n *lit:* hassle, race, rush, struggle, tussle; affray, commotion, mêlée, scrimmage; jumble, mess, muddle; hard ascent, stiff climb; *spec:* emergency take-off; (motorbike) trial. **vb** *lit:* jump, leap, race, rush, struggle; elbow, jostle, push; clamber, climb, scrabble; confuse, jumble, mix up, shuffle; encode.

scrap n *lit:* bit, crumb, fragment, morsel, part, piece, shred, sliver; leaving, leftover; junk, waste; affray, battle, brawl, fight, quarrel, row, scrimmage, scuffle, set-to, skirmish, wrangle. **vb** *lit:* abandon, discard, ditch, drop, write off; chuck out, get rid of, throw away; bicker, brawl, fight, quarrel, scuffle, wrangle.

scrape n *lit:* abrasion, dent, graze, rub, scratch, scuff-mark; depression, excavation, hollow, pit; *fig:* fix, hole, jam, mess, plight, predicament, spot of trouble; *spec:* thin layer (of butter or margarine). **vb** *lit:* abrade, dent, graze, scratch, scuff; rub, scour, scrub; file, grind, rasp; grate, screech, squeak; shave; excavate, hollow out; *fig:* put together, save up.

scratch n *lit:* abrasion, graze, laceration, mark, rip, scrape, tear; standard. **vb** *lit:* claw, etch, incise, lacerate, rip, rend, score, scrape, tear; scrawl; *fig:* cancel, delete, eliminate, rub; strike off;

withdraw. **adj** *lit:* casual, impromptu, improvised, rough.

scrawny **adj** *lit:* bony, emaciated, gaunt, lean, scraggy, skeletal, skinny, spindly, thin, underweight.

scream **n** *lit:* screech, shriek, wail, yell; *fig:* hoot, laugh, riot. **vb** *lit:* cry, holler, screech, shout, shriek, wail, yell; *fig:* be conspicuous, be loud; clash, conflict, jar.

screen **n** *lit:* divider, parclose, partition; cover, defence, hide, shield; awning, canopy, guard, shade, shelter; fence, panel, railing, windbreak; grill, mesh, raddle, sieve; grid; white surface. **vb** *lit:* keep apart, partition, separate; cover, defend, protect, shelter, shield; conceal, mask, shade; filter, sieve, sift, test; examine, scan, vet; broadcast, present, project, transmit.

screw **n** *lit:* dowel, thread; propeller; spin, twist, wind; *fig:* prison officer, warder; pay, salary, wages; jade, nag. **vb** *lit:* compress, tighten, turn, twist, wind; coerce, constrain, force, pressurize; *fig:* contort, crumple, pucker; steel, summon (up); cheat, con, defraud, swindle; foul (up), mess (up), muck (up).

scrub **n** *lit:* bath, clean, soaping, wash; brushwood, heath, veldt; runt. **vb** *lit:* bath, brush, clean, rub hard, scour, soap, wash; *fig:* abandon, call off, cancel, drop, give up.

scrum **n** *lit:* ruck, scrimmage, scrummage; crowd, crush, press; scramble, set-to, stramash, tussle. **vb** *lit:* crowd, crush, press, swarm, throng; barge, elbow, jostle, push, shove.

scrutiny **n** *lit:* contemplation, examination, investigation, observation, perusal, study; invigilation, supervision.

scuffle **n** *lit:* affray, brawl, fight, fray, row, rumpus, scrimmage, scrum, set-to, skirmish, tussle, wrangle; scrape, shuffle. **vb** *lit:* brawl, fight, struggle, tussle, wrangle, wrestle; drag one's feet, shuffle.

seal **n** *lit:* arms, colophon, insignia, logo, mark; attestation, authentication, stamp; bond, fastening, lock, weld; cap, cover, lid, top. **vb** *lit:* close (up), make airtight, plug, stop, waterproof; fasten (up); lock (in), weld (in); *fig:* authenticate, ratify, stamp, validate; conclude, consummate, finalize, settle.

search n *lit:* exploration, hunt, quest; analysis, examination, inspection, study. vb *lit:* look for; comb, examine, frisk, rifle through, scour; go over, inquire in, investigate, probe; seek out.

searching adj *lit:* discriminating, intent, keen, minute, penetrating, probing, shrewd, subtle, thorough.

season n *lit:* division, period, term, time of year; interval. vb *lit:* flavour, pep up, spice; harden, mature, toughen, train; *fig:* moderate, temper.

seasoned adj *lit:* hardened, mature, weathered; *fig:* battle-scarred, experienced, practised; well-versed.

seat n *lit:* bench, chair, pew, settee, sofa, stool; saddle; pillion; base, centre, cradle, headquarters, site; ancestral home, manor, residence; constituency, incumbency, membership. vb *lit:* install, place, set, settle; accommodate, contain, sit, take.

second n *lit:* next, other; instant, jiffy, moment, tick, trice; assistant, backer, supporter. vb *lit:* aid, assist, back, encourage, endorse, help, support; detach, lend, temporarily transfer. adj *lit:* following, next, succeeding; additional, alternative, extra, further, other; *fig:* inferior, lesser, subordinate, supporting.

secondary adj *lit:* alternative, auxiliary, relief, reserve, supporting; inferior, lesser, minor, subordinate; contingent, derivative, indirect, serial.

secret n *lit:* confidence; enigma, mystery; formula, key; in camera. adj *lit:* private, secluded, unfrequented; closet, covert, undisclosed; camouflaged, concealed, disguised, hidden; classified, hush-hush, undercover; clandestine, furtive, stealthy; arcane, cryptic, mysterious, recondite.

sect n *lit:* church, denomination, religion; faction, school of thought; philosophy; class; group, party.

section n *lit:* division, part, piece, portion, segment; branch, department; district, sector, zone; detachment, group, squad, team; *spec:* cutting, incision, operation.

secure vb *lit:* acquire, gain, get, obtain, pick up, procure; bolt, chain, fasten, fix, lock up, padlock, rivet, tie up; defend, fortify, make safe; guarantee, insure.   **adj** *lit:* defended, impregnable, invulnerable, protected, safe, unassailable; fastened, fixed, immovable, tight; confined, in custody; assured, certain, confident, sure; absolute, definite, reliable.

sedate   **vb** *lit:* anaesthetize, drug, knock out, numb, pacify, tranquillize.   **adj** *lit:* dignified, noble, stately; composed, decorous, deliberate, grave, solemn; calm, serious.

sediment   **n** *lit:* dregs, grounds, lees; loess, silt; deposit.

seduce   **vb** *lit:* beguile, entice, lure, tempt; lead astray, lead on; deflower.

see   **n** *lit:* bishopric, diocese; cathedral city.   **vb** *lit:* discern, distinguish, espy, make out, perceive, spot; behold, observe, view, watch, witness; look up, refer to; call in on, encounter, interview, meet, receive, speak to, visit; associate with, date, go out with, go steady with; *fig:* anticipate, envisage, envision, picture, visualize; be associated with, bring; experience, undergo; apprehend, fathom, get, grasp, learn, understand; appreciate, be aware of, comprehend, know, realize, recognize; deem, judge; ascertain, discover, find out, investigate; ensure, make certain, mind; consider, deliberate over, make up one's mind, reflect on, think over.

seed   **n** *lit:* grain, kernel, spore; drupe, pip, stone; blastomere, cell; semen; *fig:* beginning, germ, source, start; descendants, heirs, issue, progeny, successors; nation, race; *spec:* top-rated player.   **vb** *lit:* broadcast, scatter, sow; nip off, stone, take out; dust, powder; *spec:* classify, rate; sprinkle.

seedy   **adj** *fig:* abraded, dilapidated, faded, old, worn; scruffy, shabby, sleazy, sordid, squalid; ill, off-colour, poorly, run-down, sickly, unwell, wan.

seek   **vb** *lit:* ask, entreat, implore, petition, request; aim for, hope for, look for; hunt, pursue, search for; attempt, endeavour, strive, try.

seethe   **vb** *lit:* boil, bubble, ferment, foam, froth; *fig:* swarm, teem; fume, rage, simmer.

seize   **vb** *lit:* clasp, clutch, grab, grasp, snatch, take; apprehend, arrest, capture; repossess, take by force; appropriate, confiscate, impound, requisition, sequester; abduct, hijack, kidnap; *fig:* clog, jam, stick fast; lash down, make fast, tie up.

select   **vb** *lit:* choose, elect, opt for, pick out, single out, sort out. **adj** *lit:* choice, elite, prime, superior, top-quality, top-rated; exclusive, limited; privileged.

self-assertion   **n** *lit:* determination, dominance, insistence, masterfulness, positivity; pushiness.

self-assured   **adj** *lit:* confident, poised, self-confident, self-reliant.

self-centred   **adj** *lit:* egotistic, monomaniacal, narcissistic, self-absorbed, selfish.

self-conscious   **adj** *lit:* abashed, bashful, diffident, embarrassed, ill at ease, insecure, nervous, shy.

self-esteem   **n** *lit:* confidence, ego, pride, self-regard, self-respect.

selfish   **adj** *lit:* self-centred, self-seeking; avaricious, greedy, mean.

selfless   **adj** *lit:* altruistic, generous, heroic, magnanimous, noble, unselfish.

self-reliant   **adj** *lit:* able, capable, independent, practical, self-confident, self-sufficient.

self-respect   **n** *lit:* dignity, pride, self-esteem, self-regard.

self-satisfied   **adj** *lit:* gratified, self-congratulatory, triumphant; complacent, overconfident, smug.

self-seeking   **adj** *lit:* calculating, mercenary, opportunistic, trimming; selfish.

sell   **vb** *lit:* deal, hawk, peddle, retail, trade, vend; dispose of, put up for sale; *fig:* market, promote, put across; convert to, convince of, persuade.

send   **vb** *lit:* consign, convey, dispatch, forward, mail, post; broadcast, transmit; fling, hurl, sling, throw; fire, launch, propel, shoot; give (off), radiate; turn away; call for; *fig:* excite, intoxicate, stir, thrill.

senior adj *lit:* chief, elder, first, older, superior, upper.

sensation n *lit:* feeling; emotion; awareness, perception; effect, impression, sense; thrill; *fig:* agitation, commotion, excitement, stir; scoop; craze, fad, novelty.

sensational adj *lit:* astounding, dramatic, earth-shattering, epoch-making, exciting, fantastic, galvanizing, spectacular, staggering, stupendous, thrilling; appalling, horrifying, outrageous, scandalous, shocking; excellent, exceptional, marvellous, superb, wonderful.

sense n *lit:* appreciation, awareness, faculty, feeling, impression; air, aura, atmosphere; intuition, premonition, presentiment; discernment, imagination, logic, nous, practicability, practicality, reason, understanding; gist, implication, import, meaning, point, purport, significance, substance, use. **vb** *lit:* appreciate, apprehend, be aware of, feel, get the impression, grasp, hear, perceive, realize, scent, see, taste.

senseless adj *lit:* absurd, crazy, fatuous, half-witted, idiotic, ludicrous, mindless, nonsensical, ridiculous, stupid, unreasonable; bootless, futile, meaningless, pointless; anaesthetized, deadened, insensible, knocked out, numb, unconscious.

sensible adj *lit:* canny, down-to-earth, matter-of-fact, no-nonsense, practical, straightforward; judicious, politic, prudent, realistic; intelligent, reasonable, shrewd, sound, wise; aware, conscious, mindful.

sensitive adj *lit:* feeling, keen, perceptive, reactive, responsive; allergic; delicate, emotional, highly-strung, impressionable, nervous, tender; thin-skinned, touchy; *fig:* controversial, hot; awkward, embarrassing; embarrassed, shame-faced.

sensual adj *lit:* bodily, carnal, fleshly, physical; erotic, lascivious, lecherous, lustful, randy, sexual, voluptuous.

sensuous adj *lit:* bodily, fleshly, physical; feeling, perceptive, reactive, responsive, sensory; gratifying, pleasurable.

sentimental adj *lit:* emotional, maudlin, nostalgic, pathetic, simpering, sloppy, soft-hearted, tearful, tender.

sentry n *lit:* guard, lookout, picket, watch.

separate vb *lit:* break off, come apart, detach, disconnect, divide, keep apart, sever, split; put on one side, segregate, sort out; *fig:* break up, diverge, divorce, estrange, part company, split up. **adj** *lit:* detached, disconnected, disjointed, divided, divorced, unattached; alone, autonomous, independent, particular, single.

separation n *lit:* break, detachment, disconnection, dissociation, division, gap, severance; *fig:* break-up, divorce, estrangement, parting, rift, split.

sequence n *lit:* course, cycle, order, progression, succession.

serene adj *lit:* calm, composed, imperturbable, placid, unruffled; clear, cloudless, halcyon, unclouded.

series n *lit:* arrangement, course, order, sequence, string, succession, train.

serious adj *lit:* grave, pensive, solemn, thoughtful; determined, earnest, genuine, resolute, sincere; *fig:* crucial, difficult, important, momentous, pressing, significant, weighty; acute, critical, dangerous, severe.

serve vb *lit:* assist, attend to, help, minister to, wait on, work for; act, discharge, do, fulfil, officiate, perform; answer, be adequate, suffice, suit; deliver, dish up, distribute, provide, supply.

service n *lit:* assistance, avail, help, supply, use, utility; maintenance, overhaul, servicing; duty, employment, office, work; *fig:* ceremony, observance, worship. **vb** *lit:* check, maintain, overhaul, repair.

serving n *lit:* helping, portion.

set n *lit:* attitude, bearing, position, posture, turn; scene, scenery, stage setting; band, circle, company, crew, faction, gang, group, outfit; *fig:* assortment, batch, collection, compendium, kit, series. **vb** *lit:* aim, apply, direct, fix, install, lay, locate, place, position, put, rest, situate, stick; *fig:* agree upon, allocate, appoint, assign, determine, establish, resolve, schedule, settle; arrange, make ready, prepare; adjust, co-ordinate, regulate, synchronize; condense, congeal, crystallize, solidify, thicken; allot, impose, lay down, specify;

decline, disappear, sink, vanish. **adj** *lit:* agreed, arranged, customary, definite, established, fixed, prearranged, regular, settled; *fig:* conventional, formal, routine, stock, traditional; entrenched, firm, hardened, inflexible, rigid, strict; bent, determined, intent.

setting n *lit:* background, context, frame, scene, set, site, surroundings.

settle vb *lit:* adjust, straighten out, work out; clear up, complete, conclude, put an end to, resolve; agree, come to an agreement, confirm, fix; calm, pacify, quell, quieten, reassure, sedate, soothe; bed down, come to rest, descend, land, dwell, live, move to, reside; colonize, found, people, populate; acquit oneself of, clear, liquidate, pay; decline, sink, subside.

sever vb *lit:* break off, cut apart, part from, slice; disjoin, divide, separate.

several adj *lit:* assorted, different, diverse, many, some, sundry, various.

severe adj *lit:* austere, Draconian, hard, harsh, inflexible, oppressive, rigid, strict, unbending; cold, disapproving, dour, forbidding, grim, stern, strait-laced, tight-lipped; acute, bitter, critical, dangerous, fierce, grinding; *fig:* ascetic, chaste, plain, restrained, simple, Spartan, unembellished; arduous, demanding, exacting, punishing, rigorous, stringent, tough; astringent, caustic, cutting, satirical, scathing, unsparing.

sexy adj *lit:* arousing, cuddly, erotic, inviting, naughty, provocative, seductive, sensual, suggestive, titillating, voluptuous.

shade n *lit:* dimness, dusk, gloom, shadiness, shadow; blind, canopy, cover, curtain, screen; *fig:* colour, hue, tint, tone; dash, degree, hint, nuance, semblance, suggestion, trace; apparition, ghost, manes, phantom, spectre, spirit. **vb** *lit:* cover, darken, dim, overshadow, protect, screen, shield, veil.

shadow n *lit:* cover, dimness, dusk, gloom, protection, shelter; hint, suggestion, trace; *fig:* ghost, image, representation, spectre, vestige; blight, gloom, sadness. **vb** *lit:* darken, overhang, screen, shade, shield; *fig:* dog, follow, stalk, tail.

shady adj *lit:* cool, dim, leafy, shadowy, umbrageous; *fig:* crooked, dubious, shifty, slippery, suspicious, unscrupulous, untrustworthy.

shake n *lit:* agitation, convulsion, jerk, jolt, pulsation, quaking, shiver, tremor, vibration; *fig:* instant, jiffy, second, trice. **vb** *lit:* bump, fluctuate, jar, joggle, jounce, oscillate, quake, rock, shudder, totter, tremble, wobble; brandish, wave; *fig:* agitate, churn, rouse, stir; distress, disturb, intimidate, rattle, shock, unnerve; impair, undermine, weaken.

shallow n *lit:* flat, sandbank, shelf, shoal. **adj** *lit:* empty, flimsy, frivolous, meaningless, puerile, skin-deep, superficial, trivial, unintelligent.

sham n *lit:* counterfeit, forgery, fraud, hoax, pretence; impostor, phoney, pretender. **vb** *lit:* affect, assume, fake, feign, imitate, put on, simulate. **adj** *lit:* artificial, bogus, counterfeit, false, imitation, mock, phoney, pseudo, spurious, synthetic.

shame n *lit:* blot, contempt, derision, disgrace, disrepute, infamy, opprobrium, reproach, scandal, smear; abashment, chagrin, embarrassment, humiliation, ignominy, mortification. **vb** *lit:* abash, confound, disconcert, disgrace, humble, humiliate, mortify, reproach, ridicule; debase, defile, discredit, smear, stain.

shape n *lit:* build, contours, figure, form, make, outline; frame, mould, pattern; *fig:* appearance, aspect, guise, likeness, semblance; condition, fettle, health, state. **vb** *lit:* fashion, form, make, model, mould; *fig:* adapt, define, devise, frame, modify, plan, prepare, regulate.

share n *lit:* allotment, allowance, contribution, due, lot, portion, quota, ration, whack. **vb** *lit:* apportion, assign, distribute, divide, go halves, partake, participate, split.

sharp adj *lit:* acute, cutting, knife-edged, pointed, razor-sharp, serrated, spiky; abrupt, distinct, marked, sudden; *fig:* alert, apt, astute, bright, perceptive, quick-witted, subtle; artful, crafty, cunning, shrewd, sly, unscrupulous, wily; distressing, excruciating, fierce, piercing, sore, stabbing, stinging; clear-cut, crisp, well-defined; chic, classy, dressy, natty, smart, snappy, stylish; acrimonious, biting, bitter, caustic, harsh, hurtful, sarcastic, sardonic, scathing, trenchant, vitriolic; acid, acrid, burning, piquant, pungent, sour. **adv** *lit:* exactly, on the dot, on time, promptly, punctually; *fig:* abruptly, unexpectedly, without warning.

sharply *adv* *lit:* acutely, cuttingly, pointedly; abruptly, suddenly; aptly, brightly, subtly; cunningly, shrewdly; fiercely, piercingly; smartly, stylishly; bitterly, harshly.

shatter *vb* *lit:* break, crack, demolish, pulverize, smash; blast, destroy, devastate, impair, ruin, wreck; *fig:* dumbfound, upset.

shed *n* *lit:* cover, hut, shelter; ridge, watershed. **vb** *lit:* cause to flow, drop, let fall, pour out, spill; cast, diffuse, emit, give forth, radiate, scatter, throw; cast off, discard, moult, slough.

sheer *vb* *lit:* swerve, turn aside. **adj** *lit:* abrupt, precipitous, steep; absolute, complete, out-and-out, total, unadulterated, utter; fine, pure, see-through, thin.

shell *n* *lit:* case, husk, pod; frame, hull, skeleton, structure. **vb** *lit:* husk, shuck; barrage, blitz, bombard, strike.

shelter *n* *lit:* cover, guard, haven, refuge, safety, sanctuary, screen. **vb** *lit:* cover, defend, guard, harbour, hide, protect, safeguard, shield.

shield *n* *lit:* buckler, escutcheon; bulwark, defence, protection, rampart, safeguard, shelter. **vb** *lit:* cover, defend, guard, protect, screen, ward off.

shift *n* *lit:* alteration, change, fluctuation, modification, rearrangement, shifting, switch, veering; *fig:* contrivance, craft, dodge, evasion, move, stratagem, trick, wile. **vb** *lit:* alter, budge, displace, fluctuate, move, rearrange, remove, swerve, switch, transfer, vary, veer.

shifty *adj* *lit:* contriving, devious, evasive, furtive, scheming, slippery, tricky, underhand, untrustworthy, wily.

shimmering *adj* *lit:* gleaming, glistening, scintillating, sparkling, twinkling.

shine   n *lit:* brightness, glare, gleam, luminosity, shimmer, sparkle; *fig:* glaze, gloss, lustre, polish, sheen.   **vb** *lit:* beam, emit light, glare, glitter, radiate, scintillate, sparkle, twinkle; *fig:* excel, stand out.

shining   adj *lit:* beaming, bright, effulgent, glittering, luminous, radiant, resplendent, sparkling; *fig:* brilliant, distinguished, eminent, illustrious, leading, outstanding.

shirk   vb *lit:* avoid, dodge, duck, shun, skive, slack.

shock   n *lit:* blow, breakdown, collapse, consternation, stupor, trauma, turn; clash, collision, impact, jolt.   **vb** *lit:* appal, astound, disquiet, jar, jolt, numb, offend, outrage, scandalize, shake up, stagger, stun, stupefy, traumatize.

shocking   adj *lit:* abominable, atrocious, disgraceful, disgusting, dreadful, ghastly, hideous, loathsome, outrageous, repulsive, revolting, scandalous, sickening, unspeakable.

shoot   n *lit:* branch, bud, offshoot, sprig, sprout, sucker; current, rapids; chute, slide; shooting expedition, party.   **vb** *lit:* bud, burgeon, sprout; bolt, dart, dash, fly, hurtle, rush, speed, tear, whisk; bag, blast, bring down, open fire, zap; discharge, fire, fling, hurl, let fly.

shore   n *lit:* beach, coast, sands, seashore.   **adj** *lit:* littoral, waterside.

short   adj *lit:* abridged, compressed, concise, curtailed, laconic, pithy, summary, terse; diminutive, dumpy, petite, small; brief, fleeting, momentary; deficient, insufficient, lacking, low, scarce, sparse, wanting; abrupt, brusque, curt, discourteous, gruff, sharp, surly, terse, uncivil; direct, straight; crumbly.   **adv** *lit:* abruptly, by surprise, suddenly, unaware.

shortage   n *lit:* dearth, deficiency, famine, lack, scarcity, shortfall, want.

shorten   vb *lit:* abbreviate, curtail, cut down, diminish, lessen, reduce, trim.

shortly   adv *lit:* before long, presently, soon; briefly, concisely; abruptly, curtly.

shot n *lit:* discharge, lob, pot shot; bullet, lead, pellet, projectile; marksman, shooter; *fig:* attempt, conjecture, crack, go, guess, stab.

shout n *lit:* bellow, cry, roar, yell. **vb** *lit:* bawl, bellow, call, cry, holler, roar, scream, yell.

shove vb *lit:* barge, crowd, elbow, jostle, press, push, shoulder, thrust.

show n *lit:* demonstration, display, exhibition, exposition, fair, pageant, parade, spectacle; affectation, appearance, likeness, pretence, semblance; *spec:* entertainment, presentation, production. **vb** *lit:* appear, display, divulge, exhibit, indicate, make known, reveal; demonstrate, explain, instruct, point out, prove; accompany, escort, guide, lead; accord, bestow, confer, grant.

shower n *lit:* downfall, downpour; *fig:* barrage, deluge, fusillade, torrent, volley. **vb** *lit:* deluge, inundate, lavish, pour, spray, sprinkle.

shred n *lit:* bit, fragment, piece, scrap, sliver, snippet, tatter; *fig:* grain, iota, jot, particle, trace, whit. **vb** *lit:* cut, tear.

shrewd adj *lit:* artful, calculating, canny, crafty, cunning, sly, smart, wily; discerning, far-sighted, intelligent, keen, perceptive.

shriek n *lit:* howl, scream, screech, wail, yell. **vb** *lit:* cry, scream, screech, squeal, wail, yell.

shrill adj *lit:* ear-piercing, high-pitched, penetrating, screeching, sharp.

shrink vb *lit:* decrease, deflate, drop off, dwindle, lessen, shrivel, wither; cower, draw back, flinch, hang back, recoil, shy away, wince.

shudder n *lit:* quiver, spasm, trembling, tremor. **vb** *lit:* quake, quiver, shake, shiver, tremble.

shuffle vb *lit:* drag, scuffle, shamble; disarrange, jumble, mix, shift; dodge, evade, fidget, prevaricate, pussyfoot, quibble.

shut vb *lit:* bar, close, fasten, seal, secure, slam. **adj** *lit:* closed, confined, enclosed, excluded.

shy   vb *lit:* balk, draw back, flinch, rear, recoil, shrink, start, swerve, take fright.   **adj** *lit:* bashful, coy, hesitant, reserved, reticent, timid, wary.

sick   **adj** *lit:* ill, nauseated, queasy; ailing, indisposed, poorly; *fig:* perverted; bored, fed up, tired, weary.

sickly   **adj** *lit:* ailing, bilious, delicate, faint, indisposed, in poor health, lacklustre, languid, pallid, unhealthy, weak; mawkish, nauseating, revolting, syrupy.

sickness   n *lit:* nausea, queasiness; ailment, bug, complaint, disease, disorder, illness, indisposition.

side   n *lit:* border, boundary, edge, limit, margin, periphery, rim, verge; aspect, facet, part, surface, view; *fig:* angle, opinion, point of view, position, slant, stand; camp, faction, party, team; airs, arrogance.   **vb** *lit:* ally with, associate oneself with, favour, go along with, second, support, team up with.   **adj** *lit:* flanking, lateral; *fig:* ancillary, incidental, lesser, marginal, roundabout, secondary, subsidiary.

sidestep   vb *lit:* avoid, bypass, dodge, duck, elude, evade, skip.

sidetrack   n *lit:* shunting track, siding; *fig:* distraction, diversion, interruption.   **vb** *fig:* deflect, deviate, distract, divert.

sift   vb *lit:* bolt, filter, pan, separate, sieve; *fig:* analyse, examine, go through, screen, scrutinize.

sight   n *lit:* eyesight, vision; appearance, eyeshot, range of vision, view, visibility; display, scene, show, spectacle, vista; *fig:* blot on the landscape, eyesore, mess, monstrosity.   **vb** *lit:* discern, make out, see, spot.

sign   n *lit:* evidence, gesture, hint, indication, proof, suggestion, trace; board, notice, placard; badge, device, emblem, ensign, logo, symbol; auspice, foreboding, omen, portent, warning.   **vb** *lit:* autograph, endorse, inscribe; beckon, gesture, signal, wave.

signal   n *lit:* beacon, cue, indication, sign, token.   **vb** *lit:* beckon, gesticulate, indicate, motion, sign, wave.   **adj** *lit:* conspicuous, eminent, extraordinary, memorable, noteworthy, outstanding, significant.

significant adj *lit:* denoting, expressive, indicative, meaningful, suggestive; critical, important, material, momentous, serious, vital, weighty.

signify vb *lit:* announce, communicate, connote, convey, express, imply, indicate, intimate, mean, portend, represent, stand for, suggest, symbolize; *fig:* carry weight, count, matter.

silence n *lit:* calm, hush, lull, quiescence, stillness; dumbness, reticence, speechlessness, taciturnity. vb *lit:* cut off, deaden, gag, muffle, quieten, stifle, subdue, suppress.

silent adj *lit:* hushed, muted, quiet, soundless, still; dumb, mum, non-vocal, speechless, taciturn, tongue-tied, voiceless, wordless; implied, tacit, understood, unspoken.

similar adj *lit:* alike, comparable, congruous, in agreement, resembling.

similarity n *lit:* affinity, agreement, analogy, comparability, concordance, congruency, likeness, resemblance, sameness, similitude.

simple adj *lit:* clear, elementary, intelligible, lucid, straightforward, uncomplicated; classic, clean, natural, plain, uncluttered; pure, unalloyed, unblended, unmixed; artless, childlike, green, guileless, naive, sincere, unpretentious, unsophisticated; basic, direct, frank, honest, naked, plain, undeniable; homely, modest, rustic; brainless, dumb, feeble-minded, half-witted, moronic, silly, slow, thick.

simplify vb *lit:* abridge, disentangle, facilitate, streamline.

simultaneous adj *lit:* coincident, concurrent, contemporaneous, synchronous.

sin n *lit:* crime, error, evil, misdeed, offence, transgression, trespass, unrighteousness, wrongdoing. vb *lit:* err, fall, go astray, lapse, offend, transgress.

sing vb *lit:* carol, chant, chirp, croon, trill, warble, yodel; buzz, hum, purr, whistle; *fig:* blow the whistle (on), grass, inform (on), rat (on), spill the beans, squeal, turn in.

single vb *lit:* choose, distinguish, fix on, pick, select, separate.

adj *lit:* distinct, individual, one, only, particular, singular, sole, unique; free, unattached, unmarried; exclusive, separate, unblended, undivided, unshared.

singular   **adj** *lit:* conspicuous, exceptional, noteworthy, outstanding, prodigious, rare, remarkable, unique; curious, eccentric, extraordinary, out-of-the-way, peculiar, queer, strange; separate, single, sole.

sinister   **adj** *lit:* dire, injurious, malevolent, malignant, menacing, threatening.

sink   **n** *lit:* basin, tub; drain, sewer; marsh, pool.   **vb** *lit:* decline, descend, drop, drown, ebb, fall, founder, go down, merge, plummet, sag, submerge, subside; abate, lapse, retrogress, slump; deteriorate, die, dwindle, fade, weaken, worsen; bore, dig, drill, excavate, lay; *fig:* defeat, destroy, finish, overwhelm, ruin; stoop, succumb.

situation   **n** *lit:* locality, place, position, setting, site, spot; ball game, circumstances, plight, state of affairs, status quo, the picture; rank, station, status; employment, job, office, post.

size   **n** *lit:* amount, bulk, dimensions, extent, hugeness, immensity, magnitude, mass, measurement, proportions, range, vastness, volume.   **vb** *lit:* arrange, classify; *spec:* glaze, stiffen.

sizzling   **adj (pr.pt)** *lit:* crackling, frizzling, spitting, sputtering.

skeleton   **n** *lit:* framework; *fig:* bare bones, draft, outline, structure.

sketch   **n** *lit:* delineation, draft, drawing, etching, outline, plan. **vb** *lit:* delineate, depict, draft, draw, etch, outline, plot, represent.

skew   **adj** *lit:* askew, awry, slanting, twisted; bent, crooked, not symmetrical.

skewer   **n** *lit:* spit; nail, pin, stake; tent-peg.   **vb** *lit:* impale, spit, transfix; nail, pin, stake; peg.

skill   **n** *lit:* ability, accomplishment, aptitude, competence, dexterity, expertise, finesse, knack, proficiency, skilfulness, talent.

skin   **n** *lit:* fell, hide, pelt; coating, crust, husk, outside, rind. **vb** *lit:* abrade, bark, flay, graze, peel.

skinny adj *lit:* emaciated, scraggy, skeletal, skin-and-bone, thin, undernourished.

skip n *lit:* jump, leap, spring, trip; basket, bucket, cage, wagon; *spec:* captain (in bowling). **vb** *lit:* bounce, caper, gambol, hop, prance; eschew, leave out, miss, omit, pass over.

skirt n *lit:* kilt; border, edge, fringe, margin, outskirts, periphery. **vb** *lit:* border, edge, lie alongside; avoid, bypass, detour, evade.

slack n *lit:* leeway, looseness, room. **vb** *lit:* dodge, idle, neglect, shirk, skive, slacken. **adj** *lit:* baggy, flexible, lax, loose, relaxed; easy-going, idle, inactive, lazy, negligent, permissive, tardy; dull, slow-moving, sluggish.

slacken vb *lit:* abate, diminish, drop off, lessen, reduce, relax, slow down.

slang n *lit:* argot, cant, colloquialism, jargon, rhyming slang. **vb** *lit:* abuse, berate, call names, insult, inveigh against, rail against, revile, slander, vituperate.

slant n *lit:* camber, incline, pitch, ramp, tilt; angle, bias, emphasis, leaning, prejudice, viewpoint. **vb** *lit:* bend, incline, lean, list, slope, tilt; bias, twist, weight.

slap n *lit:* bang, clout, smack, spank, wallop, whack; *fig:* blow, rebuff, snub. **vb** *lit:* blow, clap, clout, cuff, hit, spank, whack; daub, spread.

slash n *lit:* cut, gash, laceration, rip, slit. **vb** *lit:* gash, hack, lacerate, rend, score, slit; cut, lower, reduce.

slaughter n *lit:* blood bath, bloodshed, carnage, killing, liquidation, massacre, slaying. **vb** *lit:* butcher, do to death, exterminate, kill, massacre, murder, put to the sword, slay.

slave n *lit:* drudge, serf, servant, vassal, villein. **vb** *lit:* drudge, slog, toil.

slavery n *lit:* bondage, captivity, serfdom, servitude, thraldom, vassalage.

slavish *adj lit:* abject, cringing, grovelling, low, menial, servile, sycophantic; conventional, imitative, unimaginative, uninspired.

slay *vb lit:* annihilate, assassinate, destroy, eliminate, exterminate, massacre, murder, slaughter; amuse, be the death of.

sleek *adj lit:* glossy, shiny, smooth, well-groomed.

sleep *n lit:* doze, nap, rest, slumber(s), snooze. *vb lit:* catnap, doze, drop off, drowse, nod off, slumber, snooze, take a nap.

slender *adj lit:* lean, narrow, slim, sylph-like, willowy; inadequate, insufficient, meagre, scanty, small; feeble, flimsy, remote, slight, thin, weak.

slick *vb lit:* plaster down, sleek, smooth. *adj lit:* glossy, smooth, soft; glib, plausible, polished, sophistical, specious; adroit, deft, sharp, skilful, sly, tricky.

slight *n lit:* affront, discourtesy, disdain, insult, rebuff, snub, (the) cold shoulder. *vb lit:* affront, cold-shoulder, disparage, give offence to, scorn, snub. *adj lit:* feeble, insignificant, minor, negligible, paltry, small, superficial, trivial, unimportant; delicate, fragile, lightly-built.

slim *vb lit:* diet, lose weight, reduce. *adj lit:* lean, narrow, sylph-like, thin, trim; faint, poor, remote, slender, slight.

slimy *adj lit:* clammy, mucous, muddy, oozy, viscous; creeping, grovelling, oily, servile, smarmy, sycophantic, toadying, unctuous.

sling *n lit:* strap, string; casting, hurling, throw; band, chain, loop. *vb lit:* cast, chuck, fling, heave, hurl, throw, toss; dangle, hang, swing.

slip *n lit:* bloomer, blunder, error, fault, indiscretion, mistake, oversight, slip of the tongue. *vb lit:* glide, slide, slither; fall, lose one's footing, skid, trip (over); conceal, hide, insinuate oneself, sneak; blunder, boob, miscalculate, mistake; break free from, disappear, dodge, elude, evade, get away, outwit.

slippery *adj lit:* skiddy, slippy, smooth, unsafe, unstable, unsteady; crafty, cunning, devious, evasive, false, shifty, sneaky, tricky, two-faced, unreliable, untrustworthy.

slope n *lit:* declination, descent, gradient, inclination, ramp, scarp, slant, tilt. **vb** *lit:* drop away, fall, incline, lean, pitch, rise, tilt; creep, make oneself scarce, skulk, slip.

sloth n *lit:* idleness, inactivity, indolence, inertia, slackness, sluggishness, torpor.

slow vb *lit:* check, curb, delay, detain, hold up, lag, reduce speed, restrict. **adj** *lit:* creeping, dawdling, easy, laggard, lazy, leaden, leisurely, plodding, ponderous, slow-moving, sluggish, unhurried; behind, delayed, dilatory, late, tardy, unpunctual; gradual, lingering, long-drawn-out, prolonged, protracted; dull, inactive, quiet, sleepy, stagnant, tedious, uneventful, wearisome; dim, dull-witted, dumb, obtuse, stupid, thick.

slur n *fig:* affront, blot, brand, discredit, disgrace, innuendo, insinuation, reproach, smear, stain, stigma. *spec:* legato, slide. **vb** *lit:* conceal, go through hurriedly, minimize, pass lightly over; pronounce indistinctly; *fig:* affront, disgrace, discredit, insinuate, insult, smear, stain; *spec:* slide.

sly adj *lit:* artful, clever, conniving, crafty, cunning, devious, guileful, scheming, shifty, stealthy, underhand, wily; impish, mischievous, roguish.

smack n *lit:* flavour, taste; dash, suggestion, tinge, touch, trace; sailing boat; blow, crack, slap. **vb** *lit:* box, clap, hit, pat, slap, sock, spank, tap. **adv** *lit:* directly, exactly, pointblank, right, squarely, straight.

small adj *lit:* diminutive, little, miniature, minute, petite, pint-sized, puny, tiny, undersized; insignificant, lesser, minor, paltry, petty, trifling, trivial; inadequate, insufficient, limited, meagre, scanty; humble, modest, small-scale; base, grudging, mean, narrow, selfish.

smart n *lit:* burning, pang, smarting, sting. **vb** *lit:* burn, hurt, sting, throb, tingle. **adj** *lit:* hard, painful, piercing, sharp, stinging; adept, apt, astute, bright, canny, ingenious, keen, nimble, quick-witted, sharp, shrewd; chic, elegant, fashionable, modish, natty, neat, snappy, stylish, trim; impertinent, nimble-witted, ready, saucy, witty; brisk, lively, quick, spanking, spirited.

smear n *lit:* blot, blotch, daub, smudge, splotch; defamation, libel, mud-slinging, slander, vilification. **vb** *lit:* bedaub, blur, cover, daub, dirty, rub on, smudge, spread over, stain; asperse, blacken, calumniate, malign, sully, tarnish, vilify.

smell n *lit:* aroma, bouquet, fragrance, odour, redolence, scent, whiff; fetor, pong, stench, stink. **vb** *lit:* get a whiff of, scent, sniff; be malodorous, pong, reek, stink.

smooth **vb** *lit:* flatten, iron, polish, press; allay, alleviate, calm, extenuate, facilitate, mitigate, mollify, palliate, soften. **adj** *lit:* even, flat, flush, level, unwrinkled; glossy, shiny, silky, soft, velvety; calm, equable, peaceful, serene, tranquil, unruffled; agreeable, mellow, mild, soothing; glib, ingratiating, persuasive, slick, smarmy, suave, unctuous; easy, effortless, flowing, fluent, regular, rhythmic, unbroken, uninterrupted, well-ordered.

smothered **adj (pa.pt)** *lit:* choked, stifled, strangled, suffocated; concealed, muffled, suppressed; cocooned, inundated, overwhelmed, showered.

smug **adj** *lit:* complacent, conceited, priggish, self-opinionated, self-righteous, self-satisfied.

snag n *lit:* catch, complication, disadvantage, drawback, hitch, problem, stumbling block. **vb** *lit:* catch, rip, tear.

snap n *lit:* crackle, fillip, flick, pop; bite, grab, nip; energy, go, liveliness, vigour, zip. **vb** *lit:* break, crack, give way, separate; bite, catch, grip, nip, snatch; bark, flare out, flash, lash out at, retort, snarl; click, crackle, pop; *fig:* to take a photograph. **adj** *lit:* abrupt, immediate, instant, on-the-spot, sudden.

snare n *lit:* catch, net, noose, pitfall, trap, wire. **vb** *lit:* catch, entrap, net, seize, springe, wire.

snatch n *lit:* bit, fragment, piece, smattering, snippet, spell. **vb** *lit:* clutch, grab, grasp, grip, make off with, pluck, pull, seize, stolen, wrench, wrest.

sneer n *lit:* derision, disdain, gibe, jeer, mockery, ridicule, scorn. **vb** *lit:* deride, disdain, gibe, jeer, laugh, mock, ridicule, scoff, sniff at, snigger, turn up one's nose.

snobbish *adj* *lit:* arrogant, condescending, hoity-toity, patronizing, pretentious, snooty, toffee-nosed, uppish.

snooze *n* *lit:* catnap, doze, nap, siesta. **vb** *lit:* catnap, doze, drop off, nap, nod off.

snub *n* *lit:* affront, brush-off, insult, put-down. **vb** *lit:* cold-shoulder, cut dead, humble, humiliate, mortify, rebuff, slight.

snug *adj* *lit:* comfortable, cosy, homely, sheltered, warm; compact, neat, trim.

so *adv* *lit:* as shown, in that way, in the same way; as stated; to that degree, to this degree; in such a way, to such a degree; very; very much; accordingly, for that reason, therefore; also, likewise. **cnj** *lit:* in order that, with the result that; with the intention that; if, on the condition that. **interj** *lit:* well; all right, let it be that way; is that true?

soak *vb* *lit:* damp, drench, immerse, moisten, penetrate, permeate, saturate, wet; absorb, assimilate, suck in, take in.

sober *vb* *lit:* bring back to earth, calm down, clear one's head, come to one's senses. **adj** *lit:* abstinent, moderate, temperate; calm, clear-headed, composed, cool, level-headed, rational, reasonable, sedate, serious, sound, steady, unruffled; dark, quiet, sombre, subdued.

sociable *adj* *lit:* affable, approachable, convivial, cordial, friendly, genial, gregarious, neighbourly, warm.

society *n* *lit:* community, humanity, mankind, people, social order, the public; companionship, company, fellowship; association, circle, club, corporation, fraternity, group, guild, institute, league, organization, union; élite, gentry, high society, nobs, smart set, top drawer, upper crust.

soft *adj* *lit:* creamy, doughy, pulpy, quaggy, spongy, squashy, yielding; bendable, elastic, flexible, malleable, plastic, pliable, supple; downy, fleecy, furry, silky, smooth, velvety; delicate, diffuse, dimmed, faint, low, mellow, melodious, murmured, pale, pastel, shaded, soothing, subdued, temperate, understated, whispered; compassionate, gentle, sensitive, sympathetic, tender; easy-going, lax, lenient, overindulgent, permissive, weak; comfortable, easy, undemanding; effeminate, flabby, overindulged, pampered, podgy; daft, feeble-minded, foolish, silly, soft in the head.

soften **vb** *lit:* allay, alleviate, appease, calm, diminish, lessen, melt, mitigate, modify, muffle, palliate, quell, relax, soothe, subdue, tone down.

soil **n** *lit:* clay, dust, earth, ground; country, land, region. **vb** *lit:* besmirch, defile, foul, pollute, spatter, stain, tarnish.

solemn **adj** *lit:* earnest, glum, portentous, serious, sober, thoughtful; august, ceremonious, dignified, grand, grave, imposing, momentous, stately; devotional, reverential, ritual, sacred, venerable.

solid **n** *lit:* lump, mass. **adj** *lit:* compact, dense, firm, stable, strong, sturdy, substantial; genuine, pure, real, sound; complete, unalloyed, unanimous, unbroken, united, unmixed; *fig:* decent, dependable, level-headed, reliable, sensible, sober, trusty, upright, worthy.

solitude **n** *lit:* isolation, loneliness, privacy, reclusiveness, seclusion; emptiness, waste, wilderness.

solution **n** *lit:* answer, clarification, explanation, key, resolution, unravelling; blend, emulsion, mix, solvent, suspension; dissolution, melting.

solve **vb** *lit:* clarify, clear up, crack, decipher, disentangle, elucidate, explain, expound, interpret, unfold, unravel, work out.

sombre **adj** *lit:* dark, dim, doleful, drab, dull, funereal, gloomy, grave, melancholy, mournful, sad, shadowy, shady.

somebody **n** *lit:* bigwig, celebrity, heavyweight, household name, public figure, V.I.P. **prn** *lit:* anybody, anyone, one, someone.

sometimes **adv** *lit:* at times, every now and then, from time to time, now and again, now and then, occasionally, off and on, once in a while.

song **n** *lit:* air, anthem, ballad, canticle, carol, chant, ditty, hymn, melody, pop song, psalm, shanty, tune.

soon   *adv lit:* before long, in a minute, presently, shortly; promptly, quickly; leaf, readily, willingly.

sophistication   *n lit:* finesse, poise, savoir-faire, urbanity, worldly wisdom.

sordid   *adj lit:* dirty, filthy, foul, seamy, seedy, sleazy, squalid; backstreet, base, debauched, disreputable, shabby, vile; avaricious, covetous, grasping, mercenary, niggardly, selfish, venal.

sore   *n lit:* abscess, boil, inflammation, ulcer.   *adj lit:* burning, chafed, inflamed, irritated, raw, smarting, tender; annoying, distressing, grievous, sharp, troublesome; acute, critical, dire, extreme, pressing, urgent; afflicted, aggrieved, angry, hurt, irked, peeved, resentful, vexed.

sorrow   *n lit:* affliction, anguish, distress, grief, heartache, mourning, sadness, woe; blow, hardship, misfortune, trial, tribulation, trouble, worry.   *vb lit:* agonize, bemoan, grieve, moan, mourn.

sorry   *adj lit:* apologetic, conscience-stricken, contrite, penitent, remorseful, repentant, self-reproachful; disconsolate, distressed, grieved, melancholy, sad, sorrowful; compassionate, moved, pitying, sympathetic; abject, base, deplorable, dismal, mean, miserable, paltry, pathetic, piteous, shabby, wretched.

sort   *n lit:* brand, breed, category, character, class, description, genus, ilk, kind, make, nature, order, species, style, type, variety.   *vb lit:* arrange, assort, categorize, choose, classify, distribute, divide, grade, put in order, rank, select, separate.

soul   *n lit:* life, mind, psyche, reason, spirit, vital force; being, body, individual, mortal, person; embodiment, essence, personification, quintessence, type; ardour, courage, energy, feeling, fervour, inspiration, vitality.

sound   *n lit:* din, noise, report, resonance, reverberation, tone; drift, idea, impression, look, tenor; earshot, hearing, range.   *vb lit:* echo, resonate, resound, reverberate; appear, look, seem; announce, articulate, enunciate, express, signal; fathom, probe; examine, investigate, test.   *adj lit:* complete, entire, fit, hale, healthy, intact, perfect, robust, sturdy, substantial, unimpaired, vigorous, whole; fair, just, level-headed, logical, proper, prudent, reasonable, reliable, right, sensible, true, valid, well-founded; established, proven, recognized, reputable, safe, secure, solvent, stable; peaceful, unbroken, undisturbed.

sour **vb** *lit:* alienate, disenchant, embitter, exacerbate, exasperate, turn off. **adj** *lit:* acid, bitter, sharp, tart; bad, fermented, gone off, rancid, turned; acrimonious, churlish, cynical, disagreeable, embittered, grudging, ill-tempered, peevish, waspish.

souvenir **n** *lit:* keepsake, memento, reminder, token.

sovereign **n** *lit:* autocrat, monarch, ruler. **adj** *lit:* absolute, chief, dominant, monarchal, paramount, predominant, principal, regal, ruling, supreme; effectual, efficient, excellent.

sow **n** *lit:* female hog; main trough. **vb** *lit:* disseminate, implant, inseminate, plant, scatter, seed.

space **n** *lit:* capacity, elbowroom, expanse, extent, leeway, margin, room, scope, volume; blank, distance, gap, lacuna; duration, interval, period, span, time; accommodation, berth, place.

span **n** *lit:* distance, extent, reach, spread, stretch; duration, period, spell. **vb** *lit:* arch across, bridge, extend across, link, traverse, vault.

spare **n** *lit:* extra, guest room, spare part, surplus. **vb** *lit:* afford, dispense with, do without, give, let (someone) have, manage without, part with; deal leniently with, go easy on, have mercy on, let off, pardon, refrain from, relieve from, save from. **adj** *lit:* additional, emergency, extra, free, going begging, over, superfluous, surplus, unoccupied; gaunt, lank, meagre, slender, slim, wiry; economical, frugal, modest, scanty, sparing.

spark **n** *lit:* flare, flash, flicker, glint; atom, hint, jot, trace, vestige. **vb** *lit:* excite, inspire, kindle, precipitate, set off, start, stir, trigger (off).

sparkle **n** *lit:* brilliance, dazzle, flash, flicker, glint, spark, twinkle; animation, flash, life, panache, spirit, vim, vivacity, zip. **vb** *lit:* beam, flash, gleam, glint, glitter, scintillate, shine, twinkle, wink; bubble, effervesce, fizz.

spasm n *lit:* contraction, paroxysm, twitch; burst, eruption, fit, frenzy, outburst, seizure.

speak vb *lit:* articulate, converse, discourse, express, make known, pronounce, say, state, tell, utter, voice; address, declaim, harangue, lecture, plead.

special adj *lit:* distinguished, exceptional, extraordinary, festive, gala, important, memorable, momentous, red-letter, significant, unique; characteristic, especial, individual, particular, peculiar, specific; chief, main, major, primary.

specialist n *lit:* authority, connoisseur, consultant, expert, master.

specific adj *lit:* clear-cut, definite, exact, explicit, express, particular, precise, unambiguous; characteristic, distinguishing, peculiar, special.

specifications n *lit:* details, items, particulars, requirements, stipulations.

specify vb *lit:* cite, define, detail, enumerate, indicate, itemize, mention, name, spell out, stipulate.

speck n *lit:* blemish, blot, defect, fault, flaw, fleck, mark, speckle, spot, stain; atom, bit, dot, grain, iota, mite, modicum, particle, shred, whit.

speckled adj *lit:* brindled, dappled, dotted, freckled, mottled, spotted, spotty, stippled.

spectacle n *lit:* display, event, extravaganza, pageant, performance, show; curiosity, laughing stock, marvel, phenomenon, scene, sight.

spectacular n *lit:* display, extravaganza, show, spectacle. adj *lit:* breathtaking, dazzling, dramatic, fantastic, impressive, magnificent, sensational, splendid, striking, stunning.

spectator n *lit:* beholder, eye-witness, observer, onlooker, viewer, watcher.

speculate vb *lit:* cogitate, conjecture, contemplate, deliberate, hypothesize, meditate, scheme, surmise, theorize; gamble, have a flutter, hazard, risk, venture.

speech n *lit:* conversation, dialogue, discussion, talk; address, discourse, disquisition, harangue, lecture, oration; articulation, dialect, diction, idiom, jargon, language, parlance, tongue.

speed n *lit:* acceleration, celerity, expedition, fleetness, momentum, pace, precipitation, quickness, rapidity, swiftness, velocity. **vb** *lit:* belt (along), career, expedite, flash, get a move on, hurry, make haste, press on, race, rush, tear, zoom; advance, boost, facilitate, further, help, promote.

spell n *lit:* bout, interval, period, season, stint, stretch, term, time, turn; charm, conjuration, exorcism, incantation, sorcery; allure, enchantment, fascination, magic, trance. **vb** *lit:* amount to, herald, imply, indicate, point to, portend, promise, signify, suggest.

spend **vb** *lit:* disburse, expend, lay out, pay out, splash out; consume, dissipate, drain, empty, exhaust, fritter away, squander, waste; bestow, devote, lavish, put in; fill, occupy, pass, while away.

sphere n *lit:* circle, globe, globule, orb; capacity, domain, field, function, range, scope, stratum, territory, walk of life.

spicy adj *lit:* aromatic, flavoured, fragrant, savoury, tangy; *fig:* improper, indelicate, keen, lively, piquant, pungent, salacious, showy, smart, spirited,

spin n *lit:* gyration, revolution, roll, whirl; drive, joy ride, turn. **vb** *lit:* gyrate, pirouette, revolve, rotate, twirl, twist; concoct, invent, recount, relate, tell, unfold; be giddy, grow dizzy, reel, swim.

spine n *lit:* backbone, spinal column, vertebrae; barb, quill, ray, spike, spur.

spineless adj *lit:* faint-hearted, feeble, gutless, ineffective, irresolute, lily-livered, pusillanimous, soft, squeamish, submissive, vacillating, weak, yellow.

spiral n *lit:* coil, corkscrew, helix, volute, whorl. **adj** *lit:* circular, coiled, helical, scrolled, voluted, whorled, winding.

spirit n *lit:* air, breath, life force, psyche, soul; attitude, disposition, essence, humour, outlook, temper, temperament; ardour, backbone, courage, dauntlessness, energy, enthusiasm, force, grit, guts, life, mettle, sparkle, vigour, zest; motivation, resolution, willpower; atmosphere, feeling, gist, tenor, tone; intent, meaning, purport, sense, substance; apparition, ghost, phantom, spectre, spook, sprite, vision. **vb** *lit:* carry (away), convey (off), steal (away), whisk (off).

spirited **adj** *lit:* animated, ardent, bold, energetic, high-spirited, mettlesome, plucky, sprightly, vivacious.

spit **n** *lit:* dribble, drool, saliva, spittle. **vb** *lit:* eject, expectorate, spew, splutter, throw out.

spite **n** *lit:* animosity, bitchiness, grudge, ill will, malevolence, malice, pique, rancour, spitefulness, spleen, venom. **vb** *lit:* annoy, gall, harm, hurt, needle, nettle, offend, pique, put out, vex.

splendid **adj** *lit:* admirable, exceptional, glorious, illustrious, magnificent, outstanding, remarkable, renowned, sublime, superb; costly, gorgeous, impressive, lavish, luxurious, rich, sumptuous; excellent, fantastic, fine, great, marvellous, wonderful; beaming, brilliant, glittering, lustrous, radiant.

splendour **n** *lit:* brightness, brilliance, dazzle, glory, grandeur, lustre, magnificence, pomp, renown, resplendence, solemnity, spectacle, stateliness.

splinter **n** *lit:* chip, flake, paring, shaving, sliver. **vb** *lit:* disintegrate, fracture, shiver, split.

split **n** *lit:* breach, crack, division, fissure, gap, rent, rip, slash, slit, tear; break-up, discord, disruption, dissention, divergence, estrangement, partition, rift, schism. **vb** *lit:* branch, break, burst, come apart, come undone, crack, disband, diverge, fork, give way, go separate ways, part, rend, rip, separate, slit, snap, splinter; allocate, allot, distribute, dole out, halve, partition, share out; grass on, inform on, squeal on. **adj** *lit:* ambivalent, bisected, broken, cracked, divided, fractured, ruptured.

spoil **n** *lit:* refuse, slag. **vb** *lit:* blemish, damage, harm, impair, mess up, ruin, upset, wreck; cosset, indulge, mollycoddle, overindulge, pamper; curdle, decay, go bad, go off, rot, turn.

spot **n** *lit:* blemish, blot, daub, flaw, mark, pimple, smudge, speck, stain; location, place, point, position, site; bit, little, morsel; mess, plight, predicament, quandary, trouble.   **vb** *lit:* descry, detect, identify, make out, pick out, recognize, see, sight; blot, dot, fleck, mottle, soil, spatter, splodge, stain, taint, tarnish.

spread   **n** *lit:* advancement, dispersion, escalation, expansion, increase, proliferation, spreading; extent, period, span, stretch, sweep; array, feast, repast.   **vb** *lit:* broaden, expand, fan out, sprawl, stretch, unfold, widen; escalate, multiply, mushroom, proliferate; advertise, circulate, cover, distribute, make known, promulgate, propagate, publicize, scatter, shed, transmit; arrange, array, lay, prepare.

spring   **n** *lit:* hop, jump, leap, vault; bounce, buoyancy, elasticity, flexibility, give, resilience; cause, origin, root, source, well. **vb** *lit:* bound, hop, jump, leap, rebound, recoil, vault; derive, descend, emanate, emerge, grow, originate, start, stem; burgeon, mushroom, shoot up.

spry   **adj** *lit:* agile, brisk, nimble, quick, sprightly, supple.

spur   **n** *lit:* goad, prick, rowel; impetus, impulse, incentive, motive, stimulus.   **vb** *lit:* drive, goad, impel, incite, press, prod, prompt, stimulate, urge.

spurt   **n** *lit:* burst, rush, spate, surge.   **vb** *lit:* burst, erupt, gush, jet, spew, squirt, surge.

spy   **n** *lit:* agent, mole.   **vb** *lit:* shadow, tail, trail, watch; glimpse, notice, spot.

squander   **vb** *lit:* blow, dissipate, fritter away, lavish, misuse, run through, spend, waste.

square   **n** *lit:* equilateral rectangle; number multiplied by itself; *fig:* antediluvian, die-hard, fuddy-duddy, old buffer.   **vb** *lit:* agree, conform, fit, match, reconcile, tally; balance, clear up, liquidate, pay off, satisfy, settle; adapt, align, even up, level, regulate, suit, tailor; bribe, buy off, fix, rig.   **adj** *lit:* decent, equitable, ethical, fair, genuine, honest, just, straight; behind the times, conventional, old-fashioned, strait-laced, stuffy.

squash n *lit:* crushed mass; gourd; beverage. **vb** *lit:* compress, crush, mash, pound, press, pulp, smash, trample down; annihilate, humiliate, put down, quash, quell, silence.

squeal n *lit:* scream, screech, shriek, wail, yell. **vb** *lit:* scream, screech, shout, shriek, shrill, wail, yelp; betray, blab, grass, inform on; complain, protest.

squeeze n *lit:* cuddle, embrace, hold, hug; congestion, crowd, crush, jam, jostle, press, squash, thrust. **vb** *lit:* clutch, compress, crush, grip, pinch, squash, wring; cram, crowd, force, jam, jostle, pack, ram, thrust, wedge; clasp, cuddle, embrace, hold tight, hug; bleed, extort, lean on, pressurize, wrest.

stab n *lit:* gash, incision, jab, thrust; pang, prick, twinge; *fig:* attempt, crack, endeavour, go, try. **vb** *lit:* cut, gore, jab, knife, pierce, puncture, run through, stick, thrust, transfix; *fig:* deceive, double-cross, let down, sell.

stable n *lit:* barn, shed, stall; string, stud. **adj** *lit:* constant, deep-rooted, enduring, established, firm, fixed, lasting, permanent, reliable, secure, sound, steady, sure, unwavering, well-founded.

stage n *lit:* arena, theatre; dais, platform, scaffold; jetty, pier, quay; division, juncture, lap, leg, level, phase, point.
vb *lit:* arrange, do, engineer, lay on, orchestrate, organize, perform, play, present, produce, put on.

stagger **vb** *lit:* falter, lurch, reel, sway, totter, vacillate, waver, wobble; amaze, astonish, astound, bowl over, dumbfound, flabbergast, overwhelm, shake, shock, stun, stupefy, surprise, take (someone) aback; alternate, overlap, zigzag.

stain n *lit:* blemish, blot, discoloration, dye, spot, tint; disgrace, dishonour, infamy, shame, slur, stigma. **vb** *lit:* blemish, blot, colour, discolour, dye, mark, soil, tarnish, tinge; blacken, corrupt, defile, deprave, disgrace, sully, taint.

stale **adj** *lit:* dry, fetid, flat, fusty, musty, old, sour, stagnant; antiquated, banal, cliché-ridden, common, drab, flat, hackneyed, insipid, platitudinous, stereotyped, trite, worn-out.

stall   n *lit:* compartment (in stable); booth (in bazaar); orchestra seat; stalling, standstill; delay, pretence, pretext, prevarication.   **vb** *lit:* confine (in a stall); become stuck, stop; block, delay, hedge, obstruct, play for time, prevaricate.

stand   n *lit:* rest, standstill, stay, stopover; attitude, opinion, position, stance, standpoint; base, booth, dais, grandstand, platform, rack, stage, stall, support.   **vb** *lit:* be upright, mount, place, position, put, set; be valid, continue, exist, halt, pause, rest, stay, stop; bear, cope with, countenance, endure, handle, put up with, stomach, sustain, take, tolerate, withstand.

standard   n *lit:* average, criterion, example, gauge, guide, measure, model, norm, pattern, rule, specification, type, yardstick; ethics, ideals, moral principles; banner, colours, ensign, flag, pennant. **adj** *lit:* accepted, basic, customary, normal, orthodox, popular, regular, set, staple, stock, typical, usual.

standing   n *lit:* credit, estimation, footing, rank, reputation, station, status; duration, existence, experience.   **adj** *lit:* fixed, lasting, permanent, perpetual, repeated; erect, perpendicular, upright, vertical.

stare   **vb** *lit:* gape, gawk, gaze, goggle, rubberneck.

start   n *lit:* beginning, commencement, dawn, foundation, inauguration, initiation, kickoff, onset, opening; advantage, head start, lead; break, chance, introduction, opportunity; convulsion, jar, spasm, twitch.   **vb** *lit:* begin, commence, get under way, go ahead, leave, set off, set out; initiate, instigate, kick off, originate, set in motion, create, found, institute, launch, pioneer, set up; flinch, jerk, jump, recoil, twitch.

state   n *lit:* circumstances, condition, pass, plight, position, predicament, situation; attitude, frame of mind, mood; glory, grandeur, pomp, splendour, style; bother, flap, panic, tizzy; country, federation, land, nation.   **vb** *lit:* affirm, articulate, assert, declare, enumerate, explain, expound, express, present, put, specify, voice.

station   n *lit:* depot, headquarters, location, place, position, situation; appointment, calling, grade, position, post, rank, situation, standing, status.   **vb** *lit:* assign, fix, garrison, install, post, set.

stay n *lit:* sojourn, stopover, visit; delay, halt, pause, postponement, remission, reprieve, suspension. **vb** *lit:* continue, delay, halt, hang around, linger, pause, remain, settle, sojourn, stop, tarry; lodge, put up at, visit; adjourn, defer, put off, suspend.

steady vb *lit:* balance, brace, secure, support; compose oneself, cool down, sober (up). **adj** *lit:* firm, fixed, stable, uniform; balanced, calm, dependable, level-headed, reliable, sensible, settled, sober, steadfast; ceaseless, consistent, constant, faithful, habitual, persistent, regular, rhythmic, unbroken, unfaltering, uninterrupted, unwavering.

steal vb *lit:* appropriate, embezzle, lift, misappropriate, nick, pilfer, pinch, pirate, plagiarize, poach, purloin, thieve, make off with; creep, slip, sneak, tiptoe.

steep vb *lit:* damp, drench, immerse, moisten, soak, submerge; fill, infuse, permeate, pervade, saturate, suffuse. **adj** lit: abrupt, precipitous, sheer; excessive, extortionate, overpriced, stiff, unreasonable.

stem n *lit:* axis, peduncle, stalk, stock, trunk. **vb** *lit:* arise (from), derive (from), emanate (from), issue (from), originate; check, contain, curb, dam, hold back, resist, restrain, stop, withstand.

step n *lit:* footstep, gait, pace, stride, trace, track; action, deed, expedient, means, measure, move, procedure; advancement, phase, point, progression; degree, level, rank; doorstep, stair, tread. **vb** *lit:* move, pace, tread, walk.

stick n *lit:* baton, cane, rod, staff, stake, twig, wand; *fig:* fuddy-duddy, (old) fogy, pain, prig; blame, criticism, flak, hostility. **vb** *lit:* adhere, affix, bind, cling, fasten, hold on, join, paste; insert, jab, pierce, prod, puncture, stab, transfix; bulge, jut, poke, protrude; fix, lay, place, position, put, set; clog, jam, snag, stop; linger, remain, stay; endure, get on with, stand, stomach, take, tolerate; last out, put up with; stand up for, support.

sticky adj *lit:* adhesive, clinging, glutinous, gooey, gummy, tacky, tenacious, viscous; awkward, difficult, embarrassing, nasty, thorny, tricky; clammy, humid, muggy, oppressive, sweltering.

stiff adj *lit:* firm, hardened, inflexible, rigid, solid, taut, tense, tight, unbending; austere, chilly, constrained, formal, laboured, pompous, prim, punctilious, starchy, uneasy; awkward, clumsy, crude, graceless, jerky, ungainly; arduous, exacting, formidable, hard, tough, trying, uphill; cruel, drastic, extreme, harsh, oppressive, pitiless, rigorous, severe, strict, stringent; brisk, powerful, strong, vigorous.

still   n *lit:* frame, photograph, picture; peace, quiet, stillness, tranquillity.   **vb** *lit:* distill; allay, alleviate, calm, hush, lull, quieten, settle, silence, smooth, soothe, tranquillize.   **adj** *lit:* calm, hushed, inert, motionless, peaceful, placid, quiet, restful, silent, smooth, tranquil, undisturbed, unruffled.   **adv** *lit:* even, yet; nevertheless; at that time, at this time; even to that time, even to this time; quietly, without moving.   **cnj** *lit:* but, for all that, however, notwithstanding.

stir   n *lit:* ado, agitation, commotion, disturbance, excitement, flurry, fuss, to-do, uproar.   **vb** *lit:* agitate, disturb, move, quiver, rustle, shake; arouse, excite, instigate, provoke, raise, urge; affect, inspire, thrill, touch; budge, get a move on, look lively.

stock   n *lit:* array, assortment, cache, commodities, fund, hoard, inventory, merchandise, range, stockpile, store, supply, variety; cattle, horses, livestock, sheep; breed, descent, extraction, forebears, lineage, parentage, pedigree; capital, funds, investment, property.
vb *lit:* deal in, handle, keep, sell, supply, trade in; accumulate, buy up, hoard, replenish, store up; equip, fit out, furnish, kit out, provide with, provision.   **adj** *lit:* banal, basic, conventional, customary, hackneyed, overused, regular, routine, set, standard, staple, stereotyped, trite, usual, worn-out.

stomach   n *lit:* abdomen, belly, paunch, tummy; appetite, inclination, mind, taste.   **vb** *lit:* bear, endure, put up with, resign oneself to, suffer, take, tolerate.

stoop   n *lit:* droop, sag, slouch, slump.   **vb** *lit:* bend, crouch, duck, hunch, incline, lean, squat; condescend, deign, demean oneself, resort, sink.

stop   n *lit:* cessation, conclusion, end, finish, halt, standstill; sojourn, stay, stopover, visit; bar, block, break, check, hindrance, impediment, stoppage; depot, destination, station, terminus.   **vb** *lit:* be over, break off, cease, conclude, cut short, discontinue, end, finish, leave off, peter out, pull up, quit, refrain, stall, terminate; arrest, bar, block, check, forestall, frustrate, hinder, hold back, impede, intercept, prevent, restrain, silence, stem, suspend; break one's journey, lodge, sojourn, stay, tarry.

store   n *lit:* accumulation, cache, hoard, mine, provision, reserve, stock, supply; emporium, outlet, shop, supermarket; depository, storeroom, warehouse.   **vb** *lit:* accumulate, deposit, hoard, keep, lay by, put aside, reserve, salt away, save, stock.

storm   n *lit:* blizzard, cyclone, gale, gust, hurricane, tempest, tornado, whirlwind; assault, attack, blitz, offensive, onslaught; *fig:* agitation, commotion, disturbance, outburst, outcry, row, rumpus, strife, turmoil.   **vb** *lit:* assail, assault, beset, charge, take by storm; complain, fume, rage, rant, scold, thunder; flounce, rush, stalk.

story   n *lit:* account, anecdote, chronicle, history, legend, narrative, novel, recital, romance, tale, yarn; fib, fiction, lie, untruth; article, feature, news item, report.

straight   adj *lit:* direct, undeviating, unswerving; aligned, erect, horizontal, level, perpendicular, upright, vertical; blunt, forthright, frank, outright, point-blank, straightforward, unqualified; above board, accurate, equitable, fair, honest, law-abiding, reliable, trustworthy; arranged, neat, orderly, organized, shipshape, tidy; continuous, nonstop, solid, sustained, uninterrupted; conventional, orthodox, traditional; pure, unadulterated, undiluted.   **adv** *lit:* as the crow flies; at once, directly, immediately, instantly; frankly, honestly, point-blank, pulling no punches.

strain   n *lit:* effort, exertion, force, injury, struggle, tension, wrench; anxiety, burden, pressure, stress; air, melody, theme, tune; ancestry, descent, extraction, lineage, pedigree, stock; suggestion, tendency, trace, trait; manner, style, temper, tone, vein.   **vb** *lit:* draw tight, extend, stretch, tighten; exert, fatigue, injure, overwork, sprain, tax, tire, twist, wrench; endeavour, strive, struggle; filter, percolate, separate, sieve, sift.

strange   adj *lit:* abnormal, bizarre, curious, extraordinary, fantastic, odd, peculiar, perplexing, queer, rare, singular, uncanny, weird; alien, foreign, novel, unfamiliar, untried; new to, unaccustomed to, unused to; awkward, bewildered, ill at ease, lost, out of place.

strangle vb *lit:* asphyxiate, choke, smother, strangulate, throttle; gag, inhibit, stifle, suppress.

stray n *lit:* lost animal, wanderer. vb *lit:* deviate, diverge, get sidetracked, ramble; be abandoned, drift, err, go astray, meander, roam, rove, straggle, wander. adj *lit:* abandoned, lost, roaming; accidental, chance, freak, odd, random.

stream n *lit:* beck, brook, current, river, rivulet, torrent, tributary. vb *lit:* cascade, course, flow, gush, run, shed, spout.

strength n *lit:* backbone, brawn, firmness, might, robustness, stamina, sturdiness, toughness; efficacy, energy, force, potency, vehemence, vigour; asset, mainstay, strong point, succour.

stress n *lit:* emphasis,importance, significance, weight; anxiety, hassle, pressure, strain, tension, trauma, worry; accent, accentuation, beat. vb *lit:* accentuate, dwell on, emphasize, harp on, repeat, rub in, underline.

stretch n *lit:* distance, expanse, extent, spread, tract; period, run, space, spell, stint, time. vb *lit:* cover, extend, reach, spread; draw out, elongate, expand, pull, rack, tighten.

strict adj *lit:* austere, firm, harsh, no-nonsense, rigorous, stern, stringent; accurate, exact, meticulous, particular, precise, scrupulous; absolute, complete, utter.

strike n *lit:* bang, blow, clout, hit, knock, slap, smack, wallop; stoppage, walk-out. vb *lit:* bang, beat, chastise, clobber, clout, hit, knock, pound, smack, smite, thump, wallop; clash, collide with, run into, smash into; drive, force, thrust; come to mind, dawn upon, occur to, register; chance upon, discover, find, stumble upon, unearth; assail, assault, attack, fall upon, set upon; achieve, arrive at, reach; down tools, walk out.

strip n *lit:* belt, bit, fillet, piece, shred, slip, swathe. vb *lit:* bare, deprive, dismantle, empty, loot, pillage, plunder, ransack, rob, spoil; disrobe, unclothe, undress.

stroke n *lit:* achievement, blow, feat, hit, knock, movement, pat, rap, thump; apoplexy, attack, fit, seizure, shock. vb *lit:* caress, fondle, pat, pet.

stroll n *lit:* breath of air, constitutional, excursion, promenade, ramble, walk. **vb** *lit:* amble, make one's way, mosey, promenade, ramble, saunter, stretch one's legs, toddle, wander.

strong adj *lit:* athletic, beefy, burly, hale, hardy, muscular, robust, sound, stalwart, strapping, sturdy, tough, virile; brave, courageous, determined, high-powered, plucky, resilient, resourceful, steadfast, tenacious, unyielding; acute, dedicated, deep-rooted, eager, fervent, firm, intense, keen, staunch, vehement, zealous; clear-cut, cogent, compelling, distinct, formidable, marked, persuasive, potent, telling, unmistakable, weighty, well-founded; drastic, extreme, forceful, severe; durable, hard-wearing, heavy-duty, reinforced, substantial, well-built, well-protected; bold, bright, dazzling, glaring, loud; biting, heady, highly flavoured, hot, intoxicating, piquant, pure, spicy, undiluted.

structure n *lit:* arrangement, conformation, design, form, interrelation of parts, make-up, organization; building, construction, edifice, erection. **vb** *lit:* arrange, assemble, build up, design, put together, shape.

struggle n *lit:* effort, exertion, grind, long haul, scramble, toil; battle, brush, clash, conflict, contest, encounter, skirmish, strife, tussle. **vb** *lit:* exert oneself, go all out, strain, strive, toil, work; battle, compete, contend, fight, grapple, scuffle.

stubborn adj *lit:* bull-headed, dogged, headstrong, intractable, obstinate, persistent, pig-headed, recalcitrant, stiff-necked, tenacious, unshakable, wilful.

stuck adj (pa.pt) *lit:* cemented, fastened, fixed, glued, joined; *fig:* at a loss, baffled, nonplussed; hung up on, infatuated, keen, mad, obsessed with.

student n *lit:* apprentice, disciple, observer, pupil, scholar, undergraduate.

study n *lit:* academic work, research, swotting; analysis, attention, contemplation, inquiry, investigation, scrutiny, survey; drawing, sketch; library, study. **vb** *lit:* apply oneself to, contemplate, examine, go into, meditate, ponder, read; analyse, deliberate, investigate, look into, peruse, research, survey.

stuff   n *lit:* belongings, effects, equipment, gear, kit, paraphernalia, possessions, tackle, trappings; cloth, fabric, material, textile; essence, matter, quintessence, substance; balderdash, bunkum, claptrap, humbug, nonsense, poppycock, rot, rubbish, tripe, twaddle, verbiage.   **vb** *lit:* compress, cram, fill, jam, load, pad, ram, shove, squeeze, wedge; gobble, guzzle, make a pig of oneself, overindulge.

stuffy   adj *lit:* airless, fetid, fuggy, heavy, oppressive, stifling, suffocating, unventilated; conventional, dreary, dull, musty, old-fogyish, priggish, prim, stodgy, straitlaced.

stumble   vb *lit:* fall, falter, flounder, lurch, reel, slip, stagger, trip; falter, stammer, stutter.

stunted   adj (pa.pt) *lit:* diminutive, dwarfed, small, tiny, undersized.

stupid   adj *lit:* asinine, brainless, dim, feeble-mindedness, imbecility, naive, slow, thick-headed; absurd, folly, foolhardy, inept, irresponsible, lunatic, senseless, silly.

sturdy   adj *lit:* athletic, brawny, durable, firm, hardy, hearty, muscular, robust, secure, stalwart, staunch, steadfast, vigorous, well-built.

style   n *lit:* cut, design, form, manner, technique; fashion, mode, rage, trend, vogue; approach, custom, manner, way; chic, dash, elegance, flair, panache, smartness, sophistication, stylishness, taste; affluence, comfort, grandeur, luxury; category, characteristic, genre, kind, sort, spirit, tenor, tone, type; diction, expression, phraseology, turn of phrase, vein, wording.   **vb** *lit:* adapt, cut, design, dress, fashion, tailor; address, call, dub, entitle, label, name, term.

subdued   adj *lit:* chastened, dejected, downcast, grave, restrained, sad, serious, solemn; hushed, low-key, muted, quiet, sober, soft, subtle, toned down.

subject   n *lit:* affair, business, issue, matter, object, point, question, theme, topic; case, guinea pig, participant, patient; citizen, dependant, national, vassal.   **vb** *lit:* expose, lay open, put through, submit, treat.   **adj** *lit:* exposed, liable, open, prone, susceptible, vulnerable; conditional, contingent, dependent; answerable, bound by, inferior, obedient, satellite, subjugated, subordinate.

submit vb *lit:* acquiesce, agree, bend, capitulate, comply, defer, give in, knuckle under, put up with, resign oneself, succumb, surrender, toe the line, tolerate, yield; commit, hand in, proffer, put forward, refer, tender; advance, argue, assert, contend, move, propose, propound, put, state, suggest.

substance n *lit:* body, fabric, material, stuff, texture; burden, gist, import, meaning, pith, significance, subject, theme; actuality, entity, force, reality; affluence, assets, estate, means, resources.

substitute n *lit:* agent, deputy, expedient, locum, proxy, relief, replacement, reserve, stand-by, surrogate, temp. vb *lit:* change, exchange, replace, swap, switch; act for, cover for, deputize, fill in for, stand in for. adj *lit:* acting, additional, proxy, replacement, reserve, surrogate, temporary.

subtle adj *lit:* delicate, ingenious, nice, penetrating, profound, refined, sophisticated; faint, slight, understated; artful, crafty, cunning, devious, intriguing, Machiavellian, scheming, shrewd, sly, wily.

succeed vb *lit:* flourish, make good, prosper, thrive; ensue, follow.

successful adj *lit:* best-selling, booming, efficacious, flourishing, lucky, lucrative, profitable, prosperous, thriving, top.

suffer vb *lit:* ache, grieve, hurt; bear, endure, experience, go through, put up with, sustain, undergo; be impaired, deteriorate, fall off; allow, let, permit.

suggestion n *lit:* motion, proposal, proposition, recommendation; hint, indication, insinuation, intimation, suspicion, trace.

suggestive adj *lit:* evocative, indicative, reminiscent; bawdy, blue, improper, indecent, provocative, ribald, risqué, rude, smutty, spicy, titillating.

suit n *lit:* appeal, attentions, courtship, entreaty, petition, request; costume, dress, habit, outfit; *spec:* action, case, lawsuit, proceeding, prosecution, trial. vb *lit:* agree, answer, become, befit, be seemly, conform to, do, go with, match, satisfy, tally; accommodate, adjust, fashion, fit, tailor.

suitable adj *lit:* acceptable, applicable, appropriate, apt, becoming, befitting, convenient, fitting, in character, in keeping, pertinent, proper, relevant, right, satisfactory, seemly, suited.

sulky adj *lit:* aloof, churlish, disgruntled, moody, morose, petulant, put out, querulous, sullen, vexed.

sullen adj. *lit:* glum, ill humoured, moody, morose, sulky.

sultry adj *lit:* hot, humid, oppressive, sticky, stifling, stuffy; passionate, provocative, seductive, sensual, sexy, voluptuous.

sum n *lit:* aggregate, amount, quantity, reckoning, score, tally, total, whole.

summary n *lit:* abridgment, abstract, compendium, digest, epitome, essence, extract, outline, résumé, review, rundown, summing-up, synopsis. adj *lit:* arbitrary, compact, compendious, concise, condensed, cursory, hasty, perfunctory, pithy.

summit n *lit:* acme, apex, crowning point, culmination, height, peak, pinnacle, top, zenith.

summon vb *lit:* assemble, bid, call together, convene, invite, rally, send for; call into action, draw on, gather, muster.

sunken adj *lit:* at a lower level, buried, depressed, immersed, recessed, submerged; drawn, haggard, hollowed.

sunny adj *lit:* bright, clear, luminous, radiant, sunlit, unclouded; beaming, buoyant, cheery, genial, joyful, light-hearted, optimistic, pleasant.

superb adj *lit:* admirable, breathtaking, choice, exquisite, first-rate, gorgeous, magnificent, splendid, superior.

superior n *lit:* boss, chief, director, manager, principal, senior, supervisor. adj *lit:* better, greater, higher, more advanced, predominant, preferred, prevailing, surpassing; admirable, choice, de luxe, distinguished, excellent, exclusive, first-class, first-rate, good quality, high calibre, high-class; airy, condescending, haughty, lofty, patronizing, pretentious, snobbish, supercilious.

supervision n *lit:* administration, auspices, care, charge, control, guidance, management, oversight, surveillance.

supplant vb *lit:* displace, oust, overthrow, replace, supersede, take over, undermine, unseat.

supple adj *lit:* elastic, flexible, limber, lithe, plastic, pliable.

supplementary adj *lit:* accompanying, additional, auxiliary, complementary, extra, secondary.

supply n *lit:* cache, fund, hoard, reserve, reservoir, source, stockpile, store; foodstuff, items, materials, necessities, provisions, rations, stores. vb *lit:* afford, cater, contribute, endow, furnish, give, grant, produce, provide, purvey, replenish, stock, victual.

support n *lit:* back, brace, foundation, pillar, post, prop, stanchion, stay, underpinning; aid, assistance, backing, blessing, encouragement, furtherance, help, moral support, patronage, protection, relief, sustenance; livelihood, maintenance, subsistence; backbone, backer, mainstay, supporter. vb *lit:* bear, bolster, brace, buttress, hold up, prop, reinforce, sustain, underpin, uphold; cherish, finance, foster, fund, keep, look after, maintain, provide for, strengthen, subsidize, succour, take care of, underwrite; advocate, aid, assist, back, champion, defend, forward, go along with, promote, second, side with, stand behind, stick up for, take (someone's) part; attest to, authenticate, bear out, confirm, corroborate, endorse, substantiate, verify; countenance, endure, put up with, stand (for), submit, suffer, tolerate, undergo.

suppose vb *lit:* assume, conjecture, dare say, expect, imagine, presume, surmise, take for granted, think; believe, conceive, conclude, consider, fancy, postulate, pretend.

suppress vb *lit:* check, conquer, crush, drive underground, extinguish, overthrow, quash, quench, stamp out, subdue, trample; censor, conceal, cover up, curb, hold back, keep secret, muffle, repress, restrain, silence, smother, withhold.

supreme adj *lit:* cardinal, chief, culminating, extreme, first, foremost, greatest, leading, paramount, predominant, pre-eminent, prime, principal, superlative, surpassing, top, ultimate, utmost.

sure adj *lit:* assured, clear, confident, decided, definite, positive, satisfied; accurate, dependable, foolproof, honest, indisputable, infallible, precise, reliable, trusty, undeniable, undoubted, unmistakeable; bound, guaranteed, inescapable, inevitable, irrevocable; fast, firm, fixed, safe, secure, solid, stable, steady.

surface   n *lit:* exterior, façade, facet, outside, skin, top, veneer. **vb** *lit:* appear, come to light, crop up, emerge, rise, transpire.   **adj** *lit:* apparent, exterior, external, outward, superficial.

surge   n *lit:* billow, efflux, flood, flow, gush, intensification, rush, swell, upsurge, wave.   **vb** *lit:* billow, eddy, gush, heave, rise, rush, swell, swirl, undulate.

surly   adj *lit:* brusque, churlish, crusty, gruff, ill-natured, morose, sullen, testy, uncivil.

surplus   n *lit:* balance, excess, remainder, residue, superfluity, surfeit.   **adj** *lit:* excessive, extra, odd, remaining, spare, superfluous.

surprise   n *lit:* amazement, astonishment, bewilderment, incredulity; bombshell, eye-opener, revelation, shock.   **vb** *lit:* amaze, astonish, astound, bewilder, disconcert, flabbergast, stun, take aback; catch off guard, catch red-handed, discover, startle.

surrender   n *lit:* capitulation, delivery, relinquishment, renunciation, resignation, submission.   **vb** *lit:* abandon, concede, forgo, give up, part with, relinquish, renounce, resign, waive, yield; capitulate, give oneself up, give way, quit, submit, succumb.

surround   vb *lit:* close in on, encircle, enclose, encompass, fence in, hem in, ring; *spec:* besiege, lay siege to.

surroundings   n *lit:* environment, location, milieu, neighbourhood, setting.

survive   vb *lit:* endure, hold out, last, live, pull through, subsist.

suspect   vb *lit:* distrust, mistrust, smell a rat; believe, conjecture, consider, feel, speculate, suppose, surmise, think probable.   **adj** *lit:* doubtful, dubious, fishy, questionable.

suspend   vb *lit:* attach, dangle, hang, swing; adjourn, cease, cut short, defer, delay, hold off, interrupt, lay aside, postpone, put off, shelve, stay, withhold.

suspense n *lit:* anticipation, anxiety, apprehension, doubt, expectation, indecision, tension, uncertainty, wavering.

suspicion n *lit:* distrust, doubt, misgiving, mistrust, qualm, scepticism, wariness; conjecture, guess, hunch, impression, notion, supposition, surmise; glimmer, hint, shadow, strain, suggestion, tinge, touch, trace.

swamp n *lit:* bog, fen, marsh, mire, morass, quagmire, slough. **vb** *lit:* capsize, engulf, flood, inundate, sink, submerge, swallow up, upset, waterlog; besiege, deluge, overload, overwhelm.

swear **vb** *lit:* affirm, assert, attest, declare, give one's word, pledge oneself, promise, take an oath, testify, vow, warrant; blaspheme, curse, imprecate.

sweep n *lit:* arc, curve, gesture, movement, stroke, swing; compass, extend, range, scope, span, stretch, vista. **vb** *lit:* brush, clean, clear; career, fly, glide, hurtle, sail, skim, tear, zoom.

sweet n *lit:* dessert, pudding, sweet course; confectionary, sweet-meats. **adj** *lit:* cloying, honeyed, saccharine, sugary, syrupy, toothsome; affectionate, agreeable, amiable, attractive, charming, delightful, engaging, gentle, kind, sweet-tempered, taking, tender, winsome; beloved, darling, dear, pet, precious; aromatic, fragrant, fresh, perfumed, redolent, sweet-smelling; euphonic, harmonious, mellow, silvery, soft, tuneful; gone on, keen on.

sympathetic **adj** *lit:* affectionate, caring, compassionate, concerned, kindly, understanding, warm-hearted; favourably disposed (to), in sympathy with, pro; agreeable, appreciative, compatible, congenial, like-minded.

sympathy n *lit:* commiseration, compassion, condolence(s), empathy, pity, thoughtfulness, understanding; affinity, agreement, correspondence, harmony, rapport, union, warmth.

system n *lit:* arrangement, classification, combination, co-ordination, organization, scheme, setup, structure; fixed order, practice, procedure, routine, technique, theory, usage; logical process, method, orderliness, regularity, systematization.

T

table **n** *lit:* bar, counter, stand, surface; board, fare, food; flats, mesa, plain, plateau; *fig:* chart, diagram, key, list, tabulation. **vb** *lit:* introduce, move, propose, put forward; catalogue, chart, list, tabulate.

tack **n** *lit:* drawing-pin, nail, pin; gear, harness, riding equipment, saddle; darn, temporary stitch; adhesiveness, bond; bearing, course, heading; angle, dog-leg, zigzag; *fig:* approach, method, procedure, way. **vb** *lit:* nail, pin; darn loosely, stitch temporarily; bond, glue, gum, paste, stick; change direction, veer, zigzag; *fig:* annex (to), append (on to), attach (on to).

tackle **n** *lit:* accoutrements, equipment, gear, outfit, rig, trappings; attack, block, bringing down, ruck. **vb** *lit:* apply oneself to, attack, get to grips with, grapple with, have a go at, set about, take on, undertake, wrestle with; block, bring down, fell, grab, halt, hold, pounce on, stop.

tact **n** *lit:* address, decorousness, delicacy, diplomacy, discretion, finesse, sensitivity; judgement, sense, wisdom.

tactic **n** *lit:* gambit, manoeuvre, move, ploy, stratagem, strategy; line, method, plan, policy, scheme, way.

tactless **adj** *lit:* boorish, clumsy, inconsiderate, indelicate, inept, insensitive, thoughtless, unkind; imprudent, incautious, indiscreet, undiplomatic; discourteous, impolite, rude, uncivil.

tail **n** *lit:* appendage, end, extremity; backside, behind, bottom, bum, posterior, rear, rump, seat, stern; file, line, queue, train; coda, conclusion, finale; shadower, stalker, tracker, watcher. **vb** *lit:* dog, follow, shadow, trace, track, trail; die (away), drop (off), fade (away), taper (off).

tainted **adj (pa.pt)** *lit:* blighted, contaminated, dirty, foul, infected, poisoned, polluted, soiled; blackened, blemished, branded, disgraced, dishonoured, ruined, stigmatized, sullied, tarnished.

take vb *lit:* carry (away), collect, gain possession of, get, get hold of, grasp, grip, have, hold, receive, win; bear, bring, convey, ferry, fetch, haul, lug, transport; accompany, conduct, escort, guide, lead, usher; acquire, come into possession of, obtain, procure, secure; marry, wed; arrest, capture, entrap, seize; fell, hit, kill, tackle; abduct, hijack, kidnap, run off with; abstract, liberate, misappropriate, nick, pinch, purloin, steal, swipe; deduct, remove, subtract; consume, drink, eat, ingest; accommodate, contain, have room for; *fig:* do, effect, execute, make, perform; indulge in; accept, adopt, assume, be guided by, comply with, obey; call for, demand, need, require; spend, use (up); book, engage, hire, lease, rent, reserve; buy, purchase; choose, pick, select; brook, endure, go through, put up with, stand, stomach, swallow, tolerate, withstand; bilk, cheat, con, dupe, swindle; catch, go by, travel in; believe, consider, interpret, perceive, presume, regard, see; be attractive, charm, enchant, please; learn, study; lecture in, teach; photograph, shoot, snap; *spec:* (a procedure/process may) be effective, operate, work.

tale n *lit:* account, anecdote, fable, legend, saga, story, yarn; fib, fiction, rigmarole, spiel; rumour, scandal, secret.

talent n *lit:* ability, aptitude, faculty, flair, forte, gift, knack.

talk n *lit:* address, dissertation, lecture, oration, sermon, speech; chat, chitchat, conversation, gab, gossip, natter; confabulation, conference, consultation, dialogue, discussion, parley; words.
vb *lit:* speak; chat, chatter, converse, gossip, natter, prattle, rabbit, witter; confabulate, confer, consult, discuss, parley; negotiate (about); blab, grass, spill the beans, sing, squeal.

tall adj *lit:* big, high, lanky, lofty, towering; *fig:* daunting, demanding, formidable, hard; absurd, far-fetched, implausible, incredible, ludicrous, preposterous, ridiculous.

tamper vb *lit:* fiddle (with), fool about (with), interfere (with), meddle (with), muck about (with), tinker (with).

tan n *lit:* sunburn; tannin. vb *lit:* burn, sunburn; *fig:* beat, flog, thrash, whip. adj *lit:* beige, buff, khaki, yellow-brown.

tangle n *lit:* coil, knot, mass, mesh, mess, snarl, twist; imbroglio, mix-up; labyrinth, maze. **vb** *lit:* coil, interlace, intertwine, knot, mat, mesh, snarl, twist; embroil (in), involve (in); *fig:* contend (with), cross swords (with), lock horns (with), mess (with).

tank n *lit:* cistern, container, reservoir, vessel; lake, pool; armoured vehicle.

tap n *lit:* bung, plug, stopper; bug, listening device; knock, pat, rap, touch; faucet, spout, stopcock; (on) draught; *fig:* (on) hand. **vb** *lit:* bug, listen in on; knock, pat, rap, touch; broach, draw off, open, siphon off; exploit, make use of, milk, mine, use, utilize; thread.

tape n *lit:* band, film, ribbon, strip; binding; finishing-line. **vb** *lit:* bind, secure, tie (up); record, video.

target n *lit:* butt, inner; bullseye, goal, mark, objective, quarry; prey, victim; *fig:* aim, ambition, intention, objective.

task n *lit:* assignment, charge, chore, duty, job, mission, occupation, work.

taste n *lit:* flavour, relish, savour, tang; bite, morsel, mouthful, nip, sip, snatch, swallow; appetite, fancy, fondness, inclination, liking, palate, partiality, predilection, preference; culture, discrimination, grace, judgement, refinement. **vb** *lit:* have a flavour (of), savour (of); discern, distinguish, sense; nibble, sample, sip, take a bite of, try; *fig:* encounter, experience, feel, know.

taunt n *lit:* dig, gibe, insult, snide remark; provocation. **vb** *lit:* deride, insult, jeer at, mock, sneer at, tease; provoke.

taut adj *lit:* flexed, strained, stressed, stretched, tense, tight; neat, orderly, shipshape, tidy, trim.

tax n *lit:* customs, duty, excise, impost, levy, rate, tariff, toll; inland revenue, national insurance; assessment, contribution; burden, drain, load, stress, weight. **vb** *lit:* exact a toll from, impose a levy on, levy a rate on; burden, exhaust, load down, sap, strain, try, weaken, weigh upon; charge (with), reprove (with).

teach vb *lit:* educate, enlighten, impart, inculcate, inform; give lessons in, lecture, tutor; coach, discipline, drill, instruct, school, train; demonstrate (how), show (how).

teacher n *lit:* dominie, educator, guru, lecturer, master, mentor, mistress, pedagogue, professor, tutor; coach, instructor, trainer; demonstrator.

team n *lit:* band, brigade, company, crew, gang, set, side, squad, troop, troupe; pair, span, yoke. **vb** *lit:* cooperate (with), join (up with), link (up with), unite (with).

teasing n *lit:* aggravation, badgering, baiting, gibes, mockery, needling, provocation, ragging, ridicule, taunts; carding, combing out, shredding.

technique n *lit:* art, craft, execution, knack, knowhow, proficiency, skill; manner, means, method, procedure, system, way.

teeth n *lit:* dentition, dentures, occlusion; canines, incisors, molars, premolars; fangs, tusks; cogs, projections, prongs, serrations, tines; *fig:* bite, force, power.

telephone n *lit:* handset, phone, receiver; blower; line. **vb** *lit:* buzz, call, call up, dial, get on the blower to, give one a bell, give one a call, give one a ring, phone, ring.

tell vb *lit:* acquaint of, apprise of, communicate to, divulge to, impart to, inform of, let know, make known to, mention to, notify of, say to; blab, grass, squeal; announce, proclaim, publish; depict, describe, narrate, recount, relate; command (to), direct (to), instruct (to), order (to); differentiate, discern, distinguish, identify, make out, see, understand; count, have an effect, register, weigh heavily.

temper n *lit:* consistency, density, homogeneity; disposition, frame of mind, humour, mood, nature; (lose one's) composure, cool, equanimity, self-control; fury, heat, passion, rage, tantrum. **vb** *lit:* mix, mould, work; moderate, soften; harden; check, curb, restrain; adjust the pitch of, tune.

temperance n *lit:* moderation, restraint, self-control, self-discipline; abstinence, continence, sobriety, teetotalism.

temperate adj *lit:* agreeable, clement, fair, mild, moderate, pleasant; balmy, cool, soft; calm, composed, equable, even-tempered, self-controlled, self-restrained, stable; abstinent, continent, sober, teetotal.

tempest   n *lit:* cyclone, gale, hurricane, storm, typhoon; *fig:* agitation, commotion, furore, riot, tumult, turbulence, uproar.

tempestuous   adj *lit:* blustery, boisterous, gusty, raging, stormy, turbulent; emotional, excited, feverish, furious, impassioned, intense, uncontrolled, violent, wild.

temporary   adj *lit:* bridging, fleeting, impermanent, interim; casual, passing, stand-in, substitute, transient, transitory.

temptation   n *lit:* allure, attraction, enticement, lure, pull, seduction, tantalization; bait, carrot, decoy, draw, invitation, loss-leader.

tend   vb *lit:* attend, care for, feed, keep, look after, maintain, nurse, see to, serve, wait upon; guard, protect, watch over; aim, go, lead, move, point, be biased, be inclined, gravitate, incline.

tender   n *lit:* bid, offer, proposal; coinage, currency, money, payment; supply-vehicle.   vb *lit:* give, offer, present, proffer, submit, volunteer.   adj *lit:* delicate, fragile, frail, weak; callow, green, immature, new, unripe, young; affectionate, amorous, fond, kind, loving, sentimental, soft-hearted, sympathetic; compassionate, gentle, merciful; emotional, moving, romantic, touching; aching, painful, raw, sensitive, sore.

tenderness   n *lit:* delicacy, fragility, frailty, weakness; greenness, immaturity, unripeness, youth; affection, fondness, kindness, love, sentiment, soft-heartedness, sympathy; compassion, gentleness, mercy; painfulness, rawness, sensitivity, soreness.

tense   vb *lit:* clench, contract, flex, stiffen, tighten.   adj *lit:* strained, stretched, taut, tight; *fig:* apprehensive, edgy, jittery, jumpy, keyed up, nervous, restless, strung up, wound up; nerve-racking, stressful.

tension   n *lit:* rigidity, tautness, tightness, torque; apprehension, edginess, nervousness, pressure, strain, stress, suspense.

term   n *lit:* appellation, designation, expression, name, phrase, title, word; duration, period, spell, time, while; semester, session; denominator, numerator; predicate, subject; *spec:* completion, culmination, end (of a pregnancy, of a period of grace).   vb *lit:* call, christen, designate, dub, entitle, label, name, nickname, style.

terminal n *lit:* airport, airport building; station, stop, terminus. **adj** *lit:* concluding, final, last, ultimate; endmost, hindmost, rear; fatal, incurable, lethal, mortal.

terminate **vb** *lit:* come to an end, complete, conclude, end, finish, stop; bring to an end, close, cut off, discontinue, wind up; expire, lapse, run out.

terrible **adj** *lit:* bad, grave, serious, severe; appalling, awful, dreadful, frightful, horrifying; hopeless, poor, rotten, useless.

terrific **adj** *lit:* enormous, extreme, great, intense, serious, severe, tremendous; excellent, fantastic, fine, magnificent, outstanding, superb, wonderful.

territory n *lit:* area, country, district, domain, land, manor, realm, region, tract, zone.

terror n *lit:* dread, fear, fright, panic; alarm, awe, consternation, shock; *fig:* devil, fiend, monster; scoundrel, villain; rascal, rogue, scamp.

test n *lit:* examination; check-up; analysis, assessment, evaluation, investigation; measure, proof. **vb** *lit:* analyse, assess, check up on, examine, gauge, investigate, measure, try, try out, verify.

testimonial n *lit:* character reference, commendation, reference; honorarium, memorial gift; charity match.

testimony n *lit:* evidence, submission, witness; affidavit, confession, deposition, statement; demonstration, indication, manifestation, proof, verification.

tether **vb** *lit:* lash, rope, secure, tie up; moor; attach, bind.

text n *lit:* contents, matter, words; book, reference work, source; passage, verse; motif, subject, theme, topic.

texture n *lit:* composition, consistency, quality, structure, surface; fabric, grain, weave.

then **adj** *lit:* concurrent, contemporary. **adv** *lit:* at that time; afterwards, later, presently, soon, thereafter; next, subsequently; also, besides; accordingly, consequently, in that case.

theory n *lit:* assumption, conjecture, estimate, explanation, guess, hypothesis, speculation, supposition; classification, philosophy, system.

thick n *lit:* centre, midst. adj *lit:* broad, deep, fat, substantial, wide; compact, concentrated, condensed, dense, impenetrable, opaque; crowded, jammed, packed; bristling, covered, crawling, swarming, teeming; *fig:* guttural, hoarse, husky, throaty; distinct, marked, pronounced, strong; friendly, inseparable, intimate; dim, dull, idiotic, moronic, obtuse, slow, stupid.

thief n *lit:* burglar, housebreaker, mugger, pickpocket, robber; embezzler, fraud, swindler; kleptomaniac, shoplifter; pirate, plagiarizer, rip-off merchant.

thin vb *lit:* adulterate, attenuate, dilute, water down, weaken; prune back, trim; rarefy, refine; constrict, fine down, narrow, taper. adj *lit:* attenuated, fine, narrow; bony, emaciated, lanky, scraggy, scrawny, skeletal, skinny, slender, slim, spindly; meagre, scanty, scarce, sparse; diaphanous, filmy, flimsy, see-through, sheer, skimpy, transparent, wispy; adulterated, dilute, insipid, watered down, watery, weak; rarefied, refined; *fig:* feeble, inadequate, lame, poor, superficial, unconvincing.

thing n *lit:* article, fact, item, object; affair, matter, subject, theme, topic; idea, importance, point, significance, thought; attribute, property, quality; event, incident, occasion, occurrence, phenomenon, proceedings; act, action, deed, feat, turn; apparatus, device, implement, instrument, machine, tool; belonging(s), effect(s), possession(s); *fig:* animal, creature, person; bag, hobby, pastime, preoccupation; fixation, hang-up, obsession.

think vb *lit:* brood, cogitate, contemplate, deliberate, meditate, mull, muse, ponder, reflect, ruminate; call to mind, consider, recall, recollect, remember; believe, conceive (of), hold, suppose; conclude, decide, deem, judge; assume, gather, guess, imagine, reckon, surmise; envisage, expect, presume, suspect; intend (to), plan (to).

thirsty adj *lit:* dehydrated, dry, parched; arid; *fig:* avid (for), eager (for), greedy (for), hungry (for), longing (for), yearning (for).

thorough adj *lit:* careful, conscientious, efficient, meticulous, painstaking, scrupulous; complete, comprehensive, exhaustive, full; intensive; arrant, out-and-out, sheer, total, unmitigated, utter.

though adv *lit:* for all that, however, nevertheless, nonetheless. cnj *lit:* although, despite the fact that, notwithstanding the fact that, while; albeit, yet; (as) if.

thoughtful adj *lit:* caring, considerate, helpful, kind, solicitous; contemplative, deliberative, introspective, introverted, meditative, pensive, reflective, ruminative, studious; careful, provident, prudent.

threat n *lit:* intimidation, menace, warning; blackmail; danger, peril, risk.

through adj *lit:* fast, non-stop; arterial, linking, major; completed, done, finished; breaking up, separating; bust, washed up; exhausted, spent, whacked. adv *lit:* in and straight on out; from beginning to end, from one side to the other; all the way, directly, non-stop; to the skin. prp *lit:* in and straight on out of; from beginning to end of, from one side to the other of; during the whole of, throughout; around, in, on, via; because of, by reason of, owing to; as a result of, by means of, by way of, with; done with, finished with.

throw n *lit:* bung, cast, fling, heave, hurl, lob, put, shy, sling, toss; fall; attempt, bash, go, try, turn, venture; *fig:* article, item, unit. vb *lit:* bung, cast, chuck, fling, heave, hurl, lob, put, shy, sling, toss; launch, propel; fell, floor, overturn, unseat; *fig:* catch unawares, confound, disconcert, put off altogether, screw.

thunder n *lit:* crashing, detonations, peals, rumbling; din, resonance, reverberation, roar. vb *lit:* blast, boom, crack, crash, explode, peal, rumble; resound, reverberate, roar; *fig:* bellow, shout, trumpet, yell.

thunderous adj *lit:* deafening, ear-splitting, reverberating, resounding, roaring; booming, crashing, pealing, rumbling; *fig:* dark, glowering, lowering, menacing, threatening.

thus adv *lit:* as follows, in this way; so; accordingly, consequently, hence, therefore, understandably.

tight adj *lit:* fast, firm, fixed, secure; close-fitting, hermetic, sealed;

constricted, cramped, jammed, stuck; clenched, rigid, stiff, stretched, taut, tense; impervious, proof; *fig:* neat, trim, well-built; close, even, well-matched; austere, rigorous, severe, strict, stringent; difficult, hazardous, precarious, sticky, thorny, ticklish, tricky; hard to come by, scarce; grasping, mean, miserly, parsimonious, stingy; blotto, drunk, inebriated, intoxicated, legless, pickled, plastered, smashed, stoned.

timber   n *lit:* forest, trees, woods; lumber, wood; beams, boards, joists, planks.

time   n *lit:* duration, interval, period, space, span, spell, term, while; age, date, epoch, era; day, generation, heyday, hour, season; life, lifetime, life-span; juncture, moment, stage; beat, metre, rhythm, tempo; pace, rate, speed; *fig:* chance, opportunity.   **vb** *lit:* clock, pace, rate; schedule.

tip   n *lit:* dump, refuse area, rubbish pile; apex, crest, crown, peak, point, top; cap, end, ferrule; bonus, extra, gratuity; cut, glance, snick; hint, information, suggestion, warning, wrinkle.   **vb** *lit:* cant, incline, lean, list, slant, tilt; bung, chuck, dump, empty out, pour, unload; leave a gratuity for, reward; cut, glance, snick; glue (in), paste (in).

tired   adj (pa.pt) *lit:* all in, dead on one's feet, done in, drained, drooping, exhausted, fagged, fatigued, knackered, shattered, spent, whacked, worn out; sick (of), weary (of); *fig:* clichéd, corny, hackneyed, stale, trite.

tireless   adj *lit:* diligent, energetic, indefatigable, industrious, persevering, unflagging, untiring; constant, continual, persistent.

tissue   n *lit:* cells, structure, texture; mesh, network, system, web; fabric, gauze, nylon, weave; paper handkerchief; lavatory paper, toilet roll; wrapping-paper.

toast   vb *lit:* brown, grill, heat, roast; drink the health of, drink to, salute.

together   adv *lit:* as a body, as one, collectively, in unison, jointly, mutually; at once, en masse, in unison, simultaneously; continuously, non-stop.

toilet n *lit:* bathroom, bog, closet, convenience, gents, ladies, latrine, lavatory, loo, powder room, privy, washroom, WC; ablutions, grooming, titivation, toilette.

tolerable adj *lit:* acceptable, adequate, allowable, fair, good enough, middling, not bad, passable; bearable, endurable, sufferable, supportable.

tolerance n *lit:* forbearance, indulgence, patience, sufferance; fortitude, resilience, resistance, stamina, staying power; leeway, play, swing, variation.

tolerant adj *lit:* broad-minded, complaisant, easygoing, forbearing, indulgent, liberal, lenient, long-suffering, patient, permissive.

tolerate vb *lit:* bear, endure, put up with, stand, stomach, suffer, swallow, take; accept, allow, condone, let go, let pass, permit.

toll n *lit:* charge, duty, fee, payment, tariff, tax; cost, levy, loss; chime, clang, ding, ring. vb *lit:* chime, knell, peal, ring, sound.

tomb n *lit:* burial chamber, crypt, grave, sepulchre, vault; barrow, burial mound, catacomb, cave, chamber, pyramid; sarcophagus; shrine.

tone n *lit:* air, aspect, character, effect, feel, mood, spirit, temper, tenor; emphasis, inflection, intonation, stress; modulation, pitch, timbre; note; health, strength, vigour; colour, hue, shade, tint. vb *lit:* blend (in), fit (in) well; play (down), soften (down), temper (down); brighten (up), strengthen (up).

torch n *lit:* flashlight, pocket-lamp; firebrand, sconce; arc-lamp, flame, welder; *fig:* beacon, illumination, light. vb *lit:* burn, ignite, set ablaze, set on fire.

torture n *lit:* agony, anguish, pain, suffering, torment; cruelty, sadism. vb *lit:* hurt, put on the rack, torment; *fig:* give hell, persecute.

total n *lit:* aggregate, amount, bottom line, sum, whole. vb *lit:* add up, reckon up, tot up; amount to, come to, work out at. adj *lit:* complete, comprehensive, entire, full, out-and-out, perfect, thorough, unconditional, undivided, utter, whole.

touch n *lit:* feel, feeling, physical sensation; brush, palpation, pat, stroke, tap; pressure; *fig:* effect, hand, influence; handiwork, method, style, technique; artistry, command, facility, knack, skill; acquaintance, contact, rapport; dash, hint, pinch, smattering, spot, suggestion, tinge, trace. **vb** *lit:* brush, caress, feel, finger, fondle, handle, palpate, pat, press, stroke, tap; lay hands upon; adjoin, be contiguous with, border, converge, meet, merge with, overlap; arrive at, come up to; stop over (at); *fig:* disturb, impress, move, stir, strike; affect, be pertinent to, concern, have to do with; be party to, get involved in, use; come near, compare with, equal, hold a candle to, match, rival; attain, reach; allude to, have a word (on), say something (on), speak (on); ask (for) a loan of; set (off), spark (off), trigger (off).

tough adj *lit:* all-weather, dense, durable, hard, resilient, resistant, rugged, solid, stiff, strong, sturdy, thick; brawny, hardy, iron, seasoned, stout, strapping; hard-nosed, inflexible, obdurate, obstinate, resolute, stern, stubborn, unyielding; demanding, exacting, unforgiving; aggressive, refractory, rough, violent; arduous, difficult, exhausting, knotty, laborious, strenuous, thorny, uphill; baffling, confounding, perplexing, puzzling; *fig:* bad luck, hard luck, too bad, unlucky.

tour n *lit:* excursion, jaunt, outing, trip; round-trip, sightseeing-trip; circuit, course. **vb** *lit:* do, go round, journey in, see, sightsee, travel round, visit; go on the road, play.

tower n *lit:* barbican, bastion, citadel, fortress, turret, watch-tower; belfry, dome, minaret, spire, steeple; condominium, high-riser, skyscraper. **vb** *lit:* loom, rear, rise, soar.

track n *lit:* footprints, footsteps, mark, path, scent, spoor, trace, trail; wake; course, flight-path, line, orbit, trajectory; bridle-path, footpath, lane, road; lines, rails, railway; (keep) sight (of), (lose) sight (of). **vb** *lit:* dog, follow, pursue, shadow, stalk, tail, trace, trail; hunt (down).

tradition n *lit:* convention, custom, folklore, institution, practice, usage.

traffic n *lit:* vehicles; transport, transportation; freight, passengers;

business, commerce, dealing, exchange, trade; hawking, peddling, selling. **vb** *lit:* deal (in), trade (in).

train n *lit:* locomotive, rail, railway service; caravan, column, convoy, crocodile, file; cortège, entourage, followers, retinue, suite; chain, order, progression, sequence, series, succession. **vb** *lit:* coach, condition, drill, groom, instruct, teach, tutor, school; exercise; domesticate, tame.

trample **vb** *lit:* crush, flatten, squash, stamp (on), tread (on).

transit n *lit:* carriage, passage, portage, shipment, transportation; eclipse, occultation; change, conversion, transition. **vb** *lit:* cross, traverse; go, move, travel.

transition n *lit:* changeover, turnaround; alteration, change, conversion, evolution, metamorphosis, progression, transmutation.

transmit **vb** *lit:* carry, communicate, convey, forward, impart, pass on, send, transport; broadcast, radio, relay, send out, telecast, televise.

transparent adj *lit:* clear, limpid, pellucid, see-through, sheer, translucent; *fig:* apparent, manifest, obvious, patent, plain unambiguous, visible; candid, frank, open, straightforward.

transport n *lit:* conveyance, vehicle; carriage, postage, shipment, transportation; *fig:* ecstasy, euphoria, rapture. **vb** *lit:* bring, carry, convey, ferry, fetch, haul, move, ship, take, transfer; banish, exile; *fig:* captivate, enchant, enrapture, entrance.

trap n *lit:* gin, pitfall, snare; ambush; ruse, subterfuge, trick. **vb** *lit:* catch, corner, ensnare, entrap, snare; ambush; dupe, trick.

tread n *lit:* footfall, footstep, step, stride, walk; sole; *spec:* depth, gauge, pattern (on a tyre). **vb** *lit:* plod, stamp, step, stride, tramp, trudge, walk; crush, flatten, trample.

treat n *lit:* gift, present, reward; delight, pleasure, surprise, thrill. **vb** *lit:* behave towards, deal with, handle; apply medication to, care for, medicate, minister to, nurse, tend; denature, process, purify, recycle, refine; be concerned with, discuss, examine; bargain, negotiate, parley; lay on for, pay for, stand (to).

treatment n *lit:* care, medication, medicine, remedy, surgery, therapy; handling (of), management (of), reception (of), usage (of).

tremble vb *lit:* quake, quiver, shake, shudder; judder, oscillate, vibrate, wobble.

trial n *lit:* court, hearing, tribunal; experiment, proof, test; attempt, effort, go, shot, stab, try; adversity, affliction, hardship, misery, tribulation; bane, bother, nuisance, pest. **adj** *lit:* experimental, pilot, provisional.

trouble n *lit:* anxiety, disquiet, distress, pain, suffering, tribulation, vexation, worry; bother, commotion, disorder, disturbance, row, unrest; ailment, complaint, disability, upset; care, effort, labour, pains; difficulty, hot water, pickle, predicament, scrape. **vb** *lit:* afflict, annoy, bother, disconcert, disquiet, distress, disturb, fret, incommode, inconvenience, pain, plague, upset; exert (oneself).

true adj *lit:* factual, valid, veritable; authentic, genuine, natural, pure, real; accurate, correct, exact, precise, unerring; confirmed, dedicated, faithful, firm, loyal, sincere, staunch, trustworthy, upright; reliable, sure; lawful, rightful.

tunnel n *lit:* cave, corridor, gallery, hole, passage, shaft, subway, tube. **vb** *lit:* burrow, dig, drive a shaft, excavate, mine.

turn n *lit:* angle, bend, corner, curve, deviation; coil, gyration, loop, revolution, rotation, spin, twist, whirl; change, deflection, shift; drive, excursion, outing, ride; constitutional, jaunt, saunter, stroll, walk; *fig:* go, round, spell, stint, time, try; aptitude, flair, gift, knack, propensity, talent; action, deed, gesture, service; act, performance; fright, shock, start; attack, bout, dizzy spell; cast, form, mould, shape. **vb** *lit:* arc, bend, corner, curve, deviate, go round, swerve, veer; tack, zigzag; coil, gyrate, loop, revolve, rotate, spin, twist, wheel, whirl; recoil, reverse; change direction, deflect, shift; aim, direct, point; construct, execute, fashion, form, make, mould, shape; employ, make use of, utilize; *fig:* become, get; alter (into), change (into), convert (into), render, transform (into), translate (into); go bad, go off, sour; sicken, upset; distract, unsettle; persuade, prevail upon, subvert.

U

ugly adj *lit:* frumpish, ill-favoured, plain, unattractive, unprepossessing, unsightly; frightful, hideous, horrible, offensive, repugnant, repulsive, revolting, stomach-churning; black, dark, evil, malevolent, malign, nasty, surly; dangerous, menacing, ominous, sinister, threatening.

ultimate adj *lit:* conclusive, final, last, terminal; finite, limiting; extreme, greatest, highest, superlative, supreme; most important, most significant; basic, fundamental, primary.

umpire n *lit:* adjudicator, arbiter, arbitrator, judge, linesman, referee, scorer. **vb** *lit:* adjudicate, arbitrate, judge, referee; chair, moderate, preside over.

unable adj *lit:* helpless (to), powerless (to), unqualified (to); incapable, not up to it.

unacceptable adj *lit:* impermissible, inadequate, inadmissible, insupportable, intolerable, unsatisfactory.

unaccountable adj *lit:* incomprehensible, inexplicable, puzzling; extraordinary, odd, unheard-of; not answerable (to).

unaccustomed adj *lit:* unused (to); uncommon, unusual, unwonted.

unanswerable adj *lit:* insoluble, unsolvable; conclusive, incontestable, incontrovertible, indisputable, unassailable, undeniable; unaccountable (to).

unasked adj *lit:* uninvited, unsought, unwanted; gratuitous, spontaneous, unexpected. **adv** *lit:* of one's own accord, voluntarily; gratuitously, spontaneously, unexpectedly.

unauthorized adj *lit:* unapproved, unofficial, unwarranted; illegal, unconstitutional; behind-the-scenes, private, wildcat (strike); informal, personal.

unaware adj *lit:* ignorant (of), unconscious (of), uninformed (of), unmindful (of); uncomprehending, untaught.

unbearable adj *lit:* intolerable, unendurable; insupportable, unacceptable; insufferable, unspeakable.

unbending adj *lit:* aloof, distant, formal, haughty, remote, rigid, stiff; inflexible, intractable, severe, strict, uncompromising, unrelenting, unyielding.

unbroken adj *lit:* homogeneous, intact, solid, undivided, uniform, unimpaired, whole; deep, fast, profound, sound; constant, continual, continuous, incessant, undisturbed, uninterrupted; monotonous, relentless, unremitting; unbowed, undomesticated, untamed, wild.

uncertain adj *lit:* doubtful, indefinite, indeterminate, speculative, undetermined, unpredictable; dubious, irresolute, unclear, undecided, unresolved, unsure, vague as to; erratic, fitful, precarious, unreliable, vacillating, variable; inconstant, interrupted, varying; hazy, indefinite, indistinct, vague.

unclear adj *lit:* clouded, opaque; indistinct, obscure, uncertain, vague.

uncomfortable adj *lit:* crammed, cramped, hard, ill-fitting, lumpy, painful, rough; discomfited, distressed, disturbed, pained; *fig:* diffident, ill at ease, restless, self-conscious, uneasy.

uncommon adj *lit:* infrequent, novel, rare, scarce, unusual; curious, odd, peculiar, strange, untoward; amazing, exceptional, extraordinary, outstanding, remarkable, singular, special, surprising.

uncommunicative adj *lit:* close, dumb, guarded, mute, quiet, reserved, reticent, secretive, silent, taciturn, tight-lipped, unforthcoming, withdrawn.

unconditional adj *lit:* abject, complete, full, total, unlimited, unqualified, unrestricted.

unconscious adj *lit:* comatose, fainting, insensible, knocked out, out, out cold, stunned; anaesthetized; accidental, automatic, inadvertent, instinctive, involuntary, reflex, unintentional, unpremeditated, unwitting; latent, repressed, subliminal, suppressed; ignorant (of), unaware (of), unmindful (of).

unconventional adj *lit:* eccentric, individual, irregular, nonconformist, odd, offbeat, original, unorthodox, unusual, way-out.

undecided   **adj** *lit:* inconclusive, indefinite, in the balance, unresolved, unsettled; ambivalent, dithering, in two minds, irresolute, shilly-shallying, uncertain, tentative, vacillating, wavering; debatable, moot, open.

undeniably   **adv** *lit:* beyond doubt, certainly, evidently, incontestably, incontrovertibly, indisputably, indubitably, manifestly, obviously, patently, undoubtedly, unquestionably.

under   **adj** *lit:* inferior, junior, lesser, lower, minor, subordinate; minus, short.   **adv** *lit:* below, beneath, beneath the surface; down, lower; below par.   **prp** *lit:* below, beneath; inferior to, junior to, lesser than, lower than, subject to, subordinate to; as, beneath the heading, within; less than, short of; *spec:* in (the circumstances); (a field) supporting a crop of.

undergo   **vb** *lit:* bear, endure, experience, go through, pass through, stand, suffer.

underhand   **adj** *lit:* crafty, crooked, deceptive, devious, dishonest, furtive, sly, sneaky.

underneath   **adj** *lit:* lower, under; below, beneath.   **adv** *lit:* below, beneath, down below; next to the skin, under the skin.   **prp** *lit:* below, beneath; inferior to, junior to, lesser than, lower than, subject to, subordinate to.

underrated   **adj (pa.pt)** *lit:* discounted, misjudged, sold short, underestimated, undervalued.

understanding   **n** *lit:* appreciation, comprehension, grasp, knowledge; apprising, insight, perception; belief, conclusion, view; assumption, supposition; sympathies; accord, agreement, entente, pact.   **adj** *lit:* compassionate, considerate, insightful, kindly, perceptive, sensitive, sympathetic; charitable, forbearing, forgiving, magnanimous, tolerant.

undertake   **vb** *lit:* agree (to), commit oneself (to), engage (to), promise (to); attempt, embark on, endeavour (to), set about, tackle, take on, try.

undesirable   **adj** *lit:* deleterious, disagreeable, potentially harmful, unacceptable, unpleasant, unwanted, unwelcome; antisocial, obnoxious, shabby, squalid, unattractive, unsavoury, unsuitable.

undignified   **adj** *lit:* indecorous, inelegant, unbecoming, unseemly; embarrassing, humiliating, ludicrous, ridiculous, risible, mortifying.

undisciplined   **adj** *lit:* boisterous, disobedient, naughty, obstreperous, uncontrollable, unmanageable, unruly, unschooled, untrained, wayward, wild, wilful.

undisguised   **adj** *lit:* evident, frank, genuine, manifest, obvious, open, plain, transparent, unconcealed, unfeigned, unmistakable.

undisturbed   **adj** *lit:* placid, serene, tranquil; unruffled; uninterrupted; untouched.

undo   **vb** *lit:* loose, loosen, open, unfasten, untie; annul, cancel, invalidate, overturn, quash, reverse; defeat, destroy, ruin, wreck.

undone   **adj (pa.pt)** *lit:* loosened, opened, unfastened, untied; annulled, cancelled, invalidated, overturned, quashed, reversed; defeated, destroyed, ruined, wrecked; incomplete, neglected, omitted, outstanding, unfinished.

undoubtedly   **adv** *lit:* certainly, definitely, naturally, of course, surely, unmistakably, unquestionably.

undress   **n** *lit:* deshabille, disarray, dishevelment, disorder; semi-nudity; nakedness, nudity; casual clothes, informal wear.
vb *lit:* disrobe, strip, strip off.

unemployed   **adj** *lit:* idle, jobless, laid off, on the dole, out of work, redundant; between jobs, resting.

unenthusiastic   **adj** *lit:* casual, half-hearted, lukewarm, take-it-or-leave-it, wishy-washy; indifferent.

unerringly   **adv** *lit:* accurately, exactly, infallibly, precisely, specifically.

uneven   **adj** *lit:* broken, bumpy, corrugated, lumpy, ridged, rough, undulating; fluctuating, irregular, patchy, variable, varying; asymmetrical, lopsided, top-heavy, unbalanced; one-sided, unequal, unfair.

unexpected adj *lit:* abrupt, startling, sudden, surprising; surprise, unforeseen; unasked, uninvited, unsought.

unfair adj *lit:* biased, discriminatory, inequitable, partial, prejudiced, unjust; dishonest, unethical, unprincipled, unsporting.

unfaithful adj *lit:* adulterous, deceitful, disloyal, promiscuous, two-timing; perfidious, traitorous, treacherous; *fig:* distorted, imperfect, inaccurate, unreliable; dissimilar (to).

unfamiliar adj *lit:* alien, different, new, novel, strange, unknown; unacquainted (with), unconversant (with).

unfashionable adj *lit:* antediluvian, antiquated, dated, démodé, dowdy, frumpish, fuddy-duddy, old-fashioned, old hat, outmoded, out of date, passé, unchic.

unfavourable adj *lit:* adverse, bad, negative, poor; contrary, hostile, inclement, stormy; inauspicious, unlucky, unpromising, unpropitious; inopportune, untimely.

unfit adj *lit:* inadequate (for), inappropriate (for), unsuitable (for), useless (for); ineligible (to), not cut out (to), physically unable (to), unprepared (to), unqualified (to); flabby, in poor condition, out of shape, unhealthy.

unfortunate adj *lit:* hapless, luckless, unlucky; inauspicious, inopportune, unfavourable, unpropitious; deplorable, infelicitous, regrettable.

unfortunately adv *lit:* unhappily, unluckily; inauspiciously, infelicitously; deplorably, regrettably.

unhappily adv *lit:* unfortunately, unluckily; dejectedly, despondently, disconsolately, gloomily, miserably, mournfully, sadly, wretchedly; awkwardly, badly, infelicitously, injudiciously.

unhappy adj *lit:* hapless, luckless, unfortunate, unlucky; dejected, depressed, despondent, disconsolate, gloomy, miserable, mournful, sad, wretched; awkward, inept, infelicitous, injudicious, tactless.

unharmed adj *lit:* intact, safe and sound, scatheless, undamaged, unhurt, unimpaired, uninjured, unscathed, without a scratch.

unhealthy adj *lit:* delicate, feeble, frail, puny, sickly, thin, weak; dirty, insanitary, unhygienic; corrupting, demoralizing, perverted, sick, warped.

unhesitating adj *lit:* immediate, instant, prompt, ready; resolute, steadfast, unfaltering, unswerving, unwavering.

unidentified adj *lit:* anonymous, nameless, unknown, unnamed; plain, unmarked.

unify vb *lit:* bond, combine, fuse, join, weld; amalgamate, confederate, merge; marry, wed; unite.

unimaginative adj *lit:* boring, dull, colourless, hackneyed, insipid, lifeless, pedestrian, tame, uninspired, unoriginal, vapid; derivative, plagiaristic.

unimpressed adj *lit:* apathetic, blasé, bored, impassive, indifferent, left cold, uninterested, unmoved, unperturbed, unruffled, unsurprised.

uninhabited adj *lit:* barren, desolate, empty, vacant, waste; deserted, unoccupied, unpopulated, untenanted.

uninhibited adj *lit:* free, liberated, natural, spontaneous, unselfconscious; open, unconstrained, unrepressed, unrestricted; unchecked, uncontrolled.

unintentional adj *lit:* accidental, inadvertent, unintended, unpremeditated, unthinking; involuntary, reflex; unwitting.

uninviting adj *lit:* disagreeable, offputting, repellent, repugnant, unappealing, unappetizing, unattractive, unpleasant; depressing, dismal, dreary; daunting, formidable, ominous, sinister.

union n *lit:* bond, combination, coupling, fusion, joining, linkage, suture, synthesis, weld; affiliation, alliance, amalgamation, association, coalition, confederacy, confederation, league, merger; marriage, wedlock; brotherhood, fraternity, trade organization.

unique adj *lit:* isolated, single, sole; incomparable, unequalled, unmatched, unparalleled, unrivalled; unrepeatable; *fig:* ecstatic, magic, special; characteristic, idiosyncratic.

universal adj *lit:* blanket, catholic, common, comprehensive, general, unlimited, unrestricted, worldwide; ecumenical; adaptable, flexible, versatile.

universe n *lit:* cosmos, macrocosm; world.

unknown n *lit:* anonymity, nobody, nonentity; enigma, mystery, puzzle; dark, mysterious, unexplored. **adj** *lit:* anonymous, nameless, unidentified, unnamed; obscure, unfamiliar, unheard-of, unrecognized, unsung; alien, dark, mysterious, new, strange, unexplored.

unlike adj *lit:* different, dissimilar, distinct, diverse, incompatible, unequal, unrelated. **prp** *lit:* different from, dissimilar to, distinct from, incompatible with, unequal to, unrelated to.

unlikely adj *lit:* implausible, improbable, incredible, unbelievable; not expected (to), not likely (to); unconvincing; faint, remote, slight.

unnatural adj *lit:* anomalous, odd, strange, unusual; bizarre, extraordinary, freakish, outlandish, peculiar, weird; abnormal, perverse, perverted, warped; appalling, brutish, callous, cruel, heartless, inhuman, monstrous, shocking, unfeeling; artificial, assumed, contrived, false, forced, laboured, self-conscious, stiff, stilted, strained.

unnecessary adj *lit:* inessential, needless, redundant, superfluous, surplus; pointless, useless, wasteful.

unpleasant adj *lit:* disagreeable, distasteful, irksome, objectionable, obnoxious, unattractive, unpalatable; disgusting, horrible, nasty, offensive, repellent, repugnant, repulsive, unlikable.

unpopular adj *lit:* avoided, disliked, friendless, ostracized, shunned, unwanted, unwelcome; difficult, inopportune, unfortunate, untimely.

unpredictable adj *lit:* chance, random, unforeseeable; changeable, erratic, inconstant, unreliable, variable; iffy, precarious, tricky.

unprepared adj *lit:* unready (for); caught on the hop, taken off guard; ill-considered, not thought through, unfinished, unpolished; ad lib, extemporaneous, improvised, spontaneous.

unprofitable adj *lit:* loss-making, uneconomic, unviable; bootless, fruitless, futile, unproductive, unremunerative, unrewarding, useless, valueless.

unqualified   adj *lit:* incompetent (to), ineligible (to), not up (to), unfit (to); categorical, complete, outright, total, unconditional, unreserved, unrestricted.

unreal   adj *lit:* immaterial, insubstantial, intangible, nebulous; dream, fictitious, illusory, imaginary, make-believe; artificial, false, insincere.

unrealistic   adj *lit:* artificial, contrived, false, laboured, stilted, unlifelike, unnatural; implausible, impracticable, impractical, improbable, unworkable; hopeful, idealistic, romantic, sentimental, wishful.

unreasonable   adj *lit:* illogical, irrational, nonsensical, senseless, silly; unfair, unjust, unwarranted; disproportionate, immoderate, uncalled-for, undue; capricious, erratic, inconstant, inconsistent.

unreliable   adj *lit:* irresponsible, untrustworthy; disloyal, treacherous; deceptive, uncertain, unconvincing; erratic, fallible, unsound.

unrepentant   adj *lit:* impenitent, incorrigible, shameless, supercilious, unruffled; callous, hard-bitten, indifferent, obdurate.

unrest   n *lit:* agitation, demonstration, dissension, mutiny, rebellion, sedition, riotousness; affray, commotion, disturbance, hurly-burly, tumult, turmoil; disquiet, distress, uneasiness, worry.

unsafe   adj *lit:* dangerous, hazardous, perilous, precarious, risky, treacherous, unsound, unstable; unclean, unhygienic; exposed, open, pregnable, vulnerable.

unselfish   adj *lit:* altruistic, generous, kind, magnanimous, noble, philanthropic, selfless.

unsettled   adj (pa.pt) *lit:* agitated, disordered, disturbed, flurried, restive, restless, tense, uneasy; insecure, loose, shaky, unstable, unsteady; changeable, inconstant, uncertain, variable; due, outstanding, payable, unpaid; debatable, moot, undecided, unresolved; deserted, empty, uninhabited, unoccupied, unpopulated, vacant.

unspoilt adj *lit:* genuine, intact, natural, preserved, real, unblemished, undamaged, unimpaired, untouched, wild; everyday, matter-of-fact, ordinary, unaffected, unassuming, unpretentious.

unsure adj *lit:* diffident, insecure, irresolute, uncertain, undecided; distrustful, sceptical, suspicious.

unthinking adj *lit:* careless, inconsiderate, insensitive, tactless, thoughtless, undiplomatic; inadvertent, mechanical, unconscious, vacant; impulsive, rash, reckless.

untried adj *lit:* alien, new, probationary, unfamiliar, untested; unexamined, unstretched.

untrue adj *lit:* erroneous, inaccurate, incorrect, lying, wrong; deceptive, dishonest, false, misleading, spurious; disloyal, perfidious, unfaithful; treacherous, untrustworthy; bowed, distended, distorted, not straight, off, warped, wide.

unusual adj *lit:* abnormal, atypical, exceptional, rare, singular, uncommon, unconventional; bizarre, curious, extraordinary, queer, remarkable, surprising; fishy, odd, peculiar, strange, suspicious; characteristic, distinctive, special.

unwanted adj *lit:* extra, spare, superfluous, surplus; outcast, rejected; unasked, uninvited, unsolicited, unwelcome.

unwell adj *lit:* bedridden, ill, out of sorts, poorly, sick, under the weather; ailing, indisposed, sickly.

unwholesome adj *lit:* deleterious, noxious, unhealthy; corrupting, demoralizing, depraving, perverting; ailing, pale, pallid, sickly, wan.

unwise adj *lit:* foolish, ill-advised, ill-judged, inadvisable, irresponsible, silly, stupid; impolitic, imprudent, indiscreet, injudicious, rash, reckless.

unworldly adj *lit:* idealistic, inexperienced, naive, romantic, sentimental, unsophisticated; abstract, metaphysical; ethereal, extraterrestrial; religious, spiritual, transcendental.

unworthy adj *lit:* ineligible (to), undeserving (of), unfit (to); beneath the dignity (of), disappointing (of), uncharacteristic (of); contemptible, discreditable, dishonourable, ignoble, shameful.

uprising n *lit:* coup, coup d'état, insurrection, mutiny, putsch, rebellion, revolt, revolution.

uproar n *lit:* babel, bedlam, clamour, commotion, din, furore, hullabaloo, outcry, pandemonium, racket, riot, ruckus, rumpus, turmoil.

upset n *lit:* defeat, reversal, reverse, setback; discomposure, distress, disturbance, shock; indisposition, queasiness, sickness. **vb** *lit:* capsize, knock over, overturn, spill, topple, turn over; confuse, disorder, disorganize, jumble, mix up, undo, untidy; agitate, annoy, bother, distress, disturb, fluster; best, defeat, overcome. **adj** *lit:* capsized, overturned, spilt, toppled, upside down; chaotic, confused, disordered, disorganized, jumbled, mixed up, untidy; agitated, annoyed, bothered, distressed, disturbed, flustered, hurt, put out, unhappy, worried; queasy, sick.

urban adj *lit:* city, civic, metropolitan, municipal, town.

urgent adj *lit:* compelling, compulsive, crucial, emergency, essential, exigent, imperative, necessary, pressing, vital; imploring, importunate, insistent.

use n *lit:* application, employment, operation; custom, practice, treatment, usage, way; advantage, avail, benefit, good, help, object, point, profit, service, value. **vb** *lit:* apply, employ, exercise, ply, utilize, wield; exploit, take advantage of; behave towards, treat; consume, expend, spend, take (up).

used adj *lit:* second-hand; cast-off, nearly-new, shop-soiled, worn; gumless, not mint, postmarked.

useful adj *lit:* advantageous, beneficial, effective, good, helpful, profitable, serviceable, valuable, worthwhile; adaptable, general-purpose, practical, versatile.

usual adj *lit:* common, customary, everyday, familiar, general, habitual, ordinary, regular, routine, standard, stock, typical.

V

vacancy n *lit:* job opportunity, position, post, situation; gap, room, space; emptiness, vacuum, void.

vacant adj *lit:* available, free, idle, not in use, unengaged, unoccupied; blank, empty, expressionless, inane, uncomprehending, incurious, unthinking, vacuous.

vague adj *lit:* blurred, dim, fuzzy, hazy, ill-defined, indeterminate, indistinct, loose, obscure, shadowy, unclear, unspecified, woolly; doubtful, uncertain; aimless, purposeless, random.

vaguely adv *lit:* faintly, in a way, rather, somewhat; dimly, fuzzily, hazily, indistinctly, loosely, obscurely; doubtfully, uncertainly; aimlessly, purposelessly, randomly.

vain adj *lit:* affected, bigheaded, conceited, narcissistic, ostentatious, overweening, pretentious, self-important, stuck-up, swollen-headed; arrogant, cocky, egotistical, haughty, proud, swaggering; abortive, bootless, fruitless, futile, hollow, idle, ineffectual, unavailing, unproductive, unprofitable, unsuccessful, useless, wasted; empty, pointless, worthless.

valley n *lit:* basin, combe, dale, glen, strath, vale; dell, depression, dingle, hollow; drainage area; canyon, gorge, gulch; *fig:* gutter, trough.

valuable adj *lit:* costly, expensive, precious, worth a lot; beneficial, estimable, helpful, important, profitable, useful, worthwhile; cherished, dear, prized, treasured.

value n *lit:* cost, price; evaluation, rating, worth; benefit, help, merit, profit, use, usefulness; effect, force, meaning; *spec:* duration (of a musical note); tone (in light or dark shades).   vb *lit:* assess, estimate, evaluate, rate; appraise, calculate, compute, quantify, reckon; appreciate, cherish, esteem, hold dear, prize, respect, think highly of, treasure.

vanish vb *lit:* disappear; dissolve, evanesce, evaporate, fade out, melt away.

vanity n *lit:* airs, bigheadedness, conceit, narcissism, ostentation, pretension, self-importance; arrogance, cockiness, egotism, haughtiness, pride; frivolity, inanity, triviality; emptiness, futility, hollowness, pointlessness, uselessness, worthlessness.

variation n *lit:* adapted form, development, modified form, reworking, revised form, version; alteration, change, deviation, difference, modification; divergence, diversity.

variety n *lit:* alteration, change, difference, diversity, multiplicity; assortment, medley, miscellany, mixture, range; brand, category, kind, make, order, sort, type; breed, class, species, strain, subspecies.

various adj *lit:* assorted, different, differing, divers, diverse, miscellaneous, sundry; divergent, separate; several, many.

varnish n *lit:* glaze, gloss, lacquer, shellac; *fig:* adornment, decoration, embellishment, polish; display, outward appearance, show. **vb** *lit:* glaze, gloss, lacquer, shellac; *fig:* adorn, decorate, embellish, polish; disguise.

vast adj *lit:* colossal, enormous, gigantic, huge, immense, mammoth, massive, monumental; boundless, immeasurable, limitless, unbounded; astronomical, unlimited.

vault n *lit:* catacomb, cellar, crypt, tomb; depository, safe, strongroom; arch, span; ceiling, roof; jump, leap; curvet. **vb** *lit:* hurdle, jump, leap, spring; curvet.

vehicle n *lit:* conveyance, mode of transport; means, medium; *fig:* apparatus, mechanism, organ; channel, wave.

veil n *lit:* kerchief, scarf, shawl; chador; wimple; bridal headdress; velum; film, curtain, screen; *fig:* cloak, concealment, disguise, mantle, mask; conventual vows, life of seclusion. **vb** *lit:* cloak, conceal, cover, curtain off, hide, mantle, mask, obscure, screen, shroud; *spec:* darken (in photography).

vein n *lit:* blood vessel; lode, seam, stratum; band, streak, stripe; *fig:* attitude, humour, mode, mood, strain, temper, tenor, tone; *spec:* rib (on a leaf, in an insect's wing).

veneer n *lit:* covering layer, surface; ply; *fig:* façade, front, mask, outward appearance, pretence, show. **vb** *lit:* cover, face, surface; *fig:* cover, mask, veil.

vengeance n *lit:* avenging, reprisal, retaliation, retribution, revenge, settling of scores; punishment; force, fury, severity, vehemence, violence.

vengeful adj *lit:* resentful, vindictive; demanding punishment, retaliatory, retributive, seeking revenge.

venom n *lit:* poison, toxin; bane; *fig:* acrimony, ill will, malevolence, malice, malignity, spite, virulence; acerbity, poignancy, sharpness; sting.

vent n *lit:* escape, outflow, outlet; air-duct, air intake; aperture, opening, orifice; *spec:* anus (of birds); touch-hole (in a gun-barrel). **vb** *lit:* air, express, give expression to, pour out, utter, voice; emit, issue.

venture n *lit:* attempt, endeavour, enterprise, project, undertaking; chance, fling, gamble, hazard, risk; proposition, speculation.
vb *lit:* advance (forward), plunge (into), sally (forth); attempt (to), endeavour (to), propose (to), undertake (to), volunteer (to); chance, gamble, hazard, risk, stake, wager; endanger, imperil, jeopardize; dare say, guess, suggest.

venue n *lit:* location, place, rendezvous, trysting-place, site; arena, field, pitch; scene of the crime; *spec:* hit, lunge, thrust (in fencing).

verdict n *lit:* adjudication, decision, finding, judgement, ruling; conclusion, opinion.

verge n *lit:* edge, fringe, margin, roadside, side; border, brim, brink, lip, threshold; *spec:* eaves, overhang (of a roof); shaft (of a pillar); staff of office. **vb** *lit:* be side (on to), border (on), edge (on to).

versatile adj *lit:* adaptable, flexible, reversible; handy, many-sided, resourceful; multifarious, multipurpose.

version n *lit:* form, kind, style, type; model, variant; adaptation, interpretation, reading, rendition, translation.

vertical *adj lit:* perpendicular, upright; erect; apical, at the zenith; lengthways; *spec:* harmonic (in music).

very *adj lit:* actual, express; exact, precise; identical, same, selfsame; real, true; mere, pure, sheer. **adv** *lit:* awfully, exceedingly, extremely, greatly, highly, really, terribly, terrifically, truly; acutely, deeply, profoundly.

vessel *n lit:* boat, craft, ship; container, tank; receptacle; canal, channel, duct, tube; *fig:* medium, mouthpiece, spokesperson, transmitter.

vet *n lit:* animal doctor, animal surgeon, pet doctor; zoologist. **vb** *lit:* check out, examine, review, scan, scrutinize; assess, appraise, size up, weigh up.

veteran *n lit:* old hand, professional; ex-serviceman. **adj** *lit:* long-serving, old, seasoned; battle-scarred, campaign-hardened.

veto *n lit:* negation, negative, refusal, rejection, thumbs-down; embargo, prohibition. **vb** *lit:* give the thumbs-down, negate, refuse, reject; interdict, rule out, turn down; ban, embargo, forbid, prohibit.

vibrant *adj lit:* oscillating, quivering, shivering, trembling; pulsating, resonant, resounding, thrilling, throbbing; *fig:* animated, dynamic, lively, sparkling, spirited, vivacious.

vibrate *vb lit:* oscillate, quiver, shake, shiver, tremble; pulsate, thrill, throb; resonate, reverberate; *spec:* transmit waves of (emotion).

vice *n lit:* evil, iniquity, sin, wickedness; depravity, immorality, prostitution; defect, failing, fault, shortcoming; blemish, imperfection.

vicious *adj lit:* aggressive, cruel, dangerous, diabolical, ferocious, fiendish, fierce, malevolent, malicious, malignant, mean, savage, spiteful, venomous, vindictive, violent; brutal, painful, severe.

victim *n lit:* prey, sufferer; casualty, injured party; fatality, martyr; butt, quarry, target; dupe, gull, john, patsy, sucker; fall guy, scapegoat.

victimize *vb lit:* discriminate against, persecute, pick on; be malevolent towards, be vindictive towards; cheat, con, defraud, dupe, exploit, swindle.

victorious adj *lit:* conquering, successful, triumphant, vanquishing, winning; champion, prizewinning; best.

victory n *lit:* win; success, triumph; laurels, palm, prize, trophy; conquest, supremacy.

view n *lit:* outlook, panorama, prospect, scene, sight, vista; field of vision; display, exhibition, show; *fig:* aspect, conception, idea, impression, picture; attitude, judgement, notion, opinion, way of thinking; expectation; consideration. **vb** *lit:* behold, eye, look at, observe, regard, scan, see, survey, watch, witness; examine, inspect, scrutinize; *fig:* deem, look on, think of as.

viewpoint n *lit:* position, stance, vantage point; angle, perspective; *fig:* attitude, slant, way of thinking.

vigour n *lit:* dynamism, energy, force, liveliness, pep, power, punch, snap, spirit, strength, verve, vim, vitality, zip; health, robustness, virility.

vile adj *lit:* disgusting, foul, loathsome, nauseating, offensive, repellent, repugnant, repulsive, revolting, sickening; appalling, contemptible, despicable, disgraceful, worthless; evil, immoral, perverted, shocking, sinful, wicked; abject, base, coarse, debased, low, mean, vulgar, wretched.

villain n *lit:* evildoer, malefactor, miscreant; convict, criminal; blackguard, scoundrel; libertine, rake, roué; anti-hero, baddie; *fig:* devil, monkey, rapscallion, rogue, scamp.

violence n *lit:* ferocity, fervour, fierceness, force, intensity, passion, power, severity, strength, vehemence; brutality, roughness, savagery, thuggery, wildness; boisterousness, storminess, turbulence; bloodshed, cruelty; harm, injury.

violent adj *lit:* fervent, fierce, forceful, intense, passionate, powerful, severe, strong, vehement; brutal, rough, savage, thuggish, wild; blustery, boisterous, stormy, tempestuous, turbulent; berserk, bloody, cruel, ferocious, maniacal, murderous; dangerous, harmful, injurious; agonizing, excruciating, sharp.

virgin n *lit:* maiden; damsel, young girl; spinster; madonna.
adj *lit:* chaste, maidenly; undefiled, unsullied, untouched; *fig:*
immaculate, pure; fresh, new, pristine, unused.

virile adj *lit:* male, manly, masculine, potent, red-blooded; lusty,
macho, robust, strong, vigorous.

virtue n *lit:* chastity, purity; goodness, integrity, morality, probity,
rectitude, righteousness, worthiness; good point, merit, plus, strength;
advantage, effectiveness, efficacy, potency.

virtuous adj *lit:* chaste, clean-living, pure; ethical, exemplary, good,
honourable, moral, righteous, upright, worthy.

visible adj *lit:* apparent, clearly seen, discernible, evident, in sight,
manifest, noticeable, obvious, patent, plain, unmistakable; distinct,
distinguishable; *fig:* approachable by appointment, ready for visitors;
spec: goods (in economics).

vision n *lit:* eyesight, seeing, sight; eyes, view; apparition,
hallucination, illusion, revelation; spectacle; *fig:* farsightedness,
foresight, imagination, prescience; insight, understanding; concept,
conception, idea, image, mental picture; daydream, dream, fantasy;
perfect picture, sight for sore eyes.

visit n *lit:* call; sojourn, stay, stop; excursion, trip.   **vb** *lit:* call in
on, go to see, look up, pop in on; be a guest of, stay with, stop at; go
on an excursion to, sightsee, take a trip to, tour; *fig:* afflict, assail,
attack, trouble; impose (upon), inflict (upon), wreak (upon).

visitors n *lit:* callers, guests; company; foreigners, tourists,
transients.

visualize vb *lit:* conceive, envisage, imagine, mentally see, picture;
draw up, realize.

vital adj *lit:* cardiopulmonary, living, survival; alive, dynamic,
energetic, lively, spirited, vibrant, vivacious; *fig:* cardinal, critical,
crucial, essential, fundamental, indispensable, key, necessary,
requisite.

vivid adj *lit:* brilliant, colourful, rich; bright, clear, distinct, graphic,
lifelike, realistic, three-dimensional, true-to-life; dramatic, powerful,
sharp, strong, telling.

vocal adj *lit:* articulated, oral, spoken, sung, uttered, voiced; clamorous, eloquent, loquacious, noisy, strident, vociferous.

voice n *lit:* power of speech; sound, timbre, tone; *fig:* expression, view, vote; decision; agency, medium, spokesperson, vehicle; *spec:* (part-singing) part, singer; verb-form (in grammar). **vb** *lit:* air, articulate, come out with, declare, express, say; resonate; accent, emphasize, stress.

volley n *lit:* barrage, bombardment, fusillade, hail, salvo, shower; burst, outburst, staccato rattle; *spec:* (on the) full, full toss (in cricket, tennis and football). **vb** *lit:* discharge together, fire together, sound together; *spec:* strike before (the ball) bounces.

volume n *lit:* capacity, cubic capacity; amount, bulk, mass, quantity; book, tome, work; loudness, noise, sound.

voluntary n *lit:* extempore piece, improvised piece; musical prelude; musical postlude. **adj** *lit:* discretionary, optional, spontaneous; free, unforced; honorary, unpaid; intentional, willing; independent, unaffiliated; consciously controlled, willed.

vomit vb *lit:* be sick, bring up, chuck up, heave, puke, spew, throw up; belch forth, disgorge, emit.

vote n *lit:* ballot, plebiscite, poll, referendum; suffrage; voice; choice, decision, verdict. **vb** *lit:* ballot; declare (for), opt (for); propose, recommend, suggest.

voyage n *lit:* journey, passage, trip; cruise, excursion, trip; round-trip, travels.

vulgar adj *lit:* cheap, common, commonplace, ill-bred, low, plebeian; boorish, coarse, crude, gaudy, indelicate, tasteless, tawdry, uncouth, unmannerly; debased, degraded, ignoble; native, vernacular.

vulgarity n *lit:* cliché, commonplace; crudity, ribaldry; coarseness, crudeness, indecorum, indelicacy, tastelessness, tawdriness, uncouthness.

W

wade vb *lit:* paddle (through), splash (through), walk (through); ford; *fig:* labour (through), plod (through), plough (through), toil (through); get stuck (into), light (into), tear (into).

wag n *lit:* shake, wave; comedian, humorist, jester, joker, wit.
vb *lit:* shake, wave; flutter, oscillate, rock, vibrate, wiggle.

wage n *lit:* emolument, fee, pay, payment, remuneration, salary, stipend. **vb** *lit:* carry on, conduct, engage in, prosecute, pursue, undertake.

wail n *lit:* howl, ululation, yowl; cry, moan, sob; clamour, drone, scream, whine. **vb** *lit:* bemoan, cry, howl, moan, sob, ululate, weep, yowl; clamour, drone, scream, whine.

wait n *lit:* delay, halt, hold-up, pause, rest, stop; hiatus, intermission, interval, space; ambush; carol-singer. **vb** *lit:* bide one's time, halt, hold back, hold on, pause, rest, stop, tarry; be delayed, remain, stay; attend (on), serve (at).

wake n *lit:* vigil, watch; funeral party; backwash, track, trail, wash. **vb** *lit:* awaken, be roused, come to, get up, stir; activate, arouse, reanimate, revive; *fig:* enliven, excite, galvanize, kindle, stimulate; evoke, fire, provoke.

walk n *lit:* constitutional, hike, perambulation, promenade, ramble, tramp; amble, saunter, stroll, traipse, trek, trudge; gait, pace, step, stride; aisle, alley, avenue, lane, path; pathway, trail; enclosure, pen, run; *fig:* activity, area, field, sphere; *spec:* flock (of wagtails).
vb *lit:* amble, hike, perambulate, promenade, ramble, saunter, stroll, traipse, tramp, trek, trudge; foot it, hoof it, march, step it out, stride out, yomp; inspect, pace out; advance, go, move, travel; go away, move off, withdraw; accompany, escort, take; exercise, lead.

wall n *lit:* brickwork; divider, panel, partition, screen; barricade, bulwark, fortification, palisade, rampart; barrier, fence; cliff, precipice; *fig:* obstacle, obstruction; defence; *spec:* membrane (surrounding or lining a body organ, or a cell).   **vb** *lit:* partition (off), screen (off), separate; enclose, surround; fortify; immure; *spec:* roll, squint (of eyes).

wander   n *lit:* meander, perambulation, peregrination, promenade, ramble, roam.   **vb** *lit:* drift, meander, perambulate, peregrinate, promenade, ramble, range, roam, rove, travel; deviate, digress, diverge, go astray, straggle, stray, veer off; *fig:* be led astray, err, lapse.

wandering   adj (pr.pt) *lit:* aimless, circuitous, convoluted, meandering, rambling, ranging, roaming, sinuous, tortuous, winding; drifting, itinerant, nomadic, peripatetic, travelling, vagrant, wayfaring.

wane   n *lit:* atrophy, decline, decay, dwindling, ebb, fading, falling off, shrinking, sinking, subsiding, withering; decrease, diminution, fall, lessening, lowering, tapering off, winding down.   **vb** *lit:* abate, atrophy, decline, decay, dwindle, ebb, fade, fall off, get smaller, shrink, sink, subside, wither; decrease, diminish, fall, lessen, lower; die away, draw to a close, taper off, wear off, wind down.

want   n *lit:* absence, default, demand, lack, need, requirement; craving, desire, longing, wish, yearning, yen; appetite, hunger, thirst; dearth, deficiency, insufficiency, paucity, poverty, privation, scarcity, shortage.   **vb** *lit:* desire, need, require, wish; crave, hanker for, hunger for, long for, pine for, thirst for, yearn for; be deficient in, be short of, lack, miss; seek.

war   n *lit:* battle, conflict, fighting, hostilities, strife, struggle; *fig:* contention, enmity, hostility; competition, rivalry; campaign. **vb** *lit:* battle, combat, fight, struggle; *fig:* campaign (against).

ward   n *lit:* dependant, protégé; charge; care, custody, guardianship, keeping, protection; district, division, hundred, precinct, wapentake, zone; *spec:* clinic, (hospital) dormitory, room, sanatorium; notch, slot (on a key); parry (in fencing); section (in a prison).   **vb** *lit:* guard, have custody of, keep, protect; deflect (away), fend (off), parry.

warden n *lit:* curator, executive officer, keeper, ranger, superintendent; caretaker, janitor, watchman; administrator, custodian, guardian.

warder n *lit:* guard, sentinel, sentry, watchman; jailer, keeper, prison officer; beefeater, yeoman of the guard; *spec:* baton, staff of authority.

warm vb *lit:* heat (up); melt, thaw; microwave, reheat; hot (up); *fig:* limber (up); become more friendly (to), become more sympathetic (to); excite, interest, stimulate, stir (up). **adj** *lit:* pleasantly hot; unpleasantly hot; radiating; *fig:* affable, affectionate, cordial, friendly, hearty, kind, kindly, loving, tender; lively, severe, strenuous, vigorous; ardent, earnest, enthusiastic, fervent, keen, passionate; excited, stimulated; emotional, intense; fresh, strong, vivid; irascible, sensitive, touchy; dangerous, hazardous, perilous; *spec:* close, near (in a game); rich, wealthy.

warmth n *lit:* heat, temperature; radiance, radiation, sunshine; blaze, fire, flame; *fig:* ardour, emotion, enthusiasm, feeling, fervour, intensity, passion; animation, excitement, spirit, vigour, zeal; affection, kindliness, love, tenderness; cordiality, heartiness; asperity, curtness, ferocity, sharpness.

warning n *lit:* alarm, alert, caution, notice, tip, tip-off; shot across the bows, threat; advice, notification, word; augury, omen, premonition, presage, sign; beacon, signal; attention, beware. **adj (pr.pt)** *lit:* cautionary; threatening; ominous, premonitory; *spec:* aposematic (of the coloration of organisms).

warp n *lit:* bend, distortion, twist; loop; *fig:* bias, defect, kink; perversion. **vb** *lit:* bend, be twisted, curve, distort, twist; haul, heave, hoist, winch; *fig:* misinterpret, misrepresent; pervert; *spec:* block, choke (a waterway); flood (for soil renewal).

wash n *lit:* ablution, bath, rinse, scrub, shampoo, shower; cleansing, laundering; surf, surge, swell, undertow; attrition, erosion, wear; coating, film, stain; coat, layer, suffusion; lotion, medication. **vb** *lit:* bath, bathe, launder, rinse, scrub, shampoo, shower; moisten, steep, wet; baptise, clean, cleanse; erode (away), sweep (away); *fig:* be convincing, be plausible, hold up, hold water, stick, work.

waste n *lit:* debris, dross, garbage, leavings, litter, offal, refuse, rubbish, scrap, sweepings, trash; dissipation, extravagance, loss, misuse, prodigality, profligacy, squandering; desert, outback, veldt, wilds, wilderness; destruction, devastation, havoc, ravage, ruin; *spec:* silt (in rivers); excrement, excreta, faeces, stools; urine.   **vb** *lit:* be prodigal with, blow, dissipate, fritter away, misuse, squander, throw away; atrophy, corrode, crumble, decay, diminish, dwindle, eat (away), erode, fade (away), wear (away), wither; be spent, be used up; *fig:* assassinate, kill, murder.   **adj** *lit:* extra, leftover, over, superfluous, unused; scrap, rejected, thrown away, unwanted; bare, barren, desolate, empty, uninhabited, wild; devastated, ravaged, ruined, unproductive.

watch n *lit:* chronometer, timepiece; lookout, sentry; eye, observation, surveillance; guard, vigil; period.   **vb** *lit:* eye, look at, mark, note, observe, pay attention to, stare at, survey, view; be on the alert, be vigilant, be wary of, look out (for), take heed of; guard, keep, look after, mind, protect, superintend, supervise; keep vigil.

water n *lit:* lake, ocean, river, sea; tide; rain; *fig:* amniotic fluid, blood serum, saliva, tears; urine; class, grade, quality; *spec:* clarity, lustre, transparency (of a diamond).   **vb** *lit:* damp, dampen, douse, drench, flood, hose, irrigate, moisten, ret, soak, souse, spray, sprinkle, steep; adulterate, dilute, thin, weaken; give a drink; *fig:* lacrimate, salivate.

wave n *lit:* flourish, flutter, gesticulation, gesture, shake, swing; billow, breaker, roller, undulation; oscillation, sine curve; perm; *fig:* current, flood, movement, stream, surge, swell, upsurge; epidemic, outbreak, rash, trend.   **vb** *lit:* brandish, flap, flourish, shake, stir, swing, undulate, wag; beckon, direct, gesticulate, gesture, indicate, make a sign, signal.

way n *lit:* avenue, channel, course, direction, lane, path, pathway, road, route, street, track; distance, journey, length; room, space; motion, movement, passage, progress; approach, course of action, means, method, mode, procedure, system, technique; custom, fashion, habit, idiosyncrasy, manner, practice, style, trait, usage, wont; aspect, feature, respect, sense; aim, desire, goal, will, wish; circumstance, condition, shape, state.   **adv** *lit:* far; considerably, severely.

weak *adj lit:* debilitated, delicate, effete, feeble, flimsy, frail, puny; defenceless, exposed, helpless, impotent, unprotected, vulnerable; cowardly, ineffectual, irresolute, powerless, soft, spineless; inadequate, lacking, poor, substandard; distant, dull, faint, low, muffled, quiet, slight; *fig:* invalid, lame, pathetic, unconvincing; diluted, thin, watery, wishy-washy; *spec:* fluctuating (stock market prices); regular (verb declension); unstressed (syllable).

weaken *vb lit:* fail, flag, give way, sap, soften up, temper, undermine, wane; abate, decrease, diminish, dwindle, fade, lessen, moderate; *fig:* adulterate, dilute, thin, water down; cut, debase.

wealth *n lit:* affluence, means, money, opulence, prosperity, riches, substance; fortune, lucre, pelf, property; resources; *fig:* abundance, copiousness, luxuriance, plenitude, plethora, profusion.

wear *n lit:* abrasion, attrition, depreciation, deterioration, erosion, friction damage; use; mileage, service, utility. *vb lit:* be dressed in, dress in, have on, sport; display, exhibit; abrade, depreciate, deteriorate, erode, fray, grind, rub; *fig:* bear up, endure, hold up, last; annoy, exasperate, fatigue, irk, tire (out), try, vex, weary; bring gradually (in); pass (on); accept, buy, credit, take on trust.

weary *vb lit:* drain, fag, fatigue, jade, take it out of, tax, tire, wear out; annoy, bore, burden, exasperate, harass, irk, pester, plague. *adj lit:* all in, dead beat, dog tired, done in, drained, exhausted, fagged, fatigued, jaded, spent, taxed, tired out, whacked, worn out; annoyed, bored, exasperated, irked, plagued.

weather *n lit:* atmospheric conditions, climate, elements; *fig:* normal, par; influence. *vb lit:* expose, season; harden, toughen; be discoloured, be worn; *fig:* come through, get through, last, make it, ride, ride out, surmount, survive, withstand.

weave *vb lit:* braid, entwine, interlace, lace, plait; criss-cross, intertwine, mesh; *fig:* create, make, spin, work; blend, combine; twist and turn, zigzag.

wedding *n lit:* marriage, matrimony, nuptials, solemnization of matrimony; *fig:* alliance, combination, joining, merger, union.

weep *vb lit:* blub, blubber, cry, shed tears; greet; snivel, sob; grieve (for), mourn (for); *fig:* drip, leak, ooze; exude, suppurate.

weigh vb *lit:* have a weight of, tip the scales at; bear down, burden, load; apportion (out), dole (out), measure (out); balance, hold in the balance; *fig:* be influential, count, matter, tell; consider, contemplate, evaluate, mull over, ponder, think over; insert (in), interpolate (in); get stuck (in), lay (into); *spec:* hoist up (the anchor).

weight n *lit:* heaviness; ballast, burden, load, mass; poundage, tonnage; counterpoise; lead, sinker; pendulum; dumbbell; *fig:* millstone, pressure, strain; onus, preponderance; authority, clout, importance, influence, moment, power, substance; emphasis, impact, value; force, tension; impetus; *spec:* bias (in bowls, in statistics); handicap (in horse-racing). vb *lit:* ballast, charge, load, make heavier; burden, handicap, weigh down; *fig:* add to, bias.

weighty adj *lit:* heavy, hefty, massive; burdensome, cumbersome, ponderous; *fig:* authoritative, consequential, important, influential, momentous, portentous, powerful, serious, significant, substantial; emphatic, forceful; demanding, exacting, exigent, onerous, taxing.

welcome n *lit:* greeting, reception, salutation; entertainment, hospitality. vb *lit:* give a reception to, go to meet, greet, offer hospitality to, receive, usher in; accept with pleasure, take gladly; please come in. adj *lit:* acceptable, agreeable, appreciated, desirable, gratifying, pleasing, pleasurable; *spec:* free of obligation.

welfare n *lit:* health, wellbeing; benefit, good, prosperity; *fig:* dole, social security, social services.

well n *lit:* bore, hole, shaft; pool, spring; compartment, hollow, niche, pit; *fig:* fount, source; repository, store; mine. vb *lit:* arise, rise, spring; seep, spout, trickle; flow, gush, pour, run, spurt, stream; billow, surge. adj *lit:* fine, fit, hale, healthy, robust, sound; all right, okay; fortunate, lucky; advisable, prudent; useful. adv *lit:* ably, accurately, adeptly, correctly, efficiently, expertly, proficiently, properly, rightly, skilfully, suitably; carefully, closely; comfortably, more than satisfactorily; abundantly, amply, considerably, deeply, fully, greatly, heartily, highly, profoundly, substantially, thoroughly; easily, readily; approvingly, favourably, glowingly, kindly, warmly.

wet **n** *lit:* dampness, moisture, water; drizzle, rain, storm; clamminess, condensation, damp, humidity; *fig:* drip, weakling, weed, wimp. **vb** *lit:* damp, dampen, douse, drench, flood, moisten, ret, rinse, soak, souse, spray, sprinkle, steep; baptise, dip; urinate in/on; *fig:* drink the health of, toast. **adj** *lit:* damp, dank, drenched, dripping, moist, saturated, soaked, soaking, sodden, soggy, sopping, waterlogged, watery, wringing; fluid, liquid; clammy, humid; rainy, showery; *fig:* effete, ineffectual, soft, spineless, weak, wimpish; mawkish, sentimental, soppy.

wheel **n** *lit:* hub, tyre; helm, steering column; circle, disc; change of direction, rotation, turn; *fig:* cog, gear. **vb** *lit:* gyrate, pivot, rotate, spin, swing, swivel, turn; circle, loop, spin round, whirl round; drive, push along, take, transport.

whim **n** *lit:* caprice, conceit, fancy, humour, impulse, notion, vagary; eccentricity, quirk; *spec:* horse-drawn capstan, horse-drawn winch.

whine **n** *lit:* moan, wail; drone, noise, tone; nasal timbre. **vb** *lit:* moan, wail; complain, grouse, grumble; beef, bellyache, gripe, grizzle, whinge, yowl.

whip **n** *lit:* cat-o'-nine-tails, crop, knout, lash, rawhide, scourge, switch, thong; *fig:* party manager; coachman, driver; *spec:* armature (in an electrical circuit); block and tackle, pulley. **vb** *lit:* beat, flagellate, flog, lash, scourge, strap, switch, thrash; birch, cane, leather, tan; hammer, lick; conquer, defeat, drub, overcome, overpower, rout, trounce; compel, drive, goad, incite, prick, prod, provoke, spur; force, jerk, pull, seize, snatch; dart, dash, dive, flash, fly, tear; mix, stir, whisk; appropriate, nab, nick, steal, thieve, walk off with.

whirl **n** *lit:* gyration, pirouette, revolution, rotation, spin, swirl, twirl; dizziness, giddiness; daze, dither; agitation, bustle, commotion, flurry, hurly-burly, stir; round, series, succession. **vb** *lit:* circle, gyrate, pirouette, revolve, rotate, spin, swirl, turn, twirl; reel; wheel.

whirlwind **n** *lit:* dust-devil, eddy, vortex; cyclone, tornado. **adj** *lit:* immediate, instant, lightning; hasty, rapid, speedy, swift; headlong, impetuous, impulsive.

whisk n *lit:* beater, mixer; swat; brush, flick, sweep, whip.
vb *lit:* beat, fluff up, mix, stiffen, whip; swat; brush, flick, sweep, wipe; hurry, race, rush, speed.

whisper n *lit:* low voice, murmur, undertone; rustle, sighing, susurration, swish; white sound; *fig:* breath, hint, shadow, suggestion, trace, whiff; buzz, rumour, word.   **vb** *lit:* breathe, murmur, say softly; rustle, sigh, susurrate, swish; *fig:* gossip, hint, insinuate, spread a rumour.

whole n *lit:* lot, sum, total; entirety, totality; aggregate, complete system, ensemble, total combination, unity.   **adj** *lit:* complete, entire, full, integral, total; intact, perfect, sound, unbroken, undamaged, unscathed; unabridged, uncut; better, cured, healed, healthy; all at once, in one piece.

wholesome adj *lit:* healthful, nourishing, nutritious; beneficial, hygienic; *fig:* clean, decent, edifying, good, moral, nice, respectable, uplifting, virtuous.

whore n *lit:* harlot, loose woman, strumpet, trollop; call girl, courtesan, lady of the night; hooker, hustler, prostitute, slag, slut, streetwalker, tart, tramp.   **vb** *lit:* be promiscuous, fornicate, sleep around, womanize; be a prostitute, be on the game, sell one's body, solicit, walk the streets.

wicked adj *lit:* bad, evil, impious, iniquitous, irreligious, sinful, ungodly, wrong; amoral, blackhearted, cruel, devilish, fiendish, inhuman, malevolent, malicious, malign, satanic, spiteful, vicious; abandoned, corrupt, debased, depraved, heinous, immoral, nefarious, villainous; *fig:* arch, impish, incorrigible, mischievous, naughty, roguish, sly.

wide adj *lit:* ample, broad, expansive, extensive, great, large, thick, vast; dilated, distended, outspread, outstretched; capacious, commodious, full, loose, roomy, spacious; comprehensive, encyclopaedic, sweeping; badly-aimed, inaccurate, off-target; *spec:* protein-reduced (animal feed).   **adv** *lit:* as much as possible, fully; distantly, far, expansively, extensively, remotely; aside, astray, inaccurately, off, off-target.

width   n *lit:* breadth, bulk, compass, diameter, girth, span, thickness; extent, reach; depth, latitude, range, scope, sweep.

wield   vb *lit:* apply, control, employ, exercise, handle, have at one's disposal, maintain, make use of, ply, put to use, use, utilize; brandish, flourish, hold, retain.

wild   n *lit:* natural habitat; state of nature; backwoods, desert, outback, vastness, veldt, wasteland.   adj *lit:* desert, desolate, empty, natural, uncivilized, uncultivated, uninhabited, unpopulated, virgin, waste; feral, unbroken, undomesticated, untamed; barbarous, brutish, primitive, rude; boisterous, disorderly, lawless, noisy, passionate, riotous, rowdy, turbulent, unbridled, uncontrolled, undisciplined, ungovernable, unmanageable, unruly, violent, wayward; berserk, crazed, demented, distracted, frenzied, hysterical, incoherent, irrational, mad, maniacal, possessed, rabid, raving; extravagant, fantastic, impracticable, irresponsible, madcap, preposterous, rash, reckless, unreasoned; dishevelled, scruffy, tousled, unkempt, windblown, windswept; blustery, choppy, ferocious, fierce, howling, intense, raging, rough, tempestuous; avid, batty, crazy, eager, enthusiastic, excited, fanatical, nuts, potty; *spec:* arbitrary, unassigned, unlimited (playing-card).   adv *lit:* freely, unchecked, unrestrainedly.

wilderness   n *lit:* jungle, wasteland, wilds; desert, desolation, waste; *fig:* bewildering mass, confusion, jumble, maze, tangle.

wilful   adj *lit:* conscious, deliberate, intentional, volitional, voluntary; determined, headstrong, intransigent, mulish, obdurate, obstinate, pig-headed, single-minded, stubborn, uncompromising; intractable, perverse, refractory, unmanageable.

will   n *lit:* volition; choice, decision, discretion; desire, inclination, preference, wish; intention, mind, purpose, resolve; attitude, disposition, feeling; *spec:* last wishes, testament.   vb *lit:* aim to, be going to, intend to, mean to; be determined to, be resolved to; choose, elect, opt, prefer, want, wish; command, desire, determine, direct, ordain; bequeath, endow, hand on, leave, pass on.

wilt   vb *lit:* become limp, droop, sag; dry up, shrivel, wither; *fig:* dwindle, fade, flag, wane; falter, waver, weaken.

win n *lit:* success, triumph, victory. **vb** *lit:* be victorious, come first, prevail, succeed, triumph; attain, earn, gain, make, net, reach, secure; achieve, get, obtain, receive; charm, convert, induce, persuade; *spec:* mine (coal or ore).

wind n *lit:* air, blow, breeze, draught, gale, gust; breath, puff; respiration; flatulence, flatus, gas; scent, smell; *fig:* blather, bluster, empty talk, hot air; clue, hint, inkling, intimation, rumour, suggestion, whisper; near future, offing, pipeline; *spec:* brass and woodwind (in an orchestra). **vb** *lit:* have the breath knocked out of, puff out; scent, smell, sniff; blow, sound.

wind n *lit:* angle, bend, corner, curve, meander, spiral, turn, twist, wiggle. **vb** *lit:* bend, curve, meander, snake, spiral, turn, twist, wiggle, worm, writhe; coil, curl, encircle, loop, spiral, twine (around), twist, wreathe (around); fold (around), wrap (around); key, set; roll into a ball; reel (in), winch; *fig:* excite, make tense.

winding adj (pr.pt) *lit:* circuitous, convoluted, crooked, curling, helical, looping, meandering, roundabout, serpentine, sinuous, spiral, tortuous, twisting.

winning adj (pr.pt) *lit:* conquering, successful, triumphant, unbeaten, victorious; *fig:* alluring, attractive, bonny, captivating, charming, disarming, enchanting, engaging, fascinating, fetching, pleasing, sweet, taking; influential, persuasive.

wintry adj *lit:* arctic, bleak, chilly, cold, dark, freezing, frosty, icy, piercing, raw, snowy; *fig:* distant, frozen, unfriendly.

wipe n *lit:* brush, rub, swab; lick. **vb** *lit:* brush, mop, rub, sponge, swab; clean (off), erase, expunge; dry; *fig:* snuff (out), stamp (out); *spec:* solder.

wise adj *lit:* discerning, discriminating, enlightened, erudite, knowledgeable, learned, penetrating, percipient, sagacious, sage, studied, understanding; judicious, politic, prudent, sensible, shrewd, thoughtful; aware, conscious, informed, knowing; clever, intelligent.

wish n *lit:* aspiration, hankering, hope, inclination; desire, longing, want, yearning; whim, will; bidding, entreaty, request. **vb** *lit:*

hanker, hope; crave (for), desire, long, want, yearn; bid, express a hope (for, to); will; *fig:* foist (on), pass (on).

wit n *lit:* acumen, comprehension, discernment, intelligence, judgement, perception, penetration, percipience, understanding, wisdom; ingenuity, practicality, sense; humour, quips, repartee, sense of humour, wordplay; comedian, humorist, punster, wag.

witchcraft n *lit:* black arts, magic, sorcery, spells; enchantment, supernatural power.

withdraw vb *lit:* depart, fall back, go away, leave, retire, retreat; resign, scratch; disengage, draw back, pull out; debit, draw out, extract, remove, take out; recall, retract, take back, unsay.

withdrawal n *lit:* departure, exodus, going, leaving, resignation, retirement, retreat; disengagement, separation; extraction, pulling out, removal; recall, retraction, revocation; *spec:* deprivation (of drugs).

withering adj (pr.pt) *lit:* blasting, blighting, crushing, devastating, scorching, searing, trenchant; deadly, lethal, murderous; *fig:* humiliating, mortifying, scornful, shaming.

withhold vb *lit:* detain, hold back, keep back, reserve, restrain, retain, sit on; deduct, keep; deny, repress, suppress; forbear (from), refrain (from).

witness n *lit:* beholder, bystander, onlooker; spectator, viewer, watcher; deponent, testifier; corroboration, evidence, testimony, verification. vb *lit:* behold, look on at, observe, see, view, watch; attest to, corroborate, depone, give evidence, testify, verify; authenticate, countersign, endorse.

wits n *lit:* acumen, brains, intelligence, percipience; ingenuity, practicality, sense; consciousness, faculties, senses.

witty adj *lit:* ingenious, lively, original, pointed, topical, waggish; clever; amusing, droll, funny.

woe n *lit:* anguish, dejection, depression, distress, gloom, grief, heartbreak, melancholy, misery, sorrow, suffering, tribulation, unhappiness, wretchedness; adversity, burden, hardship, misfortune, trial.

woman n *lit:* bride, lady, mistress, wife; female, girl, lass, lassie, maiden, miss; bird, chick, dame, doll, gal, girlfriend; char, domestic, female servant, housekeeper, maid, maidservant.

wonder n *lit:* curiosity, marvel, miracle, phenomenon, prodigy, rarity, spectacle; admiration, awe, fascination. **vb** *lit:* be curious, be inquisitive, inquire, query, question; conjecture, speculate, theorize, think; meditate, ponder, puzzle; be amazed, be awed, be fascinated, be flabbergasted, boggle, marvel.

wonderful adj *lit:* awesome, incredible, magnificent, marvellous, miraculous, outstanding, phenomenal, remarkable, staggering, superb; brilliant, excellent, fabulous, fantastic, great, magnificent, sensational, stupendous, super, terrific, tremendous.

wood n *lit:* xylem; forest, trees; coppice, copse, grove; planking, timber; branches, logs; *fig:* barrel, cask, keg; *spec:* bowl (in the game of bowls); club (in golf); domino.

wooden adj *lit:* ligneous, log, planking, slatted, timber; *fig:* awkward, clumsy, gawky, inelegant, rigid, stiff, ungainly; inflexible, obstinate, unbending, unyielding; blank, deadpan, emotionless, expressionless, unemotional, unresponsive; dull, muffled.

woolly n *lit:* cardigan, jersey, jumper, pullover, sweater. adj *lit:* fleecy, flocculent, woollen; hairy, shaggy; *fig:* blurred, cloudy, confused, fuzzy, hazy, imprecise, indistinct, obscure, vague; rough, uncivilized.

word n *lit:* expression, term, vocable; speech, utterance; comment, declaration, remark, statement; chat, colloquy, consultation, conversation, discussion, talk; account, information, intelligence, news; command, go-ahead, green light, order, signal; countersign; decree, edict; assurance, guarantee, oath, pledge, promise, vow; *spec:* unit of meaning (for computers). **vb** *lit:* couch, express, phrase, put, say.

work n *lit:* employment, job, occupation, profession; business, craft, line, livelihood, métier, trade; assignment, chore, commission, duty, task, undertaking; achievement, composition, creation, oeuvre, opus, performance, piece, product, production; drudgery, effort, exertion, industry, labour, slog, toil, travail; fortification; *fig:* fuss, trouble; *spec:* froth (in fermentation processes); spin (on a cricket ball).   **vb** *lit:* drudge away, labour, slave, slog, sweat, toil, travail; be employed, be in a profession, earn a living, have a job; do enough to be worth, earn; control, direct, drive, handle, manage, move, operate, ply, use, wield; cultivate, farm, till; fashion, form, knead, manipulate, mould, process, shape; accomplish, achieve, carry out, effect, execute, implement, perform; force (in), infiltrate, insinuate, inveigle, worm, wriggle; arrange, contrive, fix, pull off, swing; function, go, run, tick; *spec:* beat to windward (in sailing); ferment.

works   **n** *lit:* factory, mill, plant; acts, deeds, doings; compositions, creations, oeuvre, output, pieces, productions, writings; action, guts, insides, machinery, mechanism, moving parts.

worldly   **adj** *lit:* lay, profane, secular, temporal; carnal, earthly, earthy, fleshly, mundane, physical; experienced, knowing, politic, sophisticated, urbane; cosmopolitan; *fig:* avaricious, grasping, greedy, materialistic, selfish.

worn   **adj (pa.pt)** *lit:* frayed, ragged, tattered, threadbare; *fig:* drawn, haggard, lined; fatigued, spent, tired, wearied; hackneyed, trite.

worry   **n** *lit:* anxiety, apprehension, care, concern, misgiving, perturbation, unease; pest, plague, problem, trial, trouble.   **vb** *lit:* agonize, be anxious, be apprehensive, be concerned, be nervous, be perturbed, be uneasy, brood; be afraid, be fearful, be fretful, be frightened, fear, fret; annoy, badger, bother, distress, disturb, harass, harry, hassle, hector, importune, perturb, pester, plague, tease, unsettle, upset; attack, bite, savage.

worse   **adj** *lit:* less well, more ill; less good, more evil; more harmful, more painful, more unfavourable, more unpleasant; more incorrect; more ill-advised, more unsuitable; inferior, of lower quality, worth less; less fortunate.   **adv** *lit:* more severely; more evilly; more harmfully, more painfully, more unfavourably, more unpleasantly; more incorrectly; more ill-advisedly, more unsuitably.

worship   **n** *lit:* devotion, glorification, homage, honour, praise, prayers; adoration, adulation, love; reverence.   **vb** *lit:* glorify, honour, laud, praise, pray to, venerate; abase oneself to, make oblation to, prostrate oneself before, sacrifice to; participate in a service, praise God, praise the Lord, say devotions; adore, adulate, love; deify, idolize, put on a pedestal.

worst n *lit:* least well, most ill; least good, most evil; most harmful, most painful, most unfavourable, most unpleasant; most incorrect, most ill-advised, most unsuitable; most inferior. **vb** *lit:* beat, best, conquer, defeat, gain an advantage over, get the better of, master, overcome, overpower, vanquish. **adj** *lit:* least well, most ill; least good, most evil; most harmful, most painful, most unfavourable, most unpleasant; most incorrect, most ill-advised, most unsuitable; most inferior, of the lowest quality; least fortunate. **adv** *lit:* most severely; most evilly; most harmfully, most painfully,most unfavourably, most unpleasantly; most incorrectly, most ill-advisedly, most unsuitably.

worth n *lit:* benefit, usefulness, utility, value; importance, quality; excellence, goodness, merit, virtue; cost, price, valuation. **adj** *lit:* deserving of, meriting, meritorious of; of a value of; at a cost of, at a price of, valued at.

worthless adj *lit:* futile, ineffectual, of no use, pointless, unavailing; insignificant, paltry, rubbishy, trashy, trifling, trivial, unimportant, valueless; unusable, useless; contemptible, despicable, ignoble.

wound n *lit:* abrasion, cut, gash, graze, incision, injury, laceration, lesion, scrape, slash; *fig:* hurt, offence, shock, slight, sting, trauma. **vb** *lit:* cut, gash, graze, injure, lacerate, pierce, scrape, slash, wing; damage, harm, hurt; *fig:* cut to the quick, grieve, mortify, offend, pain, shock. **adj (pa.pt)** *lit:* coiled, curled, looped, spiralled, turned (around), twined, twisted; folded (around), wrapped (around); keyed up, set up; *fig:* excited, nervous, tense.

wrangle n *lit:* altercation, argument, disagreement, dispute, quarrel, row, squabble, tiff; affray, argy-bargy, barney, brawl, clash, dust-up, punch-up, set-to, shoving-match. **vb** *lit:* argue, bicker, disagree, dispute, fall out, have words, quarrel, row, squabble; brawl, clash, fight, scrap; *spec:* herd, tend (horses or cattle).

wreck n *lit:* hulk, sunken vessel; derelict, empty shell, husk, skeleton; destruction, ruin; *fig:* confounding, devastation, disruption, spoiling, undoing.   **vb** *lit:* lure on to the rocks, run aground, strand; break up, demolish, destroy, ravage, ruin, shatter, smash, spoil.

wring   **vb** *lit:* screw, squeeze, twist, wrench; dry, put through the mangle; extract (from), force (from), wrest (from); *fig:* coerce (from), extort (from); pain, pierce, rack, rend, tear at, wound.
spec: clasp (hands) firmly, shake (hands) warmly.

wrinkle   **n** *lit:* corrugation, crease, crinkle, crow's foot, fold, furrow, line, pucker, ridge; *fig:* device, dodge, easy method, gimmick, ploy, short cut, technique, trick; hint, tip; difficulty, problem.   **vb** *lit:* corrugate, crease, crinkle, crumple, fold, furrow, line, ruck, ruckle, rumple.

write   **vb** *lit:* inscribe, pen, put down, scribble, set down; author, compose, publish; draft, draw up, jot down, record, take down, transcribe; letter, print, spell; correspond, send a note; endorse, sign; *fig:* display, exhibit, show.

writer   **n** *lit:* author, penpusher, scribbler, wordsmith; columnist, hack, journalist, scribe; essayist, novelist, playwright, poet; littérateur, man of letters; *spec:* lawyer (in Scotland).

wrong   **n** *lit:* injury, misdeed, offence; evil, sin, sinfulness, transgression, wickedness; grievance, injustice, trespass.   **vb** *lit:* aggrieve, harm, ill-treat, ill-use, injure, offend, oppress; be evil to, sin against; deflower, seduce; cheat, defraud, do out of a right; calumniate, malign; misrepresent.   **adj** *lit:* erroneous, fallacious, false, inaccurate, incorrect, mistaken, untrue; bad, dishonourable, evil, immoral, improper, iniquitous, reprehensible, sinful, unethical, unjust, wicked; criminal, crooked, dishonest, felonious, illegal, illicit, unlawful; inappropriate, inapt, infelicitous, unsuitable; amiss, askew, astray, awry, not right; defective, faulty, out of order; *spec:* inner, reverse, under (side, surface).   **adv** *lit:* amiss, astray, awry, badly, inaccurately; erroneously, incorrectly, mistakenly.

X Y Z

xenophobic **adj** *lit:* racialist, racist; chauvinist; insular, isolationist.

Xerox **n** *lit:* copy, facsimile, photocopy, reproduction.

yacht **n** *lit:* ketch, sailing-boat, sailing-dinghy, skiff, smack; clipper, schooner, yawl; motor launch, pleasure-boat.

yearly **adj** *lit:* annual, once-a-year; annual, year-long; annual, for one year, per annum, year's. **adv** *lit:* annually, once a year; annually, for one year at a time.

yearning **n** *lit:* aching, craving, desire, hunger, longing, lust, thirst, wish.

yellow **adj** *lit:* buttercup, canary, gold, golden, honey-coloured, lemon, ochre, primrose, saffron, sandy, sulphur; jaundiced, sallow; *fig:* chicken, cowardly, craven, frightened, gutless, scared, timid.

yes **adv** *lit:* affirmative, all right, okay, roger; certainly, definitely, positively, surely; indeed so, quite so, really, that's true; affirmatively; furthermore, moreover.

yet **adv** *lit:* by now, hitherto, so far, thus far, till now, to date, until now, up to now; already, now, so soon; even, still; additionally, besides, further, to boot. **cnj** *lit:* all the same, but, however, nevertheless, nonetheless.

yield **n** *lit:* crop, harvest, produce; output, product; dividend, earnings, gain, income, profit, return, revenue, takings. **vb** *lit:* afford, bear, bring in, deliver, furnish, give, grant, produce, provide, render, supply; earn, generate, net, pay, return; accede, acquiesce, back down, bow, capitulate, cede, comply, give in, give up, relinquish, resign, submit, surrender; admit, concede, give way; bend, be pliant, flex, loosen, slacken.

young **n** *lit:* babes, children, girls and boys, juveniles, kids, youth; babies, brood, cubs, infants, issue, litter, offspring, pups, progeny, sons and daughters. **adj** *lit:* adolescent, growing, immature, infant,

junior, pre-school, pubescent; coltish, juvenile, youthful; *fig:*
fledgling, new, recently-established; green, inexperienced, raw.

youth   n *lit:* adolescence, boyhood, girlhood, immaturity,
schooldays, teens; heyday, prime; boy, lad, stripling, teenager,
youngster; teenagers, young, young generation, young people;
juvenility, youthfulness.

zeal   n *lit:* ardour, fanaticism, fervour, militancy, passion, readiness,
spirit, verve; commitment, dedication, devotion, earnestness,
enthusiasm, keenness.

zealous   adj *lit:* ardent, burning, fanatical, fervent, impassioned,
militant, passionate, rabid, spirited; avid, committed, dedicated,
devoted, earnest, enthusiastic, keen, unreserved, unstinting;
card-carrying.

zero   n *lit:* cipher, nil, nothing, nought, O; lowest point, minimum,
nadir, rock bottom; least permissible.   **vb** *lit:* calibrate; home (in
on), target (in on).

zone   n *lit:* area, district, region; band, belt, section, sector; field,
sphere.   **vb** *lit:* divide into areas, parcel out, partition, segment,
section; encircle.

Preface

Harrap's Dictionary of Synonyms is a book for both users and students of English. It is a constant reference source for the many occasions when finding the right word is essential, or when variety and interest need to be brought to writing.

The book contains an alphabetical listing of key English words. Each word's part of speech is identified, and the synonyms listed in up to three categories. First are synonyms of the literal meaning (denoted by the abbreviation *lit.*), second the figurative synonyms (*fig.*) and third, if appropriate, specialist synonyms (*spec.*). This last category includes words from the arts, sciences and technology. Where an entry represents more than one part of speech, the following order of presentation is strictly observed.

n	noun
vb	verb
adj	adjective
adj (pa.pt)	adjective (in form a past participle of a verb)
adj (pr.pt)	adjective (in form a present participle of a verb)
adv	adverb
prn	pronoun
prp	preposition
cnj	conjunction
art	(definite or indefinite) article

This consistent order of presentation is for ease and speed of access. In many cases it does not necessarily correspond with the importance or frequency of usage within the language of the parts of speech represented by the entry. The different meaning of a headword are represented by groups of synonyms separated by semi-colons.

J.O.E.C. – London, 1989.

A

abandon   n *lit:* dash, elan, recklessness, unconcern, uninhibitedness, unrestraint, verve, wildness.   **vb** *lit:* desert, evacuate, forsake, jilt, leave, leave behind, maroon, quit, relinquish, retire from, withdraw from; *fig:* abort, cede, desist, discontinue, give up, leave off, renounce, resign, stop, waive.

abbreviation   n *lit:* abridgement, condensation, contraction, curtailment, reduction, shortening, truncation.

abduct   vb *lit:* carry off, elope with, kidnap, run away with, seize, snatch; *spec:* extend (in myology); separate (in surgery).

abet   vb *lit:* aid, assist, back, be an accomplice, encourage, help, incite, prompt, second, support, sustain.

abhorrent   adj *lit:* contrary (to), detestable, disgusting, hateful, horrible, horrid, loathsome, offensive (to), repellent, repulsive.

abiding   adj (pr.pt) *lit:* constant, continuing, enduring, firm, immutable, lasting, permanent, persevering, persistent, steadfast, tenacious, unchanging.

ability   n *lit:* adeptness, aptitude, capability, capacity, competence, dexterity, expertise, facility, faculty, flair, gift, knack, power, proficiency, skill, talent.

abject   adj *lit:* contemptible, cringing, debased, despairing, despicable, fawning, forlorn, grovelling, hopeless, humiliating, ignominious, low, mean, servile, slavish, sordid, worthless, wretched.

able   adj *lit:* accomplished, adept, capable, competent, dextrous, efficient, expert, fitted, gifted, practised, proficient, qualified, skilful, skilled, talented.

abnormal   adj *lit:* anomalous, atypical, deviant, exceptional, extraordinary, irregular, mutant, odd, peculiar, queer, singular, strange, uncommon, unnatural, unusual.

abolish   vb *lit:* abrogate, annul, cancel, do away with, eliminate,

erase, expunge, get rid of, invalidate, nullify, put an end to, quash, repeal, rescind, revoke, stop, terminate, void, wipe out.

abortion n *lit:* miscarriage, stillbirth; termination; *fig:* abandonment, calling off, cancellation, freak, monster, monstrosity, postponement, travesty.

about adv *lit:* active, almost, around, close by, here and there, moving, near by, nearly, roughly, stirring, virtually. **prp** *lit:* adjacent, beside, close by, concerning, concerned with, dealing with, referring to, regarding, respecting, treating.

above n *lit:* aforementioned, aforesaid, foregoing. **adj** *lit:* aforementioned, aforesaid, earlier, foregoing, on high, overhead, preceding, previous, prior. **adv** *lit:* farther up, heavenwards, higher, in/to heaven, on high, overhead, upwards; farther up, higher, upwards; on the next level upwards. **prp** *lit:* farther up than, higher than, over; *fig:* after, beyond, more than, past, superior to.

abrasive n *lit:* grinder, scourer. **adj** *lit:* fricative, grating, scratchy, scuffing, wearing; *fig:* chafing, grating, rasping, rough, sharp.

abridge vb *lit:* abbreviate, condense, contract, cut, reduce, shorten.

abroad adv *lit:* at large, away, being spread, circulating, current, far and wide, in circulation, out of the country, outside, overseas, publicly, widely.

abrupt adj *lit:* blunt, brusque, curt, gruff, hasty, hurried, precipitate, precipitous, sharp, sheer, short, steep, sudden, terse, unexpected, unforeseen; *fig:* broken, disconnected, discontinuous, jerky, uneven; *spec:* broken off (geological stratum); sharply tapered, truncate (botanical specimen).

absence n *lit:* being away, defection, deficiency, desertion, lack, nonattendance, nonexistence, omission, want; *fig:* abstraction, inattention, preoccupation, reverie.

absent adj *lit:* away, deficient, elsewhere, gone, lacking, missing, nonexistent, not present, out, wanting; *fig:* abstracted, distracted, faraway, inattentive, oblivious, preoccupied, vacant.

absolute n *lit:* entirety, independent entity, totality, whole.

adj *lit:* autocratic, autonomous, categorical, certain, complete, conclusive, consummate, decisive, definite, downright, entire, out-and-out, positive, pure, sheer, sovereign, supreme, sure, total, unadulterated, unequivocal, unlimited, unmitigated, utter, whole; *spec:* constant, fixed, invariable (in physics); modifying, qualifying (in grammar).

absolve **vb** *lit:* acquit, clear, discharge (from), exculpate, excuse, exempt, exonerate, free, pardon, release, remit, shrive, vindicate.

absorbing **adj (pr.pt)** *lit:* arresting, captivating, engaging, engrossing, fascinating, gripping, intriguing, riveting, spellbinding.

abstain **vb** *lit:* cease, desist, forbear (from), keep (from), refrain (from), refuse, reject, stop.

abstract **n** *lit:* condensation, digest, imaginative/nonrepresentational work, outline, paraphrase, précis, résumé, summary, synopsis. **vb** *lit:* appropriate, condense, detach, isolate, outline, paraphrase, précis, remove, separate, steal, summarize, take. **adj** *lit:* conceptual, conjectural, fantastic, hypothetical, imagined, imaginative, nonrepresentational, notional, theoretical, visionary.

absurd **adj** *lit:* crazy, daft, drivelling, farcical, foolish, frivolous, idiotic, inane, irrational, jejune, laughable, ludicrous, lunatic, mad, moronic, nonsensical, puerile, ridiculous, senseless, silly, stupid.

abundant **adj** *lit:* ample, copious, luxuriant, overflowing, plenteous, plentiful, profuse, rich, teeming.

abuse **n** *lit:* derision, despoilation, disparagement, exploitation, ill-treatment, imposition, insults, invective, maltreatment, misapplication, misuse, oppression, opprobrium, vilification, vituperation, wrong. **vb** *lit:* betray, deride, despoil, disparage, exploit, ill-treat, impose on/upon, insult, inveigh against, malign, maltreat, manhandle, misapply, misuse, oppress, swear at, take advantage of, vilify, vituperate against, wrong.

abusive **adj** *lit:* cruel, defamatory, derisive, disparaging, exploitative, insulting, libellous, offensive, oppressive, rude, scathing, slanderous, vilifying, vituperative.

academic n *lit:* don, fellow, lecturer, man of letters, master, polymath, professor, scholar, student, tutor, man of letters, polymath. **adj** *lit:* bookish, conjectural, erudite, hypothetical, intellectual, learned, literary, notional, scholarly, studious, theoretical.

accelerate vb *lit:* expedite, further, go faster, hasten, hurry, increase speed, speed up; *spec:* change velocity (in physics).

accept vb *lit:* assume, bow to, defer to, receive, take; *fig:* accede to, admit, agree to, consent to, pass, recognize, stipulate, take on, undertake.

acceptable **adj** *lit:* admissible, agreeable, all right, bearable, fair, gratifying, passable, pleasing, satisfactory, tolerable, welcome.

access n *lit:* admittance, entrance, entry, means of approach, passage, path (to), road (to), way (to); *spec:* attack, onset (of illness).

accessible **adj** *lit:* achievable, approachable, at hand, attainable, available, convenient, friendly, get-at-able, manageable, nearby, on hand, open (to), possible, reachable, to hand.

accident n *lit:* blow, calamity, chance, collision, contretemps, crash, disaster, fluke, happening, luck, misadventure, mischance, misfortune, mishap, mistake.

accommodate vb *lit:* adapt, adjust, board, cater for, conform, entertain, have room for, help, house, lodge, modify, oblige, provide, put up, quarter, reconcile, serve, settle, supply.

accommodation n *lit:* adaptation, adjustment, berth, billet, board, digs, housing, lodgings, modification, place, provision, quarters, reconciliation, reservation, room, seat, service, settlement, space, supply.

accompany vb *lit:* attend, be with, come with, escort, go with, happen with, join with, occur with, supplement; *spec:* play for, provide the backing for (in music).

accomplish vb *lit:* achieve, attain, bring about, bring off, carry out, complete, do, effect, finish, fulfil, manage, perform, realize.

accord n *lit:* agreement, concurrence, correspondence, entente,

harmony, rapport, sympathy, unanimity, understanding;
fig: motivation, volition, wish.   **vb** *lit:* afford, agree (with), be
unanimous (with), confer, concur (with), correspond (with), give,
grant,harmonize (with), render.

accordingly   adv *lit:* appropriately, consequently, correspondingly,
for this reason, hence, so, suitably, therefore.

account   n *lit:* balance, bill, charge, consideration, description,
explanation, history, inventory, invoice, ledger, narration, note,
profit, recital, reckoning, record, register, report, score, statement,
story, tale, tally, worth.   **vb** *lit:* assess (to be), believe (to be),
consider (to be), deem (to be), give an explanation (for), give a reason
(for), hold (to be), reckon (to be), think (to be).

accountable   adj *lit:* answerable, comprehensible, explicable, liable,
responsible, understandable.

accumulation   n *lit:* accretion, aggregation, amassing, build-up,
coacervation, collection, conglomeration, gathering, growth, heap,
hoard, increase, load, pile, piling up, stack, stock, stockpile.

accurate   adj *lit:* correct, exact, precise, meticulous, right,
scrupulous, strict, true, unerring.

accusation   n *lit:* allegation, arraignment, charge, impeachment,
imputation, indictment.

accuse   vb *lit:* allege, arraign, blame, bring a charge against, charge,
denounce, impeach, impute, indict.

accustom   vb *lit:* acclimatize, familiarize, get used (to), habituate,
inure, train.

ache   n *lit:* anguish, longing, pain, pang, soreness, suffering,
throbbing, anguish, suffering; longing, pining, yearning.   **vb** *lit:*
be in pain, suffer; hurt, pain, put in pain, throb; feel (for), have
sympathy (for); hunger (for), long (for), pine (for), yearn (for).

acid   n *lit:* corrosive; *fig:* hallucinogenic drug; LSD.   **adj** *lit:*
corrosive; acerbic, acescent, acrid, biting, sharp, sour, tart; pungent,
vinegary; *fig:* acerbic, caustic, cutting, keen, mordant, stinging,
trenchant, vitriolic; ill-natured, ill-tempered; critical, decisive; *spec:*
silicaceous (in geology).

acknowledge vb *lit:* react to, recognize, respond to; note, notice; accept, concede, grant, profess; admit, own to; greet, hail, salute; reply to, return.

acquaintance n *lit:* associate, colleague, contact, friend of a friend, neighbour; association, familiarity, fellowship, relationship; introduction; *fig:* awareness, conversance, experience, knowledge, understanding.

acquire vb *lit:* come into the possession of, get, obtain, pick up, procure, secure; collect, gain, gather; buy, purchase; attain, win.

acquisition n *lit:* possession, property; addition, gain, prize; buy, purchase; amassing, attainment, collection, gaining, procurement.

acquit vb *lit:* absolve, clear, exculpate, exonerate, vindicate; discharge, free, liberate, release; pay off, repay, settle; bear, behave, conduct, perform.

acrid adj *lit:* acid, astringent, biting, caustic, corrosive, irritant, pungent, sharp, stinging; bitter, vinegary; *fig:* acrimonious, cutting, harsh, mordant, pointed, trenchant.

across adv *lit:* to the other side; crosswise; from side to side. prp *lit:* over, to the other side of; on the other side of.

act n *lit:* accomplishment, achievement, deed, exploit, feat, operation, performance, stroke; decree, law, measure, ordinance, statute; routine, show, turn; affectation, dissimulation, front, pose, posture, pretence, simulation. vb *lit:* function, go, move, operate, perform, take effect, work; behave, conduct oneself; impersonate, play, portray, represent; counterfeit, dissimulate, feign, imitate, pose, pretend, put it on, sham.

action n *lit:* effect, functioning, movement, operation, performance, working; activity, energy, liveliness, vigour; act, deed, move, stroke; gesticulation, gesture; mechanism, mode of operation, procedure, process; battle, clash, combat, conflict, engagement, fighting; plot, scenario, story; case, lawsuit, litigation, prosecution, suit; event, happening.

active adj *lit:* busy, doing, going, engaged, occupied, working;

functioning, moving, operative, running, ticking over; animated, brisk, bustling, energetic, spirited, sprightly, vigorous, vivacious; alert, lively, quick; enterprising, enthusiastic, hardworking, industrious, militant, zealous; *spec:* subjective (form of a verb, as opposed to passive).

activity n *lit:* animation, bustle, commotion, hurly-burly, life, motion, movement, stir; act, deed, work; exercise, exertion, work; hobby, interest, pastime, pursuit; endeavour, enterprise, project, scheme, venture.

actor n *lit:* artiste, performer, player, Thespian; impersonator, impostor, role-player; poseur, pretender, sham; agent, executor.

actual adj *lit:* authentic, genuine, literal, physical, positive, real, true; current, existing, present, prevailing.

acute adj *lit:* pointed, sharp; excruciating, fierce, intense, piercing, racking, severe, stabbing, violent; brief, shortlived, sudden; critical, dangerous, grave, serious, urgent, vital; discerning, discriminating, keen, observant, penetrating, perceptive, sensitive; astute, clever, shrewd, subtle; *fig:* at an angle, oblique; *spec:* less than a right-angle (geometry).

adamant adj *lit:* flinty, hard, steely, stony, unbreakable, unyielding; *fig:* firm, immovable, inexorable, intransigent, obdurate, rigid, unbending, uncompromising, unshakable.

adapt vb *lit:* acclimatize, adjust, conform; alter, change, modify, shape, tailor; fit, match, suit.

add vb *lit:* compute, count up, find the sum of, reckon, total, tot up; affix (to), annex, append, increase by, put next (to), put on (to); continue, go on to say.

addict n *lit:* dependant, junkie, user; adherent, devotee, enthusiast, fan, follower; buff, freak, nut. vb *lit:* habituate, hook (on), make dependent; enslave.

additional adj *lit:* extra, further, more, other, supplementary; fresh, new; appended, attached; spare.

adequate adj *lit:* enough, passable, requisite, sufficient; fair,

reasonable, satisfactory; commensurate, competent, suitable.

adjust vb *lit:* accustom, adapt, become used, be reconciled, conform, make fit; alter, change, fix, modify, reset, retune, tune; arrange, dispose, order, position, redress, regulate; accommodate, settle.

administer vb *lit:* control, direct, govern, manage, oversee, run, superintend, supervise; dispense, distribute, give, provide, tender; apply, execute, impose, mete out; *spec:* formally declare (an oath); stabilize (prices, wages).

administration n *lit:* board, control, direction, management, running, superintendence, supervision; cabinet, government, ruling party; term of office; dispensing, distribution, provision; application, execution, imposition.

admiration n *lit:* appreciation, esteem, regard, respect, veneration; delight, pleasure, wonder.

admire vb *lit:* appreciate, esteem, hold in high regard, respect, venerate; delight in, take pleasure in, wonder at; like, love.

admission n *lit:* access, admittance, allowing in, entry, introduction, passage; entrance fee, ticket price; acknowledgement, confession, disclosure, revelation.

admit vb *lit:* acknowledge, confess, disclose, let out, own, reveal; accept, concede, grant, recognize; allow, permit; allow in, let in, receive; be large enough for, have room for; permit the possibility (of).

admittance n *lit:* access, admission, allowing in, entry, introduction, passage.

adopt vb *lit:* take on, take over, take up; assume, choose, embrace, espouse, select; become a parent to, bring up, foster.

adorable adj *lit:* captivating, lovable, precious; beloved, darling; alluring, attractive, charming, delightful, wonderful.

adore vb *lit:* dote on, idolize, love, worship; revere, venerate; be crazy about, go wild about; prostrate oneself before.

adorn vb *lit:* bedeck, deck, decorate, embellish, ornament; beautify, dress, garnish, grace; festoon, garland.

adulation n *lit:* flattery, fawning, sycophancy; blarney, bootlicking, crawling, flannel, servility; acclaim, applause, genuflection, obeisance, praise.

adult n *lit:* grown-up, mature person, responsible citizen.
adj *lit:* full-grown, fully developed, grown-up, mature; ripe; *fig:* complex, erudite, intellectual; erotic, explicit, sexy.

advance n *lit:* development, headway, progress; betterment, breakthrough, furtherance, gain, improvement, promotion, step up; credit, loan; approach, overture, proposition.   vb *lit:* go forward, move on, move up, proceed, progress; accelerate, further, hasten, promote, speed; bring forward, expedite; elevate, upgrade; benefit, grow, improve, thrive; credit with, lend, loan; offer, present, put forward, submit; propose, suggest.   adj *lit:* early, prior; forward, in front.

advantage n *lit:* assistance, benefit, gain, good, help, profit, use; blessing, boon, convenience; ascendancy, dominance, edge, precedence, superiority, sway, upper hand; *spec:* one point ahead (tennis).

adventure n *lit:* enterprise, exploit, undertaking; exciting experience; readiness for anything; chance, risk, speculation.   vb *lit:* endanger, hazard, imperil, jeopardize, risk; soldier (on).

adventurous adj *lit:* daring, enterprising, intrepid, venturesome; audacious, bold, temerarious; dangerous, hazardous, risky.

adverse adj *lit:* antagonistic, hostile, inimical, opposing, unfavourable, unfriendly; contrary, negative, unfortunate, unpropitious; detrimental, harmful, injurious.

advertise vb *lit:* display, exhibit, flaunt, hype, make known, plug, promote, promulgate, publicize, publish, puff, push, tout; announce, emblazon, proclaim, signal; advise of, draw attention to, give notice of, inform about, warn of; put up for sale.

advertisement n *lit:* commercial, display, hype, notice, plug,

promotion, publicity, puff; bill, circular, classified ad, hoarding, poster, small ad.

advice   n *lit:* counsel, counselling, direction, feedback, gen, guidance, instruction, recommendation, suggestion, tip; information, intelligence, notice, notification, word; caution, warning.

advise   vb *lit:* counsel, direct, give guidance to, instruct, make a recommendation to; inform, give notice of, notify; enjoin, recommend, suggest; caution, tip off, warn.

adviser   n *lit:* consultant, counsellor, guide, mentor, teacher, tutor; coach, instructor, trainer; abetter, aide, assistant, henchman.

affair   n *lit:* circumstance, episode, event, happening, incident, matter, occurrence, question, subject, topic; business, concern, dealing, enterprise, transaction, undertaking; amour, relationship, romance.

affect   vb *lit:* act on, concern, influence, involve, relate to, touch; alter, change, disorder, disturb, modify, upset; impress, move, stir; adopt, assume, feign, pretend, put on, simulate.

affected   adj (pa.pt) *lit:* concerned, in question, involved; acted on, influenced, touched; distressed, impressed, moved, stimulated, stirred, upset, wounded; damaged, impaired, injured; artificial, assumed, feigned, insincere, pretended, sham, simulated, spurious, unnatural; camp, mincing, precious.

affecting   adj (pr.pt) *lit:* distressing, emotive, moving, pitiable, pitiful, sad, touching, upsetting; inspiring, rousing, stimulating, stirring.

affection   n *lit:* attachment, fondness, friendliness, kindness, liking, love, tenderness.

afford   vb *lit:* have the money for, be able to buy; put up with, stand, sustain, tolerate; spare; confer, furnish, give, grant, impart, provide, render, supply.

affront   n *lit:* insult, offence, outrage, slight; indignity, provocation; injury, wound.   vb *lit:* insult, offend, outrage, slight; offer provocation; abuse, injure, wound.

afraid　**adj** *lit:* alarmed, fearful, frightened, panicky, panic-stricken, petrified, scared, terrified; alarmed, in a cold sweat, jumpy, nervous, timorous, uptight; anxious, concerned, worried; browbeaten, cowed, rattled, shaken, unnerved; cowardly, chicken, yellow.

after　**adj** *lit:* later, subsequent; next, following.　**adv** *lit:* behind, in the rear; afterwards, later, next, subsequently, thereupon.　**prp** *lit:* behind, beyond, in pursuit of, to the rear of; following, subsequent to, upon; about, concerning, with regard to; according to, copying, imitating, in the style of; identically to.　**cnj** *lit:* as soon as, once, when.

again　**adv** *lit:* afresh, anew, another time, once more, one more time; back, over; on the other hand, yet; also, besides, furthermore, moreover.

against　**prp** *lit:* in contact with, on, touching, upon; abutting, adjacent to, bordering, contiguous with, next to; contrary to, counter to, in opposition to, versus; in contrast to; in anticipation of, in preparation for; for, in return for.

age　**n** *lit:* period of existence, time of life; advanced years, elderliness, senescence; majority, maturity, ripeness; generation; aeon, century, epoch, era, historical period, time; long while, years.
vb *lit:* grow old, grow up, mature, mellow, put years on, ripen; decline, deteriorate, get old.

agenda　**n** *lit:* programme, schedule, timetable; layout, list, menu, plan, scheme; *spec:* good works (in theology).

aggression　**n** *lit:* bellicosity, belligerence, hostility, pugnacity; force, violence; encroachment, infringement, invasion, raid; assault, attack, onslaught.

agony　**n** *lit:* anguish, pangs, torment, torture; pain, suffering.

agree　**vb** *lit:* be of one mind (with), concur; be consistent (with), chime, coincide, correspond, get on together, harmonize; comply, parallel, tally; assent, concede, consent, grant; *spec:* correspond in case, number or person (grammar).

agreement　**n** *lit:* accord, concord, concurrence; chorus, concert,

harmony, unison; correspondence, identity, match; arrangement, compact, pact, treaty, understanding; bargain, contract, deal.

agriculture n *lit:* agronomics, agronomy, cultivation, farming, tillage, tilling the soil; husbandry.

ahead adv *lit:* in advance (of), in front (of); forwards, on, onwards, straight on; in the lead, winning.

aid n *lit:* assistance, help, support; benefit, service, use; assistant, helper, supporter; *spec:* fund, subsidy (in feudal times and for modern charities). vb *lit:* assist, benefit, be of use to, help, subsidize, sustain; abet, second, serve, support; facilitate, further, promote.

aim n *lit:* ambition, aspiration, end, goal, intention, object, objective, target; desire, intent, wish. vb *lit:* direct (at), level (at), point (at), sight (at), train (at); aspire (to), intend (to), mean (to), plan (to), purpose (to), strive (to), try (to).

air n *lit:* atmosphere, ether, waves; empyrean, heavens, sky; breeze, wind; breath, puff; ambience, aura; bearing, demeanour, feeling, flavour, impression, look, mien, tone; expression, utterance; aria, melody, melody-line, tune. vb *lit:* aerate, circulate, dry, freshen, hang out, ventilate; *fig:* declare, disclose, divulge, expose, express, give vent to, make public, publicize, reveal, voice.

airfield n *lit:* aerodrome; airforce base; landing strip, runway.

airily adv *lit:* breezily, buoyantly, jauntily; blithely, casually, nonchalantly; ethereally, gracefully, lightly.

airless adj *lit:* close, heavy, muggy, oppressive, stifling, stuffy.

alarm n *lit:* apprehension, consternation, fear, fright, panic, trepidation; anxiety, nervousness, uneasiness; bell, danger signal, flare, hooter, siren, warning; *spec:* appel (in fencing). vb *lit:* frighten, panic, put the wind up, scare; startle, unnerve; alert, signal, warn.

alert n *lit:* alarm; warning; lookout, watch. vb *lit:* alarm, warn; inform, notify, send a signal to. adj *lit:* attentive, awake, observant, on guard, on the ball, on the lookout, on watch, ready, vigilant, wary, watchful; brisk, lively, nimble, quick, sprightly.

alien   n *lit:* foreigner, outsider, stranger; extraterrestrial, little green man, Martian; outcast; *spec:* hybrid (plant).   **adj** *lit:* exotic, foreign, outlandish, strange, unfamiliar.

alienate   vb *lit:* disaffect, estrange, set at odds, turn against; detach, disinterest, separate; *spec:* convey, sequester, transfer ownership (in property law).

alike   adj *lit:* identical, similar, uniform; akin, analogous, compatible, corresponding; equal, parallel.   **adv** *lit:* identically, similarly, uniformly; compatibly, correspondingly, in the same way; equally, to the same degree.

alive   adj *lit:* animate, breathing, conscious, living, organic; active, extant, in existence, operative, unextinguished; awake (to), sensitive (to); animated, brisk, eager, energetic, lively, spirited, sprightly, vigorous, vital, vivacious.

all   adj *lit:* every; every one of; every bit of, every part of; as much as possible, maximum, optimum; any; nothing but, only, solely.   **adv** *lit:* altogether, completely, entirely, fully, totally, utterly, wholly; exclusively.   **prn** *lit:* everyone; everything; every atom, every bit, every part, every scrap.

allege   vb *lit:* assert, aver, charge, declare, state; claim, maintain.

allegiance   n *lit:* adherence, devotion, faithfulness, fealty, loyalty.

alley   n *lit:* passage, passageway, pathway; corridor, gangway, walkway; backstreet, lane; rink.

alliance   n *lit:* coalition, confederacy, confederation, federation, league; marriage, partnership, union; association, combination.

allow   vb *lit:* give permission, permit; authorize, give leave, license; bear, stand, suffer; give, grant, provide with; admit, concede, own to; keep free, leave, spare; take into account.

allowed   adj (pa.pt) *lit:* acceptable, all right, okay, permissible; authorized, licensed, permitted, sanctioned; left over, spare; provided (for).

allure   n *lit:* appeal, attraction, seductiveness, temptation;

fascination; charm.   **vb** *lit:* attract, captivate, charm, enchant, entice, fascinate, seduce, tempt.

ally   **n** *lit:* confederate, partner; acolyte, assistant, associate, collaborator, colleague, friend; helper, supporter; accomplice, catspaw, henchman, subordinate.   **vb** *lit:* confederate (with), join forces (with), unite (with); associate (with), collaborate (with), combine (with); connect (to), relate (to).

almighty   **adj** *lit:* all-powerful, omnipotent; supreme; invincible, irresistible; *fig:* awesome, enormous, indescribable, tremendous, unspeakable.

alone   **adj** *lit:* by oneself, isolated, single, solitary, unaccompanied; apart, separate; matchless, unique; abandoned, detached, forlorn, forsaken.   **adv** *lit:* by oneself, solitarily, solo; in isolation, separately; exclusively, merely, only, solely.

along   **adv** *lit:* forwards, onwards; down; as escort, in company (with), together (with); in parallel, side by side.   **prp** *lit:* by the side of; down, down the length of.

already   **adv** *lit:* before then, by that time, previously; before now, by now, now, yet.

also   **adv** *lit:* additionally, in addition; likewise; besides, to boot, too; again, furthermore, moreover.

alteration   **n** *lit:* change, modification, reshaping; adjustment, amendment, correction, revision; difference, shift, variance; conversion, metamorphosis, transformation.

alternate   **vb** *lit:* happen in turns, take turns; interchange, rotate; oscillate, vary.   **adj** *lit:* every other, odd; interchanging, rotating.

alternative   **n** *lit:* choice, option, preference; other, second; substitute.   **adj** *lit:* other, second; substitute; different.

although   **cnj** *lit:* albeit, in spite of the fact that; while.

altogether   **n** *fig:* birthday suit, nude.   **adv** *lit:* completely, entirely, fully, quite, thoroughly, totally, utterly, wholly; all in all, all told, as a whole, collectively, generally, in general.

always adv *lit:* ever; all the time, constantly, continually, eternally, forever, perpetually, unceasingly; consistently, every time, invariably, repeatedly.

amazement n *lit:* astonishment, stupefaction, surprise; wonder.

ambassador n *lit:* emissary, envoy, plenipotentiary; diplomat, representative; consul, legate, nuncio.

ambiguous adj *lit:* equivocal, indeterminate, unclear; cryptic, delphic, dubious, enigmatic, obscure, oracular.

ambitious adj *lit:* aspiring, eager, hopeful; desirous, driving, enterprising; audacious, bold, challenging, demanding, difficult, exacting; ostentatious, pretentious, showy.

ambivalence n *lit:* equivocation, indecision, indeterminacy, irresolution, vacillation; contradiction.

ambush n *lit:* hold-up, lying in wait, stake-out, trap; mugging.
vb *lit:* bushwhack, hold up, lie in wait for, pounce on, surprise, trap, waylay.

amend vb *lit:* correct, fix, mend, rectify, remedy, repair; ameliorate, better, improve, revise.

amends n *lit:* atonement, compensation, redress, reparation, restitution.

amid(st) prp *lit:* among(st), in the middle of, surrounded by.

among(st) prp *lit:* amid(st), of; along with, in with, together with; in the middle of, surrounded by; between, to each one of; throughout.

amount n *lit:* extent, magnitude, mass, measure, number, quantity, volume; entirety, lot, sum, total, whole.   vb *lit:* add up (to), come (to).

amuse vb *lit:* be funny, divert, entertain, make laugh, tickle; keep occupied.

amusement n *lit:* diversion, divertissement; entertainment; enjoyment, fun, hilarity, laughter, merriment, mirth; game, pastime, recreation.

amusing **adj (pr.pt)** *lit:* comic, diverting, droll, entertaining, funny, hilarious, humorous, merry, witty; enjoyable, interesting.

analyse **vb** *lit:* break down, dissect, resolve; consider, examine carefully, study; assay, evaluate, test; interpret.

analysis **n** *lit:* breakdown, dissection, resolution; examination, study; assay, evaluation, results of testing; finding, interpretation; reasoning.

ancestor **n** *lit:* forebear, forefather, forerunner, progenitor; precursor; *spec:* testator (bequeathing an inheritance).

ancient **adj** *lit:* age-old, antedeluvian, antique, archaic, hoary, old, primeval, primordial; antiquated, obsolete.

and **cnj** *lit:* as well as, in addition to, plus, together with, with; furthermore, moreover; so that; in order to, to.

anger **n** *lit:* choler, exasperation, fury, ire, passion, rage, spleen, strong displeasure, temper, wrath; resentment. **vb** *lit:* enrage, exasperate, incense, infuriate, madden, outrage, provoke, rile, seriously displease.

angle **n** *lit:* corner, crook, elbow, hook; bend, curve; slant, slope, tilt; *fig:* approach, outlook, perspective; point of view, standpoint; plot, scheme. **vb** *lit:* bend, curve, tack, turn; fish; *fig:* bias, slant; fish (for), scheme (for), try (for).

angry **adj** *lit:* beside oneself, enraged, exasperated, fuming, furious, hopping mad, incensed, infuriated, irate, livid, maddened, on the warpath, provoked, raging, riled, seething, wrathful.

anguish **n** *lit:* agony, dolour, pain, suffering, torment, torture; distress, misery.

angular **adj** *lit:* cornered, hooked; pointed, sharp; *fig:* bony, gaunt, lean, rangy, scrawny, skinny; awkward, clumsy, gawky, stiff.

animal **n** *lit:* beast, creature; quadruped; *fig:* brute, monster, savage. **adj** *fig:* brutish, instinctual, lower, sensual.

animosity **n** *lit:* antagonism, antipathy, bad blood, dislike, enmity, hatred, hostility, ill will, loathing, malevolence, rancour.

annex **vb** *lit:* affix, append, attach, fasten on, join on, tack on;

appropriate, arrogate, seize, take over.

announce vb *lit:* declare, make known, proclaim; advertise, broadcast, promulgate, publish; divulge, reveal, tell; betoken, herald, portend, presage, signal.

announcement n *lit:* declaration, proclamation, statement; broadcast, bulletin, communiqué, notice, promulgation, publication; disclosure, revelation.

annoyance n *lit:* aggravation, displeasure, exasperation, irritation, vexation; bother, nuisance, trouble; bind, bore, pain, pain in the neck, pest.

anomaly n *lit:* abnormality, inconsistency, oddity, peculiarity, something strange; deviation, eccentricity, irregularity.

anonymous adj *lit:* unattested, uncredited, unidentified, unnamed, unsigned; nameless, unknown; bland, characterless, colourless, nondescript, undistinguished, unexceptional.

answer n *lit:* reaction, reply, response, return; comeback, defence, explanation, rejoinder, retort, riposte, solution; resolution. vb *lit:* react, react to, reply, reply to, respond, respond to; explain, rejoin, retort, riposte; solve; resolve.

antagonize vb *lit:* alienate, disaffect, make an enemy of, offend, rub up the wrong way; anger, annoy, irritate; counteract, neutralize, work against.

anticipate vb *lit:* await, be prepared for, expect, foresee, foretell, look forward to, predict, see coming, wait for; antedate, be ahead of, forestall, precede.

antique n *lit:* bygone, heirloom, relic. adj *lit:* antiquarian, classic, vintage; ancient, antiquated, obsolescent, obsolete, old-fashioned, outdated; aged, elderly, old.

antiseptic n *lit:* disinfectant, germicide. adj *lit:* antibiotic, hygienic, sanitary, sterile, uncontaminated, unpolluted; aseptic.

apart adj *lit:* by oneself, cut off, distant, isolated, separated; dismantled, disparate, dissected, divorced, in bits, in pieces,

separate.   adv *lit:* by oneself, independently, isolatedly, separately, to one side; asunder, to bits, to pieces.

apathy   n *lit:* disinterest, impassivity, indifference, passivity, unconcern; lethargy, sloth, torpor; coldness, insensitivity, numbness.

aperture   n *lit:* cleft, crack, fissure, gap, hole, interstice, opening, orifice, perforation, slot; chink, embrasure, eyelet, slit.

apex   n *lit:* acme, crest, crown, peak, pinnacle, point, summit, tip, top; *fig:* climax, culmination, height, zenith.

apologetic   adj *lit:* contrite, penitent, regretful, remorseful, repentant, sorry; appeasing, conciliatory.

apology   n *lit:* expression of contrition, mea culpa, regrets; *fig:* caricature (of), excuse (for), mockery (of), parody (of), travesty (of).

apostle   n *lit:* evangelist, missionary, preacher; advocate, champion, herald, messenger, propagandist, proselytizer; disciple.

appalling   adj (pr.pt) *lit:* awful, dire, disheartening, dreadful, fearful, grim, harrowing, horrific, horrifying, shocking, terrible.

apparent   adj *lit:* clear, evident, manifest, obvious, patent, plain, visible; conspicuous, overt; ostensible, outward, seeming, superficial; optical; *spec:* angular (diameter of a heavenly body); diffracted (position seen in a medium denser than air).

apparently   adv *lit:* ostensibly, superficially; outwardly, overtly, seemingly; evidently, obviously, patently, plainly.

appeal   n *lit:* entreaty, petition, plea, prayer, supplication; demand, request; allure, attraction, charm, fascination, interest; *spec:* referral to a higher court.   vb *lit:* apply (to), make a petition (to), plead (to), pray (to); make a request (to); be alluring (to), be attractive (to), be fascinating (to); *spec:* refer to a higher court.

appear   vb *lit:* be seen, come into sight, come into view, come to light, emerge, loom, manifest oneself, materialize, surface; arise, crop up, develop, occur, show up, turn up; arrive, be present, come, enter; look, seem; be clear, be evident, be manifest, be obvious, be patent, be plain; become available, be on sale, be on show, come out; act, perform.

appearance n *lit:* advent, arising, arrival, being present, coming, emergence, entry, manifestation, materialization, realization, surfacing; cropping up, occurrence, showing up, turn-up; availability, being on show, performance; air, bearing, demeanour, expression, figure, look, manner, mien, outward aspect; form, guise, semblance, shape; vision, visitation.

appetite n *lit:* hunger; desire, hankering, longing, yearning; relish, taste; room, space, stomach; *fig:* inclination, liking, readiness, willingness, zest.

applause n *lit:* acclaim, big hand, cheering, clapping, ovation; acclamation, accolade, plaudits, praise.

apply vb *lit:* bring to bear, employ, exercise, implement, practise, put into execution, operate, realize, use, utilize; appertain, be apposite, be pertinent, be relevant, be valid; commit (oneself to), dedicate (oneself to), give (oneself to), throw (oneself) in(to); appeal (to), make a petition (to), make a request (to), send in for information (to); address (to), introduce (to), put next (to); coat, daub on, put on, spread on.

appoint vb *lit:* assign, commission, nominate; arrange, choose, designate, determine, establish, fix, set; decree, direct, ordain, prescribe; equip, fit out, furnish, provide.

appointment n *lit:* assignation, date, engagement, meeting; consultation, interview, session; assignment, job, office, position, post, situation; choice, commissioning, installation, nomination.

appreciate vb *lit:* be grateful for, be obliged for, be thankful for; cherish, enjoy, esteem, like, prize, relish, value; gain, grow, increase, rise; acknowledge, be aware of, be cognizant of, comprehend, know, perceive, realize, recognize, take account of, understand.

appreciation n *lit:* gratitude, idebtedness, obligation, thanks; admiration, enjoyment, esteem, liking, relish; gain, growth, increase, rise; acknowledgement, cognizance, comprehension, knowledge, perception, realization, recognition, understanding.

approach n *lit:* access, avenue, drive, entrance, pathway; advance, coming up, drawing near, nearing; course, means, method, mode,

procedure, technique, way; attitude, way of thinking; application, overture, proposal, proposition, suggestion; approximation, likeness. **vb** *lit:* advance towards, come up to, draw near to, get close to, move towards, near; bend one's mind to, tackle; appeal to, apply to, make overtures to, sound out; approximate to, come close to, compare with, resemble.

appropriate **vb** *lit:* annex, arrogate, commandeer, confiscate, impound, make off with, possess oneself of, seize, take over; embezzle, pocket, steal; pilfer, thieve; allocate, apportion, assign, earmark, set aside. **adj** *lit:* applicable, apposite, apt, fit, fitting, suitable, suited, to the purpose, well-suited; appertaining, correct, germane, pertinent, relevant, right, timely, to the point.

approval **n** *lit:* acclaim, applause, appreciation, approbation, commendation, praise; admiration, esteem, favour, liking, regard, respect; agreement, blessing, consent, endorsement, okay, recommendation; authorization, leave, licence, permission, sanction; *spec:* sale-or-return (basis for selling).

approve **vb** *lit:* have a high opinion (of), think very well (of); agree to, commend, consent to, endorse, okay, pass, validate; authorize, give leave for, license, permit, sanction.

approximate **vb** *lit:* approach, be bordering on, come close (to), come near (to), verge on; be like, have the semblance of, resemble. **adj** *lit:* close, estimated, loose, rough, virtual; comparable, similar; adjacent, bordering, near, nearby, neighbouring.

area **n** *lit:* breadth, compass, expanse, extent, range, scope, size, width; district, locality, neighbourhood, patch, plot, region, section, sector, territory, tract, zone; department, domain, province; field, realm, sphere; arena, court, floor, space, yard.

arena **n** *lit:* bowl, court, field, ground, hall, park, pitch, ring, stadium, stage, theatre; amphitheatre, battlefield, battleground, lists; *fig:* proving-ground, testing-ground; council chamber.

argue **vb** *lit:* bandy words, dispute, fall out, fight, have an altercation, have words, quarrel, remonstrate, wrangle; bicker, disagree, squabble; debate, discuss, question; assert, claim, contend,

hold, maintain, plead; persuade (into), talk (into); imply, suggest; demonstrate, evince, exhibit, indicate, manifest, point to, show.

argument   n *lit:* altercation, clash, dispute, falling out, fight, quarrel, remonstration, row, wrangle; bickering, disagreement, squabble; debate, discussion; assertion, case, claim, contention, line of reasoning, plea, point; gist, plot, storyline, theme.

arise   vb *lit:* ascend, come up, get up, go up; get out of bed, stand up, wake up; climb, mount, soar; appear, come into sight, crop up, develop, emerge, occur, show up, surface, turn up; emanate, issue, originate, spring, stem; ensue, follow, proceed, result.

aristocrat   n *lit:* grandee, noble, patrician, titled personage; *fig:* best of its kind.

aristocratic   adj *lit:* blue-blooded, high-born, lordly, noble, patrician, titled, upper-class, well-born; pedigree; courtly, dignified, polished, refined, well-bred; arrogant, haughty, lah-de-dah, proud, snobbish.

arm   n *lit:* forelimb, upper limb; appendage, cross-piece, extension, offshoot, projection, sleeve; branch, department, division, section, sector; channel, creek, inlet, sound, strait, tributary; *fig:* authority, might, power, strength.   vb *lit:* equip with weapons, issue with weapons, provide material; activate, render active, switch on; provide with the means of attack or defence; *fig:* equip (oneself with), fortify (oneself with), protect (oneself with); *spec:* put an armature on (a magnet).

armed   adj (pa.pt) *lit:* fortified, furnished with weapons, primed, protected; activated, active, switched on; able to attack or defend; *fig:* accoutred, equipped, fitted out, provided, strengthened.

armistice   n *lit:* ceasefire, truce; peace agreement.

army   n *lit:* military, soldiers, soldiery, troops; battalions, brigades, legions; *fig:* horde, host, multitude, throng.

aroma   n *lit:* bouquet, fragrance, perfume, scent, smell; odour, whiff; redolence; *fig:* flavour, hint, suggestion.

around   adv *lit:* all over the place, everywhere, here and there; all over, throughout; in a circle; back, in the opposite direction; active,

doing, moving.   **prp** *lit:* about, encircling, enclosing, encompassing, surrounding; all over the place within, scattered in; approximately, close on; on the far side of, on the other side of.

arrange   **vb** *lit:* array, dispose, form up, group, marshal, order, organize, position, range, set out; align, classify, file, line up, rank, sort; adjust, straighten, tidy; devise, fix up, plan, schedule; contrive, determine, settle; adapt, orchestrate, score, transcribe.

arrangement   **n** *lit:* disposition, formation, grouping, order, positioning; organization; design, plan, scheme, system; adjustment, moving; agreement, compact, deal, terms, treaty, tryst, understanding; adaptation, interpretation, orchestration, score, setting, transcription, version.

arrest   **n** *lit:* apprehension, capture, detention, seizure; bust, cop; blockage, check, halt, obstruction, stoppage, suppression.   **vb** *lit:* apprehend, capture, catch, detain, take into custody; nab, nick, pinch, run in; block, check, halt, obstruct, stop, suppress; delay, inhibit, restrain, retard, slow; *fig:* absorb, engross, fascinate, grip, hold.

arrival   **n** *lit:* advent, approach, coming; appearance, entrance, entry; arising, occurrence; incomer, newcomer, visitor.

arrive   **vb** *lit:* come, show up, take one's place (at), turn up; appear, enter, make an entry, put in an appearance; *fig:* become famous, make good, make it to the top, succeed.

arrogant   **adj** *lit:* conceited, disdainful, haughty, high-handed, imperious, overbearing, presumptuous, proud, supercilious, swaggering; blustering, impudent, insolent, pretentious.

art   **n** *lit:* representation; drawing, painting; craft, craftsmanship, expertise, mastery, skill, virtuosity; facility, ingenuity, knack, talent; deftness, dexterity; artifice, craftiness, duplicity, wile.

article   **n** *lit:* commodity, item, object, thing; essay, feature, piece, story; clause, division, heading, paragraph, part, section; *fig:* matter, subject, topic; *spec:* a or the (in grammar); count (on a charge-sheet); provision (in a contract).

artificial   **adj** *lit:* man-made, synthetic; manufactured; affected,

assumed, bogus, contrived, fake, false, feigned, hollow, insincere, meretricious, mock, phoney, pretended, sham, specious, spurious, unnatural.

artist   n *lit:* aesthete; creator; cartoonist, painter, sketcher; actor, entertainer, musician, performer, showman; architect, designer, sculptor; artisan, craftsman, expert, master, virtuoso.

artistic   adj *lit:* aesthetic, beautiful, elegant, exquisite, graceful; cultured, stylish, tasteful; creative, imaginative, sensitive.

as   adv *lit:* equally, to the same degree, to the same extent; for example, like.   prn *lit:* a condition that, a fact that, which is what.   prp *lit:* in the character of, in the part of, in the role of; in the manner of, like.   cnj *lit:* during the time that, when, while; in the same way that; to the same degree, to the same extent; that the result was; because, seeing that, since; though.

ashamed   adj *lit:* conscience-stricken, embarrassed, humbled, mortified, sheepish; chagrined, crestfallen, discomfited; guilty, remorseful, sorry; bashful, shy.

aside   n *lit:* interpolation, parenthesis; digression.   adv *lit:* apart, away, off, out of the way, privately, separately; in reserve.

ask   vb *lit:* enquire, inquire, put to, quiz; seek an answer; appeal to, apply to, beg, beseech, entreat, implore, petition, request, solicit; invite; be looking for, demand, seek; call (for).

asleep   adj *lit:* dead to the world, dozing, napping, off, slumbering, snoozing; dormant, hibernating; numbed; *fig:* oblivious; inactive.

aspect   n *lit:* air, attitude, bearing, demeanour, look, mien; angle, outlook, point of view, viewpoint; facet, feature, side.

aspire   vb *lit:* be ambitious (to), be eager (to), dream one day (to), hope, long, seek, wish, yearn.

ass   n *lit:* donkey, jennet; burro, moke; *fig:* blockhead, chump, dolt, fathead, fool, nincompoop, nitwit, noodle, simpleton, twit.

assassination   n *lit:* homicide, killing, murder, slaughter, slaying; butchery, destruction, elimination, extirpation, liquidation, massacre.

assault n *lit:* attack, hit, onslaught; offensive, storming, strike; battery, beating, mugging, robbery with violence; sexual attack. **vb** *lit:* assail, attack, batter, beat, beat up, fall upon, hit, lay into, mug, punch, set upon, strike, thump; invade, storm.

assemble vb *lit:* bring together, collect, congregate, convene, round up; come together, flock, gather, muster, rally; accumulate, amass, build up; connect, fit together, piece together, put together.

assert vb *lit:* allege, aver, contend, declare, maintain, proclaim, state; press, stand upon, uphold, vindicate.

assertive adj *lit:* dogmatic, emphatic, firm, forceful, insistent, positive, self-assured, strong-willed.

assess vb *lit:* appraise, estimate, evaluate, gauge, judge, rate, size up, value; levy, tax; fix the value (at).

asset n *lit:* fund(s), good(s), holding(s), possession(s), reserve(s), resource(s); aid, benefit, boon, help.

assign vb *lit:* allocate, apportion, distribute, dole out, give out; make over (to); determine, fix, pose, set; appoint, delegate, nominate, select; accredit (to), ascribe (to), attribute (to).

assignment n *lit:* charge, commission, duty, job, mission, task; allocation, apportionment, distribution; appointment, delegation, nomination, selection; accreditation, ascription, attribution.

assist vb *lit:* abet, aid, help, serve; back, further, second, support; co-operate with.

assistance n *lit:* aid, help, succour; backing, furtherance, support; collaboration, co-operation.

assistant n *lit:* aide, helper; abettor, accessory, accomplice, henchman; backer, partner, second, supporter; collaborator, confederate. **adj** *lit:* associate, auxiliary, back-up, deputy, vice-; subordinate, under-.

associate n *lit:* ally, collaborator, confederate, friend, partner; colleague, fellow-worker; companion, mate. **adj** *lit:* ally, combine, confederate, join, league, unite; consort (with), fraternize (with), go

around (with), mix (with); *fig:* connect (with), identify (with), link (with), relate (with);

association   n *lit:* alliance, combination, confederation, federation, league; club, company, group, syndicate, union; companionship, fellowship, friendship, partnership, relationship; connection, identification, link, relation.

assorted   adj *lit:* diverse, mixed, sundry, various; arranged, classified, graded, grouped, ranged, sorted.

assortment   n *lit:* diversity, medley, mixture, selection, variety; arrangement, grouping, range, selection; classification, grading, sorting.

assume   vb *lit:* don, put on, wear; accept, acquire, shoulder, take on, undertake; appropriate, arrogate, expropriate, seize, take over, usurp; adopt, affect, feign, simulate; *fig:* believe, guess, imagine, infer, presume, suppose, surmise, think.

assurance   n *lit:* affirmation, guarantee, oath, pledge, promise, word, word of honour; certitude, confidence, conviction, poise, positivity, self-confidence; audacity, boldness, courage; insurance.

astonish   vb *lit:* amaze, astound, bowl over, dumbfound, flabbergast, stagger, startle, stun.

astonishment   n *lit:* amazement, disbelief, shock, speechlessness, startlement, stupefaction, wonderment.

astute   adj *lit:* bright, canny, clever, discerning, keen, penetrating, perceptive, sharp, shrewd; cunning, subtle, wily.

asylum   n *lit:* refuge, retreat, sanctuary, shelter; mental institution, psychiatric hospital; funny farm, loony bin, madhouse, nuthouse.

atheist   n *lit:* sceptic, unbeliever; heathen, pagan; goy, infidel.

athlete   n *lit:* sportsman, sportswoman; gymnast, runner, track-runner; competitor, contender, contestant, player.

athletic   adj *lit:* agile, energetic, fit, limber, lithe, muscular, nimble, powerful, sinewy, strong, vigorous.

atmosphere   n *lit:* air; airiness, space; *fig:* climate, conditions;

ambience, environment, feeling, mood, spirit, surroundings, tone.

attach **vb** *lit:* affix, append, connect, couple, fasten, fix, glue, join on, link, secure, stick, tie, unite; affiliate (oneself with), associate (oneself with); ascribe, assign; allocate, appoint, place, put, send.

attack **n** *lit:* assault, charge, invasion, offensive, onset, onslaught, raid, strike; bout, fit, paroxysm, seizure, spasm; calumny, criticism, denigration, spleen, vilification, vituperation. **vb** *lit:* assail, assault, charge, fall upon, invade, set upon, storm; criticize, denigrate, insult, vilify.

attain **vb** *lit:* accomplish, arrive at, bring off, fulfil, get to, obtain, reach, realize, win.

attainment **n** *lit:* accomplishment, achievement, feat, fulfilment, realization, triumph, victory, win; gift, skill, talent.

attempt **n** *lit:* bash, bid, crack, effort, go, shot, try, venture. **vb** *lit:* endeavour (to), make an effort (to), seek (to), strive (to), try (to), venture (to).

attend **vb** *lit:* be at, be present at, frequent, go to, show up at, turn up at, visit; accompany, chaperon, escort, guard, usher; serve, wait (upon); care for, look after, nurse, take care of, tend; be attached to, be connected with, follow, result from; listen (to), pay attention (to), pay heed (to); look (to), see (to).

attention **n** *lit:* awareness, concentration, consciousness, mind, notice, observation; heed; care, concern, consideration, thoughtfulness; civility, compliment(s), courtesy, gallantry, regard(s), respect(s).

attitude **n** *lit:* pose, position, posture, stance; bearing, demeanour, manner, mien; disposition, mood; approach, outlook, perspective, viewpoint.

attract **vb** *lit:* draw, induce, pull; allure, entice, lure; appeal to, charm, enchant, fascinate.

attraction **n** *lit:* draw, inducement, magnetism, pull; allure, enticement, lure; appeal, charm, enchantment, fascination.

attractive **adj** *lit:* magnetic, mesmeric; alluring, captivating, enticing,

luring, seductive; appealing, charming, enchanting, fascinating; beautiful, gorgeous, handsome, lovely.

attune vb *lit:* acclimatize (to), accustom (to), adjust (to), regulate (to), set (to).

audience n *lit:* congregation, crowd, fans, gallery, gate, house, onlookers, spectators, turnout, viewers; market, public; consultation, interview, reception.

authentic adj *lit:* actual, genuine, original, real, true, valid, veritable.

author n *lit:* writer; creator, founder, generator, inventor, maker, originator, parent, prime mover, producer.

authoritarian n *lit:* autocrat, despot, dictator, martinet, tyrant. adj *lit:* autocratic, despotic, dictatorial, doctrinaire, tyrannical.

authoritative adj *lit:* authentic, official, sanctioned; commanding, confident, decisive, definite, imperative, masterful, self-assured; dogmatic, imperious, peremptory; confirmed, factual, reliable, trustworthy, valid.

authority n *lit:* government, power, rule, supremacy; administration, board, council, local government, powers that be; connoisseur, expert, master, specialist; command, control, dominion, influence, jurisdiction, prerogative; licence, permission, sanction, say-so, testimony, warrant, word; example, precedent.

authorize vb *lit:* commission, empower, entitle, license, permit, sanction, warrant; approve, confirm, ratify, vouch for.

automatic adj *lit:* mechanical, robot, self-activating, self-propelling, self-regulating; instinctual, involuntary, reflex, spontaneous, unconscious; inescapable, inevitable, unavoidable; *fig:* habitual, routine.

autonomous adj *lit:* independent, sovereign; self-determining, self-governing.

available adj *lit:* at one's disposal, on hand, on tap, to hand, usable; free, vacant; accessible, within reach; valid.

avenge vb *lit:* repay, retaliate; get even for, take vengeance on behalf of; revenge (oneself on).

avenue n *lit:* approach, driveway, pathway, walk; boulevard; road, street, thoroughfare.

average n *lit:* mean, medium, norm, par, run of the mill, standard. adj *lit:* intermediate, medium, middle; commonplace, middling, normal, ordinary, run-of-the-mill, so-so, standard, typical, unexceptional, usual.

averse adv *lit:* antipathetic (to), indisposed (to), reluctant (to), unwilling (to); hostile (to), inimical (to), opposed (to).

aversion n *lit:* antipathy, disinclination, indisposition, reluctance, unwillingness; animosity, hostility, opposition.

avert vb *lit:* turn away; fend off, stave off, ward off; forestall, preclude, prevent.

await vb *lit:* attend on, wait for; anticipate, be prepared for, be ready for, look for, look forward to.

awake adj *lit:* aroused, aware, conscious; alert, vigilant, watchful.

award n *lit:* apportion, conferral, endowment, honour, presentation; gift, grant; prize, trophy. vb *lit:* bestow, confer, endow, give, grant, present.

aware adj *lit:* appreciative (of), apprised (of), conscious (of), informed (of), knowledgeable (of), mindful (of), sensible (of).

awareness n *lit:* appreciation, attention, consciousness, discerning, knowledge, perception, realization, recognition, sensibility, understanding.

away adj *lit:* abroad, absent, not here, out; gone, off, started; distant, far. adv *lit:* abroad, elsewhere, out; apart, aside; afar, hence, into the distance, off; *fig:* continuously, doggedly, incessantly, on and on, persistently, relentlessly, repeatedly.

awful adj *lit:* appalling, distressing, ghastly, horrible, nasty, ugly, unpleasant; bad, deplorable, dreadful, terrible; inadequate, poor, shoddy, wretched.

awkward   adj *lit:* blundering, clumsy, gawky, inelegant, inept, lumbering, ungainly; cumbersome, unmanageable, unwieldy; difficult, inconvenient, untimely; dangerous, hazardous, perilous, sticky, thorny, ticklish; compromising, embarrassing, inopportune, painful, trying, uncomfortable; disobliging, perverse, prickly, troublesome, unhelpful, unpredictable.

B

baby n *lit:* babe, infant, neonate, newborn; bairn, child; *fig:* idea, invention, pet project, plan, responsibility, scheme. **vb** *lit:* coddle, cosset, mollycoddle, pamper, pet, spoil; *fig:* humour, indulge, spoonfeed. **adj** *lit:* infant, newborn, young; *fig:* diminutive, little, miniature, minute, small, tiny; dwarf, midget, pygmy; childish, infantile.

back n *lit:* spine, vertebrae; hind part, hindquarters, posterior, rear; end, stern, tail; far end, other side, reverse; *fig:* effort, energy, power; *spec:* defender (in team games); keel, keelson (of a ship, boat); top, surface (of a river, the sea; of a vein of ore; of a bow in archery). **vb** *lit:* go backwards, regress, retreat, reverse; encourage, endorse, favour, finance, second, sponsor, subsidize, support, underwrite; abet, aid, assist, come to the help of, help; bet on, gamble on; be behind, line, reinforce, strengthen; *spec:* turn, veer (of the wind). **adj** *lit:* hind, posterior, rearward; end, hindmost, rear; distant, outlying, remote; earlier, former, old, past, previous; reverse. **adv** *lit:* retrogressively, retrospectively; again, once more; ago, in the past.

background n *lit:* context, environment, milieu, scenario, scenery, setting, surroundings; distance, obscurity, shadow; breeding, circumstances, culture, history, past, record, track record, upbringing; credentials, experience, qualifications. **adj** *lit:* environmental, residual, surrounding; accompanying, incidental, secondary.

backing n *lit:* encouragement, endorsement, favour, seconding, support; financing, funding, investment, patronage, sponsorship, subsidizing, underwriting; aid, assistance, help; confirmation, corroboration, substantiation, verification; lining, reinforcement, strengthening; accompaniment, context, setting.

backwards adv *lit:* rearwards, retrogressively; *fig:* completely, fully, thoroughly.

bacterium   n *lit:* germ, microbe, micro-organism; bacillus, coccus, schizomycete, spirochaete.

bad   adj *lit:* evil, immoral, sinful, wicked, wrong; disobedient, naughty, unruly; damaged, defective, deficient, faulty, imperfect, inadequate, inferior, poor, unfavourable, unfortunate, unskilful, unsatisfactory, worthless; erroneous, fallacious, incorrect, invalid, spurious; dangerous, distressing, gloomy, grave, grim, harmful, injurious, offensive, painful, serious, severe, unpleasant; decayed, foetid, mouldy, off, putrescent, rancid, rotten, sour, spoiled; adverse, damaging, disastrous, ruinous; ailing, ill, sick, unwell; guilty, melancholy, remorseful, sad, sorry; distressed, upset, wretched.

badly   adv *lit:* carelessly, deficiently, imperfectly, inadequately, incorrectly, poorly, shoddily, unfavourably, unfortunately, unskilfully, unsatisfactorily; evilly, immorally, sinfully, wickedly; disobediently, improperly, naughtily, outrageously, shamefully; acutely, extremely, greatly, intensely, seriously; deeply, desperately, gravely, severely.

balance   n *lit:* pair of scales, scales, weighing machine; equilibrium, equipoise; equality, equivalence, evenness, parity; composure, equanimity, poise, self-possession; stability, steadiness; difference, remainder, residue, rest; *spec:* regulator (in a timepiece).   **vb** *lit:* be poised, be stable, be steady; achieve parity, be equivalent, correspond, equal, level, match, parallel; compensate for, counterpoise, counterweight, equalize, offset; assess, calculate, compute, compare, estimate, evaluate, total, weigh, weigh up; settle, square, tally.

balcony   n *lit:* stoep, verandah; gallery, upper circle.

bald   adj *lit:* hairless; depilated, glabrous; unfledged; barren, exposed, treeless; *fig:* bare, blunt, direct, forthright, naked, plain, simple, stark, unadorned, undisguised, unvarnished.

ball   n *lit:* globe, orb, sphere; bead, drop, globule, spheroid; bullet, pellet, shot, slug; dance; *spec:* testicle.   **vb** *lit:* form a sphere, roll into a sphere; clog, entangle.

ban   n *lit:* boycott, embargo, forbidding, interdiction, prohibition, proscription; banishment, deportation, exile; anathematization, curse,

excommunication; outlawry.   **vb** *lit:* bar, debar, disallow, embargo, forbid, interdict, outlaw, prohibit, proscribe, suppress; banish, deport, exile; blacklist, veto; anathematize, excommunicate.

banal   **adj** *lit:* cliché-ridden, corny, hackneyed, pedestrian, platitudinous, stale, stereotyped, stock, tired, trite, unoriginal, vapid; commonplace, everyday, mundane, ordinary, trivial, unimaginative.

band   **n** *lit:* binding, ribbon, strap, strip; belt, tape; line, streak, stripe, vein; channel, frequency range, track, wavelength range; body, company, crew, gang, group, party, troop; ensemble, orchestra. **vb**   *lit:* affiliate, ally, assemble, associate, federate, group, join, league, merge, unite.

bandit   **n** *lit:* brigand, desperado, footpad, highwayman, marauder, outlaw, pirate, robber; crook, gangster, gunman, hijacker, kidnapper, thief; con artist, exploiter, extortioner, swindler; *fig:* enemy; *spec:* fruit machine (one-armed bandit).

bang   **n** *lit:* detonation, explosion, report, shot; boom, clap, clash, crash, pop, thud; blow, box, cuff, hit, knock, punch, slam, smack, thump, wallop, whack; *fig:* impetus, vigour, zest; buzz, kick, stimulus, thrill.   **vb** *lit:* bash, beat, hammer, knock, pound, pummel, rap, slam, strike, thump; clash, clatter, crash; detonate, explode, resound, thunder.   **adv** *lit:* abruptly, all at once, suddenly; hard, noisily, smack, violently; absolutely, directly, exactly, headlong, precisely, quite, right, squarely, straight.

bank   **n** *lit:* border, brink, edge, rim, riverside, shore, side, towpath; acclivity, embankment, mound, pile, rampart, ridge, rise, shelf; accumulation, heap, mass; depository, hoard, repository, reserve, reservoir, stock, store; funds, kitty, moneybox, money exchange, pool, savings; bar, reef, shallows, shoal; camber, incline, lean, slant, slope, tilt; array, file, line, rank, row, tier; bench, settle, work-bench, work-table; *spec:* coal-face, face (in a mine); flock (of birds); manual (on an organ).   **vb** *lit:* deposit, put into the kitty, save; amass, gather, heap up, pile up, stack; count, depend, lean, rely; camber, cant, incline, lean, pitch, slant, slope, tilt, tip; embank, enclose, surround; close over, cover, extinguish.

bankrupt   **n** *lit:* debtor, defaulter.   **vb** *lit:* break, ruin; beggar,

impoverish; liquidate, put into liquidation, put in the hands of a receiver. **adj** *lit:* broke, flat broke, indebted, insolvent, ruined; destitute, failed, impoverished; bust, on the rocks, skint, washed up; *fig:* deficient, lacking, poor.

banner n *lit:* standard; coat of arms, colours, crest, escutcheon, insignia; burgee, gonfalon, pennant, pennon; ensign, flag.

bar n *lit:* baton, batten, boom, paling, pole, rail, rod, shaft, stake, stick; handle, key, lever; bolt, latch; barrier, obstruction; counter; canteen, inn, pub, saloon, taproom, tavern; bench, court, courtroom, dock, tribunal; advocates, barristers, lawyers; band, chevron, strip, stripe; block, cake, ingot, piece; bank, reef, sandbank, shallows, shoal; ridge; *fig:* ban, embargo, prohibition, proscription; deterrent, impediment, obstacle; *spec:* bride (in lace-making); measure, unit of rhythm (in musical notation); unit of pressure (in meteorology).
vb *lit:* bolt, latch, lock, put a bar across, secure; barricade, block, exclude, keep out, obstruct, prevent; ban, forbid, prohibit; preclude. **prp** *lit:* but (for), except (for), excluding, save.

barbarian n *lit:* brute, savage; foreigner, native; hooligan, lout, ruffian, thug, vandal; *fig:* philistine; illiterate. **adj** *lit:* brutish, savage, uncivilized; foreign, native; lowbrow, philistine; crude, primitive, uncouth, uncultured, uneducated, unsophisticated; *fig:* low, uncultivated, vulgar.

barbaric adj *lit:* barbarous, brutal, cruel, inhuman, ruthless; neanderthal, primitive, savage, uncivilized; fierce, harsh, wild; coarse, crude, rough, rude, uncouth; *fig:* tasteless, vulgar.

barber n *lit:* coiffeur, coiffeuse, haircutter, hairdresser, hair stylist.

bare vb *lit:* unclothe, uncover, undress, unsheathe; disclose, expose, open, reveal; denude, strip. **adj** *lit:* denuded, exposed, naked, nude, stripped, unclothed, uncovered, undressed, unsheathed; peeled, shorn; austere, basic, cold, hard, mere, plain, severe, simple, stark, unadorned, unvarnished; literal, sheer, unembellished; blank, empty, open, vacant, void; lacking, mean, poor; barren, featureless, scrubby, treeless; abraded, worn.

bargain n *lit:* agreement, arrangement, compact, contract, deal,

pact, transaction, treaty, understanding; cheap buy, giveaway, good deal, snip, steal. **vb** *lit:* beat down, haggle, negotiate, wheel and deal; barter, exchange, swap, trade, traffic; *fig:* bank, count, depend, rely; look (for), make allowance (for), plan (for).

barrage n *lit:* bar, barrier, boom, dam; bombardment, cannonade, fusillade, salvo, volley; *fig:* deluge, hail, onslaught, rain, storm, torrent.

barrel n *lit:* butt, cask, drum, keg, tun, vat; firkin, hogshead; cylinder, revolving drum, shaft, tube; chamber, piston-chamber; *fig:* good deal, lot; *spec:* calamus, quill (of a feather); trunk (of a farm animal). **vb** *fig:* drive fast, hurtle, race, speed.

barren adj *lit:* desert, desolate, empty, unfruitful, unproductive, waste; childless, impotent, infertile, sterile; fruitless, uninformative, unprofitable, unresponsive, unrewarding, wasted; boring, dull, flat, jejune, stale, trite, unattractive, uninspiring, useless, vapid.

barrier n *lit:* bar, boom, paling, pole, rail; barricade, blockage, obstacle, obstruction; boundary, ditch, fence, wall; fortification, palisade, rampart, stockade; *fig:* check, difficulty, hindrance, hurdle, impediment, restriction, stumbling-block; defence, protection.

barrister n *lit:* advocate, counsel, lawyer.

base n *lit:* bottom, foot, foundation; bed, dais, pedestal, plinth, podium, rest, stand; basis, bedrock, core, essence, floor, grounding, heart, origin, root, source; camp, headquarters, post, station; centre, focal point, home, starting point; standard; *fig:* support; least, lowest, minimum; *spec:* alkali (in chemistry); basis of a number system (maths); stem (in botany, etymology, phonetics). **vb** *lit:* build, construct, establish, found, set up; locate, place, station; derive, ground. **adj** *lit:* basic, core, essential, original, root; central, focal, home, main, primary, principal; standard; first, starting; least, lowest, minimum; humble, inferior, lowly, menial, paltry, poor, servile, shabby, subservient, vulgar, wretched; contemptible, degraded, despicable, dishonourable, ignoble, low, mean, sordid, worthless; counterfeit, fake, forged, fraudulent; adulterated, debased, impure.

bashful adj *lit:* coy, diffident, nervous, self-conscious, self-effacing,

shrinking, shy, timid, timorous; embarrassed, sheepish; reserved, retiring; reticent.

basic *adj lit:* core, fundamental, inherent, intrinsic, original, residual, root, underlying; standard; elementary, first, starting; least, lowest, minimum; central, essential, focal, key, main, primary, principal, vital; *spec:* alkaline (in chemistry).

basically *adv lit:* firstly, fundamentally, inherently, intrinsically, originally, residually; at a minimum, at bottom, at least, at the lowest; essentially, mainly, mostly, primarily, principally.

basin *n lit:* bowl, washbasin, washbowl, washstand; bidet; dock, harbour, haven, marina, pool; delta, drainage area, flats, valley; *spec:* synclinal area (in geology).

basis *n lit:* base, bottom, footing, foundation; bedrock, core, essence, floor, grounding, groundwork, heart, origin, root, source; centre, focal point, starting point; standard; essentials, fundamentals, grounds, precept, premise, principle, rationale, reason, substance.

bat *n lit:* club, stick, willow; innings, knock; lath, plank; flittermouse, pipistrelle; *fig:* pace, rate, speed; binge, carousal, drunken spree; *spec:* disc (of clay); lump, piece (of building materials); sheet (of insulation material). **vb** *lit:* hit, rap, smack, strike, swat, whack; blink, wink; *fig:* go, race, speed.

bath *n lit:* tub, washtub; hip-bath, jacuzzi, pool, sink; ablution, dip, douche, dousing, immersion, rinse, scrub, scrubbing, soak, sponging, wash; steeping. **vb** *lit:* clean, douse, immerse, rinse, scrub, shower, soak, soap, sponge down, wash; steep.

bathe *n lit:* dip, plunge, swim. **vb** *lit:* go swimming, swim, take a dip; cleanse, dunk, give a bath, drench, immerse, rinse, soak, steep, wash; dampen, moisten, wet; be immersed, be steeped; *fig:* cover, surround; bask, be covered.

batter *n lit:* pancake mixture, sponge mixture; paste; batsman, man in; tapering slope; *spec:* damaged type (in printing). **vb** *lit:* assault, beat, belabour, buffet, dash against, lash, paste, pelt, pound, pummel, wallop; bruise, crush, injure, mangle, maul; be thicker at the top, slope inwards.

battle n *lit:* action, combat, duel, engagement, fight, fighting, fray, skirmish, war, warfare; clash, conflict, contest, dispute, encounter, struggle. **vb** *lit:* contend, fight, make war, struggle, wage war; clash, contest, dispute.

bawl n *lit:* bellow, holler, roar; cry, howl, shout, shriek, wail, yell; blubbering, crying, sobbing, wailing; caterwauling, clamour, squalling. **vb** *lit:* bellow, holler, roar; howl, shout, shriek, yell; blubber, cry, sob, wail; caterwaul, clamour, squall.

bay n *lit:* bight, cove, gulf, inlet, sound; alcove, aumbry, embrasure, niche, nook, recess; concavity, hanging valley, indentation; platform, stall, station; area, compartment, space, ward; barking, call, howl, ululation; *spec:* chestnut (horse); laurel (bush, tree). **vb** *lit:* bark (at), bell, cry, howl, ululate; corner, trap. **adj** *lit:* concave, recessed, semicircular; *spec:* chestnut, reddish-brown (horse); laurel (bush, tree).

be **vb** *lit:* exist, live; abide, continue, remain, stay; last, persist, subsist, survive; befall, come about, happen, occur, take place, transpire; become, equal, represent; go; have.

beach n *lit:* bank, littoral, shore, strand; sand, sands, seaside, shingle. **vb** *lit:* drive on shore, go aground, pull on shore, run ashore; *fig:* maroon, strand.

beacon n *lit:* fire, flare, lamp, light, signal, signal fire; light-buoy, lighthouse, navigation light; watchtower; radio guide-beam, radio mast; flashing light; *fig:* guiding light, indicator, landmark, pointer, sign, signpost; warning.

beam n *lit:* girder, joist, plank, spar, timber, trunk; ray, shaft, stream; emission, transmission; gleam; *fig:* broad smile, glow, grin, radiance; bottom, buttocks, hips; *spec:* bar, cross-piece, lever (on a pair of scales); breadth, side, width (of a ship); cylinder, roller (on a loom); shank, stem (of an anchor, a plough). **vb** *lit:* broadcast, emit, radiate, transmit; gleam, shine; aim, direct, point; *fig:* grin, smile, smile broadly.

bear n *lit:* bruin, grizzly; koala, panda; *fig:* hairy giant, shaggy person; *spec:* pessimist, seller (on the stock exchange). **vb** *lit:* bring, carry, take; convey, fetch, move, transport; drive, press, push, thrust;

have, hold, possess, sustain; assume, take on; behave, conduct; entertain, harbour, support; endure, put up with, stomach, tolerate; abide, brook; admit, afford, allow, permit; experience, suffer, undergo; bring forth, bring to birth, engender, give birth to, produce, yield; affect, be pertinent, be relevant; go, move, tend, turn, veer; give out, render; exercise; *spec:* sell (shares).

beard   n *lit:* beaver, bristles, full set, stubble, whiskers; awn, tuft; *spec:* barbel (on a fish).   **vb** *lit:* brave, confront, defy, face.

bearer   n *lit:* bringer, carrier, conveyor, messenger, porter, runner; agent, servant; holder, presenter.

bearing   n *lit:* air, attitude, carriage, demeanour, deportment, manner, mien, posture; compass point, direction; application, connection, import, reference, relation, relevance, significance; endurance, stomaching, toleration; *spec:* charge, device (on a coat of arms).

beast   n *lit:* animal, brute; creature; fiend, monster, ogre, savage.

beat   n *lit:* pulse, throb, vibration; drumming, percussion; accent, stress; measure, metre, rhythm, time; circuit, course, patrol, round; *spec:* interference pattern (in music and wave physics).   **vb** *lit:* bang, batter, buffet, cane, drub, flog, hit, lash, pound, strike, thrash, whip, whack; pulsate, pulse, throb, vibrate; drum, hammer, roar, thunder; fashion, forge, work; *fig:* best, conquer, defeat, overcome, vanquish; outdo, outstrip, overtake, overwhelm, surpass.

beautiful   adj *lit:* bewitching, enchanting, exquisite, fair, gorgeous, graceful, handsome, lovely, magnificent, radiant, ravishing, stunning.

beauty   n *lit:* attractiveness, charm, good looks, grace, loveliness, prettiness, pulchritude; advantage, benefit, good feature, major attraction; charmer, corker, cracker, dish, dreamboat, goddess, good-looker, lovely, peach, stunner.

because   cnj *lit:* by reason (of), on account (of); for the reason that, in that, since.

become   vb *lit:* change into, develop into, grow into, turn into; come to be, get, turn; be appropriate to, be fitting to, behove, suit; adorn, grace, set off; be the fate (of).

bed n *lit:* berth, bunk; mattress, pallet; litter, palliasse; resting-place; bottom, floor, foundation, substratum; stratum, vein; border, garden, patch, plot, row; *fig:* marital rights, sexual relations; *spec:* layer (of farmed oysters). **vb** *lit:* be accommodated, lodge, put up, settle (down); hit the sack, lie, sleep; have sex with, make love with, sleep with; stratify, lay down, set down; implant, insert, plant, plant out, put in.

before adv *lit:* ahead, in front; earlier, in the past, previously; by now, sooner. **prp** *lit:* ahead of, in front of; in the sight of; earlier than, prior to; sooner than; in preference to; superior to.

beg vb *lit:* beseech, entreat, implore, petition, plead with; ask for alms, ask for charity; *spec:* cry (off); evade, sidestep (the question).

beggar n *lit:* mendicant, tramp, vagrant; supplicant; bankrupt, pauper.

begin vb *lit:* commence, start; inaugurate, initiate, launch, open, set about; embark on, set out on; create, found, institute, originate; appear, come into being, emerge, spring.

beginning n *lit:* commencement, onset, start; inauguration, initiation, launch, opening; outset; birth, creation, foundation, institution, origination, root(s); appearance, arising, dawn, emergence; fountainhead, source. **adj (pr.pt)** *lit:* first, inaugural, initial, leading, opening, original, primary; incipient, rudimentary.

behalf n *lit:* account, part, side.

behave vb *lit:* act, conduct oneself, handle, operate, perform, work; act properly, be mannerly, be polite; react.

behaviour n *lit:* activity, comportment, conduct, manners; action, handling, operation, performance; reaction, responsivity.

behind n *lit:* backside, bottom, derrière, posterior, rear, seat, stern; arse, bum. **adv** *lit:* at the back, in the rear; afterwards, farther back, following, subsequently; in detention, in reserve; late, overdue, slow; in arrears, in debt. **prp** *lit:* at the back of, beyond, to the back of; after, following, subsequent to; later than, slower than; responsible for; backing, supporting.

being   n *lit:* existence, life, living; entity, essence, substance; constitution, nature; attendance, presence; creature, individual, organism.   **adj (pr.pt)** *lit:* existent; contemporaneous, continuing, present.

belief   n *lit:* confession, credo, creed, doctrine, faith, persuasion, tenet; conviction, feeling, impression, opinion, understanding, view; reliance, trust; (beyond) acceptance, (beyond) credence.

believe   vb *lit:* confess, have faith (in); credit; be convinced (that), hold (that); place one's trust (in), trust; consider, deem, think; conjecture, guess, imagine, presume, reckon, suppose.

believer   n *lit:* adherent, devotee, disciple, proselyte.

belong   vb *lit:* appertain (to), attach (to), pertain (to), relate (to); be affiliated (to); be connected (with), go together (with).

belongings   n *lit:* gear, effects, junk, paraphernalia, possessions, stuff, things.

below   adj *lit:* beneath, underneath; downstairs, lower; later, subsequent; inferior, lesser.   adv *lit:* beneath, under, underneath; down, downstairs, lower; downstream; hereafter, later.   prp *lit:* beneath, lower than, under, underneath; inferior to, less than, subordinate to, unworthy of.

bench   n *lit:* form, pew, seat; counter, work-table; frame, platform, trestle-table; judiciary, magistracy, tribunal.

bend   n *lit:* buckle, fold, warp; angle, corner, curve, turn; stoop; fastening, knot.   vb *lit:* bow, buckle, fold, warp; curve, swerve, turn, veer; lean over, stoop; flex, mould, shape; *fig:* influence, persuade, sway.

beneath   adv *lit:* below, under, underneath; lower.   prp *lit:* below, lower than, under, underneath; inferior to, less than, subordinate to, unworthy of.

benefit   n *lit:* advantage, gain, good, help, improvement, profit, use; dole, grant, unemployment grant, welfare; charity performance.
vb *lit:* be good for, do good to; advantage, aid, further, serve; be advantaged, be assisted, gain, profit.

benevolent adj *lit:* beneficent, benign, charitable, considerate, generous, humane, kindly, philanthropic, well-disposed.

bent n *lit:* bias, inclination, leaning, penchant, preference, propensity; tendency, trend; flexion, torque; ability, endurance; *spec:* type of grass. **adj** *lit:* bowed, buckled, folded, twisted, warped; angled, curved; crooked, hunched, leaning, stooping; *fig:* determined (on), insistent (on), intent (on), resolved (on); criminal, dishonest, fraudulent, unscrupulous; deviant, kinky, perverted.

berth n *lit:* bed, bunk, cabin, couchette, place, seat; sleeping-place; anchorage, dock, mooring, quay, wharf; *fig:* job, position, post, situation; leeway, room, sea-room, space.

beside adv *lit:* additionally, also, further, furthermore, in addition, moreover, too. **prp** *lit:* adjoining, alongside, bordering, by the side of, contiguous with, next to; *fig:* compared to/with, in comparison with; *spec:* not pertinent to, unrelated to (the point).

besides adv *lit:* additionally, also, further, furthermore, in addition, moreover, too; likewise, similarly; else, otherwise. **prp** *lit:* as well as, in addition to, over and above; apart from, barring, excepting, other than, save.

best n *lit:* finest, flower, greatest, number one, optimum, supreme, top; elite, favourite, pick; champion, first, victor, winner; utmost. **vb** *lit:* beat, conquer, defeat, outdo, surpass; outwit. **adj** *lit:* finest, foremost, greatest, highest, optimum, supreme, top; favourite; champion, first, leading, victorious, winning; most advantageous; most fitting. **adv** *lit:* most, supremely; most correctly, most efficiently, most thoroughly; most advantageously; most attractively, most fittingly.

bet n *lit:* gamble, risk, speculation, wager; ante, pledge, stake; *fig:* alternative, choice, course of action, route; belief, guess, opinion, supposition. **vb** *lit:* gamble, punt, risk, speculate (on), stake (on), wager; *fig:* be certain, be sure.

betray vb *lit:* double-cross, sell out; divulge, give away, reveal; inform on, tell on, unmask; ensnare, entrap, seduce, undo; be disloyal to, deceive; desert, forsake, leave in the lurch; *fig:* let slip, manifest, show signs of.

betrayal   n *lit:* double-cross, give-away, sell-out; disclosure, divulgence, unmasking; entrapment, seduction; violation; disloyalty, deception, duplicity, perfidy, treachery, treason; desertion, forsaking, ratting.

better   vb *lit:* ameliorate, enhance, forward, further, improve; amend, correct, rectify; beat, cap, defeat, outdo, top.   **adj** *lit:* finer, greater, higher, preferable, superior; more useful, more valuable; more apt, more suitable; more expert, more skilled; more intense; cured, healthier, progressing, recovering, stronger, well again. adv *lit:* more (than); in a superior way, more advantageously, more usefully, more valuably; more aptly, more suitably; more expertly, more skilfully; more fully, more intensely.

between   prp *lit:* betwixt, intermediate to, in the middle of; within the range separating; connecting, joining, linking; through the combined action of; in the joint possession of.

beware   vb *lit:* be careful (of), be wary (of); be on one's guard (lest/that).

beyond   adv *lit:* at a distance, behind, farther away; past.   **prp** *lit:* across, behind, on the farther side of, over, to the farther side of; later than, past; above, besides, more than, outside; *fig:* out of the reach of, too much for the comprehension of.

bias   n *lit:* leaning, partiality, predilection, predisposition, prejudice; diagonal, oblique; weighting.   vb *lit:* influence, predispose, prejudice, slant, weight.

bid   n *lit:* offer, proposition, tender; *fig:* attempt, effort, endeavour, try.   vb *lit:* make an offer, tender; call; greet, say, wish; ask, invite; command (to), direct (to), order (to), tell (to).

big   adj *lit:* colossal, enormous, gigantic, great, huge, hulking, immense, large, massive, sizable, substantial, tremendous; adult, elder, grown-up; full, loud; pregnant (with); *fig:* important, influential, powerful, prominent, valuable; altruistic, benevolent, generous, liberal, magnanimous, noble, princely; arrogant, boastful, conceited, pompous, pretentious.

bill   n *lit:* account, invoice, reckoning, score, slate, tally;

advertisement, broadsheet, circular, handout, leaflet, poster; inventory, list, programme, schedule; law, measure, proposal; banknote, note; beak, neb; cleaver, pick. **vb** *lit:* charge, invoice, put on the slate; advertise, announce, give advance warning of, stick posters up over; *spec:* touch beaks of birds).

binding n *lit:* casing, cover, covering, jacket; border, edging, trimming; ski-fastening. **adj** *lit:* indelible, irrevocable; compulsory, obligatory.

bird n *lit:* feathered friend, fowl; *fig:* bloke, chap, guy, person; chick, doll, girl, girlfriend; porridge, stretch, term, time; barracking, booing, raspberry.

birth n *lit:* accouchement, delivery, labour, parturition; nativity; ancestry, blood, breeding, family, lineage, parentage; *fig:* beginning, creation, dawn, emergence, genesis, inauguration, origination.

biscuit n *lit:* cracker, cookie, nut, savoury; crispbread.

bit n *lit:* bite, chip, crumb, fragment, morsel, scrap, slice; part, piece, section, segment, small amount; coin; bore, drill; curb, mouthpiece, snaffle; *fig:* little, minute, moment, second, while.

bite n *lit:* dentition, occlusion; grasp, grip; nip, prick, puncture, sting; morsel, mouthful, nibble, snack; *fig:* acidity, corrosiveness; kick, piquancy, punch, spice; attempt, bash, go, try; answer, reaction, response. **vb** *lit:* chew, chomp, clench, gnaw, masticate, munch, nibble, nip; grind, grip, puncture, rend, seize, sting, tear; corrode, eat into, erode, wear away; cut, pierce; be caught, take the bait; *fig:* be effective, take effect; react, respond, snap (at); annoy, bother.

bitter adj *lit:* acescent, acid, acrid, astringent, harsh, sour, tart; *fig:* acrimonious, hostile, rancorous, resentful, sulky, sullen; caustic, fierce, sharp, stinging, virulent; biting, freezing, intense, piercing; distressing, galling, grievous, heart-rending, painful.

black adj *lit:* dusky, ebony-coloured, jet, swart, swarthy; dark, raven, sable; dim, inky, murky, stygian; dirty, filthy, foul, grimy, soiled; *fig:* depressing, foreboding, funereal, hopeless, mournful, ominous, sombre; evil, malignant, villainous, wicked; lowering, morose, resentful, sullen, sulky; aggressive, hostile, menacing,

threatening; banned, boycotted, embargoed, strike-bound.

blackout n *lit:* dizzy spell, faint, loss of consciousness, swoon; epileptic fit; electricity cut, power failure; *fig:* censorship, silence, suppression.

blame n *lit:* accusation, censure, charge, recrimination; culpability, guilt; *fig:* fault, liability, responsibility.   vb *lit:* condemn (for), find fault with (for), hold responsible (for), rebuke (for), reproach (for).

blank n *lit:* emptiness, space, tabula rasa, vacuity, vacuum, void; gap, hiatus; empty sheet, white page; *spec:* bullseye, inner, white (on a target).   adj *lit:* bare, empty, plain, pristine, unmarked, unused; white; uncut, unformed, unshaped; *fig:* bewildered, confounded, dumbfounded, nonplussed; deadpan, expressionless, impassive, lifeless, uncomprehending, vacuous.

blanket n *lit:* coverlet, rug; *fig:* carpet, coat, covering, film, layer, sheet.   vb *lit:* carpet, coat, cover, envelop, spread oneself over; cloak, mask, obscure, veil.   adj *lit:* all-inclusive, comprehensive, general, universal.

blast n *lit:* gust, squall, storm, wind; blare, honk, hoot, peal, wail; blow, jet; bang, crash, detonation, eruption, explosion; pressure-wave; *fig:* outburst.   vb *lit:* blare, blow, hoot; blow up, detonate, explode, shatter; demolish, destroy, smash, wreck, zap; kill, ruin, shrivel, wither; *fig:* be scathing about, flay, pan, slate; abuse, curse, swear at, vilify; *spec:* smoke (marijuana).

blatant adj *lit:* brazen, flagrant, glaring; conspicuous, obvious, overt, pronounced; clamorous, loudmouthed, noisy; garish, gaudy, loud, ostentatious.

bleak adj *lit:* bare, barren, exposed, gaunt, open, windswept; chilly, cold, raw, windy; cheerless, colourless, depressing, discouraging, gloomy, sombre.

bleed vb *lit:* lose blood, shed blood; lose sap; leak, ooze, seep, trickle; draw blood from; draw sap from; catheterize, drain, leech, siphon off, squeeze; *fig:* blackmail from, extort from; ache (for), feel (for), have pity (for); *spec:* go off the edge of the page (of illustrations).

blend n *lit:* amalgam, combination, compound, fusion, mixture, synthesis; merging, shading; harmonization. **vb** *lit:* amalgamate, combine, compound, fuse, mingle, mix, synthesize; merge (with); go well (with), harmonize (with).

bless **vb** *lit:* consecrate, hallow, make holy, sanctify; commend to God's grace, invoke divine favour upon, make the sign of the cross over; make fruitful, make happy, make joyful, make prosperous; adore, extol, glorify, praise, worship.

blessing n *lit:* benediction, benison; consecration, invocation; grace, thanksgiving; *fig:* approval, backing, encouragement, favour, sanction, support; benefit, gift, possession, present; boon, godsend, help, piece of luck, stroke of good fortune.

blind n *lit:* louvres, shutter, slats; canopy, shade; carousal, drinking spree, pub-crawl; *fig:* cover, device, façade, feint, front, mask, ploy, pretext, pretence, ruse, screen, stratagem. **vb** *lit:* put out the eyes of; be too bright for, dazzle; *fig:* keep in the dark, render oblivious (to), stop from seeing. **adj** *lit:* sightless, unseeing; *fig:* dead-end; inattentive (to), indifferent (to), insensitive (to), oblivious (to); dark, dim, hidden, obscured; unreasoning, unthinking. **adv** *lit:* ad lib, extempore, off the cuff, straight off, unseen; through instrumentation only.

block n *lit:* barrier, blockage, impediment, obstacle, obstruction, stoppage; bar, brick, cube, ingot, piece; building, site, square; anvil, base, platform, support, table; pulley; *fig:* group, row, set; book, pad, ream; bounce, head. **vb** *lit:* bar, check, halt, impede, obstruct, stop; bung, choke, clog, plug up, stuff up.

blockade n *lit:* barricade, barrier, obstruction; encirclement, investment, siege. **vb** *lit:* barricade, fortify, obstruct, secure; besiege, cut off, encircle, isolate.

blood n *lit:* gore; plasma, serum; claret, cruor; ancestry, birth, descent, extraction, family, genealogy, lineage, pedigree, stock, strain; kindred, relations, relatives; *fig:* juice, sap; anger, passion, temper; death, murder; disposition, feeling, temperament; buck, blade, dandy, spark; aristocracy, nobility, royal family. **vb** *lit:* smear with gore; *fig:* initiate (into), introduce (into).

bloom n *lit:* blossom, flower; blossoming, flowering, opening; glaucescence, powdery surface; cloudiness, milkiness; *fig:* fragrance, freshness, perfection, prime, radiance; blush, flush, rosiness; *spec:* aggregation, mass (of plankton). **vb** *lit:* blossom, burgeon, flower, open; *fig:* flourish, prosper, succeed, thrive; be fragrant, be radiant.

blossom n *lit:* bloom, flower; flowers, scented petals. **vb** *lit:* bloom, burgeon, flower; *fig:* come into one's own, flourish, lose one's reserve, mature, show what one can do.

blow n *lit:* blast, gale, gust, wind; bang, belt, buffet, clip, clout, clump, knock, punch, smack, sock, thump, thwack, wallop, whack; *fig:* calamity, catastrophe, disappointment, disaster, setback, upset; (at a) stroke. **vb** *lit:* fan, gust, puff, waft, whirl, whistle; blast, buffet, sweep, whisk; breathe hard, exhale, pant; pipe, play; blare, hoot, sound; *fig:* exhaust, spend, squander, use up; divulge, reveal, tell; *spec:* lose, miss (one's chance); melt (a fuse); spout (of whales).

blue vb *lit:* bleach, dye white; *fig:* exhaust, spend, squander, use up. **adj** *lit:* aquamarine, azure, cerulean, cyan, indigo, turquoise, ultramarine; gunmetal; cold, frozen, numb; under-oxygenated; *fig:* dejected, depressed, downcast, doleful, glum, melancholy; depressing, dismal, unpromising; bawdy, erotic, indecent, obscene, smutty; *spec:* flattened, seventh (note in music).

blunt vb *lit:* dull, take the edge off; *fig:* dampen, deaden, muffle, soften, weaken. **adj** *lit:* dull, flat; *fig:* bluff, forthright, frank, plain-speaking, outspoken, straightforward; explicit, forceful.

blur n *lit:* blot, smear, smudge, splodge; blear, fog, haze, mist, vagueness; streak. **vb** *lit:* blemish, blot, smear, smudge; cloud, darken, obscure, soften; unfocus; flash, streak.

blush n *lit:* flush, glow, reddening, suffusion; bloom, rosiness. **vb** *lit:* colour, crimson, flush, redden, suffuse; be ashamed (at), be mortified (at).

board n *lit:* joist, panel, plank, timber; lath, slat; card; table; catering, food, meals, provisions; committee, council, directors, trustees; arena, platform, stage, surface. **vb** *lit:* plank (over), shutter, timber (over); cater for, feed, provide meals for; billet, lodge, put up, quarter; enter, get on, mount.

boast n *lit:* brag, vaunt; joy, pride, pride and joy, treasure.
vb *lit:* brag, talk big; blow one's own trumpet, crow, vaunt; be proud of, flatter oneself on; *fig:* exhibit, have, own, possess.

boastful adj *lit:* big-headed, bragging, conceited, egotistical, vaunting.

boat n *lit:* craft, ship, vessel; canoe, cutter, dinghy, ketch, launch, sloop, yacht, yawl; cruiser, liner; ferry.

body n *lit:* figure, form, frame; build, physique; being, human, mortal, person, soul; cadaver, corpse, mortal remains; torso, trunk; fuselage, nave; *fig:* bulk, core, main part, majority, mass; essence, matter, substance; density, firmness, fullness, opacity, solidity; band, collection, company, group, set.

bog n *lit:* fen, marsh, morass, moss, quagmire, slough, swamp; *fig:* convenience, Gents, Ladies, latrine, lavatory, loo, privy, toilet.

boil n *lit:* abscess, carbuncle, furuncle, pimple, pustule, spot, stye. **vb** *lit:* steam, vaporize; cook, poach; evaporate; agitate, bubble, churn, foam, seethe; *fig:* be incensed, fulminate, fume, hit the roof, rage, rant.

bold adj *lit:* audacious, brave, courageous, daring, fearless, intrepid, valiant; flirtatious, forward, shameless; brash, cheeky, impudent, saucy; *fig:* bright, conspicuous, loud, showy, striking, vivid; forceful, lively, spirited.

bolt n *lit:* bar, catch, latch, peg, pin, rod, slide; arrow, dart, quarrel; dash, runner, sprint; stroke of lightning, thunderflash; *spec:* roll (of cloth). **vb** *lit:* bar, fasten, latch, lock, peg, pin, secure; dash, flee, fly, run for it, sprint; gobble, gorge, guzzle, stuff, wolf; *spec:* run to seed (of a plant).

bomb n *lit:* explosive device, mine, shell; lava-ball; *fig:* nasty shock, unwelcome surprise; fortune, lot of money; success, treat. **vb** *lit:* blitz, blow up, bombard, detonate, shell; *fig:* fly, hurtle, race, rocket, speed.

bond n *lit:* adhesivity, stickiness, tackiness; cement, glue, gum, mortar; binding, chain, cord, fastening, fetter, manacle, rope, shackle;

molecular force; affinity, attachment, link, tie; agreement, contract, covenant, pledge, promise; guarantee, security, surety; debenture, promisory note; *spec:* style, technique (in bricklaying). **vb** *lit:* cement, fasten (together), fix (together), fuse, glue, gum.

bonus n *lit:* bounty, commission, dividend, extra, gratuity, honorarium, premium, reward; perk; rake-off, share of profits; prize, winnings; windfall.

book n *lit:* publication, tome, volume; work; archive, chronicle, ledger, log, record; libretto, script. **vb** *lit:* enter, insert, log, post, put down, record, register, write down; engage, line up, reserve, schedule; take the name of; check (in).

boost n *lit:* encouragement, furtherance, help; expansion, hike, hoist, improvement, increase, lift. **vb** *lit:* advance, encourage, foster, further, help; add to, enlarge, expand, hike up, hoist, improve, increase, lift, promote, support.

boot n *lit:* heavy shoe, wellie, wellington; kick, punt; luggage compartment, trunk. **vb** *lit:* shoe; kick, punt; chuck (out), kick (out), throw (out); avail, be of use, profit; *spec:* access, insert (a computer program).

border n *lit:* boundary, brink, edge, frontier, limit, margin, rim; flower-bed; edging, fringe, hem, trimming; outskirts. **vb** *lit:* adjoin, be adjacent to, bound, delimit, front on, march with; edge, fringe.

bore n *lit:* hole, shaft; barrel, calibre; *fig:* drag, nuisance, pain, pest; chore, thankless task. **vb** *lit:* drill, mine, penetrate (into), pierce (into), sink a shaft (into), tunnel (into); *fig:* bother, fatigue, tire, weary.

boredom n *lit:* ennui, having nothing to do, listlessness, monotony, tedium, tediousness, tiresomeness.

boring adj (pr.pt) *lit:* dismal, dull, flat, humdrum, insipid, monotonous, mundane, numbing, ordinary, soporific, stale, stultifying, tedious, tiresome, uninteresting, wearisome.

borrow vb *lit:* have the use of; have, use, utilize; adopt, appropriate, copy, derive, imitate, pilfer, pirate, plagiarize; *spec:* make allowance for (the terrain in golf).

bosom n *lit:* breast(s), bust; chest; *fig:* emotions, feelings, heart, sentiments; centre, midst. **adj** *lit:* close, dear, intimate.

boss n *lit:* knob, ornament, stud; chief, employer, foreman, gaffer, leader, manager, master, overseer, supervisor.

bother n *lit:* annoyance, inconvenience, irritation, nuisance, problem, vexation; commotion, disturbance, fuss, to-do. **vb** *lit:* annoy, be a nuisance, inconvenience, irritate, pester, plague, vex; go to the trouble (to), make the effort (to); blast, damn.

bottom n *lit:* base, basis, floor, foundation; underneath, underside; arse, backside, behind, bum, posterior, rear, rump, seat; hull, keel; *fig:* core, heart, root, source. **adj** *lit:* base, fundamental, ground, lowest, ultimate.

bough n *lit:* branch, offshoot; shoot, stem; twig.

boundary n *lit:* border, edge, extremity, fringe, frontier, limit, line, margin, termination; *spec:* four (in cricket).

bountiful adj *lit:* beneficent, generous, liberal, munificent; ample, copious, plenteous, plentiful, prolific, unstinting.

bout n *lit:* contest, encounter, fight, round; period, session, spell, stint, time.

bow n *lit:* bend, bob, inclination, kowtow, nod; curve, distortion, warp; fore, front, prow, sharp end; looped knot. **vb** *lit:* bend (low), bob, incline, kowtow, nod; curve, distort, hunch, warp; play the violin; *fig:* defer (to), give in (to), surrender (to), yield (to); crush, oppress, subdue, weigh down.

bowl n *lit:* basin, dish; container, pot, vessel; hurl, pitch, throw; ball, wood. **vb** *lit:* fling, hurl, pitch, throw; roll.

box n *lit:* carton, case, package; chest, crate, trunk; receptacle; bang, blow, buffet, clip, clout, punch, wallop; *fig:* inset, rectangle; goal area, penalty area; cabin, hut, lodge; jock, protector; *spec:* (Christmas) gratuity, tip. **vb** *lit:* enclose, insert, pack into; confine, pen; fight, spar, trade punches; bang, buffet, clip, clout, punch, thump, wallop.

boy   n *lit:* adolescent, lad, son, stripling, young man, youth; bloke, chap, fellow, guy.

brain   n *lit:* central nervous system, cerebral hemispheres, cerebrum, grey matter; intellect, mind; common sense, intelligence, nous, wit; *fig:* genius, mastermind, prodigy; expert; highbrow, scholar; control system, guidance system.

brake   n *lit:* check, constraint, curb, decelerator, rein; bracken, ferns, thicket, undergrowth.   **vb** *lit:* check, constrain, curb, decelerate, halt, rein in, slow, stop.

branch   n *lit:* bough, offshoot; shoot, stem; twig; arm, limb; *fig:* ramification; department, office, part, section, subdivision, subsidiary.   **vb** *lit:* diversify, divide, fork, ramify, spread (out); develop, expand, increase, proliferate.

brand   n *lit:* colophon, hallmark, label, logo, mark, sign, stamp, symbol; class, kind, make, sort, type, variety; *fig:* imputation, slur, stigma, taint.   **vb** *lit:* label, mark, sign, stamp; *fig:* call, mark down as, stigmatize as.

brandish   **vb** *lit:* flourish, swing, wave about, whirl, wield; display, exhibit, flaunt, hold (in front of).

brawn   n *lit:* beef, muscle, muscularity, robustness, strength, vigour.

breach   n *lit:* break, cleft, fissure, gap, hole, rift, split; infraction, infringement, transgression, violation; alienation, difference, division, estrangement, separation, variance; breaking of the waves, surf.
vb *lit:* break, crack, fracture, make an opening, rend, split; infringe, transgress against, violate.

bread   n *lit:* loaf; *fig:* food, livelihood, nourishment, provisions, sustenance; cash, funds, money.

breadth   n *lit:* latitude, span, width; beam; area, compass, extent, measure, range, scale, scope, size, spread, sweep; liberality, openness; integrity, totality.

break   n *lit:* crack, fracture, rupture, snap; breach, cleft, fissure, gap, hole, rent, rip, tear; alienation, divergence, estrangement, separation, split; division, parting, severance; breather, halt, intermission,

interval, pause, recess, rest, stop; *fig:* chance, opportunity; piece of luck, stroke of good fortune; alteration, change, difference; *spec:* ad lib, cadenza (in a musical performance); dawn (of day); run (of points in billiards/pool/snooker); spin (on a ball). **vb** *lit:* come apart, crack, fracture, rupture, snap; crush, fragment, powder, shatter; breach, leave a gap in, make a hole in, rend, rip, tear; interpose, separate, split up; divide, part, sever; be intermittent; disconnect; discontinue, leave (off), stop, take a breather, take time (off); interrupt; interpolate (in), put one's oar (in); infract, infringe, transgress against; overwhelm, subdue, tame, undermine; degrade, demote, dismiss, ruin; *fig:* disclose, divulge, impart, let out, reveal, tell; appear, emerge, erupt forth; *spec:* beat, better, exceed, outdo, top (a record); cure (a habit); cushion, soften (a fall); escape from (prison); leave (cover); run (for it); spin (of a ball on bouncing); unfurl (a flag); violate (a promise, one's parole).

breast n *lit:* bosom, bust, chest; mammary gland; boob, bristol(s), dug, knocker(s), pap, tit; udder; nipple, teat; mound, rounded hill; *fig:* conscience, heart, mind, soul. **vb** *lit:* reach with the chest; *fig:* confront, engage with, meet, oppose.

breath n *lit:* animation, life; exhalation, inhalation, respiration; gasp, pant; breeze, flutter, puff, waft; aroma, odour, perfume, scent; *fig:* hint, suggestion, suspicion, whisper.

breathe vb *lit:* exhale, inhale, respire; blow, gasp, pant, puff; *fig:* murmur, say softly, sigh, whisper; infuse (into), inject (into).

breed n *lit:* family, lineage, pedigree, stock; class, kind, race, sort, species, type, variety. **vb** *lit:* multiply, proliferate, procreate, propagate, reproduce; cultivate, farm, raise, rear; bring up, educate, train; *fig:* beget, cause, create, generate, occasion, produce.

bribe n *lit:* backhander, bait, carrot, enticement, greased palm, inducement, kickback. **vb** *lit:* buy, get at, grease the palm of, pay off, suborn.

bridge n *lit:* crossover, span, viaduct; flyover, overpass; catwalk, gantry; bond, connection, link; *spec:* navigation centre (on a ship); support (for the strings on a violin, for a cue, or for a pair of

spectacles); top (of the nose).   **vb** *lit:* go over, lie across, span, straddle; connect, join, link.

brief   **n** *lit:* outline, précis, summary, synopsis; argument, contention; case, statement; summons, writ; *spec:* (papal) epistle.   **vb** *lit:* advise, bring up to date, fill in, give a rundown, inform; instruct, prime; précis, summarize.   **adj** *lit:* concise, short, succinct; outline, thumbnail; brusque, curt, sharp, terse; fleeting, momentary, short-lived, transitory.

bright   **adj** *lit:* brilliant, dazzling, effulgent, glittering, glowing, intense, luminous, resplendent, scintillating, shimmering, shining, vivid, white; clear, pellucid, translucent, transparent; blazing, cloudless, fair, sunny; *fig:* astute, clever, ingenious, intelligent, imaginative, inventive, practical, quick-witted, shrewd; cheerful, encouraging, favourable, happy, jolly, optimistic, promising; animated, lively, vivacious; glorious, illustrious, magnificent.

brilliant   **adj** *lit:* bright, dazzling, effulgent, intense, luminous, lustrous, radiant, resplendent, shining, very white; coruscating, glittering, scintillating, twinkling; glamorous, grand, magnificent, splendid; *fig:* excellent, expert, extremely intelligent, highly gifted, masterly, very talented; glorious, illustrious, magnificent.

bring   **vb** *lit:* carry, convey, deliver, fetch, take, transport; advance, forward, present, proffer; conduct, escort, guide, lead, steer; turn (about); cut (down), shoot (down); *fig:* induce (to), persuade (to), prevail upon (to); compel (to), force (to), oblige (to); carry (off), pull (it off); command, earn, net, sell for.

brink   **n** *lit:* clifftop, edge, sheer edge; bank, brim, verge; *fig:* point, threshold.

brisk   **adj** *lit:* bustling, busy, energetic, lively, sprightly, spry, vigorous; bracing, exhilarating, invigorating, keen, sharp; piquant.

bristle   **n** *lit:* hair, whisker; prickle, spine, thorn.   **vb** *lit:* horripilate, prickle, rise, stand on end; *fig:* bridle, flare up, recoil; crawl (with), swarm (with), teem (with).

brittle   **adj** *lit:* crisp, rigid, taut, tense; fragile, friable; *fig:* edgy, nervous, stiff; cool, stilted; unstable.

broad adj *lit:* thick, wide; ample, free, generous, extensive, large; capacious, open, roomy, spacious; *fig:* comprehensive, encyclopaedic, sweeping, universal; liberal, permissive, progressive; uninhibited, unrestrained; blue, coarse, indecent, indelicate, vulgar; *spec:* accented (dialect); clear, full (daylight).

broadcast n *lit:* programme, transmission. vb *lit:* air, radio, relay, televise, transmit; announce, circulate, noise abroad, proclaim, publish; disperse, disseminate, scatter, sow, seed, spread.

brown vb *lit:* fry, roast, sauté; seal in the stove. adj *lit:* bistre, dun, sepia, tan, umber; auburn, brunette, chestnut, hazel; dark, dusky, tawny; bronzed, tanned; chocolate-coloured, coffee-coloured.

bruise n *lit:* contusion, discoloration; sore spot, tenderness; dent, indentation. vb *lit:* contuse, discolour; damage, injure, wound; crush, pound, powder.

brush n *lit:* besom, broom; bristles, hair; bushy tail; bushes, scrub, thicket, undergrowth; abrasion, bump, contact, friction, glance, graze, scrape; *fig:* confrontation, encounter, skirmish, tussle; *spec:* (electrical) contact. vb *lit:* clean, dust, sweep; paint; bump, make contact with, glance off, scrape; caress, flick, stroke, touch.

brutal adj *lit:* bestial, callous, cruel, inhuman, merciless, relentless, ruthless, savage, unfeeling; harsh, repressive, rigorous, severe, stern, strict, tyrannical; coarse, gross, rude.

brute n *lit:* animal, beast; *fig:* bully, ruffian, sadist, savage, thug; barbarian, boor, lout, yobbo.

bubble n *lit:* bead, drop, globule; blister, vesicle; *fig:* lame duck, speculative venture. vb *lit:* boil, effervesce, fizz, seethe; babble, gurgle, murmur, ripple.

buckle n *lit:* catch, clasp, hasp; bend, bow, distortion, fold, kink, warp. vb *lit:* do up, fasten, lace up, latch, tie up; bend, bow, crumple, distort, fold, kink, warp.

budget n *lit:* exchequer, finances, funds, resources; allocation, cost specification, estimate, sum set aside; financial programme. vb *lit:* allocate, cost, estimate; set aside a sum (for); plan one's fiscal affairs.

bug n *lit:* bed-louse, beetle, creepy-crawly, insect, midge; bacterium, germ, microorganism, virus; infection; concealed microphone; *fig:* defect, fault, gremlin, snag; craze, fad, rage. **vb** *lit:* plant a microphone on; tap; *fig:* annoy, disturb, irk, pester, plague.

build n *lit:* body-shape, figure, frame, physique. **vb** *lit:* construct, erect, make, put up; create, form, fashion, mould; amass, assemble, collect, put together; base, establish, found; augment, develop, expand, extend, increase.

building n *lit:* construction, edifice, erection, structure; block, house.

bulge n *lit:* lump, protuberance, swelling; dilation, distension; blister, bump, cyst, wen; broadening, expansion, thickening; corporation, eminence, overhang, protrusion; *fig:* fluctuation, temporary increase, rise. **vb** *lit:* dilate, distend, expand, project, protrude, stick out, swell.

bulk n *lit:* immensity, magnitude, size, volume; body, majority, major proportion, mass, most part; cargo, hold. **vb** *lit:* expand, swell (up); amass (up), pile (up); broaden (out), thicken (out); loom (large), stand out (large).

bulky adj *lit:* big, hulking, immense, large, massive; cumbersome, heavy, ponderous, unwieldy, weighty.

bull n *lit:* ox; *fig:* buyer, speculator; bunkum, nonsense, rubbish, twaddle; bullseye, inner, target; drill, spit and polish; *spec:* full-grown male (elephant, moose, seal, walrus, whale, etc.); (papal) decree, edict.

bullet n *lit:* ball, pellet, shot, slug; cartridge, casing.

bully n *lit:* blackmailer, intimidator, persecutor; oppressor; ruffian, thug, troublemaker. **vb** *lit:* browbeat, bulldoze, domineer. intimidate, oppress, push around, terrorize.

bump n *lit:* bang, blow, collision, crash, impact, jolt, shock, thump; contusion, knob, lump, nodule; bulge, swelling. **vb** *lit:* bang into, collide with, crash into, jolt, knock into, strike, thump; bounce, jar, rattle, shake; *fig:* run (into); kill (off).

bun n *lit:* cake, muffin, roll, pastry, scone; coil, knot, mass.

bunch n *lit:* bouquet, bundle, clump, cluster, handful, parcel, posy, sheaf, spray; batch, collection, pile; knot, tuft; band, crowd, gang, group, mob, party, team. **vb** *lit:* assemble, cluster, concentrate, congregate, crowd together, group, pack together; clench, contract, knot.

bundle n *lit:* batch, bunch, collection, group, pile, stack; bale, bolt, mass, package, parcel, roll; knot, node; *fig:* lot. **vb** *lit:* batch up, collect together, group, pile up, stack; bale, pack up, parcel together, roll up, tie up; *fig:* hurry, hustle, push, shove, thrust.

bunk n *lit:* bed, berth, cot, sleeping-place; balderdash, claptrap, hooey, humbug, junk, nonsense, piffle, rubbish, stuff and nonsense, tosh, twaddle; *fig:* (do a) legger, (do a) runner.

burden n *lit:* encumbrance, fardel, load, weight; cargo, freight; *fig:* millstone, onus, responsibility, strain, stress, worry. **vb** *lit:* encumber, load, weigh down; saddle (with); *fig:* handicap, make difficult for, oppress, penalize, worry.

burglar n *lit:* housebreaker, raider, sneak thief; intruder, trespasser, robber.

burglary n *lit:* breaking and entering, housebreaking, larceny, theft; break-in, robbery.

burial n *lit:* interment; funeral, obsequies.

burn n *lit:* brand, scorch, singe; firing, launch, lift-off, thrust; fast ride. **vb** *lit:* be on fire, blaze; ignite, kindle, light, set alight; glow, smoke; brand, char, cremate, incinerate, singe; oxidize; *fig:* consume, expend, use; hurt, smart, sting; be inflamed, be passionate, smoulder with desire (for), yearn (for).

burst n *lit:* emission, outpouring, transmission; eruption, gust, rush, surge; acceleration, sprint, spurt; breach, break, rupture, split; blast, discharge, explosion, salvo, volley; display, shower. **vb** *lit:* blow up, explode, fly apart, puncture, rupture, shatter; barge (in), rush (in); break (into), snap (into); break (out), erupt; flood, gush, overflow, spout; implode. **adj (pa.pt)** *lit:* flat, punctured, ruptured; blown up, exploded, shattered; breached, broken, holed.

bury vb *lit:* inhume, inter, lay to rest; dig in, embed, plant, sink;

fig: conceal, cover up, hide away; engross, immerse, preoccupy.

bus n *lit:* charabanc, coach, double-decker, single-decker, tram; *fig:* banger, car, heap, wreck; aeroplane, kite; *spec:* (electrical) distributor.

bush n *lit:* hedge, shrub, woody plant; forest, jungle, thicket, wilds; outback, scrub, veldt.

business n *lit:* commerce, industry, manufacturing, marketing, trading; company, concern, firm, organization; craft, job, line, métier, occupation, profession, trade, work; deals, transactions; assignment, duty, function, responsibility; affair, issue, matter, topic.

bust n *lit:* bosom, breasts, chest, figure; head and shoulders, statue; arrest, cop, raid. **vb** *lit:* break, burst, rupture, shatter; bankrupt, impoverish, ruin; arrest, catch, cop, raid. **adj (pa.pt)** *lit:* broken, burst, ruptured, shattered; bankrupt, broke, impoverished, ruined; arrested, caught, raided.

busy adj *lit:* active, exacting, full, strenuous; engaged, engrossed, fully employed, occupied, preoccupied; hard at it, industrious, labouring, toiling away; *fig:* fussy, officious; interfering, meddlesome, prying; *spec:* over-detailed, restless (in art).

but cnj *lit:* however, nevertheless, on the other hand, still, yet; except (for/that/to), save (for/that/to); unless.
adv *lit:* just, merely, no more than, only, simply.

butcher n *lit:* slaughterer; killer, slayer; sadist, torturer. **vb** *lit:* slaughter; carve, cut up, dress, joint; cut down, kill, slay; *fig:* botch, make an utter hash of, mutilate, travesty.

button n *lit:* boss, knop, rivet, roundel, stud; bellpush, disc, key, knob, pad; bud; *spec:* chin (in boxing).

buy n *lit:* purchase; acquisition; bargain. **vb** *lit:* pay for, purchase; invest in; acquire, procure, secure; bribe, pay (off), square; *fig:* accept, believe, credit, grant.

buyer n *lit:* emptor, purchaser; client, customer, habitué, patron; agent, purchasing manager, stock manager, supplier.

by **adv** *lit:* at hand; beyond, past; aside, away. **prp** *lit:* along, alongside, beside, close to, near; past, through, via; on, over; because of, through the means of, through the use of; the invention of, the work of; in proportion to, in relation to, with respect to; times; before, prior to; according to; to the extent of; *spec:* called, of, under (the name).

C

cabin n *lit:* bothy, but-and-ben, chalet, cottage, hovel, hut, lodge, shack, shanty, shed; berth, deckhouse, quarters, room.

cabinet n *lit:* case, closet, commode, cupboard, dresser, locker; administration, assembly, council, ministry; apartment, boudoir, chamber.

cable n *lit:* chain, cord, flex, line, wire; hawser, rope; telegram.

café n *lit:* cafeteria, coffee bar, lunchroom, restaurant, snack bar, tearoom.

cage n *lit:* enclosure, pen, pound. **vb** *lit:* confine, coop up, fence in, immure, impound, incarcerate, lock up, restrain, shut up.

cake n *lit:* bar, block, cube, loaf, mass, slab. **vb** *lit:* bake, cement, coagulate, congeal, consolidate, dry, encrust, harden, ossify, solidify, thicken.

calculate vb *lit:* adjust, compute, consider, count, determine, estimate, figure, gauge, judge, rate, reckon, value, weigh, work out; design, intend, plan.

calculation n *lit:* computation, estimate, estimation, figuring, forecast, judgement, reckoning; caution, circumspection, contrivance, deliberation, discretion, foresight, forethought, planning, precaution.

call n *lit:* cry, hail, shout, signal, whoop, yell; announcement, appeal, demand, invitation, notice, plea, request, ring, summons, supplication, visit; cause, grounds, justification, occasion, reason, urge. **vb** *lit:* announce, arouse, cry, hail, rouse, shout, waken, yell; assemble, bid, contact, convene, gather, invite, muster, phone, rally, ring up, summon; christen, describe as, designate, dub, label, name, style, term; appoint, declare, decree, ordain, order, proclaim, set apart; consider, estimate, regard, think.

calling n *lit:* career, line, mission, occupation, profession, province, pursuit, trade, vocation, walk of life, work.

callous adj *lit:* apathetic, cold, hard-boiled, hardhearted, heartless, indifferent, insensitive, inured, obdurate, thick-skinned, torpid, uncaring, unfeeling, unsusceptible, unsympathetic.

calm n *lit:* calmness, hush, peace, quiet, repose, serenity, stillness, tranquillity. vb *lit:* hush, mollify, placate, quieten, relax, soothe. adj *lit:* halcyon, mild, pacific, peaceful, placid, quiet, restful, serene, smooth, still, tranquil, windless; collected, composed, cool, dispassionate, equable, impassive, imperturbable, relaxed, undisturbed, unemotional, unexcited, unflappable, unruffled.

camp n *lit:* bivouac, camp site, encampment, tents. adj *lit:* affected, artificial, effeminate, mannered, ostentatious, postering.

can n *lit:* canister, cylinder, tin, tube.

cancel vb *lit:* abolish, abrogate, annul, call off, countermand, delete, do away with, efface, eliminate, erase, expunge, obliterate, quash, repeal, repudiate, revoke; compensate for, counterbalance, make up for, neutralize, nullify, offset.

cancellation n *lit:* abandonment, abolition, annulment, deletion, elimination, quashing, repeal, revocation.

candidate n *lit:* applicant, claimant, competitor, contender, contestant, entrant, nominee, runner, solicitant.

canopy n *lit:* awning, covering, shade, tester.

canteen n *lit:* bar, cafe, dining-hall, mess, refectory, restaurant; cutlery drawer; billy-can, flask, hip-flask, water container.

cap n *lit:* cover, lid, seal, top; detonator; head-dress. vb *lit:* beat, better, complete, cover, crown, exceed, excel, finish, outdo, surpass, top, transcend.

capable adj *lit:* able, accomplished, adept, adequate, apt, competent, efficient, experienced, gifted, proficient, qualified, skilful, susceptible.

capacity n *lit:* amplitude, compass, extent, range, room, scope, size, space, volume; ability, aptitude, brains, capability, efficiency, faculty, power, strength; appointment, function, office, position, post, role, service, sphere.

cape n *lit:* cloak; headland, peninsula, point, promontory.

capital n *lit:* assets, cash, finances, funds, investment(s), means, money, property, resources, stock, wealth, wherewithal.   **adj** *lit:* cardinal, central, chief, controlling, foremost, important, leading, main, overruling, paramount, pre-eminent, prime, principal, vital; excellent, fine, first-rate, splendid, superb.

capsize vb *lit:* invert, keel over, overturn, tip over, turn turtle, upset.

capsule n *lit:* lozenge, pill, tablet; case, pericarp, pod, receptacle, sheath, shell, vessel.

captain n *lit:* boss, chief, commander, leader, master, number one, officer, (senior) pilot, skipper.

captivate vb *lit:* allure, attract, beguile, charm, dazzle, enamour, enchant, enthral, fascinate, infatuate, lure, mesmerize, win.

captive n *lit:* convict, detainee, hostage, internee, prisoner, slave.   **adj** *lit:* caged, confined, enslaved, imprisoned, incarcerated, locked up, restricted, subjugated.

capture n *lit:* apprehension, arrest, imprisonment, seizure, taking captive, trapping. **vb** *lit:* apprehend, arrest, bag, catch, secure, seize, take prisoner.

car n *lit:* automobile, motor, motorcar, vehicle; cable car, coach, (railway) carriage, van.

carafe n *lit:* decanter, flagon, flask, jug, pitcher.

caravan n *lit:* column, cortege, train; mobile home, trailor, van, wagon.

card n *lit:* playing card, post card, visiting card; wire brush; *fig:* means, plan; character, crank, joker.

care n *lit:* affliction, anxiety, concern, disquiet, hardship, pressure, responsibility, stress, tribulation, trouble, vexation, worry; attention, caution, circumspection, consideration, forethought, heed, meticulousness, pains, prudence, regard, vigilance; charge, custody, guardianship, management, ministration, protection, supervision, ward. **vb** *lit:* be concerned, feel interest; like, want, wish; mind.

career n *lit:* calling, life work, occupation, pursuit, vocation; course, passage, path, procedure, progress, race. **vb** *lit:* bolt, dash, hurtle, race, rush, speed, tear.

careful adj *lit:* accurate, cautious, circumspect, conscientious, discreet, fastidious, painstaking, precise, prudent, punctilious, scrupulous, thoughtful, thrifty; alert, attentive, concerned, mindful, particular, solicitous, vigilant, wary.

careless adj *lit:* absent-minded, cursory, forgetful, heedless, incautious, indiscreet, negligent, perfunctory, remiss, thoughtless, unconcerned, unmindful, unthinking; inaccurate, irresponsible, lackadaisical, neglectful, offhand, slipshod, sloppy; artless, casual, nonchalant.

caretaker n *lit:* concierge, curator, custodian, janitor, keeper, superintendent, warden. **adj** *lit:* holding, interim, temporary.

carnage n *lit:* blood bath, butchery, havoc, holocaust, massacre, mass murder, shambles, slaughter.

carnival n *lit:* celebration, fair, festival, fête, fiesta, holiday, jamboree, jubilee, merrymaking, revelry.

carpenter n *lit:* cabinet-maker, joiner, wood-worker.

carpet n *lit:* floor covering, rug. **vb** *lit:* cover (wall to wall); *fig:* call to account, rebuke, reprimand, reprehend, summon, tell off, tick off.

carriage n *lit:* conveyance, delivery, freight, transport; cab, coach, vehicle; *fig:* bearing, behaviour, conduct, demeanour, deportment, gait, manner, mien, posture.

carry vb *lit:* bear, bring, convey, haul, lift, lug, move, relay, take, transport; accomplish, effect, gain, win; drive, impel, influence, motivate, spur, urge; hold up, maintain, shoulder, stand, support, sustain, uphold; broadcast, communicate, display, stock.

cart n *lit:* dray, tumbril, vehicle, wagon. **vb** *lit:* bear, carry, heave, haul, lug.

carton n *lit:* box, case, container, pack, packet.

carve vb *lit:* chip, chisel, cut, engrave, etch, fashion, grave, incise, indent, mould, sculpt, slice, whittle.

case n *lit:* box, cabinet, canister, capsule, carton, cartridge, casket, chest, container, crate, holder, receptacle, suitcase, trunk; casing, cover, envelope, folder, jacket, sheath; circumstance(s), context, contingency, dilemma, event, plight, predicament, situation, state; example, instance, occasion, occurrence; *spec:* action, dispute, lawsuit, proceedings, process, suit, trial.

cash n *lit:* banknotes, bullion, coinage, currency, dough, funds, money, ready money, resources, wherewithal. vb *lit:* give cash, obtain cash.

cashier n *lit:* accountant, bank clerk, bursar, purser, teller, treasurer. vb *lit:* break, cast off, discard, discharge, dismiss, expel.

cask n *lit:* barrel, keg, tun, wooden vessel.

casket n *lit:* box, case, chest, coffer.

castle n *lit:* chateau, citadel, donjon, fastness, fortress, keep, peel, stronghold, tower.

casual adj *lit:* accidental, chance, contingent, incidental, irregular, occasional, random, unexpected, unforeseen, unintentional; apathetic, blasé, cursory, informal, lackadaisical, nonchalant, offhand, perfunctory, unconcerned.

casualty n *lit:* loss, sufferer, victim; accident, calamity, catastrophe, contingency, disaster, misadventure, misfortune, mishap.

cat n *lit:* feline, grimalkin, moggy, mouser, pussy, tabby.

catalogue n *lit:* directory, index, inventory, list, record, roll, roster, schedule. vb *lit:* alphabetize, classify, file, index, list, register.

catastrophe n *lit:* adversity, affliction, blow, calamity, devastation, disaster, fiasco, mischance, misfortune, mishap, reverse, tragedy, trial, trouble.

catch n *lit:* bolt, clasp, clip, fastener, hook, latch; disadvantage, drawback, hitch, snag, stumbling block, trap, trick. vb *lit:* apprehend, arrest, capture, clutch, ensnare, entangle, entrap, grab,

grasp, grip, seize, snare, take; detect, discover, expose, find out, surprise, take unawares; contract, develop; discern, hear, perceive, sense.

category n *lit:* class, classification, department, division, grade, grouping, heading, list, rank, section, type.

cause n *lit:* agent, creator, genesis, mainspring, maker, originator, producer, root, source; agency, aim, basis, consideration, end, grounds, incentive, inducement, motivation, object, purpose, reason; attempt, conviction, enterprise, ideal, movement, undertaking.
vb *lit:* begin, bring about, create, effect, generate, incite, induce, lead to, motivate, occasion, precipitate, provoke, result in.

caution n *lit:* alertness, care, circumspection, deliberation, discretion, forethought, heed, prudence, vigilance; admonition, advice, counsel, injunction, warning. **vb** *lit:* admonish, advise, tip off, urge, warn.

cautious adj *lit:* alert, cagey, careful, circumspect, discreet, guarded, judicious, tentative, vigilant, wary, watchful.

cave n *lit:* cavern, cavity, den, grotto, hollow. **vb** *lit:* hollow out, make into a cave.

cavity n *lit:* crater, dent, gap, hole, hollow, pit.

cease **vb** *lit:* break off, come to an end, conclude, culminate, discontinue, end, fail, finish, halt, leave off, refrain, stay, stop.

ceiling n *lit:* roof; maximum altitude; peak, summit, top, upper limit.

celebrate **vb** *lit:* commemorate, commend, eulogize, exalt, extol, honour, laud, observe, praise, proclaim, rejoice, reverence, toast.

celebration n *lit:* carousel, festival, festivity, jollification, jubilee, merry-making, party, revelry; anniversary, commemoration, honouring, observance, remembrance, solemnization.

celebrity n *lit:* bigwig, dignitary, luminary, name, megastar, personage, personality, superstar, VIP; distinction, fame, glory, notability, pre-eminence, prominence, renown, repute.

cell n *lit:* cavity, chamber, cubicle, cytoplasm, dungeon, stall; caucus, group, nucleus, unit.

cellar n *lit:* basement, bunker, crypt, vault; salt container.

cement n *lit:* adhesive, binder, concrete, glue, gum, paste, plaster, sealant. **vb** *lit:* attach, bind, bond, combine, glue, gum, join, plaster, seal, solder, stick together, weld.

cemetery n *lit:* burial ground, churchyard, graveyard, necropolis.

centre n *lit:* bull's-eye, crux, epicentre, focus, fulcrum, hub, middle, nub, nucleus, pivot. **vb** *lit:* cluster, concentrate, converge, focus.

ceramics n *lit:* earthenware, porcelain, pottery, terracotta.

ceremony n *lit:* commemoration, function, observance, parade, service, show, solemnities; ceremonial, decorum, etiquette, form, niceties, pomp, protocol.

certain adj *lit:* assured, confident, convinced, positive, satisfied, sure; conclusive, irrefutable, plain, true, undeniable, unequivocal, unmistakable, valid; bound, definite, destined, inescapable, inevitable, inexorable; decided, established, fixed, settled; constant, dependable, reliable, stable, steady, trustworthy, unquestionable; express, particular, precise, specific.

certificate n *lit:* authorization, credential(s), diploma, licence, voucher, warrant.

certify vb *lit:* ascertain, assure, authenticate, confirm, corroborate, endorse, guarantee, notify, testify, validate, verify, vouch.

chain n *lit:* bond, coupling, fetter, link, manacle, union; progression, sequence, series, set, string, succession, train. **vb** *lit:* bind, confine, enslave, fetter, handcuff, manacle, shackle, tether, trammel, unite.

chair n *lit:* bench, seat, sedan, throne; authority, chairperson, office; metal socket (in railway).

chairperson n *lit:* chair, director, presider, speaker, toastmaster.

challenge n *lit:* confrontation, dare, defiance, provocation, test,

trial, ultimatum.   **vb** *lit:* accost, arouse, brave, call out, confront, dare, defy, demand, dispute, object to, provoke, question, require, summon, tax, test.

champion n *lit:* challenger, conqueror, defender, nonpareil, patron, protector, title holder, victor, vindicator, warrior, winner.
vb *lit:* advocate, back, defend, fight for, support, uphold.

chance n *lit:* likelihood, occasion, odds, opening, opportunity, possibility, probability, prospect, scope; accident, coincidence, contingency, fate, fortuity, luck, misfortune, providence; gamble, hazard, jeopardy, risk, speculation, uncertainty.   **vb** *lit:* befall, betide, come to pass, happen, occur; endanger, gamble, hazard, jeopardize, risk, stake, venture, wager.   **adj** *lit:* accidental, casual, contingent, fortuitous, incidental, random, unforeseen, unintentional.

change n *lit:* alteration, difference, innovation, modification, permutation, revolution, transition, vicissitude; conversion, exchange, substitution; break, diversion, novelty, variety.   **vb** *lit:* alter, convert, fluctuate, modify, reform, reorganize, shift, transform, vacillate, vary, veer; alternate, barter, exchange, remove, substitute, swap, trade.

channel n *lit:* canal, conduit, duct, furrow, groove, gutter, main, passage, strait; *fig:* approach, avenue, course, means, path, route, way.   **vb** *lit:* conduct, convey, direct, guide.

chapel n *lit:* kirk, meeting house, mission, oratory, place of worship.

chapter n *lit:* clause, episode, period, phase, section, stage.

character n *lit:* attributes, calibre, complexion, disposition, individuality, nature, personality, quality, reputation, temperament, type; honour, integrity, rectitude, uprightness; eccentric, oddity, original; cipher, emblem, figure, glyph, hieroglyph, letter, pictograph, logo, rune, sign, symbol; part, portrayal, role; fellow, guy, individual, sort, type.

characteristic n *lit:* attribute, feature, idiosyncrasy, peculiarity, quality, trait.   **adj** *lit:* distinctive, distinguishing, idiosyncratic, individual, singular, specific, symptomatic, typical.

characterize vb *lit:* brand, distinguish, identify, indicate, mark, represent, stamp, typify.

charge n *lit:* accusation, allegation, indictment; assault, attack, onslaught, rush, sortie; burden, care, custody, duty, responsibility, trust, ward; amount, cost, expenditure, expense, payment, price, rate; command, direction, exhortation, injunction, mandate, order, precept; *spec:* anion, cation, ion, unit of electricity. vb *lit:* accuse, blame, impeach, incriminate, indict; assail, assault, attack, rush, storm; afflict, burden, commit, entrust; fill, instil, load, suffuse; bid, command, enjoin, exhort, instruct, require.

charitable adj *lit:* benevolent, generous, lavish, philanthropic; considerate, favourable, humane, kindly, lenient, magnanimous, sympathetic, understanding.

charm n *lit:* allure, appeal, attraction, enchantment, fascination, magnetism, spell; amulet, fetish, talisman, trinket. vb *lit:* allure, attract, beguile, cajole, captivate, enamour, enchant, enrapture, fascinate, please, win over.

chart n *lit:* blueprint, diagram, graph, plan, table. vb *lit:* draft, graph, outline, plot, sketch.

chase n *lit:* hunt, pursuit, race. vb *lit:* drive, expel, hound, hunt, pursue, run after, track.

chasm n *lit:* abyss, breach, cleft, crater, crevasse, fissure, gorge, hiatus, hollow, ravine, rift, void.

chat n *lit:* chatter, gossip, heart-to-heart, natter, talk. vb *lit:* chatter, gossip, jaw, natter, rabbit (on), talk.

cheap adj *lit:* bargain, cut-price, economical, inexpensive, low-cost, reasonable, sale; common, inferior, paltry, shoddy, tatty; contemptible, despicable, mean, scurvy, vulgar.

cheat n *lit:* deceit, deception, fraud, rip-off, swindle, trickery; charlatan, con man, dodger, double-crosser, impostor, rogue, shark, trickster. vb *lit:* bamboozle, beguile, con, deceive, defraud, do, dupe, fleece, hoax, hoodwink, rip off, swindle, take in, trick; baffle, check, deprive, foil, frustrate, prevent, thwart.

check n *lit:* examination, investigation, scrutiny, test; control, curb, hindrance, impediment, limitation, obstruction, restraint; blow, disappointment, frustration, reverse, set-back. **vb** *lit:* compare, enquire into, examine, inspect, look at, make sure, note, probe, scrutinize, test, verify; arrest, bar, control, curb, delay, halt, hinder, impede, limit, obstruct, restrain, stop, thwart; blame, chide, rebuff, rebuke, reprimand, scold, tell off.

cheerful adj *lit:* animated, blithe, buoyant, cheery, contented, enthusiastic, happy, jaunty, jolly, merry, sparkling, sprightly, sunny.

chemist n *lit:* apothecary, dispenser, druggist.

chest n *lit:* thorax; case, casket, coffer, crate, strongbox.

chew vb *lit:* bite, crunch, gnaw, grind, munch; *fig:* mull over, ponder, reflect upon, ruminate, weigh.

chic adj *lit:* elegant, fashionable, modish, smart, sophisticated, stylish.

chicken n *lit:* fowl, hen, rooster; coward, cowardy custard, sissy, yellow-belly; challenge, dare. **vb** *fig:* cowardly, frightened, pusillanimous, scared, timid.

chief n *lit:* boss, chieftain, commander, head, leader, manager, master, ringleader, ruler, superintendent. **adj** *lit:* capital, cardinal, especial, foremost, highest, key, leading, main, paramount, predominant, pre-eminent, prevailing, primary, principal, supreme, uppermost, vital.

child n *lit:* baby, brat, infant, issue, juvenile, kid, minor, nipper, offspring, toddler, tot, youngster.

childhood n *lit:* immaturity, infancy, minority, youth.

childish adj *lit:* immature, infantile, juvenile, puerile, simple, young.

china n *lit:* ceramics, crockery, porcelain, pottery, service, tableware.

choice n *lit:* alternative, option, pick, preference, say, selection, variety. **adj** *lit:* best, dainty, elite, exclusive, exquisite, hand-picked, precious, prime, prize, rare, special, superior, uncommon, valuable.

choose vb *lit:* adopt, designate, desire, fix on, opt for, pick, prefer, see fit, settle upon, single out, take, wish.

chop n *lit:* dismissal, sacking, the axe, the boot, the sack. vb *lit:* axe, cut, fell, hack, hew, lop, sever, truncate.

chorus n *lit:* choir, choristers, ensemble, singers; refrain, response, strain; accord, concert, harmony.

chronic adj *lit:* deep-seated, incessant, incurable, ineradicable, ingrained, persistent.

church n *lit:* abbey, cathedral, chapel, kirk, meeting house, minster, mission, synagogue, temple; congregation, denomination, sect.

cigarette n *lit:* ciggy, fag, gasper, smoke.

cinema n *lit:* films, motion pictures, movies, picture palace.

circle n *lit:* band, circumference, cordon, cycle, disc, lap, loop, orb, perimeter, revolution, ring, sphere; area, bounds, circuit, compass, enclosure, orbit, range, region, scene; assembly, clique, company, fraternity, group, set, society. vb *lit:* belt, circumnavigate, coil, compass, encircle, enclose, envelop, gird, revolve, ring, rotate, surround, whirl.

circulation n *lit:* currency, distribution, spread, transmission; circling, flow, rotation.

circumstance n *lit:* condition, contingency, detail, event, fact, factor, incident, occurrence, particular, position, situation.

citizen n *lit:* burgher, denizen, dweller, inhabitant, resident.

city n *lit:* conurbation, metropolis, municipality, town.

civic adj *lit:* communal, community, local, municipal.

civil adj *lit:* civic, domestic, home, municipal, political; accommodating, affable, courteous, courtly, obliging, polite, refined, urbane, well-mannered.

civilization n *lit:* advancement, cultivation, culture, enlightenment, progress, refinement, sophistication; community, people, society; customs, mores, way of life.

civilized adj *lit:* cultured, enlightened, humane, polite, sophisticated, urbane.

claim n *lit:* affirmation, allegation, assertion, call, petition, pretension, privilege, request, requirement, right. **vb** *lit:* allege, assert, call for, demand, exact, insist, maintain, profess, require, uphold.

clarify vb *lit:* clear up, elucidate, explain, resolve, simplify; cleanse, purify, refine.

clarity n *lit:* clearness, definition, explicitness, intelligibility, lucidity, precision, simplicity.

class n *lit:* caste, category, classification, department, division, genre, grade, group, kind, order, rank, set, sort, species, status, type, value. **vb** *lit:* categorize, classify, codify, designate, grade, rank, rate.

classify vb *lit:* arrange, catalogue, categorize, codify, file, grade, rank, sort, systematize.

clause n *lit:* article, chapter, paragraph, part, section; heading, item, point, provision, specification, stipulation.

claw n *lit:* nail, nipper, pincer, talon, unguis. **vb** *lit:* dig, lacerate, mangle, maul, rip, scrape, scratch.

clean vb *lit:* cleanse, disinfect, dust, launder, mop, purify, rinse, scrub, sponge, sweep, wash, wipe. **adj** *lit:* flawless, fresh, hygienic, immaculate, laundered, pure, sanitary, spotless, unblemished, unsoiled, washed; antiseptic, clarified, decontaminated, purified, sterilized, unadulterated, unpolluted; chaste, decent, good, guiltless, innocent, moral, respectable, undefiled, upright, virtuous; delicate, elegant, neat, simple, tidy, uncluttered; complete, conclusive, decisive, entire, perfect, thorough, total, unimpaired, whole.

clear vb *lit:* clean, erase, purify, refine, tidy (up), wipe; break up, clarify, brighten; absolve, acquit, exuse, exonerate, vindicate; free, liberate, set free; disengage, disentangle, extricate, loosen, open, rid, unblock, unload; jump, leap, miss, pass over; earn, gain, make, reap. **adj** *lit:* bright, cloudless, fine, halcyon, light, shining, sunny,

HARRAP'S ENGLISH STUDY AIDS

In the same series:

ENGLISH GRAMMAR
★ Comprehensive grammar of modern English
★ Ideal reference for all users of English
ISBN 0 245-54746-0

ENGLISH VERBS
★ 1,000 phrasal verbs with definitions and examples
★ Index to verb patterns and forms
ISBN 0 245-54745-2

BASIC ENGLISH VOCABULARY
★ 2,000 frequently used words
★ Thousands of other words formed from the main words
★ Exercises and key
ISBN 0 245-54747-9

ENGLISH SPELLING
★ Nearly 30,000 alphabetical entries
★ Colour-coded to identify common spelling mistakes
ISBN 0 245-54832-7

ENGLISH USAGE
★ Over 4,000 alphabetical entries
★ Practical guidance on all aspects of usage
ISBN 0 245-54830-0

MINI ENGLISH DICTIONARY
★ 125,000 words and meanings
★ Phonetic transcriptions
ISBN 0 245-54587-5